W9-ACJ-703

# Essays in Self-Destruction

# Essays in Self-Destruction

Edwin S. Shneidman
Editor

Science House, Inc. New York

First Edition

Library of Congress Card Number 67–27406

To
the Memory of
HAROLD M. HILDRETH
Devoted Godfather
to the
Scientific and Humanitarian Study
of
Self-Destruction in Man

# Contents

# Preface

What greater pleasure than to play host to a distinguished group of gracious guests, each of whom is an old friend. Happily, that is my fortunate role in this pleasant venture. Perhaps the only greater possible delight lies in sharing with a known and unknown host of readers the rangeful spread of "tarts and beef and potatoes" that these contributors have, as perfect guests, brought to a banquet that they themselves so abundantly provided. All I did was furnish the hall. They, from first to last, supplied the viands and catered to our most exacting needs. It goes without saying (but nonetheless merits explicit expression) that it is to them that I am to the utmost indebted.

Since 1958, in the likely city of Los Angeles, at a new and unique operation called the Suicide Prevention Center,[1] a band of scientists

[1] The Suicide Prevention Center has been supported by grants (1958-1962, 1962-1969) from the National Institute of Mental Health, U.S. Public Health Service. Sentiments of gratitude and appreciation are felt by each member of the SPC team toward the NIMH, especially toward the late Dr. Harold Hildreth who, before and since its inception, was the guiding spirit of the Suicide Prevention Center project. The present NIMH grant is administered through the University of Southern California, specifically through the Department of Psychiatry (of which Dr. Edward Stainbrook is Chairman) of the School of Medicine (of which Dr. Roger Egeberg is Dean). Drs. Stainbrook and Egeberg, as well as Dr. Clayton Loosli, former Dean, have all been actively helpful supporters of the Suicide Prevention Center program, and it is a pleasure here to express our warm feelings to each of them. From the inauguration of the Center in 1958 until September 1966, Dr. Norman L. Farberow was Co-Director with me; subsequent to that latter date, when I left Los Angeles to become Chief of the newly-established Center for Studies of Suicide Prevention at the National Institute of Mental Health in Chevy Chase, Maryland, Dr. Farberow and Dr. Robert E. Litman have been Co-Directors of the Los Angeles Center.

and clinicians, including psychoanalysts, psychologists, psychiatric social workers, and volunteers have pitted their own life's energies against the thanatopic impulses of those in the community who, while suffering unendurable emotion, have sought to end their own lives; and, even more importantly, these same experts have attempted systematically to study the actual phenomena of self-destruction in its very process. All this is to say that each contributor to this volume of essays has been associated directly with one common enterprise. The kind of conceptual cement which holds this book together (and justifies the publication of these essays in one volume) is not only the contributors' common interest in a unifying topic but happily also a shared association with some aspect of the activities of the Los Angeles Suicide Prevention Center.

To be specific: Of the twenty-six contributors (including the writer of the Foreword), nine were Fellows at the Center for the Scientific Study of Suicide (CSSS), a special study and research unit at the Suicide Prevention Center. The CSSS Fellows represented in this book are: Kresten Bjerg (1962–1963), Warren Breed (1965–1966), Jacques Choron (1965–1966), James Diggory (1964–1965), Harold Garfinkel (1963–1964), Gerald Heard (1964–1965), Stephen Pepper (1964–1965), Harvey Sacks (1963–1964), and Elsa Whalley (1962–1963).

The Center for the Scientific Study of Suicide was established (in 1962), spurred by my feeling that what this field needs most is ideas and with the thought that there ought to be, as an on-going part of the Suicide Prevention Center, at least a small unit of two or three Fellows representing, over the years, a productive variety of fields and disciplines, such as sociology, political science, psychology, anthropology, philosophy, logic, linguistics, etc. I sought especially those individuals who had not previously published on the topic of suicide and who thus might, by virtue of their ostensible lack of trained incapacities, be looked on to bring fresh insights and new concepts to the emerging area of suicidology. Such individuals were invited to the CSSS for what was hoped would be to them a challenging assignment, namely "to contemplate suicide" for one year. In large measure, this book was initiated by their responses and is built around their contributions.

Seven contributors are members of the National Advisory Board of the Suicide Prevention Foundation, Inc. This Foundation was established in 1961 as a nonprofit, tax-exempt, scientific and educational organization supported by public funds and associated with the Suicide Prevention Center. Its major functions relate primarily to support of research and training aspects of the suicide prevention activities. The members of the

National Advisory Board represented in this volume include Theodore Curphey, Louis Dublin, Paul Friedman, Harold Garfinkel, Lawrence Kubie, Karl Menninger, and Henry Murray. (Harold Garfinkel has also been a Fellow at the Center.)

Five of the contributors have been visitors to the Suicide Prevention Center or have lectured there. These include Mel Faber, Neil Kessel, Talcott Parsons, Halmuth Schaefer, and Avery Weisman.

Two of the contributors are Consultants at the Suicide Prevention Center: Mamoru Iga, who is Sociologist Consultant, and Louis Dublin, who is Senior Consultant. (Dr. Dublin is also a member of the National Advisory Board.)

Finally, four of the contributors—Norman Farberow, Robert Litman, Norman Tabachnick and myself—were directly affiliated with the Los Angeles Suicide Prevention Center as members of the staff.

Each word in the title of this book was meant to convey something about the scope of the volume. "Essays" implies that the chapters are discursive, contemplative, expository; that they advertently employ the essay form. Very few of them are designed to be statistical reports of empirical and experimental studies. The word "essay" also has the meaning of an attempt or a trial and, by extension, a foray, an adventure, an advance or a thrust. These are admittedly uncommon meanings of the term, but they are nonetheless meanings which in the present context ought to be considered.

It is of more than casual importance for the understanding of the spirit in which this book was conceived to note that the term "self-destruction" is meant to convey the notion that whereas the book, coming as it does from the activities of a suicide prevention center, certainly touches upon and even explicitly deals with suicidal behaviors, it is not limited to discussions of overt suicide but also includes presentations of a wide range of self-damaging and self-negating aspects of human behavior, including partial death, attrition of the personality, surrender of parts of the self, etc.; in short, it takes as its province any of the diminishing, reductive, truncating, or inimical patterns of life—the dark side of man—that a reader is likely to encounter in his professional consultations, his literary explorations, his social life, or within himself.

This book is not in the genre of a "how to" book. Its highest aspiration is to present some selected frontiers of thought which are directly or indirectly related to the universally important topic of self-destruction in man. Had there been a contributor who had chosen to write on the topic of "the long and protracted era of ferocity and anguish" in which we now perilously live (that is to say, the topic of *global* self-destruction), I would have welcomed his essay to this volume—but there was none, so that topic is not represented. I mention this because some readers may find other lacunae, conspicuous omissions of favored topics, in this book. This collection of essays is not offered as a comprehensive package, but rather as a sampling of the topic of self-destruction—delectations for the whetting, if not the satisfaction, of the appetite.

As can be seen from the Table of Contents, the contributions are divided into four sections. Selection of these particular four categories is meant to reflect, as well as possible, the beliefs apparently supported by the majority of the contributors and enthusiastically shared by the Editor that the study of self-destructive behaviors is mainly the study of human personality and, further, that a comprehensive study of personality has at least some of the following characteristics:

1. It permits the intensive study of a few persons or single persons, including historical and literary figures, as well as the now fashionable study of small aspects of large numbers of human or infrahuman subjects; and it also permits (if not requires) the study of individuals' sentiments, values, beliefs, philosophies and "world hypotheses." Part I of the book, "Literary and Philosophic Essays," is meant to reflect these beliefs.

2. It views the individual within the context of his meaningful (and often stressful) dyadic relationships and, further, within the context of his social class memberships, as constantly engaged in the task of "doing sociology" in the ordinary events of his everyday life. Part II, "Sociological and Ethnographic Essays," presents these aspects of the total study of man.

3. It requires personality to be seen in terms of its present (paridictive) cross-sectional aspects as well as its past (postdictive) lifelong processes, both of which should include something of the psychodynamic history of the individual, his fantasies and aspirations, and his personal ontology. Also, the proper study of man includes, compassionately, study of prophylaxis and remediation of his maladaptive patterns as well as admiration and praise for his adaptive ways. The "Psychological and Psychiatric Essays," Part III, represent some of these aspects of personality study.

4. A growing science of personology requires techniques for identifying and classifying dimensions and parameters of personality and for identifying and describing some of the more useful units and dimensions

within these classifications. It should ever seek novel multidisciplinary affiliations and groupings as well as new classifications based on fresh and unconventional conceptualizations. All this points to the crucial importance of developing "good theoretical formulations of significant problems which can be tested by appropriate data or utilizing data in such a way as to generate new theoretical formulations." Some of these beliefs are reflected in Part IV, "Taxonomic and Forensic Essays."

Specific appreciations for permission to use the contributions which appear in this volume by Lawrence Kubie, Talcott Parsons, and Neil Kessel—from the Williams and Wilkins Company, the Office of Social Research of the Equitable Life Assurance Society of the United States, and *The British Medical Journal*, respectively—are cited in the initial footnote of these three chapters. And I would be more than remiss if I did not give great thanks to Mrs. Kay Smith and Miss Barbara Tabor for their substantial assistance in helping me prepare the manuscript for the publisher, and to Lee J. Glober, M.D., for his help in the preparation of the Name Index.

The illustration on the jacket of this volume was drawn by the eminent California artist, Leon Saulter.

E.S.S.

*Chevy Chase, Maryland*
*November, 1966*

# Foreword

Who wants to read about suicide? Not I, many would say. And not just ignorant people who cannot read, or hell-bent-for-pleasure people who do not want to read. Some serious-minded people avoid the subject. Self-destruction is a terrible thing; it is tragic that there are such desperate or pitiable or lonely people; our hearts bleed for them, but other problems face us that we can do something about.

And there's the rub. Many intelligent people don't know that there *is* something to be done about suicide and self-destruction. How can we spread this news? How can we get people to realize that suicide is only a dramatic, individual example of human self-destructiveness and that we can and must combat it?

The universality of self-destructiveness is obvious in history, in sociology, in psychiatry, in the day-to-day behavior of people and nations. The crucial problem is how to increase self-control and maintain a vital balance of instinctual urges and reality offerings. Scientists are thinking about these things today, and making progress toward that goal. The new discoveries in physics, expressed in atoms, bombs and space flights, or in microbiology, are better known to the public than the new discoveries in psychology and the social sciences—or even the old facts of psychology and the social sciences appearing in new clothes. This book endeavors to fill that gap.

These essays by over a score of authorities sparkle with interesting facets. Only a better understanding of all the factors involved in self-destruction can effectively diminish the incidence of this human cataclysm. These essays go far in that direction. We owe much to Edwin Shneidman and to his colleagues at the Suicide Prevention Center who have persistently kept before the public the importance of thinking about suicide and self-destruction, and to their researches, which have deepened our knowledge.

KARL A. MENNINGER, M.D.

*Topeka, Kansas*
*June, 1967*

# CONTRIBUTORS

Kresten Bjerg, Mag. Art, is Research Assistant, Psychological Laboratory, University of Copenhagen.

Warren Breed, Ph.D., is Professor of Sociology, Newcomb College, Tulane University.

Jacques Choron, Ph.D., D.S.Sc., is a Lecturer in Philosophy, New School of Social Research, New York City.

Theodore J. Curphey, M.D., is Chief Medical Examiner-Coroner, County of Los Angeles; Clinical Professor of Pathology at the medical schools of the University of Southern California, the University of California at Los Angeles, and the Loma Linda University.

James C. Diggory, Ph.D., is Professor and Chairman of the Department of Psychology, Chatham College, Pittsburgh, Pennsylvania.

Louis I. Dublin, Ph.D., is Second Vice-President and Statistician (retired), Metropolitan Life Insurance Company.

M. D. Faber, Ph.D., is Assistant Professor of English, University of Victoria.

Norman L. Farberow, Ph.D., is Co-Director of the Los Angeles Suicide Prevention Center; Principal Investigator, Veterans Administration Central Research Unit for the Study of Unpredicted Death; Clinical Professor of Psychiatry (Psychology), University of Southern California School of Medicine.

Paul Friedman, Ph.D., M.D., is a practicing psychoanalyst; member of the New York Psychoanalytic Society; Attending Staff, Mount Sinai Hospital, New York City.

Harold Garfinkel, Ph.D., is Professor of Sociology, University of California at Los Angeles.

Gerald Heard is historian, philosopher, lecturer.

Mamoru Iga, Ph.D., is Professor of Sociology, San Fernando State College, California.

Neil Kessel, M.D., Cantab., F.R.C.P., D.P.M., is Professor of Psychiatry, University of Manchester.

Lawrence S. Kubie, M.D., is Visiting Professor of Psychiatry, Jefferson Medical College of Philadelphia; Clinical Professor of Psychiatry, University of Maryland School of Medicine; Lecturer in Psychiatry, The Johns Hopkins University School of Medicine.

Victor Lidz, A.B., is Research Assistant, Department of Social Relations, Harvard University.

Robert E. Litman, M.D., is Chief Psychiatrist, Los Angeles Suicide Prevention Center; Clinical Professor of Psychiatry, University of Southern California School of Medicine.

Karl Menninger, M.D., is Dean, The Menninger School of Psychiatry; Chairman of the Board of Trustees, The Menninger Foundation; Senior Consultant, The Stone-Brandel Center, Chicago; and University Professor at Large, University of Kansas.

Henry A. Murray, M.D., Ph.D., is Emeritus Professor of Clinical Psychology, Department of Social Relations, Harvard University.

Talcott Parsons, Ph.D., is Professor of Sociology, Department of Social Relations, Harvard University.

Stephen C. Pepper, Ph.D., is Emeritus Mills Professor of Intellectual and Moral Philosophy and Civil Polity, University of California, Berkeley.

Harvey Sacks, L.L.B., Ph.D., is Lecturer, Department of Sociology, University of California at Los Angeles.

Halmuth H. Schaefer, Ph.D., is Chief of Research, Behavioral Research Laboratory, Patton State Hospital; Adjunct Associate Professor of Psychology, Claremont Graduate School, Claremont, California.

Edwin S. Shneidman, Ph.D., is Chief, Center for Studies of Suicide Prevention, National Institute of Mental Health, Chevy Chase, Maryland; Lecturer in Psychiatry, The Johns Hopkins University School of Medicine; formerly Co-Director, Los Angeles Suicide Prevention Center; Professor of Psychiatry (Psychology), University of Southern California School of Medicine.

Norman D. Tabachnick, M.D., is Associate Chief Psychiatrist, Suicide Prevention Center; Associate Clinical Professor of Psychiatry, University of Southern California School of Medicine.

Avery D. Weisman, M.D., is Assistant Clinical Professor of Psychiatry, Harvard Medical School; Director of the Psychiatric Consultation Unit, Department of Psychiatry, Massachusetts General Hospital.

Elsa Whalley, Ph.D., is Associate Professor of Psychology, Fairleigh Dickinson University, Rutherford, New Jersey.

**Part I**

# LITERARY AND PHILOSOPHIC ESSAYS

From a certain point of view, the current disciplines relating to the psychological and sociological study of man represent attempts to reformulate within the contemporary language of science what philosophers and poets have, in their own special language, written about for centuries. A comprehensive study of self-destruction in man should include contributions both from the literary and the philosophic traditions. The essays in this section include not only chapters about the writings of specific philosophic minds (including Buddha, Shakespeare, Morris, and several others) but also—viewing personality as a dynamic system—a chapter which examines the dynamic role of changes in attitude toward life itself over the extended psychological history of a specific individual (Melville) and a chapter which examines the general (and important) question of the role of philosophy in the ongoing life of any individual.

Henry Murray's essay, in many ways, sets the tone for the entire volume. He illustrates a number of crucial characteristics of the self-destructive man from the wealth of his intense knowledge of Herman Melville. And what is to be especially noted is that it is not of overt suicide that Professor Murray writes—such as the death of Melville's eldest son Malcolm—but rather of the moiety of Melville's last forty years, "the great refusal," Melville's half-death and his inner dialogue with the specter of annihilation. It is precisely these suicidal equivalents, the inimicalities of life—superbly described and expounded in Dr. Murray's paper—that are the prototypical topics of this book.

Mel Faber has, in his chapter, combined his professional interests in Shakespeare and the topic of suicide. Insightfully, he focuses on both the metaphoric and ambivalent aspects of suicide. His explication of each of Shakespeare's suicides, within the setting of sixteenth and seventeenth century lore as well as contemporary psychological and psychiatric knowledge, provide, in one exciting verbal panorama, increased information about

Shakespeare, his chief protagonists, the topic of self-destruction, and human nature in general.

Jacques Choron's chapter is a condensed history of philosophic thought, an index, as it were, of philosophy from the point of view of "Death." Specifically, his general topic is that of death as the "Muse" or inspiration of philosophic thought. Man's concern with his naughtment and, conversely, his immortality has been the catalyst of much of his most systematic (and certainly his most serious) philosophic work. The variety of philosophic arguments in relation to death is an especially interesting thread through philosophic history which Dr. Choron traces for us in his chapter. There is, of course, an obvious relationship between this chapter and that of Professor Pepper: Dr. Choron's chapter is historical in its sweep and Dr. Pepper's is more discursive and contemporary in its perspective. They might very well be juxtaposed in reading this volume.

Gerald Heard is a man of omnivorous interests, as anyone knows who is acquainted with him at all. When I approached him about the possibility of his writing a chapter, he responded by saying that he had, for a long time, wanted to write a paper on Buddha and self-destruction. His chapter, characteristic of his multifaceted approach, is an historical, biographical, philosophical discussion of the nuances of Buddhism and the subtleties of self-destruction, with a clear synthesis in the conclusion of the chapter pointing toward a particular "way of life," of which Gerald Heard is a vocal espouser and a shining example. Although this chapter is comprehensive, inviting our attention to the various types and aspects of Buddhist ethics, it is openly partisan. It is thus all the more interesting to compare it with Dr. Whalley's chapter, in which a number of different philosophic "ways of life" are described.

Elsa Whalley is a student of Charles W. Morris, the famed American scientistic philosopher. Her chapter, although focussed around the topics of values and conflicts among competing values, is primarily a systematic presentation of one aspect of Morris' work, specifically his "ways to live," relating to the historically important philosophies of life. Data from factor analytic computations and cross-cultural studies are presented, and their implications for understanding self-destructive behaviors are delineated. In her chapter, Dr. Whalley brings to this volume findings and suggestions which provide a broad and useful overview for philosophic understanding.

Stephen Pepper's essay is not about any historical or literary person; it is rather a philosophic essay, complete within its own rights. Further, it is in many ways an unusual philosophic essay in that it clearly sets the limits for unadulterated intellection or pure reason, arguing for the "dynamic effectiveness" of a philosophy of life. More than that, it urges the distinction between rational and irrational self-destruction—with the obvious implication that there are rational suicides. But Professor Pepper reserves his strongest argument for an exhortium away from organized creed and dogma and for individual flexibility and an openness to revise one's philosophy in tune with contemporary changes and current trends.

# 1. Dead to the World: The Passions of Herman Melville

Henry A. Murray

This being the very first of the planned series of scientific lectures under these auspices,[1] you have every reason to expect positive reinforcement of your locomotions to this place by hearing some authoritative intellectual news about suicide or its prevention. And so I start with fear and trembling lest the confidence you surely have in the judgment of the president of the Suicide Prevention Foundation be somewhat shaken by your encountering on this platform a nonauthority with a far-fetched title and subtitle, neither of which have any apparent relevance to the substance of your shared interests. For this, Dr. Shneidman is initially to blame, since it was he who, at an unenlightened moment a year and a half ago, invited me to address you on this occasion. I would attribute the invitation to his preternatural trust in the potentialities of his friends, which very occasionally inclines him to an act of folly—coupled with my inability to say No with a bang, or even with a whimper, when it comes to a request from him.

Fearing that you, being entirely unaware of its creative consequences, might focus on Dr. Shneidman's act of folly and hold it up against him, I have been prompted to preface this lecture with a very short true story, a kind of informative and inspiring parable, which will prove to you that your confidence in Dr. Shneidman's wisdom should be higher, rather than lower, than it has been. The moral of the parable can be expressed in a variety of ways. La Rochefoucauld's maxim that "a man who lives without folly is not so wise as he thinks" is pertinent but a little off-center. Closer to the gist of the matter would be: worthy of admiration is the man who can transmute the lead of folly into the gold of unexampled wisdom. You may choose your own wording after you have heard the story which begins more than a year ago at the moment that it dawned on Dr. Shneidman that for the opening lecture of this series he was saddled with a speaker whose scientific knowledge of suicide was confined to the writings of the staff of the Suicide Prevention Center. He saw the absurdity of my crossing the continent to bring honey to the very beehive from which it was extracted, and he saw me as entangled in a double bind from which I could neither withdraw with honor nor emerge with credit; and I even suspect that compassion, a professional compassion, was aroused in him by viewing me as a potential suicide, that is, as heading toward a suicide of whatever reputation I may laboriously have gained for talking out of knowledge more than out of ignorance. Faced by this predicament what do you think my dear old friend decided he should do? What would you have done? Nothing, I would wager, so unprecedented and so uniquely creative as *his* solution of the problem, which was to sit down and write, especially for my benefit, a substantial and exciting paper entitled "Orientations Toward Death,"[2] which consisted of two major parts, in each of which I was presented with an open route out of my dilemma.

In the first part Dr. Shneidman expanded the whole realm of the Foundation's concern by including a variety of phenomena whose relation or similarity to suicide or to a suicidal tendency had heretofore been overlooked, and, by so doing virtually permitted me to follow suit and choose as a topic certain other states, also analogous in some respects to suicide, which I am subsuming under my main title "Dead to the World." And then Dr. Shneidman, as if doubtful of my readiness to seize the suggestions he had proffered, wrote a terminal part to his paper which he called "An Example of an Equivocal Death." In this essay he invaded a region in which I had proprietary rights and provided the missing keystone to the arch which I had started a dozen years ago in the name of an old satanic friend of mine, the immortal Captain Ahab. Here he was saying in effect: "You see I am showing you, in case you can think of nothing else to talk about, that Herman Melville would be an acceptable topic to your patrons in Los Angeles." This explains my subtitle. In short, the timely publication of Dr. Shneidman's paper in two parts provided me with a frame reference for a lecture to be delivered here; and if you are not impressed by the creative intelligence and generosity involved in this resourceful act of his, you are not deserving of so great a president. So much for my preamble, a parable that may be more instructive than anything to come.

In the paper I have mentioned, "Orientations Toward Death," Dr. Shneidman stressed the importance of distinguishing between the wish for a permanent cessation of conscious life (a veritable suicide) and a wish for temporary cessation (or interruption) of conscious life. He pointed out that some people who have killed themselves and some who appear to have intended but failed to kill themselves did not actually commit suicide or attempt suicide, because in neither case did they deliberately intend an absolute termination of their lives. Their intention was no more than an urgently felt necessity to stop unbearable anguish, that is, to obtain relief by interrupting for awhile the stream of suffering. In view of the existence of this motivational state, Dr. Shneidman suggested that attention to other forms of interruption, such as sleep, might provide "fresh leads and new insights into suicidal behavior." Aha! I said to myself at this point, if sleep would be a suitable topic for a talk at the Suicide Prevention Center, or SPC for short, why not some other related condition, such as a temporary or permanent cessation of a part of psychic life—the cessation of affect (feeling almost dead), for example—or the cessation of an orientation of conscious life—the cessation of social life (dead to the outer world) or of spiritual life (dead to the inner world), for example—or, instead of restricting oneself to two concepts—cessation (to stand for no life at all) and continuation (to stand for ongoing living processes)—it might be well to take account of different degrees and of changes of degrees of life—near-cessation (as good as dead) or a trend toward cessation (diminution).

When I chose the phrase "dead to the world," I was thinking of a variety of somewhat similar psychic states characterized by a marked diminution or near-cessation of affect involving both hemispheres of concern, the inner and the outer world. Here it is as if the person's primal springs of vitality had dried up, as if he were empty or hollow at the very core of his being. There is a striking absence of anything but the most perfunctory and superficial social interactions; output as well as intake is at a minimum. The person is a nonconductor. To him the human species is wholly uninviting and unlovable, a monotonous round of unnecessary duplicates; and since everything he sees and every alternative opportunity for action seems equally valueless and meaningless, he has no basis for any choice. In fact, to make even a small decision and to execute it calls for an exhausting effort. Sometimes, he unresistingly and automatically falls in with somebody else's decision; but he is more likely to respond to suggestions with a blanket No, keeping his thoughts hidden from others behind a deaf-and-dumb reserve, the impenetrable wall of a self-made prison.

I was thinking particularly of Melville's forty-year withdrawal from his society—the "Great Refusal" as Weaver called it[3]—and of a patient of mine who resembled Melville in this respect but whose cessation of affect was more total, suffering as he was from what we used to call the "feeling of unreality." His sensations and perceptions of nature and of people he encountered were unusually acute and vivid, but he did not experience other persons as animate beings: they resembled puppets, automatons, mechanical contrivances without any feelings or desires to which anyone could appeal. He saw eyes that were as bright as the glass eyes of a manufactured doll, but he received no intimations of a soul, or consciousness, behind these eyes. Primitive people and children spontaneously animate the inanimate—see a man in the moon who follows them on their walks, as Piaget has described; but here was a man who reversed the process; he inanimated the animate. All empathy was dead in him; he was inert as a stone, unmoved by any of the events or confrontations which moved others.

Then I thought of *The Stranger*, that landmark book by Camus in which the psychic condition of a man who is untouched by his mother's death is hauntingly portrayed. This condition of affectlessness—which has been expertly analyzed by Nathan Leites[4]—was almost immediately recognized as representative for our time, representative at least of the root mood of an articulate depth-sensitive minority, the Ishmaels of today. This brought to mind scores of other modern authors of whose views of the contemporary world Melville's writings were prophetic; their obsession with darkness, death, and leanings toward self-destruction epitomized in Malraux's affirmation: man is dead. But none of these seemed quite so revealing as Meursault, the nonhero of *The Stranger*, whose outburst of antitheistic rage near the end of the story showed that a volcano of resentful passion had been simmering all along beneath that crust of emotional inertia. What had once looked like an apathetic indifference to the surrounding world, an all-pervasive ennui, could now be more dynamically understood as an alternative to murder, namely ostracism of mankind contrived by an unforgiving heart that had been turned to stone by experiencing an intolerable offense.

At this point what psychoanalyst could resist coming forth with a battery of concepts to explain it all?—say, as nothing but a perseveration of the child's global reaction to his mother at a time when she quite literally constituted the child's whole known world and its culture. In the case of Camus as well as of Melville, for example, there is evidence that a virtually deaf-and-dumb, ostracising mother generated resentment in the child which was followed by a reciprocal, retaliative withdrawal. A conventional psychoanalyst would be likely to assume, if he were confronted by a patient in whom this state of being had persisted into adulthood, that it was his office to get his patient to look homeward, and like an angel melt with ruth. Once having reconciled himself to either his mother or his father, as the case might be, the patient would more readily become reconciled to the culture in which he was imbedded and less reluctantly adjust to it. But if the culture—society and its churches—was actually inimical to the realization of the fullest potentialities of an individual's personal life, as Melville and Camus believed it to be, the question is, should a man who saw the culture as the Enemy be persuaded by the implications of a seductive professional technique to throw in his sponge and surrender to it?

I have been talking about a diminution or cessation of feeling, one component of consciousness, on the assumption that this condition is somewhat analogous to a cessation of the whole of consciousness. If the cessation of feeling is temporary it resembles sleep; if it is permanent (a virtual atrophy of emotional life) it resembles death, the condition of the brain and body after the home fires of metabolism in the cortex have gone out. In a feelingless state the home fires are still burning but without glow or warmth. The implication here is that an intensive, detailed study of affective states in connection with suicidal phenomena should be fruitful in "fresh leads and new insights." This seems too obvious to require mention. For what is suicide in most instances but an action to interrupt or put an end to intolerable affects? But do we know all we need to know about the nature of intolerable affects? Is there not more to learn about the different varieties of feelings, combinations of feelings, and temporal sequences of feelings which are conducive to suicide on the one hand or, on the other hand, make suicide unthinkable?

As one standing-stone for my proposal let me quote from William James, whose books and letters abound in all sorts of uncommon common sense. "Individuality," he affirms, "is founded in feeling; and the recesses of feeling, the darker, blinder strata of character, are the only places in the world in which we catch real fact in the making, and directly perceive how events happen and how work is actually done."[5] Not very long after the avowal of this judgment, John B. Watson's swift invasion and conquest of a good deal more than half of the terrain of American academic psychology, committed James to such an outcast state that one leading physiological psychologist announced—to the President of Harvard, of all people—that Professor James had done more harm to psychology than any man who had ever lived. But there are indications that the exile of James and of feelings as phenomena worthy of investigation was only temporary. They have recently named the Cambridge habitat of the behavioral sciences William James Hall, and throughout the country there have been an increasing number of studies of those negative affects—anxiety, anger, resentment, and guilt—whose vicissitudes and dynamics were revealed to us by Freud and his successors, Dr. Franz Alexander for one. And now, to do justice to some of the feelings and emotions omitted by psychoanalysis, we have the prospect of the completion in the near future of the intricate three-volume work by Silvan S. Tomkins, *Affect, Imagery, Consciousness.*[6] Besides, there is burgeoning in this country, as an antithetical reaction to strict behaviorism, an enthusiastic though still amorphous aggregate of phenomenological, existential, and humanistic psychologists who question the assumption that evolutionary processes fashioned human nature for the special advantage of technocratic behaviorists of this century, setting forth all its most important determinants on the surface and leaving nothing of any consequence inside. In short, a concentrated study of affects in relation to suicidal inclinations would have a sufficient array of facts and theories to start with and should break new ground, provided the investigators were prepared to make much finer distinctions than current terminology, or even the English language, permits, envisaging as an ideal, let us say, the power of an Indian (Hindu) language to differentiate, as we learn from Coomaraswamy, "three hundred and sixty kinds of the fine emotions of a lover's heart."[7]

We might start by asking what gross affects familiar to us all have been found to be associated with suicide? The results of one research will be sufficient for my present purpose. In a systematic statistical study of the case histories of neuropsychiatric male patients at Veterans Hospitals, of which 220 had committed suicide and 220 had not committed suicide, Farberow, Shneidman, and Neuringer found that the suicides were characterized by (1) more crying spells, (2) more fist fights and violent episodes, (3) more severe depressions, and (4) more periods of withdrawal and mutism. Furthermore, (5) they escaped from the hospital more often.[8]

Of these SPC categories, the fourth—withdrawal and mutism—(best exemplified, perhaps, by a schizophrenic catatonic state) is evidently the closest to the concept of "dead to the world" as defined earlier, a correspondence that gives me sufficient provisional ground for the surmise that manifest affectlessness constitutes not only a partial interruption or cessation of social life but also a condition which predisposes its victim or initiator, as the case may be, eventually to terminate his life. With this hypothesis in mind, we might be well-advised to look for whatever dynamic relationships may subsist between manifest affectlessness, or "dead to the world," and each of the other affective states that were found to be correlated with an intentioned suicide. What was the temporal sequence of these various emotional conditions and acts in each of the 220 cases? In ordinary life the order of experienced affects depends to a large extent on the unpredictable vagaries of fortune—the occurrence of events entirely outside a person's control, the kinds of situations he happens to encounter, whether because of good or bad luck he succeeds or fails in this and that endeavor, how he is treated by others, and so forth. But since a hospital environment is likely to be relatively stable and since the affects of a neuropsychiatric patient are more apt to be determined by his internal rather than by his external environment, it is possible that regularities would be found among short (micro) or longer (meso) processions of emotion in each subject, or in each type of subject, or even in the majority of subjects. A micro temporal study would be one in which expressions of emotion were recorded consecutively from moment to moment or from occasion to occasion; whereas a meso temporal study would concern itself only with the more striking changes that occur from day to day. A patient's entire stay in the hospital might be said to constitute a macro temporal unit. Since affects do not occur in vacuo but always in relation to an internal or an external confrontation (or *press*), or to a mixture of the two, an investigation of this sort would call for recordings of both aspects of each interior emotional transaction.

Now, in connection with this idea that very detailed studies be made (first in a hospital setting and then in other settings) of the sequence of affective states during free associations on certain selected or unselected topics, as given by people who are suspected of entertaining suicidal inclinations, it occurred to me that a roughly analogous study might be made of micro, meso, and macro cycles of affective transactions in the works of certain Romantic authors, authors whose credo encourages them to give vent in apt and telling words to emotions of all sorts. I need not tell you the name of my first choice among eligible authors. A comprehensive study of this sort would be a prodigious undertaking and even a condensed report of the findings would take at least an hour to read. So I decided on a crude macro survey of Melville's whole works and a few micro analyses, restricting myself to the four negative affects and the one action which the SPC had found to be correlated with suicide in neuropsychiatric subjects—crying spells, fist fights and violent episodes, depressions, withdrawal and mutism, and leaving the hospital. Out of this, of course, came a very distorted impression of the range of feelings in Melville's writings as well as in his personality, for in the early phases of his career as an author he was a veritable hive of spontaneous positive emotions—zest, mirth, affection, joy, admiration, and compassion. After about three years of exuberant authorship, however, these brighter and for him lighter states of being were invaded and submerged by a tide of negative affects, roughly of the nature of those mentioned by the SPC. Finer differentiations of the negative affects described in Melville's writings were not made, since my aim was to come out with categories which seemed to correspond to those which the SPC had found to be correlated with suicide in males.

The order of the negative (distressful, hostile, desperate, joyless) emotional states which I found most characteristic in micro, meso, and macro analyses of Melville's works is generally as follows:

1. *Pitiful forlornness, deprivation, distress, and grief* (which I am taking as the nearest equivalent of the SPC's *crying spells* and maybe of one form of the SPC's *depression*). The expressive prototype of pitiful forlornness is the cry of the child at birth, forcefully expelled from its comfortable habitation, and later, in its helpless state, when it is momentarily alone and hence deprived of what it hungers for: contact, food, and love. In one way or another it is saying: "Poor me, I am suffering and nobody I care for cares for me." Then as well as later the implication is that the world (the mother, the beloved one, whoever "counts") is indifferent, cold, and heartless or that the one who counts is absent, dead, or unattainable. Here we may be reminded of Shakespeare's "I all alone beweep my outcast state. And trouble deaf heaven with my bootless cries"; of Whitehead's "God the Void"; of Rilke's "Who, if I cried, would hear me among the angelic orders"; and of Keats's sonnet to Fannie Brawne, "I cry your mercy—pity—love! . . . in pity give me all, Withhold no atom's atom or I die." Descriptions of various degrees of this affective state are conspicuous throughout Melville's writings from the very first paragraph of his first book, *Typee,* to the last page of his posthumous *Billy Budd.*

Grief deserves a separate category; but for present purposes I am regarding it as an accentuation, deepening, and prolongation of deprivation (lack or loss) distress. It belongs to the family of depressed states which includes melancholy, that essential component of Romanticism dating from Rousseau, the "apostle of adversity," who, by way of Byron's poetry, had a lasting effect on Melville, which began in his adolescence. Melville distinguished a gradation of feelings running from pensiveness "whence comes sadness" (both of which were associated in him with more pleasantness than unpleasantness) through several degrees of melancholy and sorrow to the "far profounder gloom" of grief, or woe. Melville, who had been "rubbed, curried, and ground down to fine powder in the hopper of an evil fortune," firmly believed that "that mortal man who hath more of joy than sorrow in him, that mortal man cannot be true—not true, or undeveloped. With books the same. The truest of all men was the Man of Sorrows, and the truest of all books is Solomon's, and Ecclesiastes is the fine hammered steel of woe." Note that in this sentence Melville links Jesus, whose mission was to bring glad tidings of life after death, with the unchristian prophet-author (not Solomon as Melville assumed) of Ecclesiastes, who affirmed that belief in immortality is vain—"all is vanity." This opposition of dissonant figures, both venerated by Melville, manifests the force of his conviction that "there is a wisdom that is woe," and is made possible only by the image of Jesus, as the Man of Sorrows, hanging on the cross, the woeful worldly outcome of his unworldly wisdom. Even the atheistical "moody stricken Ahab" is described as standing before the officers of the *Pequod* "with a crucifixion in his face; in all the nameless regal overbearing dignity of some mighty woe." Generally speaking, woe is apperceived as sufficient justification for almost any form of conduct. In Ahab's case, however, we are warned that *his* woe is not the woe that is wisdom but the "woe that is madness." The woe that is madness takes us to my next category.

I have put the present category—which embraces a series of states running from a mild pitiful forlornness to a profoundly depressing sorrow—first in order, because in Melville's works sequences of expressed negative emotions most commonly start with affects of this nature. Characteristic is his description in *Redburn* of his melancholy mood when as a boy he left home for his first sea voyage. Perhaps his mother, he tells us,

> thought me an erring and wilful boy, and perhaps I was; but if I was, it had been a hard-hearted world and hard times that had made me so . . . Cold, bitter cold as December, and bleak as its blasts, seemed the world then to me; there is no misanthrope like a boy disappointed; and such was I, with the warm soul of me flogged out by adversity.

But this same class of affects, as we shall see, is also prominent at the end of Melville's major books, indeed at the end of all tragic narratives. It includes the determinants of Aristotle's pity, the pity that is excited in a spectator's heart in the last act of a dramatic tragedy, a passion that may be intensified if the defeated hero gives vent to a heart-searing expression of his anguish, such as Mark Antony's "I am dying, Egypt, dying," and Christ's "My God, why hast thou forsaken me?"

2. *Extrapunitiveness* (blaming others), *anger, hate,* and *physical aggressiveness* (which is my nearest equivalent to the SPC's *fist fights and violent episodes*). This is a category that embraces the affects, words, and acts which in Melville's writings are most likely to follow, or even accompany, the cluster of feelings just described. The prototype of this fusion would be a child at birth or a very hungry child whose cries are more suggestive of an angry protest or furious complaint than they are of piteous helplessness. The transition from the first category to this, my second category, that is, from a forlorn "poor me" reaction to a howling rage, can be nicely illustrated by the opposition of two excerpts from Melville's works. The first comes from the opening paragraph of *Typee,* the very first lines that Melville ever penned and published in book form:

Six months at sea! Yes, reader, as I live, six months out of sight of land; . . . Weeks and weeks ago our fresh provisions were all exhausted. There is not a sweet potato left; not a single yam. Those glorious bunches of bananas which once decorated our stern and quarter-deck have, alas, disappeared! and the delicious oranges which hung suspended from our tops and stays—they, too, are gone!

After going on in this vein for two more pages, Melville tells us that the course of the "land-sick ship" has at last been shaped to the Marquesas. "Hurrah! . . . the Marquesas . . . Naked houris—cannibal banquets—groves of cocoa-nuts," and so forth. Now he is like a hungry but trustful child who is rendered patient by the confident prospect of close contact with the nurturant mother in the near future—a lovely houri and a cannibal banquet. But in one second a child's mood can change from this state of being into one of fierce intolerance, as is metaphorically represented in an excerpt from *Mardi* in which the author celebrates ecstasies of grief-rage as source of the greatest creativity:

He knows himself, and all that's in him, who knows adversity. To scale great heights we must come out of lowermost depths. The way to heaven is through hell . . . Howl in sackcloth and in ashes! . . . The lines that live are turned out of a furrowed brow. Oh! there is a fierce, a cannibal delight, in the grief that shrieks to multiply itself. That grief . . . pities all the happy.

When we come to *Moby Dick,* the whole tragic conception of which was born out of a "furrowed brow," we find that the grief-rage which made its first appearance in *Mardi* (described in words that would be fitting for a hungry child momentarily howling for its absent mother) has become a consolidated, all-pervasive tragic state coupled with a dedicated, vengeful hatred that is ruling the personality of the proud, satanic Captain Ahab, for whom all evil, we are told, was:

visibly personified, and made practically assailable in Moby Dick. He piled upon the whale's white hump the sum of all the general rage and hate felt by his whole race from Adam down; and then, as if his chest had been a mortar, he burst his hot heart's shell upon it.

Here is the essence of my second category carried by Ahab to an extravagant and irrational degree. The occurrence of such an intense, all-embracing, global emotion (not appropriate, as Starbuck pointed out, to the realities of the existing circumstance) is evidence of its origin in infancy when first the mother and then the mother and the father actually constituted their son's entire world and the apparent determinants of his fate. The same can be said of Ahab's antecedent state of mind, the consuming morbid grief which bred and seemed to justify his rage.

Considering the unparalleled abundance of oral imagery throughout Melville's works, his reference to Adam in the excerpt just quoted from *Moby Dick* is consonant with the possibility that the boy-hero's first consequential trauma was that of weaning (at the age of twelve months) or its equivalent, a virtual expulsion from the paradise of his mother's embracing arms, up until then monopolized, this deprivation being dynamically related to an impatient, howling impulse to bite his mother's proffered apple-breast and eat of it with "cannibal delight." This hypothesis is supported by our knowledge that Herman had three teeth at the unusually early age of three months. What Melville described as "the half-wilful over-ruling morbidness at the bottom of his nature," I would attribute to this earliest of deprivations subsequently reinforced, time and time again, by his mother's all-too-obvious preference for his more promising older brother, her first-born child, and by her own seasons of unresponsive moody melancholy. "She hated me," Melville said in his old age. This is but a fragment of the evidence I have to offer to support the thesis that Melville was beset in his deeps by matricidal as well as parricidal inclinations and that the white whale upon which Ahab has been prompted to "burst his hot heart's shell" embodies the rejecting mother and the world she stands for, as well as the punishing father and the God *he* stands for, all of these being powerful and imperative components of the author's imprisoning conscience, or superego.

In view of the form of injury to which Ahab is reacting with such fury—the white whale's oral amputation of his leg—every good Freudian, I surmise, would identify the whale with the child's mythological images of the castrating father, generated by a terror of this punishment for incestuously possessing the beloved mother in his dreams. Since Herman Melville enjoyed and suffered from the most patent and protracted (overt as well as covert) Oedipus complex I have ever encountered in print or practice; and since his works, especially *Mardi*, are studied with castration imagery, I have no hesitation in agreeing with this orthodox formula, despite the fact that to me its ritualistic repetition in every case, however vaporous the evidence, has become almost unbearably banal. It happens that there is a remarkably close correspondence between psychoanalytic theories and the dynamic forms of Melville's imagination, almost as if Freud had had this amazing writer constantly in mind during the composition of his theoretical system. Nearly everything essential to the system is amply illustrated in Melville's life and works; and, furthermore, it is apparent that in many instances Melville was conscious or half-conscious of the import, in a psychoanalytic sense, of what he was communicating.

As roots of the explosive fury which Melville eloquently expressed in a sublimated form while composing *Moby Dick*, I have mentioned only the matricidal and parricidal dispositions of infancy, the overt actuation of which in any recognizable form was inhibited for many years, we can be certain, by the dread of losing love from a parent on whose affection the boy's security and happiness depended. There is evidence at hand which indicates that little Herman's inward development conformed in most respects to Freud's conception of the usual sequence of events: the ambivalent (loved and hated) father served as a model for the development of a personified conscience which in its early stages was as punitive as the God of Calvinism. This brings us to my third category.

3. *Intrapunitiveness, remorse, guilt, depression, bad conscience,* and *need for punishment* (my nearest equivalent to the SPC's *depression*). This refers to any kind or degree of self-punishment subsequent to the actual or imaginal execution of a forbidden act. If a child has a nightmarish dream of being pursued, attacked, overpowered, or injured by a furious creature of some sort, man or beast, this is susceptible of various interpretations. But only one of these possible interpretations is relevant to the

category I am discussing here, namely, the one which states that these assaults are guilt-bred imaginations of punishments coming at the termination of a dream, the first repressed strip of which portrayed the commitment of a forbidden act. In contrast to concealments of this nature, we are offered in the allegorical *Mardi* for the first time in Melville's writing the vivid spectacle of a crime perpetrated by the hero: the murder of a warlike old priest who was guarding a tent in which a beautiful maiden was held captive. Knowing that his father's name was Allan Melville, we prick up our ears first when the author refers to the priest as Old Aaron and then again when he tells us that his actual name is Aleema. The hero justifies his killing and his escaping with the maiden in his arms by saying that since Aleema was wickedly intending to sacrifice her to the gods, his own act was the virtuous one of "rescuing a captive from thrall." But then, suspecting his real motive, he is smitten with remorse, and for the rest of his journey among the islands of Mardi, he is pursued by the avenging furies in the persons of three sons of the old priest (Melville's three brothers?). I would suppose that this oedipal fantasy was derived from an early season of childhood near the onset of a period of tormenting conflict between an extraggressive instinct (category 2) and an intraggressive father figure (category 3). Evidently, this civil war within the boy's psyche was at least partially resolved by a change in the apperception and evaluation of the internalized father figure: God the enemy became God the friend. We gather that at seven years of age Herman was his devoted father's most "beloved son," a boy with "a docile and amiable disposition" who soon decided to follow in his parent's footsteps and become a merchant. We are told in the autobiographical *Pierre* that after his father's death when he was twelve, the author-hero was sustained in the conduct of his adolescent life by an exalted image of his departed sire enshrined in his soul's innermost retreat. "Not to God had Pierre ever gone in his heart, unless by ascending the steps of that shrine, and so making it the vestibule of his abstractest religion."

Here we have a striking example of the loving deification of a once partly hated father figure. In this instance it was chiefly as the immaculate exemplification of chastity and purity, a figure "without blemish, unclouded, snow-white, and serene," that the father of the author-hero of *Pierre* was raised to the status of a Christian saint. Here the important point is that by this conversion of feeling, the once ambivalent father figure became wholly univalent; and the conflict between instinct and conscience was brought to an end, because from then on, it would not be the boy's fear of punishment that would dictate his renunciation of instinct ("conscience doth make cowards of us all") so much as his ambitious resolution to be as perfect as his father. The dependence of the eighteen-year-old Pierre Glendinning (and of his creator, I am sure) on an unsullied image of his parent is sufficient explanation of the tumult Pierre experiences when he learns of the existence of an illegitimate sister, a premarital by-blow of his supposedly chaste father. Thus suddenly bereft of an exemplar to support the edifice of his character and give meaning to his life, Pierre feels that he has been deserted, struck down in a flowering season of his youth by father, Fate, and God, and his first reaction is one of utter desolation (category 1). And then Melville, announcing that a vigorous young man is "not made to succumb to the villain Woe," has his hero rise from the chair in which he has been sitting alone in his room, and murmur to the unhearing All:

Myself am left, at least, With myself I front thee! Unhand me all fears . . . Fate, I have a choice quarrel with thee, thou art a palterer and a cheat; thou hast lured me on through gay gardens to a gulf . . . I will be a raver, and none shall stay me! I will lift my hand in fury, for am I not struck? I will be bitter in my breath, for is not this cup of gall? . . . all piety leave me;—I will be impious, for piety hath juggled me, and taught me to revere, where I should spurn. . . . (category 2)

To understand the magnitude of this reaction we need, once again, Freud's concept of "the return of repressed," in this case, the first explosive return in actual life of the long-submerged hatred whose genesis and history in Melville I have already briefly traced in connection with its second (more sublimated) return fourteen years later while writing *Moby Dick*. But, in addition to all this, it is important to recognize that the collapse of young Melville's unifying, personified ideal resulted in a disastrous regression to that state of obsessional conflict (categories 2 and 3) from which he had previously emerged and from which he would never extricate himself completely. Thenceforth his self would be divided as Captain Ahab's body was divided by the livid scar which ran down his skin from the top of his head. That Melville attributed the genesis of this condition to the just-mentioned stunning disillusionment of worship described in *Pierre*, and that his potent father, Fate, and God were furiously blamed for inflicting it on him is indicated in the chapter entitled "The Candles," where the hero Ahab, addressing the tripointed trinity of flames in a tone reminiscent of the hero Pierre, exclaims:

Oh! thou clear spirit of clear fire, whom on these seas I as Persian once did worship, till in the sacramental act so burned by thee, that to this hour I bear the scar; I now know thee, thou clear spirit, and I now know that thy right worship is defiance . . . No fearless fool now fronts thee . . . Come in thy lowest form of love, and I will kneel and kiss thee; but at thy highest, come as mere supernal power; and though thou launchest navies of full-freighted worlds, there's that in here that still remains indifferent. Oh, thou clear spirit, of thy fire thou madest me, and like a child of fire, I breathe it back to thee . . . But thou art but my fiery father; my sweet mother, I know not. Oh, cruel! what has thou done with her? (category 2)

So far I seem to have presented a superfluity of utterances illustrative of the return of Melville's long-repressed rage and extraggression (category 2) and a paucity of examples of the intraggressive superego forces that for years succeeded in repressing them (category 3). This disproportion of space devoted to the two warring sides of our author's divided self has been dictated by the fact that up to this point in Melville's writings the extraverted forces have been vociferous and eloquent and the intraverted forces relatively silent; and this being the case, demonstrations of the potency of what was previously repressed provide us with the best available measure of the strength of the united body of punishing repressors, symbolized by the unconquerable white whale. Later on in *Pierre* there are numerous avowals of the anguish of guilt, and it becomes apparent that Ahab's moody melancholy had been a depressing combination of grief (category 1) and a bad conscience (category 3). But in *Moby Dick* and earlier, perhaps our best indication of the power of the compound of intraggressive forces in Melville's personality is the fact that all the really critical extraggressive intentions of his heroes are, as Shneidman made plain in Ahab's case,[9] patently suicidal or sacrificial. In other words, the idea of being killed is invariably linked with that of killing from the very outset, as when Melville says in *White Jacket* that: "The privilege, inborn and inalienable, that every man has, of dying himself, and inflicting death upon another, was not given to us without a purpose. These are the last resources of an insulted and unendurable existence."

Characteristic transitions from one category to another are succinctly condensed in the famous opening paragraph of *Moby Dick*. (*a*) Categories 1 and 2 (deprivation distress leading to grief-rage): "Call me Ishmael" ("whose splintered heart and maddened hand," Melville tells us, "were turned against the wolfish world"). (*b*) Category 3 (guilt, depression, need for punishment): "Whenever I find myself growing grim about the mouth; whenever it is a damp, drizzly November in my soul; whenever I find myself involuntarily pausing before coffin warehouses, and bringing up the rear of every funeral I meet." (*c*) Category 2 (anger, extraggression): "and especially whenever my hypos get such an upper hand of me, that it requires a strong moral principle to prevent me from deliberately stepping into the street, and methodically knocking people's hats off." (*d*) Category 4 (egression): "then, I account it high time to get to sea as soon as I can. This is my substitute for [category 3] pistol and ball. With a philosophical flourish Cato throws himself upon his sword; I [category 4] quietly take to the ship."

4. *Egression* and *desertion* (my nearest equivalent to the SPC's *leaving the hospital*). Physically considered, locomotion has two aspects: going some place and leaving some place. Although one of these two (attraction or repulsion) is ordinarily decisive and foremost in the consciousness of the locomotor, there may be times when the trend of his conduct becomes ambiguous even to himself, as when Ishmael was suddenly confounded by the impression that the *Pequod* was "not so much bound to any haven ahead as rushing from all havens astern." It is this second aspect of locomotion that I am stressing here and labeling "egression," which may be defined for present purposes as a person's intended departure from a region of distress, chiefly with the aim of terminating with relief the pain he has been suffering therein. In the last excerpt quoted from *Moby Dick*, Melville gives us to infer that the distressing condition which in 1840 he, as Ishmael, hoped to terminate by going on a long whaling journey was that of an obsessional conflict between a diffuse homicidal rage and a suicidal depression (categories 2 and 3). That in Melville the simpler state of deprivation distress (category 1), engendered by maternal indifference, was sufficient to instigate egression is exhibited in a juvenile effusion written in 1839, just prior to his first departure from home for a short voyage to Liverpool and back. In this story (with a distinctly Oriental flavor) the hero, after finally gaining access to the inner chamber of a resplendent, melancholy, queenly beauty, sinks on one knee and, bowing his head, exclaims: "Here do I prostrate myself, thou sweet Divinity, and kneel at the shrine of thy peerless charm." Receiving no response, he covers her passive hand with burning kisses and asks whether his passion is requited:

> Speak! Tell me, thou cruel! Does thy heart send forth vital fluid like my own? Am I loved,—even wildly, madly as I love?" She was silent; gracious God! What horrible apprehension crossed my soul?—Frantic with the thought, I held her from me, and looking in her face, I met the same impassioned gaze; her lips moved—my senses ached with the intensity with which I listened,—all was still,—they uttered no sound;

I flung her from me, even though she clung to my vesture, and with a wild cry of agony I burst from the apartment!—She was dumb! Great God, she was dumb! Dumb and Deaf!

This is the way the story ends: deprivation distress, "agony" (category 1), with a touch of anger, "I flung her from me" (category 2), followed by a precipitous egression, "I burst from the apartment" (category 4). Two weeks after the publication of this fantasy in a local gazette, Herman left his widowed mother with whom he had been living in Lansingburgh, New York, and set forth in a troubled state of mind on the voyage dramatized in *Redburn*. His description of the behavior of the "sweet Divinity" is consonant with what I have said earlier about Mrs. Melville's inferable, customary attitude toward her adoring second son; and his hero's agonized reaction to it reminds one of Freud's statement that some people, especially narcissistic schizophrenics, hunger for such volumes of love that neutrality or indifference (deafness and dumbness) in another person is interpreted as hate, and hate is hated.

I have defined "egression," in the most general terms, as an intended departure from a region of distress, but more pertinent to our present topic is the genus of egressions that is marked by the outcrossing of the established boundary of a territorial, social, and/or cultural domain within which a person is conventionally expected or legally required to abide and play a role; and, therefore, by an egression of this import, the egressor runs the risk, maybe of pursuit and capture, maybe of punishment, maybe of social ostracism or at least of somebody's disapproval, and maybe, with or without one of these outcomes, a guilty conscience (in which case we have the states of category 3 following the action of category 4). The prototype of all these is "running away from home" in childhood.

Before he got himself married and tied down at the age of twenty-eight, Melville had a record of about seventeen egressions—from schools, jobs, home, country, and ships—but, as far as we know, veritable guilt was associated with none of them except, to a slight extent, with his desertion of the *Acushnet*, as described in *Typee*, and with his first temporary desertion of his home and mother, as described in *Redburn*, and, then, to a much greater extent, with his second, more absolute desertion of his home and mother when he left for New York in 1840 and later for the South Seas, a desertion for which he was severely criticized by at least one member of his family. Like many intended suicidal acts which involve the desertion of the perpetrator's closest, bonded persons, egressive desertions call for moral justifications or excuses of some sort, and these—as given, for example, in Melville's works—are no doubt susceptible to classification in terms of the species of logic that Dr. Shneidman has defined[10] and so should constitute suitable material for the exercise of his special talent in performing analyses of this type.

Melville's mode of thought, as he fictionally revealed it, is to have his hero become extrapunitive before he acts—to have him see the victim of his intended egressive (category 4) or aggressive (category 2) course of conduct as, in some respect, malevolent: The captain of the *Acushnet* is a tyrant who fails to provide enough good fodder for his crew; Aleema, the priest, is planning to sacrifice an innocent maiden he is holding in captivity; the mother is deaf and dumb to her son's affectionate entreaties; the white whale was prompted by malice when he devoured Ahab's leg (omitting the fact that Ahab was the original aggressor); Pierre's father is branded as an unpardonable sinner because of a single amorous affair four years before his marriage; and Pierre's haughty mother is said to be exiling him from his home ground to wander in a heartless world like an Ishmael without a maternal Hagar to console him (isolating the plain fact that Pierre has voluntarily expelled himself by an unexplained action which, so far as she could see, was both mad and cruel). By thus incriminating his opponent at the outset, the hero's urgent drive to action is not only made morally excusable but is rushed through the barrier of conscience on a wave of moral indignation. Not till after the deed is done does the other side of self come up with all the morbidly depressing dispositions of category 3. And then in *Pierre*, after this second, guilty phase has nearly run its course, Melville returns to the affectional state from which he started as a child—the desolation and piteous forlorness of category 1. Near the end of the novel, he speaks of the soul of the man who has radically egressed from home and faith as being born from the "world-husk," yet still craving for the sustenance it once enjoyed within the husk, "the support of its mother the world and its father the Deity." And then he tells us that the hardest and most grievous hour in the life of such a man comes, if it comes at all, when both the maternal world and the paternal God reject him and despise him. "Divinity and humanity then are equally willing that he should starve in the street for all that either will do for him." Here Melville is virtually saying to his mother and her world and to his father and his God: "Thou shouldst love and honor thy son with all thy heart and with all thy mind; but instead thou hast cruelly disowned him." In reply, the four targets of his indictment might have said in unison: "Out of your all-consuming, selfish narcissism you demanded the impossible, a complete monopoly of love and honor, *all* or *nothing*; and when you realized that you were not fated to have *all*, you choose *nothing* as next best, and made certain that you would end with *nothing* by madly disowning and detesting us." Granting the validity of this interpretation, we can see that egression not only may be, as it is in many cases, an expedient substitute for total suicide (insofar as it results in a surcease of pain), but ultimately, in some rare cases, may constitute a wilful, partial suicide by taking the egressor beyond the tolerance of his fellowmen and of his own conscience, or, in other words, to the point where he is as good as dead in the affections of the world and of the "personified impersonal," and *they* are as good as dead in *his* affections.

5. *Affectlessness* (one variety of "dead to the world," my nearest equivalent to the SPC's *withdrawal and mutism*). This is a latecomer in Melville. Not till after *Moby Dick* do we get unmistakable premonitory signs of its approach, especially in *Pierre* where several profound experiences leading to affectlessness are perspicaciously and movingly communicated. By cutting the world dead and living entirely within his own mind, a person may become emotionally dissociated from all the established values that regulate social interactions.

> In those Hyperborean regions, to which enthusiastic Truth, and Earnestness, and Independence, will invariably lead a mind fitted by nature for profound and fearless thought, all objects are seen in a dubious, uncertain and refracting light. Viewed through that rarefied atmosphere the most immemorially admitted maxims of men begin to slide and fluctuate, and finally become inverted . . . But the example of many minds forever lost, like undiscoverable Arctic explorers, amid these treacherous regions, warns us entirely away from them; and we learn that it is not for man to follow the trail of truth too far, since by so doing he entirely loses the directing compass of his mind; for arrived at the Pole, to whose barrenness only it points, there, the needle indifferently respects all points of the horizon alike.

This passage could be taken as an anticipation of the state of mind underlying today's widespread philosophy (if you will) of absurdity: everything is meaningless and purposeless, and hence there are no standards whatever in terms of which one can distinguish the better from the worse; maybe what was once better is really worse, and what was worse is really better, like Saint Genet. Another anticipation is the image of the hollowness of modern man bereft of passion, faith, and aspiration. Melville's hero, Pierre, has been exploring his unconscious:

> Ten million things were as yet uncovered to Pierre. The old mummy lies buried in cloth on cloth; it takes time to unwrap this Egyptian

King . . . By vast pains we mine into the pyramid; by horrible gropings we come to the central room; with joy we espy the sarcophagus; but we lift the lid—and no body is there!—appallingly vacant as vast is the soul of a man!

Melville accounts for this state, in some measure, by saying that Pierre had been giving himself up, "a doorless and shutterless house for the four loosened winds of heaven to howl through," or, in psychological terms, he had been submitting to a flood of intoxicating passions and stirring archetypal images upsurging from the id, a succession of hot explosions which had ultimately left him cold and hollow as a "burnt-out crater," as if he had had in view from start to finish the passage in Revelation (3:16) which announces: "So then because thou art lukewarm, and neither cold nor hot, I will spew thee out of my mouth." Melville's image of a "burnt-out crater" could hardly be improved upon as a symbol of affectlessness, or dead to both worlds, a pathetic state which he touchingly set forth, as viewed from the outside, in "Bartleby, the Scrivener," a long short story composed in 1853, a year after the reception of a host of blockheaded and malicious feedbacks to the publication of his *Pierre*.

Since the concept of "dead to the world" has already been briefly expounded in this paper, and since, in another context,[11] I have communicated all that I have to say about "Bartleby," at this point I shall merely report, for the benefit of those who have not read it, that in this novella Melville presents us with an unforgettable portrayal of the near immobility and speechlessness of a forlorn young man whose spirit has been reduced to that last tenable position of individuality and pride, at which the embattled self insists on nothing but its inalienable right to say "No" to the whole world, or, in Bartleby's case, a mild "I would prefer not to." The attorney asks his clerk:

> "Will you tell me, Bartleby, where you were born?"
> "I would prefer not to."
> "Will you tell me *anything* about yourself?"
> "I would prefer not to."

And so it goes until the very end when Bartleby dies with his reticence unconquered and his privacy intact. The prototype of this condition of the soul is the morose, unresponsive apathy of a child, often an institutionalized child, who has been traumatically separated from his mother at a critical age, or of a child who has been severely deprived of maternal concern at home and on entering the hospital is given the diagnosis of FTT (failure to thrive) and the prescription of TLC (tender loving care) to be administered by the nurses. Still closer to the state depicted by Melville is that of schizophrenic catatonia coupled with the defiant No of the negativistic boy of about eighteen months. There is pride in it which seems to be saying to the mother with vengeful punitiveness: "Since you have been persistently, insultingly, and unforgivably deaf and dumb to my entreaties, I shall from now on be deaf and dumb to you in kind and may you suffer as I have!" In the specific case of the non-hero Bartleby, the conclusion is inescapable that both his passive social death (his refusal to engage in human reciprocities) and his passive total death (his final refusal to take nourishment) were intentional and wilful, and, as it happens, it is only from this period of his life that we have an indubitable record of suicidal inclinations invading the stream of consciousness of Bartleby's creator.

The thread of fateful continuity that runs through the whole procession of negative states and emotions which we have been surveying is Melville's craving for the responsive, undivided, utter love of somebody whom he loves with his whole heart. Since this vision of affectional mutuality—the golden haven on the attainment of which his felicity depends—was never actualized for long enough to unify his being (because of internal and external impediments), what I have had to exhibit to you in this paper consists of hardly anything but a variety of reactions to the frustration of this craving in different situations, dating from childhood when love was fixated on his mother: piteous forlornness, desolation, grief-rage, fantasies of suicidal homicide, suicidal depression, egression as a substitute for suicide, egression as an intentional social suicide, and eventually, after several cycles of these grievous dispositions, a burnt-out crater, dead inside as well as outside. Not relevant to my topic were countless expressions of happier states—delectable humor, admiration or compassion for certain characters, celebrations of many shapes of beauty—which alternated with the doleful affects I have mentioned; and then—in this case not irrelevant to my topic but not mentioned in the SPC report—there was another state which succeeded the affectlessness portrayed in "Bartleby," and that was what I have called *disgust, bitterness, sardonic humor*, the temper of which the *Confidence Man* was wrought.

And now in ending, let me present to the members of the SPC for the exercise of their interpretive powers the following sequence of psychic states. The essence of Melville's outlook in *Mardi* (1849) can be credibly represented, I would say, in these words: "If I fail to reach my golden haven, may my annihilation be complete; all or nothing!" Two years later in *Moby Dick*: "I foresee my annihilation, but against this verdict of Fate I shall hurl my everlasting protest." In *Pierre* (1852): "I am on the verge of annihilation but I can't make up my mind to it." In 1856, to Hawthorne in Liverpool: "I have pretty much made up my mind to be annihilated;" and in *Billy Budd* (1891): "I accept my annihilation." Did this last station of Melville's pilgrimage constitute a victory of the spirit, as some think? an ultimate reconciliation with God at the end of a lifelong quarrel? or was it a graceful acquiescence to the established morality and conventions of his world with Christian forgiveness toward those who had crushed him in their name? or a forthright *willing* of obligatory? or was it an acknowledgement of defeat? a last-ditch surrender of his long quest for a new gospel of joy in this life? or was it a welcoming of death?

> My towers at last! These rovings end,
> Their thirst is slaked in larger dearth:
> The yearning infinite recoils,
> For terrible is earth.

## REFERENCES


1. This paper, in slightly modified form, was originally delivered by Dr. Murray at Bovard Auditorium, University of Southern California, October 6, 1963, as a Special Lecture sponsored jointly by the University and by the Suicide Prevention Center. On that occasion, Dr. Murray was introduced by his old friend, the late Dr. Franz Alexander. [Editor's note]
2. E. S. Shneidman, "Orientations Toward Death: A Vital Aspect of the Study of Lives," in R. W. White (ed.), *The Study of Lives* (New York: Atherton Press, 1963).
3. R. M. Weaver, *Herman Melville, Mariner and Mystic* (New York: George H. Doran Company, 1921).
4. "Trends in Affectlessness," in C. Kluckhohn, H. A. Murray, and D. M. Schneider (eds.), *Personality in Nature, Society, and Culture* (New York: Alfred A. Knopf, Inc., 1953).
5. *The Varieties of Religious Experience* (New York: Longmans, Green & Co., Inc., 1902), p. 501.
6. New York: Springer Publishing Co., 1963.
7. A. K. Coomaraswamy, *The Dance of Shiva* (rev. ed.; New York: Noonday Press, Inc., 1957).
8. N. L. Farberow, E. S. Shneidman, and C. Neuringer, "The Socio-Psychological Matrix of Suicide," unpublished report (Los Angeles: Central Research Unit, Veterans Administration Center, 1962).
9. Shneidman, *op. cit.*

10. E. S. Shneidman, "Psycho-Logic: A Personality Approach to Patterns of Thinking," in J. Kagan and G. Lessor (eds.), *Contemporary Issues in Thematic Apperceptive Methods* (Springfield, Ill.: Charles C. Thomas, Publisher, 1961).
11. H. A. Murray, "Bartleby and I," *Kent State Melville Papers* (Kent, Ohio: Kent State University Press, 1965).

# 2. Shakespeare's Suicides: Some Historic, Dramatic and Psychological Reflections

M. D. Faber

Karl Menninger once remarked that "a monistic interpretation of human motivation is inadequate to explain the observed facts." Shakespeare would have agreed—from the very beginning. For although the young Shakespeare, poet-playwright of *Venus and Adonis* and the *Comedy of Errors,* had not yet thoroughly polished the mirror he was to hold up to nature, he was sufficiently in touch with reality to create human beings who were not artificially driven, who were not, as Menninger put it, "monistically motivated." True, a number of his seedtime characters fail to meet our present specifications or fail to satisfy our aesthetic and psychological palates, but, and this is the point, his suicides are not among these. For all her brine and glibness Lucrece is ultimately believable, and for all their stylized lines Romeo and Juliet strike home. Why?

If recent investigations of suicidal individuals have taught us anything they have taught us this: In only a very small number of instances does death appear to be the sole or even the chief aim of the agent-victim. In the words of one authority:

> Most of us, when we think about suicide, think about the . . . goal in the behavior and automatically assume that this is death. Closer scrutiny reveals, however, that this purpose is probably present in only a small proportion of the total number of persons who engage in suicidal behavior.[1]

But if death is not the aim, or at least the *unique* aim, of those who harm themselves, what is? A few preliminary remarks may help to point the way and, at the same time, still the agitations of the curious. Speaking for the staff of the Suicide Prevention Center at Los Angeles, Edwin Shneidman has remarked: "We believe that most suicidal behavior involves a gamble with death . . . dependence on the role of the 'significant other' . . . and it is acutely ambivalent."[2] That is to say, such behavior ordinarily constitutes a method, albeit extreme, of coping with reality, or what the victim takes reality to be. Thus it can be, and paradoxically most often is, life-oriented as well as death-oriented, the outcome of an emotional-intellectual impasse at which energy is simultaneously invested, once again paradoxically, in both this world and in its absence. The key concept then, the concept which will underlie this survey as a whole, is "ambivalence." With that concept in mind we may turn to the beliefs of another age, an age in which some arresting, unforgettable plays were written.

The best way to get at Renaissance attitudes toward suicide is to clear away certain misconceptions, misconceptions so deeply ingrained in the minds of Western man as to have assumed the rank of historical commonplaces. The first of them runs as follows: In Shakespeare's day Christians regarded suicide as a damnable sin against the laws of God and His church, and since the vast majority of Englishmen were Christians, suicide was generally regarded as a sin. The second of them, which is slightly more lethal than the first because it is slightly more accurate, has this to say: Although suicide was considered a damnable sin in Shakespeare's day, the famous self-murderers of antiquity were sometimes admired and even openly praised on the grounds that they flourished during a pre-Christian era which could not be expected to reflect the laws of God and His church. The third and last misconception says simply that the revival of classical learning that took place during the fifteenth and sixteenth centuries undermined the age-old prohibitions of the Church and allowed suicide to be "reborn." Those who express this view often make it appear as though Shakespeare's contemporaries considered themselves to have been duped for about a thousand years and were therefore resolved to make up for lost time. As was suggested, all of these opinions are erroneous; they are wrong because the scholarship behind them is either incomplete or inaccurate. A more thorough investigation of Renaissance attitudes toward suicide will bring us to some very different conclusions, conclusions which should help us to focus more sharply upon both Shakespeare's tragic craft and our own persuasions.

If we are to get off to a right start we would do well to listen closely to the following remarks made by a Renaissance preacher who was popular while Shakespeare was at the height of his career. "There be two sorts of voluntarie deathes," says the Reverend Mr. Tuke, "the one lawful and honest, such as the death of Martyrs, the other dishonest and unlawful, when men have neyther lawfull calling, nor honest endes, as of Peregrinus, who burnt himselfe in a pile of wood, thinking thereby to live forever in mens remembrance."[3] What Tuke is telling us here, and his words point up the irreparable flaws in all the views just described, is that the act of suicide is not *per se* a sin, but only when the motivation behind it is sinful. Thus we cannot generalize; we cannot speak of suicide with a capital S and expect to achieve accuracy. We must break the issue down into what might for convenience' sake be called its motivational contexts and then proceed, as cautiously as possible, from there.

Tuke continues to point the way; for when he says "there be two sorts of voluntarie deathes" he touches upon an essential truth which might be worded thus: Suicide has never been greeted with indifference; invariably it stimulates responses which are, depending on what provoked or appeared to provoke the deed, either sympathetic or unsympathetic, favorable or unfavorable, positive or negative, or any two opposing words you choose. Why do I say, "appeared to provoke"? Because, to put it bluntly, we no longer "believe" in suicide in quite the same way that Shakespeare's contemporaries believed in it. When an honorable Elizabethan, for example, declared his preference of death to dishonor and proceeded to destroy himself in the face of a predicament which was sure to compromise his honor, his contemporaries were apt to regard his suicide as the product of his devotion to honor. Today, however, such a suicide would probably call forth responses composed not of words like "honor" or "reputation" but of words like "ego" or "self-concept" or "rigidity." From the psychoanalytic point of view, tragic heroes may still fool themselves but they may no longer fool audiences as easily as they once did. Obviously there is loss as well as gain in this. But I am anticipating. My chief concern here is to indicate briefly the motivational contexts in which self-murder was apt to call forth positive responses from Tudor Englishmen and the contexts in which it was apt to call forth just the opposite.

The motivational context of martyrdom has already been touched upon and little more need be said of it;[4] for everywhere in the literature of the day one finds this kind of suicide wept over, lauded, and vigorously recommended: "Martyrs in all ages are much to be admired, and that being indued with true fortitude, did most willingly embrace their deaths," wrote Henry Crosse in 1603,[5] and the fiery Cleland four years later exhorted his fellow Englishmen "to dye a thousand times," rather than renounce even one tenet of the faith.[6] Nor was Cleland less insistent with regard to patriotic suicide.

From one standpoint, Renaissance England was Tudor England and the Tudors made a great to-do about loyalty to one's prince and one's country. In this they were at one with ruling families everywhere and at all times: indeed, even during the much misunderstood Middle Ages, a period in which ecclesiastical loyalties ostensibly predominated, to destroy oneself for the welfare of the realm was urged by kings and clerics alike.[7] Renaissance attitudes may be summarized in the following passage from Elyot's influential patchwork *The Governour* (1531). Referring to an ancient Greek monarch who destroyed himself in an effort to preserve his people, Sir Thomas exclaims, "O nobel Codrus, howe worthy had you ben (if god had bene pleased) to have aboden the reparation of mankynde, that, in the habite and religion of a Christen prince, ye moughte have showed your wonderfull benevalence and courage, for the saulfegarde of Christen men, and to the noble example of other princes."[8] Thus, in the early sixteenth century we have a Christian humanist enthusiastically presenting a pagan self-murder to his countrymen and urging them to follow suit if and when the occasion should arise. One could cite a dozen passages similar in spirit and content.

At this point the reader has probably surmised that the religiously or patriotically motivated suicide might be labeled what Durkheim called "altruistic suicide." The fact is that altruistic self-murder was universally admired in Shakespeare's England. Whether one destroyed himself for the sake of his friend,[9] his master,[10] his spouse,[11] his nation, or his faith, he was sure to be extolled. In the words of Arthur Golding, words which may be said to summarize Renaissance feeling in this matter, to embrace "certaine death" for a "good cause" is to be "esteemed hardie, valeant, and manly-minded."[12] Golding's attitude is not so very different from our own; certainly the general public is apt today to find something of value in altruistic suicide and to express its respect and admiration on this score. Regarding the suicide of love, however, one cannot say precisely the same thing.

Were I to kill myself this evening with amorous expressions on my lips I doubt very much whether the coroner or the police officer in charge would find anything to admire in my end. Probably it would be regarded as the unfortunate result of neurotic dependency needs, or the ego's inability to bear thwarting, or an excessively masochistic personality. In Shakespeare's day, however, such a death would have been regarded as exclusively unfortunate only by some; a great many others would have found in it evidence of loyalty, of devotion, of fathomless sincerity; for in former times the act of suicide was a traditional exit for the bereaved or unsuccessful lover, a literary convention with a pedigree extending back to the inception of the popular romance, and something that, on the stage at least, was calculated to beget not only tears but respect as well. Take, for example, the following scene from John Webster's *The Devil's Law Case.* (ca. 1617). Standing over the bodies of two young gentlemen who have just displayed their eagerness to bleed for her love, Jolenta, the emulative heroine, remarks: "Well, these are perfect lovers." And when she is asked why they are perfect lovers, she replies: "It has ever been my opinion, / That there are none love perfectly indeed, / But those that hang or drown themselves for love."[13] In Jolenta's opinion we have the essence of an attitude that had long since become a force in Western literature. I am not, of course, suggesting that any Renaissance youth who destroyed himself upon losing his beloved or on being repulsed by her would have been admired, and nothing but admired, by everyone. Certainly particular lovers begot particular responses, some of which were far more sympathetic than others. What I am suggesting is that it was possible in Shakespeare's day for love suicide to stimulate a current of positive emotion in the breasts of the theatergoing public. Such currents were apt to be engendered by the suicide of honor as well.

Every age has its clichés. "Haste makes waste," "better late than never," and "too many cooks spoil the broth" are, it seems, some of ours. Of the sixteenth century's favorite phrases, many of which correspond in spirit and in substance to those just cited, one of them lays claim to our special interest, and that one is "death before dishonor." Everywhere in the literature of the day the investigator comes upon this maxim in one form or another. Grimaldus' influential *Counsellor,* for example, maintains that any individual who aspires to the title of gentleman "maketh choise rather to die, then dishonour his life with reproch"[14]; and Lodowick Bryskett in his *Discourse of Civill Life* asserts that "it is the part of a stout heart, for a man to kill himselfe rather then to suffer shame or servitude."[15] Explicit and convincing as these citations are, it should be made clear that honor suicide was not entirely free of ecclesiastical censorship; it is possible to find in Tudor printed matter outspoken disapproval of such an exit from life. But it is also possible to find Elizabethans openly defying "devines" who would tarnish the memory of famous honor suicides with the stigma of ungodliness.[16] The point is that honor suicide, like love suicide, religious suicide, or patriotic suicide, was capable of evoking positive responses from Shakespeare's contemporaries. And the same may be said for the suicide of chastity, which will be dealt with more fully when we come to *The Rape of Lucrece.*

Was there, then, any suicide which was apt to beget the disapproval and the outrage, as well as the shock, of sixteenth-century Englishmen? Certainly. Suicide prompted by despair, a sense of sinfulness, or a lack of hope invariably sparked negative reactions. Such suicides implied a distrust in God's mercy or an unwillingness to atone correctly for previous misdeeds and were considered unutterably and even unpardonably sinful. The trouble is that students of the period tend to extrapolate general conclusions from remarks directed exclusively toward this kind of self-murder. In the words of Dublin, "The motives behind suicide are as varied as the number of people who solve their problems in this way."[17] We must be careful to avoid talking about Renaissance attitudes toward suicide as if the deed were motivated only by despair. What is the point of all this historical material? Simply that Shakespeare's contemporaries were able to respond positively as well as negatively to suicidal spectacles.

Shakespeare exploited this ability; like Aristotle, who spoke, as everyone knows, of pity and fear, Shakespeare took the tragic moment, which on many occasions was the suicidal moment, to be conflictual or ambivalent. He was not willing to round out his efforts with an entirely negative or depressing spectacle, to leave the audience only horrified at the close of the play, as a purely despair-filled self-murder might leave them. Nor was he willing to conclude on a purely positive note, for Shakespeare did not believe that a tragic close lay in either of these formulas. Rather, it lay in a spectacle which was at once positive and negative, one which simultaneously horrified and elevated, which forced the onlooker to thrill and sympathize and blossom out on the one hand and to shudder and gape and draw back on the other. I am not implying that Shakespeare followed Aristotle consciously; he probably never read the *Poetics*. What I am implying is that Aristotle got at the essence of tragic conclusions and that Shakespeare got at it too. There is only one essence.

At this point we are in a good position to get on with the business of the psychology of Shakespeare's suicides: We know something about modern views, which might be called scientific; something about Elizabethan views, which might be called moralistic; and something about the essence of Shakespeare's tragic craft. Only two further points need to be made. The first has been implicit in all that we have said thus far and can be stated explicitly this way: Because suicide inevitably gives expression to what prompts it, because it is the culmination and radical embodiment of particular emotions, because it is, in short, the anagram of motivation, it becomes, from the literary angle, a metaphor. If patriotism stands behind it then it speaks, on the stage, for patriotism; if despair stands behind it then it is fated to speak for despair, and so on for whichever catalyst happens to be at work.

The second point has to do with ambivalence and concerns the following problem: If Shakespeare's contemporaries were prone to think of suicide monistically, to regard this one as prompted by honor and that one by despair, as they obviously were, then would they not have been in a poor position to appreciate Shakespeare's suicidal conclusions, which depend for their effectiveness on the presence of ambivalent emotions? But it is precisely *because* they were prone to think about suicide monistically that Shakespeare's contemporaries were apt to react strongly to suicide at the Globe. In other words, they were prepared to marvel at the truth of Shakespeare's depictions and to recognize deep within themselves the inadequacy of their own persuasions. They were ready to have their eyes opened, and Shakespeare was the man to open them.

A favorite subject of European artists throughout the fifteenth and sixteenth centuries was the suicide of Lucrece: time and again drawings and paintings depicted this Roman gentlewoman falling upon a sword or thrusting a sizeable dagger into her breast. And in 1540 when Englishmen went in search of a busy publisher by the name of Thomas Berthelet, they were sure to find him in his Fleet Street printing shop, which had above its door a large sign of Lucrece making an end of herself in the manner just described. Elizabethan printer Thomas Purfoote announced that his wares were to be purchased "in Paules Churcheyarde, at the signe of Lucrece," and even inserted miniatures of that woman's gory demise into the books he handled. Why all the enthusiasm for this ancient self-murderess? Because for Medieval and Renaissance Europeans her voluntary end gave succinct and dramatic expression to deep-rooted feelings about the preciousness of chastity. "The Church it selfe is resembled to a woman without spot or blemish,"[18] cried Greene in 1587 and Count Lewis of *Courtier* fame maintained, "in women honestie once stained doth never returne againe to the former estate."[19] But Elizabethans were only following an ancient tradition here. Christianity had for centuries beaten the drum for chastity, going so far as to canonize a couple of women who preferred to kill themselves rather than be defiled by lustful and disrespectful men. Even Augustine, that great enemy of voluntary death, could not withhold his sympathy on this score.[20] Thus the suicide of Lucrece, which was celebrated by ancient writers almost immediately after its occurrence, became to subsequent centuries a metaphor for chastity and inspired this kind of doggerel from an Elizabethan poet named Yates:

Lo . . . The Matron slewe her selfe,
because she would not have:
A body for her spouse unchaste,
but brought it to the grave.
Oh Virgins let this be a glasse,
to shew you honest life:
Remember how that Chastitie,
did rest in her most rife. . . .
One night Sir Morpheus did leade,
and then unto me shewed:
How Lucrece sate in heaven above
her seate was there bestowed.[21]

These lines tell us much: they tell us, for example, that heaven has room for suicides when they kill themselves for the right reasons, that a pagan self-murderess might be to Christian virgins an emulative figure, and finally, that Lucrece killed herself because "she would not have a body for her spouse unchaste." This last point brings us to the psychology of her end.

Yate's eminently simple, black-and-white explanation is a typically Renaissance one. Lucrece, after having been defiled by her house guest Sextus Tarquinius, decides to kill herself because she does not want her husband Collatinus to have a stained wife on his hands; that is all there is to it. Those who took up Shakespeare's poem did so with this in mind and could not have been very surprised at what their eyes beheld; for Shakespeare, in the main, reflects the traditional view. I say in the main because, when we examine his poem closely we find amid the largely colorless whole some fascinating glimmerings of things to come. Notice, for example, these lines that the heroine, in the midst of her decision to kill herself, addresses to her absent spouse:

"My honour I'll bequeath unto the knife
That wounds my body so dishonoured.
'Tis honour to deprive dishonour'd life;
The one will live, the other being dead:
So of shame's ashes shall my fame be bred;
  For in my death I murder shameful scorn:
  My shame so dead, mine honour is new-born.

"Dear lord of that dear jewel I have lost,
What legacy shall I bequeath to thee?
My resolution, love, shall be thy boast,
By whose example thou reveng'd mayst be.
How Tarquin must be us'd, read it in me:

Myself, thy friend, will kill myself, thy foe,
And for my sake serve thou false Tarquin so.

"This brief abridgement of my will I make:
My soul and body to the skies and ground;
My resolution, husband, do thou take;
Mine honour be the knife's that makes my wound;
My shame be his that did my fame confound;
And all my fame that lives disbursed be
To those that live and think no shame of me."[22]

It does not take a great deal of reflection here to realize the twofold or ambivalent nature of Lucrece's avowed intention. She is not interested only in dying; she is also interested in resurrecting through death the late-defiled honorable wife of Collatinus. That is to say, she is driven, in large measure, by what the suicidologist would probably call magical thinking.

When investigators juxtapose the words suicide and magic they are attempting to bring home to the reader the idea that suicide "is not pre-eminently a rational act pursued to achieve rational ends, even when it is effected by persons who appear to be eminently rational. Rather, it is a magical act, actuated to achieve irrational, delusional, illusory ends."[23] Voluntary death, they go on to say, may be regarded "not only as a surcease from pain in this world . . . but also as an act whereby one acquires powers, qualities, and advantages not possessed in the living state."[24] This kind of thinking, as Shneidman makes clear, involves an illogical split in the individual's orientation toward his own self and forces the student to distinguish between the $I_s$ which refers "to the person's own experiences, his pains and aches, and sensations and feelings," and the $I_o$ which refers to the individual "as he feels himself thought of or experienced by others."[25] Clearly, what Lucrece is planning here is get rid of her $I_s$, which she has come to regard negatively as a result of strong guilt feelings (ll. 1023 ff.) and immortalize her $I_o$, which, as she anticipates its future glories, is already affording her a measure of relief. The illogicality of all this lies, of course, in the fact that as a dead body she could not be affected by world opinion. But in her present state such a consideration has no significance for her; she is willing to destroy herself forever that the intangible being she enjoys in others' eyes might survive and flourish. "Good name in man and woman . . . is the immediate jewel of their souls," says Iago: "Who steals my purse steals trash." Lucrece discards the trash in order to preserve the jewel—her reputation in the world. And, be it noted, she does so where others can see her; for it is only when her husband arrives home, surrounded by illustrious friends, that she actually accomplishes her death: To ensure the preservation of $I_o$ the suicide must be public. In all of this—her rigid self-concept, her concern with the opinion of others, her capacity for guilt, her devotion to an ideal—Lucrece looks forward to the suicides of Shakespeare's full maturity. And most of all, she looks forward to them in that her end expresses not only a desire for death but a passionate concern for life as well. It is as if the mighty opposites Freud spied at the heart of things were vigorously at work here too, in the rhetorical apprentice piece of a budding genius.

This is not the place to enter into a discussion of Shakespeare's sources; still, with regard to an understanding of Romeo and Juliet's voluntary ends, one point must be made. In Brooks's *Romeus and Juliet,* Shakespeare's chief and perhaps sole source for the play, the lovers destroy themselves that they might reunite immediately in an afterworld which for centuries had provided a special sanctuary for youthful lovers come to tristful ends.[26] But Shakespeare will have none of this; so completely does he depart from his source material here that his lyric tragedy contains not a single hint of the reunion motif. This departure points our way; indeed, it might be regarded as the key to the understanding we are seeking, especially regarding Romeo. Let us pursue the matter further.

That love suicide is commonly provoked by the longing for "reunion in death with the lost loved one" is common knowledge. As a matter of fact, Moss and Hamilton include it in an ancillary way among what they take to be the three "coexisting unconscious or partially conscious determinants of suicide: (*a*) A promise or hope of greater future satisfaction [in] the form of a permanent reunion in death with a lost loved one, the forcing of attention or satisfaction otherwise unobtainable from the present environment, or the pleasure of spite or revenge. (*b*) Hostility or rage directed toward important persons upon whom blame [is] placed for present frustrations, which because of guilt, fear, or anxiety [becomes] self-directed. (*c*) An expression of hopelessness and frustration—a relinquishing of any prospect of gaining necessary satisfactions from the present environment. . . ."[27] When we abstract the longing for reunion from this list of determinants we are left with a causal scheme which succinctly reveals what I take to be chief catalysts in Romeo's, and to a lesser extent in Juliet's, suicide and which adumbrates what I take to be the effect Shakespeare was seeking here. For we must understand that by the play's last act Romeo has taken just about all one can be expected to take and has taken it for the most part in good or at least in sympathetic grace. An ignorant, bestial family feud has repeatedly gotten between him and his loved one; he has endured gibes, threats, insults, banishment, and, for his ardent temperament, one of the most painful frustrations imaginable; and now he is asked to endure the sudden, inexplicable death of his bride. A world that, for whatever reasons, affords its inhabitants such miserable fortunes is simply not worth abiding. "I defy you stars," cries Romeo just as he decides to die, and in that cry we have much of what is driving him; to put it somewhat more crudely, his suicide is, in large part, an obscene gesture directed toward the world and the world's authorities. There is in it the spite, the revenge, the rage, the hostility referred to earlier, and there is in it also the frustration and hopelessness mentioned by Moss and Hamilton.

It may seem paradoxical to speak of a self-murderer as one who desires not so much to die as to cease living; but if we are to come close to an understanding of Romeo and Juliet we must pursue this line of thought, for "in some cases," to quote Shneidman, "it seems that the person's intention [is] not to embrace death but rather to find surcease from external or internalized aspects of life."[28] Now in contrast to what we have been saying so far, this applies to Juliet somewhat more than it applies to Romeo, for when she awakens in the tomb of her family she does not think about defiance or the cruelty of the fates; she thinks only about getting out of a world in which Romeo no longer dwells. She is not really interested in death; she kills herself simply because she recognizes at once that suicide is the only way for a young girl to get out of the world; if it could have been accomplished by pronouncing a few magic words, then she would have pronounced them; any way at all, so long as she might succeed. As has been said, all of this applies, though in a somewhat milder way, to the poisoned young man stretched out upon the floor below her. And it is in this aspect of their self-inflicted deaths that we find a tragic paradox characteristic of suicide generally: Romeo and Juliet do not want to die so much as they do not want to live without each other.

Shakespeare's contemporaries would have called this "fidelity" and found it not entirely unattractive. There may be some today who find it so. However, what Elizabethans would have found unattractive, or even shocking, is the desperate, willful defiance in Romeo's final posture, and what there is of that in Juliet's. Thus Shakespeare's tragic ending here is in keeping with his tragic endings elsewhere. Because his protagonists are not motivated monistically, because there is something positive as well as negative in their ends, we are able to leave the performance charged with the pity and the fear spoken of so long ago by Aristotle. The same may be said for *Julius Caesar*, Shakespeare's next tragedy and one in which voluntary death again rounds out the action.

In the words of Dr. Shneidman, "Suicidal and/or dying behaviors do not exist *in vacuo,* but are an integral part of the life style of the individual."[29] When the newspapers tell us, as they sometimes do, about the man who destroyed himself because he lost a fortune on the stock exchange, or because he lost his wife, or his job, or his prestige, they are offering us a superficial explanation of the matter; for how are we to explain the man who reacts quite stoically to the loss of his money or his job or his wife? To understand an act of voluntary death we are obliged to understand the motivational dynamics behind it, for it is these which will guide us to a knowledge of the individual's "life style." Accordingly, when Cassius has his servant run him through on the plains of Philippi, it is not enough to point to the imminence of military defeat in explanation of the deed; we must know more, and, as might be expected, Shakespeare's characterization does not thwart our knowledge.

What is really bothering Cassius, bothering and even threatening him throughout the course of the play, is the realization that Caesar

> Is now become a god, and Cassius is
> A wretched creature, and must bend his body
> If Caesar carelessly but nod on him. (I.ii.116–118)

For if there is anything Cassius cannot stand, it is the notion of his own inferiority; indeed, so lofty is his self-concept and so deep-rooted his fear of disgrace that he would prefer plain, blunt death to a situation which compromised his estimation of himself and his position in the world. As Antony tells us by implication in his famous choral speech (V.v. 68–75), Cassius' plans for Caesar are hatched by "envy" not patriotism, and everything Cassius says and does throughout the course of the play substantiates this notion. To put it briefly, Cassius hacks at Julius because Julius is rising higher than Cassius; that he would also like his power goes without saying. As for students of self-murder, they would probably call Cassius a "striver," and they would probably go on to point out that this type of individual frequently turns up in psychiatric institutions where his suicidal conduct is considered to be a desperate effort to maintain his self-concept even unto death.

Nowhere is Cassius' fear of abjection brought out more vividly than in the first scene of Act III when it looks as though Popilius Lena is revealing the conspiracy to Caesar on the steps of the Senate-House. Says Cassius to those about him:

> Casca, be sudden, for we fear prevention.
> Brutus, what shall be done? If this be known,

> Cassius or Caesar never shall turn back,
> For I will slay myself. (19–22)

To which Brutus replies:

> Cassius, be constant. (22)

Thus the merest hint of failure is enough to bring the hilt to Cassius' palm. His mind is simply unable to support the consequences of "prevention." Imagine Caesar taking Cassius by the scruff of the neck and maligning him as a despicable turncoat; perhaps something of this sort flashes through his mind as he watches the mysterious Popilius advancing toward Caesar. In any case, Brutus might well advise him to be constant, for his conduct here directly presages his conduct at Philippi.

Just as Cassius misconstrues the actions of Popilius before the Senate-House in Rome, in the play's last act, he also misconstrues the actions of Titinius as reported by Pindarus. Sending the trusty Titinius to his camp in order to determine whether it contains friendly or hostile troops, Cassius calls upon Pindarus to observe his (i.e., Titinius') reception. "My sight was ever thick," he offers in the way of explanation. Now if Shakespeare sometimes wrote symbolic lines this is one of them; for Cassius' shortsightedness brings him directly to his death, just as it brought him to the murder of Caesar which triggered the events leading to his death, and just as it always kept him from seeing things as they are. Indeed, Cassius' lofty self-concept might be thought of as the product of his shortsightedness, of his inability to look beyond himself; and it is his frantic attempt to protect that self-concept which in the last analysis catalyzes his demise. For when Pindarus reports that Titinius has been seized, Cassius, again projecting his fear of abjection into events which admit of more than one interpretation, immediately assumes he has been seized by hostile hands. The opposite, of course, is true, but Cassius has already called for death. Such a death would not have pleased Shakespeare's contemporaries, who believed all the difference in the world existed between one who relinquished his life in order to regain or preserve his honor (Lucrece, for example) and one who did so to escape fearful circumstances. From the dramatic point of view, however, this is no great failing, for Brutus and not Cassius is the hero of this play.

That murderous wishes are apt to exact from the psyche the same self-punitive toll as murderous deeds has become a commonplace truth in Western psychology; it is a truth, however, which has for centuries dwelt at the heart of Western religious and ethical systems. To become a sinner one has only to think sinfully; the doing is more or less superfluous. When Brutus enters the first act of *Julius Caesar* he is already suffering from the exactions of his conscience. Why? Because he has already spent a good many hours pondering the fate of one whom he loves and admires, and because he possesses, in contrast to Cassius, a conscience which can only be characterized as rigorous, exacting, and stern. Thus our first glimpse of Marcus Brutus is a glimpse of a man who has lost his mirth, who is "vexed . . . with passions of some difference" (I.ii.39–40); who is, in short, "with himself at war" (46).

The depth of Brutus' guilt-fed melancholy is pointed up in the second act where Portia speaks of the "sick offence" (II.i.268) within her husband's mind, outlines in a few well-chosen words his strange behavior, and lovingly reproaches him for his gloomy, solitary ways. But it is not until after the murder of Caesar that Brutus settles into his most rigid posture. Refusing to admit he has done wrong, refusing to discharge his conscience through "confession," Brutus becomes increasingly "sick" (IV.iii.144) until his sickness finally culminates in sharp hallucinations. Needless to say, these take the form of Julius Caesar. In such a psychological context no one can be surprised at the ring of his final syllables:

> Caesar, now be still;
> I kill'd not thee with half so good a will. (V.v.50–51)

Brutus' last words constitute, of course, a confession of guilt; they tell us that Caesar has never been "still," that his image, his spirit, has continuously hovered in Brutus' mind, that the sore of remorse has ceaselessly rankled in his brain. But they tell us a good deal more; they tell us that Brutus was never really convinced of the justice of the conspiracy in which he took part, that he stabbed his "best lover" with doubt in his heart, that he betrayed his conscience. The ambivalence in all of this is clear. Brutus not only kills himself but kills also that part of himself which could destroy an individual who loved and trusted him; he strives through self-murder not only to destroy the Brutus who faces the shame of defeat but also to resurrect the Brutus who flourished before thoughts of murder flourished, whom chains and loud denunciations would destroy forever. Shakespeare's audience would have thrilled to the man's unwillingness to continue on in disgrace and shuddered at his refusal to repent for his past sins. *Othello* is in sight.

We have already said something about the relationship between suicide and magical thinking; however, some further clarification on this score, along with an introduction of Shneidman's notion of the post-ego,[30] which bears directly on matters of magic, will lead us to a more exact appreciation of the nature of Othello's voluntary end. According to one authority, "much of the activity of . . . suicidal persons constitutes an appeal, directed specifically to persons within their environment, with a definite aim of causing some change in the attitudes and feelings that are being expressed to them. Essentially this amounts to an appeal for a reestablishment of the former symbiotic relationship."[31] Now if Othello is anything when the play begins he is a man of justice and honor who has striven long to achieve eminence and prestige in the eyes of those around him. His reputation is his most cherished possession; whenever he opens his mouth his utterances breathe forth his high, but by no means unfounded, estimation of himself. Recent criticism has come to recognize the significance of this, and *Othello* may now be considered not so much a tragedy of jealousy as a tragedy of outraged pride; for when Desdemona "falls," Othello's reputation falls with her. This is the point Iago presses home; this is the spot he finds most vulnerable and goads with devilish subtlety. But Desdemona has not, of course, fallen, and when Othello discovers that he has killed an innocent, that he has deposited his soul into the hands of a villain, that he has harkened to the promptings of his baser nature, he realizes his honor is on the verge of being lost forever. The final indignity, however, comes when Lodovico, representing the elders of Venice, strips him of his office and makes as though to lead him off to prison. The exigent is indeed at hand.

In his last speech Othello juxtaposes for the benefit of those around him his present degeneration with his past greatness:

> Soft you; a word or two before you go.
> I have done the state some service, and they know 't.
> No more of that. I pray you, in your letters,
> When you shall these unlucky deeds relate,
> Speak of me as I am; nothing extenuate,
> Nor set down aught in malice. Then must you speak
> Of one that lov'd not wisely but too well;
> Of one not easily jealous, but being wrought,
> Perplex'd in the extreme; of one whose hand,
> Like the base Indian, threw a pearl away
> Richer than all his tribe; of one whose subdu'd eyes,
> Albeit unused to the melting mood,
> Drop tears as fast as the Arabian trees
> Their medicinal gum. Set you down this;
> And say besides, that in Aleppo once,
> Where a malignant and a turban'd Turk
> Beat a Venetian and traduc'd the state,
> I took by th' throat the circumcised dog,
> And smote him—thus. [*Stabs himself*] (V.ii.338–356)

Clearly, if we define post-ego as the "concern of the living individual with his own after-death reputation, survival, heritage, impact, image, memory, influence—those aspects of him which 'live' after his cessation,"[32] we cannot but recognize Othello's preoccupation with his own post-ego here. For he kills himself not only with the aim of destroying a monstrous villain but of reviving a noble Moor. In brief, Othello kills the Moor of Venice that the Moor of Aleppo might live on. His suicide may therefore be regarded as an "appeal, directed specifically to persons within [his] environment, with a definite aim of causing some change in the attitudes and feelings that are being expressed to [him]." Needless to say, the logic which brings him to the proposition that the self must die in order that a "better" self might flourish is the product of the severe emotional crisis through which he has just passed.

It might be emphasized that this crisis is charged with remorse as well as reputation, for I am by no means suggesting that Othello's last act is the product of his "honor" and nothing more. Undoubtedly the searing feelings of guilt which rip through him as he gazes down upon the body of his lifeless bride help to bring the dagger to his hand and to drive him to what Shakespeare's contemporaries called "Judas' repentance." What I am suggesting is that Othello's feelings of guilt operate within him by attacking his self-concept, by tearing down the internal edifice he has striven so long to erect; *that* is how his conscience works, and that is why we may say his conscience ultimately impels him to the magical act of resurrection which terminates his life. As Elizabethans saw it, there was something to admire and something to abhor in such an act. Othello's unwillingness to live on in disgrace would have impressed the majority of those who paid their penny at the entrance to the Globe, whereas his unwillingness to repent in the conventional Christian way would have shocked them to no small degree. Ambivalent suicides, motivated dualistically, spark conflictual feelings in the breasts of beholders. Is Lady Macbeth's suicide of an identical nature?

We must first of all remember that some commentators might think it presumptuous to speak of Lady Macbeth as a suicide at all. We do not actually see her kill herself and the report of her death can be taken two ways depending upon the significance one attaches to the words "as 'tis thought" in line 70 of the play's last scene. For if we take these words to mean "so goes the rumor" then we cannot with assurance speak of the woman's self-murder. If, however, we take them to mean "in accordance with the common suspicion," and there is no reason not to do that, we can.

Like Brutus and Othello before her, Lady Macbeth is a person of rigorous, exacting conscience; and one of the play's sharpest ironies is that neither she nor her husband is really cut out for murder. In the early acts, just prior to the deeds of blood in which she directly or indirectly participates, the woman calls upon certain "spirits" to "unsex" her, to "stop up th' access and passage to remorse," to still all "compunctious visitings of nature" (I.v.39 ff.)—in short, to freeze her conscience and temporarily inactivate her capacity for guilt. But her herculean effort, again ironically, only speaks for the strength of the conscience she is attempting to still; even as she goes about her chilling business (II.ii) hints of its capacity for punishment peep through (II.ii.13–15); and by the time the sleepwalking scene rolls around, the wall of repression which she had successfully reared shortly before the murder of King Duncan has come down as low as it can come. Plagued by guilt-ridden fears of discovery, by recurring hallucinations, by profound dejection, she glides unladylike into the realms of schizophrenia, the victim of a conscience as savage as any depicted to mankind by a creative artist. Her suicide, of course, constitutes the final savageness. In the words of Karl Menninger, "The power of the conscience is believed to be derived from a portion of the original aggressive instincts which, instead of being directed outward to take destructive effect upon the environment, are converted into a sort of internal judge or king. . . . It is as if that part of the destructive instinct retained within the ego had to carry on within the microcosmos of the personality an activity precisely comparable to that which the ego is directing toward the macrocosmos outside. If the individual directs an attack of a certain nature upon some person in the environment, the conscience, or super-ego, directs an attack of the same nature upon the ego. This formula is well known to us in social organization in the form of the *lex talionis*. . . ."[33] Thus Lady Macbeth, like her destructive forebears Brutus and Othello, comes in the end to destroy herself; but certainly there is not in her death the positive qualities which informed the ends of the Roman and the Moor.

As we turn to the tragedy of *Antony and Cleopatra* the wheel of self-murder comes again full circle, for the last pair of suicides Shakespeare offers to the theater are, like the first, love suicides. It would be a mistake, however, to structure our analysis on this fact alone, because the differences between the two pairs of lovers, particularly with regard to the motivation of their ends, far outweigh the similarities. For example, the notion of reunion, conspicuously absent in *Romeo and Juliet*, plays a crucial role in the later tragedy. Too, the catalyst of honor, with its obvious correspondence to our present ideas of post-ego and $I_o$, has almost nothing to do with the Italian play but a great deal to do with the Roman one. In short, whereas *Romeo and Juliet* is a love story, *Antony and Cleopatra* is both a love story and an empire story.

In this way, Antony is impelled toward self-murder by two overriding considerations. On the one hand, his armies have been utterly defeated by the forces of Caesar and he, their general, will surely be led in triumph through the streets of Rome unless he puts some sharp instrument to good use. On the other hand, his military defeat is followed almost immediately by a report of Cleopatra's death. Thus the two things that matter most to him, his reputation in the world of Rome and his pleasure in the world of Egypt, are removed irrevocably in an instant. But perhaps I should not say irrevocably, for as Antony sees it both of these items are still within his grasp and the way to get at them is self-inflicted death.

Just before he instructs his servant to destroy him Antony speaks as follows to the audience alone:

> I will o'ertake thee, Cleopatra, and
> Weep for my pardon. So it must be, for now
> All length is torture; since the torch is out,
> Lie down, and stray no farther. . . .
> I come, my Queen! (IV.xiv.44–50)

Clearly, to paraphrase Batchelor, the wish to become reunited with the loved one has overridden the will to live: suicide has become, as it so often does, "a means of gratification."[34] But this gratification is not related to the Queen of Egypt alone; for Antony, by killing himself, also permits his "former fortunes" to live on. He does not die "basely" or "cowardly" but, as he puts it, "valiantly" (IV.xv.51–59), and he tells those around him to be sure and remember that. Like Lucrece, Brutus, and Othello before him, Mark Antony cannot reconcile certain things with his self-concept and for that reason he elects to die.

The same, of course, is true of Cleopatra who, when Caesar's intention of displaying her to the shouting multitudes of Rome becomes clear, describes suicide to her servant as "the way / To fool their preparation, and to conquer / Their most absurd intents" (V.ii.224–226), and those who have perused the play with care will be quick to agree upon the absurdity of Cleopatra's absorbing any kind of disgrace whatsoever. For although her fear of death or, more accurately, the pain of death, is great, her devotion to her self-concept is even greater. As a matter of fact, there is something almost obstinately infantile about much of her behavior throughout the course of the play, something which is by no means irrelevant here and which calls to mind these words of Menninger: "There is still another way in which the life instinct finds satisfaction, paradoxically, in self-inflicted death. It depends upon that deadliest of erotic investments, narcissism. To kill oneself instead of being executed or slain by fate, is to retain for oneself the illusion of being omnipotent, since one is even by and in the act of suicide, master of life and death. Such omnipotence fantasies, for all that they have been extolled by poets and schizophrenics, are none the less to be regarded as infantile relics. They presuppose or assume the certainty of a future life, a reincarnation—so that such a suicide is not, in the conscious interpretation of the victim, a real death. The same dereistic fantasy is operative when suicide is elected to . . . demonstrate . . . devotion. . . ."[35] Now Cleopatra's final speeches, in which she explicitly refers to her "immortal longings," her "liberty," and her desire to "meet the curled Antony" who is to praise her for her noble deed, combine with her final wish to have her crown placed upon her head and her most lavish robes draped upon her shoulders to corroborate the truth of Menninger's view. The bereaved Queen of Egypt, having just preserved her internal reflection from the machinations of young Caesar, is off again, in splendid attire, to meet Mark Antony upon the river Cydnus. How could it, from her point of view, be otherwise?

The conclusion of *Antony and Cleopatra* marks a departure from Shakespeare's usual formula in that the protagonists are impelled toward self-murder by overwhelmingly positive catalysts: love and honor. The explanation for this, which I have fully developed elsewhere,[36] lies, as I see it, in the nature of the protagonists themselves. That is to say, Antony and Cleopatra, in contrast to Shakespeare's earlier tragic figures—Brutus and Othello, for example—are so lacking in positive qualities throughout the course of the action that the playwright was simply unwilling to inject a negative note into their final scenes. In a word, he saw that his most effective conclusion would lie in bringing essentially negative characters to essentially positive ends and evoking thereby a sudden and shocking sense of waste or bereavement from the members of his audience. To borrow a phrase of Farnham's, Shakespeare's conception of tragic conclusions changed somewhat here because he was at the outer limits of his "tragic frontier."[37] This does not mean, of course, that his *psychological* depiction of suicide marks a departure. On the contrary, a little reflection will surely uncover the ambivalence in both Antony's and Cleopatra's self-inflicted deaths. The departure I am referring to is thus a purely dramatic one effected for the kind of purely dramatic reasons which are rooted firmly in the Renaissance ethical milieu.

A word should now be said about *Hamlet* and *King Lear*, for no discussion of this kind would be complete without some mentioning of these plays. The first thing to be noticed is that they focus not so much upon people who afflict and destroy as upon those who are afflicted and destroyed. That is to say, whereas Brutus, Othello, and the terrible Macbeths unleash their destructive urges onto the innocent and come in the end to turn these urges onto themselves, exemplifying in the process the tendency of the conscience to reward aggression with self-recrimination, Hamlet and Gloucester feel the cuts of the aggression of others and, as a result, come perilously close to renouncing the world. Take, for example, Hamlet's famous first and fourth soliloquies.

In these speeches the Prince of Denmark reveals his attraction to self-murder. Precisely why does he desire death? Much, perhaps too much, has been written on this score since Freud placed his memorable footnote in the pages of his essay on melancholia. In his view, and the views of his many followers (Jones, for example, in *Hamlet and Oedipus*), Hamlet is suffering from a distortion of the Oedipus complex. He unconsciously loves his mother and this love blocks expression of anger toward her for marrying his uncle. His desire to destroy himself is, in reality, the inwardly directed expression of his inabilities to express anger and to wreak vengeance upon the forbidden object toward whom he feels intense but repressed love, namely Gertrude. In a word, Hamlet cannot "get up" his feelings toward his mother for having hastily united with his uncle and is therefore on the verge of committing, to use Shneidman's phrase, "murder in the one hundred and eightieth degree."

Let us look briefly at this view of Hamlet's death. Hamlet's melancholia is the product of profound disillusion, the result of his unwillingness to accept the fallen world. Hamlet, it may be said, is a man who is much discontented at having his feet in the muck of Denmark and his head among the stars. He is a man who is quite willing to accept the world as it "should be" or "ought to be" but certainly not as it is. Such things as adultery, homicide, hypocrisy, drunkenness, usurpation, and even death, things which swirl with vigor and reality about him, are not at all to his liking. In this way, Hamlet's one great task is not of revenge but acceptance. Indeed, until he accepts the fallen world and himself as a part of it, he will be unable to accomplish his own destiny. To put it another way, Hamlet is so busy learning how to endure that he has no time for revenge. This is not the place, of course, to chart the progress of his transformation and his short-lived spiritual victory; one need only say that by the time the final scenes are upon us, the discomfited youngster of the first and fourth soliloquies has learned to look death and corruption in the eye, has learned to keep what ought to be from blotting out what is, has learned to spy a providence in a tiny sparrow's fall, has learned, in short, to die, and for that reason can, in the full sense of the word, *live* just long enough to right his father's wrongs.

The struggle at the heart of *Hamlet*—the struggle of acceptance and endurance—is also to be found at the heart of *King Lear*. Indeed, from this perspective, the later play may be regarded as a spiritual extension and intensification of the earlier one. However, the man who wants to get out of life in *Lear*, the Duke of Gloucester, suffers not only great spiritual distress, as does Hamlet, he suffers great physical distress as well. By the time he makes his suicide attempt he has undergone just about all a man can be expected to undergo and there is nothing very complicated about his psychological state. In the words of Shneidman, "The choice of suicide over an existence in which the life pattern has been totally disrupted, the body image attacked, the self-concept severely strained, and all familiar interpersonal relationships practically destroyed seems, on the face of it, understandable."[38] Certainly it seems so to Gloucester—whose pessimistic leanings come out early in the play—as he stumbles over the heath toward the Dover cliffs. But the issue is, of course, whether or not there is anything—any thought, any consideration, any code or system of conduct—that should restrain a man from destroying himself even when to do so seems, on the face of it, understandable. In the seventh scene of the fourth act of *Lear*, Edgar resolves this issue in a way that calls to mind the sternness, even the starkness, of the Old Testament, particularly the Book of Job. The precise nature of that resolution is not our business here, but it might be said in passing that in his most personal and passionate work Shakespeare seems unable to reconcile himself to the idea of self-murder as a convenient escape from earthly ills. Men, no matter how miserable their lot, must endure; and it is only through endurance that the riches of the spirit may be won.

Thus far we have been talking of suicide in a more or less conventional manner, for by it we have meant any willful or voluntary relinquishing of life, any openly self-destructive gesture or situation for which the agent-victim can be held ultimately responsible. In a word, we have been talking about suicide as men have always talked about it—in antiquity, in the Renaissance, and in the current age. What I would like to emphasize here, however, is that such talk is no longer sufficiently inclusive; indeed, it does not even begin to describe the variety of human behavior that should be characterized as essentially suicidal in nature. Briefly, we can no longer, from the psychological point of view, regard the alcoholic, the dope addict, or the ascetic, as qualitatively distinct from the man who flings himself in front of a train or puts a bullet through his head. In *all* of these cases self-destruction is at work, in *all* of them the individual is undermining his existence, shortening it, repudiating it, abusing it in one way or another. Not every suicide takes place in a moment, or a day, or even a month; as a matter of fact, where ambivalence is particularly strong and a relatively stable tension maintained between self-destructive and self-preservative forces a suicide may be enacted gradually over a period of years. Think, for example, of the man who slowly drinks himself to death or of the man who becomes involved in a never-ending stream of "accidents" until one accident finally finishes him for good. No; our awareness of unconscious determinants and of the variety of guises they may assume forbids us from continuing to think of suicidal behavior as exclusively and obviously "intentioned."

In his valuable "Orientations Toward Death"[39] Shneidman attempts, among other things, to achieve a more meaningful classification of self-destructive conduct and arrives at the following conclusions. Such conduct is either "intentioned," as in the case of Romeo who knows quite well what he is about; "contra-intentioned," as in the case of Richard III who seems perfectly willing to kill himself at the behest of Lady Anne but is actually only posturing (*R.III*, I.ii); and "subintentioned," as in the case of Desdemona who is driven by unconscious motivations not to commit suicide but to "permit suicide," to employ again an expression of Shneidman. I would like to round this chapter out with a brief analysis of her "case."

We have already said a few words about martyrdom, but some further clarification would be wise, I think, at this point. According to Menninger:

> . . . the components of the self-destructive urge in . . . martyrdom are . . . identical with those which we found to determine actual suicide: the self-punitive, the aggressive, and the erotic. Evidently, however, these are in different proportions. For that death is postponed is evidence of some greater degree of neutralization by the erotic element, a neutralization which would seem to vary greatly in different instances. The precise nature of the interplay between these vectors can be studied in a few examples, insufficient in number to permit of generalizations beyond those already implied: in chronic suicide [which may be taken here to mean subintentional suicide, although the two concepts are not precisely equivalent] the erotic elements are stronger, the destructive elements relatively weaker, than in direct and immediate suicide.[40]

The "objective observer," concludes Menniger, cannot but come to recognize martyrdom as "explicit self-destruction."[41] Others would refer to it as a "passive kind of suicide" in which cultural sanctions play a significant role.[42] But regardless of the nomenclature employed, the predilection for martyrdom must be regarded as ultimately suicidal.

Now, as we have seen, Shakespeare's contemporaries, although lacking in psychoanalytical knowledge, were inclined to regard martyrdom thus—to call once again upon the Reverend Mr. Tuke:

It may be demanded, whether the death of Christ and of the holy Martyrs may be called voluntarie, seeing they died at the command and by the execution of others. I answere, their death was voluntarily but not with wicked willfullnesse sustained of them. For Christ could have saved himselfe, when hee suffered himself to be apprehended, condemned, and executed . . . so the martyrs would willingly embrace the fire, rather than dishonour God by cowardize, and loose their soules by Apostacie.[43]

Thus martyrs, in spite of the voluntary nature of their ends, were sure to experience "triumph in heaven"[44] during the sixteenth century; the touch of martyrdom which is, as we shall see, so visible in Desdemona's character would have made her particularly precious to Elizabethans.

We must remember here that the ideal Renaissance wife was willing to embrace self-destruction for her husband's sake; that she was willing to carry her loyalty to the furthest possible extreme; that she was willing, in short, to become Love's martyr. Alcestis, the classical matron who voluntarily perished in an effort to preserve her husband's life,[45] mirrored the aspirations of the age. Again and again Tudor printed matter referred Elizabethan ladies to her deed, exhorting them to duplicate it if the need should arise. "I shall hope to have a wife . . . who with Alcest will bee content to lose her life to preserve her [husband],"[46] wrote Pettie in 1576, and countless writers would have agreed with him,[47] for within this psychological context voluntary death constituted a shining accomplishment, a precedent for all good wives to follow. Thus, to achieve perfection in Shakespeare's days a woman had to have a touch of the martyr within her. Desdemona is a reflection of this standard. She is unutterably precious because her desire for life is relative rather than absolute.

But we should also be careful to note here that the urge toward martyrdom admits of various degrees of intensity. At the one extreme, the individual "actually causes himself to be the victim of cruelty at the hands of circumstances or another person."[48] At the other extreme, he merely submits to what would ordinarily be regarded as unpleasant or even intolerable, manifesting in the process a "devotion to [his] convictions" which is "greater than [his] loyalty to reality."[49] Now the latter extreme most vividly describes this side of Desdemona's personality. To maintain that she "actually causes her own destruction" is to make chaos out of the play: Iago's continual presence diminishes Othello's responsibility quite enough. No; Desdemona's "convictions" regarding Othello's character simply usurp her "loyalty to reality." In other words, her loyalty to her husband is absolute.

Desdemona's very first words point up her fidelity to the Moor. "Here's my husband" (I.iii.185), she informs her father, and her willingness to follow that husband across wide seas and through tempests is soon made clear. Not until Act III, however, does she explicitly reveal her great capacity for self-sacrifice: We are aware of her loyalty throughout the play; we become aware of her sacrificial tendencies only upon the verge of the crisis. Promising to aid him in his suit, Desdemona tells Cassio:

> My lord shall never rest; . . .
> I'll intermingle everything he does
> With Cassio's suit. Therefore be merry, Cassio;
> For thy solicitor shall rather die
> Than give thy cause away. (III.iii.22–28)

And indeed her constant harping upon Cassio's suit, as well as her cry: "Alas! he is betrayed and I undone" (V.vii.76), contributes significantly to the tide of passion that eventually sweeps her away. These lines, it may be said, foreshadow, or anticipate, the usurping urge for martyrdom which comes to govern Desdemona's behavior. Her interest in Cassio's welfare is sufficiently strong to stir a mild self-destructive feeling within her. To blossom fully, the self-sacrificial side of her nature needs only the catalyst of conjugal devotion.

Desdemona believes her "noble Moor" to be ". . . true of mind and made of no such baseness / As jealous creatures are . . ." (III.iv.27–28). Nothing will persuade her to relinquish or even modify this belief. She endures a torrent of harsh, unwarranted epithets (IV.ii), a cruel, insulting slap (IV.ii), a violent, murderous attack upon her person (V.ii), and still she refers to the Moor as "my kind lord" (V.ii.125). Hard upon Othello's distracted ranting over "The handkerchief," Emilia quite naturally demands: "Is not this man jealous?" (III.iv.99). For a moment Desdemona is befuddled and admits: "I ne'er saw this before" (III.iv.100). A moment later, however, she absolves him from such a charge and even chastises herself for doubting his noble nature.

> Beshrew me much, Emilia,
> I was, unhandsome warrior as I am,
> Arraigning his unkindness with my soul;

But now I find I had suborn'd the witness,
And he's indicted falsely. (III.iv.150–154)

Struck upon the mouth in front of the Venetian delegation, Desdemona speaks her thoughts aloud. "I have not deserv'd this" (IV.i.251), she says, and, martyrlike, leaves the stage with sad eyes and bowed head. When Othello, nearly mad, weeps in her presence she immediately takes the blame upon herself. "Am I the motive of these tears . . .?" (IV.ii.43), she asks. Having been branded the "cunning whore of Venice" by her husband, Desdemona says in brief soliloquy:

'Tis meet I should be us'd so, very meet.
How have I been behav'd, that he might stick
The small'st opinion on my least misuse? (IV.ii.107–109)

Very revealing lines; they indicate just how thoroughly Desdemona has come to realize the unjustness of Othello's behavior. Yet, she remains perfectly faithful in spite of that realization. Indeed, she is concerned only with recapturing Othello's goodwill (IV.ii.149). Regardless of consequences she will continue to love him. Even the threat of death lacks the power to alter her loyalty. In her own words:

Unkindness may do much;
And his unkindness may defeat my life,
But never taint my love. (IV.ii.159–161)

The possibility of a martyrdom has by this time become quite distinct, for Desdemona's words reveal a willingness to die rather than retract the slightest measure of devotion. Othello's unkindness cannot even "taint" her love, let alone quench it. There is in her instructions to Emilia a dismal note of fatalism:

Prithee, tonight
Lay on my bed my wedding sheets, remember. (IV.ii.104–106)

When Othello commands her:

Get you to bed on th' instant. . . . Dismiss your
attendant there. Look't be done,

Desdemona dutifully replies: "I will, my lord" (IV.iii.8–10). Can it be she has an inkling of his intentions? Emilia is quite startled to learn of Othello's injunction. "Dismiss me!" she cries in disbelief. And in spite of the fact that something foreboding floats through that cry, Desdemona fails to regard it. Othello must by no means be displeased. If to avert death means displeasing him, then death must not be averted. When Emilia announces that the wedding sheets have been placed upon the bed, Desdemona remarks:

> All's one. Good faith, how foolish are our minds!
> If I do die before thee, prithee, shroud me
> In one of these same sheets. (IV.iii.23–25)

Yes, Desdemona does have an inkling of Othello's intentions, but she continues to obey him nonetheless. Her self-destructive tendencies have simply usurped her volition; she will continue to love the man, continue to believe in him, in spite of all. She says to Emilia:

> My love doth so approve him,
> That even his stubbornness, his checks, his frowns,—
> . . . have grace and favour in them. (IV.iii.19–21)

Clearly, her loyalty to Othello—to that which, in her mind, he represents—has become greater than her loyalty to reality.

At this point, Desdemona manifests a quality often found in the martyr's personality: self-pity. On the verge of "weeping" (IV.iii.59), she sings the sad song of Barbary which tells of a loyal, much abused young lady and of a man lacking gentleness and faith. "Good-night, good-night" (IV.iii.105), she says to Emilia as the scene draws to a close. It will be her last night and she knows it.

Confronted with the reality of death Desdemona cowers. This is perfectly understandable. Her self-destructive urges have not taken the most extreme form; she has not actually brought about her own demise. The thoroughly fanatical martyr can look toward the blaze or heaven with bliss in his heart. The less-than-fanatical martyr might very well tremble in the face of the heat or the roaring. No doubt a good many have done so. When death stalks into Desdemona's bedroom it does not sport a particularly pleasant countenance. It is large and dark; its eyes roll; it seems somehow entranced; it gnaws its nether lip. Desdemona is afraid and pleads for her life. "Have . . . mercy . . .!" (V.ii.58), she cries, but mercy, it seems, is too much to ask. Her last words are her most revealing.

When Emilia inquires: "O, who hath done this deed?" (V.ii.123), Desdemona, on the verge of expiring, replies:

> Nobody; I myself. Farewell!
> Commend me to my kind lord. (V.ii.125–126)

Desdemona's desire for martyrdom is here confirmed by her own death wish. She claims to have killed herself and by that claim explicitly reveals the self-destructive tendencies in her personality. Then too, she carries her self-sacrificing loyalty to the furthest possible extreme by taking upon herself the burden of Othello's guilt. If departing from the world as a self-homicide can benefit her husband, then she will depart from the world as a self-homicide. Desdemona maintains her unquestioning loyalty down to her final breath. Although her "kind lord" has murdered her, she will continue to serve him in whatever way she can. Othello in his blindness cannot, of course, grasp this, and one of the play's most painful moments is when he rewards her Christ-like generosity with the appellation "liar" (V.ii.129).

Desdemona's behavior today would no doubt be regarded as psychologically unsound. The following quotation may be taken, I suppose, as a representative example of what a clinician might say about it: "It is important to realize how passive, paralyzed, indifferent, submissive and suicidal people can become under circumstances which demand the utmost activity if self-preservation is to be accomplished. Like the bird standing stock-still as the snake approaches, man may surrender passively to what he dreads. The suicidal riddance-reaction liberates him from the tension of anticipation."[50] Those opposed to psychological analyses would probably be prone to look upon her as contemptibly weak or stupid. Few, in any case, would regard her as strong or consider her behavior exemplary. But then, nearly four centuries have intervened between Shakespeare's day and our own. To a Renaissance audience, Desdemona's self-destructive urges would have expressed the depth of her loyalty and devotion. As a wife she would have been considered no less than a treasure. Undoubtedly many would have spied in her conduct the divine self-sacrifice of the holy martyrs, perhaps of Christ himself. In others her behavior would have called to mind the loyalty of Alcestis or various other classical suicides whose conjugal devotion knew no mortal bounds. In everyone her attitude, her words, and her bearing would have aroused deep sympathy and admiration. Thus Desdemona's suicidal tendencies set the seal upon her infinite worth. She dies, like all martyrs, having decided upon the "preservation of the ideal" at all costs.[51]

As a final word, I would like to say that I have advertently avoided working up one all-inclusive definition of suicide and then applying it wholesale to Shakespeare's characters, because such a definition might not only force distortions but might dissatisfy, from a purely theoretical point of view, many of those interested in self-destruction. For the plain fact is that we do not yet have all the answers; we are still in what might be called the formative stage, faced with innumerable stones which will eventually have to be turned, and we are groping through the formidable miasma of our own projections. In short, the why of suicide is vastly different for different investigators. We do know that suicide is ordinarily engendered by ambivalent states of feeling, that it expresses dramatically the creative and destructive tendencies which seem to inform the human psyche, and that it is the product of forces which have been long at work within the individual. The rest is silence.

## REFERENCES


1. Norman L. Farberow, "Suicide: The Gamble With Death," unpublished paper presented to the Los Angeles County Psychological Association, May, 1962, pp. 1–2.
2. "Suicide," in *Taboo Topics*, Norman L. Farberow (ed.) (New York, 1963), p. 39.
3. *A Discourse of Death* (London, 1613), p. 21.
4. The final section of this chapter will treat the subject of martyrdom somewhat more fully.
5. *Vertues Common-wealth* (London, 1603), Eiii$^{r-v}$.
6. James Cleland, *The Institution of a Young Noble Man* (London, 1607), p. 132.
7. Henry Fedden, *Suicide* (London, 1938), p. 162.
8. Ernest Rhys (ed.) (New York, 1907), p. 153.
9. See Ludowick Lloyd, *The Pilgrimage of Princes* (London, 1573), p. 177; George Whetstone, *An Heptameron of Civill Discourses* (London, 1582), Xiv$^{r}$; Matteo Bandello, *Certaine Tragicall Discourses* (1567), Robert L. Douglas (ed.) (London, 1898), I, p. 55; Pierre La Primaudaye, *The French Academie* (London, 1594), II, p. 138.
10. See Francis Bacon, "On Death," in *Essays and New Atlantis* (New York, 1942), p. 8; *The Warres of Cyrus* (London, 1594), Ciii$^{v}$; John Norden, *The Mirror of Honor* (London, 1597), p. 41.
11. See Lloyd, p. 199; George Pettie, "Admetus and Alceste," in *A Petite Pallace of Pettie His Pleasures* (1576), Herbert Hartman (ed.) (Oxford, 1938), p. 143.
12. *Politicke, Moral, and Martial Discourses* (London, 1595), p. 74.
13. In Alexander Dyce (ed.), *Works* (London, 1830), II, p. 46.
14. Laurentius Grimaldus, *The Counsellor* (London, 1598), Mvi$^{r}$.
15. London, 1606, p. 183.
16. George Whetstone, *The Honorable Reputation of a Souldier* (London, 1585), Cii$^{v}$.
17. Louis Dublin and Bessie Bunzel, *To Be Or Not To Be* (New York, 1933), p. 4.
18. Robert Greene, *Penelope's Web* (London, 1587), Eiv$^{r}$.
19. Baldassare Castiglione, "The Courier" (1561) in Burton Milligan (ed.), *Three Renaissance Classics* (New York, 1953), p. 274.
20. *The City of God*, Bk. I, chap. 17.
21. James Yates, *The Chariot of Chastitie* (London, 1582), Jiii$^{r-v}$.

22. "The Rape of Lucrece" in W. A. Neilson and C. J. Hill (eds.), *The Complete Plays and Poems* (Cambridge, Mass., 1942), p. 1361, ll. 1184–1204. Hereinafter references to Shakespeare works will be to this edition.
23. Charles W. Wahl, "Suicide as a Magical Act," in Edwin S. Shneidman and Norman L. Farberow (eds.) *Clues to Suicide* (New York, 1957), p. 23.
24. *Ibid.*, p. 27.
25. Edwin S. Shneidman, "Suicide, Sleep, and Death: Some Possible Interrelations among Cessation, Interruption and Continuation Phenomena," *Journal of Consulting Psychology*, XXVIII (April, 1964), 102–103.
26. Paul Siegel, "Christianity and the Religion of Love in 'Romeo and Juliet,'" *Shakespeare Quarterly*, XII (Autumn, 1961), 371–392.
27. Leonard M. Moss and Donald F. Hamilton, "Psychotherapy of the Suicidal Patient," in *Clues to Suicide*, E. S. Shneidman and N. L. Farberow, (eds.) (New York, 1957), p. 100.
28. Edwin S. Shneidman, "Orientations Toward Death," in Robert W. White, (ed.) *The Study of Lives*, (New York, 1963), p. 211.
29. *Ibid.*, p. 206.
30. "Suicide, Sleep, and Death," *op. cit.*, p. 103.
31. Norman L. Farberow, "Suicide: The Gamble With Death," unpublished paper.
32. Shneidman, "Suicide, Sleep, and Death," *op. cit.*, p. 103.
33. *Man Against Himself* (New York, 1938), pp. 52–53.
34. I. R. C. Batchelor, "Suicide in Old Age," in *Clues to Suicide*, p. 147.
35. *Op. cit.*, pp. 70–71.
36. See my *Suicide in Shakespeare*, unpublished doctoral dissertation, University of California, Los Angeles, 1964, chap. 10.
37. Willard Farnham, *Shakespeare's Tragic Frontier* (Berkeley and Los Angeles, 1950).
38. "Suicide," pp. 35–36.
39. Edwin S. Shneidman, "Orientations Toward Death," *op. cit.*, p. 211.
40. *Op. cit.*, p. 142.
41. *Ibid.*, p. 143.
42. See Norman L. Farberow and Edwin S. Shneidman (eds.), *Cry for Help* (New York, 1961), p. 302.
43. *Op. cit.*, p. 20.
44. William Vaughan, *The Golden Grove* (London, 1600), Fvii[r].
45. See Euripides' play *Alcestis*.
46. *Op. cit.*, p. 146.
47. See, for example, Lloyd, *op. cit.* p. 199; Charles Gibbon, *The Praise of a Good Name* (London, 1594), p. 9.
48. Menninger, *op. cit.*, p. 83.
49. *Ibid.*, p. 91.
50. Joost A. M. Meerloo, *Suicide and Mass Suicide* (New York, 1962), p. 46.
51. Portions of this section first appeared in *Literature and Psychology* (Fall, 1964).

# 3. Death as a Motive of Philosophic Thought

Jacques Choron

It is one of the peculiarities of the contemporary philosophical scene that philosophers, with the exception of the few existentialists, completely ignore the subject of death.

It is the purpose of the present essay to elucidate, as far as possible, the reasons for this state of philosophic affairs and to show that the disregard of death is not necessarily the last word in philosophic wisdom. Perhaps such an inquiry will also help to remind those interested in the various problems arising in connection with the fact of death of the wealth of insights and ideas about death available in the writings of some philosophers of the past and the present.

The issue of whether or not death is a "legitimate" theme for philosophic reflection is perhaps best approached by examining a proposition that is more than simply the opposite of the one that ignores death, for it boldly asserts that death is the real motive of philosophic thought. The reference is, of course, to Arthur Schopenhauer's thesis set forth in the second volume of his *The World as Will and Idea*.[1] Schopenhauer writes:

> Death is the true inspiring genius, or muse of philosophy. . . . Indeed, without death men would scarcely philosophize. The brute lives without the proper knowledge of death. In the case of man the terrifying certainty of death necessarily entered with reason. But as everywhere in nature with every evil a means of cure, or at least some compensation is given, the same reflection which introduces the knowledge of death also assists us to metaphysical points of view, which comfort us concerning it. . . .

All religious and philosophical systems are principally devoted to this end, and are thus primarily the antidote to the certainty of death. . . .

In order to decide whether and to what extent Schopenhauer's assertion may be true, it is necessary first to establish in what sense one can speak of death as "the inspiring genius" of philosophy, and then, if possible, to find a criterion that would allow us to determine unequivocally that in that sense "death" is indeed the muse, or at least one of the muses, of a given philosophy.

However, before turning to these questions, we shall consider briefly man's "discovery" of death. Schopenhauer's view of this discovery is too simple. Actually, "the terrifying certainty of death" was the result of a long process that, as far as it can be reconstructed, consisted of two stages. At first, man conceived of death not as a necessary end of life but as a separate "thing" that might or might not come in conflict with life. One could be killed or die of disease (brought on by a curse), but death was not thought to be inevitable. Once its inevitability had been understood and accepted, death was still merely an interruption of life, more precisely, a change in the mode of existence. Only much later did the suspicion arise that death could be total annihilation. Even then it remained limited at first to a definite area. Thus, in the speculative thought of ancient Egypt there is still the certainty of a full-blown afterlife, whereas in that of Mesopotamia death means an almost complete destruction of personality.

The discovery that death may be total annihilation is relatively recent. The Gilgamesh epic, which contains the moving description of the event that led to this insight, is barely four thousand years old. Gilgamesh's shock and despair at the sight of the corpse of his beloved friend culminates in fear of dying and the sense of the utter vanity of life. But whereas Gilgamesh's search for immortality failed, other peoples of antiquity either preserved their original belief in an afterlife or were able to convince themselves that it nevertheless existed, in spite of all evidence to the contrary. However, ideas of an afterlife were not uniformly optimistic. In particular, where conditions became more difficult and precarious, as in the last millennium B.C. in Egypt, pessimism about life on earth either made death as total destruction seem a welcome release or spilled over into a pessimistic view of the hereafter. And when philosophy began in the Greek colonies on the coast of Asia Minor in the sixth century B.C., the prevailing view was that the dead led a listless existence as bloodless shadows in the bowels of the earth. At the same time, as most authorities concur, the ancient Greeks were keenly conscious of mortality. This consciousness darkened their outlook on life and their speculative thought. Yet there is no evidence that death was the moving force behind early philosophic thought. Rather, the Ionian philosophers were stimulated by their curiosity and their desire to understand the "origin" of things, not so much in the sense of initial condition as in the sense of the sustaining or "first" principle of all that exists.

It is true that the second philosopher on record, Anaximander (611–547 B.C.), speaks not only of the "coming into being" but also of the "perishing of things." His famous fragment, the first original philosophical text so far known to us, is too short, and its true meaning too obscure, to allow the conclusion that death was of special concern to him. But this may well have been the case with Heraclitus (533–475 B.C.)—among whose 126 known fragments no less than 16 deal with death and immortality.

Death occupies an important place in the thought of Plato, but the widespread notion that he defined philosophy as "meditation on death" is incorrect. He says in *Phaedo* that "the true votary of philosophy is likely to be misunderstood by other men; they do not perceive that he is always pursuing death and dying; and if this is so, he has had the desire of death all his life long. . . ."[2] This passage is made more explicit by another, where Socrates tells Simmias that "the true philosophers are always occupied in the practice of dying, wherefore also to them least of all men is death terrible." It is clear from the term *practice* that "pursuing death and dying" and the "desire of death" have nothing to do with a predilection for nonbeing, and the confusion referred to above arose from a mistranslation of the word practice, or more correctly *rehearsal*, as "meditation." What is meant by rehearsal of dying, however, can be properly understood only in the light of Plato's concept of death as the liberation of the immortal soul from the body and his view of the body as an obstacle to the attainment of true knowledge. Only when the soul is no longer hampered by the body can it arrive at true knowledge. Therefore the real philosopher in his search for truth longs for the liberation of his soul and rehearses dying by constantly trying to approach the ideal state when his body is already out of the way and his soul is free. Since he thus becomes familiar with death, he is not afraid of dying.

It is not these pronouncements but rather Plato's eagerness to marshal arguments for the immortality of the soul that seem to indicate his concern with death. Aristotle relates that, as a youth, Plato came under the influence of Cratylus, a disciple of Heraclitus, who was said to have been even more distressed by the spectacle of change than his master. But Aristotle does not mention that Plato himself was similarly affected; he merely reports that "the discovery that all sensible things are ever in a state of flux" led Plato to the conclusion that "since there is genuine science its object must be something other than flux." In addition, there are Plato's own statements (in *Theaetetus*, 155 D) that "philosophy begins in wonder" and (In *Timaeus*, 47 C) "the sight of day and night and the months, and the revolutions of the years, have created number, and have given us a conception of time; and the power of enquiring about the nature of the universe; and from this source we have derived philosophy." Thus, even though Plato was sufficiently concerned with death to devote to it and to the problem of immortality a whole dialogue, *Phaedo*, and the beginning and the end of *The Republic*, it would be going too far to assert that his concern with death was excessive.

However, it is quite likely to be true of Epicurus. He considered the fear of death and the fear of the gods to be the greatest afflictions of mankind. In the *Garden*, his disciples argued about which of the two fears is the greater evil. Epicurus's philosophical effort is mainly directed to overcoming the fear of death, and he does this by asserting that the soul is mortal since, like the body, it consists of atoms, albeit especially smooth ones. Since the soul dissolves at death, there is no sensitivity after one is dead: "When I am, death is not, and when death is, I am not." In short, the atomism of Democritus is being embraced as an explanation of the true nature of things best suited for the purpose of proving that there can be no pain and suffering in death and that it is "nothing to us."

The Stoics of the Roman Empire turned to philosophy for help in facing death and dying. In "On the Shortness of Life" Seneca (4 B.C.–A.D. 65), for whom immortality was merely a fond hope and not a certainty, recommends the study of great philosophers "because they will teach you how to die." And Marcus Aurelius (A.D. 121–180) exalts philosophy as the one thing by which man is able to conduct himself in living and dying:

> [It] consists in keeping the demon within man free from violence and unharmed, superior to pains and pleasures . . . accepting all that happens and all that is allotted . . . and finally waiting for death with a cheerful mind, as being nothing else than a dissolution of the elements. . . . For it is according to Nature, and nothing is evil which is according to Nature.

Philosophy for Marcus Aurelius, as well as for the other Stoics of that period, especially Epictetus (A.D. 60–120), was not only a doctrine but a mental discipline, the goal of which was the attainment of *apatheia*, the supreme indifference to pain and, of course, to death. It is this apathy that perhaps compensates for the inadequacies of the doctrine when it comes to facing death. No doubt, death looms large in the Stoics' thoughts; several of Seneca's essays and many of his letters deal with death, and Marcus Aurelius's *Meditations* are to a considerable extent meditations on death. For all this, the Stoics saw the aim of human existence in the attainment of perfect virtue and believed that the sage can even enjoy perfect bliss in spite of the shortness of life and the prospect of eventual dissolution. What seems to have oppressed Marcus Aurelius was not so much a fear of death as a recognition of the transistoriness of all things; if he suffered from fear of death at all, it was a much weaker emotion than his feelings of boredom and his belief in the vanity of existence.

When Stoic philosophy was revived in the late Renaissance by Michel de Montaigne (1533–1592), he discussed the proposition "that to philosophize is to learn to die," the title of Chapter XX of the first part of his *Essays*. Montaigne admitted that he was troubled by attacks of dread of dying and that he turned to Seneca's remedy against it, which consisted in constantly thinking of it. Gradually, he came to realize that the remedy was worse than the affliction and decided that "it is wrong to trouble life with our concern with death, and to trouble death with our concern with life." Like the Stoics before him, Montaigne advocates "giving in" to Nature, "the Great Mother of us all," and comes to the conclusion that "if we have known how to live properly and calmly, we will know how to die in the same manner."

Montaigne's confidence in Nature is shared by his contemporary, the philosopher-poet Giordano Bruno (1548–1600) who, in the poem that serves as a preface to his *Infinite Universe and Worlds*, asks: "Who gives me wings and removes my fears of death and torture?" He finds consolation in his vision of the infinite universe—incidentally, a triumph of creative imagination that anticipates the cosmology of the twentieth century, with its millions of solar systems and multitude of inhabited worlds. Precisely because the universe is infinite, there is no "emptiness" in it that could engulf things. It is a *plenum* and, "Nature cries with a loud voice against the madness of the dread of dissolution. Neither bodies nor souls should fear death, since both matter and form are absolutely constant principles." Thus, Bruno overcomes his dread of death by convincing himself that it is but a stage in the eternal process of "cosmic metabolism."

The reaction of Blaise Pascal was the very opposite of Bruno's cosmic enthusiasm. He complained that "the silence of this infinite expanse frightens me," and his concern with death was even more pronounced than Bruno's: "There is nothing more real than death, nor more terrible." It has been suggested that all the references to the horrible aspects of death ("the last act is atrocious") are not expressions of his own feelings but are used rhetorically to impress the freethinkers, the *esprits forts* of his times, and to convince them of the truth of revealed religion. But if one considers Pascal's known anxieties, this view is difficult to maintain, and it is more than probable that his reaction to death came from the depth of his torment.

So far, the inordinate concern with death appears to be the earmark of thinkers who are not considered philosophically "important."[3] But we find it also in Descartes, Spinoza, Hume, and Hegel. There is evidence that Descartes' search for "the truth in sciences" was to a large extent prompted by his passionate interest in longevity and the eventual conquest of bodily death. It is only gradually and with great reluctance that he gave up his hopes in this respect, but he stubbornly clung to belief in the immortality of the soul, which held an enormous importance for him. There exists a revealing letter to his friend Constantin Huygens, written on the occasion of the death of Huygens' daughter:

> I am sure . . . that you know all the remedies to appease your sorrows, but I cannot abstain from telling you of one which I have found to be very powerful, not only to make *me bear patiently the death of those I loved,* but to *prevent me from fearing my own,* although I belong to those who love life very much. It consists in the view of the nature of our souls, of which I believe I know so clearly that they outlast the body, and that they were born for joys and bliss much greater than those we enjoy in this world . . . for I recognize in us an intellectual memory, which is certainly independent of our body. [Italics added]

Spinoza is persistently cited as an example of a "true" philosopher because of his purported indifference to death. This reputation, as shall be shown, is based on a misinterpretation of his famous proposition that "a free man thinks of nothing less than death." And although to say that Spinoza desired not to think of death, and never ceased to think of it is an exaggeration, one cannot doubt that he thought of it a great deal. It is significant that in *On the Improvement of Our Understanding,* where he states the aim of his philosophizing to be the attainment of perfect happiness, he argues that "things commonly pursued by men are vain and futile" because they "bring no remedy that tends to preserve their being, but even act as hindrances, causing death not seldom of those who are possessed by them." And he refers to "innumerable cases of men who have hastened their death through overindulgence in sensual pleasure." Therefore, his well-publicized frugality and continence must be seen in the light of his concern with death. This concern is further evident in the attention he gives to the problem of mastering the fear of death.

David Hume, who astonished his friends and irritated his enemies by his composure in the face of "imminent dissolution" and wrote a brilliant rebuttal of the doctrine of the immortality of the soul, was intensely afraid of death. But his death fear was of the kind Epicurus set out to cure and that afflicted many people particularly in the "age of faith," namely, the fear of what comes after death. A contemporary, Lord Charlemont, reports that when Hume fell seriously ill at the age of thirty-seven, "he talked with much seeming Perturbation of the Devil, of Hell and of Damnation."

Hegel was keenly and painfully aware of death. The *Aphorisms*, written by the young Hegel, state, "The highest that has to be transcended is death." At thirteen, he was deeply affected by the loss of his mother, and, in later life, he never became reconciled to the death of his only daughter. According to the outstanding Hegelian scholar Alexandre Kojève, "the idea of death plays a momentous role in the philosophy of Hegel."

Hegel's one-time disciple Ludwig Feuerbach, who later became an opponent of Hegelianism, anticipated some of the most original thoughts about death found among contemporary thinkers. Both his first and last writings dealt with the problem of immortality, and he became perhaps the most outspoken champion of its denial in the nineteenth century. He finds that "Nature is not avid of life," and he foreshadows Freud's theory of the "death instinct" in his insistence that there is not only an instinct of self-preservation but also one of destruction. Feuerbach also advances views, found later in Heidegger, that death is not a sudden catastrophe but is bound up with life from the very first and that awareness of death is a means toward the knowledge of Being.

Contrary to widespread opinion, the philosophers of "existence," although they all deal at length with the subject of death, differ widely in the intensity of their concern with it.

The problem uppermost in Heidegger's mind is not death but the "meaning of Being." He does assign a most important role to the anxiety of death, through which he discovers that Being is "veiled" in Nothingness. But in spite of this, and in spite of his view that "authentic" existence "takes death upon itself" and in this way attains "anxiety-ridden freedom for death," there seems no justification in describing his philosophy as a meditation of death.

Sartre's main concern is human freedom. His position with respect to death, and his disagreement with Heidegger on this matter, is best conveyed in his own words: "Far from being my own possibility, death is a contingent fact, which, as such, escapes me in principle. . . . I cannot discover my death, nor wait for it, nor take an attitude toward it, for it reveals itself as undiscoverable, as that which disarms all expectations. . . . Death is a pure fact, like birth; it comes to us from the outside. . . ."[4] Death is not, as for Heidegger, inherent in life but a stranger to it. Man is not "free for death" but a "free mortal," who can despise it.[5] It is interesting, however, that while Sartre was formulating his philosophy during the German occupation of France, death was very much on his mind. In the *Republic of Silence* he reports that at the time "Exile, Captivity and especially death . . . became for us the habitual objects of our concern."

It is the "religious existentialist" Gabriel Marcel who seems to be obsessed with his own death. But then it turns out that he is not so much preoccupied with this as with the death of his loved ones. "The idea of a solitary and narcissistic survival is, for me at least, deprived of all significance." It is "in the perspective of the death of the other, the beloved" that Marcel finds a basis for belief in immortality. That problem presents itself to him as the question "whether destruction can affect that which makes a person a being with which I can establish this particular relationship [of loving]"; for, "to love a person is to say: you shall not die." For Marcel, death is the springboard of an absolute hope. "A world where death is absent would be a world where hope would exist only in an embryonic state." When death is envisaged "on its true plane, that of mystery," it loses its terrifying aspect and ceases to be seen as an evil. It becomes the threshold of another dimension, another birth: "the existential moment coincides with the eternal instant and death itself appears as an accomplishment."

Karl Jaspers, however, cannot go along with the doctrine of immortality because it is dependent on "proofs," and he holds that all arguments in its favor are fallacious. What actually can be proved is mortality. Jaspers revives the definition of philosophy as "learning to die," although for him it is not the only definition. "If philosophizing is learning to die . . . learning to live and learning to die are one and the same thing.[6]

This view is rooted neither in the beneficial effect that the awareness of death has on moral conduct of life nor on the favorable influence of a morally good life on the psychological preparedness for death, as it was for the later Stoics. It is based on Jaspers' concept of "limit," or "ultimate," situations, one of which is that one has to die. The awareness of limit situations leads to the experience of the "Encompassing," Jaspers' term for God, where "infinite calm" is attained, in which success or failure, living or dying, become irrelevant. Significantly, as in the case of Sartre, Jaspers has a special reason for concern with death. Because of a bronchial deficiency that according to a medical authority condemned him to death before the age of thirty, he has lived most of his life under the immediate threat of death.

What emerges from this survey is that a concern with death is not necessarily always provoked by a fear of death or dying. There are at least three different ways in which death can become the object of concern and conceivably even a muse of philosophy. Although it is primarily the fear of one's own death that triggers the search for consolation, very often the stimulus is the death of those near and dear to us, as Shakespeare says, the "love-destroying death." And there is also "the thought of frustration and final unreason" that death arouses and that makes one revolt against it and seek reassurance in a metaphysical point of view.

Fear of one's own death can, of course, assume various forms. In addition to the fear "that I may cease to be" (Keats), which is found in Montaigne, Bruno, Pascal, and Descartes, it also takes the form of the fear of what comes after death, the fear of Epicurus and Hume. Finally, it can be the fear of the process of dying when, in Paracelsus' words, "not death is the torture, but torture is where death begins." This is a variant of death fear also found in Montaigne, who confessed that "it is not death but dying which alarms me."

As to concern over the death of our loved ones, it is particularly strong in Hegel and Marcel. Nicolai Berdyaev, too, writes in his autobiography, "I am not prone to the fear of death, as for instance Tolstoy was, but I have felt intense pain at the thought of death, and a burning desire to restore to life all those who died."

The feeling of the utter meaninglessness of life that the thought of death as possible total annihilation is known to provoke in many people is perhaps most clearly expressed in Ecclesiastes: "Man's fate is a beast's fate. One fate befalls them both; as the one dies, so the other dies . . . both are vanity . . . both sprang from dirt, and to dirt both return. . . . What does a busy man gain from all his toil? What is the use of all my wisdom?" (Eccles. 2:16; 3:9; 3:19).

Marcus Aurelius must have felt this when he wrote, "The whole body is subject to putrefaction and what belongs to the soul is a dream and vapor, and life is a warfare and a stranger's sojourn and after fame is oblivion." Usually, this feeling is expressed by philosophers in connection with arguments for the belief in immortality. Fichte writes, "should this life not prove entirely vain and ineffectual, it must at least have relation to a future life, as means to an end." The outstanding Plato scholar A. E. Taylor has said that without immortality "our life is blind and our death fruitless." The English pragmatist F. C. S. Schiller insists that "one need not be violently enamoured of one's own life to feel that if the chapter of life is definitely closed by death, despair is the end of all its glories."

It is irrelevant here whether this reaction to death is, as some claim, "unphilosophical," since we are concerned with the fact that it not only exists but is also quite frequent, even among philosophers.

The various ways in which death can become the object of concern vastly increases the scope of the possible applicability of Schopenhauer's thesis. It must be admitted, however, that the inordinate concern with death found in some philosophers does not as yet constitute sufficient evidence to conclude that death was the motive of their philosophies. The most that can be said is that there is a great probability that it was one of several motives. In either case, a positive assertion is possible only when direct and unequivocal acknowledgement on the part of the philosopher himself exists.

Such a direct acknowledgment, for example, was made by Cicero, who confessed that it was the death of his daughter Tullia that made him turn to philosophy. According to this criterion, even the fact that Schopenhauer formulated the thesis in question does not make it certain that it applies to him. What can be considered such an acknowledgment is rather the autobiographical report that as a youth of seventeen he was "possessed by the sorrows of the world as Buddha was in his youth at the sight of illness, old age and death."

It is necessary, however, to go a step further and inquire into the reliability of even such a criterion as the direct acknowledgment by the philosopher himself, especially when the fear of death is involved, since according to Freud, "the fear of death is an analogue to the fear of castration and involves an interplay between the ego and the superego." Thus it can be maintained that when a philosopher assumes that fear of death ("the terrifying certainty of death") is the motive of his philosophizing, he is mistaken, since it is not really death he is afraid of. Admittedly, this statement refers to neurotic fear of death, not to *Realangst*, but it appears certain that in some of the instances examined the former was present.

In evaluating the implications of Freud's views with respect to Schopenhauer's thesis, one must consider that his position is based, in part at least, on his assumption that fear of death is not a primary fear and on the curious fact that "no one believes in his own death . . . in the unconscious every one of us is convinced of his own immortality."[7] But even if one agrees that fear of death is not a primary anxiety, it does not necessarily have to be so in order to be a stimulus to philosophizing. As to the psychological fact that no one really believes in his own death, it is counterbalanced, as Schopenhauer has pointed out, by the conscious knowledge of mortality. The disbelief in our mortality is daily challenged and refuted by the death of strangers and even of those close to us. It is noteworthy in this connection that Max Scheler held that there is in all of us an "intuitive certitude of mortality" and that Paul Landsberg speaks of the "experience of death," which is most pronounced when a beloved person dies.[8]

In any event, Freud's views are not shared even by many psychoanalytically oriented psychologists, who consider death to be a basic fear.[9] Thus, there is a good possibility that when a philosopher insists that he is motivated solely by a disinterested search for truth, he may not be aware that he is "inspired" by the fear of death. This may well be the meaning of Schopenhauer's emphasis on the epithet "true" when speaking of death as the "true inspiring genius of philosophy." As an unconscious motive, however, nothing short of a psychoanalytic exploration could determine whether or not it is indeed present in a given instance, and this would obviously preclude the possibility of determining with absolute certainty the verification of Schopenhauer's thesis as far as all philosophers of the past are concerned.

But fear of death, as has been seen, is not the only way in which "death" can motivate philosophy. Freud himself seems to confirm Schopenhauer's thesis, for the latter spoke not only of philosophical but also of religious systems as "antidotes to the certainty of death." Discussing the origin of religious ideas, Freud says that they are "born of the need to make tolerable the helplessness of man . . . defending himself against the crushing supremacy of nature—earthquake, whirlwind, flood, disease and *above all the painful and insoluble riddle of death*." And he continues: "The Gods . . . must exorcise the terrors of nature, they must reconcile one to the cruelty of fate, *particularly as shown in death. . . .*"[10] This amounts to saying that the fact of death is a preeminent motivating force in generating religious ideas. By extension, this would apply also to philosophical speculation, insofar as it has concerned itself with "ultimate" problems of human destiny. But whereas the terrors of natural phenomena have been successfully neutralized or eliminated by the scientific explanation and mastery over them, the "painful and insoluble riddle of death" is still very much with us. It continues to cause people to "get" religion, to meditate on death, and to search for "comforting metaphysical points of view."

It would seem fair to say, then, that there is undoubtedly an element of truth in Schopenhauer's thesis. Even if only in a very few instances death appears as the sole or primary motivation of philosophical reflection, in a considerable number of cases it is more than probable that it is one of the motives, a sufficiently strong one to have made death a major theme of philosophy.

In the light of these findings, the complete disregard of death in most contemporary philosophy is perplexing, especially since the intense preoccupation with death in contemporary literature seems to be more than the expression of personal idiosyncracies of the writers, and in some measure reflects also the concerns of their readers. Before the reasons for the present avoidance of the topic can be elucidated, previous eclipses of death from philosophic reflection will have to be traced.

It is interesting that philosophic thought, which we are accustomed to associate with destructive criticism of belief in an afterlife, played the opposite role in antiquity, The teachings of Pythagoras and Plato present a more attractive view of man's destiny after death than the traditional mythico-religious notions prevalent among the ancient Greeks. For example, whereas the Elysian Fields were strictly limited to the blessed and the heroes and immortality was believed to be the privilege of these select few, these two philosophers, on the contrary, taught that it was the attribute of each and every soul.

Plato's doctrine of immortality suffered a severe blow when his great disciple Aristotle subjected the platonic theory of ideas, on which some of the most important arguments for immortality were based, to a severe critique. Aristotle's own views on the subject were, to say the least, ambiguous. Alexander of Aphrodisias, the most outstanding ancient commentator on him, even maintained that the true position of the master was a categorical denial of personal immortality. As a result, Aristotle's disciples gradually despaired of the possibility of arriving at a clear-cut decision on the matter of immortality and therefore felt that concern with the problem was idle. Thus the first instance of a deliberate disregard by philosophers of a basic issue arising from the fact of death is found among the Peripatetics.

A similar situation arose in connection with the teachings of Epicurus. This is ironical, inasmuch as death was a central concern of his philosophy. His famous remedy for the fear of death made meditation on it appear unnecessary since, at least in theory, everyone could follow his injunction to "become accustomed to the belief that death is nothing to us." Once rid of the fear of death, and of gods, everyone could live like Epicurus himself, "entrenched against all the secret attacks of Fortune . . . and when the time comes for us to go, we will leave life spitting contempt on life and on those who vainly cling to it, and crying aloud in a glorious triumph song that we have lived well." The liberating effect of his argument against the fear of death must have been considerable. Three hundred years after Epicurus's death, his Roman disciple Lucretius Carus glorified him as the greatest benefactor of humanity for helping it to get rid of "the dread of Acheron."

Even though Epicurus's argument is even today considered conclusive by many people, some of his contemporaries already had noted that it is effective only when the fear of death takes the form of fear of the hereafter,[11] which was the case with most people of his time. It is of no avail against the other death fear, more frequent in our day, which is the fear of ceasing to exist. In these instances, even the belief in the immortality of the soul is merely a second-best solution compared with the Christian doctrine of the resurrection of the body.

For this reason, once the Christian answer to death was proclaimed to the world, especially to a world pervaded by a sense of doom and oppressed by the thought of final annihilation in death, philosophical reflection about death lost its raison d'être. And, of course, any deviation from Christian dogma gradually became more and more dangerous.

When philosophy ceased to be the handmaiden of theology, as far as death is concerned it was faced with the challenge, already familiar from antiquity, of dispelling the nightmarish aspects of death and dying that obsessed man in the late Middle Ages. The rediscovery of the works of Aristotle and acquaintance with the commentaries on them of the great Arab philosopher Averroës (1126–1198) supplied the necessary ammunition for this task. In the second half of the thirteenth century, Siger of Brabant, the leader of the Averroists, challenged the views of Thomas Aquinas, particularly those he held on the immortality of the soul, and taught that individual men are mortal—only the race is immortal. Siger's condemnation and subsequent assassination by his secretary did not put an end to the controversy. Pietro Pomponazzi's *De immortalitate animae* (1516) decisively influenced the future philosophical position on the matter. He disagreed with the Thomist as well as the Averroist interpretations and declared the problem of the immortality of the soul to be "neutral," that is, the truth or falsity of it could not be demonstrated by natural reason. Pomponazzi's subsequent denial of heretical intentions and his assurance of strict adherence to the dogma of bodily resurrection did not diminish the impact of his neutralism on philosophic thought. There is little doubt that it contributed to the radical change in emphasis from the medieval *memento mori* to the *momento vivere* of the Renaissance, at which time many philosophers accepted the doctrine that the individual soul merged after death with its divine source. This is essentially the view of Bruno and of Spinoza. Of course, not everyone was satisfied with that kind of immortality,[12] and Descartes and Leibniz, among others, took up the defense of the doctrine of personal immortality. However, David Hume's refutation of it left an indelible imprint on the subsequent treatment of the problem, and when, in addition, it became expedient to denounce the doctrine of immortality as a "priestly lie" that stands in the way of political and social progress, the view of death as total annihilation was promoted by the French Encyclopaedists and materialists. This could not but result in a drastic reduction of the concern with death in philosophical thought. If dying was still a "problem," it was so only because it became fashionable to die "well," that is, nonchalantly, and with appropriate last words if possible.

All the while, important changes were taking place in the philosophical enterprise itself. Before turning to them, a few words should be said about Spinoza's purported responsibility for the elimination of death from philosophy. Actually, it is not his famous proposition that "a free man thinks of nothing less than death and his wisdom is a meditation of life not of death" but, as we have already mentioned, its misinterpretation that has, if at all, played this role. It is true that Spinoza did not want to think of death, but he well knew that this was not an easy task. One has first to become free, that is, master of one's emotions, in order to be able not to think of death. The proposition is therefore not an admonition to cease such an idle pursuit as meditation on death but an affirmation of the beneficial results of becoming free, or wise, which in turn is possible only through attainment of "higher" knowledge. Actually, Spinoza comes to terms with death only after having thought about it a great deal and after having constructed a philosophical system in which death is shown to be necessary and just when seen "under the aspect of eternity."

Whatever Spinoza's importance was in bringing about the disregard of death in philosophy, this position became prevalent only since the middle of the nineteenth century and was largely owing to the impact on philosophy of the spectacular advances of the physical and biological sciences. In some philosophers, these discoveries awakened the desire to make philosophy "exact" in its own right. For others, the examination of the foundations of science opened a new and fertile field of investigation. These positivist trends were strongly favored by the growing surfeit with metaphysical speculation, as a consequence of which philosophers were neither inclined nor expected to concern themselves with ultimate questions of human destiny.

The contemporary philosophical scene, particularly in the English-speaking countries, shows an increasing positivist trend, which expresses itself in an even greater narrowing of the scope of philosophy. The "analytic" and neopositivist philosophers see it as linguistic analysis, be it of an ideal scientific language (Rudolf Carnap) or of "ordinary" language (G. E. Moore), and consider philosophical questions as insoluble pseudo-problems that can only be "cured" by showing that they are "meaningless" (Wittgenstein), that is, "intersubjectively unverifiable."

However, there are still various attempts to reassert the more traditional conception of philosophy as "understanding the world." But if the analytical thinkers exclude death because of a narrow view of the task of philosophy, the traditionalists disregard death for the opposite reason. Interested as they are in "totality," in Being, or in Nature in general, man and his death appear to them of little importance. Typical is the remark of Nicolai Hartmann that only "self-tormenting metaphysicians" waste their time meditating on death and speculating about immortality. If only man would relinquish his narcissism and see himself as what he is—a mere drop in the stream of universal happenings—he would stop making a fuss about his having to die.

This view is challenged by the philosophical anthropologists and the existential philosophers. They well remember Pascal's comment that although man is a "trifling thing," he is nevertheless great, because he knows his own weakness as compared with the overwhelming might of the universe. For them, man is the measure of all things, in the sense that what he experiences directly as his very essence is the key to the secrets of reality. Methodologically they are all followers of Schopenhauer, who discovers the thing-in-itself as Will through insight into the true nature of his own body. Moreover, the uniqueness of each individual human being is a basic fact. And it is this that makes death a worthy, and even an all-important, topic of philosophic thought.

It is mainly for this reason that Sidney Hook takes to task the philosophers of existence in his presidential address to the American Philosophical Association, "Pragmatism and the Tragic Sense of Life" (1959). He reasserts the definition of philosophy as pursuit of wisdom and reproaches the existentialists for being unduly preoccupied with death. He is obviously worried that meditation on death will distract attention from the moral and social problems besetting mankind. He writes:

Agony over death strikes me as one of the unloveliest features of the intellectual life of our philosophic times, and certainly unworthy of any philosophy which conceives itself as a quest for wisdom. It has never been clear to me why those who are nauseated by life, not by this or that kind of life, but any kind of life, should be so fearful of death.

It is not clear whom exactly Hook has in mind, except perhaps Tolstoy and Unamuno, the only ones he mentions by name, since there is no "agony over death" among the philosophers of existence. And as far as Hook's last remark is concerned, to see merely a logical contradiction in, for instance, St. Augustine's confession "*taedium vivendi erat in me gravissimum et moriendi metus*" is to miss an important fact about man's attitude toward life and death—its ambivalence. Furthermore, it is difficult to agree with Hook when he denies the tragedy of death by stating that "death as such is not a tragic phenomenon." He seems to forget that death as such is an abstraction and that it is the merit of the philosophers of existence to have pointed out that death is always concrete, the death of someone, and therefore always affects someone tragically.

In a recent article, "Mistaken Attitudes Toward Death," Corliss Lamont[13] agrees with Hook that "death . . . does not in itself justify the conclusion that man's life as a whole is tragic" but points out that "Death . . . is a blow of such magnitude and finality that it is always a thing of tragic dimensions—to the person who dies, or his intimate survivors, and usually both." He concludes by stating:

The mature philosopher never attempts to mask the tragic aspects of death. But he is not preoccupied with death; nor does he permit it, on account of the heartache and crisis it causes, to overshadow in his philosophy the other phases of human existence . . . he looks at death with honesty, dignity and calm, recognizing that the tragedy it brings is inherent in the great gift of life.

No matter how gratifying it is to find that death is being taken seriously by a nonexistentialist philosopher, and no matter how wholeheartedly one may agree with Lamont's balanced view that death should not be ignored, nor should concern with it monopolize philosophy, one cannot but feel disappointed that he never faces the real problem in connection with it. To call other attitudes to death mistaken is a rather questionable approach. It is hard to see on what grounds a craving for death should be condemned, if this view is held sincerely. If one chooses to forgo the pleasures of being a grandparent and is not too eager to wait until he becomes eligible for old-age benefits, it is his own business. And although society may suffer a loss, death is after all a private matter. The most that can be said is that this attitude is socially undesirable, although sociologists worried about the burdens imposed on the economy by the growing number of "senior" citizens will deny even this.

To consider the revolt against death mistaken is even less justified. Such an attitude may be more fitting for a philosopher than looking at death philosophically, at least until he has arrived at a metaphysical point of view that would provide reasons for viewing the prospect of death with calm and dignity. Primarily because he neglects the differences in intensity of the reluctance to die, Lamont overlooks the importance of a philosophical Weltanschauung that answers, at least to the satisfaction of the philosopher himself, the ultimate questions. Instead, Lamont speaks of the mature philosopher. Maturity is, however, a greatly abused concept that usually serves the purpose of avoiding a coming to grips with basic issues, and it is particularly sterile here since one of its definitions is that a mature person is one who has made his peace with the necessity of having to die. Thus, the question *how* one becomes mature with regard to death is left open, unless what is meant is that this is something that happens with advancing age, when an acquiescence to the inevitable gradually emerges. Of course, this is also a solution, but preferably, a true philosopher, in addition to acknowledging the tragedy death brings in its wake, ought to recognize the need for a philosophy that would both assist in living untroubled by the knowledge of death and help in facing it calmly. This can only be a philosophy that can refute the apparently inescapable conclusion that if death is total annihilation, human life is a mere "episode between two oblivions." For if it is true that death does not make man's whole life a tragedy, it seems to make it a farce.

The quest for a philosophy that could overcome the nihilistic implications of death should not be misconstrued as equivalent to turning philosophy into a meditation on death. On the other hand, however, the fact that most contemporary philosophers are able to avoid thinking of death either because they can happily reconcile their philosophical activities with traditional religious answers to death or because they are genuinely indifferent to it or, finally, because they are afflicted with what Scheler called metaphysical thoughtlessness (metaphysischer Leichtsinn) does not do away with the problem created by man's knowledge that he is mortal. This knowledge is part of the human condition, and not to take it into account when dealing with the improvement of humanity is to simplify and to misunderstand it. Thus, the pragmatist's goal, as stated by Hook, of "enlarging human freedom by the arts of intelligent human control," important as it is, does not allow for the probability that improvement in social and economic conditions will inevitably sharpen the consciousness of mortality. Perhaps the preoccupation with death in contemporary literature ought to be seen as indicative that something of the kind is already taking place. Moreover, the fact that man alone among two million species knows that he has to die may have a deeper significance. Perhaps it denotes a break in the evolutionary process in the sense that the knowledge of death foreshadows the death of the human race or even the end of all life on earth. Perhaps this is too pessimistic an implication. Knowledge of death may on the contrary serve the purpose of preserving the human species. Meanwhile, for the individual it is the source of anguish and frustration.

It is true that most people seem to be able to live without being unduly troubled by such knowledge, and some will die calmly even without a comforting philosophy. Thus the need for it may not be as urgent as it may appear to those who seek it. Moreover, to find an answer to the question of the ultimate meaning of human existence that, while in accord with scientific knowledge of the world, would make sense of life condemned to total annihilation seems so far to be a hopeless undertaking. And yet the search for such a consoling vision of man's destiny is not only the pain but also the glory of all true philosophizing.

## REFERENCES

1. This second, supplementary volume appeared in 1843, twenty-five years after the publication of the first volume.
2. Jowett translation.
3. Thus Bruno is not even listed in the index to Bertrand Russell's *History of Western Philosophy*; Montaigne's name is mentioned twice without anything being said about his ideas; and the only information about Pascal is that "he sacrificed his magnificent mathematical intellect to his God, thereby attributing to Him a barbarity which was a cosmic enlargement of Pascal's morbid mental tortures" (p. 768).
4. *L'Etre et le Neant*, p. 630.
5. Sartre's companion, Simone de Beauvoir, on the contrary, is oppressed by the thought of death, which makes her feel that her life and work are senseless and utterly vain. (See Volume III or her autobiography *La Force des Choses*.)
6. *Einführung in die Philosophie*, 1953, p. 121. [*The Way to Wisdom,*

trans. Ralph Mannheim (New Haven, Conn.: Yale University Press, 1959)].

7. In *Thoughts for the Times of War and Death* Freud writes: "The psychoanalytic school could venture the assertion that at the bottom no one believes in his own death, or to put the same thing in another way, in the unconscious every one of us is convinced of his own immortality." In fact, only the second part of this statement can be credited to the perspicacity of the psychoanalytic school, since the first assertion has been made before. To mention but two, Seneca wrote: "You live as if you would live forever; the thought of human frailty never enters your head." And Schopenhauer: "Man does not really receive death into his living consciousness." There are several variations of this thesis in Freud, one of them being, "The unconscious knows nothing of our own death. . . . It follows that no instinct we possess is ready for a belief in death." We do not want to insist here on the incongruity of speaking of the unconscious not knowing of death, as if it "knows" anything at all. More important, however, is how this ignorance can be squared with Freud's concept of the death drive. If it exists, then the unconscious ought to know of death, and there is an instinct that not only is ready for the belief in death but is "death."
8. Paul Landsberg, *L'Experience de la Mort* (Paris, 1933).
9. For details, see my *Modern Man and Mortality* (New York: The Macmillan Company, 1964).
10. *Future of an Illusion*; (italics added).
11. For details see my *Death and Western Thought* (New York: The Macmillan Company, 1963), p. 285.
12. As Madame de Staël remarked when this view was revived by the Romantics, "that the individual return to the Whole, this kind of immortality has a frightening similarity to death."
13. *Journal of Philosophy* (1955), 62: 29–36.

# 4. Buddha and Self-Destruction

GERALD HEARD

Why include Gautama Siddhartha, the Buddha, the founder of the greatest religion of the East, as one whose attitude toward self-destruction is worth enquiry? Albert Schweitzer, a modern, authoritative, world-famous religious figure, in his survey of the great religions of the world, has divided them into two categories: The West's, which are hallmarked as "life-accepting"; and the East's, which are as easily and distinctively marked (branded might be the better word) as "life-rejecting."

This dichotomy is, of course, too simple. During all its formative generations, Christianity was undeniably apocalyptic. That is, Christians believed that the world was about to be destroyed. As E. N. Burkett of Cambridge University, one of the most eminent authorities on the pristine Apocalyptic phase of Christianity (from A.D. 30 to 200), put in a phrase the mood and outlook of that Church's attitude toward life and its forecast of the future of human self: All Christians during those half-dozen generations went on being firmly convinced that "they were living in a world in which there would be no grandchildren." And Christianity's great defector and rival, Islam, also accepted Christianity's conviction that at any moment the phenomenal world could be more than liquidated, it could be completely volatilized—unbelievers shot down into Hell, true believers shot up into a Heaven packed with "houris."

We should not be surprised that Buddhism, Christianity, and Islam, the three great world religions, are otherworldly and so, in our terms, life-denying. They are the religions of private conscience. That is to say, they mark a psychological "shore line": they show that a sharp break, a "faulting," has taken place in the human psyche. Before, religion was wholly and only a tribal matter. For example, if a member of the group broke the taboo structure, then not only was he himself killed out of hand, but the same fate was meted out to his wives and children—one instance being the slaughter of Aachan and all his family because Aachan concealed some of the spoil he had looted in the sack of Jericho.

The rise of personal conscience meant two things. First, this conscience would of necessity be a bad conscience, for specific private guilt appeared, and guilt is the negative mood that succeeds the previous negative mood, shame. The second result of finding that one has a personal conscience is that, besides feeling guilty, this new human mood is one of despair. What can I do to get out of and escape from my guilt? Shame I might hide. But guilt is not only *in* me; far worse, it is indelible. It is imprinted in my mind: nay more, it is instinctive. It is as inborn for me to offend against the social traditional moral law as it is for me to think for myself, to have a deep voice or blue eyes.

The religions of private conscience, therefore, had little hope that keeping the traditional taboos would make you lucky. Anyone who was observant soon saw that the meticulous ritualist had as many accidents and misfortunes as he who scamped his prayers. Nor did they hope that by "taking arms against a sea of troubles," taking things into one's own hands, one could tidy up the fabulous tangle heaped all around man.

As for the notion that "one increasing purpose runs, / And the thoughts of men are widen'd with the process of the suns,"[1] such a notion of inherent progress, as J. B. Bury established in his volume *The Idea of Progress*,[2] apparently was never even enunciated (although Seneca, in one of his reflections, suggests the possibility) until the beginning of the Eighteenth Century.[3]

Indeed, we may say that once men became fully reflective (for example, when man's place for empathic learning, the theater, was turned by the first Puritan from the traditional fertility religion performances to the performance of tragedy), it was the supreme master of this new theme and style, Sophocles, who made his chorus chant (as the basic conclusion and moral of all their descriptions of how heroes perish because of their fatal inbred pride, hubris): "Happy are those who die young [he himself lived to exceed 90], but only truly blessed are those who never were born." So much for the master feeling tone of the bright Hellenes.

Why then waste any further time discussing whether or not Buddha believed in self-destruction. Is not Buddhism, of all the religions of private conscience and personal guilt, the most consistently life-rejecting and therefore suicide-commending? Christianity and Islam both have made terms with life and reinterpreted their harsher pristine statements about predestination and eternal torment.

But surely Buddhism has been grimly consistent? Only those who abandon all life; only those who desert home and keep that strict celibacy which ensures race suicide; only these can escape the wheel of suffering, the perpetual rebirth into this world, which is a blind, uncontrollable cycle; only these can escape this body which, because of its inborn cravings of greed, must result in fatal suffering, in the ignorant repetition of those drives which ensure for everyone futile misery.

Certainly it was a natural conclusion for those who first found themselves up against (and so started to study) this vast and stubborn religion. From the very start they found they were confronted with some odd questions. No one who had taken the trouble to master the two tongues in which the huge mass of Buddhist canonical literature is written, Pali and Pali's parent language, Sanskrit, doubted that those who constructed these systems out of the postulates of their founder's teaching were minds of advanced intelligence, high logical capacity, and argumentative subtlety. And yet they seemed from the start to have left unanswered a question both basic and obvious—a question of such cardinal importance that if left aside unanswered and even unraised must seem to show that these religious philosophers were either curiously simple or simply lacked the courage to push a basic argument to its logical conclusion. For if life in the body is for everyone an inescapable misery and, however many tempting preliminary moments it may have, these are only the bait of the trap which in the end inflicts cruel punishment on all, then why not advise suicide? Some sects of other religions have. Some splinter groups of the Cathars, usually called in the West the Albigensians (for in the Thirteenth Century they were strongly centered round the Midi city of Albi), on occasion committed group suicide. As late as the "true believer" movement in the Russian Orthodox Church these persecuted groups would gather together in their meeting houses and perform a group holocaust. And in the ancient Mexican pantheon there was a special goddess of suicide who promised those who followed her example (she is shown hanging from a tree branch) that they would enjoy a uniquely favorable paradise.

But there can be no manner of doubt that, throughout its history, Buddhist teaching specifically denied each and every member of the "Sangha," the Buddhist church, this apparent shortcut of suicide.[4]

Is there any way to solve this puzzle? Western scholars who began research into Buddhism started with that great half of Buddhism, the *southern* school which was based in Ceylon and called itself the Theravadin school, which ("thera" meaning monk) stressed the point that only the lifelong celibate could attain Nirvana. And not only was this, the southern school (which spread along the coast to Burma through Malay, Cochin China, and so up into southern China), more accessible geographically, it was also emotionally less daunting than the other great half of Buddhism, the *northern* school, which called itself Mahayana.

Theravadin Buddhism is more practical and less subtle than Mahayana Buddhism. It clung to an explicit teaching: the one appeal the monk may and must make is that he can teach and show that life as man lives it is pain and that pain can be stopped only by finding out how to stop all involuntary feeling. From this premise was deduced the conclusion that because Buddha left no statement about what happened to consciousness when this painless person at last died, there was therefore nothing that survived. This is the *an-ata* doctrine of the southern school; and, as *ata* is the Pali word for what in Sanskrit is *atman*—that is, pure egoless spirit—therefore nothing of any sort exists and carries on, and so it can reincarnate if the monk has wholly quenched—"blown out" is the literal meaning of Nirvana (Sanskrit) or Nibbana (Pali)—all desire.

This surely looks like a death wish, a roundabout way of suicide. The northern school was more thorough and penetrating in its analysis of the subtle problem and its answer to the obvious retort, "Why not kill yourself?"

First they asked, "What is this self?" Is the crude dualism of an ego mind in a material body an adequate inventory of the psychosomatic spectrum? They had little difficulty in demonstrating that the mind-body was a complex lamination of psychophysical shifting states and fluctuating balances; that selfconsciousness was only one superficial state of mind; that there were far profounder and more powerful states of concentration (for example, hypnosis) and that mind went far deeper than the unreflective, unselfexamining man knows or can imagine. And, conversely, that body was just as baffling with its growth capacity, its homeostasis, its matrix of emotions, its ultrasubtle energy fields and radiations. They also covered their flank against the attack of the simpler, cruder southern dogma (which charged the northerners with deviationism by watering down the teaching of the master) by quoting that when he lay dying and was asked, "Did you teach personal survival?" the Buddha answered back, "Did I say that?" Determined to pin him down on one of the horns of this dilemma, they questioned, "Did you teach extinction?" and again came the counter question, "Did I say that?"

In short, we may say that there was no inconsistency in teaching a life of indefatigable exploration of "the Beyond which is within" and also insisting that for the beginning of such basic research a whole lifetime is a little span. Suicide in this frame of reference is then clearly a mistake. Conversely, when the practitioner-trainee had made contact with his entire psychophysical spectrum and knows his full self, then he will know when, by cooperating with the fulfilled task, he can achieve a voluntary because a wholly understood, informed, and intended parturition—as the pre-dragonfly, having completed and crawled up out of its native submerged way of living, casts its husk and functions with new faculties in a new and higher environment.

There is a further reason for regarding as gravely mistaken our customary view of Buddhism and the teaching of its Founder.

If Buddhist ethics were as grossly, crudely, and completely obsessed with nothing but an egotistic craving to escape personal physical suffering and this suffering was the one thing that mattered, then why did they bother with a lifetime of skilled abstinences? Why not avoid the long and weary disciplined straining toward a final cessation of physical pain? If there is no spirit that survives the death of the body; if epiphenomenalism is the truth; if "when the lamp lies shattered," its oil spilt, and soaked up by the earth, when the flame of its combustion must vanish; what possible opposition can there be to—indeed is not every argument in favor of—instant analgesia, complete and total anaesthesia, final extinction? For "every bondsman in his own hand bears the power to cancel his captivity."

We have also seen that there is one obvious reason why these first Western scholars so misjudged this great world religion that they assumed they were competent to evaluate—and invalidate—and so felt justified to censure and dismiss because of its antisocial teaching of "holy selfishness."[5]

Modern Western scholars first came in contact with southern Theravadin Buddhism. And they found it (as its self-named character shows) wholly celibate in its aims. So these Western nineteenth-century scholars should not be blamed for regarding its key teaching, the "an-ata" doctrine, as one that taught as its entire aim a Nirvana that meant extinction, a "blowing out."

But here we must mention a factor that turned Western scholars against northern Buddhism. This great school significantly called itself the Mahayana school, that is, the teaching of the "Great Vehicle" or "Raft." Thus it contrasted with the purely monastic southern school, that school which the northern Buddhists with some contempt called "Hinayana" Buddhism, that is, "the Little Vehicle." We have also seen that northern Buddhism was less accessible for study. For while Theravadin Buddhism tenaciously held its own along the coastal lands from Ceylon to southern China, all Buddhism in India was driven north by a reviving Brahmanism until Mahayana was confined to a northern slip of India—Nepal today, for instance. (Evidently Theravadin Buddhism was wiped out in India proper.) Caught between Islam's pressure from the west and northwest, Mahayana was forced up into Tibet where it combined with an "animistic" autochthonous religion (*Bon*) to become Lamaistic Mahayana Buddhism, and where it stood its ground with its capital at Lhasa until crushed by Chinese Communism.

But inaccessibility was not the only obstacle that prevented Western scholars from understanding this richly complex religion. It is a curious fact that northern Buddhism's life-acceptance turned European scholars against it more than the life-rejection of the southern school had made these same scholars reject the Theravadins for their lack of social conscience. Western puritanistic scholars felt a certain patronizing sorrow toward those who practiced life-rejection. That such discipline, such noble personal denial, should have so sorry a goal was felt to be sad, a kind of perverse nobility. But when eminent advocates of Buddhist studies came to study northern Lamaistic Mahayana Buddhism, their feeling of sad superiority quickly turned into disgust, despite the fact that it was northern Lamaistic Mahayana Buddhism that demonstrated that its school differed from the life-rejecting, purely monkish views and practices of the southern Theravadins.

Today we can understand the disgusted bewilderment with which these nineteenth-century puritanical scholars viewed a teaching that had a subtler, more penetrating, and more comprehensive view of the life force and its purpose in man than ever Freud or Jung attained. For these linguistic scholars found that Lamaistic Mahayana Buddhism had been amalgamated with Tantra.[6] To nineteenth-century scholars this looked as horrible as it seemed unbelievable. How could such a depraved alliance take place? Today, however, we not only can understand intellectually how this fusion came about, we can envisage how such an alloy could serve as a suicide preventive and, more, a psychophysical therapy which not only prevents suicide but points toward a more highly developed philosophy and way of life, one that can train the psychophysical emotions (the training of which has been so gravely neglected by our society, with our overdeveloped and overtrained forebrain, which produces hypertrophied powers).

First, glance at the process of all Buddhism: The Buddha himself took the first step away from a total life-rejection religion. He began by practicing fakir mortifications (practiced, for example, by the Jains, a Dravidian life-rejecting faith) which taught that since all action in this life produced suffering, every deed marked up more evil karma that in this and succeeding lives would produce more suffering. Therefore abstain from all deeds. The world is evil, the body evil. "Ahimsa" ("harmlessness") is not compassion: it is keeping so detached that nothing can catch you and drag you back. This is true holy selfishness. Buddha did not say the body was evil. Indeed, he saw it as an essential primary instrument to be properly used, so that full freedom and complete comprehension might be attained. It must, then, be kept as a well-trained horse, not as a wild beast to be tormented.[7]

His monks were to have sufficient food—all strenuous, debilitating fasts as well as any other body-damaging mortifications were forbidden. They were to wear enough cover. They were to rest and sleep and meditate where they would have right protection from the weather. If, then, life was not evil, what was the root of the grave trouble, "the dislocation," the Dukkha? Not the body but the mind. "All that we are is what we have thought" is the key proposition of probably the most influential of all the shorter Buddhist classical texts, *The Dhammapada*. Correct the mind and, first of all, not only will your conduct be right but, secondly, your whole body will begin to function better and obey better your rational and dedicated intelligence. Today, psychosomatic medicine would not only accept but advocate this view. But Buddhism takes a third step and makes a third promise to the dedicated trainee. The corrected mind is like a corrected lens. Not only can behavior and metabolism there, and there alone, be made truly correct; the way the mind's eye perceives and conceives will continue to improve, so that all the old misconceptions and ignorances are righted so that it is possible to see what should be done and perceive where to go and how to get there. This presupposes the willingness and freedom (liberation) to perform in perfect accordance with a wholly realistic, wholly comprehensive vision.

But as Buddhist thought, practiced with this powerful formula, penetrated ever more deeply into the depths of the mind, into the abyss of the "Beyond Within," it began to ask, "If it is mind that has made all forms and every body, what has made the *human* mind (and, looking at animals, for instance, *any* performing mind) too often function so poorly, so badly, so destructively, so perversely, blindly, and ignorantly?" Early Buddhism declined to deal with this riddle, usually called the problem of evil. The Buddhas must have thought about it carefully and no doubt concluded that the first thing, the essential initial step, was to get people training to control and use their minds.

Nor does there seem any doubt that after some generations, perhaps centuries, of intensive thought being given to this problem, "What caused all this evil, what spawned all this bad karma?", these penetrating thinkers began to focus on a source below and before the mind. The mind made mistakes, misconceptions, misbirths because the *will*, the desire to be conscious, had taken a wrong turn. As it aimed rightly to become self-conscious in the right sense of that word, that is, as it strove to become reflectively intensified in its awareness, it fell into, contracted into, the restraint of wrong self-consciousness. The base of all evil, many Buddhist texts diagnose, is "the wish for separate existence." Intensity banished extensity. The ego, the sharp point of private apprehension, tore itself from its total field. It contracted until it was totally alienated from its fellows, and all life, each and every separate life, was shut up, self-shackled, hoodwinked in its misunderstood body.

Meanwhile, Vedanta (Brahmanism), with its apparel of yogas, by means of which it experimented with consciousness-changing exercises (breath control, the limited environment, etc) and consciousness-changing drugs, was also approaching a similar concordat between body and mind. The false dichotomy between flesh and spirit, which had dominated all ethical theory and method since the rise of the religions of private, post-mortem salvation, was now losing the divisive power it exercised through the guilt-obsessed conscience. At about the same time, Buddhism and Brahmanism (the religion out of which Buddhism had grown) both began to conceive that attempting to dilate consciousness by repression was dangerous in its means and perverse in its aim. It became evident to the practitioners and theorists of both religions that it was by skilled expression, by athletic release, that men could experience a realistic "metanoia," that is, a radical extension of consciousness. This world and the body in which and from which man viewed this world were neither an illusion nor a snare. The world was still only partly apprehended. And by developing the body-mind as an organic whole, the wholeness of the world would be increasingly apprehended, and the nature and character of man would conversely be realized as the growing edge of the life process.

Tantra, then, was the final development of Brahmanism, as Lamaistic Mahayana was the final development of Buddhism. It was a natural and inevitable coalescence of two convergent streams of theory and practice.

However, both had to undergo rejection and persecution. The constant attack of crude, militaristic, persecutory Islam had repeatedly tried to crush Brahmanism. When, with Akbar, the Moguls established their suzerainty over a large part of India, this able ruler, finding that he could not enforce a puritan ethos on Brahmanism (which was rooted in fertility tradition), offered toleration to all the other religions, which he called "Religions of the Book". [For example, Christianity, Judaism, and even Vedanta (since its "Bible" could be said to be the *Vedas* and the *Upanishads* and its basic discipline was celibacy)].

However, because he considered its life-acceptance obscene, Akbar persecuted Tantra with the utmost brutality. We always misrepresent those whom we resolve to destroy. Even Brahmanists accepted scandalous accounts of Tantric depravities (as the Roman world accepted its government's scandal propaganda against the new Christian religion).

Tantra, therefore, had to go underground in India, as Lamaistic Mahayana Buddhism had had to take refuge in Tibet. However, with the rediscovery of clues to these highly evolved versions of the pretragic, preblood fertility religions, we are now beginning to understand that here lies a true life-accepting praxis, a psychophysical group therapy.[8]

In short, we may conclude that, as Buddhism developed, in the end it discovered a psychophysical group therapy (similar to the Tantra that Brahmanism had developed and the "Adamite" underground sect that had—as Hieronymous Bosch shows in his great chart-picture "The Garden of Earthly-Delights" which hangs in the Prado Museum in Madrid—sprung up from a sub-Christian root). It was a therapy whereby three things might be achieved or at least attempted. First, by regressional experience, as the childhood layer of experience is thus brought up again into consciousness, the specific sexual guilt angst can be greatly reduced and possibly eliminated. Second, by such psychosomatic mood-changing, basic thanatophobia can be modified. And third, as psychosomatic exercises reduce the "psycho-membrane" (called in Sanskrit "forgetfulness," in Greek "lethe," and today "repression") which screens the midbrain from conscious dialogic intercourse with the forebrain, the midbrain (with this "psycho-membrane" removed) can inform the forebrain whenever the general metabolic slant of the total organism indicates that the appropriate period has arrived when the physique is ripe to be shed. Conversely, with a forebrain so instructed, the self-conscious persona, the mature elder being can, without any thanatophobia, achieve voluntary, intentional, and informed death. The achievement of such integral comprehension (as Radhakrishnan has named it) is the only valid and effective method of tackling suicide. For if we are to develop any method that can be really efficacious, we must be able to answer far better than we have the argument that the sane and responsible person who plans suicide uses against the current persuasions and arguments that we usually put forth to make him reconsider his decision.

For all we are doing is talking to gain time. We are not doing what we should and could—that is to inform the "case at issue" what his natural term of life is.

We could begin to do this by finding out what is the life expectancy of the particular genetic stocks from which the individual's ancestry is composed; and next to diagnose the stage and degree of completion-elimination at which a thorough physicopsychological study could show the particular person had now arrived. Once we had obtained this basic information (obviously necessary if any adequate advice is to be given), with this basic diagnosis and prognosis in hand we could proceed to the second step, treatment, with far greater hopes of better success than has yet been achieved (especially with the elderly and those suffering from incurable disease). For, as the obstetrician-trainers in natural childbirth during the trainees' pregnancies do, so the preventer of the impulsive, irrational and irresponsible person who considers suicide could and should initiate the dialogue between the person's forebrain that reasons and consciously plans (for instance, to interfere with the life persistence that keeps him surviving) and the midbrain that (through the vagus nerve, for example) controls the "pace-making" of the vitals, those rhythms (now in Western man wholly involuntary) which keep the body alive even when the mind feels profoundly convinced it should be gone.

Such then is our present knowledge of the psychosomatic trainings which Buddhism and its kindred systems of mind training (such as the Taoistic, Jain, Lamaistic, Sufi, and some Greek Orthodox and Coptic sects) attempt. To call these processes autosuggestion, or autohypnosis, may define, but it does not instruct. This enlarged awareness and control, by blending the selfconscious foremind with the psychosomatic field is, we now know, demonstrable. It can be called self-destruction, if destruction of its shell by the chick is self-destruction. Premature breaking of the shell means death to the immature chick but not to the mature one. Too long retention in the shell or the womb means degeneracy. The psyche retained in the body when it should be free does also degenerate, as we know to our cost and sorrow. The Buddha, or rather *a* Buddha, (because Buddhism believes that there have been and there must be a series of such men) does not mean someone arrested in a somnolent trance.

On the contrary, the word means "one who has woken up." The rest of us, they say, are the sleepwalkers. Our whole society lives in a self-induced illusion in which we move with a fatal irrationality and unawareness of the actuality of our present condition, as does a totally instinctual insect or a deeply hypnotized subject. Such semantic accuracy may help us diagnose our problem of the qualities of death and the qualities of the self that bring about death. It may help us understand more about the many objectives and goals for which this vague word "death" stands, has stood, and can come to stand: more about the many methods and procedures whereby the hierarchy of selves which compose the microcosm called a psychosome, and its projected sheath, its society, practice life and death (from the most self-centered schizoid constituent to the worldwide nationalistic wars, the global, ideological, "liquidating" crusades, and the faiths of life rejection).

The actual study and practice of the most advanced Buddhist methods of mind-body training might give us a method of total integration which at last would provide us with a therapy that could prevent all ignorant self-destruction by demonstrating to the individual how he may, by such trained integration, intentionally fulfill and consciously complete his whole life process.

It is obvious then that if we are to state briefly the answer to the question of what was the Buddha's attitude to self-destruction, that answer cannot be given unless and until we understand what we mean by the word "self" which we use so crudely in our still rather raw-minded society on which the psychological (or better, the psychophysical) revolution is now breaking. We are beginning to grasp the fact that the enormous distortion in our perceptions (and still more in our conceptions) is caused by the crudity of our unexamined assumptions as to what we are, how we react, and how we may consummate ourselves.

Nor is this merely an academic correction of a mistaken translation, an amend made to a powerful and history-changing genius whom we have dismissed as an escapist at best, more probably a shirker, that put back man's progress to a better life by directing thought away from action, the individual away from society, and the mind away from the race and the biological destiny which the self-conscious intellect could fulfill.

Today our suicide rate is shocking and, gravest cost, it takes its greatest toll among the informed. For we have no answer to the basic questions of meaning, intention, purpose. "Why should I do anything for posterity? What has posterity ever done for me?"

Within the mechanomorphic frame of reference there is no truthful, scientifically honest answer.

And simultaneously we have a steadily aging population. This means (for we have ample evidence) that as these advanced-age groups multiply and extend their tenure they become ever more expensive to keep, ever less worth their expense. In contrast, in some societies even until today (for example, Japan) there have been advanced-age groups which were neither unwanted by their juniors nor themselves just clinging to life out of fear of death.

Our problem and the cure of this tragic absurdity lies, of course, in the fact that we have produced a society which, in spite of the fact that survival is extended, has all its values fixed on the prepsychological prizes, goals, and ends of an immature animal. This is the inevitable result of having overeducated the forebrain to a capacity to produce physical power and physical health without psychological content, a deluge of means without any channels of meaning and directives of worthy significance.

We know now, however, that it is our untrained emotions that lead to these grotesque and futile results. And we know that these, the emoters, the drivers of life, can be trained. It was tragic that the keepers of these techniques of mind training, the teachers of emotive athleticism, mood mastery, and psychophysical directives, were stung to demonstrate their abilities to show an alien Western church allied with an alien commercialism that in "trial by ordeal" they could display an expert control, the challenge of which none of our churchmen (with their boasted list of canonized martyrdoms) dared take up any more than our "tough" trained military "elites" ventured to offer themselves as champions for and on our side.

Yes, Buddha did believe in the destruction of the false self, the fancy image we publish of ourselves. His aim was, and his method still can make it possible, to shatter this mendacious mask so that the only true life-acceptor, life-controller, and life-advancer, the true self of whom the *persona* is the willing instrument, can emerge.

## REFERENCES

1. From *Locksley Hall,* by Alfred Lord Tennyson, in *The Selected Poetry of Tennyson* (New York: Random House, Inc., 1951).
2. London: Macmillan & Co., Ltd., 1920.
3. The objective of the pristine civilization was the *reverse* of progressive; that is, it was to keep everything, to the smallest detail, exactly as it was. See Henri Frankfort, *Ancient Egyptian Religion* (New York: Columbia University Press; 1948).
4. The startling display of self-immolations performed in Vietnam by Buddhist monks is certainly a grave violation of the rule, the Dharma. For not only was suicide condemned: any such display of superhuman power, even an act of spiritual (hypnotic?) healing comes under the sweeping excommunicatory interdict of "The Blessed One" in his well-known saying, "By this shall you know that a man is not my disciple in that he attempts to perform a miracle." All display of psychic power (which is forbidden not only by Buddhism but by its successor in India, Vedanta) is stated to be a specific obstacle to liberation and enlightenment because it makes the practitioner selfconscious, vain, and venerated by the ignorant.
5. That actual phrase, it is worth noting, was coined and employed approvingly by St. Jerome (A.D. 340–420) when he commended "the Desert Fathers," those eremites and extreme ascetics who in thousands, during those critical centuries from the middle of the third century to the rise of Islam, deserted Western civilization on its most exposed flank, the Niles-Euphrates front.
6. For further information on Tantra, see the article on Lamaism by Rhys Davids in *Encyclopaedia Britannica,* 1911 ed., vol. xvi, p. 98.
7. See the saying attributed to the Buddha, "He that is in the saddle of a horse from which he must not dismount will not unduly strain his steed."
8. See also Wilhelm Fränger, *The Millennium of Hieronymous Bosch* (London: Faber & Faber, Ltd., 1952). In this work Dr. Fränger traces the life-accepting underground which, in spite of the frantic persecution by the Christian blood religion, managed to survive the Middle Ages.

# 5. Values and Value Conflict in Self-Destruction: Implications in the Work of C. W. Morris

Elsa A. Whalley

The writer's stimulating year at the Center for the Scientific Study of Suicide was spent investigating the role of personal life-philosophies in self-destructive inclinations and attempts.[1] In a society which claims to value life above all else, suicidal desires and acts pose sharp ethical and moral problems to both those who contemplate and those who observe them. To the social scientist they set difficult but not impossible research tasks. Values as motivating forces have become legitimate objects of investigation. There remains, nevertheless, considerable disagreement as to precisely what they are and how they can best be studied.

Charles Morris's approach to values, and the results of empirical studies based upon it, was an important aspect of the theoretical framework which guided my own explorations. In the first half of this essay I shall attempt to present—necessarily in capsule form—some basic elements of that framework and the findings. The second half is devoted to their implications for the topic of this volume and a consideration of the extent to which my interviews with patients of the Suicide Prevention Center supported my inferences.[2]

The reader should interpret my observations as possible "hypotheses for hypotheses." Admittedly impressionistic, these reflections may nonetheless be useful to others who pursue this intriguing topic.

## Values, Signs, and Behavior

Morris finds meaning in the term "value" only insofar as it refers to valuing behavior—in his terminology "preferential behavior."[3] His position is a development of that of John Dewey, who grounds "value" in "selective-rejective behavior."[4] Preferential behavior may also, Morris suggests, be identified with Murray and Morgan's "positive and negative conative trends."[5]

Since the preferential behavior of humans is generally mediated by symbols, Morris argues that a scientific theory of values (axiology) must be grounded in a scientific theory of signs. His work in values is directly based upon his "Semiotic," which has been acclaimed as a firm base for a scientific signs theory.[6]

Semiotic recognizes four basic kinds of signs, each corresponding to a major function of signs in behavior.[7] Distinguishing between *designative, appraisive,* and *prescriptive* signs is essential for the social scientist, whose work generally falls in the field Morris has called "pragmatics"—the analysis of relationships between signs and their users. *Designative* signs are informative, signifying "properties of objects or events which affect sense organs or other instruments of discrimination." The *appraisive* sign signifies the position of something in a series of objects or acts "ordered in terms of its interpreter's preferential behaviors." (The "interpreter" is the *agent* of the sign process.) Such signs dispose their interpreters "to preferential behavior toward what is signified." They are the result of a process of "evaluation," which is essentially, as Morris writes, "determining what preferential status will be accorded to something or other insofar as it is carried out by signs." *Formative* signs, which indicate how signs should be put together (as in formal linguistic systems), do not concern us here.

The ambiguity of the language of values is a frequent source of difficulty, for crucial terms such as "good" may be used either designatively or appraisively.

> . . . to say that an object is "good" is to signify *either* that it falls in the upper range of a series of objects ordered in terms of the preferential behaviors accorded to them by the interpreter of the sign, *or* to signify that the object reduces the need of some organism.[8]

The practical relevance of distinguishing among the modes of signifying is illustrated by the statement "suicide would be a good solution."

The communicator himself may be uncertain of the sense in which he intends the term "good." The communicatee is therefore still less certain and may respond inappropriately. Or the communicator may intend the term appraisively, while the communicatee believes it is meant merely designatively. Is the statement merely a description of the perceived need-reducing capacity of the act? Does it refer to the position of this action within the sign-user's current hierarchy of preferred behaviors—a position reached after a process of evaluation?

Verification of both kinds of signs is achieved through observations, but of different types. Designative signs are confirmed by studying the properties of objects or events "discriminable by effects on the sense organs of other subjects," i.e., by consensual validation. Appraisals are verified by observing relations between signs and action—by observing the preferential status given the object or event in action. Responses of observers who wish to verify the signs used by others will, therefore, depend on their analysis of the kind of sign being used. An assumption that every communication which has any self-destructive content has some appraisive aspects seems to underlie the therapeutic approach of the Suicide Prevention Center, which insists that the therapist resonate to the "cry for help."

*Prescriptive* signs are used incitively, to direct behavior rather than to dispose toward it. The road signs "school children" and "hairpin turn" may sound designative, but in the context of automobile driving they have definitely prescriptive intent. Much psychotic behavior might be described as confusing modes of signifying-interpreting as designative or confusing appraisive terms as prescriptive and vice versa. Such a person might hear the statement "suicide is a good plan" as having prescriptive intent directed at himself, when it was intended merely designatively.

A major conflict has waged among philosophers and social scientists with respect to the applicability of scientific methods to the study of values. Like Dewey, Morris takes the position that this is not only entirely possible but essential. Since both types of signs are confirmed by observation, scientific methods of control are equally applicable. This conviction undergirds Morris' "experimental humanistics"—an effort to discover general laws of preferential behavior by empirical studies of appraisive signs.

In discussing the meaning of "value," Morris reminds us that it is crucial to distinguish among three usages of the term. "Value" may refer to "the preferred," to "conceptions of the preferable," or to "the preferable." The "preferred" (*operative values*) is the actual direction of preferential behavior toward objects or events. "Conceptions of the preferable" (*conceived values*) are preferences for symbolically indicated objects. The "preferable" (*object values*) is that which is desirable whether or not it is preferred or conceived of as preferable. Morris points out that

> . . . all three usages have been explicated with respect to some form of the term "prefer"—value as the preferred, value as a conception of the preferable, value as the preferable. . . . What is preferred (operative values) can be found through a study of preferential behavior. What is conceived to be preferable (conceived values) can be studied through the symbols employed in preferential behavior and the preferential behavior directed toward symbols.[9]

The main contrast is between the "preferred" and the "preferable," the "esteemed" and the "estimable." Morris seems to give a kind of independent status to "object values," but he insists that they cannot be defined without reference to preferential behavior that ultimately defines the value field.

To concern ourselves with "object value" would involve us in an ancient philosophical debate, far too complex to be considered here. Behavioral science methodology limits us to examining values in their concrete, particular, relativistic manifestations—as operative or conceived values. Distinguishing between the two kinds of values is practically useful as well as theoretically important. Conflicts and discrepancies between these within a culture are often causes of intraindividual conflict (one kind of "anomie"). Inconsistencies between these types of values are both symptoms and causes of intraindividual conflict and interpersonal tension. I have tried to consider such conflicts with respect to self-destructive acts.

## The Formal Model

In *Paths of Life,* C. W. Morris analyzed seven major religious and ethical systems in which he discerned three basic dimensions of value which seemed to correspond to overarching tendencies in personalities.[10] He called these the *dionysian, promethean,* and *buddhistic* components. The *dionysian* (*d*) component of personality refers to tendencies "to release and indulge existing desires." The *promethean* (*p*) component consists of "active tendencies to manipulate and remake the world." The *buddhistic* (*b*) aspect comprises "those tendencies in the self to regulate itself by holding in check its desires."

Seven patterns result from varying strengths of components. Six have counterparts in historical cultural systems, while the seventh has not yet been realized. Morris calls this the "Maitreyan Way" after a legendary Indian figure. In the diagrammed profiles below, dionysian, or *d*, refers to a value-component, while "Dionysian" refers to a way of life involving all three components in a certain order. This is also true of *p* and *b*.[11]

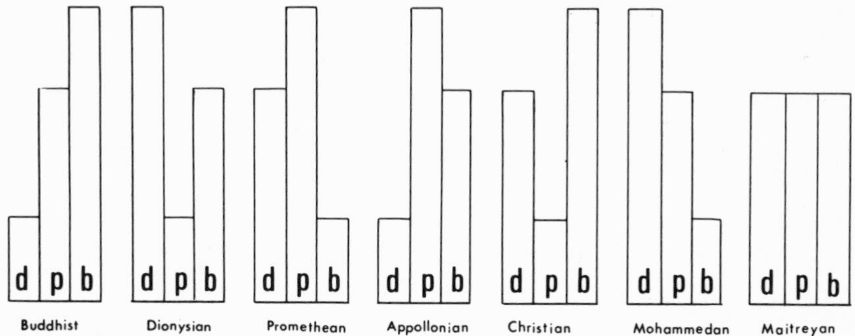


Morris assumed that the relative strength of the three components differed in individual personalities as well as in the content of religious and ethical systems and that there was a relation between personality types and favored "strategies for the conduct of life." This hypothesis and others stemming from it have been tested by him and his coworkers in a series of studies.

"Ways to Live," the instrument created to operationalize the model, consists of thirteen paragraphs. The first seven state the major patterns indicated above. Ways 11, 12, and 13 are statements of "pure types," while Ways 8, 9, and 10 describe orientations implied in written reactions to the pilot version. Respondents express their liking for each Way on a seven-point scale and then rank them from most to least liked. Space permits listing only the identifying phrase for each Way and the ethical or religious system which best represents it.[12]

1. "Nothing in excess"—preserve the best that man has attained. *Apollonianism. Confucianism.* (Aristotle)
2. "Independence of persons and things"—simplify the self; overcome desires by self-knowledge. *Buddhism.* (Gautama Buddha)
3. "Sympathetic concern for others"—stress helpful love for other people above self and all else. *Christianity.* (Christ)
4. "Festivity and solitude in alternation"—abandon the self to release of desire, and thus rejuvenate the self. *Dionysianism.* (Nietzsche)

5. "Group activity, group enjoyment"—join together to attain a corporate goal. *Mohammedanism.* (Marx)

6. "Man the eternal maker and remaker"—take the initiative against the social ills; struggle against them with science and technology. *Prometheanism.* (Dewey)

7. "Dynamic integration of diversity"—balanced activity, enjoyment, contemplation; stress flexibility, multiplicity, unified in and through diversity. *Maitreyan Way.* (Morris)

8. "Carefree wholesome enjoyment"—prefer the simple unsophisticated pleasures of senses, living. *Epicureanism.* (Epicurus)

9. "Wait in quiet receptivity"—nonaggressive receptivity to cosmic powers. *Taoism.*

10. "Vigilant, manly self-control"—do all you can; expect little of the universe. *Stoicism.*

11. "Meditation on the inner life"—pure type of "Becoming" orientation; pure "buddhistic".

12. "Active, daring, adventuresome deeds"—pure type of "doing" orientation; pure "promethean".

13. "Let yourself be used"—pure type of "being" orientation; pure "dionysian".

## Empirical Value Patterns

With this instrument, a considerable body of data has been accumulated describing cross-cultural patterns of value preferences and a series of sociological and psychological correlates. I shall summarize only those findings which seem to carry direct implications for the problem at hand.

### *Cross-Cultural Factors and Scales*

Preferences for the several "Ways to Live" were collected from students in the United States, India, and Nationalist China, and independent factor analyses were performed on the three sets of data. Five factors were extracted from the American material,[13] which reappeared—with slight differences—in the other analyses. The factors are described below, together with the Ways, with highest positive and negative loadings on each:

Factor A: Social Restraint and Self-Control
The stress is upon responsible, conscientious, intelligent participation in human affairs. The orientation is primarily moral. There is an awareness

of the larger human and cosmic setting in which the individual lives and acceptance of the restraints which responsibility to this larger whole requires. The accent is upon the appreciation and conservation of what man has attained rather than upon the initiation of change. The antithesis of the trait is unrestrained and socially irresponsible enjoyment. (i.e., Factor E) (High positive loadings: Ways 1, 10; High negative 4; Secondary positive, 3)

Factor B: Enjoyment and Progress in Action

The stress is upon delight in vigorous action for the overcoming of obstacles. The emphasis is upon the initiation of change rather than upon the preservation of what has already been attained. The temper is one of confidence in man's powers rather than of caution and restraint. The orientation is outward to society and to nature. The antithesis of the trait is a life focused upon the development of the inner self. (i.e., Factor C) (High positive: 12, 5, 6; High negative, 2)

Factor C: Withdrawal and Self-Sufficiency

The stress is upon a rich inner life of heightened self-awareness. The self rather than society is the focus of attention. The emphasis is not one of self-indulgence, however, but is rather upon the simplification and purification of the self in order to attain a high level of insight and awareness. Control over persons and things is repudiated, but not deep sympathy for all living things. The antithesis of the trait is mergence of the self with the social group for group achievement and enjoyment. (i.e., Factor B) (High positive: 11, 12; High negative, 5; Secondary small positive, 9)

Factor D: Receptivity and Sympathetic Concern

The stress is upon receptivity to persons and to nature. The source of inspiration comes from outside the self, and the person lives and develops in devoted responsiveness to this source. Since there are only two high positive and no high negative loadings on this factor, Factor D is not as sharply defined by the Ways as are the other factors. But a stress upon responsive and devoted receptivity is clearly a mode of orientation different from that represented by any other factor. (High positive loadings, 13, 9; secondary, 3)

Factor E: Self-Indulgence (or Sensuous Enjoyment)

The stress is upon sensuous enjoyment, whether this enjoyment be found in the simple pleasures of life or in abandonment to the moment. The emphasis upon social restraint and self-control characteristic of Factor A is rejected. The antithesis of the trait is responsible submission of one's self to social and cosmic purposes. (i.e., Factor A) (High positive, 8, 4; High negative, 10, 13)[14]

In the Chinese data, *B* splits into two factors. $B^1$ seems to be oriented toward the specific problems of persons and society, whereas $B^2$ seems to lack this focus. Both stress activity and are clearly related to the *B* factor in the Indian and American analyses.

*D* does not appear in the Chinese analysis. This is thought to result from the translation of Way 13, which loads highest on *D* in the American and Indian analyses. Way 13 stressed receptivity less in the Chinese translation than in the English version used in India and the United States.

The factors were sufficiently alike and stable in the three analyses to conclude that a common "value-space" with similar dimensions underlies the responses of individuals in apparently dissimilar cultures.

> Put in terms of spatial metaphor, it is as if persons in diverse cultures employ five common coordinates in locating the place of conceptions of the good life in value-space. Or using a musical example, it is as if persons in various cultures have in common five major tones in the musical scales on which they compose different melodies. The value dimensions here isolated can, in any case, serve as points of orientation and comparison for further studies of the dimensionality of the value domain.[15]

Psychological scaling methods applied to this material and ratings made in Norway and Japan revealed similar scales in the five cultures, justifying creation of a common interval scale. The scale value of every Way in each culture was then recalculated on the cross-cultural scale. Factor scores were also calculated by multiplying the scale value of a Way in a given sample by the factor loading and summing the results. Scale values and factor scores are used for cross-cultural and intra-cultural comparisons. With consistent cross-cultural dimensions and an interval scale, genuine "measurement" of values has been attained. (See Table 1.)

The content of the factors and the reported patterns of scores for the Ways and the factors suggested that they might contain clues to the dynamics of self-destruction. One of my early impressions at the Suicide Prevention Center was that the specific values of patients did not differ remarkably from those I had encountered in nonsuicidal patients and in nonpatients. Except for the denigration of their own lives (and thus, by implication, "life" itself to a degree), their manifest values could be described—at least superficially—in terms of generalized American standards and goals: work-achievement, "getting along," security, and so

Table 1

Factor Scores For Five National Groups*

| | A | B | C | D | E | Mean |
|---|---|---|---|---|---|---|
| U. S. | 0.43 | 0.47 | −1.35 | −0.87 | 0.35 | −0.19 |
| Norway | 1.09 | 0.32 | −0.82 | −0.11 | −0.12 | 0.07 |
| India | 1.55 | 0.72 | −0.40 | 0.30 | −0.20 | 0.39 |
| Japan | 0.93 | 0.30 | −0.33 | 0.10 | −0.07 | 0.19 |
| China | 0.81 | 0.96 | −1.49 | 0.45 | −0.51 | 0.04 |
| Mean | 0.96 | 0.55 | −0.88 | −0.03 | −0.11 | 0.10 |

* Morris, *Varieties of Human Value*, p. 44.

forth. Granted that attempting to live up to the inherent contradictions in the American ideology often results in inner tension and a sense of failure, still it rarely leads to self-destruction. Since it did not seem the answer would be found at the level of concrete goals and values, I hoped that some light would appear by examining a body of material which described the latent structure of a "value-domain," which had been defined by individual preferences for extremely broad, historically relevant "strategies for the conduct of life."

## *Cross-Cultural Value Variations*

Morris does not believe it possible to separate definite Eastern and Western patterns. The ratings of the three Asiatic countries have much in common, as do those of the two Western ones. Nevertheless, there are important within-group differences. In some ways, the choices of Norwegian students resemble those of Japanese and Indians more than those of Americans. Contrasts between the two Western groups become particularly interesting when we recall that, among Western countries, Norway has one of the lowest suicide rates.

Dublin examined the 1959 and 1960 international suicide rates to see if Durkheim's hypothesis regarding the effectiveness of religion as an antisuicidal agent still holds. He found that it does hold up very well, for rates in predominantly Catholic countries tend to be low and those in predominantly Protestant ones tend to be high.[16] We have arranged Dublin's figures in the following table, in which the place of Norway as one of the "Protestant exceptions" is clear. (See Table 2)

Comparative factor scores show that the order of scores for Norway is *A* (social restraint and self-control), *B* (enjoyment and progress in

Table 2

Suicide Rates for Protestant and Catholic Countries
(*From L. I. Dublin*)

| *Predominantly Catholic: Low rates* | | *Predominantly Protestant: High Rates* | |
|---|---|---|---|
| Irish Free State | 3.0 | West Germany | 18.7 |
| Spain | 5.2 | West Berlin | 33.3 |
| Italy | 6.3 | Sweden | 17.4 |
| Greece | 3.8* | Denmark | 20.3 |
| *Catholic "Exceptions": High Rates* | | *Protestant "Exceptions": Low Rates* | |
| Austria | 23.0 | Northern Ireland | 4.4 |
| France | 15.9 | Norway | 6.4 |
| Hungary | 24.9 | Netherlands | 6.6 |

(United States: 10.6)

* The doctrinal position of the Greek Catholic Church resembles that of the Roman Catholic.

action), *D* (receptivity and sympathetic concern), *E* (self-indulgence and sensuous enjoyment), and *C* (withdrawal and self-sufficiency). All factor scores are moderate. In terms of these factors Norway occupies a middle-of-the-road position.

Comparing the factor scores for the two Western groups, we find a very high valuation of social responsibility and self-restraint (factor A) in Norway and a very low development of this factor in the United States. Norwegian students are oriented more positively toward interpersonal receptivity and concern (factor *D*) and toward self-awareness and self-insight (factor C) than are Americans. On the other hand, they are oriented less toward achievement through personal initiative (factor *B*) and much less toward the gratification of personal desires (factor *E*). The most marked differences are between the scores on factor A (self-restraint and social control) and factor *E* (self-indulgence and sensuous enjoyment). The results suggest that in these factors we may find a key to the marked difference in the rates of self-destruction. At the same time, contrasts in the other factors suggest that any one or all may play a part.

### *The American Value Pattern*

It will be seen that factor A (social restraint and self-control) and factor *D* (receptivity and social concern) are lower, whereas factor *E* (self-indulgence and sensuous enjoyment) is higher in the American material than in any other. Factor *B* (enjoyment and progress in action) has a slightly higher score within the American pattern. The lowest score is for factor *C* (withdrawal and self-sufficiency).

These scores reaffirm the demise of the "Protestant Ethic" as a directive force in the lives of Americans—at least young Americans. Just the reverse pattern would be predicted from that ethic. What appears here is an activist, "other-directed," hedonistic viewpoint.

Clearly, a self-centered value system in which the gratification of personal desires is salient and inward self-development has a low status leaves the person susceptible to intense frustration by the outer world, which is seen as the source of supply.

The low place of factor *D* (receptivity and social concern), which includes Way 3, a translation of the Christian ethic, is notable. Way 7 ("dynamic integration of diversity") ranked highest among the choices of American students. Since this includes the values represented by all five factors, but none to an extreme degree, it has no high positive or negative loading on any of the factors. Morris sees the high place of Way 7 as indicating a desire to balance self-indulgence with social responsibility. He cautions that the structure of the American value pattern is very complex and cannot be understood solely from the factor scores.

## *Psychological Correlates*

Correlations, at the $p < .01$ level in some cases, have been established between the value factors and the personality variables as measured by such instruments as the Thurstone Temperament Test[17] and the Cattell 16-Factor Personality Test.[18] None of the correlations is large enough to warrant identifying any of the value factors with any of the personality factors. Factor A (self-restraint and social control) and factor *E* (self-indulgence and sensuous enjoyment) appear to be less related to personality variables than the other three factors.

Morris regards the Thurstone factors—since they are derived from items referring to long-term preferences—as close to the level of operative values. To the extent that they can be so considered, he finds a congruence between operative values and conceived values as indicated by the value factors and concludes that temperamental differences definitely enter into the ratings of the Ways. In a lesser study, a similar congruence was seen between preferences for the Ways and certain of the Cattell variables.[19]

If temperament traits and ethical style tend to be associated, then lack of congruence between them could certainly be a source of internal discomfort. The possibility that in extreme cases the effort to live by, to live up to, and to live with incompatible value systems might lead to self-destruction is another implication to be considered.

Certain Ways seem to be related more strongly to personality variables than are others. Those entering into factor A (social restraint and self-control) and factor *E* (self-indulgence and sensuous enjoyment) seem to be more independent of temperament than Ways entering into the other factors.

Ways to Live and the familiar Allport-Vernon Scale of Values[20] tap different though related aspects of value. It will be recalled that the Allport-Vernon categories were originally based on the Spraenger typology and validated by occupational groups. Because many items emphasize social and occupational role behavior, Morris thinks of the Allport categories as closer to the level of operative values than the Ways.

In an analysis performed by Morris on material collected by this writer, mean Allport-Vernon scores were compared for subjects who rated a given Way positively and those who rated it negatively. Ways were combined according to the five factors.[21] Significant positive relationships were found between factors A (social restraint and self-control) and *D* (receptivity and social concern) and Allport's "social" and "religious" categories. Factor *B* (enjoyment and progress in action) proved to be associated with the "economic" category. Factor C (withdrawal and self-sufficiency) was positively associated with the "aesthetic" and "religious" and factor *E* (self-indulgence and sensuous enjoyment) with "theoretical" and "economic" scales.

Relationships between the "religious" category and three of the factors suggest the intriguing possibility that high scorers on this scale may do so out of at least three broad ethical orientations. If this were so, it might clarify the self-destructive acts of people who consider themselves "religious" and who score high on this particular measure.

In one orientation, "religiosity" would be associated with a moralistic sense of social responsibility (high factor A). A second would involve strong sensitivity to others (high factor *D*). In the third, "religiosity" would be accompanied by intensive self-awareness and an effort to develop the self inwardly (high factor C). Both of the first orientations could have high scores on the "social" scale, but the significance of the scores would be quite different.

## Sociological Correlates

The factors prove to be associated with a number of social background indices, among which size of childhood community is especially relevant. When American respondents were grouped by the size of community in which they had spent their childhoods, those raised in the largest cities (over 500,000 population) has significantly higher scores on factor C (withdrawal and self-sufficiency) and lower ones on factor A (self-restraint and social control). Scores on factors *B* (enjoyment and progress in action) and *D* (receptivity and social concern) were also lower. "Outer-oriented" factors tend to be rejected: maintaining the social fabric, receptivity and enjoying interaction with others, manipulating the external world. "Inner-oriented" values tend to be accepted: privacy, self-sufficiency.

Compared with those raised in smaller communities, persons raised in large cities tend to prefer "strategies for living" which are congruent with descriptions of the "anomic" individual and the clinical picture of depression. This is certainly not to conclude that the whole "big-city" group fits those categories, but merely to point up the similarity between the value profiles and syndromes described as suicidogenic.

One of the major complaints of several older patients interviewed at the Suicide Prevention Center was social isolation. While age and economic difficulties played a part in creating this situation for some, for others it seemed to be largely self-determined. The isolated person may be motivated by evaluations of society of which he is only dimly aware, they are so deeply embedded in the urban-life orientation which one patient called "defensive living." Several patients expressed a wish to live in smaller communities where they felt they might be closer to others and less anonymous. These same people had rejected the friendly advances of their immediate Los Angeles neighbors because they "didn't want to get too involved with their problems or they with mine."

## Implications for Understanding Self-Destructive Behavior

The value scales, factor scores, and cross-cultural and intracultural findings are measures of conceived values. Deviating from these patterns obviously is not the same as deviating from normative behavior or personality patterns, nor is conforming to them. To give assent to propositions about life does not mean one would in fact prefer to live by those propositions, nor that one lives by them.

The manifest ideology of American culture, grounded in the Judeo-Christian religious tradition, expressly prohibits the "suicidal solution" in any circumstance. The person who even considers its utility as an "escape hatch" already separates himself from the cultural value system, for the preferability of life over death is perhaps the one value in which the ideology is consistent.[22] (Wars are justified by saying that losing a certain number of lives will lead to saving a greater number or by the semantic "ploy" of saying that the "life" which would be led under conditions of conquest would "not really be life.")

In some instances a deviant valuation of life is clearly associated with other kinds of cognitive and behavioral deviance, but this is not always so. Presumably, in Western culture (where Eastern "altruistic suicide" is not socially sanctioned) no one commits suicide when he is at ease in the world. To that extent, all suicide efforts have something in common with the neuroses and psychoses and it may be worthwhile to examine the values of clinic patients.

### *Values and Psychotherapy*

In *The Open Self*, Morris suggested that there might be "healthy" and "pathic" expressions of each of the Ways to Live. Healthy expressions "permit the continued growth of the self in a direction which offers it widening satisfactions" while pathic ones block this growth "by giving partial satisfactions which keep the self from moving forward." As an illustration, he suggested that those who strongly preferred the Taoist Way 9 might under stress tend toward depression, whereas those drawn strongly toward the Promethean Way 6 might tend toward paranoia. Evidence of relationships between preferences for the Ways and body type was a source of Morris's thinking at that time.[23]

Morris and his associates (working at the Hacker Foundation Clinic in Los Angeles) administered Ways to Live to three groups of fifty persons each: outpatients, spouses or closest friends of patients, controls. Eighteen patients had been diagnosed as "neurotic," twelve as "psychotic" (all schizophrenic), seventeen as "personality disorder," three as "psycho-physiological problem." Ratings for severity of disturbance were also available. *D*'s and correlations between means were used as measures of deviation.[24]

The value profiles of all groups were generally similar. Differences between groups were smaller than intercultural differences. *D*'s between neurotics and psychotics were larger than those between patients and controls.

### *Gross Similarity*

These findings indicate that we should not expect the general values of people who appear bent on self-destruction to be *grossly* different from the general American pattern—except for devaluation of their own lives. This was the case with Suicide Prevention Center patients with whom I talked. Most accepted the normative valuation of "life per se" while devaluing their own lives. They seemed undisturbed by this apparent contradiction, justifying it merely by the statement that "things are different for me." This is an indication of the sense of separateness which was shown in many ways.

We would anticipate that self-destructive persons will include adherents to value patterns described for subgroups in the United States and that their choices may be conditioned as much by sociological factors (age, sex, urban background, etc.) as by emotional state.

Studies of suicide have generally separated out known psychotics. The wisdom of this practice is obviously confirmed here. Still, it is apparent that even the schizophrenic patients are not entirely out of touch with the conceived values of the society—at least insofar as they have learned them. Of course, we do not know what idiosyncratic meanings these statements had for them. (This is true of the responses of all individuals.)

### *Value Rejection*

Despite general similarity, there are important differences between patients and controls and within the patient group, especially between neurotics and psychotics. Patients liked the instrument as a whole much less than did controls. (Average ratings were lower, tending toward the "dislike" pole.) "Total liking" scores were higher for neurotic than for psychotic patients.

Adopting a group's ideology is the initial step in participating in its life. A pluralistic society offers a wide range of alternative ideologies and groups. These findings confirm the belief that mental illness is in a sense an "antisocial" phenomenon.

Viewing suicide with Durkheim as partly a result of the weakening of social control by normative beliefs, one would anticipate still stronger rejection in a suicidal population. The "total liking" scores might appear as follows:

Highest  Nonsuicidal normals
         Suicidal normals[25]

| | |
|---|---|
| | Neurotic, nonsuicidal |
| | Neurotic, suicidal |
| | Psychotic, nonsuicidal |
| Lowest | Psychotic, suicidal |

Data collected on patients at the Suicide Prevention Center on the Ways are quantitatively meager. Since they were embedded in another instrument, results are only generally comparable. They are offered as the merest hints of possibilities; there are only nine cases.

The Ways are included in a 62-item 5-part instrument on life philosophies, which uses a 5-point scale (—2 to +2) of "agreement-disagreement" (rather than "liking").[26] "Total agreement" could range from —26 to +26. The scores of patients ranged from —9 to +8, with an average "total agreement" for the group of —2.5. This is only slightly negative, but the mean for the original group on the 62-item test was almost precisely neutral (—.02).[27]

Six of the nine patients had negative total agreement scores and only three, positive ones. Six disagreed with more Ways than they agreed with. This skewing toward the negative pole resembles the attitudes of the other patients. The 117 choices (13 choices each for 9 persons) give an expected frequency of 29 in 3 categories and 30 in one if equally distributed. (Respondents were strongly discouraged from using the (?) category.) The choices were distributed thus:

| | |
|---|---|
| Strongly agree | 17 |
| Moderately agree | 32 |
| Moderately disagree | 31 |
| Strongly disagree | 31 |
| Can't decide | 6 |

Of the 117 choices, 62 are negative valuations and only 49 positive. Moderate categories are used with equal frequency but there are fewer choices in the extreme "agreement" category. (Both extreme categories were avoided in our earlier study.) This very sketchy material suggested that Suicide Prevention Center patients are also rejecting the Ways.

In the cross-cultural studies many American students found all the Ways unsatisfactory and also did not wish to formulate personal alternatives, arguing that "life must not be restricted."

Is this attitude being expressed by patients with greater intensity? Or is their rejection based on experienced failure of attempted life philosophies to gratify their desires? Both attitudes seem to be involved. The Suicide Prevention Center group was considerably older than the students. The only patient whose comment resembled those described for the American students was the youngest, a married student in her late 20s. She wrote:

The paths listed seem to me based on intellectual reasons rather than innate desire, while I think any way of life, because a person has a feeling for it at the moment, should be *the* way of life. It should not have to be rationalized as performing a function either for oneself or others . . . to say I choose a way of life because it provides the most good for society and for me is not "living" but serving out a self-imposed sentence . . . my point is that I would like to be able to live "emotions" rather than because of LOGIC . . . *no* predetermined METHOD is a good reason for LIFE.

Ways to Live become "reason for Life." Any questionnaire becomes a projective test under the right circumstances!

Among the other patients there was consensus that it *was* desirable to have a philosophy of life and try to live by it. However, all said they had not found such a satisfying philosophy themselves. They were "still looking"—with different degrees of zeal and hope. Most were uncertain if they would find a satisfying view but had some slight hope.

The one patient who said that she was no longer looking for a philosophy of life because she had no hope of finding it, yet thought that people who had "something to believe in" were much more fortunate than those who did not, was the only one who committed suicide.

### *Uncertainty, Conviction, Idiosyncrasy*

In the Hacker Foundation Clinic study, the patients' scores were more variable than those of controls and more Ways received extreme ratings. We have noted the "extremism" with respect to "dislike" categories.

A peculiar constellation of extremism, variability of attitude, uncertainty, and idiosyncrasy seemed to characterize the interview responses of Suicide Prevention Center patients. During the first interviews, they were unusually reluctant to express any opinions or beliefs whatsoever—to commit themselves on even the least controversial of subjects. However, this quickly disappeared with encouragement and they proceeded to use the interviews as a (obviously pleasurable) podium. They presented views which were at once uncertain and vague yet strong in a singular kind of conviction. This was the conviction that, no matter how confused they might be at the moment, when they did "get clear," they would not—and must not—end up with *ordinary* viewpoints. Repeatedly, the theme appears that "I am not a person who accepts run-of-the-mill opinions." These patients—who admittedly had not been doing well with their own "solutions"—were intensely determined not to adopt the ways others had found satisfactory.

The wish to be different is certainly a common theme in neurosis, but it stood out here with great clarity. It seems as if these people—failing to achieve a greatly desired individuality in their lives—were determined at least not to die ordinary deaths.

The life philosophies that patients did describe were extremely fragmentary and internally inconsistent as well as vague. They seemed to be composed of discrete elements adopted from science, religion, philosophy that were ill-digested and not at all integrated into an organized view. There seemed to be a kind of stubborn eclecticism operating without an ability to use pragmatic tests of ideas.

This kind of eclecticism is neither surprising nor unusual among Americans. It is usually, however, subordinated to some general system—religious or otherwise. Only two or three people were trying actively to organize isolated values and beliefs into an inclusive system. These were patients who (after being rescued from an attempt) had begun to think their childhood religious training might be readopted and used as an organizing principle to give direction to their lives.

### *How Crucial Is Factor A?*

Scores on factor A (self-restraint and social control) differentiated patients in the Hacker Foundation study more than other measures. Patients had significantly lower scores than controls, with the difference more marked for psychotic than neurotic, and for female than male patients. Severity of disturbance was inversely correlated with the factor score. Patients, especially males, tended significantly more often to choose values which were more "egocentric" than "social." Neurotics were more inclined to choose ways involving interaction.

These results, the Norwegian pattern and the value profiles for urban-reared people, predicted low liking for the Ways represented in factor A and for nonegocentric ones on the part of the self-destructive group.[28] Interviews and case histories show a highly narcissistic quality in the attempts, even those made with low rescue possibilities, and in the completed suicide.

Foolhardy though it is to comment in print on nine cases, we shall do so for the reader's possible interest. "Total agreement" scores for our group (sum of individual agreement ratings) for individual Ways gave Way 7 ("dynamic integration of diversity") a clear first place. The group is "ideologically normal" in an important aspect.

Way 1 ("nothing in excess") was a clear second. Way 3 ("sympathetic concern for others") was third with a somewhat lower score but still at the positive end of the continuum. Way 11 ("meditation on the inner self") was most rejected, followed closely by Way 2 ("independence of persons and things") and then Way 12 ("active, daring adventuresome deeds") and Way 4 ("festivity and solitude in alternation") with equal scores. The scores pile up at the disagree pole, but the three most agreed upon and four least agreed upon are clear.

Surprisingly, two of the three accepted Ways fall at the very "social" end of the egocentric-nonegocentric continuum, and three of four rejected Ways at the "egocentric" pole.

Looked at in terms of the factors, the Ways to which most assent was given have high loadings on factor A (self-restraint and self-control) except for Way 7, which did not have high loadings on any of the factors. Way 3 ("sympathetic concern for others") also has a high loading on factor *D* (receptivity and social concern). Of the disliked Ways, one, Way 4, has negative loadings on factor A. The other most rejected Ways, 11 and 2, both load high on factor C (withdrawal and self-sufficiency). Way 12 is the extreme promethean attitude, with positive high loadings on factor *B* (enjoyment and progress in action). It is rejected, but so is Way 2, with a high negative loading on that factor. Like other results for factor *B*, this is ambiguous. This group seems to be assenting most to Ways involved positively with two other-oriented factors (*A* and *D*) and disagreeing with one involved negatively in such a factor. It seems to be disagreeing with Ways contributing positively to a self-oriented factor (C).

If the factors do not separate self-destructive people from the rest of the population, that is itself informative. Our meager data indicate that—for the large part—these patients respond as other Americans. Ranking the Ways by the total agreement scores for each, we compared them with Morris's reported figures for over 2,000 American women (six out of nine were women). Our little group follows the United States female pattern closely in major respects. Ways 7, 1, 5, 2, and 11 fall, respectively, into first, second, fourth, twelfth, and thirteenth places in both instances.

However, the patients' responses give much higher place to Ways 3 and 9, much lower to Way 12, and slightly lower to Ways 4 and 8.

Returning to the definitions of the Ways, we find the patients were especially drawn to the Christian (3) and Taoist (9) Ways and away from the pure promethean (12), Epicurean and Dionysian Ways. Considering the formal model, we find that the Christian Way has a fairly high buddhistic component. Way 9, the third-ranking Way, expresses the Taoist counsel of "nonagressive receptivity before the cosmic powers," also a buddhistic attitude. This counterbalances the rejection of Ways 2 and 11. The rejected Epicurean Way emphasizes enjoyment of "simple unsophisticated pleasures." In this it has a strong dionysian component, which is the major aspect of the rejected Dionysian Way. The disliked Way 12 is an emphatic statement of the promethean component.

The responses resemble those of American women except for a greater preference for the philosophical quietism expressed in the Taoist Way, for interpersonal receptivity and responsibility, and less responsiveness to gratification of sensuous demands and active efforts to remake the world.

Are these the responses of frustrated prometheans or have these always been "passive-dependent characters"? To what extent is the orientation genuinely receptive and to what extent merely passive? It is impossible to say. To what extent did the responses reflect reactions to the unsuccessful attempt? There are suggestions that they do so to a great degree. Are they telling us that they have become more receptive to the world because their strenuous efforts to reshape it to their hearts' desires were futile?

We must return to the elusive factor A. Must it be ruled out as a contrasuicidal force? Not at all. We could argue that the results speak in favor of that hypothesis. Possibly it is the very strength of factor A that keeps this an "attempter" group rather than a "completer" group. They are deeply involved in the social organism—on one level at least. They have deviated sharply in an important operative value, but their view of reality, their "conceptions of the desirable" are those of highly socialized persons. This was not the case with the psychotics. (We cannot say to what extent the Suicide Prevention Center patients' responses are those of neurotics.)

All our calculations and comparisons are merely ways of "playing games with the data." The real facts are to be found in the interviews, where we find so clearly stated the attitudes summed up in these little numbers. In our conversations we heard repeatedly the patient's awareness of his own confusion, vagueness, inconsistency, and unproductive modes of thinking and evaluating. We heard his attempts to bring himself to a quiet place, slow down, look around, find out what it was all about, and perhaps get close to other people at last. We heard his awareness that he had not found the answer to the riddle by hectic efforts and was trying to open himself to new answers, though it was hard to shake off his old habits of reasoning and valuing. *Stop the World—I Want to Get Off!*—the title of a recent Broadway musical—perfectly expresses this theme. When patients came to the Suicide Prevention Center, they seemed to have learned that they could not—because they really did not want to—get off, and the world would not stop. Their liking for the Taoist Way seems to say that they now wanted merely to have it slow down a bit so that they could take a deep breath and get ready for a new try. And this time they would not try to make it by frantic struggling but by balance, control, order, predictability, reasonableness, and "waiting in quiet receptivity."

Let us hope that philosophical objectivity—not psychological depression—is speaking in the attraction to the Taoist Way. Until we learn more about values and valuing, we must rest with the conclusion that there is no suicidal Way of Life other than misuse of the guidelines available to all of us. Whatever Ways they choose, we hope these people can learn to use them creatively, as healthy rather than pathological "strategies for living."

## REFERENCES

1. My deepest appreciation to Dr. Edwin S. Shneidman for making this possible. My thanks to Drs. Norman Farberow, Robert Litman, Norman Tabachnick, and the staff of the Suicide Prevention Center for their cooperation. Kresten Bjerg, Jack Hattem, and Joseph Scheitzach were challenging and insightful colleagues at the Center. My greatest debt is to the patients who entrusted their private views of the universe. I hope the research interviews, like the therapeutic ones, made the world seem a little less cold and hostile.
2. Extensive interviewing—extending in some instances to 20 to 25 hours—was conducted with three men and nine women patients. Therapy priorities precluded controlled selection of subjects. All had made serious attempts. One woman realized her suicidal intent during the course of contact. All were self-referred, and none was designated as psychotic. Ages ranged from early 20s to late 60s, and all socioeconomic and educational levels were represented. Structured instruments measuring religious attitudes, personal life philosophies, values, life goals, and alienation were also administered.
3. C. W. Morris, "Axiology as the Science of Preferential Behavior," in Ray Lepley (ed.), *Value, A Cooperative Inquiry* (New York: Columbia University Press, 1949), pp. 211–222.

4. John Dewey, "A Theory of Valuation," *International Encyclopedia of Unified Science* (Chicago: University of Chicago Press, 1939), II, (4), 27; "The Field of Value," in *Value, A Cooperative Inquiry*. pp. 64ff.
5. Henry A. Murray and Christiana D. Morgan, "A Clinical Study of Sentiments, *Genetic Psychology Monographs*," 32: 3–149 and 153–311, 1945.
6. C. W. Morris, "Foundations of the Theory of Signs," *International Encyclopedia of Unified Science* (Reprinted as bound volumes; Chicago: University of Chicago Press, 1955), I, part I, 78–137; *Signs, Language and Behavior* (Englewood Cliffs, N. J.: Prentice-Hall, Inc., 1946, and 2d ed.; New York: George Braziller, Inc., 1955).
7. The four types of signs correspond roughly to the four "functional problems" which Bales believes must be solved by all action. The informational use relates to the "adaptive problem," the valuative to the "expressive problem," the incitive to the "instrumental," and the systemic to the "integrative problem." See R. F. Bales, *Working Papers in the Theory of Action* (New York: The Free Press, 1953).
8. Morris, "Axiology as the Science of Preferential Behavior," p. 222.
9. C. W. Morris, *Varieties of Human Value* (Chicago: University of Chicago Press, 1956), pp. 9–12.
10. New York: Harper & Row, 1942, and 2d ed.; New York: George Braziller, Inc., 1956).
11. Morris, *Varieties of Human Value*, pp. 2–3.
12. *Ibid.*, pp. 13–17.
13. C. W. Morris and Lyle V. Jones, "Value Scales and Dimensions," *Journal of Abnormal and Social Psychology*, 51: 523–535, 1955.
14. Morris, *Varieties of Human Value*, pp. 27ff.
15. *Ibid.*, p. 185.
16. Louis I. Dublin, *Suicide: A Sociological and Statistical Study* (New York: The Ronald Press Company, 1963), pp. 19–20, 74–79, and 211.
17. *Thurstone Temperament Schedule and Examiner's Manual* (Chicago: Science Research Associates, 1949).
18. R. B. Cattell, *The 16-Factor Personality Test* (Champaign: Institute for Personality and Ability Testing, 1949).
19. *Varieties of Human Value*, p. 99.
20. G. W. Allport and P. E. Vernon, *A Study of Values* (Rev. ed.; Boston: Houghton Mifflin Company, 1951).
21. To correspond with other sections of the research instrument, in which the Ways were included, a five-point ordinal scale was used. The experimental group was somewhat higher in "theoretical" and "aesthetic" and lower in "economic," "political," and "social" scores than the standardization population for the Allport-Vernon Scale of Values.
22. Elsa A. Whalley, "Values and the Suicide Threat," *Journal of Religion and Health*, 3: 261–269, 1964. This contains some of my thinking about the implications of employing the "suicidal hypothesis."
23. Detailed discussion of those findings and confirming evidence in later work has been omitted for lack of space to do them justice. Evidence of relations between value factors and temperament variables has already been

mentioned. Morris has described in detail his methods of somatotyping and his findings regarding body type and the value factors, temperament and body type, and body type and clinical diagnoses. See *Varieties of Human Values*, pp. 121–130, 139–143, 148–153, and 158.

24. Bernice T. Eiduson, C. W. Morris, and D. O'Donovan, "Values of Psychiatric Patients," *Behavioral Science*, 4: 297–312, 1960.
25. This is a debatable category, defined as persons who contemplate, attempt, or succeed in self-destruction—whose histories give no evidence of prior chronic or recurring difficulties in solving adaptive problems at crucial life stages and in crucial life areas.
26. Elsa A. Whalley, "Individual Life-Philosophies in Relation to Personality and to Systematic Philosophy: An Experimental Study" (Unpublished Ph.D. dissertation, University of Chicago, 1955). "Views of the World," which includes Ways to Live, is described in full.
27. Unfortunately, total agreement scores are not available for subsections. It is hard to say how much "negativity" the Ways contributed to the Views of the World scores.
28. From an unpublished study by Charles E. Osgood, Charles Morris, and Edward Ware, reported in Eiduson, Morris, and O'Donovan. The order of the Ways on an "egocentricity-sociality" factor continuum is: 2, 4, 12, 6, 13, 11, 5, 10, 9, 7, 8, 1, 3.

# 6. Can a Philosophy Make One Philosophical?

STEPHEN C. PEPPER

The meanings of the terms in the title above are quite different, even though one is grammatically the adjective form of the other. "A philosophy" generally means a set of beliefs held by a person, his philosophy of life. "Being philosophical" generally means an attitude of emotional balance in a situation, particularly in the face of disappointment or frustration, a willingness to accept the reality of a situation and make whatever practical adjustments are required. The question of our title then amounts to this: Can a set of concepts keep a person, or help keep him, emotionally balanced in relation to the reality of a situation in which he becomes involved? This is a refined application of a broader question: What control, if any, does a person's thought have over his emotions or actions?

Though these seem simple questions, they become increasingly involved the further one goes into them. The first spontaneous answer is: Of course thought controls actions. We have evidence of this every day. We have the idea of buying a car or building a house, and following that idea we carry out the appropriate acts. If it is a house we are thinking of, an architect is engaged to realize our idea. He questions us in order to formulate our idea in greater detail, and then with his technical knowledge he articulates it into plans and elevations, which can be read by a contractor who, in turn, organizes the physical acts required to actualize the house. This whole complex enterprise consists in an ordered sequence of thoughts controlling an ordered sequence of acts toward the realization of a concrete physical goal. The process also controls a sequence of needs, desires, and drives which in a broad sense constitute the dynamic emotional factors in the enterprise. In formulating the plans, the architect draws out and integrates a variety of needs and desires of his client, adjusting them to the funds available. The planning necessarily controls their integration. Moreover, the plans are projected into the social community subject to the rules of the society for the payment and contracting of such a job. The rules control the emotional inducements of the contractor and his subcontractors and laborers to carry the plans out effectively. From such evidences there can be no question that thought can control human actions and emotions.

However, there are other occasions when the emotions appear clearly to control the ideas. This is obvious whenever basic drives—hunger, thirst, micturition, sex, pain, fear, anger, and the like—emerge with intensity. As hunger increases, associations go more and more to thoughts of food. Similarly with the others. On such occasions the emotions charge the instrumental plans that present themselves for the satisfaction of the needs and desires, and these plans can control the succeeding actions; but the plans themselves are controlled for their dynamics by the needs and drives that charge them.

It is the complexity of human life arising from countless occasions of such mingled emotional and intellectual control that gives rise to those sets and schemes of guiding concepts which we call philosophies. They are more or less comprehensive plans of living. The less comprehensive ones with a special emphasis on the human problems are commonly known as philosophies of life. The completely comprehensive ones are known as philosophies unqualified, or metaphysics, or world hypotheses. The former are entirely practical in intent. A philosophy of life presents a plan for human living. But a world hypothesis may be offered purely for intellectual comprehension. Nevertheless, a philosopher's principal motivation for developing a world hypothesis may be the practical one of presenting a comprehensive theory of the world as the ultimate evidential support for a way of life included within it.

This is quite obviously the motivation underlying all, or nearly all, of Plato's writing. Remember that the guardians of his Republic were to be fully educated, with the most advanced knowledge of mathematics and dialectic (that is, metaphysics), in order to have the wisdom to govern and direct policy in his society. The teleological pattern of Aristotle's philosophy suggests the same motive. The philosophy of the Stoics and Epicureans was avowedly practical. Lucretius expressly states that he is writing *On the Nature of Things* in order to dispel man's false fears and superstitions by the light of rational understanding.

For if men could see that there is a fixed limit to their sorrows, then with some reason they might have the strength to stand against the scruples of religion and the threats of seers. . . . This terror then, this darkness of the mind, must needs be scattered not by the rays of the sun and the gleaming shafts of day, but by the outer view and the inner law of nature.[1]

Thomas Aquinas's world view was an intellectual justification of the Catholic Christian religion as *the* way of life—so successfully done that it was accepted as the orthodox doctrine by the Church. Spinoza blazoned the practical significance of his monumental system by entitling his book *Ethics*. Hobbes did the same by entitling his book *The Leviathan*, which meant "the great society." The earlier sections of Hume's *Treatise* give one the impression of being preliminary to the later sections on his ethics. And though it cannot be said that Kant wrote his *Critique of Pure Reason* as a support for his *Critique of Practical Reason* and his *Metaphysics of Morals*, it is obvious that he was so aghast at the first apparent ethical implications of the result of the former critique on the presuppositions of physical science that he wrote the latter to show that a parallel metaphysical procedure could justify the presupposition of current morality—namely, an ethics of freedom and universal good will toward men. Among prominent recent philosophers who have been concerned with supporting a practical way of life by imbedding it within a comprehensive metaphysics are, conspicuously, Whitehead in all his later writings and Dewey.

The question can now be raised as to how effective these comprehensively well-based philosophies have been in practical human action. They have without much question guided the lives of the philosophers who developed them and likewise their followers, for these philosophies gather men into schools or movements which can be traced in the histories of philosophy.

These schools are not numerous, for along with the requirements that they be both comprehensive and sound, their adequacy is judged on the basis of their handling of the facts of scientific observations and human relationships and values. There are four such movements that exhibit a high degree of adequacy. The first is generally known as *naturalism* and is associated with Lucretius, Descartes, and the modern scientific naturalists. The second, often called *realism*, is associated with Plato, Aristotle, the scholastics, and modern logical formalists. The third, generally known as *objective idealism*, is associated with Hegel and the modern exponents of organic relationships, recently exemplified by Brand Blanshard and in part by Whitehead. The fourth is generally known as *pragmatism*, or contextualism and is particularly associated with Peirce and Dewey and their followers. If to these are added *mysticism* and *animism* which, though easily shown inadequate as comprehensive philosophies, reach far back into primitive cultures and are still appealing, we have virtually all dominant types of conceptual organization that have acted as guides to human action and still do. Each of these offers a practical philosophy of life.[2]

Some of these philosophies offer many philosophies of life. A sign of inadequacy in a philosophy is that it supports a number of mutually incompatible philosophies of life. This is a striking characteristic of animism. Since most religious creeds have animistic presuppositions—some more and some less—this accounts in considerable degree for the irreconcilability of religious disputes.

However, even setting animistic influences to one side, the philosophical situation exhibits at the present time inherent conflicts among philosophies of life. Suppose we take just the four relatively adequate philosophies first named. Even if each supported just one consistent philosophy of life—which might be conceded if we do not insist on consistency to the smallest detail—we still have four mutually contrary guides to action. Since none has a definite edge over the others in intellectual adequacy, none can be chosen on purely rational grounds as preferable to the others.

However, this can be said: if any one of these is chosen and a person guides his life by that alone, he would be following a rational pattern, which could be expected to support his decisions as far as the adequacy of the philosophy goes—and this we are assured is quite a long way.

My own conclusion in a study I made of these philosophies is that the most reasonable thing for a man to do is to acquire a sympathetic understanding of each of these relatively adequate philosophies and then find their applications to whatever problem is seriously troubling him. He will often find that they all agree on the practical solution for this particular problem. Where they disagree, he will find the core of the problem clearly exposed, and this itself will be a guide for his actions. For it is rare that the four relatively adequate philosophies will not show a balance of joint judgment in some definite direction. But most men prefer rational consistency to wisdom of judgment, and the former is an excellent second best choice if the philosophy chosen is a relatively adequate one. A man at least may know what his acceptable reasons are for every act he performs, and so may his friends.

If a whole society does this, the same follows. It would be pursuing a rational course, and everyone in the society would know where he stood with regard to everyone else. The reasons one person would give for his decisions, he could expect to be the reasons that other persons would accept as good reasons. So, a number of people could discuss policy with the assurance that at least their presuppositions were the same in relation to the evidence on hand.

Now this is more or less what does happen in the development of cultural patterns in relatively isolated or culturally insulated societies. A cultural pattern is a set of rules (that is, concepts with social sanctions attached to them) to which conformity is demanded of the persons belonging to the society. Normally, in practice the conformity is guaranteed largely by the process of acculturation. One set of rules determines for members of a given society what actions are proper in the kinds of situation that usually arise.

We know now that societies over long periods of time have become stabilized by this process, even when the guiding pattern represented a philosophy of life far from adequate in terms of the relatively adequate philosophies listed above. The inadequacies are not simply because of a watering down of a relatively adequate philosophy but more often because of a mixture of incompatible philosophies. However, I pass over the cultural patterns of primitive societies which, as John Ladd showed in his study of the Navaho moral code,[3] may have close affinities with the philosophy of life of one of our most sophisticated schools, namely the individual hedonism of philosophical naturalism. The medieval Western society in its feudal-ecclesiastical structure was an effective combination of Christian animism and Platonic-Aristotelian realism. The succeeding Protestant democracies of Europe and America have been combinations of naturalistic individualism with strains of animism, medieval realism, and lately an innoculation of pragmatism. The astonishing stabilizing pattern of the modern communist movement—calling itself dialectical materialism—is a strange mixture of Hegelian idealism and mechanistic naturalism.

The relatively adequate philosophies combined with other less adequate ones do find their exemplifications in cultural patterns and corresponding philosophies of life; and through the acculturation of individuals and social sanctioning, they do control human actions.

Another point also comes out. That is that we cannot afford to neglect entirely any of the relatively adequate philosophies. It would be ideal if we could bring them together in some sort of nonconflicting way. Perhaps this may yet be done. In the meantime, I think we should be tolerant of any relatively adequate philosophy of life for an individual's or a society's guidance. The great enemy of this simple maxim is dogmatism.

Before going further, I wish to refer to another approach to the same problem—the problem of how far conceptual patterns control human action. I refer to the work of Charles M. Morris on "Ways of Life." The remarkable thing is that in approaching the matter from a totally different angle and using quite different methods, he reaches results very close to those I have been summarizing above. In a number of works—*Paths of Life* (1942), *The Open Self* (1948), *Varieties of Human Value* (1956)—he makes an intensive empirical study of philosophies of life, based mainly on questionnaires. These questionnaires were distributed to large numbers of individuals of different nationalities and cultural backgrounds—Americans, Norwegians, Japanese, Chinese, Indian. The results were submitted to factor analysis.[4]

His final questionnaire, after much preliminary testing, was based on thirteen briefly described ways of life. These yielded five factors through statistical factor-analysis techniques. These five factors, plus a synthetic way of life which Morris calls the Maitreyan and which he evidently regards as the most adequate, correspond closely to the four relatively adequate philosophies I named above, plus mysticism, which I regarded as one of the most appealing but too lacking in scope to be considered even relatively adequate.

The five factors, together with the ways of life with which they were associated in the factor analysis, are:

1. *Formism or realism*: related to way 1, Apollonianism and Confucianism ("nothing in excess"); way 3, Christianity ("sympathetic concern for others"); and way 10, Stoicism ("manly self-control")

2. *Contextualism, pragmatism*: related to way 5, Mohammedanism ("group activity, group enjoyment"); way 6, Prometheanism ("man the eternal maker and remaker"); and way 12, doing orientation ("active, daring, adventuresome deeds")

3. *Mysticism (Buddhistic)*: related to way 2, Buddhism ("independence of persons and things"); and way 11, "becoming" orientation ("meditation on the inner life")

4. Mysticism (Taoist): related to way 9, Taoism ("wait in quiet receptivity"); and way 13, "being" orientation ("let yourself be used")

5. Naturalistic hedonism: related to way 4, Dionysianism ("festivity and solitude in alternation"); and way 8, Epicureanism ("carefree wholesome enjoyment").

In addition, organistic, objective idealism can be related to Morris's way 7, Maitreyan way ("dynamic integration of diversity").

These correlations of Morris's five factors of ways of life with the four relatively adequate world hypotheses of my analysis plus mysticism are admittedly rough; but so also are Morris's ways of life.

The correspondence is about as close as possible; and I take it as a sort of confirmation of the view that the four relatively adequate world hypotheses with their philosophies of life have a wide and permeating application as intellectual guides for human thought and action. To these must be added mysticism as a deeply appealing philosophy, even though it is not intellectually adequate—indeed it is a philosophy that is openly anti-intellectual.

One may wonder why animism, another highly inadequate philosophy with an intense human appeal, does not figure in Morris's results. I suspect the reason is that interpretations of it are so exceedingly varied. Its concepts of spirits and their imaginary actions yield so many myths that are all equally justifiable in animistic terms that no settled animistic way of life comes to the surface.

What about religion and science as guides to life? It will be observed that among Morris's ways of life several of the major religions find a place—Buddhism, Taoism, Mohammedanism, Christianity, and Confucianism—but are stripped of all animistic appendages and sectarian rituals. What turns a conceptual way of life into a religion is perhaps largely a matter of intensity of belief, faith, and dogmatism.

As regards science, this is an historically recent name for a collection of special areas of research with institutionalized methods of observation, experiment, and analysis. It has become almost a way of life under the name of positivism. But positivism tends to take on a characteristic that automatically removes it from a way of life—namely, a denial of concern with human values. In my judgment this also automatically removes it from the group of relatively adequate philosophies, since values are a subject matter too massive and insistent to be ignored. When positivists relent and begin to concern themselves with values, they find that their interpretations of the human enterprise, including the activities of the special sciences, coalesce with those of one or another of the four relatively adequate philosophies—but not ever, however, with mysticism. Positivism and mysticism, from opposite poles, are thus alike in exhibiting an inadequacy of scope.

Having made this rapid survey of the ways in which sets of concepts seem to have a guiding influence on human action, we are now in a position to consider their application to a single person—particularly to a person who finds himself in practical difficulties and is seeking guidance about what to do. Immediately we must point out that our examination up to this moment has been concerned almost entirely with matters of intellectual guidance. Yet at the outset we stated our problem as not a purely intellectual one but one having equally to do with emotions. Our question was whether a set of concepts could keep a person emotionally balanced in view of the reality of a situation in which he found himself. The rationalists across the centuries have unanimously said yes. What else indeed could be expected to hold the emotions in harmony? Perhaps, on the long view, they are right. But the conclusion is far from obvious. There have been dissident voices across the ages. There have been champions of faith and for the reasons of the heart, champions of power, complaints of the hopeless in the toils of temptation, and subterfuges of addicts. Reasons of the intellect sometimes have a pale and feeble look.

I want to commit myself to a certain hypothesis at this point, one with which some psychologists will not agree but which has been gaining steadily in acceptance and which I think will eventually be proved correct. This is that the dynamics of human action is one thing and the intellectual channeling of it another—the hypothesis that there are no, or very few, dynamics or drives intrinsic to thought. All the dynamics (or nearly all) come from drives and (in the wide sense) the emotional side of the personality.[5]

This hypothesis, if correct, is important for our present subject. It sets certain limits to rational guidance. It means that we cannot assume that correct reasoning from a set of true concepts will always be effective in leading a man to act reasonably. It means that a philosophy will not necessarily make a man philosophical. It does not by any means imply, however, that philosophy cannot be efficacious. It implies only that there are limits to its efficaciousness which have nothing to do with its truth or adequacy. This conclusion may pertain directly to the general topic of our volume, which is self-destruction.

I do not propose to argue for the above hypothesis in this paper. That would be an essay in itself. I only want from now on to show its bearing on the problem of suicide for those who accept it.

To begin with, I think it leads to a distinction between what could be called rational and irrational grounds for suicide. This suggests that all suicides need not be regarded as irrational. Incidentally, the wide acceptance of the view that all suicides are owing to depression or other emotional conditions beyond the rational control of the victim is strong evidence for the hypothesis I am advocating. But in suggesting the possibility of rational suicides, I am opposing the opposite extreme of granting no efficacy to the conceptual channelling. A rational suicide would be one that is based on a dynamic demand for sound logical and evidential grounds for actions or for an equivalent in rationally accepted institutionalized authority.

Such dynamic rational grounding of action is to be distinguished from rationalization. Rationalization is the finding of plausible reasons for strong impulses (often unconscious) to justify one's action. Dynamically charged rational activity is in its less complex instances simply problem-solving by whatever instrumental acts seem best available to reduce the tensions. In more complex instances, as in scientific inquiry, the acts are mediated by logical, mathematical, and experimental procedures which have gained men's confidence as reliable tools for guiding instrumental action. These rational tools are charged with the dynamics of the problem motivating the scientists. The rational tools have no intrinsic dynamics in themselves. The same is the case with the philosophies we were considering earlier.

Here is where a man's philosophy of life relates to the problem of suicide. How much influence does a man's philosophy of life have upon the releasing or the restraining of suicidal impulses? We are assuming that a set of concepts cannot of itself instigate dynamic impulses. However, if a person is caught in a serious predicament loaded with conflicting impulses of fear, love, hate, loyalty, and respect for obligations, law, and other such, the dynamics of these impulses could charge a philosophy of life in which this person has gained confidence and effectively guide him to a decision. The philosophy of life would function in this instance just as the rules of scientific procedures guide a scientist to his results. The decision would be rational even if it were for an act of suicidal self-sacrifice or at the risk of death. And the philosophy of life would clearly be responsible for that decision. There is just one important qualification: the decision could not be regarded as *entirely* rational if the philosophy of life that led to this decision was not itself as rational or reasonable as possible. This means, according to our earlier discussion, that the philosophy must be as adequate as any available to the person confronted with the problem.

Another way in which a philosophy of life may acquire dynamic effectiveness is if it becomes a cultural institution with which a person has become identified through the action of acculturation. A person who deliberately acts in conformity with the demands of his cultural pattern in the solution of a problem loaded with conflicting impulses can hardly be said to be acting other than rationally. But here again the same qualification may be made that was made above; his decision would not be regarded as entirely rational unless the culturally institutionalized philosophy was itself as rational as possible.

The rationality of a suicidal act is thus a matter of degree. I think we must grant that any act of self-destruction is rational if it is voluntary and deliberate and wholly determined by factual conflicts of a situation that was considered with the guidance of a philosophy of life. It would be rational whether the guiding philosophy was the man's own choice or creation or one that he had acquired through acculturation. However, the degree of rationality of the act would depend on the degree of rationality of the philosophy which was guiding the person's deliberations.

Insofar as Indian widows were conforming to their culture in throwing themselves on their dead husbands' funeral pyres, they were minimally rational in their acts. But the institutionalized philosophy of life that sustained that custom was of questionable adequacy. A person who is considering how to act in an intensely conflicting situation cannot be regarded as making the most rational decision, unless he has been as critical as possible of the philosophy that is guiding his decision. If the philosophy is institutionalized as a political ideology or a religious creed, he must think critically about the institution in order to acquire maximum rationality of judgment. This principle is clear enough even if in practice it is enormously difficult to fulfill.

The main conclusion we are reaching is that acts of self-sacrifice may be rationally performed even to the point of voluntary self-destruction. This is clear in cases of death or risk of death incurred in the line of duty—for firemen, policemen, soldiers, lifesavers, coastguardsmen, sea captains on sinking ships, and even for laymen who find themselves in comparable positions. This conclusion seems to me clear also in situations in which an argument can be made for the advisability of induced death, as in hopeless cancer cases in which the patient takes the final decision into his own hands. These are all instances of what I would call rational suicide.

What then would be irrational suicide? These would be cases for which efforts for prevention are obviously in order. These would seem to be cases based on serious emotional disturbance, in which rational guidance is cut off, or largely cut off, by the intensity of the emotional conflicts. In most such cases, I suspect that the emotional impulses are beyond the person's voluntary control, being in the region of the inhibitions of the unconscious. Here whatever reasoning there is takes the form of rationalization, and a person's perceptions of the reality of the situation are either blanked out or interpreted to fit his emotional projections instead of used to test his hypotheses and imaginations. To the person, it seems that the only way out is suicide; whereas to a psychologically trained outsider it is evident that the problems are of the person's own making because of his lack of insight into his own motivations and twists of interpretation. By careful professional help such persons may gain insight into the nature of their impulses and acquire a correct awareness of the reality of their situation and thereby gain a capacity for rational intellectual guidance for their actions. The therapist may often have to do much more. He may have to give them the support that they may have been lacking until they are able to stand on their own feet. He may even have to build up a stable inner core of integrated character (ego strength as it is often called) with which the person can then build on further and function effectively in his environment.

For such suicide-prone persons when their suicide impulses are strong, it would seem that a philosophy of life could have only a minor restraining effect. Even the institutionalized creed of a church to which the person belonged would have little effect. This seems to be borne out in the statistics of Catholic versus non-Catholic suicides. Though there are more non-Catholic suicides, the proportion of Catholic suicides is large. To these should be added the suicides from strict Protestant churches of Calvinistic or high Episcopalian sects which proscribe suicide with religious sanctions as severe as those of the Catholic Church. To render the statistics comparable, comparison should be made between strict Christian churches and permissive, individualistic ones. Furthermore, like the unreasonable Catholic prohibitions against birth control, the Catholic prohibition of all suicide may restrain some devout Catholics from performing what in the foregoing discussion we found could be regarded as rationally well-justified suicide.

It may be added that some suicide-prone persons with an extreme capacity for imaginative rationalizations could well invent a philosophy of life for themselves which sanctioned and encouraged suicide. Schopenhauer's philosophy of life notoriously does this and he has had many followers. Not infrequently we read in the newspapers of suicides reported to have taken an intense interest in Schopenhauer's philosophy. His philosophy, it should be noted, is a form of mysticism. Let me remind the reader that in my previous review of the relatively adequate philosophies, I referred to mysticism as a model of a philosophy which suffered from inadequacy of scope. For consistency we shall have to admit that a suicide based on mystic premises exhibits an act of extreme minimal rationality, since a person performs it on the basis of a highly systematized philosophy of life, whereas such an act is at the very outer rim of rationality, beyond which is nothing but rationalization. Often we suspect that a suicide's interest in such a philosophy is a rationalization.

Edwin S. Shneidman recently conducted an informative series of conferences with suicide-prone subjects and inquired about their philosophies of life. He asked each of them in a disarmingly informal manner the following questions: (1) What is your philosophy of life? (2) What is the purpose of life? (3) Is that a real tree (or chair, and so forth)? (4) What are the tests of reality or of truth? (5) What is your idea of causation, chance, decision?

In all he interviewed six subjects at the Suicide Prevention Center. The first question seemed to mystify or be misunderstood by most of these subjects. One man (the most disorganized of the group) replied, "Passive indifference. I don't seem to care about anything." But to the second question he answered, "Health in the normal way, happiness, good, accomplishments." Pressed further he stated that he was a "strictly dogmatic Catholic," expected to see people after death in "heaven, hell, or what. If I find happiness, I don't know what form it will take."

About the tree, his belief that it was real was based on its "form, shape." His belief in the hereafter was based, however, on "intellectual conviction and faith."

Luck, he said, played no part in his life; but as for being "preordained," he did not believe in it at all. Asked about cause and effect, he replied, "Vague in my own mind what you mean." He was sure he had no right to commit suicide.

This sort of vagueness about a philosophy of life, perception, tests of truth, and cause and effect ran through the answers of all these subjects except one. She, along with two of the others, was an agnostic—though she went to a Unitarian church with which she felt loosely connected.

Her answers, which exemplify the opposite extreme from those of the man quoted above, went like this: As to her philosophy of life, she was Unitarian, although raised Methodist. "Never believed in God, but always sort of wished I could." As for afterlife, "Nothing." As for purpose of life, it was "human relationships, to love and be loved." Taken more broadly, "Life is purposeless. It just happened." To Shneidman's inferring, "You are an adventitious circumstance of biological roulette," her reply was, "Yeah, I think it was just a question of which sperm got to the ovum first. An awful lot of ova there who didn't get any sperm at all, but I think it was strictly chance." Referring to the birth of her child she said, "I was delighted with him." And to the question of whether she thought of him as arbitrary, "I don't feel any lack about the fact that this is biological." About immortality, her reply was, "Improbable." About the reality of the tree, "Accepted," but "No explanation of the origin of the world." She found no difficulty with the notion of infinity in connection with space and time for the world.

Her comments on suicide were vivid: "I think suicide is one of the greatest things to keep you going. If you knew you couldn't die, I think the world would be unbearable. . . . I think it's great. . . . I think it's a completely moral justifiable thing that nobody need do, but if you are miserable yourself and you're not doing anybody any good, I think it's great." On Shneidman's asking if her suicide would not put her "skeleton in the grandchildren's psychological closet," she recognized that "this kind of scar will be very bad."

Asked if she felt her life was entirely within her hands, she replied yes. Pressed further about whether this would be so if she were in a depressed state, she admitted that "you perceive only those things you care to perceive. But I think it's my right." Shneidman then asked, "What about the decision itself? Granted that you have the right." Her answer: "The decision, will I be able to make an intellectual decision about an emotional thing? Probably not. I think it will be an emotional decision, not an intellectual one."

This woman in these last few words just about summarizes the conclusions of the present paper. She has a rather well developed naturalistic philosophy of life, which does, as Hume convincingly shows in his essay "Of Suicide," grant to a man on the basis of a naturalistic, individualistic ethics a right to end his life if he finds such an act is one that will maximize the satisfactions of all concerned. "A man who retires from life," he wrote, "does no harm to society: He only ceases to do good. . . . I am not obliged to do a small good to society at the expense of a great harm to myself."[6] The woman whose comments we have just quoted is simply stating the same thesis, that under certain justifiable conditions an act of suicide is rationally justified if it conforms to an adequate philosophy and is performed after careful rational deliberation. However, she also sees that in a state of depression a person is most likely to act irrationally, and suicide under such motivation is not rationally justified. The decision then is "not an intellectual one."

The obvious conclusion is that under the latter circumstances the suicide should be prevented if possible and that the most skillful therapeutic techniques should be employed to place the person emotionally driven in this way without benefit of rational channelling and control of his actions in a position to have insight into his emotional conflicts and lethal drives—in short, to convert him so far as possible into an integrated personality in adjustment (though not necessarily in literal conformity) with his social and physical environment. As part of this remedial work, it would be beneficial to provide him with an adequate philosophy of life for long-term guidance of his emotional impulses.

The woman we are speaking of had such a philosophy. But she evidently did not have full insight into her emotional conflicts and the depression resulting from them. And she recognized that in the emotional stress and dominance of a depression, her philosophy of life would probably be powerless to guide her to "an intellectual decision." Hence she needed psychological help to save her from the irrevocable consequences of an irrationally motivated act.

Her situation seemed to be similar to those of the other four patients except for their much greater lack of philosophical guidance. From their replies none of them showed evidence of an explicit conception of a way of life. Their answers were fragmentary, although paradoxically often quite firm and dogmatic. My suspicion is that their responses were guided by better articulated philosophies of life than they knew they had. They were responding from dogmas that were deeply imbedded in their personality structures by acculturation. This came out clearly in the case of the man who accepted on faith and authority the whole Catholic creed: he was unable to tell in detail what this philosophy of life involved, even with respect to the objects of perception or cause-and-effect. The same can less clearly be surmised of the others, even of those who were "free thinkers" and agnostics (perhaps the more so because they were so definitely agnostic). Embedded in their personalities by the acculturation of their American environments is some kind of philosophy of life which would come out in action whenever these unexpressed dispositions happened to get touched. But again, such institutionalized philosophies were as powerless as was the explicit philosophy of the woman quoted above to channel action rationally in the stress of a state of emotional disturbance.

The rational guidance of a philosophy of life is available only to a relatively well-integrated personality whose unconscious conflicts (such as he has) do not overpower his voluntary actions. To such a man an adequate philosophy would be his safest guide through life. And to my mind, for all who are in a position to acquire it, an explicit philosophy is a guide greatly superior to a purely institutionalized ideology or creed. For even when not inadequate, the latter is rigid and dogmatic, whereas the former may be flexible and open to revision. Particularly in these days of rapid social and technological change, it is highly important for men to acquire a philosophy that is adequate for comprehending such changes and for recommending reasonable adjustments to them or effective ways of guiding them to beneficial ends.

## REFERENCES

1. Trans. Cyril Bailey, Bk. I.
2. These world hypotheses and their sources of evidence and cognitive justification are taken up in the author's *World Hypotheses* (Berkeley: University of California Press, 1942).
3. *The Structure of a Moral Code* (Cambridge, Mass.: Harvard University Press, 1957).
4. For the form of much of this summary I am indebted to a report by Dr. Elsa A. Whalley presented at a staff meeting of the Suicide Prevention Center, Los Angeles, on Oct. 26, 1962.
5. In support of this hypothesis, I refer to K. B. Madsen's book *Theories of Motivation* (Cleveland: Howard Allen, 1964; Copenhagen: Munksgaard, 1964). The most influential recent writer to develop a dynamic theory of cognition is D. O. Hebb in his *The Organization of Behavior* (1949). But since 1955 he has felt obliged to change his view, mainly on the evidence of certain physiological data. In an article in the *Psychological Review* (62: 243–54, 1955) he writes: "Psychologically, we can now distinguish two quite different effects of a sensory event. One is the *cue function* guiding behavior; the other, less obvious but no less important is the *arousal* or *vigilance* function. Without a foundation or arousal, the cue function cannot exist . . . arousal in this sense is synonymous with a general drive state, and the conception of drive therefore assumes anatomical and physiological identity . . . the drive is an energizer but not a guide . . . Thus I find myself obliged to reserve my earlier views and accept drive conception." To this quotation from Hebb, Madsen adds, "It should finally be added that this conception of 'drive' is in agreement with the conception now gradually dominating psychology" (p. 187). In his summary chapter Madsen states: "As a consequence of the previous discussion, I would suggest that '*motivation variables*' should be defined as synonymous with '*dynamagenic function variables*' and as a consequence of this I would define '*cognitive variables*' as synonymous with '*directive* function variables' " (p. 306).
6. This is quoted from S. E. Sprott, *The English Debate on Suicide from Donne to Hume* (La Salle, Ill.: The Open Court Publishing Company, 1961), p. 133. This detailed scholarly account of the century-long debate on the transition from the medieval to the modern Western cultural pattern and its more naturalistic philosophy of life is most illuminating and pertinent to the topic we have been discussing.

## Part II

# SOCIOLOGICAL AND ETHNOGRAPHIC ESSAYS

A new sociology of suicide is aborning. Some of its manifestations are evidenced in the chapters contained within this section, which—concerned with much more than the conventional sociological characteristics of suicide among various groups—examine how suicidal individuals, the significant-others of suicidal individuals, professional workers at a Suicide Prevention Center, municipal officials, including medical examiners and coroners, and many others, partake in the sociology of creating what is then called "self-destruction."

Talcott Parsons and Victor Lidz have written a sociological treatise delineating some aspects of the place of death in the attitude system of contemporary American society, including an examination of some of the religiocultural roots of these attitudes and their relation to the total social structure. They relate changes in concepts toward death to demographic changes in aging and longevity and to changes in the meaning of death within the context of a cultural evolutionary series. In this regard, they trace the role of death in the development of Christianity, often using an economic analogy to illuminate their thoughts. Throughout, they treat death as an index of many related features of our current society and culture.

Harold Garfinkel examines the practices whereby suicidal deaths are certified. His goal is to delineate several features of practical actions as problematic phenomena. He builds his chapter around three concepts: That the work of certifying the cause and mode of death engages a variety of interested parties in developing (consistent, reproducible) features of indexical expressions and actions; that these demonstrable rational properties of indexical expressions and actions are organizational phenomena; and that as such they consist, for the members, of managed, ongoing accomplishments subject to every exigency of organizationally situated conduct.

Warren Breed takes two concepts as his special fields of interest: The kinds of interpersonal social relationships that members of society experience (as opposed to the organization of society, groups within society, or the psychic functioning of the individual); and the notion of "loss." He elaborates these concepts with interview data from survivors of some 250 suicides in New Orleans over the last decade. He concludes by stressing the importance of combining all these concepts in a comprehensive interactional approach to the study of suicidal phenomena.

Harvey Sacks has written an ethnographic study of suicidal conversational activities taken from telephone dialogues, giving us a sociological study in depth of the operational meanings of "the search for help," and of "no one to turn to." Within the context of these ideas, he has established rules for definition and has given us a number of telling verbatim illustrations in explication of these rules.

Mamoru Iga points out that suicide in Japan, in spite of rather high rates for certain subgroups (women, rural inhabitants, and the distinctly young and old people), has not been given the intensive attention it deserves. His paper, using data collected by Dr. Kenshiro Ohara on young people who have attempted suicide in Kamakura, emphasizes especially the factors of dependency, self-inflation, and insecurity, as these factors operate within the Japanese suicidal adolescent, the Japanese adolescent in general, the Japanese family, and the Japanese social structure. From his own bicultural life, Dr. Iga draws conclusions about the causal nexus of suicidal phenomena, including (in a comprehensive way) sociological, psychological, phenomenological, and interactional causes.

Louis Dublin, speaking out of the wisdom of his eighty-some years, issues a straightforward challenge to the public health profession, specifically to health officers and to mental health authorities, to take initiative and participate actively in programs of suicide prevention. He believes that suicide prevention is primarily a public health problem and that its neglect by the public health profession has existed far too long.

# 7. Death in American Society*

Talcott Parsons and Victor Lidz

The present paper will examine the basic patterns of orientation toward death in American society, their cultural roots, and their relations to the social structure. We hope also to suggest problems for further research, as social science clearly lacks crucial knowledge about the subject, as well as to shed light upon some related aspects of American society and culture, e.g., attitudes toward life purposes or strivings and toward aging, problems occasioned by the increasing proportion of older people in our population and by the high incidence of suicide, and the nature of current funeral practices.

We shall begin with a foil—the widespread view that the realities of death are characteristically met with "denial" in contemporary American society,[1] an opinion that seems dubious to us. Usually cited as evidence of this opinion are practices such as embalming, the elaborate dressing of corpses, and the use of cosmetics upon them, as well as more extreme ones such as concern with coffins' impermeability to decay and the seeming apathy of many terminal patients about their diseases.

Such practices are commonly interpreted as indications that Americans are "going soft," becoming progressively less capable of facing the harsh reality of the actual world. In such interpretations, reality and harshness are often equated, whereas the pleasant things of life are considered not very "real." Americans are said, then, to live in a world of illusion, con-

* This chapter is based in large part on a working paper written by the senior author as one of a series of studies supported by the Office of Social Research of The Equitable Life Assurance Company of the United States and is reproduced here with permission.

structing elaborate defenses against intrusions of reality. Our handling of death is considered only one striking manifestation of a general deplorable tendency.[2]

This paper will present an alternative view, namely that American society has institutionalized a broadly stable, though flexible and changing, orientation to death that is fundamentally not a "denial" but a mode of acceptance appropriate to our primary cultural patterns of activism. We cannot develop our argument until we have reviewed some of the salient characteristics of American society and have discussed some aspects of death and dying. However, it seems appropriate to register immediately a basic difficulty of the denial hypothesis: it would be very anomalous for a society that has no thoroughly institutionalized scientific values to adopt an attitude so drastically discrepant with the realism of science in an area so close to biology and medicine.

Death is a "natural" phenomenon rooted in the conditions of the biological existence of man and all the higher organisms. Moreover, modern biological science has established that death is not only inevitable among higher organisms but is also a *positive* factor in species' adaptations within the broader physical and organic system.

The differentiation between germ plasm and somatoplasm, which is the crux of the mortality of the higher organisms, enhances both stability and variability of genetic materials in adaptational terms. Bisexual reproduction favors controlled genetic variation by combining two independent genetic lines to produce a new, unique genetic constitution in practically every individual of the offspring generation. However, if the resulting adaptive changes are to accumulate with much efficiency, the parental generation must die off so that its genetic materials can be replaced by those of the offspring. Hence death is positively functional for biological adaptation.[3]

The death of the individual human personality seems to be similarly functional for the sociocultural system to which it belongs. Human kinship systems tend to ascribe reproduction and its correlate in the sociocultural system, the socialization process, to each other, though there is certainly some independent "play" between the two. Through its structuring of marital selection and family maintenance, a kinship system determines both what organic-social components in the society are combined for perpetuation and how the resultant offspring are submitted to the primary learning processes that introduce them to members within the continuing society. In maturing through the life cycle, a new generation comes to internalize the cultural patterns of the society as communicated by the parental generation.[4] It then becomes important that the older generation be "on the way out" so that its offspring can "take over" the controlling positions of the society, perhaps especially those of reproduction and socialization, and can be free to innovate, both socially and culturally.[5] Like genetic patterns, the cultural patterns communicated to specific offspring seem to vary with both generation and the particular "lines" in the kinship system which the parents represent. Clearly, death plays an important part in the genesis and utilization of new variations in the cultural patterns that will have adaptive significance for the society.

Thus death must be regarded as a fundamental aspect of the human condition, not only by us in our roles as social scientists but by all men as members of their various social groups. All who attain even a moderate longevity must undergo the strains of losing at least some persons to whom they have been closely attached. And, by virtue of being human and being oriented in action by long-accumulating, complex symbol systems, all will have anticipatory knowledge of, and must contemplate, their own deaths. Furthermore, it seems that mortality must always be a particularly important example and trenchant symbol of the finitude of the concrete human being. It is the barrier to omnipotence and the limit to capacities that simply cannot be overcome but must be adjusted to and accepted.

Because death inherently has such critical meaning for humans, it must be given an important position in the "constitutive symbolism" of all viable religious systems. In terms of its own fundamental patterns of orientation, each culture must attribute some "ultimate" meaning or reference to death. If a religion is to remain a workable, institutionalized complex, it can *never* simply deny the ultimate relevance of such a basic condition, although it can (and must) select among the many possibilities which are viable within the human condition, including some rather extreme ones.[6] It must provide a framework for interpreting death that is meaningful and appropriate, in relation to other elements of the culture, for defining attitudes regarding both the deaths of others and the prospect of one's own death. Closely associated with such a framework, of course, are the conventions for occasions of death, particularly the complex of funeral practices.[7]

Some massive facts indicate that modern Western society stands very far along in a major evolutionary development in the biological-demographic sphere. It is well known that "nature" is generally prodigal with the potentials of reproduction at the lower levels of evolution. Among the lower species, the ratio of ova produced to ova fertilized is exceedingly high, as is the ratio of fertilized ova to those which develop into mature organisms. The general evolutionary trend is toward reducing these ratios and increasing the species' "investment" in the probability that particular organisms will perpetuate its patterns.[8] For example, the long periods of gestation and postnatal care that characterize mammals are evidence of this trend. Man has a particularly prolonged gestation period and a relatively extreme postnatal dependency, but he also has a generally high rate of successful maturation (and reproduction). Modern societies seem to accentuate this development within the broad range of possibilities that comprises the biologic basis of the human condition.

Most striking is the recent prolongation of the individual life and concomitant reduction in the ratio of, first, conceptions and, then, live births to completions of a relatively maximum life cycle. The dramatic demographic fact is that in modern societies life expectancy at birth has approximately doubled in the last century, from in the thirties to about seventy years. However, this has occurred without a marked change in the typical maximum life span—the proportion of centenarians has increased little, if at all. The essential fact, then, is that a substantially larger proportion of a birth cohort, or cohort of young adults, lives to approximate completion of the life cycle. Premature death, relative to a normality of attaining "old age," has been enormously reduced.

This broad development comprises a gain in control over the effects of death in that we need not fear its caprices so acutely now that we have fair (statistical) assurance of living out our most active days. Nevertheless, in some other senses the problem of death has concomitantly come to be posed even more massively and trenchantly.

Modern societies contain a rapidly increasing class of persons who have attained old age. Over 9 percent of the American population is now over 65 years of age, as opposed to only 4 percent only 60 years ago.[9] A very large proportion of these people have completed their more obvious and important life tasks, as valued by the ordinary criteria of our society. In general, they have retired from their occupational jobs, and their children have matured and become independent and have families of their own. By the nature of their social positions, they are "on the way out" and are living "in the shadow of death," having entered what is—by most *institutional* criteria—a terminal period of their lives. Thus, there is a relatively large group institutionally placed so that, in some sense, it must rather directly confront the problem of inevitable death. Moreover, this situation affects a much wider group, as those associated with the aging, particularly their children, must prepare to lose them in the relatively near future.

Both for the individual as he faces death and for the social groups intimately attached to him, the problem of the *meaning* of death is coming in a new sense to be concentrated about death occurring as the completion of a normal life cycle. This central, irreducible problem is becoming disentangled from the problem of adjusting to deaths that occur earlier in the life cycle, particularly in infancy and early childhood, which was much more general in the premodern period.

This development may be regarded as differentiating two aspects of the historic problem of death: that stemming from the inevitability of death and that pertaining to deaths which are potentially subject to some kind of human control. We generally value very highly efforts to minimize deaths of the latter type and are particularly upset by such deaths when they do occur. This seems to be the underlying reason why we feel deaths in automobile accidents to be so shocking and their rates to warrant so much public concern. Similarly, lapses in control over avoidable deaths that we now take for granted are experienced as especially disturbing—e.g., the great international concern over the recent Zermatt typhoid epidemic. Similarly, a major rise in deaths due to smallpox or plague would be highly traumatic, very largely because it is now so completely unexpected and considered to be unnecessary.

This basic differentiation within the complex of orientations toward death has some important correlates. We have come to expect that death will occur primarily among the old and only rarely in other groups. Parents no longer frequently experience the deaths of young children, nor do they ordinarily expect that they will. Similarly, the death of young adults, once so closely associated with tuberculosis, is now relatively uncommon—Violetta and Mimi, though characters still as tragic as when *La Traviata* and *La Boheme* were composed, no longer represent a common fate. The fact that people killed in automobile accidents are often the young probably contributes greatly to our concern over such deaths.

With the prevention of premature death being so heavily and broadly emphasized, difficult problems of meaning are raised by instances in which death either is deliberately imposed or could be avoided through greater care. Significantly, the imposition of capital punishment has been declining, even in proportion to convictions for capital crimes, and is being opposed by widespread movements to abolish the death penalty altogether. Similarly, the contemporary world has newly developed general and intense convictions about the ethical unacceptability and irrationality of war.

Death also has a very broad, if complex, association with suffering and violence. On the one hand, it is an ultimate severity on the scales of punishment, violence, and suffering. On the other hand, it is just as ultimate a release from them. Our modern concerns with control clearly bear upon these scales, and the minimization of suffering in general has certainly become highly valued. The deliberate imposition of physical suffering through torture has generated very great humanitarian opposition, so much so that torture is now almost considered basically unacceptable in the main Western tradition, no matter how "good" its cause may be. Throughout our era, torture has been a major focus of the moral objection to totalitarian regimes. Increasingly, the aggressive employment of violence for overt political ends seems to be attracting opposition of a similar moral generality, except in the cases of certain extreme situations. The most massive developments in the control of suffering, however, have been those in modern medicine. These are salient, not only in the prevention and cure of disabling diseases but also in the reduction of the physical suffering that is involved in illness, including mortal illness. Anesthetics and narcotics have been the most important means for this accomplishment (note that even those who are alarmed by contemporary American attitudes toward death object very little to such "denial" of pain) and have enabled modern man almost to exclude physical suffering from the problems which death inevitably presents.

Thus, modern institutions differentiate three components of the more diffuse problem of death from the core phenomenon of "inevitable death": "premature" death that can be avoided by human measures; deliberately imposed death; and the physical suffering that dying may entail. The modern tendency has been to mobilize control measures to minimize the undesirable impact of each of these three components. In a sense, all three comprise the "uncertainty" of death, as distinguished from its inevitability, and it is this adventitious uncertainty that we strive to control. Although it is unlikely that any of the three components will ever be completely eliminated, all have already been sufficiently reduced to be distinguished clearly from the category of the inevitable "natural" death of all individuals. They need be involved in only a small and varying minority of deaths—they are no longer constitutive components of "man's fate." Moreover, when they occur, they may be seen as "irrational" relative to the "normal," natural aspects of death.

Here we may note how radically these ideas contrast with most pre-modern orientations toward death. Many primitive societies evidently regard *all* deaths as a result of the adventitious play of human or magical factors and lack a clear conception of "natural death." Deaths can then be warded off or adapted to on some combination of political and religio-magical grounds, but they cannot be foci of distinct cultural complexes that discriminate between their "ultimately" and scientifically meaningful aspects. Most of the classical civilizations adopted a rather fatalistic attitude toward death and illness, when early in life as well as in old age.[10] They regarded the loss of a large proportion of a population cohort before maturity as quite normal. Furthermore, they would have considered any very elaborate efforts to save the dying and to mitigate suffering as interference with Divine provision. Thus, the modern development of both a pattern for valuing the prolongation of life and a highly rationalized schema for identifying the controllable components of the death complex must not be taken for granted.

The comparative evidence suggests that the concomitant emergence in modern societies of the two general developments we have noted, the prolongation of actual life expectancy and the orientation toward controlling the "adventitious" components of the death complex, can hardly be fortuitous. It suggests that we should view the modern, differentiated orientation toward death as a component of a much broader orientation system which emphasizes dedication to activity that can be expected on rational grounds to maximize human control over the *conditional* elements of the life situation. A major tradition of sociological research, stemming largely from Max Weber's comparative studies in religion, has shown that such a general orientational system, which may be conveniently called instrumental activism, characterizes modern Western civilization, particularly American society,[11] and underlies much of the modern day's rather spectacular reconstruction of the human condition.[12] A major theme in our analysis as it develops will be that American attitudes and practices regarding death can be interpreted very generally as elements of that reconstruction.

This bears directly on our rejection of the view we have set as a foil, that American attitudes tend to "deny" death. Instrumental activism is a rational orientation in that, when specified to a particular sphere of action, it can develop the type of control that it values only by accurately recognizing the facts and conditions of the relevant situation. Here, the development of science that it has fostered is evidently prototypical—surely science is not grounded primarily in fantasies that deny basic realities of the empirical world, no matter how problematic is any sense in which it simply reflects these realities. It would seem that the modern orientation toward controlling the adventitious aspects of death must involve a very similar realism, both because of its interpenetration with science (e.g., medicine) and because of its need for highly rationalized means for meeting human strains. However, it is evident that the orientation of control cannot apply to the "inevitable" aspect of death, which is its core phenomenon, in quite the same sense. Rather, the differentiation between the adventitious and inevitable aspects of death has rendered the latter still more irreducible—something that must be faced still more squarely than ever before. The sense in which such facing of death has been incorporated in the value pattern of instrumental activism is extremely complex; it can be treated only after we have considered the "ultimate" meaning that Western tradition has given to the fact of death.

As noted above, the biological integration between the mechanism of procreation and the mortality of the individual must be paralleled at (or extended to) the sociocultural levels of the organization of action systems. In a complex society such as our own, the instrumentalities for effecting such integration must be highly ramified, because the means of facing death must articulate with a great variety of functionally distinct structural contexts and discrete concrete structures. It will be helpful, therefore, to examine briefly the much simpler forms that such instrumentalities take in primitive societies before considering the consequences of the extreme complexity of American society in regard to its attitudes and practices concerning death.[13]

An ancestral cult seems to be a universal among the most primitive societies as well as a common structure in certain types of more advanced societies, in which it adopts a somewhat different form. In the primitive societies, it integrates the kinship status of the individual (which must bear *some*, if a highly variable, relation to his actual filiations and hence to his "place" in the system of procreation and mortality) with the ultimate meaning of his life and, obversely, his death, in an especially direct manner. It gives sacred meaning to the order of kinship statuses but is structurally limited in generating and interrelating categories of the sacred to a rather simple isomorphism with the kinship system.[14] This compresses both the temporal and eternal fate of the individual into a *single* basic framework for developing meaning and defining identity. Within this framework, there is only a minimal distance between the sacred and profane, the eternal and temporal.[15] Elements of contingency, which might make the death of an individual "problematic" in a modern sense, have only a minimal degree of freedom to operate independently and to generate independent, individualized meanings.

Thus societal community is conceived, religiously, as extending in time both before birth and after death. Among the Australian aborigines, for example, birth is regarded as some kind of incarnation of "souls" from the ancestral water holes, and death is regarded as the return of the "souls" to their proper pools. Indeed, the dead, who are also the "to be born," seem to comprise a kind of sacred "upper class" of the society. Deaths are always thought to be *imposed* by human action, by effects of the sacred "souls," or by both through the mediation of black magic. A concept of "natural death" seems to be virtually absent, as is the concept of a "natural order" that could make its causes intelligible.[16]

In such societies, both life and death tend strongly to be "one possibility" things,[17] bounded sharply by ascribed totemistic-kinship references so far as the general elements of the *meaning* of a life are concerned. The fundamental inflexibility of these references is reflected in the prescriptive quality of the institutional means of facing death. A death is overwhelmingly the concern of just the particular kinship and totemic groups of the dead, which must adjust to their changed relations with the sacred "upper class," a ritual matter that generally involves rigidly fixed practices. These rites symbolically transfer the dead (or dying) person from his status in the living collectivity to his status in the corresponding collectivity of the dead. They generate the stereotyped ultimate meaning of the death. There is relatively little institutional "room" for more individualized social or personal reactions to the death.[18] Above all, the death cannot stimulate responses that break through the kinship nexus *level* of social responsibilities or derive their meaning from transcendental references.

With social evolution, extensive areas of social structure are freed from ascriptive embeddedness in a diffuse kinship-religious *nexus* of the primitive type. Nevertheless, kinship organization, in close relation to a set of religious commitments, remains the focus of the system of orientation toward death. There does not seem to be any society—as distinguished from special, subsocietal religious or military orders—in which a death is not normally the concern of the next of kin in the *first* instance. Even in a society such as ours, in which the important associations of an individual generally ramify very far beyond kin, close relatives almost always take the leading role in, and hold primary responsibilty for, the arrangements that must be made after a death. To a considerable degree, this situation is ensured by strong legal provisions concerning the *rights* of the close kin. Deaths, like other major points of transition in the personal life cycle, remain occasions upon which the central significance of the nuclear family in the personal attachments of the individual is conspicuously demonstrated, along with the solidarity of more extended kin groups. Nevertheless, in proportion to a society's degree of differentiation, the relevant kin groupings comprise less the only social system of observance upon occasions of death and more the core from which radiates a series of social networks, their number and type depending upon the prominence of the deceased.

That the family retains its central position in social functioning upon such occasions is clearly owing to its primordial characteristics. The depth and diffuseness of its members' personal investments in their family roles, and the particularistic integration among them, make this the area of social structure in which the loss of a member is ordinarily apt to cause the most severe disturbance, with the most diffuse effects. Moreover, kinship is the structural context in which the individual is "rooted" as a human social actor. It provides the interpersonal mechanisms for effecting the society's generational continuity and hence must be *specially* concerned with birth and death. Therefore, the fact that the efforts to absorb the effects of the loss of a member of society are concentrated in the family is to be expected.

Since the universalistic sectors of society must be structured very differently—in a manner ordinarily making the status of a particular individual inherently less problematic—particular deaths are not likely to concern them crucially beyond the actual associational networks of the deceased. Perhaps the major consideration here is that in large, highly ramified social systems the individual is a very small unit. Unless he fills an especially important position, it is unlikely that anything that happens to him, including death, could raise critical problems for the system. The enormous importance of deaths of heads of state seems to be grounded in the breadth of their spheres of association, which are comprised of whole societies—or more than that. Such a situation can be contrasted with the very restricted importance to the society of the deaths of most ordinary citizens. It then becomes clear that deaths are not specially and inherently problematic in the universalistic sectors, but are only so in relation to the statuses of the deceased.

As societies become more modern, kinship structures cover a diminishing proportion of the individual's role involvements. In very primitive societies, questions of "who" a person is can be answered almost exclusively in kinship (and ascribed religious) terms. In modern societies, differentiated elements pertaining to occupational and community roles are generally more important components of an individual's identity. The articulations between the various role involvements, however, are always problematic, at both the personality and the social-system levels. Furthermore, the problems tend to become particularly salient upon occasions of transition and adjustment—perhaps prototypically at deaths.

We cannot analyze the orientational bases underlying such articulations in American society until we have examined certain fundamental qualities of its religious heritage. At this point, it is more important to clarify somewhat the nature of the highly differentiated universalistic sector of American society. A proper analysis can hardly be attempted here; we can call attention only to the more pertinent outstanding characteristics.

Modern Western societies, generally, have developed far-reaching degrees of *differentiation* between the religious and secular aspects of society. Most radically in the United States—if due allowance is made for the special status of religion in Communist societies—this has entailed the secular structures' emergence to increasing prominence. Although particularly evident in the economy, this is also basically true of all levels of political organization and the major bases of community-type association. In these sectors of the social structure, the grounds of participation in roles have very generally been differentiated from particular religious loyalties, commitments, or performances. Obversely, the religious system has been opened to an indefinite number of denominational collectivities, each organized as a purely voluntary association.

As the secular structures of the society become further differentiated upon the basis of their "freedom" from religious involvements, role–pluralism becomes increasingly characteristic of the individual's participation in the societal system. A given individual participates in each sector of the society by virtue of involvement in a role which is independent of his roles in other sectors. In general, all individuals will then have unique "personal" complexes of role participations.

A society having such a complex role structure can manage to "place" its people in roles that fulfil their aspirations and its operational requirements only by developing very considerable *mobility*. In general, mobility is a rather direct consequence of the maintenance of universalistic standards for allocating aspirants among the desirable roles. It enables the individual to change his "location" in territorial, occupational, community, stratification, ethnic, and other contexts as he commits himself to specific roles.

Together, role-pluralism and mobility tend strongly to *pluralize* the internal structures of the various societal sectors, perhaps especially the various (including local) community structures. That is, each sector comes to contain great varieties of substructures which differ from one another in their typical goals and their characteristic organizational patterns. Many problems of sheer complexity arise in this situation, perhaps the most acute developing where highly specialized units of one sector must acquire "factors" of their operations from the maze of highly specialized units of other sectors. The complexities of institutionalizing markets through which economic units can obtain labor and through which households can obtain consumer goods may be taken as prototypical here.[19] The stabilization of processes that can regulate such complicated interchanges among sectors *and* maintain order among the highly various units of given sectors requires the firm institutionalization of such highly generalized mechanisms as money-credit, political power, status and influence, and religiously grounded commitments as well as a societal code of rules for their use.[20]

Among these mechanisms, the one that mediates the *commitments* of units of action *to act* in specific categories of social situations is of focal concern here. Basically, we are interested in how units maintain (or change) their commitments when faced with problems posed by the deaths of persons in various positions within the society. We may regard two considerations as primary. First, generalized forms of commitment have their importance in action insofar as they can actually bind the relevant unit to paths of action which make real differences in its relations with other units. Second, these differences basically involve the unit's "holdings" of money and credit, power, status and influence, and future opportunities to make commitments. The *making* of commitments by a social unit must, therefore, involve calculations in terms of the consequences of such commitments upon these realities. The fact that a unit exists—and must meet the exigencies of its existence—in a society of the type sketched above greatly affects the kinds and degrees of commitments it can make, precisely because that society constitutes the *reality* it "knows."

For example, a family that experiences the death of the head of its household might typically be confronted with the following problems: It must appropriately symbolize its commitments in the contexts of its membership in a specific religion, its solidarity with a distinctive ethnic group, its sense of belongingness in the American community, its involvements in the occupational system, its generalized status in the stratification system, and its position within its network of kin. Yet, it must limit expenditures and the acquisition of obligations to the resources at its command, whether available through the economic market or only through more particular channels such as friendship and association, in the light of its other commitments and needs for resources. In contemporary American society, these decisions must be made largely without the benefit of traditionalized standards. This is only a selective (perhaps minimal) list of problems and does not focus upon such common, even though special, ones as those posed by the effects of mobility—e.g., the family members not knowing securely what is expected of people of their status because it is new and "strange" to them. The differences between the situation of a family which must make such problematic decisions and that of a primitive kinship group, which has the significant elements of its mourning rites fully prescribed, are obviously very great.

A particularly salient characteristic of American society is that personal decisions—such as those just listed—are generally made within thoroughly *privatized* contexts, ones institutionally defined as almost exclusively the "private matters" of the individuals involved. Such decisions are especially critical for establishing, maintaining, and symbolizing the social unit's fundamental *patterns* of individual value commitment as it engages in various types of action, subjecting the integrity of its values to the risk of disruption. In a highly pluralized society, where each individual has unique role involvements and unique grounds for evaluating them, the personal meaningfulness of value-commitment patterns can be maintained only if social units can make their private decisions with relative freedom from "official" or "public" pressures, which cannot, in general, be notably understanding of personal matters.

The individual units must integrate their various commitments under the "supervision" of their own consciences, and the elements of the "public" affected by the decisions must rely upon the general quality of the plurality of private consciences. Thus, we had best turn to the structuring of private consciences in order to understand American orientations toward death.

Early Christianity, by combining certain Hebrew and Greek cultural elements, developed a basically new degree of differentiation in the socio-cultural structuring of the individual conscience. Since this was based on emphasis on the salvation of the individual soul, it very fundamentally involved problems of orientation toward death.

To be sure, this development was strongly conditioned by the advanced autonomy of the individual under the Roman Empire and its legal order. The early Christians pledged their faith to Christ and joined the radically *associational* church (then sharply segregated from the rest of society) *as individuals.*

However, it was the sacrificial death of Jesus that was the founding act of Christianity. A significant reason for its becoming "symbolic" in so massive a way was its clear relation to *all* the components of the death complex discussed above. It was a thoroughly human, biological death; it was deliberately imposed, being an execution; it was attended by great suffering; and it was a very premature death of a vigorous leader of men. Therefore, it presented a particularly stinging problem of meaning, involving perhaps the worst possible combination of the problems of death.

At the same time, Jesus's death was conceived of not only as an end like any other death but also as a critical beginning. Still more important than the belief in Jesus resurrected, "sitting on the right hand of God," was the idea that this event founded the Christian Church. The Church was believed to be both the mystical body of Christ and a human collectivity, which continued the role of its Founder in mediating between the divine and human worlds. Fulfillment of the responsibilities of membership in this collectivity guaranteed the individual that his death would not be "the end" but the basis of "eternal life." Thus the Church comprised a framework, which was concurrently social and extra-social ("supernatural"), for giving meaning to both temporal life and its germination.

In a sense not true of either Judaism or Greco-Roman religion, the religious individualism of Christianity dissociated the basic spiritual welfare of the individual from his particular position in the broader society in which he was born, lived, and died. Especially in the early days of the Church, the Christian tended strongly to cut himself off from the primordial securities of pagan society. For example, if he was a Jew by birth, he would strive to receive salvation within the new framework of Christian obligations rather than be "received back into the bosom of Abraham" upon death. Similarly, the element of kinship and its obligations was sharply downgraded, basically because a person encountered his "eternal" fate strictly as an individual within the Church.[21]

It is a crucial fact, however, that a member of the Church could attain salvation only by participating in the sacraments. These constituted a mechanism which, with the automatism of magic, purported to mediate to the individual within the human order the ultimate benefits that only the transcendental order of the Father could bestow. Moreover, Church doctrine began increasingly to assert that salvation could be obtained only through the performances of duly authorized priests under conditions regulated by the Church hierarchy. The individual Church member could not face his God directly, at least not in regard to such an ultimate matter as his own salvation.

After the extraordinary societal retrogression that followed the disintegration of the western Roman Empire, the medieval institutional system gradually emerged, based on a conception that Troeltsch called the *Christian Society*.[22] This constituted the Church's very sophisticated adaptation to conditions in which the secular authorities were themselves Christians rather than pagan "Caesars" with whom involvement was to be avoided. As a result of this situation, Christianity was clearly placed between a Scylla and a Charybdis. On the one hand, when the "authorities" were Christian—with whom one associated in the Church and who shared one's ultimate references and purposes—one was well obligated to take an active interest in their worldly concerns and not merely "render" them a residual loyalty. Perhaps the fusions of secular and religious concerns and efforts involved in the Crusades are prototypical here. On the other hand, it was extremely difficult to maintain the Christian pattern of "other-worldliness" in concern and orientation if, pragmatically, one were to counter Christian tradition and accept the fundamental legitimacy of worldly obligations and entanglements. Essentially, these difficulties were resolved by transforming the Christian society, in its religious aspects, into a two-class system. The truly (radically) Christian religious life was lived only by members of the segregated religious orders, who comprised an upper class relative to ultimate, transcendent matters. The broad masses of the laity—no matter how pious some among them might be—lived under comparatively secular conditions which the "natural law" designated as being of a lower order, only illumined and leavened by, not articulating with, divine grace. By administering the sacraments to all, the secular clergy provided integration between these levels, to be sure. Nevertheless, there was a critical sense in which this was only a *partially* Christian society.

The great significance of the Reformation was that it collapsed this two-class system. The laity came to be included in the religious upper class; in a critical sense, "every man became a monk," even though certain previous requirements of monasticism, such as celibacy and obedience to a *human* authority, were dropped when the altered framework of religious meaning and purpose deemphasized their value. The requirement of poverty was perhaps the last of these to gain thorough transformation. Of course, it had long been permitted for the Orders, as supernaturally grounded corporations, to become rich insofar as they were considered faithful trustees for the common good. As Weber has stressed, however, the Reformation made it possible for the individual to take over this trusteeship function, if he was religiously justified.[23]

The religious framework of the Reformation also generated pronounced increments in the valuation of *activism* as a pattern of social action, in the sense sketched above. A dual implication underlay this development. First, the justified society derived its meaning from the mission, ordained by direct divine mandate, to establish a Holy Community as *the* vehicle for implementing God's design for man. Secondly, the individual who contributed to the Holy Community through his *worldly* "calling" was upgraded to a position of the highest possible moral standing. On this basis, the *whole* society gained the potential of becoming truly and fully Christian. Both the society as a whole and its individual members could become "instruments of God's will."

As Protestantism developed, increasingly salient became the fact that these gains in the ultimate standing or justification of the society and the individual were, very essentially, *potentials,* not secure or inherent qualities. In order to preserve the sense in which action poses moral dilemmas—an essential means in all complex sociocultural systems of guarding social order against the effects of "antinomianism" or "gnosticism"—individuals had to be regarded as "free" instruments of God and hence as prone to imperfect performances for which they were responsible. Such responsibility was conceived in quite radical terms and concerned precisely the ultimate matter of salvation. The eradication of the medieval two-class system involved the elimination of the supernatural grounding of the visible Church and its capacity to assure salvation through its sacraments. The true Church became "invisible," the mystical association of the elect, who were, in principle, unidentifiable by mere humans. There were, then, no secure, ascriptive grounds (such as membership in the Catholic Church) on which a Protestant could assure himself that he would certainly be saved. Rather, it became a matter of *conscience* that he use the offer of grace so to perfect himself as an instrument of God that he would be saved.

In his innermost self, then, the justified Protestant can gain a sense of security only by relying upon the judgment of his faithful conscience as he orients himself to his tasks in the world.[24] By no means need this judgment be insensitive to the judgments of fellow Christians, but, to be authentic, it must be genuinely rooted in the individual's own conscience. This deep grounding of individuality and conscientiousness gradually led Protestant culture to differentiate complexes of morality more sharply from strictly religious principles than had the Catholic (or any other) tradition.[25] These cultural complexes were to regulate the diverse *commitments* to the increasingly differentiated sphere of moral action, and were hence to assure the intrinsic quality of contributions to the task area of worldly activity insofar as this was presumptively dedicated to the mission of building the Holy Community. This broad development had major implications for problems about the meaning of death.

With respect to the Protestant basis, doing God's will in a secular calling could not, in the early or medieval Christian sense, be considered "living the life of sin" from which one could gain release only by assuming a special religious status. Secular life, if it was "righteous," actually came to be sanctified. By implication, the individual who lived conscientiously, i.e., who performed his Christian duties in his secular callings, was believed to be in fact doing God's will. A God who was "reasonable" could not then punish him for doing his best. It came to be felt that the death of a conscientious individual could not typically be interpreted in terms of fear of hellfire and divine wrath. Rather, there was greater hope for fulfillment of the Christian desire for an "eternal life" having the meaning of a reward for good work, perhaps classically expressed as "well done, good, and faithful servant."

Although this orientation toward the core meaning of death seems to represent the central developmental tendency of Protestantism, it emerged on a scale that included two deviating orientations. One was an "inflationary" bent, which was "Arminian" in its milder form and "Antinomian" in its more extreme form. It involved a susceptibility to sanctimonious self-righteousness and the conviction that accepting social responsibilities need not involve serious moral dilemma or the risk of incurring moral guilt. The other was a "deflationary" tendency, which was basically fundamentalist in form. It asserted that the individual was so completely dependent on God that he must radically restrict his autonomous moral responsibility because of his basic incapacity to act in morally acceptable ways. Moreover, it was strongly pessimistic concerning the possibility that the worldly conditions of action were to become ultimately valuable, doubting that God willed that they should. While the inflationary view regarded the religious as "saints" bound for a very happy eternity upon their deaths, the deflationary orientation viewed death as an impending horror for nearly all and greatly to be feared.

It is our view that certain derivatives of these religiously "deviant" orientations are still prominent in American society and culture—and not only in orientations toward death. Very generally, they seem to comprise the major patterns of orientational change with which Americans respond to strains lodged at various points in the action system. Yet, it must be recognized that they are grounded in the same basic structuring of the conscience-commitment mechanism as the more normative orientation. They seem to be modes of trying to close off *risks* to the security of certain social units that are inherently generated by the operation of that mechanism.

The emergence of a moral complex supporting the Protestant level of activism also exerted strong pressure toward differentiating the components of the death complex, as discussed above. As an instrument of the divine will, the individual had an ultimate value, so that no unnecessary sacrifice of his capacities could be sanctioned religiously. From this viewpoint, control was needed over matters of sickness and death because ill health was a hindrance to ultimately sanctioned effective performance; premature death was a waste of assets for building the good society; and suffering could not easily be reconciled with the mandates to be instrumentally effective and to accept divine rule joyfully. The desirable death was that of the person who had lived a whole life through and legitimately avoided these hindrances to achievement and contribution.

There is a very striking transition in Western history, from the "Christian pessimism," which emphasized the hopeless entanglement of "sin and death" in terrestrial life, the inevitable presence of overwhelming evil in the human condition, and a dependence of man on divine grace so absolute that only religious devotions could possibly alleviate his suffering, to the more modern optimism of activity intended to achieve the religiously desirable and of conviction that what is good by the criteria of the faith cannot generally occasion the most terrible punishments. Insofar as the latter provides the setting for contemporary American orientations toward death, it offers little foundation for any very basic "denial" of the reality of death.

The first generation of New England Puritans experienced death as an important opportunity for reaffirming the basic commitments of the involved individuals, families, and communities in profoundly religious terms. Yet, the ritualization of the occasion, especially of the funeral, was sharply deemphasized, for fear that ceremony would lead to a "Popish" practice of sanctification through the flesh. Ascetic funerals were seen as preserving the Protestant belief that the visible Church could not grant salvation to individuals through its sacraments.

Funerals, then, were very simple.[26] A plain coffin was made by a man of the family or a close friend, and the body of the deceased was washed and plainly dressed, usually by the women of the family. The burial generally took place in the churchyard and in the presence of the minister. Afterwards, there would often be a short service of prayers in the church. The clergy seems generally to have made considerable effort to limit observances of community mourning to this ascetic minimum, as seemed most appropriate to people so preoccupied with death's meaning as a birth into everlasting life. However, there was considerable evidence of strain in the funeral patterns, focusing upon the people's complaints about the uneventful quality of the community observances.

By the end of the seventeenth century, this strain had generated a more complex set of funeral practices, characterized by a relatively clear-cut differentiation between the religious and secular contexts of meeting the problems posed by death.

On the religious side, funeral sermons were often made particular high spots in the life of the religious community. Yet, the asceticism was continued in precisely this context. The sermons posed the meaning of death in very stern terms and generally dealt at length on the particulars of the life of the deceased, on his faults and errors as well as his achievements, especially in the moral context. People of conscience were to be stimulated by such sermons to awareness that their deaths would occasion the severe judgment of their worldly deeds.

The secular aspects of funeral practices were developed quite extensively in this period. The recently deceased were commonly memorialized by notices in the newspapers, the printing of mourning handbills containing poems or remarks about them, the circulation of mourning rings and gloves by their families, street processions of their mourners and fellow church members, and sizeable gatherings of their kin and friends. Although such observances were often criticized as distasteful or irrational, they seem not to have had the Popish effects that were feared, largely because of their considerable differentiation from specifically religious contexts of meaning. Their symbolism concentrated on the deceased's achievements within the community and on the community's problem of having to continue without him. They were clearly not ceremonial efforts to assure his salvation or directly to symbolize his ultimate value by accounting his worldly attainments.

The same basic pattern of funeral practices was maintained through the early years of the Republic. As the country grew richer and the society became structurally more complex, however, the practices grew more elaborate, and the more elaborate versions were extended to more of the populace. This made the supplying of funerary goods increasingly profitable and brought increasing numbers of craftsmen into the business. Various types of craftsmen were often involved, the chief ones evidently being carpenters who made coffins, upholsterers who supplied black drapery for the homes of the mourners, and liquor merchants who provided drinks for the gatherings. It seems that the increasingly complicated funeral arrangements were made either by members and friends of the family or by church sextons, some of whom may have made this a business in order to supplement their salaries.

In the second and third decades of the nineteenth century, certain businessmen in the populous areas of the East (calling themselves undertakers in accord with earlier English usage) began to offer the service of arranging funeral proceedings, so that mourners need not be concerned with such matters. These undertakers were generally craftsmen supplying funerary goods who had recognized a demand for additional services that would earn greater profits.

During this period, the market for funerary goods and services evidently did not extend very far from the chief population centers into the countryside. They could not be supplied, nor could there be much demand for them, in the more rural and poor areas. Nevertheless, deaths were generally major occasions for community gatherings in the rural areas also. Soon after a death—particularly of a man who was the head of a family—and often in conjunction with the burial, a large number of the family's local acquaintances would congregate. On these occasions, people would honor the deceased in their small talk and brief speeches, reassure the deceased's family of the community's sympathy and support (sometimes economic), and reforge the solidarity of the community—which could pose important problems if the community had just lost a leader or the chief of a faction. The family of the deceased organized and played host to these gatherings, which could often be quite a burden: much food and drink could be consumed, and there could be considerable property damage. Even when the actual materials of the funeral (e.g. the coffin) were frugal, the family often spent rather heavily to have a notable occasion for honoring the individuality and worldly achievements of the deceased with a supportive gathering of his associates and for symbolizing its commitment to him. In terms of their general meaning, then, these customs evidently adhered to much the same pattern as the more elaborate ones of the cities.

In the sixty years following the Civil War, the undertaking profession became rather fully institutionalized throughout the nation, greatly affecting the funeral arrangements in practically all areas. Funeral homes, as places for preparing bodies for burial and for holding certain of the funeral ceremonies, were established in large numbers for the first time. As the funeral directors organized into extensive professional associations and as large national firms came to dominate the manufacture of caskets, embalming fluids, hearses, and other funeral goods, national markets with national product standards emerged. For the first time, numbers of large privately owned, often commercially operated, cemeteries were established on the peripheries of the large cities and towns, replacing the older ones located in the city churchyards as the typical burial places.

These developments crystallized a complex funeral industry that closely articulated with the society's various community structures, focusing about the funeral director's position in the local community and the relationship of the market to the national community. Moreover, this industry seems to have developed in response to several aspects of the social change that America was undergoing at that time, especially the enhancement of mobility and pluralism.

The organization of the market for funeral goods and services in terms of nationally institutionalized product standards assured that relatively appropriate funeral arrangements were broadly available throughout the country. The advertising of the period indicates that the "status symbol" import of funeral goods and services was felt to have its significance relative to popular commitments to the national community. For example, Grant's burial in a special brand of casket was widely noted in newspaper accounts and greatly aided the sale of caskets of that type throughout the country. Also, patriotic references were commonly used in naming brands of caskets, hearses, etc., to lend them distinction. The development and popularization of embalming techniques and of heavy, strong caskets was a response to the need to preserve the body, if the funeral was to be postponed until relatives and friends could gather from distant places. Furthermore, this made it possible to elaborate and individualize the funeral arrangements. Here, the new degree of differentiation in the market for funeral goods and services enabled funerals to be better suited to the particular social (e.g., ethnic, class, religious) conditions of the deceased and their families. The rapid style changes in hearses and caskets that first emerged in this period seem particularly noteworthy in this regard. They enabled people to be stylish and to demonstrate themselves to be "up" with national trends. The emergence of funeral homes was especially important because it enabled people, especially those who lacked large homes, to hold much larger wakes and permitted funeral arrangements to proceed with more efficiency and less inconvenience to the mourners.

Embalming and the use of elaborate caskets deserve our further attention, largely because of their continued importance in American funerals. Embalming was first made practical just before the Civil War and was first widely used to preserve dead soldiers who were being shipped home for burial during the war. As embalming rapidly became a common procedure in the late nineteenth century, two themes were prominently used to advertise it. First, it was said to preserve bodies long enough for distant people to come and "pay their last respects." This shows clear linkage with the problems created by the great mobility of the time. Second, it was claimed to be an important sanitary measure, articulating with the strenuous efforts emerging in that period to control the "adventitious" components of the death complex through public health measures. There seems never to have been much real concern with "preserving" bodies over extended periods in a manner that would have "pagan" implications. Strong, heavy caskets were used initially as aids in keeping corpses inoffensive until they were buried and hence stood upon the same bases of evaluation as embalming. Indeed, both were evidently accepted popularly as basic advances of modern technology relevant to funerary observances. However, the casket was soon established as the major "status symbol" involved in the typical funeral, apparently because it was so directly associated with the body of the deceased at the wake or funeral. As the deceased comprised the center of attention at funeral observances, it was important to a society of mobile, "achieved" relationships that his remains be well presented, particularly in the status terms that reflected his worldly attainments.[27] This pattern of meaning also focused upon the family's intention of affording the best it could in order to demonstrate before the community its love, respect, and commitment to the deceased, as well as to symbolize the family's status in the community. It is important to note here that funeral directors have generally tried to offer varieties of caskets, distinctive by style as well as cost, so that their clients can demonstrate taste and expressive sensibility, not just wealth.

Among contemporary funeral practices, perhaps the most important tendency is toward stabilizing the differentiation between the religious and secular—or, more accurately expressed in this instance, the privatized and community—contexts of handling death problems. Increasingly, the more religiously ultimate and emotionally intense aspects of the problems raised by a death are managed at religious services, at the actual burial, or at special gatherings of particularly close kin and friends. A distinct wake or memorial service, involving a much more extensive gathering of the deceased's associates, tends to focus more sharply on the worldly achievements of the deceased and his standing in the community. The nature of this basic differentiation must be kept in mind if the meaning of practices occurring in one context or the other is to be correctly gauged.

The pluralistic structure of American society makes it inherently more difficult to generalize about the privatized contexts of funeral observances, because they give structural primacy to the particular commitment patterns of the chief mourners, including especially religious and ethnic commitments. Clearly, observances within this sphere vary greatly between, for example, Jewish and Catholic or Negro and Yankee groups. In the community sphere, however, there has been a notable tendency for certain generally "American" practices to hold primacy over particularistically linked practices, even when the latter are in evidence, as they frequently are at wakes or memorial services. This is probably a "functional requirement" of obtaining community support for the deceased's family under conditions in which the associates of the deceased have varied religious and ethnic allegiances. Yet, these more public observances should not be regarded (as they often are) as comprising the totality of American funeral practices—the more privatized observances present a less uniform pattern and are less evident, but neither their importance nor the profundity of their religious grounding should be underrated.

It seems best to focus the present analysis upon the open-casket wake, the major community[28] observance in roughly 90 percent of American funerals, because it has become so controversial in recent years.[29] Most arguments to the effect that Americans tend to deny the reality of death are framed with considerable reference to the practices it commonly involves.

The contemporary wake, being an elaboration of the pattern that originated in the late nineteenth century, centers about the presentation of the deceased to his former associates. Typically, the corpse is not only embalmed and placed in an expensive, often ornate, casket, but also "restored," decorously dressed-up, surrounded by an elaborate floral display, and perhaps posed in a "lifelike" manner.

At least two complexes of meaning seem to underlie the practices of the newer type of wake. First, there seems to be a strong tendency in our individualistic, activistic society to want the deceased to appear in a manner that makes his former active capacities recognizable. Clearly, such an appearance can facilitate the wake's function of symbolizing and honoring the worldly attainments of the deceased. Beyond that, however, it seems also to facilitate the specific acts—"giving our last respects to" or "saying good-bye to" the deceased—through which this function is accomplished and solidarity with the family of the deceased is demonstrated. Second, these changes involve an important extension of the "control" orientation toward the suffering component of the death complex. Perhaps the crux of this matter can be posed as a question: if the sick and dying should not suffer, why then must the bereaved mourners? Therefore, an effort is made not to exacerbate the problems of mourning, perhaps particularly by not calling attention to the suffering, loss of capacity, or mutilation which the deceased underwent in dying. Far from relating to denial of death, however, this extension of our orientation toward suffering seems to articulate with an enhancement of the obligations upon mourners to do their "grief work" efficiently and thoroughly, so that they may soon resume their own life tasks. Perhaps it is this general upgrading of the individual's obligations to mourn that comprises the most basic change in the whole field of handling problems of death that has emerged in the last fifty years or so.

It seems important to note that the major changes in the wake during the last half-century involve primarily the mode of presentation of the deceased and the decoration of the funeral parlor rather than the actual patterns of interaction at the wake. If there are important changes in the latter, they seem to involve only some relaxation in formality, some lessening of the religious involvements of the occasion, and some gain in people's control over their behavior. Therefore, it would seem unlikely that any very fundamental change in orientations toward death (e.g., from mastery to denial) is involved in the specific changes noted in the foregoing paragraphs.

Nevertheless, there is much evidence that significant portions of the American population show elements of strain and orientational distortion in planning and holding funerals. Such distortion seems to follow both inflationary and deflationary patterns, but with inflation being more prominent. Its most common manifestation is overspending on funeral observances relative to the normative requirements arising from the various aspects of the social standing of the deceased and his family. Such overspending may arise from convictions that elaborate observances can fundamentally improve the worldly status of the family or can affect the ultimate well-being or even the salvation of the deceased's soul.[30] The deflationary tendency is based on beliefs that funeral observances "do nothing" except expend the resources of the family of the deceased and rests on a broader American tendency to distrust action that lacks clearly demonstrable instrumental value. In recent years, this tendency has crystallized a growing movement proselytizing for low-cost, minimal funeral arrangements planned in advance of the death. The strained quality often present in this movement is clear in the great concern for funerary matters displayed by its members, despite the claim that funeral observances are basically unimportant.

The genesis of the more prevalent, inflationary pattern is particularly interesting in sociological terms. It seems to be grounded in certain "anomic" effects of the pluralistic diversity of ethnic, religious, class, occupational, etc., loyalties that enter into the integrative structures of contemporary society. People who are disoriented about the relative appropriateness of different funeral arrangements and feel conflict among the distinct pressures of their various loyalties tend to "make sure" that they will make proper decisions by overfulfilling their commitments. This tendency is especially marked among the social groups that, relative to their expectations and frequently to other groups, have been deprived of expected (often formerly held) positions of positive prestige or leadership—though not necessarily very high ones. Southern California, with its large population of people who are disappointed by what they have *not* gained from that land of opportunity (even though they may have gained many things), and who feel "up-rooted" as a consequence of having left their "home" communities, is perhaps the area of the country most permeated with this tendency. Members of the transitional generations in particular ethnic groups, who often become super-Americans in reaction to feelings of ambivalence about their identities as "ethnics" and as "Americans," also seem particularly susceptible to inflation in funeral practices.

These patterns of strain are very familiar to sociologists, but primarily because of their tendency to generate *deflation* (fundamentalism or rightism) in the political sphere.[31] It seems that, in a broad way, inflation in such private areas as that of funeral observances correlates with deflation in the area of public, collective action.[32] Evidently, a personal feeling that one has "lost" more than one has "gained" from contemporary processes of social change frequently stimulates a romanticization of past social conditions and, within the American context of individualistic values, an idealization of the capacities of the individual and an image of the "true" individual as operating in opposition to social processes. This broad ideological position, then, can generate both deflation in collective, political action and inflation in the assertion of the status strivings of individuals and family units. Inflated funeral observances, whether in privatized or community contexts, fit the latter type of case.

It is notable that funeral directors, the most influential group in establishing style and taste in funerary matters, generally fall into population categories which are very susceptible to political deflation and individualistic inflation. Many of them feel obliged to hold a difficult ideological balance between maintaining firm ethnic identities and adhering to a robust Americanism in order to keep the trust of their clients—who are often made more sensitive to such matters by the strains of handling a death. Funeral directors tend to be moderately upwardly mobile in status terms yet are deprived of the degree of social prestige that accrues to such professionals as doctors and lawyers. In recent years, most have found their businesses more limited in growth than most of the economy by the heavy saturation of their trade relative to the demand for their services. Finally, many funeral directors are quite concerned about the "unfair" limitations placed upon their private lives and families by the nature of their work—e.g., many are afraid to drink at social events because it might reflect badly on their morality or reliability, especially if they are suddenly called to work; and many believe they are often excluded from membership or leadership in prestigious clubs or social circles because of their professional contact with the tabooed dead.

The ideological positions of the funeral directors' professional associations and journals follow the pattern we would expect. Politically, they have adhered conspicuously to the values of God, America, individualism, motherhood, etc., while being suspicious of almost all expansion in governmental activities, especially welfare regulations, that might affect their businesses. Regarding funeral observances, they have quite constantly advocated the increasing elaboration of goods and services, frequently to the point of attempting to legitimize the new usages on highly "inflationary" grounds. Moreover, funeral directors often seem to play upon the guilt feelings of clients in order to inflate commitments to do the "best" for the deceased and the social standing of the family.[33]

The actual effects of the funeral directors' inflationary advice is exacerbated by certain ambiguities in the institutionalization of the funeral director's role that permits a degree of "exploitation" of the clients. Simply put, the funeral director (much like the pharmacist) is both a business man and a professional in the same role. As critics have emphasized, the funeral director is offering certain goods and services for sale, the profit in which he is interested varying directly with the value of his sales. But, as the funeral directors' associations have long emphasized, the funeral director is also a professional in that he must make decisions on behalf of clients which rather inherently cannot knowledgeably be made by the clients themselves. In recent years, there has been an increasing tendency to develop this aspect of the role. For example, funeral directors have tried to simplify as far as possible the arrangements to which clients must attend: many advertise that making one phone call is all that the client need do. However, it is clear that the funeral directors' ideology and interests often motivate them to undermine the professional structuring of their role and sell the client more than he wishes or can appropriately use. Further, the funeral director is in a good position to exploit certain profession-like aspects of his relation with the customer: preneed arrangements aside, the customer is unlikely to shop around to find the funeral home giving the best deal; the grief-stricken, particularly those afflicted by the sudden death of a near relative (and it is rare that we are fully prepared for a death), can often be badly taken by one who plays upon their disorientation and guilt feelings.

It should be clear, then, that many strains and inflated orientations operate within various contexts in the general sphere of funeral observances. These often give rise to practices that are strikingly disharmonious with general American orientational patterns, particularly in certain of their symbolic meanings. However, these seem to operate through quite particular mechanisms that are known to promote deviating (not deviant in the usual sociological sense) patterns of very special types. They do not justify claims that American orientations toward death have changed in any very general or fundamental manner. Perhaps we can buttress this claim by examining the case of a death that occurred in very different circumstances, ones not quite so subject to inflationary mechanisms, at least at this time and in this context.

In treating American attitudes and practices concerning death, we have put principal emphasis upon contexts in which deaths are primarily the private matters of the family, friends, and close associates of the deceased. In a large-scale, pluralistic society, no very large fraction of the population, even of most local communities, can be concerned with the death of an ordinary citizen. However, the deaths of prominent public figures are public events and throw a somewhat different light on the whole death complex of the society. Because the assassination of President Kennedy was a peculiarly dramatic case and will be fresh in the memories of our readers, a brief account of its impact seems appropriate for our analysis.

Since Kennedy was the fourth President of the United States to be assassinated, the risk had been well recognized in the century since Lincoln's death. However, it had been two-thirds of a century since the last presidential assassination, so the shock was tremendous, not only throughout the nation but throughout the world. Adding greatly to the shock was the fact that this death was far from one that completed a fulfilled career. It struck down a vigorous man in early middle-age—all the more poignant because Kennedy, as the youngest of American Presidents and as a particularly dynamic person, had become a symbol of youth's promise in high office.

It will be remembered that the blow struck about noon on a Friday in November, in Dallas, Texas, where the President had been making a very successful political tour. He was dead within minutes of arrival at the hospital. Furthermore, the assassination was made as "senseless" as possible by the fact—or so it then appeared to an overwhelming majority—that it was the work of a completely isolated individual (and perhaps an insane one) who acted from obscure motivation, not political consideration or participation in an organized movement.

The event precipitated the whole complex of strong emotional reactions which Durkheim and Malinowski have so perceptively described. There was disbelief, horror, a disposition to accuse, anxiety about future developments, and pity and sympathy for the victim and his bereaved family, especially his attractive, fortitudinous young widow and two small children. Nevertheless, the overwhelming response was realistic, but at the same time it was cathartic in that grand-scale emotional reaction took place in a highly ritualized form. Within an hour of the certification of the death, Johnson had taken the oath of office as President and had begun the return to Washington, with the body and the widow. As soon as the funeral observances were completed, he addressed a joint session of Congress, especially stressing the continuity of his policies with those of President Kennedy.

The funeral was a state occasion in the fullest sense. Dignitaries attended from all over the nation and the world, perhaps the most notable figure among them being General de Gaulle. The lying-in-state, first in the East Room of the White House and then in the Rotunda of the Capitol, with its enormous public participation, the funeral service, and the burial were all conducted with the highest dignity. The coverage of radio and, especially, television—which was both thorough and highly dignified—made it possible for the whole nation to participate in a manner never before known. Moreover, this participation was enormous—an unprecedented proportion of the population devoted itself almost entirely to the national mourning until the funeral ended on Monday afternoon.[34]

We have stressed the realism in the general reaction, above all in the orderly continuation of the affairs of state under the leadership of the new President. Perhaps equally impressive was the general restraint of the public in managing not to search for "plots" and political involvements behind the assassination—it should be remembered that the assassin had resided in the Soviet Union.[35] There was also strong ritual support of the bereaved, and placement of Mrs. Kennedy and her children in a very special symbolic position. Probably there has never been another occasion in which bereavement has been so widely and poignantly shared by millions and in which a family has thereby become a symbolic focus for a bereaved nation and, beyond that, a bereaved world.

This is one aspect of the reaffirmation of solidarity, one which funeral ceremonies typically effect. Another aspect, however, was especially significant in this case. Kennedy was the first Roman Catholic to be elected President of the United States; his election had signalled a major advance in the inclusion of non-WASP elements into the status of full membership in the American societal community. In this context too, then, a special air of tragedy and martyrdom hung over the event in that he, of all recent Presidents, should have been assassinated.

Kennedy's funeral crucially symbolized the new ecumenical status of the American community in relation to the religious affiliations of its members. In a sense, death is ultimately "private," and in death John F. Kennedy reassumed his private status, which, among other things, included his standing as a good Catholic. It was taken for granted that he should have a Catholic funeral, conducted by his parochial priest, Cardinal Cushing of Boston. However, this was the first occasion of such importance and poignancy to bring the full implications of the American system of denominational pluralism, with its peculiar balance between the public and private statuses of religion, in such sharp focus.

At the funeral, which was seen by millions over television, the Cardinal symbolized this situation. As the pastor of the dead President and the Kennedy family, he was the appropriate person to conduct the rites of burial. At the same time, he was also the religious spokesman of the American national community. The first role was exclusive in that one cannot be both a Catholic and a Protestant *as an individual*. But the second role was not exclusive in this sense, for the societal community (in America) is neither Catholic nor Protestant nor Jewish, but comprises *all* of these. Given the Protestant background of American society, however, it was new and crucially important that a Catholic priest should assume the role of community spokesman at a time of crisis—as a rabbi may also be called upon to do sometime in the future.

In keeping with the national and international significance of the occasion, the congregation in the Catholic cathedral in Washington was entirely interdenominational, with President Johnson, a Protestant, occupying the place of honor next to the Kennedy family. Very likely, Catholics were in a minority within the cathedral, as they certainly were in the television audience. It is interesting in this connection that, when Mr. Johnson first left Washington as President, about two weeks after the Kennedy funeral, he attended the funeral of former Senator Lehman of New York, conducted by a rabbi in a Jewish temple.

The ritual meaning of the Kennedy funeral lay in the fact that, as President, Kennedy was not only the Chief Executive of the United States government, but also the first citizen of the American national community. His death was a great blow to the integrity of that community. It evoked not only private grief but also a great demonstration of emotion on a national basis that combined appropriate reaction to the crucial loss with a reassertion of national solidarity and will to sustain the basic national tasks fundamentally as before. This demonstration seems to have proceeded in broad accord with the general orientation which we have outlined as the basic one in American society and with the American principles of popular participation in political and community affairs. Above all, despite the profundity of the emotional disturbance and reaction, there was relatively little trace of "denial" or even sentimentality, especially in the critical cathartic observances of the first several days. A bit speculatively, we hold that the death of President Kennedy, being in a sense sacrificial, had an effect on national affairs that has well transcended the shock and loss it immediately occasioned. It seems that the sweeping outcome of the 1964 presidential election, with the assertion of a center-to-left solidarity by the great majority of the nation, can be partly attributed to a solidarity associated with a common national experience of the meaning of Kennedy's life. Perhaps the accelerated pace with which the nation, until it was slowed by too deep an involvement in the Vietnamese War, pursued certain goals to which Kennedy had been dedicated, particularly in civil rights and other matters of internal affairs, was associated with the sacrifice.[36]

In view of the purpose of this volume, we will conclude our paper with a brief discussion of the manner in which attitudes toward suicide fit into orientations toward death which we have been analyzing.

Available evidence indicates that suicide is tenth on the list of common "causes" of death in the United States, claiming at least 20,000 lives every year. Since this amounts to almost 11 deaths per 100,000 people every year, there can be little doubt that suicide poses a very great, unsolved problem for the American orientation toward reducing "adventitious" deaths.[37] The predominant types of suicide seem to involve, in Durkheim's terms, not only "anomic" but also "*egoistic*" elements.[38] The latter arise when institutionalized pressures assert ultimate imperatives for the individual to accept a very high order of responsibility. Such pressures have been very powerful and prevalent in societies within the "ascetic Protestant" tradition, arising from their structuring of the *conscience* mechanisms.

We have stressed that modern society has differentiated the death complex into the components which are inevitably grounded in the human condition and those which are "adventitious." The primary criterion of adventitiousness has been openness to human control, primarily through measures of medicine and public health but also through many other factors, such as safety measures. Acting upon the ascetic activism of the value pattern, our society has tended strongly to institutionalize the means of reducing adventitious deaths. Yet, the enhanced capacity to save and prolong lives can be a two-edged sword in certain contexts; the shift from the relative fatalism of earlier societies to contemporary instrumental activism raises very acutely the problem of the meaningfulness of the alternative open to every individual to terminate his own life deliberately. An individual's decision to take his life comprises a tragedy with inherent social involvements in a society that is strongly committed to reducing "premature" death in general.

To be sure, Durkheim stressed the strength of the moral objection to suicide in all the main Western religious traditions. In particular, he stressed that, since this factor is common to Catholic and Protestant groups, it cannot account for the important differences in suicide rates between them. In general terms, a strong objection to suicide is associated with the basic Christian—and, in a modified sense, Jewish—conception that man is placed on this earth to carry out a divinely ordained mission and that he may not presume to shirk his task so long as he has life and strength. By contrast with many other cultures, Western civilization, despite its many bloody episodes, has clearly had a special conception of the sacredness of human life.[39]

The conception of the sanctity of life relates integrally to the modern stress on the importance of individuality, which also has strong religious bases. The main theme of this individualism is not permissiveness for self-indulgence but a sense of mission and obligation to act with maximum responsibility in contributing to the good society. It is essentially this theme which underlies the strong sentiment that, in general, an individual may not take his own life, much as he may not take the lives of others.

In the earlier phases of Western civilization, this sentiment was enforced with a rigor that we would now consider almost barbaric in severity. Thus, the suicide was denied all religious rights in death, including that of burial in consecrated ground. In general, however, severity has yielded to the individualizing trends of the great cultural movements of the modern era. These have increasingly stressed the rights of the responsible individual to autonomy, including, as we have noted, his rights to be guided by his own conscience in the management of his life and his rights to have his ultimate responsibilities treated as his *private* affair. It is only logical that this reasoning should extend to the individual's termination of his own life, at least under certain kinds of circumstances.

Moreover, various modern denominations, particularly the "liberal" Protestant ones, have come to regard the classification of the saved and the damned as applying not to total personal entities but to components of them. Specific individuals, then, participate in *both* categories in different degrees and ways, though with various risks and uncertainties. This definition of the ultimate situation makes it appear much less likely that an individual will be ascribed to either category in any simple sense by virtue of particular acts, even so drastic an act as suicide.[40] This seems to have two important consequences for the problem of suicide. On the one hand, it increases the risk that suicides will actually be committed because it makes meaningful a more "charitable," if not quite permissive, attitude toward suicide. On the other hand, it increases the ultimate motivation to develop active controls over suicide (e.g., through mental health programs for those who have made suicide attempts) because the suicidal person is no longer defined as inherently reprobate and undeserving of efforts to "save" him.

The recent increase in our knowledge of unconscious motivation has perhaps reinforced these developments. It has become almost a commonplace that most, if not all, individuals have "death wishes" directed at both "significant others" and themselves. Hence suicide, regarded as a consciously deliberate act, must be considered as the limiting case along a common and deeply grounded range of variation—the case in which death wishes for oneself (cf. Freud's famous *Thanatos*) gain full ascendancy over one's personality.[41]

Moreover, the importance of this complex extends to a great many deaths which ostensibly occur from organic causes, considerably blurring the boundaries of the very concept of suicide. The phenomenon of accident proneness is particularly striking as a type of "indirect" self-destruction. However, there also seem to be numerous other more subtle mechanisms, especially of the type that we call psychosomatic. Perhaps it no longer seems too radical to claim that there is a suicidal component in a very large proportion of ordinary deaths. The important question, then, is not whether such a component exists, since in almost any case it may, but when and under what circumstances it plays a crucial role. In a large proportion of deaths of the relatively aged, there is probably an important sense in which the individuals have "unconsciously" decided that it is time for them to die.

These considerations apply throughout the field of illness as well as to actual deaths. What we have called premature death—whatever the agency responsible for it—may be regarded as withdrawal from otherwise possible performances of social roles. In a sense, illness is just a temporary or partial case of the same thing. To be sure, we ordinarily apply the concept of illness only when the relevant individual does not responsibly decide to withdraw but the disability causing him to withdraw "happens" to him. However, this does not preclude the possibility that one component in the illness is an unconscious wish to be ill that cannot be controlled by deliberate decision. Such a component is implied in the concept of "secondary gain" as an element in motivated illness and resistances to recovery.

The basic social attitudes in this field have become greatly complicated in recent years. Illness is clearly an *undesirable* state—insofar as it is actually desired, even unconsciously, it is deviant. Nevertheless, it is not, like crime, to be punished. The sick person is to be treated with compassion and helped to recover, his disability and suffering being regarded in a crucial sense as "not his fault." However, he has a clear obligation to recover if possible and to cooperate with therapeutic agents in aiding his recovery.[42]

It seems to us that the problem of suicide in our society is also deeply embedded in this broad context. Like illness, it must certainly be generally disapproved in ordinary cases. Yet, specific circumstances may warrant a conditional relaxation of the standards of undesirability—as may be involved in the treatment of given instances of motivated illness.

Excepting the crucial difference of the finality of death, we may clarify this point by comparing suicide with divorce. We certainly regard persons as irresponsible who enter a marriage without the intention of making it permanent. If persons of good faith become entangled in irresolvable conflicts which are injurious to their spouses, their children, and themselves, however, divorce is commonly approved as the best way out of a bad situation. If a divorced person seems to have done his best to make his marriage work, he is given another chance, not punished, despite his previous failure. Similarly, an individual's decision to end his own life does not usually become a basis for bitter condemnation. Rather, we generally respond with compassion and an attempt to understand the intolerability of the difficulties in which he was entangled. There is often a conditional concession that suicide may have been the best way out for the person involved.

At the same time, responsible agents in the society will almost always make strenuous attempts to dissuade prospective suicides from ending their lives. If there is a presumption of pathology, such coercive measures as commitment to a mental hospital are generally applied in order to prevent a suicide attempt. The rationale here is that "if he were in his right mind, he would reconsider."

Clearly, there is a crosscutting of institutional themes: the individual is considered to be responsible and autonomous, holding some kind of right to make all personal decisions, including the drastic decision to take his own life;[43] yet, the suicide is considered to be in the role of illness, with the presumption that he is subject to irrational compulsions which the society should prevent. At present, we cannot assess the relative importance of these components, either in the general field of mental illness or for suicide particularly. However, we can conclude that, even though severe mental illness is surely involved in a very large proportion of the suicides in our society, insofar as they are egoistic suicides in Durkheim's sense, the broader cultural component should not be ignored.

Insofar as it is closely related to illness, suicide comprises, in the first instance, a *release* from an intolerable situation of intense suffering. Yet, suicide may also involve two underlying types of meaning which should not be understressed. One is the suicidal individual's feeling that his work is done, and that it does not make sense to linger on. This seems to be typical of suicides among the aged, particularly those who feel that they are a burden to others. However, it also occurs among younger people who despair that they have become such total failures that they cannot be redeemed.[44] The other type of meaning is that in which suicide is conceived of as a special symbolic act or demonstration, e.g., of protest or the expiation of guilt. A famous instance is the Japanese institution of hara-kiri. However, it should not be supposed that this type is entirely absent from our society. A sacrificial component is so importantly grounded in externally imposed death by the Christian tradition that its self-imposition cannot be disregarded as providing a meaning complex for suicide.

## REFERENCES

1. Herman Feifel states that "denial and avoidance of the countenance of death characterize much of the American outlook," by way of summarizing a predominating theme in the book he edited, *The Meaning of Death* (New York: McGraw-Hill Book Company, 1959), which contains contributions by many distinguished people in a variety of disciplines. Quotation is from p. xvii.
2. Perhaps the most sociological discussion of funeral practices and such a hypothetical general trend is Peter Berger and Richard Lieban, "Kulturelle Wertstruktur und Bestattungspraktiken in den Vereinigten Staaten," *Kölner Zeitschrift für Soziologie und Sozialpsychologie,* No. 2, 1960.
3. See George Gaylord Simpson, *The Meaning of Evolution* (New Haven, Conn.: Yale University Press, 1949).
4. See Talcott Parsons, *Social Structure and Personality* (New York: The Free Press, 1964), especially chap. 4.
5. S. N. Eisenstadt has probably made the most important contribution to the understanding of problems in this field. See his *From Generation to Generation* (New York: The Free Press, 1956).
6. Max Weber's *Sociology of Religion* (English ed.; Boston: Beacon Press, 1963) is probably still the best single statement of the broad analytical position we are taking toward religion.
7. These last paragraphs are intended to give death its due in terms of its general implications for action systems. We wish to note, however, that our account is quite distinct from that of much current existentialism, which seems to claim that, very generally, life purposes and a great many life activities gain their meaning *only* from being contrasted with and opposed to death. Analytically, this seems extreme and perhaps hinges upon a rather pejorative use of the term "meaning."
8. See Simpson, *op. cit.*
9. M. Gendell and H. L. Zetterberg, A *Sociological Almanac for the United States,* 2nd ed. (New York: Scribner's, 1964), p. 42.
10. Buddha, we may recall, viewed sickness, old age, and death, with their attendant suffering, as the aspects of this world that led him to recognize the need for adopting a radical other-worldly orientation.
11. The best statement on the characteristics of the pattern of instrumental activism that is yet in print is given in Talcott Parsons and Winston White, "The Link Between Character and Society," chap. 8 in *Social Structure and Personality.* It should be clear that we are referring to a general orientational pattern that can be specified, in principle, to all contexts of social action. We are *not* simply talking about the "scientific" orientation.
12. Cf. Talcott Parsons, *The System of Modern Societies,* forthcoming.
13. We are developing here the view that the "death complex" is a universal that, like the "family," can be found in all societies. In the primitive societies, it is diffusely embedded in other structures, much like the kinship

system. In the more evolved societies, it assumes greater structural autonomy, in a sense very parallel to the modern nuclear family.

14. This point is well developed by Claude Levi-Strauss in *Totemism* (Boston: Beacon Paperbacks, Beacon Press, 1963).
15. This concept of "distance" was developed by Henri Hubert and Marcel Mauss in their *Sacrifice: Its Nature and Function* (English ed.; Chicago: University of Chicago Press, 1964).
16. Cf. W. Lloyd Warner, *A Black Civilization* (rev. ed.; New York: Harper & Row, 1958).
17. We have taken the concept of "one possibility" from "Religious Evolution" by Robert N. Bellah (in the *American Sociological Review*, June, 1964), who has adapted it from W. E. H. Stanner's articles "On Aboriginal Religion" in *Oceania*.
18. Cf. Warner, *op. cit.*, and Robert Hertz, "Death" in *Death and the Right Hand* (New York: The Free Press, 1960).
19. See Talcott Parsons and Neil J. Smelser, *Economy and Society* (New York: The Free Press, 1960).
20. The present concepts of generalized media and mechanisms have been developed by Talcott Parsons in the papers "On the Concept of Political Power" (*Proceedings of the American Philosophical Society*, June, 1963) and "On the Concept of Influence" (*Public Opinion Quarterly*, Spring, 1963).
21. Cf. A. D. Nock, *Conversion* (London and New York: Oxford University Press, 1933).
22. Our account of early and Medieval Christianity, particularly, rests heavily on Ernst Troeltsch's *The Social Teachings of the Christian Churches* (New York: Harper Torchbooks, Harper & Row, 1960).
23. Max Weber, *The Protestant Ethic and the Spirit of Capitalism* (New York: Scribner's Paperback Library, Charles Scribner's Sons, 1958).
24. The most important recent work on the understanding of the ascetic Protestant conscience is that of Perry Miller. Perhaps the best brief statement is the essay "The Marrow of Puritan Theology" in his *Errand into the Wilderness* (New York: Harper Torchbooks, Harper & Row, 1964).
25. In framing our discussion here, we are considerably indebted to the doctoral thesis of Johannes J. Loubser, *The Development of Religious Liberty in Massachusetts* (Harvard University, 1964). Richard Niebuhr's *The Kingdom of God in America* (New York: Harper Torchbooks, Harper & Row, 1959) is also a basic work on the extension of the activistic pattern from religious to other social contexts.
26. The facts on the history of funeral directing in the United States have been taken primarily from Robert Habenstein and William Lamers, *The History of American Funeral Directing* (Milwaukee: Bulfin Printers, 1962). LeRoy Bowman's *The American Funeral* (Washington, D. C.: Public Affairs Press, 1959) has also been helpful. The interpretive framework is largely our own, although the works of Miller and Loubser have proven particularly helpful in a variety of respects.
27. For broader sociological interpretation of the status-conscious elements in American patterns of consumption, see Winston White, *Beyond Con-*

*formity* (New York: The Free Press, 1961) and Seymour Martin Lipset, *The First New Nation* (New York: Basic Books, Inc., 1963).

28. It is a community observance in our terminology because it is generally open to those members of the community who feel themselves affected by the loss of the deceased, who wish to pay their respects to him, or wish to show their support of his family. In the case of a prominent figure, a great many people may wish to attend or send some message. A wake is generally not privatized in the sense of being open only to the very close friends and kin of the deceased and of being an occasion which less closely related people could not appropriately attend.
29. Cf. Bowman, *op. cit.*; Jessica Mitford: *The American Way of Death* (New York: Simon and Schuster, Inc., 1963); Ruth Mulvey Harmer: *The High Cost of Dying* (New York: Collier Books, The Macmillan Company, 1963). The last two books, while very helpful descriptively, hardly meet sociological standards of analysis and objectivity.
30. It is our impression that inflation grounded in the latter conviction is more common among Catholics, who believe in a much less absolute and more easily affected line between the saved and the damned.
31. See Daniel Bell (ed.), *The Radical Right* (Garden City, N. Y.: Doubleday & Company, Inc., 1963), especially the chapters by Talcott Parsons and Seymour Martin Lipset.
32. The converse is probably also true, that certain inflated orientations toward matters in the public sphere correlate with deflated orientations toward funeral observances. However, the relevant problems have not been well enough studied to yield any very firm hypotheses in the present context.
33. See Mitford, *op. cit.*, and Bowman, *op. cit.* These works also give considerable information on the institutionalization of the funeral director's role.
34. There were also innumerable special observances; for example, the Saturday evening concert of the Boston Symphony Orchestra. The program had been completely changed to one of funeral music, culminating with the Beethoven "Eroica" Symphony with its magnificent funeral march; and there was no applause.
35. Sociologically, it is particularly interesting that convictions about "plots" have gained much wider currency in Europe than in the United States.
36. A more tangible sequel, on a smaller scale, was an assertion of religious and social solidarity in Boston. Exactly two months after Kennedy's death, on January 22, 1964, Cardinal Cushing officiated at a memorial Requiem High Mass in the Catholic cathedral in Boston. Its unusual feature was that the Mozart *Requiem* was played by the Boston Symphony Orchestra, which had never played in a religious service before and which has long been a citadel of Protestant upper-class Boston. The congregation was representative of all faiths, and clergymen of all faiths, including at least one rabbi, marched in the procession and sat in the sacristy.
37. Louis I. Dublin, *Suicide: A Sociological and Statistical Study*. (New York: The Ronald Press Company, 1963); Andrew Henry and James Short, "The Sociology of Suicide" in Edwin S. Shneidman and Norman L. Farberow (eds.), *Clues to Suicide* (New York: McGraw-Hill Book Company, 1957).

38. Emile Durkheim, *Suicide* (New York: The Free Press, 1951).
39. Thus, the statement attributed to Mao Tse-tung, rightly or wrongly, that a nuclear war would not be serious for China, because even if half its population were destroyed, there would still be over 300 million people left, has been considered very shocking in the West.
40. In some countries at least, Catholic suicides are now almost routinely certified by their parish priests as having been insane, so that they need not be denied the rites of the Church. Cf. Franco Ferracuti, "Suicide in a Catholic Country," in Shneidman and Farberow, *op. cit.*
41. This seems to be the central theme which various authors in Shneidman and Farberow, *op. cit.*, and in the other book they have edited, *The Cry for Help* (New York: McGraw-Hill Book Company, 1961), are attempting to articulate. It must be clear, however, that this refers to the type of decision—and to its context of meaning—which the suicide is presumed to have made. It is not a "factor" in the analytical explanation of how and why suicide occurs.
42. See the articles in the section on "Health and Illness" in Talcott Parsons, *Social Structure and Personality.*
43. There are some important limitations upon this. For example, a soldier, who holds the public obligation to defend his nation, has considerably less right to take his own life, because he would be in a sense deserting and might touch off morale problems, e.g., an epidemic of suicides.
44. This has probably been best analyzed by Herbert Hendin in his *Suicide and Scandinavia* (Garden City, N. Y.: Anchor Books, Doubleday & Company, 1965) and in "Suicide: Psychoanalytic Point of View" in *Cry for Help.*

## GENERAL NOTE

Some recent studies have demonstrated much "denial" of death to exist in at least one social situation, namely the relation of medical personnel to terminal patients. Two problems are involved, the inability of hospital staffs to aid dying patients in readying themselves and their personal relationships for debility and death, and a tendency for doctors to continue "treating" their patients, in ways that involve great discomfort and cost for both patients and their families, well after there can be any realistic hope for significant recovery of faculties. Since these problems focus sharply about a particular institutional situation, we do not feel that their existence detracts from our analysis of the general American orientation toward death. We suggest that the element of denial is evidence of a well localized, if severe, structural strain regarding the boundaries between the orientation toward controlling the adventitious aspects of death and the orientation toward the inevitable aspects of death, as they are specified to the norms of medical practice. The elements of strain and denial can probably be reduced only by enlarging the sphere within which control of the suffering of family and friends as well as of the patient, rather than the delaying of death, comes to be seen as ethically the predominant concern of medical treatment. A movement in this direction seems already underway, partly under the impetus of recent sociological findings about the effects of denial upon patients. Since this movement seems to us to be strongly grounded in the general modern orientations toward death, we predict that it will eventually supplant the elements of denial that many claim are the more basic phenomena. The studies mentioned above are: B. G. Glaser and A. L. Strauss, *Awareness of Dying* (Chicago, Aldine, 1965); D. Sudnow, *Passing On; The Social Organization of Dying* (Englewood Cliffs, Prentice-Hall, 1967); and John Hinton, *Dying* (Baltimore, Penguin, 1967), which is a British study.

# 8. Practical Sociological Reasoning: Some Features in the Work of the Los Angeles Suicide Prevention Center

Harold Garfinkel

The purpose of this chapter is to treat "certification practices" of the Los Angeles Suicide Prevention Center (SPC) as an occasion for reflections about practical actions and practical sociological reasoning in order to formulate several of their features as problematic sociological phenomena. Insofar as these phenomena exhibit characteristic properties of their own, they constitute a legitimate area of inquiry in themselves. The certification practices of the Suicide Prevention Center provide an experience with which these phenomena may be examined.

The plan of the chapter is as follows: Practical action and sociological reasoning are characterized in the first part in sections devoted to features of "common-sense situations of choice" learned about elsewhere but which are repeated in the circumstances and practices of the SPC; to singular features of SPC accounting practices; and to some structural equivocalities in SPC accounts. These remarks are then used as a context for the second part in which three problematic features of practical sociological reasoning are formulated.

## Practical Sociological Reasoning

### *Doing Accounts in "Common-Sense Situations of Choice"*

The SPC and the Los Angeles Medical Examiner-Coroner's office joined forces in 1957 to furnish coroner's death certificates the warrant of scientific authority "within the limits of practical certainties imposed by the state of the art." Selected cases of "sudden, unnatural death" that were equivocal between suicide and other modes of death were referred by the Medical Examiner-Coroner to the SPC with the request that an inquiry, called a "psychological autopsy," be made.[1] Subsequently, in joint consultation, the mode of death is decided and a proper title for the death is entered on the death certificate.

The practices and concerns of SPC staff to accomplish their inquiries in common-sense situations of choice repeated the features of practical inquiries that were encountered in other situations: studies of jury deliberations in negligence cases; clinic staff selections of patients for out-patient psychiatric treatment; graduate sociology students' coding of the contents of clinic folders into a coding sheet by following detailed coding instructions; and countless professional procedures in anthropological, linguistic, social psychiatric, and sociological inquiry.[2] The following features in the work at SPC were recognized by staff with frank acknowledgement as prevailing conditions of their work and as matters to consider when assessing the efficacy, efficiency, or intelligibility of their work and SPC testimony added to that of jurors, survey researchers, and the rest: (1) There was an abiding concern on the part of all parties for the temporal concerting of activities; (2) there was a concern for the practical question *par excellence*: "What to do next?"; (3) there was a concern on the inquirer's part to give evidence of his grasp of "what anyone knows" about how the settings in which he had to accomplish his inquiries work and a concern to do so for actual occasions when decisions were to be made by his exhibitable conduct in choosing; (4) matters that at the level of talk might be spoken of as "production programs," "laws of conduct," "rules of rational decision-making," "causes," "conditions," "hypothesis testing," "models," and "rules of inductive and deductive inference" in the actual situation were taken for granted to consist of recipes, proverbs, slogans, and partially formulated plans of action; (5) inquirers were required to know and be skilled in dealing with situations "of the sort" for which "rules of rational decision-making" and the rest were intended so that they would "see" or, by what they did, insure the objective, effective, consistent, complete, and empirically adequate; i.e., the rational character of recipes, prophecies, proverbs, and partial descriptions in actual use of the rules; (6) for the practical decider, the actual occasion as a phenomenon in its own right exercised overwhelming priority and decision rules or theories of decision-making were without exception subordinated in order to assess the rational features of the occasion rather than those of the rules; and finally, and perhaps most characteristically, (7) all of the foregoing features, together with the inquirer's system of alternatives, his decision methods, his information, his choices, and the rationality of his accounts and actions were constituent parts of the same practical circumstances in which inquirers did the work of inquiry—a feature that inquirers, if they are to claim and recognize the practicality of their efforts, know of, require, count on, take for granted, use, and *gloss*.

## *SPC Accounting Practices*

The work by SPC members of conducting their inquiries was part and parcel of the day's work. Recognized by staff members as constituent features of the day's work, their inquiries were thereby intimately connected with the terms of their employment, various internal and external chains of reportage, supervision, and review, and similar organizationally supplied "priorities of relevances" for assessments of what "realistically," "practically," or "reasonably" needed to be done and could be done, and how quickly, with what resources, seeing whom, talking about what, for how long, and so on. Such considerations furnished the "we did what we could, and for all reasonable interests here is what we came out with" its features of organizationally appropriate sense, fact, impersonality, anonymity of authorship, purpose, reproductibility—i.e., of a *properly* rational account of the inquiry.

Members were required in their occupational capacities to formulate accounts of how a death for all practical purposes *really* happened. "Really" made unavoidable reference to daily, ordinary, occupational workings. Members alone were allowed to invoke such workings as appropriate grounds for recommending the reasonable character of the result *without necessity of furnishing specifics*. On occasions of challenge, ordinary occupational workings would be cited explicitly, in "relevant part." Otherwise such features were disengaged from the product. In their place an account of how the inquiry was done made the how-it-was-actually-done out as appropriate to usual demands, usual attainments, usual practices, *and* to usual talk by SPC personnel in speaking as *bona fide* professional practitioners about usual demands, usual attainments, and usual practices.

One of several titles (relating to *mode* of death) had to be assigned to each case, being legally possible combinations of four elementary possibilities—natural death, accident, suicide, and homicide.[3] *All* titles are so administered in order to withstand the varieties of equivocation, ambiguity, and improvisation that arise in every actual occasion of their use; but these titles are so administered that they *invite* that ambiguity, equivocality, and improvisation. It is part of the work not *only* that equivocality is a problem—is *perhaps* a problem—but also that practitioners are directed to those circumstances in order to *invite* ambiguity, equivocality, improvisation, temporizing, and the rest. It is not that the investigator, having a list of titles, performs an inquiry that proceeds stepwise to establish grounds for electing among them. The formula is not "here is what we did and among the titles as goals of our research *this* title finally interprets in the best fashion what we found out." Instead titles are continually postdicted and foretold. An inquiry is apt to be guided heavily by the inquirer's imagined settings in which the title will have been "used" by one or another interested party, including the deceased; the inquiries do this in order to decide from whatever "datum" might have been searched out that which can be used to mask the situation if that needs to be done—or they equivocate, gloss, lead, or exemplify, and so on. The prevailing feature of the inquiry is that nothing about it remains assured except the organized occasions of its uses. Thus a routine inquiry is one that the investigator uses particular goblins to accomplish, and he depends upon particular goblins to recognize and to recommend the practical adequacy of his work. Viewed with respect to practices for making it happen, a routine inquiry is not one that is accomplished by rules. It seems much more to consist of an inquiry which is openly recognized to have fallen short; but its adequacy is acknowledged in the ways it falls short, and no one offers or calls particularly for explanations of its shortcomings.

What members are *doing* in their inquiries is always somebody else's business, in the sense that particular, organizationally located, and locatable persons acquire an interest as a result of an SPC member's account of whatever it is that might have been reported to have "really happened." Such considerations contribute heavily to the perceived feature of investigations, namely, that they are directed in their course by an account for which the claim will have been advanced that it is correct for all practical purposes. Thus one of the investigator's tasks is to render an account of how a particular person died in society that is a reasonable one for all practical purposes.

"What really happened," over the course of arriving at it as well as after the "what really happened" has been inserted into the file and the title has been decided, may be chronically reviewed as well as chronically foretold in light of what might have been done or what will have been done with the decisions. On the way to making a decision, what might come from it is reviewed and foretold in light of its anticipated consequences. *After* a recommendation has been made and the coroner has signed the death certificate the result can still be "revised," as they say. It can thus become a decision that needs to be reviewed "once more."

Inquirers wanted very much to be able to give the assurance that they could arrive at the end with an account of how the person died that would permit the coroner and his staff to withstand claims by arguing that the account was incomplete or that the death happened differently from—or in contrast to or in contradiction of—what members to the arrangement "claimed." Reference here is neither only nor entirely to complaints of the survivors. Such issues are dealt with as a succession of episodes, most of which are settled fairly quickly. Greater contingencies consist of enduring processes that result from the fact that the coroner's office is a political office. Its activities produce continuing records of its activities; and records are subject to review as products of the scientific work of the coroner, his staff, and his consultants. Office activities are techniques for accomplishing reports that are scientific for all practical purposes, and they involve "writing" as a warranting procedure, for the report by reason of being written proceeds into a file. That the investigator "does" a report is thereby made a matter for public record, for the use of some other only partially identifiable persons. Their interest in why or how or what the inquirer did would have in some relevant part to do with his skill and entitlement as a professional. But investigators also know that other interests will inform the "review," for the inquirer's work will be inspected to see its scientific-adequacy-for-all-practical-purposes as professionals' socially managed claims. Not only for investigators but for all sides there is the relevance of "what was really found out for all practical purposes," which consists unavoidably of how much can one find out, how much can one reveal, how much can one mask, how much can one conceal, and how much can one hold as none of the business of some important persons, *investigators* included. All investigators acquire an interest by reason of the fact that as a matter of occupational duty they are making written reports of how for all practical purposes a person really died and really died *in* the society.

Decisions have an unavoidable consequentiality. By this is meant that investigators need to say *in so many words* what really happened. The important words are the titles that are assigned to a text to recover that text as the title's "explication." But what an assigned title consists of as an explicated title is at any particular time for no one to say with any finality, even when it is proposed "in so many words." In fact, *that* it is proposed in so many words, *that*, for example, a written text was inserted into the file of the case, furnishes grounds that one can invoke in order to make something of the "so many words" that will have been used as an account of the death. Viewed with respect to patterns of use, titles and their accompanying texts have an open set of consequences. Upon any use of texts it remains to be seen what can be done with them, what they will come to, what remains to be done "for the time being" pending the ways in which the environment of that decision may organize itself to "reopen the case," "issue a complaint" or "find an issue," and so on. Such ways for SPC'ers are, as patterns, certain; but as particular processes for making them happen, they are in every actual occasion indefinite.

SPC inquiries begin with a death that the coroner finds equivocal as to *mode* of death. They use the death as a precedent by means of which various ways of living in society that could have terminated with the death are searched for and read "in the remains"—in the scraps of this and that, such as the body and its trappings, medicine bottles, notes, bits and pieces of clothing, memorabilia: anything that can be photographed, collected, and packaged. Other "remains" are collected too: rumors, passing remarks, and stories—material in the "repertoire" of whomever might be consulted through the common work of conversations. These "whatsoever" bits and pieces that a story or a rule or a proverb might make intelligible are used to formulate a recognizably coherent, standard, typical, cogent, uniform, planful, i.e., a professionally defensible, and thereby for members, *recognizably* rational account of how the society worked to produce these remains. This point will be clearer if the reader consults a standard textbook in forensic pathology. In it he will find the inevitable photograph of the victim with a slashed throat. Were the coroner to use that "sight" to suggest the equivocality of the mode of death he might say something such as this: "In the case where a body looks like the one in that picture, you are looking at a suicidal death because the wound shows the 'hesitation cuts' that accompany the great wound. One can imagine these cuts are the remains of a procedure whereby the victim first made several preliminary trials of a hesitating sort and then performed the lethal slash. Other courses of action are imaginable, too, and so cuts that look like hesitation cuts can be produced by other mechanisms. One needs to start with the actual display and imagine how different courses of action could have been organized such that *that* picture would be compatible with it. One might think of the photographed display as a phase-of-the-action. In any actual display is there a course of action with which that phase is uniquely compatible? *That* is the coroner's question."

The coroner (and SPC'ers) ask this with respect to each *particular case*, and thereby the work of achieving practical decidability seems almost unavoidably to assume a prevailing and important characteristic. SPC'ers must accomplish that decidability by considering the "this's": They have to start with *this* much; *this* sight; *this* note; *this* collection of whatever is at hand. And *whatever* is there is good enough in the sense that whatever is there not only *will* do but *does*. One makes whatever is there do. By this is not meant that an SPC investigator is too easily content or that he does not look for more when he should. What is meant rather is that the "whatever" it is that he has to deal with is what will be used to find out, to make decidable the way that society operated to produce *that* picture, to have come to *that* scene as its end result. In this way the remains on the slab serve not only as a precedent but as a goal of SPC inquiries. *Whatsoever* SPC members are faced with must serve as the precedent by means of which they read the remains in order to see how the society could have operated to have produced what it is that they have "in the end," "in the final analysis," and "in *any* case." What the inquiry can come to is what the death came to.

### *Structural Equivocalities of Practical Accounts*

The structurally equivocal features of the methods and results of both lay and professional sociologists of making practical activities observable were epitomized by Helmer and Rescher,[4] who point out that when members' accounts of everyday activities are used as prescriptions for locating, identifying, analyzing, classifying, making recognizable, finding one's way around in comparable occasions, the prescriptions are lawlike, spatiotemporally restricted, and "loose." By loose is meant that though they are intended as conditional in their logical form, "the nature of the conditions is such that they can often not be spelled out completely or fully." The authors cite as an example a statement about sailing-fleet tactics in the eighteenth century. They point out that the statement carries reference to the state of naval ordnance as a test condition.

> In elaborating conditions (under which such a statement would hold) the historian delineates what is typical of the place and period. The full implications of such reference may be vast and inexhaustible; for instance . . . ordnance soon ramifies *via* metal working technology into metallurgy, mining, etc. Thus, the conditions which are operative in the formulation of an historical law may only be indicated in a general way, and are not necessarily, indeed, in most cases cannot be expected to be exhaustively articulated. This characteristic of such laws is here designated as *looseness*. . . .
>
> A consequence of the looseness of historical laws is that they are

not universal, but merely quasi-general in that they admit of exceptions. Since the conditions delimiting the area of application of the law are often not exhaustively articulated, a supposed violation of the law may be explicable by showing that a legitimate, but as yet unformulated, precondition of the law's applicability is not fulfilled in the case under consideration.

Consider that this holds in every *particular* case and not from logical necessity, i.e., not by reason of the meaning of "quasi-law" but because of the investigators' actual, particular practices. According to these practices one uses such a formulation and counts it a correct formulation despite the fact that the conditions under which one might specify its appropriate or proper or correct use on *that* particular occasion would have been relaxed, yet the result and the usage considered adequate. Accordingly, Helmer and Rescher point out:

> The laws may be taken to contain a tacit caveat of the "usually" or "other things being equal" type. An historical law is thus not strictly universal in that it must be taken as applicable to all cases falling within the scope of its explicitly formulated or formulable conditions; rather, it may be thought to formulate relationships which obtain generally, or better, which obtain "as a rule."
>
> Such a "law" we will term *quasi-law*. In order for the law to be valid it is not necessary that no apparent exceptions occur, it is only necessary that, if an apparent exception should occur, an adequate explanation be forthcoming, an explanation demonstrating the exceptional characteristic of the case in hand by establishing the violation of an appropriate, if hitherto unformulated, condition of the law's applicability.

These and other features can be cited for the cogency with which they describe SPC members' certification practices. Thus: (1) Whenever a member is required to demonstrate that an account analyzes an actual situation he invariably makes use of the practices of "et cetera," "unless," and "let it pass" to demonstrate the rationality of his achievement. (2) The definite and sensible character of the matter that is being reported is settled by an agreement that reporter and auditor make with each other to furnish one another with whatever unstated understandings are required. Much of what is actually reported is therefore not mentioned. (3) During the time required for their delivery, accounts are apt to require that auditors be willing to wait for what will be said in order that the present significance of what has been said will have become clear. (4) Like conversations, reputations, and careers, the particulars of accounts are built up step-by-step over the actual uses of and references to them. (5) An account's materials are apt to depend heavily for sense upon their serial placement, upon their relevance to the auditor's projects, or upon the developing course of the organizational occasions of their use.

In short, the recognizable sense, fear, methodic character, and impersonality of SPC accounts are not independent of the socially organized occasions of their use. Their rational features *consist* of what members do with and what they "make of" the accounts in the socially organized actual occasions of their use. SPC accounts are reflexively and essentially tied for their sense to the socially organized occasions of their use, for they are *features* of the socially organized occasions of their use.

## Some Problems Dealing with the Practical Accomplishment of Rational Action

### *Objective and Indexical Expressions*

Properties that are exhibited by accounts (by reason of their being features of the socially organized occasions of their use) are available from studies by logicians as the properties of indexical expressions and indexical sentences. Husserl spoke of expressions whose sense cannot be decided by an auditor without his necessarily knowing or assuming something about the biography and the purposes of the user of the expression, the circumstances of the utterance, the previous course of the conversation, or the particular relationship of actual or potential interaction that exists between the expressor and the auditor.[5] Russell observed that descriptions involving them apply on each occasion of use to only one thing, but to different things on different occasions.[6] Such expressions, wrote Goodman, are used to make unequivocal statements that nevertheless seem to change in truth value.[7] Each of their utterances, "tokens," constitutes a word and refers to a certain person, time, or place but names something not named by some replica of the word. Their denotation is relative to the speaker. Their use depends upon the relation of the user to the object with which the word is concerned. Time for a temporal indexical expression is relevant to what it names. Similarly, just what region a spatial indexical expression names depends upon the location of its utterance. Indexical expressions and statements containing them are not freely repeatable; in a given discourse, not all their replicas therein are also translations of them. The list can be extended indefinitely.

Virtually unanimous agreement exists among students of practical sociological reasoning, both laymen and professionals, about the properties of indexical expressions and indexical actions. Impressive agreement exists as well that (1) although indexical expressions "are of enormous utility" they are "awkward for formal discourse"; (2) a distinction between objective expressions and indexical expressions is not only procedurally proper but unavoidable for whosoever would do science; (3) without the distinction between objective and indexical expressions, and without the preferred use of objective expressions, the victories of generalizing, rigorous, scientific inquiries—logic, mathematics, some of the physical sciences—would fail, and the inexact sciences would have to abandon their hopes; (4) terms and sentences can be distinguished as one or the other in accordance with an assessment procedure that makes decidable their character as indexical or objective expressions; and (5) in any particular case only practical difficulties prevent the substitution by an objective expression of an indexical expression.

In philosophers' studies the distinction and substitutability are motivated by a search for and a concern with theories of consistency proofs and computability of terms and sentences. Areas in the social sciences where the promised distinction and substitutability occurs are countless. These are supported by and themselves support immense resources which are directed toward developing methods for the strong analysis of practical actions. Promised applications and benefits are immense.

Nevertheless, wherever studies of practical actions are involved the promised distinction and substitutability of objective expressions for indexical expressions remain programmatic in every particular case and on every actual occasion in which the distinction or substitutability must be demonstrated. In every actual case without exception conditions will be cited that a competent investigator will be required to recognize such that in *that* particular case the terms of the demonstration can be relaxed and the demonstration nevertheless be counted an adequate one.

For "long" texts, or "long" courses of action, for events where members' actions are features of the events that their actions are accomplishing, or wherever tokens are not used or are not suitable as proxies for indexical expressions, the programs' claimed demonstrations are satisfied as matters of practical social management. The distinction and substitutability are always accomplished *only* for all practical purposes, and thereby the first problematic phenomenon is recommended to consist of the reflexivity of the practices and attainments of science in and of the organized activities of everyday life, which is an essential reflexivity.

### *The Essential Reflexivity of Accounts*

SPC members' practical theorizing is sober, serious business. Their concerns are for what is decidable "for practical purposes," "in light of this situation," "given the nature of the actual circumstances," and the like. SPC members are acutely aware that the practices that make up their work circumstances are the same measures whereby a suicide rate is produced. Further SPC practices are treated by its personnel as somewhat approximating scientifically adequate procedures. Accounts with the use of which each problematic death is made out under the auspices of "the case" are treated as being some approximation of "what really happened." Suicide rates are treated as being in some approximation to "real suicide rates."

SPC members cite the relevance of practical considerations to their work of sociological theorizing as defects of their work. Such defects are also invoked as challenges or sources of the virtues in their work. Their brag consists of reciting the frustrations that nature and man impose on the tasks of doing science while certifying cause and mode of death. In its terms *how* they are doing *what* they are actually doing is glossed: "We are, after all, doing the best we can, which is better than most."

It is the case for the members of the SPC just as it is for jurors and for professional sociological researchers that practical circumstances and practical actions refer to many organizationally important and serious matters: to resources, aims, excuses, opportunities, tasks, and of course, to grounds for arguing or foretelling the adequacy of procedures and the findings they yield. One matter is excluded from the SPC members' interests: practical actions and practical circumstances are not in themselves *a* topic, let alone a sole topic, of their inquiries; nor are their inquiries addressed to the tasks of sociological theorizing undertaken to formulate what these tasks consist of as practical actions. In no case is the investigation of practical actions undertaken in order that SPC personnel might be able to recognize and describe what they are doing in the first place. Least of all are practical actions investigated in order to explain to practitioners their own talk about what they are doing. Indeed, SPC personnel find it altogether incongruous to consider seriously that they be engaged in the work of certifying mode of death in such a way that they would concert their efforts with a person seeking to commit suicide so as to assure the unequivocal recognition of "what really happened."

To say they are "not interested" in the study of practical actions is not to complain, nor to point to an opportunity they missed, nor is it a disclosure of error, nor is it an ironic comment. Neither is it the case that because SPC members are "not interested" that they are "precluded" from sociological theorizing. Nor do their inquiries preclude the use of the rule of doubt, nor are they precluded from making the organized activities of everyday life scientifically problematical, nor does the comment bear on the difference between "basic" and "applied" interests in research and theorizing.

What does it mean then to say that they are "not interested" in studying practical actions and practical sociological reasoning? And what is the import of such a statement?

There is an aspect of accounts of singular and prevailing relevance in that it restricts the other features to their specific character as recognizable properties of practical sociological inquiries. It consists in this: With respect to the problematic character of practical actions and the practical adequacy of their inquiries members take for granted that a member must at the outset "know" the settings in which he is to operate if his practices are to serve as measures to bring particular, located features of these settings to recognizable account. They treat as the most passing matter of fact that members' accounts of every sort in all their logical modes, with all of their uses and for every method for their assembly, are constituent features of the settings that they make observable. SPC members know, require, count on, and make use of this reflexivity to produce, accomplish, recognize, or demonstrate the scientific adequacy for all practical purposes of their procedures and findings.

Not only do SPC members, like jurors and others, take that reflexivity for granted, but they recognize, demonstrate, and make observable for each other the rational character of their actual—and this means their occasional—practices while respecting that *reflexivity* as an unalterable and unavoidable condition of their inquiries.

When I propose that SPC members have no interest in studying practical actions I do not mean that members have none, little, or a lot of it. That they are not interested has to do with reasonable practices, with plausible arguments, with reasonable findings—with "accountable for all practical purposes" as a discoverable matter, exclusively, only, and entirely. To be interested would consist of undertaking to make the reflexive character of practical activities observable—to examine the artful practices of rational inquiry as organizational phenomenon without thought for correctives or irony. SPC members, and members wherever they engage in practical inquiries, though they would like to, *can* have none of it.

### *The Analyzability of Actions in Context as a Practical Accomplishment*

In indefinitely many ways SPC inquiries are constituent features of the settings they analyze. In the same ways, their inquiries are made recognizable to members as scientifically adequate for all practical purposes. Thus, that deaths are made accountable for all practical purposes are practical organizational accomplishments. Organizationally, the SPC consists of practical procedures for accomplishing the rational accountability of suicidal deaths as recognizable features of the settings in which that accountability occurs.

In the actual occasions of interaction such an accomplishment is for members omnipresent, unproblematic, and commonplace. For members doing sociology to make this kind of accomplishment a topic of practical sociological inquiry seems unavoidably to require that they treat the rational properties of practical activities as "anthropologically strange." By this I mean to call attention to reflexive practices such as the following: when by his accounting practices the member makes familiar, commonplace activities of everyday life recognizable *as* familiar, commonplace activities; when on each occasion that an account of common activities is used, that they be recognized for "another first time"; when the members treat the processes and attainments of "imagination" as continuous with the *other* observable features of the settings in which they occur; and when proceeding in such a way that at the same time that the member "in the midst" of witnessed actual settings recognizes that witnessed settings have an accomplished sense, an accomplished facticity, an accomplished objectivity, an accomplished familiarity, and an accomplished accountability the organizational hows of these accomplishments are unproblematic, are known vaguely, and are known only when done skillfully, reliably, uniformly, with enormous standardization, and as an unaccountable matter.

The accomplishment consists of doing, recognizing, and using ethnographies. In unknown ways that accomplishment is a commonplace phenomenon for members. And in the unknown ways that the accomplishment is commonplace it is an awesome phenomenon, for in its unknown ways it consists of (1) members' uses of concerted everyday activities as methods with which to recognize and demonstrate the isolable, typical, uniform, potential repetition, connected appearances, consistency, equivalence, substitutability, directionality, anonymously describable, planful—in short, the rational properties of indexical expressions and indexical actions, and

(2) the analyzability of actions in context, given not only that no concept of context in general exists, but that every use of "context" without exception is itself essentially indexical.

The recognizedly rational properties of their common sense inquiries—their recognizedly consistent, methodic, uniform, or planful character—are *somehow* attainments of SPC members' concerted activities. The rational properties of their practical inquiries *somehow* consist in the concerted work of making evident from fragments, from proverbs, from passing remarks, from rumors, from partial descriptions, from "codified" but essentially vague catalogues of experience, and the like, how a person died in society, and of doing so for deaths from enormously diversified settings of everyday activities. *Somehow* is the problematic crux of the matter.

## Programmatic Considerations

The earmark of practical sociological reasoning wherever it occurs is that it seeks to remedy the indexical properties of members' talk and conduct in order to demonstrate the observability of organized actions. Endless methodological studies are directed to the tasks of providing a remedy for indexical expressions, for their properties are pervasive and obstinate nuisances to members in their abiding attempts, with rigorous use of ideals, to recover common conduct and common talk with full structural particulars.

The properties of indexical expressions and indexical actions are ordered properties. These consist of organizationally demonstrable sense, facticity, methodic use, and agreement among "cultural colleagues." Their ordered properties consist of organizationally demonstrable rational properties of indexical expressions and indexical actions. Those ordered properties are ongoing achievements of the concerted commonplace activities of investigators. The demonstrable rationality of indexical expressions and indexical actions retains over the course of its managed production by members the character of ordinary, familiar, routinized, practical circumstances. As process and attainment, the produced rationality of indexical expressions consists of practical tasks subject to every exigency of organizationally situated conduct.

For the study of the foregoing problems, the following interpretive policies are recommended:

1. Let the SPC, like any setting, be viewed as self-organizing with

respect to the intelligible character of its own particular, actual, perspectively located appearances as appearances of a social order. Like any setting, the SPC organizes its activities to make its properties as an organized environment of practical activities detectable, countable, recordable, reportable, analyzable—in short, accountable. Its organized arrangements consist of various methods for accomplishing the accountability of its organizational ways as a concerted undertaking. Every claim by SPC practitioners of effectiveness, clarity, consistency, planfulness, or efficiency, and every consideration for adequate evidence, demonstration, description, or relevance obtains its character as a phenomenon from the corporate pursuit of this undertaking and from the ways in which its various organizational environments by reason of their characteristics as organizations of activities "sustain," "facilitate," "resist," etc., these methods for making their affairs accountable matters for all practical purposes.

In exactly and only the ways that SPC is said by its members to be organized it consists of members' methods for making evident to each other their settings' ways as clear, coherent, planful, consistent, chosen, knowable, uniform, reproducible connections—i.e., as rational connections. In exactly the way that SPC personnel are members to organized affairs, they are engaged in serious and practical work of detecting, demonstrating, and persuading through displays on the ordinary, actual occasions of their interactions the appearances of consistent, coherent, clear, chosen, planful arrangements. In exactly and only the ways in which the SPC is said by its members to be organized its activities consist of methods whereby its members are provided with accounts of the setting as countable, storyable, proverbial, comparable, picturable, representable—i.e., accountable events.

2. Of course, not only the SPC but any actual occasion of activity whatsoever can be examined for the feature that "choice" among alternatives of sense, of facticity, of methodic practice, of cause, of communal agreement among "cultural colleagues," and of practical actions is a project of members' actions. When such a possibility is used as a prescription for search and interpretation it turns up inquiries of every imaginable kind, from coroner's inquests to experimental astrophysics, all of them alike in claiming our interest in them as socially organized, artful practices. Every way of doing inquiry without exception acquires its eligibility for our interest from the various ways that the social structures of everyday activities furnish contexts, objects, resources, justifications, and topics. The work of doing water witching, mathematics, chemistry, and sociology, as well as the psychological autopsy, whether done by lay persons or professionals, would be addressed according to the policy that every

feature of sense, of fact, and of method for every particular case of inquiry is the managed accomplishment of organized settings of practical actions; further, that particular determinations in members' practices of consistency, planfulness, relevance, or reproducibility of their practices and results are acquired and assured only through particular, located organizations of artful practices. Every kind of inquiry without exception would consist of organized artful practices whereby the rational properties of indexical expressions—of proverbs, advice, partial description, elliptical expressions, passing remarks, fables, tales, and the rest are demonstrated. The demonstrable rationality of indexical expressions and indexical actions is an ongoing achievement of the organized activities of everyday life. And here is the heart of the conjectural matter. The managed production of this phenomenon in every aspect, from every perspective, and in every stage must retain the character for members of serious, practical tasks, subject to every exigency of organizationally situated conduct.

## REFERENCES

1. The following references contain reports on the psychological autopsy procedure developed at the Los Angeles Suicide Prevention Center: (1) Theodore J. Curphey, "The Forensic Pathologist and the Multidisciplinary Approach to Death," a chapter in this volume; (2) Theodore J. Curphey, "The Role of the Social Scientist in the Medicolegal Certification of Death from Suicide," in Norman L. Farberow and Edwin S. Shneidman (eds.), *The Cry for Help* (New York: McGraw-Hill Book Company, 1961); (3) Edwin S. Shneidman and Norman L. Farberow, "Sample Investigations of Equivocal Suicidal Deaths," in *The Cry for Help*; (4) Robert E. Litman, Theodore J. Curphey, Edwin S. Shneidman, Norman L. Farberow, and Norman D. Tabachnick, "Investigations of Equivocal Suicides," *Journal of the American Medical Association,* 184; 924–929, 1963; and (5) Edwin S. Shneidman, "Orientations Toward Death: A Vital Aspect of the Study of Lives," in Robert W. White (ed.), *The Study of Lives* (New York: Atherton Press, 1963), reprinted in the *International Journal of Psychiatry,* **2**;167–200, 1966.
2. Reported in the author's *Studies in Ethnomethodology* (Englewood Cliffs, N. J.: Prentice-Hall, Inc., 1967).
3. The possible combinations include the following: natural, accident, suicide, homicide, possible accident, possible suicide, possible natural, accident-suicide undetermined, natural-suicide undetermined, natural-accident undetermined, and natural-accident-suicide undetermined.
4. Olaf Helmer and Nicholas Rescher, *On the Epistemology of the Inexact*

*Sciences,* P–1513 (Santa Monica, Calif.: RAND Corporation, Oct. 13, 1958), pp. 8–14.

5. Marvin Farber, *The Foundation of Phenomenology* (Cambridge, Mass.: Harvard University Press, 1943), pp. 237–238.
6. Bertrand Russell, *Inquiry into Meaning and Truth* (New York: W. W. Norton & Company, Inc., 1940), pp. 134–143.
7. Nelson Goodman, *The Structure of Appearance* (Cambridge, Mass.: Harvard University Press, 1951), pp. 287–298.

# 9. Suicide and Loss in Social Interaction

Warren Breed

The many ways to study sources of suicide can be categorized along four dimensions:

1. The sociocultural organization of the society and the extent of "integration" it displays.

2. The groups and strata within the society and how they are interrelated in cooperation, competition, or conflict, and the manner in which individuals are attached to these groups and strata.

3. The kinds of interpersonal social relationships that members of the society experience.

4. The intrapsychic structure and functioning of the individual person; how he developed from childhood and how he adapts to stresses coming from the first three dimensions.

Many psychologists operate mainly with dimension 4, for this indeed is their area of specialization. Durkheim,[1] on the other hand, tried to eschew this level completely (although he found himself there from time to time and beat a swift retreat). His favorite was dimension 1, from which eminence he argued that his chief interest was in suicide rates as indices of greater or lesser societal integration. Demographers can be found working in dimension 2, with an actuarial focus on the comparative suicide rates of old and young, male and female, urban and rural dwellers, and the social classes of which they form a part, the several zones of the city, the races and ethnic groups, and so on.

The study of all four dimensions is required for our growing understanding of the phenomenon of suicide. If dimension 1 is "sociological" and dimension 4 is "psychological" and those in between are "social psychological," so be it. Single attacks and joint attacks, quantitative and qualitative attacks from all quarters, all can make their contributions.

In this essay I will claim special interest in dimension 3, the interpersonal level. I believe that this has been the least studied of the four. Why this is so is difficult to understand, for it would seem evident that interpersonal social relationships are "obviously" of paramount significance to the human being, but all of this obviousness may be spurious if it is so little studied and discussed.

This state of affairs is due, I believe, to the plain fact that most psychologists are trained to define dimension 4 as their domain, whereas sociologists have been accustomed to work at the first two levels and simply have not gotten around to analyzing suicide—among other things—at the interpersonal level of daily life. Both psychologists and sociologists have done considerable empirical and theoretical work in dimension 3 with respect to many behaviors other than suicide; there is no reason to delay the attempt to apply its relevance to the phenomena of suicide.

## Loss in Suicide

One can begin by noting that several writers on suicide have used the same notion: the notion of "loss." To be specific, we can turn to Part II of *The Cry For Help*.[2] Here nine men review their own theories and the theories of others (Freud, Adler, Horney, etc.), and refer to a wide range of other works on suicide as well. Seen most broadly, the idea of loss is present in all nine essays, although the exact word is not found in all. Some speak of "deprivation," "rejection," "frustration," "depression," and so on, so that I feel something very general, if not universal, is present. To quote examples:

". . . the identification of the ego with the incorporated love object takes place . . . and this object becomes lost, either in reality or in fantasy." (Futterman on the Freudian viewpoint)[3]

"The loss may be of a person, money or position." (Hendin on the psychoanalytic point of view)[4]

"In Mary he lost the only woman with whom he truly felt superior as a man . . ." (Ansbacher on the Adlerian point of view)[5]

"Rado has critically improved Freud's theory . . . the depressive episode is initiated by a real or imagined loss, which is related to earlier real injury or loss." (Green on the Sullivanian point of view)[6]

"What he had lost was something that never could be restored . . . He had lost a deep sense of validity for the way he had once ordered his world." (Kelly)[7]

"The earlier (1918) Freudian formulation of hatred expressed toward a rejecting or abandoning (lost) introverted love object falls in this category." (Farberow in the Summary)[8]

This recital is intended only to show that several authorities on the intrapsychic life of suicidal persons have cumulated—whether by consideration of earlier theory or by independent observation—enough interest in the area of loss to constitute a point of departure for the analysis of sources of suicide. Even Durkheim considered the individual person from time to time and in several instances used a generalized notion of loss: the soldier who kills himself at the slightest disappointment; the artist whose work goes unappreciated; the businessman gone bankrupt.

The basic question can be put, "What is lost?" I will start from this point, using interview materials concerning some 250 suicides in New Orleans over the last decade.[9] Relatives, friends, neighbors, employers, coworkers, and physicians were asked numerous questions about the suicide person, especially about the latter years of his life. Thus relatively rich materials are available with which to study loss in suicide.

Taking Hendin's statement as our tentative text ("The loss may be of a person, money, or position"), it is clear that these three losses are certainly apparent in cases of suicide. This is a point of departure: Man loses something and commits suicide. But once expressed so crudely, one feels that he is begging the question. So we reformulate the question: "How does this or that loss effect what kind of person so that he will commit suicide?"

In exploring this question one can say, in brief, that the loss can take many forms but that three forms predominate. These are job ("position"—mostly among men); person (usually the mate, and most frequently among women); and something more general that I will call "mutuality." One or more of these kinds of losses occurs, but the process is not over. Many persons—perhaps all of us—encounter such losses. Two further steps seem to be taken by the person who eventually kills himself. First, he must become aware of the loss and feel it, in the sense of being embarrassed or humiliated by it. This involves the awareness that other people notice the loss (dimension 3) and the awareness (whether accurate or not) that other people recognize the failure. Second, the individual's particular psychic structure must impel him to suicide rather than to some less final course of adaptation. This last is a process within dimension 4, the province of the psychoanalyst or psychologist.

We may now proceed to the interview materials concerning loss.

## *Loss of a Position*

In an earlier paper on suicide among white New Orleans males aged twenty to sixty, I reported the high frequency of unemployment and downward vertical mobility.[10] Of 103 men, only 52 were working full time just before they committed suicide. Measures of intergenerational and work-life mobility showed a great deal of downward "skidding," especially among the lower-class suicides. For the white-collar men, the difficulty was not in high frequencies of downward mobility per se, but more than half had experienced a decrease in income during the last two years of their lives. Taking all these forms of loss, about 75 percent of the men had suffered some form of drop in "position."

Some of the men, it is true, had kept their class position or moved up in the prestige hierarchy, but even among these, there were cases in which the man had missed an expected promotion, had been assigned to a smaller office, or had retired before age sixty while still able to work. The great majority of these men, then, probably felt acute dissatisfaction with their own work performance and may easily have guessed that other persons defined them as failures in their main life role.

Illustrations in individual cases are plentiful; a few examples will suffice: a Navy officer, ambitious and devoted to duty, is discharged from the service because of an accident to his ship; a policeman, fired for accepting a bribe, takes a job as guard with lower pay and prestige; a business consultant fails to secure more than a few clients; a real estate salesman, who "used to get a kick out of a sale," gradually loses interest in work—"he seemed to give up"; a barber's shop is closed down by the sanitary inspector; a man who became construction superintendent during the war is unable to keep such prestigious work in peacetime and feels it keenly; a lawyer for a large corporation is passed over for promotion for more than ten years; a veteran with minor war injuries feels insecure because he cannot make an adequate living; a plumber, unable to continue in his trade because of hand injury, is reduced to clerking in a small family store; a former bank teller working at odd jobs sees men he had supervised becoming officials; and many more. The loss here is of a position, a position that had conferred identity and prestige upon the man.

*Loss of a Person*

The typical case here is that of the woman who has lost her husband. It may be a loss pure and simple—the husband has left the home. Also, it may be that the woman only *feels* her husband has been lost to her—he pays her little or no attention, for various reasons, or is seeing another woman. Or it may be that she "lost" him only in aspirations: she had hoped to find a husband but failed in the attempt. The saying "She died of a broken heart" is not at all inapplicable in many of these cases.

Quantitative data, coded from interviews, is available for 89 New Orleans white females between the ages of eighteen and sixty. Of these, 57 percent were married, 7 percent had never married, 10 percent were widows, 17 percent were divorced or separated, and 9 percent were living with a man out of wedlock. Several additional attempts at coding marital dimensions yielded the following: 39 percent were judged to have problems "almost entirely" in relation to the mate, and others showed this problem in combination with other family disturbances; only 24 percent were seen as married with "good" husband-wife relations and no illicit affairs reported; and of those with some kind of family problem, 50 percent were rated as having experienced the major problem with relation to a man in the same age bracket (whether present or absent), plus others who had this problem in combination with other difficulties. In contrast for this same group, health was seen as "the major problem" for only 10 percent of the suicides, and "job" (her own or her husband's) for 3 percent. This last figure indicates, perhaps surprisingly, that the great source of male suicide applies only infrequently to women, that the prestige gained from occupational, economic, and "class" status is much less applicable to women than to men, at least as seen in suicide statistics.

Loss of a man by a woman can, of course, take many forms. Several of these forms will be described somewhat along the dimension of "social distance."

At one extreme is the woman who never married, never even got to know a man well. Several cases appear in our files. Death here tends to come between the ages of thirty and forty. Only one did not wish to marry; she had a form of hemophilia and chose not to marry, let alone have children. The others probably aspired to marry but were unable to find a man. Some were not attractive physically, others lacked social skills. One case was that of a thirty-seven-year-old woman who never married but among whose effects was found literature from a lonely hearts club.

Aborted romances constitute the next category. The man draws away, and the anguish felt by the woman can be of sufficient strength to result in suicide. These women are usually also over thirty. One was forty when dating a man who married someone else; friends said she was never the same for the three years she lived after that. Included in this category may be a divorced woman as well; the unsuccessful search for a second husband can be depressing too. Another example is the case of a nursing student whose husband, a soldier, left her within a few weeks of marriage. She never saw him again.

Frequently, the wife feels her husband does not love her. She has evidence in the fact that he seldom stays home for long and never takes her out. Friends of one woman called the hubsand an "ogre" who paid her no attention; another woman would cry a great deal because her husband kept her "penned up" at home. Several women slowly became disillusioned with their husbands because the husbands continued to avoid them. The husband may be a traveling man or he may work in the community. In one case of the latter type, drunkenness in the husband contributed to the wife's "aggravation" or "disgust," to quote respondents. In a similar case, the wife's marital distress was increased by the fact that one son had been sent to jail.

Another group of women shared the experience of learning that the husband was seeing one or more other women. One of these, described by a friend as a most attractive and charming person, had a husband who had several other women simultaneously "on the string." One discovered that her sister's son was her husband's child; and another killed herself two weeks after learning of her husband's infidelity, according to the husband's mother. In another case, the husband heard a shot in the next room and went in to be told by his dying wife, "You don't love me anymore." Soon thereafter he married the woman he had been seeing.

The threat of separation preceded several suicides. In one instance, a neighbor told the interviewer that the wife had told her of threats to leave made by the husband, "who never took her out." In a case of one common-law union, the man had locked the woman, who drank heavily, out of their house several times. Neighbors reported that he had told them he was getting sick of her and that after her death he was at home much more often and seemed to be much happier. The question of "blame" will not be raised here. For present purposes it is enough that the rejected individual apparently *feels* that he has suffered a loss. In the last-mentioned case, two neighbors, one a male and the other a female, both sided with the male and agreed that the woman exhibited a great deal of unattractive behavior as well as clear statements of guilt and self-blame while worrying publicly about her mate's waning affection.

A variation on these forms is the case of the wife who is for one reason or another extremely jealous of the husband without apparent justification. One woman would, according to the neighbors, drive to the husband's place of work during the lunch hour, especially "during that time of the month." In cases of this type the woman tended to show more pathological behavior than in the cases given above.

Finally, one suicide involved an extremely attractive woman who had been married three times, always to sailors, and concurrently had been a prostitute. Two friends independently described her as beautiful but brazen about her beauty and her flaunting of it. "She would make Salome and Jezebel ashamed," one said. At thirty-four, however, she felt she was going downhill, "a butterfly turned into a moth." She felt the sailors were abandoning her "like rats from a sinking ship." Rather than endure this state, she took her life. For her, apparently, the loss was her beauty and her ability to attract not any one man but numbers of them.

All of these cases share more than an element of tragedy. They demonstrate the wide variety of losses women may experience with relation to the marital condition. Moving to a more theoretical ground, one might say that these materials indicate the vital significance of a social role: the role of wife in the life of American women. For a woman, to play adequately the role of wife may overshadow any other single aspect of her life. What other role would compare with it? To be a mother, of course, is closely associated with being a wife, but evidence from our study does not show motherhood to be as crucial as wifehood. The same conclusion applies to the role of "class position." Recall that "job" accounted for only 3 percent of the "major problems" among the female suicides. The interview materials indicate that only seldom does downward mobility or work failure—her husband's or her own—become a principle source of female suicide. Intergenerational downward mobility in this sample differs little from the female population at large. Some of the suicides' husbands were doing less than well occupationally, but interviews do not contain statements that this inadequacy was felt as bringing shame or humiliation to the wife. His success or failure at work, in other words, does not seem to "rub off" on her to any appreciable extent.

Men and women in our society, then, have quite different life-experience "reasons" impelling them to suicide. For men, the primary loss revolves about work, and for women, it revolves around the man. This recalls Freud's answer (although it is not sex-specific) when he was asked what he thought a normal person should be able to do well. Freud is reported to have said, "*Lieben und Arbeiten*" (To love and to work).[11]

Having drawn this rather strong conclusion from our data, I hasten to add that marital problems also plague men who commit suicide. They suffer more of a combination of work-marriage problems than do women. One man, a house painter who "skidded" to the job of peddler, was pictured by his brother as having "died of a broken heart" because of his wife's departure, although he did not take his life for several years thereafter. A hotel bell captain was "never the same" after he found the young woman he was dating already married. "Nagging wives" were implicated in the suicides of four men. It is among this group that the data point most clearly to the "aggression" against another person. In the most extreme of these cases, the husband was said by a close friend to have lost two high-paying jobs because of his wife. His hatred was shown in the fact that he left in his dresser two insurance policies made out to his wife, both having been allowed to expire shortly before.

### *Loss of Mutuality*

Whereas loss of position or mate may happen abruptly or gradually, the third type of loss, of mutuality, may have occurred at any time, from childhood on. This is the least specific of the three types. Seen most broadly, it could embrace the other two, but this would serve no useful purpose. Rather, mutuality will refer not to the specific loss of any one person but to a weakening of mutual social relationships in general. As a type it is much like Durkheim's "egoistic" category, in which the individual lacks bonds and ties to other persons and does not share a community of sentiments with others. Usually, the individual's "personality" has been characterized either by shyness, a lack of gregariousness, introversion, or strong "self-consciousness," or he has evidenced traits which are found to be aggravating or insulting to other persons.

Quite a few of the suicides were described as having been obnoxious to others. Some apparently had so comported themselves for years, while others had started to do so only shortly before their suicide. In the latter event, the loss of a person or a position often triggered the disliked behavior. Both male and female suicides show these signs.

One man, for example, was said by his son to have been "just plain hateful." The son's wife, present during this portion of the interview, added, "Put that down; it's the best way to describe him." The man had enjoyed parties but liked getting into fights—"the bigger the better," the son said. A woman was called by her former husband "a vile person;" he added that she had moved around a great deal and always failed to adjust to others.

Several of the suicides do not merit the appellation "obnoxious," but they were unable to tolerate the other person's opinion in the give and take of ordinary social communication. One woman "thought she knew it all"; in an argument she would insist she was correct even though clear alternative opinions were possible. A businessman likewise insisted his view on all subjects was correct. "He was terribly arrogant, always referring to his college background (although I believe he had been there for only a year), and if a topic came up he wasn't interested in, he'd find reason to leave. I finally stopped talking to him," the suicide's former next-door neighbor said.

Closely related to these cases are the "Johnny One-Note" people, as one of them was called. Their one topic of conversation was frequently the errant husband. One of these was a thirty-eight-year-old woman separated from her husband for a year. He had been a heavy drinker, and she had become one too, to accompany him, but the relationship worsened until they separated. "Basically she was a gregarious person," a relative said, "but she was sort of shunned after a while because everyone knew what she would talk about. She was bitter, pessimistic, talked about her unhappy marriage." Another woman, in ill health, "would phone me up and say the same things over and over for an hour. I tried to avoid her."

Some were described as unpredictable and hard to get along with. One social-climbing woman was called a snob by her sister. "She was awfully hard to get along with at times, and she had an ugly disposition." Of another woman a friend said, "One day she'll talk to you real nice, the next day she was all clammed up." A third woman, one of the rather rare cases of downward mobility, lived in a subdivision built by her father. (Her husband was a bakery driver.) She would enter the home of a new neighbor and criticize the furnishings as being below standard for her father's tract. A neighbor said, "She came in and told me I'd paid too much for my furniture, and besides, it didn't look good."

Others simply had a difficult time being friendly with people. A thirty-two-year-old single man had never been very sociable but did become engaged; the girl broke the engagement and he became more and more morose and solitary. "He lost his courage," the mother said, telling how he would come home from work and lie on his bed most of the evening. From the interview it was clear that he talked little even to his mother. Of a woman in her forties, her neighbor said, "She didn't mix too well.

She had a friend down the street and me, and that's about it. The lady in back stopped talking to her, and that bothered her." The woman was kindly and never seemed nervous, but she had no friends. Another woman's sister said, "She couldn't talk. I was the only one she confided in. She'd never get expressive—it would just be a statement of fact. She implied things rather than expressing herself."

Loss of mutuality as used here covers a wide area. The common characteristic, as seen in these suicides, resides in the inability of the individual to maintain satisfactory social relationships with others. Loss here does not mean that a sudden change has taken place, although in many cases a person with good social relationships began to lose the previous quantity and quality of contacts in the period prior to suicide. Also the loss of "expected" mutuality, or the kind of social life the individual aspired to, might be included in this category.

## Interaction Theory and Suicide

Proceeding from observed cases of suicide, we have documented particular kinds of losses suffered by the suicide person before his death. There have been losses of position, person, and mutuality. The latter two clearly point to social relationships; the first involves social relationships indirectly through loss of a position—frequently an occupational position—and therefore the individual's ability to lay claim to legitimate role performance *as seen by other persons*. Each loss can now be seen as having both an objective and a subjective aspect.

Let us return to the four dimensions along which suicide can be approached. Our data are only remotely understandable with the Durkheimian dimension 1, and we do not have sufficient intrapsychic information to make meaningful headway by way of dimension 4. Likewise, the second dimension of group and strata does not promise immediate explanatory power, because the individuals were members of various formal groups and all social classes. It is dimension 3, then, the area of interpersonal relationships, that we will pursue. The question asked here is, what are the differences in interpersonal relationships between suicides and nonsuicides in all classes, all sexes, all groups—among all persons?

What is needed is a social-psychological mechanism which links the four dimensions. We may assume the existence of relevant features of society, culture, group, strata, and individual functioning for all members of this society, including the suicides. These structures, while of course not identical for each member of society, are relatively constant for individuals playing roles in society. The variable is the fact of loss for the suicide person. The needed mechanism must identify a general process whereby the individual suffering loss places a particular kind of meaning to his loss, so that he decides he is better off dead than alive.

The mechanism I wish to suggest brings into action the process of self-evaluation, as mediated through the individual's taking the role of other persons toward himself and, in these cases, resulting in a negative self-conception. This theory is associated with James, Baldwin, and Cooley ("the looking glass self") and especially with George Herbert Mead,[12] founder of the "symbolic interaction" school. It assumes that one attitude central to the human being is his attitude toward himself and that he must maintain, on balance, a favorable self-conception. The source of this attitude is his estimate of the assessments other persons make of him. He infers these assessments by the perceptual clues others give off about him, and his behavior is influenced accordingly. Not only specific persons but also "the generalized other" affects the individual's self-conception; this in Mead's terms is "the organized social process of which he is a part." Many times the individual need not wait to judge the others' assessment of his behavior if it is culturally clear what the standards are; he can anticipate their reactions.

Thus other persons act as "social controls" over the individual. If, for example, behavior pattern *A* elicits approval from others, he will tend to continue such behavior so as to gain social approval and maintain a favorable self-image. If however his behavior *B* is met with what he infers as disapproval, he is faced with a serious problem. He can do one of several things: he can change his behavior, remove himself from similar situations and the disapproving persons, decide the other persons are incorrect in their assessment, or make a number of other adaptations, one of which is to entertain a negative self-conception. Since the latter adaptation tends to bring anxiety, the individual who finds himself unable to shift from the disapproved behavior *B* (such as performing up to cultural expectations in work or family) and is also unable to take any other than the latter adaptation experiences mounting strain. As applied to the suicides, I am speculating that they have followed this path. When a man loses his job role or a woman loses her marital role, less latitude for choice remains as well as less gratification and reward in the form of response and recognition from others. With a blurring of identity and a constricting of role choices, the individual loses confidence in himself, and this is communicated to others. The process is a downward spiral. The resulting strain eventually becomes too much to bear.

Since the early theorists, some empirical work has been attempted to test portions of the theory. Studies by Miyamoto and Dornbusch[13] and by Reeder, Donohue, and Biblarz[14] have shown that the individual's self-conception is related to the attitudes other persons hold toward him. Investigation of attitudes generally tends to suggest that some attitudes held by individuals are intense, central, consistent, and stable, and that the attitude toward the self is one of these.[15] Applied to personal pathology, Rosengren, studying boys who were receiving long-term psychiatric hospital treatment, concluded that the boys who responded positively to treatment were also the ones who showed improved ability to infer the attitudes of the generalized other toward themselves.[16] These were "boys whose self-functions more nearly approximated Mead's ideal." Roughly the opposite was true for boys who did not meet this ideal. Reckless, Dinitz, and Murray, although not showing the process of self-image formation, found that sixth-grade boys described by teachers as "good" (not potential delinquents) also possessed "good" self-conceptions and were thus presumably insulated against deviance.[17]

In addition to these empirical studies, Rose, Wallace, and Breed have theorized that self-conception should be related to deviant behavior. In presenting an interactional theory of neurosis (especially involutional melancholia) Rose uses Cooley and Mead to argue that continued adverse reactions to the individual, received from other persons, result in a series of blows to the self-conception which lead to anxiety sufficient to render the individual unable to perform roles.[18] "A depreciated or 'mutilated' self is a major factor in the development of a neurosis, we hypothesize, because an individual's ability to accept strongly held values of any kind and to act effectively to achieve these values is a function of his conception of himself—a conception that he is an adequate, worth-while, effective, and appreciated person." Wallace[19] has "shame" following the anxiety resulting from a poor self-image; he uses the verb "to gaslight"—apparently taking it from the film in which Charles Boyer "makes" Ingrid Bergman ill by planting "her" mistakes for her to contemplate. (Interestingly, just the reverse of this Meadian process is suggested by Kinch, who reviews the possibly apocryphal story of the boys who conspired to date the homely coed, who thereupon became more attractive and interesting—their actions required a change in her self-conception and thus a change in her behavior.[20]) I have attempted a "structural-interactional" hypothesis of suicide,[21] an effort which is being elaborated here. Working mainly in dimension 4, Diggory has studied "self-esteem" among suicidal persons.[22]

In all of these theoretical studies the Meadian process provides a link between loss—or the gap between aspirations and achievements—and objective sociocultural factors and subjective dispositions within the individual.

One question will doubtless occur to the reader. All human beings suffer losses—many of them losses as serious as those which afflict the suicides. Why do they not commit suicide? For one reason, the loss may not be accompanied by the other elements of the process outlined above. Basically, the typical individual who has suffered a loss indeed feels it keenly, and he may experience a blow to his self-conception through his recognition of his own failure and his inferred or anticipated loss of "face" in the eyes of other persons. Yet he has numerous other possible alternative adaptations: he may vow to try harder next time, reduce his level of aspirations, engage in other mechanisms of ego defense, such as repression, projection, or rationalization, or drift into other deviant modes of behavior, such as Merton's innovation, ritualism, rebellion, or various forms of retreatism. In any event, he refuses to define himself as a terminal failure and enters a new phase, which he and others will again evaluate as to success or failure. It is clear that questions of individual "personality" must be asked at this point. Numerous ideas can be found in *The Cry For Help*; [23] perhaps most closely related to the present thesis are the presentations by Hendin and Kelly on depression, dependence, rejection, and threat.

The form of analysis given above has emphasized an interactional dimension while probably slighting a second contemporary sociological approach to deviant behavior called the structural form. This second mode of analysis is best exemplified by Merton's theory of Social Structure and Anomie, which holds that deviant behavior follows from a disjunction between the cultural structure and the social structure.[24] Briefly, Merton says that when a social structure (as seen in an individual's low class or ethnic position) blocks the achievement of the individual's goals, the resulting strain may bring the individual to one or another form of deviant behavior mentioned above.

Nothing in these data on loss in suicide requires a rejection of Merton's hypothesis. Many of the losses, indeed, show these properties. In the last decade, however, numerous works have sought to isolate the process by which the individual comes to define himself as deviant and proceeds to undertake deviant acts, as an individual or in groups.[25] These studies have all found the interactional approach useful—as have I. We can now talk about "interactional strain" as well as "structural strain." Merton's emphasis, especially in his earlier works, largely skipped over dimension 3. The "goal" he imputes to individuals tends to be defined in terms of the entire society, whereas the interactional approach focusses on the smaller "generalized other" or community that they live in from day to day. Put another way, whereas the structural school calls the loss one of "prestige," the interactional approach deals with a loss of "esteem" as well. In this usage, prestige refers to a position as evaluated by the entire society, whereas esteem is conferred for role performance as assessed by the concrete individuals who know the individual personally. In either case, as Merton points out, the very "success" goal institutionalized by the society becomes a source of individual strain.

The use of four levels of analysis, rather than one or two, seems important if we are to achieve a more comprehensive understanding of suicide. Only when we begin to ask about the *process* of suicide can we understand the meaningfulness of each of the several dimensions. Durkheim dwelt too little on dimensions 3 and 4, and psychologists were equally unhelpful in other than dimension 4. As for the particular process theory I have suggested, it remains to be tested. In addition to studying suicide, variations could be attempted with other forms of deviant behavior, such as mental illness and alcoholism. Studies of schizophrenia and "isolation" or "alienation" would fall within this approach. And most certainly, sociologists, psychologists, and psychiatrists should combine their efforts to analyze each of the four dimensions and to relate them into a more complex and meaningful whole.

## REFERENCES

1. Emile Durkheim, *Suicide* (1897) (New York: The Free Press, 1951).
2. Norman L. Farberow, and Edwin S. Shneidman, *The Cry For Help* (New York: McGraw-Hill Book Company, 1961).
3. *Ibid.*, p. 171.
4. *Ibid.*, p. 184.
5. *Ibid.*, p. 216.
6. *Ibid.*, p. 223.
7. *Ibid.*, p. 269.
8. *Ibid.*, p. 299.
9. This research was supported by a grant from the National Institute of Mental Health. I would like to acknowledge the very helpful assistance given by Jane Ledford.
10. Warren Breed, "Occupational Mobility and Suicide Among White Males," *American Sociological Review,* **28**:179–188, 1963.
11. Erik H. Erikson, *Childhood and Society* (New York: W. W. Norton & Company, 1950), p. 229.

12. George H. Mead, *Mind, Self and Society* (Chicago: University of Chicago Press, 1935). See also Arnold M. Rose (ed.), *Human Behavior and Social Processes* (Boston: Houghton Mifflin Company, 1962).
13. S. Frank Miyamoto, and Sanford M. Dornbusch, "A Test of the Interactionist Hypothesis of Self-Conception," *American Journal of Sociology,* **61**:399–403, 1956.
14. Leo G. Reeder, George A. Donohue, and Arturo Biblarz, "Conceptions of Self and Others," *American Journal of Sociology,* **66**:153–159, 1960.
15. Theodore M. Newcomb, Ralph H. Turner, and Philip E. Converse, *Social Psychology* (New York: Holt, Rinehart and Winston, Inc., 1965), chap. 5.
16. William R. Rosengren, "The Self in the Emotionally Disturbed," *American Journal of Sociology,* **66**:454–462, 1961.
17. Walter C. Reckless, Simon Dinitz, and Ellen Murray, "Self Concept as Insulator against Delinquency," *American Sociological Review,* **27**:744–746, 1956.
18. Arnold M. Rose, "A Social Psychological Theory of Neurosis," in Rose, *op. cit.,* pp. 537–549.
19. Anthony F. C. Wallace, *Culture and Personality* (New York: Random House, Inc., 1963), pp. 182–184.
20. John W. Kinch, "A Formalized Theory of the Self Concept," *American Journal of Sociology,* **68**:481–486, 1963.
21. *Op. cit.*
22. James C. Diggory, and Doreen Z. Rothman, "Values Destroyed by Death," *Journal of Abnormal and Social Psychology,* **61**:205–209, 1961.
23. Farberow and Shneidman, *op. cit.*
24. Robert K. Merton, *Social Theory and Social Structure* (New York: The Free Press, 1957), chaps. 4 and 5.
25. For example: Howard S. Becker, *Outsiders* (New York: The Free Press, 1963); Richard A. Cloward, "Illegitimate Means, Anomie, and Deviant Behavior," *American Sociological Review,* **24**:164–176, 1959; Edwin M. Lemert, *Social Pathology* (New York: McGraw-Hill Book Company, 1951); and Talcott Parsons, *The Social System* (New York: The Free Press, 1951), chap. 7.

# 10. The Search for Help: No One to Turn to

Harvey Sacks

## I

I shall aim to construct a description of how the conclusion a suicidal person may reach (that he has no one to turn to) may be reproducably provided for. The aim may be satisfied by (1) locating the collections of membership categories in terms of which the search for help is properly formulated; and by (2) describing the ways such collections are used to determine whether there are eligible persons available.[1]

For the materials at hand,[2] two category collections seem crucial. They may be called: (1) a collection of paired *relational* categories called *R*, and (2) a collection (called *K*) constructed with reference to special distributions of *knowledge* obtained about how to deal with some trouble (here "suicidalness").

The collection of relational categories *R* is composed of such pairs of categories as: husband-wife, parent-child, neighbor-neighbor, friend-friend, cousin-cousin, stranger-stranger, etc. We find that the following rule provides for whether a pair of categories is a member of collection *R*: Any pair of categories is a member of collection *R* if that pair is a "standardized" relational pair which constitutes a locus for a set of rights and obligations concerning the activity of giving help.

To say that the pairs are standardized is to say the following: (1) If any Member X knows his own pair position with respect to some member Y, then X knows the pair position of Y with respect to himself. X also knows that if *Y* knows what pair position *Y* has to X, then*Y* knows what pair position X has to Y. (2) If any Member *N* (neither X nor Y) knows what X feels is *X*'s pair position to Y, then *N* knows what pair position X feels *Y* has to X. *N* also knows that X considers that if *Y* knows that X stands to *Y* in the pair position X supposes, then *Y* feels that Y stands to X in the pair position X supposes. *N* knows too that the converse holds for Y. *N* knows further, as do X and Y, what the rights and obligations are that obtain between X and *Y* given a convergence in their determination of their respective pair positions.

Since it is altogether central to the use of *R* in the search for help that it has the sort of standardization we have proposed, let us here and now locate what, in the materials, the formulation permits us to observe.

By virtue of the features of the standardization of *R*, any two Members, without regard to the pair positions they employ to locate each other, and, therefore, even if not acquainted prior to the given conversation, are able to assess the treatment any third Member expectably will (1) give one of them, if one of them is suicidal and the third Member's pair position to that one is determined, or (2) get from any other Member, if it is someone other than one of the two who is suicidal and if the pair relation of that third and any other Member is determined.

With the foregoing we can then partially provide for some of the most recurrent occurrences of our materials. That is; the various pairs of conversationalists are able to assess the expectable behavior of variously categorized third persons where one participant to the conversation, and sometimes both, know only the pair position of the third persons whose expectable behaviors are being assessed. Such occurrences are then observably orderly across the various pair positions from which they are done.

Collection *K* is composed of two classes (professionals and laymen). Since *K* will be little considered in this paper, only a minimal characterization will be offered. First, both *K* and *R* can categorize any population of one or more Members. As to *K* itself: (1) All those occupational categories for which it is correct to say that Members of them have special or exclusive rights for dealing with some trouble(s) are occasional occupants of *K*'s class (professionals). (2) For any given trouble for which such an occupation exists as 1 above locates, that occupation constitutes the category exclusively occupying the (professional) class, where all who are not Members of it are undifferentiatedly occupants of the *K* class (laymen). Thus, for any given trouble incumbency in one of the classes excludes incumbency in the other.

II

In focussing on collection *R*, it might be asked: How is it that when a search for help is being engaged in, the relevance of collection *R* is provided for? The formulation is, however, erroneous. For, as we shall observe, the very propriety of search for help is provided for by the rights and obligations which are organized by reference to collection *R*. Our initial task is then to show how features of collection *R* provide for the propriety of occurrence of a search for help.

For some pairs of categories:

1. X (a suicidal person, a programmatic incumbent[3] of some pair positions) has a right to turn to Y (a programmatic incumbent of alternative pair positions) for help. Hence, any Member has a programmatic right to undertake a search for help, i.e., at least to determine whether any pair positions to whose programmatic incumbents he has a right to turn are occupied by actual incumbents.

2. If X chooses to undertake a search for help, and if that search involves telling those sought out who he is, X is obliged to turn to incumbents of these categories on the basis of what it is that is wrong with him and what he makes out the causes of his suicidalness to be. Incumbents of these categories have it as a right that X not turn to incumbents of other categories.

3. If X sees that the alternative to searching for help is suicide, then X is obliged to seek help as an alternative to suicide. It is a right of incumbents of these classes that X seek help as an alternative to suicide.

These three rules provide for the propriety of the search for help, where the alternative to seeking help is suicide. They provide also for its permissibility. They provide further that if the search is undertaken, it will, properly, be from categories to which the obligation to undertake a search is owed, that is, that helpers will be sought.

Since the rules provide from whom help may and may not be sought, they can be seen to distribute the categories of collection *R* into two subsets: *Rp* and *Ri*. Those categories which the rules locate as "categories whose incumbents are proper to turn to" are members of *Rp*, and those which the rules locate as "categories whose incumbents are not proper to turn to" are members of *Ri*.

It seems that subset *Rp* is properly used in an orderly fashion—that there is a proper sequence in the use of its categories—and, furthermore, that rules 1 to 3 hold not only with regard to the subset *Rp* but also with regard to the proper sequence for going into *Rp*. Then: If there is an incumbent of some "first-position" category, with respect to any incumbent of some "second-position" category, the rules provide that the incumbent of the first position and not the second should be turned to.

Given the foregoing, and with respect to collection *R*, we are in a position to pose at least the form of the searcher's problem: "Anyone" means "any incumbent of a pair position in subset *Rp*," and "no one" means "no incumbent of a pair position in subset *Rp*." For any search then, the problem is: Are there available persons who are incumbents of some pair position which is a member of the subset whose incumbents are properly turned to for help?

Assuming for the moment what we have yet to establish, that incumbency and availability are separate problems, we may observe: If for some suicidal person there are no incumbents of *Rp*, then the rules provide only that he is not obligated to turn to anyone for help; the rules do not provide, given that eventuality, that he cannot properly turn to anyone else.

With the preceding discussion we have established (if that discussion is descriptive) the correctness of the assertion that it is not the case that the search for help provides the relevance of collection *R*. Instead, the fact of suicidalness provides the relevance of a set of rights and obligations organized by reference to collection *R*. Collection *R* and the rights and obligations organized by refenence to its categories provide the propriety of engaging in a search for help. As has been further indicated, collection *R* does more than that. It provides for the permissibility of the search and also the procedure for doing that search. But of these latter more will be said in the ensuing.

## III

Let us now see how the apparatus we have constructed out of our materials may permit us to analyze their production. Let us see how the foregoing categories and rules of use provide for the reproducible occurrence of a variety of actually occurring pieces of conversation. Let us see further how solutions may be constructed to the problem we initially posed: How is it that the conclusion "I have no one to turn to" may be reproducibly provided for?

First of all, the fact that *R* classifies any population (of one or more people) and the obligations to seek help and the rules for searching for helpers are formulated in terms of its categories operates to provide that *R* is used to make an initial classification of the recipient, of the phone conversations we are examining, by the suicidal caller. Thus the recipient can be categorized by reference to categories organized in some other collection (for example, *K*). Suicidal callers recurrently talk of the recipient as a "stranger." Also nonsuicidal callers recurrently report that it is by reference to the categories of R that a suicidal person came to locate them as someone to turn to for help.

Such categorization is made "even though" (as we may put it) it may be that given the category employed to locate the recipient, the recipient is thereby—by reference to the subsets of *R*—formulated as improper to turn to.

If the recipient is not a member of *Rp*, it may be noticed that explanations which involve reference to *Rp* features are offered without being sought or are sought, and when sought, are offered without being treated as irrelevant or improper.

(1) Suicidal woman: No request for an account has been made by the recipient. "My sister came over on Sunday and she talked to me and I called her now to talk to her and she told me to please call these people and tell me what they say."

If an account has not been offered, then as an alternative to requesting one, the recipient may, by reference to the standardization of *R*, construct an account himself. He may infer the account, employing the feature of *R* where the fact of a contact having been sought with someone in *Ri* is treated as indicative of the situation of a caller with respect to *Rp*.

(2) S1 Have you ever been married, Miss M——?
C1 No.
S2 And you're out here kind of on your own and things not going well?
C2 That's it.
S3 You have no one out here?
C3 Well, I have cousins, but you know they're cousins. They're third or fourth cousins . . . .

It is extremely important to see that as our formulation proposes, the caller may treat his having made the call as improper without regard to the fact that the recipient is one who holds himself out as proper to be called quite independently of the regulations of *R*. Impropriety of a contact and the unwillingness of a recipient are quite separate matters. The fact that some persons or classes of persons are willing to give help, hold themselves out to give help, or propose their special competence to give help does not make them proper to turn to if with respect to *R* they are Members of *Ri*.

(3) C1 Maybe it was a mistake to call. I don't know. But I mean . . .
S1 Why do you think it might be?
C2 Well, you know, it seems to reach out for help from strangers . . . . I don't know. It seems to be very—like I shouldn't do it. Like my family and my friends don't help me, I mean why should I go to a stranger for help, you know?
S2 Sometimes you need professional help.
C3 Well I'm going to tell you something. I have tried for many many years to get my family to help me. To understand and make myself clear to them. Try to tell them exactly what I was, and what I was trying and they refused to listen and oh, everything's all mixed up and now I've been just thrown over to my grandmother's and of course I'm—oh I don't know.
S3 Well, you know sometimes when the people close to us don't come through when we need them, we get sort of hopeless and feel as if no one will.
C4 Well, that's exactly how I feel. I feel today as though I would just like to go out and say to hell with the whole thing and just flash away and be gone with me. That's exactly how—you know I shouldn't of called you to start with. I mean, I wanted to, I really wanted to. I thought maybe I might get a few answers, but I shouldn't have, because I feel as though it's a deceit. I really do.

The fact of the standardization of *R*, and of the relevance of its categories in the search for help provides for discourse between Members about the categories and their incumbents "even though" the participants to the conversation are previously unacquainted with it. The collection of categories provides a set of topics. For one, the question of whether there are incumbents of these categories may be considered, where (1) the relevance of consideration of whether there are incumbents is not seen as problematic, and (2) the way in which the fact of there being (or not being) incumbents is dealt with is not in itself disorderly.

It is recurrently observable in the materials that the assessments of expectable behavior (of third persons, nonparticipants to the conversation) turn on the determination of the pair positions in *R* of the Member whose expectable behavior is being assessed. It is not the case that such discussions proceed by reference to Members formulated as "somebody" or to formulations by reference to collections other than *R*. Sometimes neither participant to the conversation is acquainted with those they are talking about, but the pair-position information still seems adequate to them to provide assessments of expectable behavior. Given the pair-position information, those who feel that they have information about the incumbent inconsistent with the inferences pair-position knowledge provides, feel, as do those they are conversing with, that pair-position inferences are not simply superseded if "special knowledge" is held back. Instead, special argumentation is required, and it may be insisted that the special knowledge will turn out to be incorrect whereas the pair-position inferences will not. The inferences that pair-position knowledge provides are then to be treated seriously, even if their correctness is to be denied. Acquaintanceship does not obviously provide superseding knowledge.

If it is the suicidal person who is a third party to the conversation (i.e., not a participant) then their expectable reaction to proffered help is assessable. Again, in doing such assessment, the regulations with regard to *R* are relevant. The caller will recurrently propose that it is not expectable that the help of a "stranger" will be accepted, that further, the suicidal person would be much disturbed to know that an outsider has been consulted. In several cases the caller proposed that the proper strategy would be for them to tell the suicidal that it is a "friend" who has been sought out and who ought to be contacted.

The standardization of *R* and the rules for distributing categories into its subsets provide one sense of one solution to the problem of this paper. A sense of "no one to turn to" is: For the subset *Rp* for some Member A, there are no incumbents of *Rp* categories.

The standardization only provides the sense of a solution. The possibility that such a situation may occur for some Member is another order of fact, one whose possibility is provided for by reference to quite a different apparatus. For some societies the removal of an incumbent from a category, say the death of a husband, is the occasion for the operation of machinery which involves some other Member taking that place, if such another who is eligible is available. Among the Bemba, for example: "When a man dies his name, his kinship duties and his hereditary bow are passed on to his sister's son or to her grandson through a daughter. The heir actually becomes the dead man in a social sense; he adopts the kinship terms the latter used, calling, for instance, 'maternal nephew' the person he would previously have called 'brother.'"[4] Again, among the people of the Shtetl: "If a man dies childless his unmarried brother is obligated to marry the widow in order to perpetuate the line. Neither the widow nor the brother may marry anyone else without a formal release from the other."[5] Such machinery seems largely absent in this society. The fact that this absence is of special importance because a variety of relations which Members treat, where the slots of a unit are filled, as named person–named person and not unit member–unit member relations, turn out, upon the occurrence of a pair being rendered incomplete, to have been or to now become unit member–unit member relations. A widow finds that her friends are no longer her friends when she no longer has a husband and she then finds that she has lost (even) more than her husband by his death (or, in the case of divorce, by the divorce). Conversations include such interchanges as:

(4) S1 How long have you been feeling the way you're feeling now? Since Christmas? [Her husband left her then for another.]
C1 Yes.
S2 Before?
C2 No, I had hope before Christmas. I had hope. I thought that a love such as mine could overcome anything. I felt I had everything there was in my love. And now it's turned against me. I don't feel like I have anything anymore. Nobody gives a damn, in other words.
S3 Nobody what?
C3 Gives a damn. What's the use?
S4 How about friends? Have you friends?
C4 I have friends. So-called friends. I had friends, let me put it that way.
S5 But you feel that since he left, everything . . .
C5 It's just like rats deserting a sinking ship. Nobody wants to talk to anybody that's in the condition I'm in. They all have their own family, their own problems. They all have their own husbands.

## IV

Let us proceed now to develop another way that the conclusion "I have no one to turn to" may properly be arrived at. It seems that with the assertion of "I am suicidal" (as one assertion that can stand as a request for help) the offering of an account, an explanation, is a proper accompaniment. One basis for the request for help being accompanied by an account may be formulated. The basis seems to be of far more general relevance than the situation of suicidalness.

When the Members' action, such as giving help, is conditioned by their being informed of the presence of some state (1) which cannot independently be determined to be present, and (2) the assertion of which is not definitive in terms of its correctness (i.e., is made improperly, as a joke or a lie), then Members feel that they may be placed in a situation where the request is made without proper basis. Members' orientation to possible misrequests in such situations is exemplified by the "Cry Wolf" fable.

In the case of suicidalness, Members consider that the claim of suicidalness may be misasserted.

(5) (the former girl friend in regard to an avowed suicidal man)
S1 Do you know if he's had this kind of mood before?
C1 Not like that, no. But I mean as I tried to mention before, at first I thought that this was all part of an act. I mean not act, I shouldn't use that word. But it's just, he tries everything, you know, to patch things up and so . . .

This fear of what we may call the subversive use of a claim of suicidalness is clearly not without basis. For example, note the following conversation between a man referred to the clinic and a staff member.

(6) S1 What did you do?
C1 It was an impulse because my wife was going to leave me, but it was only to steer her into going into reconciliation court. Do you understand what I mean?
S2 Yes, what did you do?
C2 I tried to shoot myself
S3 How did you do it?
C3 I took the gun and loaded it, and tried to fire it.
S4 Then what happened?
C4 It went off, but actually I didn't aim it at myself. Maybe I can explain it better. It was to let her know that I had intentions of doing that.

. . . . .

S5 Well, what do you think about what you did?
C5 I got her to reconciliation court.

There is a variety of ways that have been developed for dealing with this possibility of a subversive use of the request for help; one way is the following: Members feel that they may determine whether to help and what help they ought to give on the basis of whether or not an adequate and determinable present ground exists. Members feel that they may decide whether or not some proposed fact exists by determining whether or not its proposed explanation exists and is adequate.

(7) The following quotation from a quite different area (it is part of an arbitration decision) may exemplify this procedure. (Ford-UAW Arbitrations, Case A-70, Harry Shulman, arbitrator)

> The story of the other discharged employees approaches the bizarre. Twelve of them testified before me. Each of them claims to be a completely innocent bystander wholly at a loss to understand why he was picked up for discharge. None of them admits being part of the crowd in any of the demonstrations. None of them admits even the normal curiosity of an innocent bystander. Each claims that he knew very little about the cause of the stoppages and cared even less after learning the cause. Each claims that when the lights went out, or the lines stopped, he asked his foreman what to do and, upon being told to stay or go home as he pleased but that his time stopped in any event, he left for home. One of the men, a lively young boxer, asserts that, after seeing the crowd and the excitement, he calmly repaired to a warm comfortable spot and went to sleep. He did this, he asserts, on two of the three days (being absent on the third) and slept the peaceful sleep of the just until the excitement completely quieted down. All, it seems, were veritable angels above and beyond contagion by the excitement in the Department. Now there unquestionably were serious stoppages in Dept. 84 on Nov. 5th, 6th and 8th. There were vociferous and angry men milling around and demanding action. Who were the incensed men who did take part? Who were the angry men whom it was so difficult to get back to work and who were so incensed that, as the Union claims, they turned against their own committeemen and even assaulted two of them? How indeed were these 14 chosen?
>
> The Union advanced no explanations. There is no suggestion that these men were chosen by lot; and even such a method would normally be expected to catch some of the guilty. And there is no basis whatever in the evidence to suppose that the men were selected because of any personal animosity against them—with the slight possible exception of one man. Nor were the men generally regarded as "trouble-makers" of whom the Company would be glad to be rid.
>
> The Company's explanation is simple and without any contradiction other than the incredible stories related by the men themselves. The labor relations conciliator, with the help of his assistant, took the names or badge numbers of the most active men in the crowds that demonstrated in his office. This accounts for twelve of the fourteen . . . Under these circumstances I cannot give credence to the men's protestations of innocence.

In short, Members consider that they may choose among proposed competing facts by deciding that the (possible) fact is present for which there is an adequate explanation, and the (possible) fact is not present for which there is not an adequate explanation. Hence, when giving help is properly conditioned by the presence of some state which is not independently determinable to be present by the one who ought to give help, the requirement that the request be accompanied by an account seems to be directed to permitting a determination to be made of whether the state is indeed present.

One who is contemplating the use of *R* to get help may then be faced with having to announce both his grounds and why he is suicidal. He may thereby be faced with having to consider the various treatments he may receive given the announcement of his grounds—the account. Therefore, it is not merely the claimed fact of suicidalness which determines what *Rp* Members ought to do. The account of suicidalness provides those sought out with an account for their own response. That is, the suicidal Member's account provides *Rp* Members with grounds for their own response. A procedure is then available for assessing what potential helpers may expectedly do. The suicidal Member may consider the various actions that the potential helper may take for which the suicidal's account stands as the potential helper's proper account. The suicidal may use such a procedure in a circumscribed fashion, by reference to the standardization of proper actions that the potential helper may take when given some account as the account of those actions.

We may recall that if there is a first Member of *Rp* available the suicidal ought to turn to that Member for help. Hence, the suicidal may use the procedure just noted with reference to the first Member. Suppose the suicidal person is a married woman. For such a one, the first Member of *Rp* is her husband. Suppose further that the account of her suicidalness involves the fact that she has been seduced into having an affair with another man (say, to keep as the prototype one which we have found in a suicide note, an acquaintance of her husband). She may then consider the various actions her husband may take when given her adultery as the grounds of his action. On the one hand, he might treat the fact of her suicidalness as adequately accounted for and give her help. On the other, he might treat the fact of her adultery as an adequate ground for a breach in their relationship, for getting a divorce.

She faces then the following dilemma: On the one hand, the fact that she is married and suicidal means that her husband is the one to turn to for help. On the other, what she shall tell him may operate so as to take him out of the slot that established him as the first one for her to turn to. He is there (perhaps) so long as she does not speak; once she does, he may no longer be there. In that sort of dilemma she may well see that there is no one to turn to, whereas, she is obliged to turn for help, to turn to him, and he is available.

The prototype may readily be generalized. If a suicidal Member's account of his suicidalness is some action that for the first Member of *Rp* stands as an adequate ground for a breach (e.g., of divorce, or disownment, or breaking-off, or indeed of death), then the suicidal person may, employing the categories according to the rules of use we have constructed, find himself in the dilemma described above and may see and report that "I have no one to turn to." The caller in the following is suicidal and homosexual.

(8) S1 Well I understand what these pressures are on you. Is there anyone you trust, anyone who can take care of you, because right now you need some taking care of. You need somebody to move in and take over.

C1 The only people I know are people just like myself. I don't have any regular friends.

S2 Well what about people just like yourself?

C2 They give me all kinds of things and they . . .

S3 What about your doctor?

C3 I don't have a family doctor.

S4 Well, somebody prescribed those pills.

C4 Well, he's just a doctor. I only called him up.

S5 You never saw him?

C5 A long time ago, for a little thing. I don't know him that well.

S6 You think he'd take over?

C6 I don't know.

S7 What about your parents?

C7 I can't tell them. I'd rather kill myself than tell them.

S8 You can't tell them what?

C8 Anything.

S9 Not even that you're suffering and need to be in a hospital?

C9 No.

S10 But they must have eyes. They probably have been sitting around worrying about this for a long time now.

C10 No. They haven't.

S11 I'd like to call them up and talk with them.

C11 I don't want them to know.

S12 I certainly wouldn't tell them anything that you told me. I'd just tell them that you're suffering, and that you're in bad shape, and you're thinking of killing yourself, and you need to be in the hospital, and I'd want them to get you there. You willing to have them know that?

C12 I don't want them to know anything. My dad's got heart trouble, and my mother ain't very good.

S13 And your mother what?

C13 And my mother isn't in good health either. If you called them and told them anything . . .

S14 I don't know. I've talked to a lot of people and I think I can handle them so they won't fall over or anything. But you certainly need somebody to take care of you right now. I think this is part of the big problem, that you have no relationships, you got nobody you can lean on. That's true isn't it?

C14 Yeah. The only thing I can lean on right now is the floor.

S15 I think, well, what I've found from my experience is that people usually come through better than you think they will, even a stranger will come through for you if you say I'm sick and I've got to get to the hospital, but in any case, I would like to talk with your parents about this. You can be sure I won't tell them anything about your sexual problems, and I'm sure they're worried about your coming home drunk every night.

C15 They don't know. They're always in bed.

S16 Are they not very bright?

C16 They're all right. They've done too much for me, actually.

Having proposed that there are correct ways of arriving at the statement that there is "no one to turn to" the reader may ask whether for us any assertion of that conclusion leads only to the problem of how to show that the assertion is correct. There are, apparently, incorrect assertions of this type. Members recognize assertions as incorrect, and our analysis permits their location.

(9) S1 Now you say you are contemplating suicide?

C1 That is right. I have been contemplating it now for three months. But I finally reached the end of my rope, I think.

S2 You think that the only pressure on you is financial?

C2 That is right. I don't think I'm insane. In order to think of suicide, I understand you've got to be insane.

S3 That's not necessarily true. Suppose we talk about your financial condition then.

C3 It's in a muddle, that's all. When I say it's in a muddle there is no embezzlement involved. It's just a lot of money that I have borrowed and I can't meet my obligations. A lot of it is personal, dear friends of mine, and a good portion I owe to the bank. The payments are due, and it's just pressing me and I have no other alternatives. I can't turn anywheres—that is, I still could. I could still go to friends of mine, but I've got a lot of pride and I don't want to do that anymore.

For Members, the fact that a breach may properly occur when the suicidal's account is given does not necessarily mean that it will. However, when suicidal persons do try to find out if it will, the attempt to find this out meets with special difficulties.

The problem is as follows: (1) There are known to be maxims which suggest that there are some actions that might cause a breach, but do not. This would cover cases of unmarried pregnant daughters. Although parents might propose in general that pregnancy of unmarried girls is terrible and that drastic actions, such as disowning, should be taken for those who get "that way," if a daughter is in such a situation, then the maxim proposes, to quote its use in one of the conversations, "parents close ranks around her, and give her the care she needs." There are such maxims for many "breach-usable" actions, but: (2) They seem uniformly to be maxims for which there are no procedures available to determine whether, on any given occasion of their relevance, it will be the breach or the maxim that will characterize the relevant *Rp*'s actions.

How *Rp* will behave does not seem readily enough determinable as a condition of informing them (or not) of an action upon which they may proceed to act in drastically different ways. The various ways that one in such a situation may attempt to find out what will be done are manifestly inadequate. They involve, for example, getting a discussion going on the matter in general or on current occurrences not within the given relational unit. For these, the proper conversational response seems to involve suggesting that a breach would be proper, whether one would resort to it or not were the proposed situation confronting him.

(10) S1 Is there anyone who you can lean on or turn to?

C1 Not in a situation like this.

S2 There is no one who knows what you're going through?
C2 No, and nobody—I'll explain this to you. I share an apartment with a fellow who is very close. However, this isn't the sort of thing I want to go into with him.
S3 Why?
C3 Well, let's say that this fellow is a very positive thinking type.
S4 Sort of aggressive . . .
C4 Very aggressive type of person, and well, for one thing, this would rather dunk him and he's always had a great deal of faith and—you name it, and he has leaned against me a number of times. Now for me to turn around and tell him this had been going through my mind and so forth and so on.
S5 You don't think he'd understand?
C5 He would understand it, but it would mean that he'd feel that he couldn't lean upon me or trust me or so forth to the degree that he has been doing.
S6 I don't quite follow that jump in reasoning. You feel that if he finds out you have a weakness or that you're feeling upset or despondent, that you would shake his faith in you?
C6 Yes. This is my feeling.
S7 Now sometimes we don't evaluate the people around us very well, and sometimes they respond better to a situation than we might imagine. But that's just a guess. I don't know him.
C7 Well, I have sort of tried to evaluate the situation as far as he is concerned; shall we say, by dropping subtle hints and referring to other people and so forth and so on, and this is the attitude that I get.
S8 He doesn't think much of anyone who feels that way?
C8 No. He's apt to consider them very weak and not able to handle problems and so forth and so on. And I don't want to create that impression in his mind that such a thing would happen to me.
S9 You'd rather be dead?
C9 Quite frankly, I think yes.

## V

It is apparent that central to the foregoing possibility is the rule of orderly use of *Rp* and its correlate. If a first position of *Rp* has an incumbent, then the fact that a suicidal person has a good warrant for not turning to them does not mean that turning to some second-position incumbent is thereby made proper.

The orderly use of *Rp* has a set of consequences which we shall collect in this section. Some of them have been mentioned or suggested earlier. First, on the occurrence of a death that officials feel might be suicidal, those who are concerned about determining whether or not it was attempt to locate and interrogate Members whom they feel might have relevant information. It does seem that *Rp* and the rules of its use provide officials with the how of such an investigation. It does seem that they use device *R* such that, knowing no more than the dead person's name, they can feel confident about who it is—that is, the potentially available possible persons—that they need to discover and contact in order to determine if the death was suicidal. Officials can suppose that if it is a suicide, and if there are Members of *Rp* available, then the dead person would (according to the rules of *Rp*) have informed the Members—some at least—that he was suicidal if he was. *Rp* is routinely used in this way by the police and coroners.

(11) [From a police report] "After we had completed our investigation at the hospital, we proceeded to the location and contacted victim's husband and her two sons. Upon questioning them, they repeated to the undersigned that it was their opinion that victim had probably died of natural causes; that she had never threatened or attempted suicide, and that they felt that the capsule found near the body had nothing to do with her death."

(12) [From a coroner's report] "It is felt that the person who should be contacted is Mr. R's wife, who, however, is in New Mexico, apparently permanently."

The fact that the first-position member is standardized is obviously crucial to officials. The specifics of the standardization are that it is expected that the fact of a first-position Member is something determinable by use of the dead person's name, so parent or spouse is sought and furthermore considered an exclusively appropriate repository; that is, if either exists, then the question of the success of an inquiry turns first on his availability. The fact of their unavailability seems to have as its consequence that the inquiry proceeds without further use of R, that is, without seeking to locate persons who might otherwise know whether a declaration of suicidalness was made. In short, officials consider the fact that locatable persons with whom they are unacquainted may be specified and that it is expectable that these persons will have information about the possible suicidalness of a currently dead person. *R* provides for that specification.

First-position Members may be seen to agree with officials that if someone had been suicidal he would have used *R* in its proper fashion to inform first-position Members of the fact of their suicidalness. Thus they conclude that if a possible suicide did not inform them that he was suicidal, then the death is not to be seen as suicidal. The fact that they may propose that they were not so informed recurrently constitutes the basis for a claim on their part that a decision that the death was suicidal should not be made or should be reversed.

(13) [From a letter asking coroner to reverse a decision of suicide] "I know this may seem just a nuisance to you, but as I said I can't explain how much it means to me not to have my mother's memory marred by there being any question of her death. I also do not ever want any of her grandchildren, of which there are thirteen, to ever know or feel there was ever any doubt in her death, because I know there couldn't have been.

"My husband spent some time with her that evening and she was in good spirits. She went to work Saturday in the morning and worked till 4:30 PM. She stayed and had coffee with one of the women and was in good spirits. Later in the evening she talked to the lady in the connecting apartment, telling her how badly she felt *physically* and that she intended moving in with me and making her home with us. Later that evening my sister-in-law called her on the phone and she was coughing a lot and felt very tired but was completely herself mentally and she said she felt so bad she was going right to bed and try to get some rest as she had to be to work very early Sunday morning. . . ."

(14) [From a coroner's report] "I called Mrs. P., to arrange an appointment. She said that her husband never talked about suicide, and it was not like him to commit suicide."

When a non-first-position incumbent is either turned to or happens on to information about suicidalness, then, even if he is unacquainted with first-position incumbents he feels that his proper course of action consists in either locating and informing a first-position incumbent of the presence of the state or advising the suicidal person that a first-person incumbent should be sought out.

(15) C1 I wonder if you could give me a little bit of advice. Last Saturday I had a neighbor and friend who came over. She

was very desperate about a family situation, and she told me that she just didn't want to live any more, and I really didn't take her seriously, but while she was here she took 20 sleeping pills.

S1 At your home?

C2 Yes. This was on Saturday—oh about 5 o'clock, I'd say, and so I have advised her to—I didn't know that she did this, you know, because it was when I went out of the room. And I had advised her to go and see a relative. I thought it could give her more help than I could. You know, to stay with, everything . . .

It may be that there is an extremely important consequence of the proper orderly use of *Rp*. To wit: if first-position Members fail to give help, it is not to be expected that any further-position Members will do so.

## VI

We have observed that both *R* and *K* can categorize any population. Since the rules organized with reference to *R* provide for the propriety and the procedure of the search for help for suicidalness and since in reference to *R* one who is, in reference to *K*, a "professional" is also (in our materials) a "stranger," i.e., a Member of *Ri*, the question must be posed: How is it that suicidal persons, or those they turn to for help in reference to *R*, come to treatment calling a professional's help proper?

Since it seems that the restriction to use of *Rp* is an obligation that the suicidal have to *Rp*, several procedures consistent with the nonviolation of that obligation may be found.

Members of *Rp* may tell the suicidal that they ought to turn to a professional (See Sec. III, quotation 1).

Members of *Rp* on being turned to for help may themselves seek out a professional.

If there are no Members of *Rp* then and whereas turning to a "stranger" may not involve turning to one who owes help, it is at least not improper.

(16) S1 Let me ask you another thing. We're very interested here. We get calls from people who often are very reluctant to give their names or just don't. Why is that? What prevents you or what makes you hesitate?

C1 Well. One feels like such a goddamn fool, you know?

S2 Why?

C2 I'm well over 21, and I should, you know, if I had a sister or a brother, or a husband or somebody to talk to that person. But I feel like such an idiot when you have to call up a stranger and say will you please let me talk to you.

In this case one is not replacing *R* with *K* but using *R* beyond a point where one has claims to get help.

If there are Members of *Rp*, then perhaps one does not violate his obligations to them if when he seeks out a nonmember he does it anonymously, i.e., without revealing who he is and thereby without revealing who his *Rp* are. Such an agency as the Suicide Prevention Center finds that suicidal persons who call it for help often will not give their names.[6] Perhaps this can be partially accounted for by the fact that in contacting a stranger they are violating the rules of *R* if they inform the stranger of their names. If a contact is made under these constraints, then it is obvious that a recipient who seeks to extend the contact to a therapy relation faces a special task. While we shall not consider here in detail how a professional can extend the contact in such a situation, an outline of a solution may be sketched.

Just as the appropriateness of *R* provides for the inappropriateness of *K*, so the appropriateness of *K* provides for the inappropriateness of *R*. Those who with reference to *R* are Members of *Rp* are likely with reference to *K* to be Members of *Ki*, where *Kp* is professionals and *Ki* laymen for any given trouble for which *K* is relevant.

The task of a professional, contacted initially as stranger, who seeks to provide for both the propriety of his having been sought out and a transformation of his status into the exclusively appropriate category of one to have been sought out is then to show the suicidal person that his trouble is one for which the profession has special and exclusive competence, so it is not merely not improper to turn to them, but also *Rp* cannot give help.

(17) S1 Well, let's get something straight. Anybody can get into a spot that he can't get out of by himself, where he needs some outside help.

C1 Yeah, so then we have to call strangers to get some help?

S2 Yes. If you break a leg, you wouldn't think anything of calling a doctor to have him help you.

C2 Yes, but that's different. But your own family should help you, don't you think?

S3 Maybe they should but they're not . . .

C3 Yeah. But I really do think, I mean . . .
S4 Actually I don't think your family could help you with this. I think this is something you're going to have to struggle out of inside yourself, and you will need professional help with this.
Now are you afraid this means you're crazy?
C4 No. I don't really think that I'm crazy.

Since the conclusion "no one to turn to" is arrived at by reference to *Rp*, it might be supposed that the replacement of *R* by *K* would in principle undercut the possibility of arriving at the conclusion. However, to remove the appropriateness of *R* may serve to undercut the obligatory character of the search for help. Furthermore, insofar as the use of *K* is seen as not merely conditional on need of help, but need of help plus ability to pay, those who lack the latter might see themselves in even a weaker position if they saw *K* as exclusively appropriate.

(18) S1 Well, certainly you need some help. There is a lot that can be done for this kind of problem.
C1 Like what? Like spend about forty-five dollars an hour by going some place like a psychoanalyst, which I don't have. I haven't been able to work for a year and a half.

## REFERENCES

1. The materials for this chapter were collected and a good deal of the analysis was done during the year I was a Fellow at the Center for the Scientific Study of Suicide. I am greatly indebted to that institution and to its director, Dr. Edwin Shneidman, for the financial and other support afforded me. Further analysis and the various drafts were written thereafter with financial support made available to me, under a grant from the U. S. Air Force, AF-AFOSR-757-65, by Professor Harold Garfinkel, principal investigator. I would like also to thank L. Churchill, E. Schegloff, and D. L. Weider for their criticisms of earlier drafts. The Department of Sociology, U.C.L.A., provided me with the time for pursuing these researches.
2. The materials analyzed consist of verbatim telephone conversations between staff members of The Suicide Prevention Center and a caller who is either suicidal or calling in reference to someone who is suicidal. In the quotations included in the text, S is a staff member and C is the caller. By the term "categorization device" we shall intend: Any "collection of membership categories," containing at least one category, which

may be applied to some population, containing at least one Member, so as to provide, by the use of some rules of application, the pairing of at least a population Member and a categorization-device member. A device is then a collection plus rules of application. The term "collection" is used only for some group of categories which Members do group together. When "member" is used with an uppercase first letter it refers to a user of the categorization device or one whom it is used on; when with a lowercase first letter it refers to a category, that is, a member of some collection.

3. It is the case that, for collections like *R*, if the collection is relevant then all of its categories are thereby relevant, whether or not some of them are actually occupied by an incumbent. For this reason we talk of "programmatic incumbents."
4. A. I. Richards, *Chisungu* (London: Faber & Faber, Ltd., 1956), pp. 38–39.
5. Mark Zborowski and Elizabeth Herzog, *Life is With People* (New York: Schocken Books, Inc., 1962), p. 289.
6. Norman Tabachnick and David J. Klugman, "No Name—A Study of Anonymous Suicidal Telephone Calls," *Psychiatry*, **28**:79–87, 1965.

# 11. Japanese Adolescent Suicide and Social Structure

Mamoru Iga

## Introduction

Suicide in Western countries has been studied rather extensively, but Japanese suicide has been analyzed neither extensively nor intensively in spite of its importance. Japan is unique in its very high suicide rates for females, rural areas, and for both young and old people. In all categories of age groups 15–19 and 20–24 for both sexes, Japanese suicide rates for 1952–1954 were more than two and a half times the rates reported for the country with the next highest rate.[1] In contrast with the suicide rates of 8.7 and 2.6 per 100,000 in 1955 for American 20- to 24-year-old males and females, respectively, the comparable figures for Japanese were 84.8 and 47.2, respectively.

The purpose of this chapter is to shed some light on Japanese suicide by analyzing suicide attempts in Kamakura (a city of 100,000, located about 30 miles southwest of Tokyo) from both psychological and sociological viewpoints. It will attempt to describe and analyze: (1) the psychological model of the suicide-attempting youth in Kamakura; (2) the social-structural model of their families; (3) the psychological model of Japanese youth in general; and (4) the social-structural model of Japanese society.

The hypotheses underlying the study of these four levels of models are: (1) suicide-attempting subjects show a higher degree of dependency, self-inflation (groundless self-assertion), and insecurity—which in this chapter are regarded as the basic elements of suicidal motivation; (2) the families producing suicidal subjects are characterized by disintegration and disadvantageous parent-child relations, which produce insecurity and provide little support for suicidal victims; (3) the high suicide rates of Japanese youth are at least partly explained by the similarity between suicidal and general youth in Japan with respect to the elements of suicidal motivation; and (4) Japanese social structure contains factors which make for a high degree of dependency, self-inflation, and insecurity in individuals.

Contributive causes of suicide are many: physical and mental illnesses, economic plight, altruism, alienation, the wish to meet the loved one in the next world, glorification of suicide, etc. Sociologists have studied suicide in relation to social structure, in terms of social solidarity and status integration.[2] The immediate cause of suicide, however, is not simply environment, whether physical, cultural, or social. Henry and Short discussed the relation between suicide and social environment (e.g., economic depression) in terms of the psychological concept of hostility against oneself; and Dublin maintained that "suicide is essentially a personal reaction," explaining it in psychological and psychiatric terms.[3] Henry and Short did not explain, however, what kind of perception of the situation makes for hostility against oneself, and Dublin did not analyze the victim's psychology in relation to his own immediate situation.

In order to explain suicide in its immediate situation, it seems to be necessary to analyze intervening factors between social structure and the individual's psychology, such as value conflicts, their effects upon his perception of the world, and consequent wishes or felt needs which motivate his action. Suicide studies require knowledge of what kinds of social conditions are perceived in what ways by an individual of what type of personality, resulting in what kinds of behavior.

One kind of perception conducive to suicide seems to be what Horney calls basic anxiety—diffuse fear as a reaction to the world which is perceived as unreliable, unfair, and merciless.[4] When an insecure individual perceives society in this way, two reactions—dependency and self-assertion—seem to become dominant for coping with a difficult situation. When the situation does not improve, conflicts between dependency and a wish for self-assertion intensify through the "neurotic trend toward perfectionism" and result in heightened insecurity.[5]

When the conflict between interstimulating wishes for dependency and for self-assertion becomes intensified because of insecurity, the consequence seems to be self-inflation, or the wish for "presenting to the self and to others qualities or achievements for which there is no adequate foundation."[6] A corollary of self-inflation is the wish to impose oneself upon others. When an object of self-inflation is not available because of fear of retaliation, fear of the loss of love, or some other reasons, hostility—a crystallized resentment—may be directed toward oneself rather than another. High suicide rates of Japanese youth suggest that Japanese social structure produces and intensifies a need for dependency, wish for self-assertion, and insecurity, without providing effective institutional outlets for hostility. It may be that the individual differences with regard to susceptibility to suicide lie in the different patterns of each of the three elements within the individual.

Self-assertion, dependency, and insecurity seem to correspond to Menninger's basic elements of suicide—the wish to kill (derived from hatred), the wish to be killed (stemming from guilt, masochism, and feeling of worthlessness), and the wish to die (derived from helplessness and despair).[7] The primary difference seems to be that the former categories are more oriented to specific social objects and therefore provide the link between psychological conditions and social structure. In addition, there seem to be more available tools for quantification of self-assertion, dependency, and insecurity.

We now turn to a discussion of dependency, self-inflation, and insecurity in relation to the four models given at the beginning of this paper.

## A Modal Personality Type of Suicide-Attempting Individuals in Kamakura

Kenshiyo Ohara, a Japanese psychiatrist, studied suicide attempts in Kamakura during the period from April, 1951 to August, 1959.[8] In his first study, 21 suicidal males and 23 suicidal females were compared with 50 applicants for the Japan Air Academy and 50 nurses at Jikei Medical School by use of the Thurstone test and *shinjoshitsu-kensa* (Temperament Test), which is used at most medical schools and hospitals in Japan. The average ages for the four groups are 27, 26, 27, and 24, respectively. In his second study, 26 suicidal males (average age, 23) and 29 suicidal females (average age, 21) were compared with 404 university, 261 high-school, and 249 junior-high-school students, 98 air force personnel (average age, 22), 94 nurses (average age, 21), and 149 randomly selected ordinary citizens (average age, 24 for males and 23 for females). For the second study the Yatabe-Guilford personality test was used.

In relation to Ohara's study it might be pointed out that (1) despite the fact that he entitled his article "A Study of the Factors Contributing to Suicide," factors in suicide attempts are not necessarily factors in actual suicide; (2) tests administered to those who attempt suicide may not show the temperament of the subjects under normal conditions; (3) in the two studies, different groups were studied with different tools, which results in poor comparability; and (4) the selection of control groups is not adequate because the suicidal and the control groups are not always comparable on major relevant factors; for example, in one case air force personnel and nurses are compared with suicidal subjects. But in spite of these difficulties, Ohara's data are still the most empirically based and reliable data on Japanese suicide available at present.

### *Dependency*

The first factor in suicidal motivation—dependency—may be analyzed on two levels: dependency for task performance and emotional dependency.

1. Dependency for Task Performance. According to the *shinjoshitsu-kensa* (Temperament Test), both male and female suicidal subjects are significantly different from control groups in *muryoku-sei* (lack of endurance) ($X^2=15.0$ for males; 27.6 for females; $P<.001$ for both).[9] This finding suggests that suicidal subjects are deficient in the capability and effort needed for problem-solving. Thurstone tests show significantly lower scores for suicidal than for control males on *D* (capability of taking initiative and responsibility); and both suicide-attempting males and females show significantly lower scores on V (capability of enjoying strenuous projects).[10]

Dependency may cause economic difficulties that, in turn, produce family problems. Therefore, it may be that although a great proportion of Japanese suicidal attempts involve economic and family troubles, a considerable proportion of these troubles result more basically from the dependency of suicidal persons.

2. Emotional Dependency. The second kind of dependency is emotional involvement. Emotional dependency upon family members seems to be indicated by answers to the question "Why is suicide bad?" Whereas 4.1 percent of college control subjects, comparable with suicidal subjects in age, state that suicide is bad because it makes parents and siblings sad, the comparable figure for the suicidal group is 14.5 percent ($X^2=8.6$. $P<.01$). The close similarity between the proportion (14.5 percent) for the suicidal group with an average age of 22 and the proportion (15.3 percent) for the junior-high students with an average age of 15 may imply the immaturity of the suicidal individuals. Emotional dependency as indicated by overconcern with the social object's reaction seems to be particularly strong among suicidal females. They show

significantly higher scores on *kakan-sei* (over-sensitiveness with suspicious trend) ($X^2=30.7$; $P<.001$), although there is no significant difference between suicidal and control males on this item.

Emotional dependency is related to De Vos's concept of "role narcissism," which he proposes as the major cause of Japanese suicide.[12] It is defined as "the over-involvement with one's social role which has become cathected by him as his meaning of life," i.e., the ego is dependent upon others for the meaning of life; hence, his strong concern with the others' reaction and with his own appearance. This concern with one's own appearance is related to the second factor of suicidal motivation in this chapter—self-inflation.

### *Self-Inflation (Groundless Self-Assertion)*

An operational index of self-inflation is a high degree of self-assertion plus ineffectual self-control. The need for self-assertion seems to be indicated by greatly higher scores for suicidal males and females than control subjects on Co (lack of cooperativeness) in combination with Ag (aggressiveness) on the Yatabe-Guilford tests.[13] This tendency is particularly marked in suicidal females, who show significantly higher scores on both *jiko-kenji-sei* (self-manifestation) and *sokuko-sei* (inclination toward immediate action) ($X^2=16.2$ and 6.2; $P<.001$ and $P<.01$, respectively). These findings seem to show that Japanese females whose personality is characterized by self-manifestation and immediate action are more likely to have difficulties because these qualities are not ordinarily expected from female roles in Japan.

The lack of effective self-control is shown by *bakuhatsu-sei* (explosiveness), on which female suicidal subjects show significantly higher scores than the comparable control group ($X^2=6.2$; $P<.02$). Suicidal females also show significantly higher scores on *kibun-ihatsu-sei* (inclination to flare up easily) ($X^2=10.3$; $P<.01$).

These findings seem to be supported, partly at least, by experiences of the contemplation of *iede* (running away from home), a form of self-assertion. Whereas the percentage of control-group members who had contemplated *iede* was 30.5, 65.5 percent of suicidal subjects did so ($X^2=27.2$; $P<.001$).

### *Insecurity*

The third factor in suicidal motivation is insecurity. The insecurity of suicidal persons seems to be indicated by higher scores on D (worries over possible misfortune), C (frequent shift of mood), I (inferiority feeling), N (nervousness), and O (lack of objectiveness; taking things personally) of the Yatabe-Guilford test and lower scores in E (emotional stability) and S (sociability) of the Thurstone test.[14]

A case history translated from an article by Ohara, Aizawa, and Shimizu illustrates the interaction between the need for dependency, the wish for self-inflation, and insecurity:[15]

Shinichiro W. was the fifth of seven children in a farming family in Shizuoka Prefecture. After graduating from high school, he joined a *Jieitai* (self-defense army) in Sendai, about 200 miles from his home. He had served in the army after World War II for two and a half years before his suicide attempt. He was obedient, reserved, industrious, unsociable, and *kage-benkei* ("bully at home but gentle outside").

He fell in love with Reiko S., a twenty-three-year-old nursing assistant. She was beautiful but vain and conceited. She was once chosen as beauty queen of the city and enjoyed many admirers. Somehow Shinichiro made her believe that he was from a wealthy family, and he won her over several competitors. Wanting to marry her, he asked for his eldest sister's opinion, as he was accustomed to do. The sister was a telephone operator at a hospital near their parents' home. She favored the marriage and obtained a nursing job for Reiko at the hospital.

One day she took Reiko and Shinichiro, who had returned on leave, to their parents' home for the purpose of introducing the prospective sister-in-law to their family. The parents were not pleased with their son's choosing his wife without consulting them, but they yielded to the wish of the young people. In accordance with the sister's suggestion, it was decided that Reiko could commute to the hospital from the parents' home on the ground that the future bride should become accustomed to the customs of the parents-in-law. The father also secured the promise of a clerical job for Shinichiro at the hospital in preparation for the time when he would be released from the army.

Reiko formed friendly but flirting relationships with several men, which were not pleasant for Shinichiro's family members. Partly because of her conceited and exploitive personality and partly because of her verbal complaint to outsiders that her fiancé's family was not as wealthy as she believed, conflicts developed between her and Shinichiro's family, including the eldest sister.

Wishing to go back to Sendai, she sent a telegram for Shinichiro to return and settle the matter. When he came back, his family members were cold to him, and he could not get *kozukai* (petty cash) which his parents would give to him when he returned from the army. He did not have much money, nor did Reiko. They spent the night on the beach and at a railway station. The deadline for returning to the barracks became overdue, and Shinichiro had no idea how to get the railway fare to Sendai. He asked Reiko to get sleeping pills. When she brought a bottle of 200-tablet *brobarin,* he swallowed about two-thirds of the contents. Upset with the situation, Reiko took the rest.

Ohara summarized the personality traits of suicidal subjects as: lack of ego differentiation; lack of will and endurance; lack of efforts to solve their own problems; lack of a realistic definition of the situation; emotional instability and withdrawal; a considerably high degree of self-examination, regret, and disappointment about past deeds; and the awareness of the necessity for one's own efforts.[16]

These psychological characteristics of suicide-attempting Japanese today are quite different from the type of suicide with which Japan has been identified—the altruistic suicide in Durkheim's typology. The altruistic suicide is characterized by a mystical feeling of being engulfed in something that is regarded as the real essence of life. Since World War II, the Japanese seem to have lost this sense of mystical dedication to a cause. When a suicide appears to have occurred because of shame or a wish to maintain family honor, such sociologistic motives seem to be used as instruments for satisfying a more basic psychologistic motive (e.g., hostility, wish for escape, etc.). We can say, following Devereux, that subjective motives may seek and find an ego-syntonic outlet in a sociologistic motive.[17] Such traditional Japanese suicide as *harakiri* for honor may be regarded as biologically nonadaptive (i.e., against biological survival) but subjectively adaptive (i.e., the victim himself may have thought that he, or his name actually, would live forever because of his biological death). This idea of subjective adaptation seems to correspond to what Shneidman calls "post-self."[18] Present-day Japanese suicide typically seems to be for the purpose of adjustment to fear or hostility (tension reduction) rather than adaptation (survival), because "relatively few modern Japanese believe in or are concerned with life beyond death."[19]

Japanese suicide today does not seem to fall into the category of egoistic suicide either, because egoistic suicide is characterized by a retreat that is far from the meaning given by the society and which is without a sustaining individualistic sense of one's own purpose. Many Japanese suicides seem to reveal too strong a concern with the reaction of others for "the meaning given by the society" to be called egoistic.

The third type of suicide in Durkheim's typology is anomic; it appears to be applicable to many Japanese suicides at present. De Vos's concept of "role narcissism," or "overinvolvement with one's social role which has become cathected by him as his meaning of life," is useful. When this type of person experiences the sudden disruption of his life pattern by economic, social, or political upheaval, he is an easy victim of suicide. Because of difficulties involving his inflexible personality under such circumstances, he may want to "escape the necessity to redefine himself"[20] or to escape from his damaged self image.

## Social-Structural Model of the Families Producing Suicide-Attempting Young Japanese

We have seen that the Japanese youths in Kamakura who attempt suicide seem to be characterized by a combination of intense dependency, self-inflation, and insecurity. It is assumed that this personality type of suicidal individual is related to certain family situations and that the family situation producing suicide attempts will show the lack of integration and disadvantageous parent-child relationships (including lack of understanding and intimacy), all of which lead to insecurity in suicidal individuals and to lack of support from family members.

Ohara analysed the families of 82 suicide-attempting individuals for the incidence of suicide, mental disease, *shinkei-suijyaku* (nervous breakdown), *shinkeisho* (neuroses), epilepsy, *henjin* (eccentric person), and *iede* (running away from home).[21] He found at least one of the above abnormalities occurring in 25.6 percent of families producing individuals who attempted suicide as compared with their only 8.3 percent of 1,472 control families ($X^2=29.47$; $P<.001$). Whereas 0.7 percent of families of the control group produced more than two of the above abnormalities from a family, 7.3 percent of the suicidal group did so ($X^2=14.4$; $P<.001$); and whereas only 1.6 percent of the control group showed the incidence of suicide among family members, 6.1 percent of the suicidal group did so ($X^2=4.51$; $P<.05$). The above differences are assumed to represent the transmission of disadvantageous family atmosphere to suicidal victims.

One of the important factors in a disadvantageous family atmosphere is the absence of parents. The percentage of families with neither the biological father nor mother living with the subject at the age of 17 was 10.9 percent for the suicidal and only 0.9 percent for the control group ($X^2=25.9$; $P<.001$). This finding is supported by the percentage of families in which neither father nor mother took care of the subjects before the latter's grammar-school age, the percentage being 13.4 for the suicidal and 3.1 for the control group ($X^2=15.2$; $P<.001$).

Where there were parents who took care of the children, the family situation producing suicidal individuals was characterized by more stressful parent-child relations. This may be inferred from the frequency of, and reasons for, *iede* (running away from home); and by authoritarian parent-child relations with a concomitant lack of understanding and intimacy.

Suicidal persons significantly more frequently contemplated *iede* than nonsuicidal subjects. The percentages of persons who had contemplated *iede* were 65.5 and 31.5 for the suicidal and the control groups, respectively ($X^2=27.2$; $P<.001$). It may be assumed that there are common causes between suicide attempts and the contemplation of *iede* by the suicidal subjects. As reasons for the contemplation of *iede,* the largest proportion (31.9 percent) of suicidal subjects gave "rebellion against the family"; 23.5 percent, "longing for freedom"; and 19.2 percent, "family disharmony." Other reasons given were "being scolded" (10.6 percent) and "failure in test, at school, and at work" (4.1 percent). These figures apparently represent a close connection between suicide attempts of Japanese youth and family problems.

The stressful family situation also seems to be indicated by too authoritarian relations with a resulting lack of understanding and intimacy between parent and child. The criticism of the father as *kagebenkei* (smiling outside and bullying inside home) was given by 19.2 percent of suicidal subjects as compared with 9.0 percent for the control group ($X^2=3.96$; $P<.05$). The close similarity between the suicide group with an average age of 22 (10.9 percent) and the junior-high-school group (11.2 percent) on the father "restricting freedom too much" is noticeable compared with 5.5 percent for college control-group members, who are comparable in age with the suicide subjects. This may represent the interaction between an immature personality and an authoritarian family atmosphere for the suicidal victims.

A frequent criticism against the mother among the suicidal subjects was: "Mother did not treat father right." The percentage was 12.7 for suicidal cases as against 5.7 percent for the control group. Although the difference is not statistically significant, the chi-square value of 3.27 is very close to the 5 percent significance level and appears to show a tendency of the mothers involved in suicidal cases toward a "bossy" attitude, which violates the expected role of a gentle, kind, and self-sacrificing mother. When the father is strong and loving, the family may not produce suicide, which is consistent with what Meerloo says.[22] However, in such an authoritarian society as Japan, there tends to be a lack of understanding and intimacy between father and child; the mother is often the only source of love and security for children. Nevertheless, *kakatenka* ("petticoat government") is not rare among Japanese. When the mother not only fails as the source of affection but also assumes an authoritarian role herself, the child may suffer from rebellion against the source of love and security.

Usually the authoritarian mother is associated with a weak father who suffers from a sense of inadequacy because he has failed to achieve the ideal social expectation of male superiority. Also the authoritarian mother frequently has a strong desire for success. When this type of mother projects her ambition onto her child, her expectations for him may become unrealistic, especially if she concentrates all her hopes and wishes on the child's success. Under these conditions the pressure upon the child may be unbearable. This is a particularly important factor in Japanese suicide, because, as De Vos found, the sense of guilt of Japanese youth is not as much related to violation of conscience, as in Western culture, as to failure in satisfying maternal expectations.[23]

The mother's failure as a source of love and security coupled with a weak father as a cause of suicide attempt is exemplified by the following case history:[24]

Subject: Female, aged 16, factory worker. Stubborn, extrovert, gay.

Father: 54, factory worker. Sincere, but reticent and reserved, leaving family matters entirely to his wife.

Mother: 53, nagging and peevish, short-tempered, domineering.

After graduating from a junior high school, the subject worked as a clerk. Because of her repeated love affairs, she was not regarded highly by her company, and her family was rather antagonistic toward her.

One morning when she returned from staying out overnight, she was forcibly taken by her mother to a physician for a "proof of immorality," although she was in her menstrual period. After this humiliating incident, she attempted suicide by taking 100 sleeping pills. When she was awakened, her siblings sneered at her inability even to die.

When an unrequited love affair motivated her to attempt suicide again, none of her family came to the hospital to see her. She said, "I cannot trust people; I don't know genuine parental love."

This case history shows not only disadvantageous parent-child relations but cold reactions of the family to suicidal victims, evidencing little psychological support from the family. In Ohara's study of 23 suicide-attempting cases which were taken to hospitals in Kamakura during a 5-month period in 1960, the reaction of the families, including both parents, was recorded for 15 cases. There were four cases in which parents "worried" about the victims. In one case, only the mother worried; and in three cases, only the older brother did. In the remaining seven cases no family members (including parents) showed any compassionate concern for the suicidal victims.[25]

In summation, we notice a considerable extent of family disintegration in suicide cases. The lack of concern, understanding, respect, and responsibility of family members toward suicide victims seems to characterize families that produce suicide attempts. On the other hand, family integration and honor (including success) are still ideal norms of Japanese families, as is the authoritarian stratification by age and sex within the family. For attaining the goals of family integration and honor, such values as propriety, obligation, and achievement of family goals are strongly upheld; and children are disciplined to conform to these norms by force (physical punishment) and fear (negative informal social sanction or withdrawing of assistance). Paternalism is another method of keeping children in line. Japanese society teaches children that whatever parents may do to them arises from parental wishes for their better future, so that if children do not conform to parental expectations, they should feel shame or guilt. There is a strong pressure to censure rebellious children even when parents are noticeably wrong. Where a member endangers family integration and honor, the result is a sense of shame and hostility directed toward the "disgraceful" member.

The typical response of suicide-producing families to strain caused by a "misbehavior" of their family member seems to be first shame and then suppression and hiding of the disturbing element. When the disturbing element (i.e., the suicidal subject's behavior) goes beyond their control, they become hostile toward the "culprit" who disgraces the family honor and finally withdraw their support from him. This is the way that insecure Japanese show that they are not "bad"; they are not responsible for the deviant's "shameful" behavior. Society's reaction is evidently more important to them than their own family member. This response pattern is shown in the indifferent or hostile attitudes of parents toward suicidal victims in Ohara's study reported above.

## The Psychological Model of Japanese Youth

From the above, it would seem that the suicide-producing family situation is characterized by disintegration and disadvantageous parent-child relations, which leads to insecurity and lack of support for persons in need. Although the difference in family situation affects the individual's susceptibility to suicidal motivation, the high suicide rates of Japanese youth suggest that the essential elements of suicidal motivation are shared by a large proportion of Japanese youth. What then are the typical personality patterns of the general youth in Japan?

### *Personality Structure—Mode of Relating to Social Object*

The basic mode of Japanese youth of relating themselves to social objects seems to be characterized by (1) dependency, lack of identity, and strong concern with the others' reaction; (2) a narcissistic wish for self-inflation; (3) insecurity and deep seated pessimism; and (4) masochism, indicated by guilt, shame, and easy embarrassment.

Dependency and lack of identity are indicated by such expressions as *ware ga nai* ("no self"), which is proposed by Ohara as a major factor in the high rate of *oyako shinjyu* (parent-child suicide); and *jibun ga nai* ("egolessness") and *amae* (the wishes to be loved and for dependency), as given by Doi as major factors in mental disturbances of Japanese youth.[26] As Doi maintains, *amae* is the key for understanding Japanese personality. The need for social relatedness which has been pointed out by other writers on Japanese personality[27] seems to derive from *amae*. Caudill points out two characteristic patterns of Japanese emotion: an "emphasis on non-sexual satisfaction" and conscious "denial of pleasure and emotion."[28] These two emotional patterns also appear to be rooted in the basic wishes to be loved and for dependency, because the emphasis on sexual satisfaction and on pleasure and emotion tends to make individuals more competitive, to disrupt the group life, and consequently to hamper the satisfaction of the basic wish of *amae*. It is somewhat surprising that dependency indicated by the emphasis on "collateral" (or group) relations is more marked among young Japanese than among the older generation, whereas the individualistic orientation is more noticeable among the older than the younger generation, as shown by Caudill and Scarr.[29]

Another characteristic of Japanese youth is narcissism. "The optimism and self-confidence of Japanese youths are well-established facts," and "hankering after fame is common among Japanese youths." However, Stoetzel thinks that Japanese self-confidence "tends toward wishful thinking, to the illusion that what one desires must necessarily be true . . . thinking of the power one will acquire when grown up, and of the status, quite different from what it is now, to which one will attain."[30] This wishful thinking may be interpreted psychologically as a narcissistic regression to the belief of infantile omnipotence. One of the important indications of narcissism is a strong concern with one's own appearance. The Japanese, as De Vos points out, are "unduly preoccupied with standards of excellence. . . . They worry about how they appear to others, and sometimes less obviously, they worry about how they appear to themselves."[31]

When *amae* (the infantile desire for primary love) is frustrated, narcissistic regression occurs. As Doi implies, *amae* and narcissism coexist in an immature Japanese personality.[32] When intense self-love cannot be satisfied, a profound pessimism may result—more deep-seated than the surface optimism. Many Japanese youth lack confidence in their own capability to solve their own problems, as represented by their strong wishes for dependency and for group affiliation together with their tendencies to avoid responsibility. Although Japanese youth "feel that they ought to take part in the life of the community . . . at the same time they feel that they are unfitted to undertake this task," and they tend to "evade the issue when asked for details" regarding how to participate in community life.[33] Sofue's projective tests (used by Stoetzel[30]) show the inclination of Japanese youth to see the tragic aspects of life. Their insecurity is further evidenced by a large proportion of those studied by Stoetzel who show passivity and resignation (three-fourths), a strong fear of illness (one-fourth), and the feeling of despair (28 percent of males and 19 percent of females). In industrial areas, such as Yawata, the number of persons showing despair amounted to 64 percent.[34]

Another characteristic of the Japanese mode of relating to others is masochism, which seems to be a result of the combination of dependency, self-inflation, and insecurity. Masochism is basic to the Japanese virtue of patience or endurance. Their patience derives from "an unconscious equation underlying cases of moral masochism that present suffering will be repaid in future triumph."[35]

### *Unifying Principles—Mode of Approaching Social Objects*

With a personality type characterized by dependency, self-inflation, insecurity, and masochism, the typical methods for Japanese youth to approach others seem to be conformity, self-effacement, and avoidance. The highest value of Japanese culture is loyalty and propriety. Group loyalty for them means "not only identification with group goals but a willingness to cooperate with the other members and to respond to group consensus enthusiastically,"[36] which leads to conformity.

When inferiority and conformity combine, self-effacement seems to be a dominant social technique. Self-effacement may take the form of politeness and humility. To present oneself as inferior is at least safer than self-assertion, which may make for frustration later. Besides, self-effacement on the part of inferiors boosts the ego of authoritarian superiors. By utilizing this tendency, the subordinate may satisfy the need for dependency. On the other hand, the lack of self-effacement on the part of subordinates may be regarded as *namaika* ("bumptious") by superordinates and invite disapproval or punishment.

The avoidance of a new experience which might cause frustration is common among Japanese. This is predictable upon consideration of their concern with "face" and their deep-seated insecurity, especially lack of self-confidence.

### *Response to Strain*

The typical responses of Japanese to strain seem to be (1) acceptance, (2) escape, and (3) compensatory and identification defenses. Acceptance may take the form of resignation (e.g., fatalism) or regression, such as narcissistic self-inflation (e.g., boasting of groundless achievement or unrealistic ambition). Escape may be escape from difficulty or from a damaged self. As Stoetzel noticed, "one of the commonest mechanisms is that of escape, and certain signs of escapism are clearly discernible in relations of Japanese."[37] Suicide is a socially acceptable form of escape. A politician's suicide may not only "purify" his misconduct but also elicit a great amount of sympathy and even praise for his "integrity."

Compensation takes various forms, such as gossiping and finding scapegoats in inferiors, making the inferiors more susceptible to suicide. One typical Japanese form of compensation for tension reduction is the rather obsessive interest in physical pleasure—eating, drinking, bathing, and sexual activity. Traditionally, the wife has never been the primary object of erotic pleasure; hence the "emphasis on other than sexual satisfaction" in marital relationships; but activity with professionals (prostitutes, *geisha*, and waitresses) has been highly cherished by many Japanese males.[38] The Japanese liking for artistic activities or objects also may be regarded as a displaced wish for self-expression. Mild illness is a customary defense mechanism for getting attention among Japanese. Suicide also may be regarded as a Japanese way of self-expression and an attention-getting mechanism.

Identification with someone or something underlies Japanese loyalty to their groups. Emperor worship, the concept of *shinkoku* ("Divine Nation"), and the emphasis on group honor are examples of this type of identification. Many Japanese endured difficulties, poverty, and wars for their emperor worship, nationalism, or family honor. Identification not only provided the ego with an ideal to strive for but also furnished a defense for tension reduction. It is essential to Durkheim's concept of the altruistic suicide. Identification, however, seldom seems to lead to suicide of present-day Japanese. This assumption appears to be substantiated by Ohara's characterization of suicide-attempting Japanese as reported above.

In summary: The typical personality of Japanese youth as described by Stoetzel, Vogel, and others can be summarized as follows: (1) Mode of relating to others characterized by dependency, self-inflation, insecurity, and masochism; (2) mode of approaching others characterized by a value set on conformity and collectivity orientation, together with self-effacement and avoidance; and (3) response patterns characterized by acceptance (e.g., resignation, regression), escape, and compensation. These traits correspond to the personality characteristics of suicide-attempting subjects summarized by Ohara, as cited above. The difference between the suicidal and nonsuicidal Japanese youths seems to be in the intensity of these traits possessed by particular individuals. But the similarity between the two categories of Japanese youth is one of the major causes of their high suicide rates.

## Suicide Attempts and Japanese Social Structure

If Japanese young people generally show dependency, self-inflation, and insecurity, then the high suicide rates of Japanese youth suggest that the social structure in that country produces and reinforces these elements of suicidal motivation. Their high suicide rates also suggest the social structure's influences over the personality of people forming the social environment of suicidal individuals. Let us consider each one of these elements in order.

### *Influences of Social Structure upon Suicidal Motivation*

1. Dependency and Japanese Social Structure. The basic unit of Japanese society is a solidarity group, whether family, school, firm, or power group. Japanese tend to follow the goal set for them by parents and leaders. The habit of asking advice for goal attainment is very strong and expected even among adults. This dependency seems to be produced by socialization in infancy and later by the effects of social structure, especially of occupational structure, upon personality.

2. Dependency Produced by Socialization. The effects of Japanese

socialization upon dependency have been pointed out by several writers.[39] Especially marked are (1) incessant physical contact and proximity of mother and child, such as holding the baby on the mother's back and sleeping and bathing together frequently, even at early school ages; (2) the inculcation of fear of the outside, strangers, and ghosts, with the assurance that children will be safe as long as they are with the mother; and (3) early indulgence, with little disciplining and much praise. The indulgence of the child is largely due to Japanese social structure. The mother's position is precarious, yet she is held responsible for the child's behavior, even though she does not have clear authority for laying down rules. The cry of children often infuriates the authoritarian father, who blames the mother for her inefficiency. The best way for her to win the child's cooperation without making a commotion is by praise, flattery, and indulgence. "Bribery" with goodies is common. In addition, the child is the only object for unrestrained expression of the mother's affection in a formalistic authoritarian society, especially when the relationship between her husband and his mother is particularly close. Such extremely close mother-son attachment has been reported as a characteristic of Japanese culture by Caudill.[40]

The father too has a precarious position, because in an authoritarian society he too is often a victim of exploitation by his superiors. Inferiors provide scapegoats for superiors to compensate for their frustrations. When the frustrated father takes his spite out on his children, the mother oversympathizes with them because of her own position as a victim of suppression. When she cannot verbally show her sympathy with them, she overacts in behavior. The father himself may feel embarrassed by his exploitation of the children for his tension reduction and then be indulgent in order to counteract his own embarrassment.

3. Dependency Produced by Occupational Structure. In the United States the occupational institution is anchored to competency and competition; in Japan it is anchored to loyalty and dependency. Loyalty and dependency are cultivated not only by socialization but also by the occupational structure. The effects of occupational structure upon personality may be analyzed on three levels: (1) Dependency is required for adjustment, (2) dependency is rewarded with security, and (3) violation of dependency is punished.

*Requirement of dependency.* When group solidarity is the basic value and authority is "right," then dependency is required for the individual's adjustment. Large Japanese firms, which are less paternalistic than are smaller ones, obtain dependent but competent employees by two methods: the employment of fresh graduates from "good" universities, who were reared in "sound" families; and the requirement of an introduction, personal connection, and, if necessary, investigation of personal background. More important than an employee's competency in any particular tasks is his capability to merge into the social system of a particular company.

The importance of this method of securing employees is evidenced by the great economic difficulty experienced by children of divorced or widowed mothers. As Vogel found, they generally fail to secure preferable jobs because of three rationalizations by company administrators: a fatherless boy would not have been given proper disciplining and "moral" training; he is apt to be dishonest because of his greater need for money; and he will be a greater burden on the company if he is hired, because a firm ordinarily assumes some responsibility for the welfare of its workers and their families.[41] The most important reason for this practice seems to be that children reared under economic and family difficulties will more likely be resentful toward society, and this attitude may affect other workers against the company.

*Reward for dependency.* As long as workers are loyal to the company and satisfactory to management, they are secure. More than half of the sixty administrators studied by Whitehill and Takezawa stated that "even under the condition of serious and prolonged decline in business, the worker can look to the company for a good deal of employment security—remaining employed either at normal pay, or at shorter hours with less take-home pay."[42] The large company often obtains for the retiring loyal worker a position at another company under its influence. Children of retiring loyal workers usually receive preference in employment.

Another form of reward for loyalty is that the basic criteria for payment are length of service and rank, followed by age and family size. Competence constitutes only a small part of the criteria for security or promotion.[43] Rewards for loyalty also include a variety of fringe benefits, such as company housing either at no charge or at special low rent to employees; recreational programs, such as staff trips at the company's expense; a cooperative system of purchases; health insurance provided by the company; and free company bathhouses, which provide an opportunity for social association of workers and their families. Abegglen found that the work group in Japan is quite different from the work group in the United States and more nearly akin to American family groups in terms of motivation and reward.[44]

*Punishment on violation.* The importance attached to introduction and to personal connection and the investigation of the applicant's background function as deterrents to disobedience. In addition, various forms of informal negative sanction are used for social control—for example, postponement, avoidance, vagueness, and ignoring. These forms of informal sanction are very effective because of the great sensitivity to social pressures among Japanese. De Vos interprets this sensitivity as derived from underlying infantile fear of abandonment.[45] It is also related to the decreased prospect of security once one becomes the object of social censure in Japan, primarily because of the difficulty of finding jobs.

4. Self-Inflation and Japanese Society. The characteristics of narcissism—vanity, conceit, craving for prestige and admiration, a desire to be loved with an incapacity to love others, withdrawal from others[46]—seem to be very common among not only "insecure" but also normal Japanese. This narcissistic personality is rooted in socialization and the high value on achievement. The high value on success is generally true among Japanese regardless of class. Japanese farmers were found (by use of the Thematic Apperception Test) to be "very much concerned with getting ahead and have always had aspiration characteristic of the middle class."[47] Hero worship has been traditionally prevalent and intense among young Japanese. The narcissistic desire for success seems to be different from the nonnarcissistic one in that the former lacks in (1) the wish for development in one's own potentiality—physical, social, emotional, and intellectual—and in the awareness that success is a by-product of self development; and (2) in the capability for realistic definition of the situation and for scheduling to select immediate goals which will facilitate the attainment of ultimate goals. The lack of realistic definition of the situation on the part of suicidal individuals was found by Ohara, as reported earlier in this chapter.

The intense desire for success is largely due to the Japanese mother's projection and compensation. Since the mother's status rises and falls according to her child's success or failure, her wish for self-assertion is channeled through the child's success in education, especially in examinations.[48] Her own achievement drive is projected to the child, or the child is used as compensation for her frustration. The high value on competition and achievement is expressed in many subtle forms, such as intense shame-avoidance demands, strong concern for praise, and a marked liking for decorations, formal titles, and verbal deference.

5. Insecurity and Japanese Society. When dependency and wish for self-assertion are both strong, the discrepancy between them will cause insecurity. But insecurity alone may also cause the discrepancy. What social structural factors make for insecurity in Japanese youth? Authoritar-

ian social relations imply the ever-present threat of exploitative aggression by superiors, whether father or employer. Superiors may take out their spite on inferiors at their whim. The threat of economic insecurity is real to most Japanese. Lower-class people seldom have secure jobs. Even though middle-class husbands may have secure jobs, wives and children seldom get additional income, not only because of limited opportunity but also because of social stigma against working middle-class wives and children. Security crumbles quickly when some emergency occurs, because of lack of developed social-welfare services by the government.[49] Unemployment is a constant threat under an authoritarian system where the superior's whim can ruin the individual's security, although the unemployment rate in Japan is always distorted by underemployment and "returning to the family work." Once unemployed, a person seldom thereafter obtains a respectable job. Even if fortunate enough to find a new job, "he will have to start again at the bottom, with a low salary and with little hope of rapid promotion."[50]

An important factor in Japanese social structure that produces insecurity is the vital importance of entrance examination to "good" universities. As Vogel says, in a society "where one has no place to turn in time of need, and welfare is provided by neither the government nor the family nor personal connections, the large firm assumes a critical importance, because it provides security as well as income."[51] However, entrance into a large firm is determined by graduation from, and entrance into, a "good" university, which, in turn, requires a high-class position at all levels of schooling. Japanese children and youth are generally in incessant competition for a higher standing at all times. The competition between parents, particularly mothers, for a higher position for their children is extremely intense.[52] Often the mother's affectional reward to them is contingent upon their standing at school.

The insecurity of Japanese youth is much more deeply rooted than simply economic or educational. Historical traditions and conventional child-rearing practices appear to be still affecting the personality of Japanese people today.

The insecurity of Japanese is historical. Their living for a long time under the strict police system of the Tokugawa regime with collective responsibility not only for family members but also for neighbors and villagers conditioned them to refrain from self-expression. Espionage and severe punishment, which characterized the Tokugawa administration, frightened people into "taking their proper places." The privilege of *samurai* (retainers to feudal lords) who could kill commoners with impunity[53] made the latter cautious not to say anything that might incur even a slight hostility in samurai. Samurai himself was in the same precarious situation in relation to his equals and superiors. The Japanese saying, *Mono ieba kuchibiru samushi akino saze* (Opening lips, we feel autumn wind cold) implies that any statement may be unfavorably interpreted, and therefore to be silent is wisest.

Japanese insecurity is also rooted in their child-rearing practices. The discontinuity in cultural conditioning[54] which occurs therein may partly explain their insecurity. Their infancy is a period of indulgence, which causes security and developing expectations in the child that others are always on the watch to satisfy his needs. When later these expectations are not satisfied and he is thereby frustrated, insecurity prevails, leading to narcissistic self-infatuation. The disciplining of the child in toilet control, bowing to visitors, walking, speaking, etc., increases with age. There is strong competition among parents to show how well their children have been trained in early infancy. As a result, when the autonomy that such behavior requires is imposed upon an infant before his neuromuscular system is ready to assume it, he often forms a sense of inadequacy, which leads to insecurity.

Insecurity is heightened by the authoritarian relation between father and child. The father tends to exploit age differences by using the child as a scapegoat upon whom he can take out his spite. In many cases "disciplining" by an insecure father is a compensative aggression. Unreasonable and inconsistent punishment leads to resentment and defiance in the child, who, being forbidden to express his antagonism toward the father, develops anxiety and insecurity in relation to authority figures in general. This exploitation may be frequent, for under the authoritarian social system the father himself is a scapegoat for his superiors to utilize. If the mother assumes the disciplinarian role, as we often see in Japanese families, the child experiences insecurity primarily because of a lack of any source of love and affection. This is particularly true with middle-class children, because their opportunity for spontaneous self-expression is much more limited than it is with upper- or lower-class children.

Another derivation of insecurity in Japanese youth may be a failure to learn a wider range of effective techniques to approach superiors other than by conformity and submission. Japanese youth tend to use some defense mechanisms, especially compensatory scapegoating and identification, but they seem to lack more positive mechanisms with which to attack problems directly. The narrow range of social techniques and adjustment mechanisms, with a resultant inflexibility, leads to insecurity.

*Effects of Social Structure upon Social Environments Conducive to Suicide*

Thus far, this chapter has described the characteristics of Japanese social structure—the primary goal of integration, the stratified social system with paternalistic authoritarianism, an emphasis on virtues conducive to social control (conformity, obligation, propriety, group loyalty, etc.)—and has emphasized the types of defense mechanisms which reduce tension without endangering social order, e.g., scapegoating and identification. These characteristics contribute to high suicide rates not only because of their effects upon need for dependency, wish for self-inflation, and insecurity of suicidal persons but also because of their effects upon the personality of people surrounding suicidal victims. These effects may be analyzed on two levels: first, effects on the personality of governmental leaders, and second, effects on the public.

1. The Governmental Indifference to The Individual's Welfare. Ohara lists the lack of governmental concern with the individual's welfare as the primary cause of *oyako-shinjyu* (parent-child suicide).[55] Historically, when survival in fights with enemies was the primary goal, the basic principle for Japanese rulers was control by force and fear. They thought that wealth made people independent and difficult to control while education made people critical of society and dangerous for rulers. Consequently Japanese governments in pre-modern days not only were indifferent to the public welfare but tried actively to keep the masses poor and ignorant. Even in modern Japan social education has been concerned with teaching conformity and propriety for social integration rather than individual development and welfare. We cannot expect this long tradition to change rapidly simply because of technological modernization in recent years. As recently as after World War II, to the complaint that poor people could not afford to buy their staple food (rice), a minister of finance (who later became premier) answered that the poor did not have to eat rice; cheaper grains were available. This attitude of governmental leaders toward the public welfare will be better understood when we know the typical personality type of governmental officers in Japan.

Assuming that the work situation or occupational role more likely molds the personality of persons engaged in it to fit the ideal type of personality required for the best performance in that occupation, we can expect a high correlation between the basic characteristics required for an occupation and the typical personality type of those engaged in it. Quigley and Turner in 1956 cited five forces in Japanese politics which were traditional but also operating currently.[56] They are: (1) dynasticism and Emperor worship; (2) dualism, or the coexistence of Emperor worship and rule under the actual power holder; (3) militarism, or the glorification of the *samurai* code, with an emphasis on duty and self-sacrifice; (4) bureaucracy; and (5) group consciousness. These five characteristics of Japanese politics fairly well indicate the personality structure, unifying principles, and response patterns of government officials in that country.

Japanese bureaucracy seems to reveal the personality type of Japanese leaders. Japanese governmental officers are highly bureaucratic in terms of specialization, formalization of roles, and a hierarchy of authority. They are not, however, simply bureaucratic but "bureaucratic despots in their relation to the masses."[57] To the Japanese, bureaucracy is largely the method by which governmental officials avoid responsibility by distributing it to elders, advisers, councils, and other officers, in order to shield themselves from criticism. As Quigley points out, the coexistence of "high ambition" with the inclination to "seek and enjoy the exercise of power" on the one hand and the immature wish to avoid responsibility on the other seems to be the most important feature of Japanese governmental officers and politicians.[58]

Authority has been maintained by the effective socialization of children to conformity, endurance, and self-sacrifice, severe punishment for violation, and strong informal control by gossiping and ostracism together with the fear of espionage. Although the maintenance of authority is much more difficult since World War II, because of the general Americanization of Japan, the basic attitudes of Japanese leaders toward governmental policy seem to follow the traditional line. Group consciousness of bureaucratic officials makes for clique politics. They fight against any outsiders who may threaten their vested interests, even though they are also sometimes suspicious of one another. Clique politics based on *oyabun-kobun* (parent role-child role) relationships is evident even today.

When the personality of governmental officials is characterized by exploitation, conservatism, militarism, and suspicion of and hostility toward outsiders, we cannot expect from them much concern for the public welfare. This assumption is confirmed by the quotations from Vogel already referred to (see chapter notes 49 and 51).

Many governmental leaders of Japan seem to be from middle-class families. Because individuals with special skills and knowledge from whatever class were indispensable for the survival of lords (and faction leaders in modern days) in incessant competition with enemies and rivals, there resulted a relatively high degree of social mobility for competent individuals who possessed the skills that were required by the leaders. Nevertheless, partly because of the fact that higher-status achievers are mostly from the middle-class families which incorporated samurai values, and partly because of the great adjustability and conformity of Japanese, this type of individual who is successful generally dissociates himself from the interests of his former membership group.

2. Individual's Lack of Concern for Others' Welfare. The basic characteristic of Japanese people is insecurity, as already discussed in detail, which means that the search for security takes precedent over other concerns in their lives. Ohara holds that *ware ga nai* (no self) means *tsumi ga nai* (no sin).[59] People merge into a group, losing individual will. Without individual will, people are not responsible for helping others in need; it is the group (or the government) that is responsible for it. Inkeles, Haufmann, and Beier, comparing Russian and American personalities, maintain that Russians are quicker to admit their weaknesses and difficulties, and they expect government to be responsible for them, which makes governmental assistance obligatory.[60] This seems to be true with Japanese too. They feel sympathetic with suicidal victims for their difficulties, but they do not tend to take any action to help. As a consequence, they may feel guilty for not taking any action, but then rationalize their behavior by blaming the government.

The characteristic responses of many Japanese toward the person in need seem to be a combination of suppressed resentment against society and cathartic pleasure. Since they themselves are victims of the strictly formalized society under authoritarian rulers, they consciously or unconsciously feel resentful. With the probable exception of left-wing radicals, the resentment, however, is seldom expressed against a superior. In general, resentment is dissolved by the cathartic pleasure experienced when an insecure individual hears about others' misfortunes, feeling that "after all, we are still happier than some others." The principle of relative deprivation operates. It is probably for these reasons—an underlying resentment against an authoritarian society, pleasure obtained from others' misfortune, and a guilt feeling for not helping victims who deserve sympathy—that Japanese often glorify suicide, especially double love-suicide cases.

## Conclusion

The primary cause of suicide is not social structure, population characteristics, or physical settings, as many sociologists have analyzed; nor can suicide be explained only by psychological concepts, such as depression, the wish to die, thanatos, man against himself, etc. Each, however, is an important contributive cause. The causal nexus of suicide is the perceived meaning of the situation by the actor, where the perception of meaning is determined by the interaction between personality and social-structural factors.

This chapter first described the modal personality type of suicide-attempting youths in Kamakura and illustrated the interaction between the elements of suicide—dependency, self-inflation, and insecurity—by a case history. Second, it analyzed the structure of families producing suicidal subjects in terms of family structure, unifying principles (e.g., values), and patterns of responses to strain. Next, the "ideal" personality type of Japanese youth in general was discussed in order to see its similarity in personality traits to that of suicidal individuals. The similarity explains, at least in part, the high suicide rates for Japanese youths. Finally, this chapter analyzed the typical social structure of Japanese society in relation to the forces producing and reinforcing the basic elements of suicidal motivation—a need for dependency, the wish for self-inflation, and the presence of insecurity. The effects of social structure upon the personality of governmental leaders and of the public in general were also considered as factors in the high suicide rates of Japanese youths.

If dependency, self-inflation, and insecurity are the essential elements of suicidal motivation, it should be possible to predict, with additional information on attitudes about suicide and death, which individuals are more susceptible to suicide, since the measurement of these traits can be accomplished by use of psychological inventories and scales. Also any change in suicide rates can be roughly predicted by measuring the modal personality type of representative samples in terms of these traits.

In order further to study Japanese suicide and its relation to social structure, we should study a larger number of suicidal subjects and compare them with control groups that are representative in age, sex, region, class, and urbanity. In addition to the modal personality type and case histories of suicide attempts, as used in this paper, future studies should analyze also (1) action of suicide, e.g., what, when, who, how, etc.; (2) documentary expression of suicidal intent, e.g., will, letter, note, diary, etc.; and (3) reconstructed personalities and situations immediately before the suicidal act through interviews with their "significant others," as exemplified by the "psychological autopsy" method used by the Suicide Prevention Center of Los Angeles.[61] In addition, the degree of lethal intention of the subject should be measured by a comparable technique, such as the Suicide Potentiality Assessment Form used by the Suicide Prevention Center.[62]

In order to study the effects of culture upon suicide, cross-cultural studies should be made by use of standardized definitions and methods, in terms of differential attitudes toward death and suicide and of the degree of social stress and strain together with institutional outlets for aggressive impulses.

## REFERENCES


1. Mamoru Iga, "Cultural Factors in Suicide of Japanese Youths with Focus on Personality," *Sociology and Social Research*, **46**:75–90, 1961.
2. E. Durkheim, *Suicide*, trans. J. A. Spaulding and G. Simpson, (New York: The Free Press, 1951); J. F. Gibbs, and W. T. Martin, "Status Integration and Suicide," *American Sociological Review*, **23**:140–147, 1958.
3. A. F. Henry, and J. F. Short, *Suicide and Homicide* (New York: The Free Press, 1954); L. E. Dublin, *Suicide: A Sociological and Statistical Study* (New York: The Ronald Press Company, 1963), p. 153.
4. K. Horney, *New Ways in Psychoanalysis* (New York: W. W. Norton & Company, Inc., 1939), p. 74.
5. *Ibid.*, p. 77.
6. *Ibid.*, p. 99.
7. Karl Menninger, *Man Against Himself* (New York: Harcourt, Brace and Company, Inc., 1938), p. 359.
8. "Jisatsu no Yooin ni Kwansuru Kenkyu" (A Study of the Factors Contributing to Suicide: From The Standpoint of Psychiatry), *Seishin-shinkeigaku Zasshi* (*Psychiatria et neurologia Japonica*), **63**:107–166, 1961.
9. For statistical comparisons the present writer used the chi-square formula from Sidney Siegel, *Nonparametric Statistics* (New York: McGraw-Hill Book Company, 1956), p. 107.
10. Ohara, *op. cit.*, p. 111.
11. *Ibid.*, p. 104.
12. G. A. De Vos, "Role Narcissism and the Etiology of Japanese Suicide," paper read at the International Conference of Social Psychiatry at London, 1963.
13. Ohara, *op. cit.*, p. 143.
14. *Ibid.*
15. K. Ohara, S. Aizawa, and M. Shimizu, "Jyoshi no Seishin-Igaku-teki Kenkyu" (A Psychiatric Study of Double Love Suicide), *Seishin Shinkeigaku Zasshi*, **64**:762–780, 1962.
16. Ohara, *op. cit.*, p. 163.
17. G. Devereux, "Two Types of Modal Personality Models," in Neil J. Smelser and William T. Smelser (eds.), *Personality and Social Systems* (New York: John Wiley & Sons, Inc., 1963), p. 29.
18. E. S. Shneidman, "Suicide, Sleep, and Death: Some Possible Interrelations among Cessation, Interruption, and Continuation Phenomena," *Journal of Consulting Psychology*, **28**:95–106, 1964.

19. G. De Vos, and H. Wagatsuma, "Psycho-cultural Significance of Concern over Death and Illness among Rural Japanese," *International Journal of Social Psychiatry*, **5**:5–19, 1959.
20. De Vos, *op. cit.*, p. 21.
21. Ohara, *op. cit.*, p. 122.
22. J. A. M. Meerloo, *Suicide and Mass Suicide* (New York: Grune & Stratton, Inc., 1962), p. 139.
23. G. A. De Vos, "The Relation of Guilt toward Parents to Achievement and Arranged Marriage among the Japanese," *Psychiatry*, **23**:287–301, 1960.
24. K. Ohara, and H. Mashino, "*Jisatsu* to Katei-Kwankyo" (Suicide and Family Environments), *Seishin-igaku* (*Psychiatry*), **3**:775–783, 1961.
25. *Ibid.*, pp. 778–779.
26. T. Doi, "Amae—A Key Concept for Understanding Japanese Personality Structure," *Psychologia*, **1**:1–7, 1962.
27. Hajime Nakamura, "Japanese Emphasis upon Social Activities," in *The Science of Thought* (Tokyo: The Institute for the Science of Thought, 1954); Y. Scott Matsumoto, "Contemporary Japan: The Individual and the Group," *Transactions of the American Philosophical Society*, vol. 50, pt. 1, 1960.
28. W. Caudill, "Observations on the Cultural Context of Japanese Psychiatry," in M. K. Opler (ed.), *Culture and Mental Health* (New York: The Macmillan Company, 1959), p. 221; "Patterns of Emotion in Modern Japan," in R. J. Smith, and R. K. Beardsley (eds.), *Japanese Culture* (Chicago: Aldine Publishing Company, 1962), p. 129.
29. W. Caudill, and H. A. Scarr, "Japanese Value Orientations and Cultural Change," *Ethnology*, **1**:53–91, 1962.
30. J. Stoetzel, *Without the Chrysanthemum and the Sword*, A UNESCO publication (New York: Columbia University Press, 1955), p. 224.
31. De Vos, "Role Narcissism," p. 34.
32. Doi, *op. cit.*, p. 3.
33. Stoetzel, *op. cit.*, pp. 287, 209, and 218.
34. *Ibid.*, pp. 215, and 219.
35. De Vos, "Role Narcissism," p. 27.
36. E. F. Vogel, *Japan's New Middle Class* (Berkeley: University of California Press, 1963), p. 147.
37. Stoetzel, *op. cit.*, p. 220.
38. F. Henriques, *Prostitution and Society* (London: MacGibbon & Kee, 1962), p. 311.
39. G. A. De Vos, "Deviancy and Social Change: A Psychocultural Evaluation of Trends in Japanese Delinquency and Suicide," in R. J. Smith and R. K. Beardsley, *op. cit.*, p. 153–171; E. F. Vogel and S. H. Vogel, "Family Security, Personal Immaturity, and Emotional Health in a Japanese Sample," *Marriage and Family Living*, **23**:161–166, 1961.
40. Caudill, in *Culture and Mental Health*, p. 221; also "Around-the-Clock Patient Care in Japanese Psychiatric Hospitals: The Role of the Tsukisoi," *American Sociological Review*, **26**:204–214, 1961.

41. Vogel, *op. cit.*, p. 18.
42. K. M. Whitehill, Jr., and S. Takezawa, *Cultural Values in Management-Worker Relations: Japan, Gimu in Transition* (Chapel Hill, N. C.: University of North Carolina Press, 1961), p. 86.
43. J. C. Abegglen, *The Japanese Factory: Aspects of the Social Organization* (New York: The Free Press, 1958), p. 128.
44. *Ibid.*, p. 70.
45. De Vos, "Relation of Guilt," p. 288.
46. Horney, *op. cit.*, p. 88.
47. De Vos, in *Japanese Culture*, p. 163.
48. E. F. Vogel, "Entrance Examinations and Emotional Disturbances in Japan's New Middle Class," in *Japanese Culture*, pp. 140–152.
49. Vogel, *Japan's New Middle Class*, p. 15.
50. *Ibid.*, p. 18.
51. *Ibid.*, p. 19.
52. Vogel, in *Japanese Culture*, p. 148.
53. H. S. Quigley, and J. E. Turner, *The New Japan: Government and Politics* (Minneapolis: University of Minnesota Press, 1956), p. 11.
54. Ruth Benedict, "Continuities and Discontinuities in Cultural Conditioning," in C. Kluckhohn, H. A. Murray, and D. M. Schneider (eds.), *Personality in Nature, Society and Culture* (New York: Alfred A. Knopf, Inc., 1954), pp. 522–531.
55. K. Ohara, K. S. Aizawa, M. Shimizu, and H. Kojima, "Oyako-Shinjyu no Bunkashiteki Kenkyu" (On Parent-Child Suicide: A Study of Cultural History), *Memorial Issue for Prof. Kora*, Jikei University School of Medicine, 1964, pp. 418–426.
56. Quigley and Turner, *op. cit.*, chap. I.
57. *Ibid.*, p. 11.
58. *Ibid.*
59. Ohara, Aizawa, Shimizu, and Kojima, *op. cit.*, p. 435.
60. A. Inkeles, A. E. Hanfmann, and H. Beier, "Modal Personality and Adjustment to the Soviet Socio-Political System," *Human Relations* (Ann Arbor, Mich.: The Research Center for Group Dynamics), **11**:9, 1958.
61. R. E. Litman, T. Curphey, E. S. Shneidman, N. L. Farberow, and N. Tabachnick, "Investigations of Equivocal Suicides," *The Journal of the American Medical Association*, **184**:924–929, 1963.
62. N. D. Tabachnick, and N. L. Farberow, "The Assessment of Self-Destructive Potentiality," in N. L. Farberow and E. S. Shneidman (eds.), *The Cry for Help* (New York: McGraw-Hill Book Company, 1961), pp. 60–77.

# 12. Suicide: A Public Health Problem

Louis I. Dublin

The suicide problem has been neglected far too long by the public health profession. I know of very few health officers who have assumed administrative responsibility for the control of this condition in their community as is required by law and as they have for most other important causes of sickness and death. A few papers on suicide have from time to time been prepared by public health workers, but, so far as I can discover, none has outlined a definite program of suicide prevention as an administrative health function. Some years ago, Dr. G. M. Crocetti of Johns Hopkins University presented a discussion of some public health aspects of suicide, but the burden of his argument was that there were too many uncertainties and too many unexplored areas to permit a worthwhile program to be undertaken by the health authorities.[1] Moreover, he felt such a program, if launched, would not receive the support of the community.

No one could be more aware than I, who have worked in this field for more than thirty years, that much more knowledge concerning the causes and preventability of suicide is greatly needed. The point I wish to make in this paper[2] is that we already have a mass of data on this problem, however imperfect it may be, which suggests a field of public health activity that has been allowed to lie fallow far too long. Even the limited achievements thus far offer enough promise of success to justify the launching of a campaign by the public health profession. I believe that a concerted effort on our part, working with other interested professional groups, would be the surest guarantee that the gaps in our knowledge would be filled all the sooner. We shall learn more by working than by bewailing our ignorance. Let trial and error, born of actual experience, be our guide.

To be sure, many potential suicides have been treated by individual psychiatrists and psychologists and their conditions have been relieved. We do not know their number, whether their improvement was temporary or long-lasting, or the effects of this or that method of therapy on the general picture of suicide in the community. It is obvious, however, that this very costly approach can reach only relatively few of those who can profit from treatment, and these few are not always those who most need such intensive care. What mass efforts have been made to reduce the incidence of suicide have been launched, with one major exception, by voluntary associations, working with very limited resources of funds or personnel and altogether without official sanction or support. These associations have made only limited contributions to the main problem, carrying no official responsibility to see the whole job done. They have not been able to draw on community funds in a continuing budget or to draw upon all the resources of their community, including volunteers and private agencies which have special skills.

The one outstanding agency in the United States concerned with suicide prevention—the Los Angeles Suicide Prevention Center—has indeed made most important additions to our knowledge of the factors underlying the psychological phenomena of suicide. It has identified the very important presuicidal warning signals which should help bring patients under treatment; it has perfected techniques for handling less hazardous cases by telephone until the emergency has passed; and it has shown in many other significant ways how to serve a limited number of individuals under suicidal stress. But this organization has likewise operated without official cooperation or support from the city of Los Angeles. Its greatest contribution has been to do research on some phases of the problem rather than to work out a feasible and efficient municipal administrative practice that would be applicable to other communities. In fairness it should be said that such an objective never was or could be its primary goal.

Suicide is nevertheless a health problem of great importance. Although seriously and consistently underreported, it is already listed among the first ten, and at some ages among the first three, causes of death. There are each year not less than 25,000 suicides in the United States. The abortive attempts at suicide are much more numerous, the best estimate being around seven or eight attempts for each completed case. On this basis, there are probably from 175,000 to 200,000 attempts in the United

States each year. Nor are these attempts to be dismissed lightly; they are all cries for help: many, very desperate appeals. Because they involve young people for the most part, their numbers accumulate over the years. I estimate that today there are not less than two million persons alive in the United States who have a history of one or more such attempts. These people with this searing emotional experience constitute a pool from which the completed suicides of succeeding years are largely drawn. The record clearly shows that a sizable fraction of completed suicides have made previous attempts.

Equally important is the fact, as demonstrated in many countries, that this condition lends itself to intelligent efforts at control. Interest in suicide prevention is growing. In the United States, in addition to the Suicide Prevention Center at Los Angeles, there is an increasing number of smaller agencies, including Rescue, Inc. in Boston, the Friends in Miami, the San Francisco Suicide Prevention, Inc., and a few more in other centers of the country. In England, the work of the Samaritans in London is expanding rapidly to other centers because it meets a growing public need with a measure of success. So also is the work in Vienna, Berlin, and more recently in Milan. It is still too early to estimate the success of these efforts in lives saved and individuals restored to productive work and to normal places in their families and communities. There can be no question, however, that these efforts are effective and that they have the capacity for greater usefulness as facilities and trained personnel increase and as more effective leadership is developed. This certainly was the keynote of the meeting held in 1963, in Copenhagen, by the Working Conference on Suicide Prevention attended by some 80 leaders in the field, both from Europe and America. The consensus of the meeting was that suicide would come under increasing control, very much as tuberculosis has, if a persistent and well-considered campaign were directed against it.

This is the time when the health workers and especially the health officers of the country should step into the picture and play their part. It is they who carry the power and the legal responsibility for protecting and advancing the public health. There can be no question that suicide is, to a degree at least, a preventable condition. Up to now, it has been passed up by the public health authorities. If it has been served at all, it has been, as I have already pointed out, by a variety of unofficial agencies sporadically and on an emergency basis. The record shows that a large number of suicidal individuals see their physicians sometime during the year of the fatal act, but often it is to little or no useful purpose, because their telltale symptoms are not recognized as warnings and as appeals for help in their emotional distress. Many of the attempters come to the attention of the police or fire departments of their communities. Others find their way to the poison control centers in the emergency wards of our general hospitals, of which we now have 500 in our cities. We may assume that they receive good emergency care at these centers, but unfortunately this is usually where the service stops. After a few hours or days, these patients are generally returned to their homes and to the same frustrations and tensions which have led to their despair.

The basic difficulty is that the suicide problem has not been thought through and accepted by any one publicly supported community agency as its major responsibility. In metropolitan areas we usually have the necessary skills and services, such as the mental health centers, the psychiatric social workers, the emergency hospital wards, the competent psychiatrists and psychologists, the interested volunteers, and so on. We have them all, but generally speaking their services have not been coordinated and organized into an effective working plan. It has been rather a case of the right hand not knowing what the left hand was doing.

The fact is that fifty years ago we were very much in the same situation with our tuberculosis problem as we are now with suicide. Most of the service the patient received was from the local general practitioner or the social worker in voluntary agencies. Few health departments were organized to give effective service in finding cases, guiding them to hospitals and sanatoriums, following them up on their return—in a word, in taking responsibility for the management of the problem as a community function. But once the way was shown, the movement spread all over the country, and what had seemed like an impossible job was accomplished. Today, tuberculosis is no longer one of our major health concerns.

Because of his authority and central position in the community, the health officer is, in my opinion, the key man in the present fluid suicide situation. It is he who can best bring order and purpose into the program of suicide prevention. He can bring the interested groups together, the official as well as the voluntary agencies, and work out an effective organization. Such a plan of organization might operate along the following lines: A small central bureau of the department might be set up as a clearing and record office to which all cases would be referred, whether by physicians, psychiatrists, hospitals, social workers, the police, firemen, or others. It should be the function of the bureau staff to follow the cases and to see that they receive the necessary care until they can safely be dropped from the record. Public health nurses are admirably fitted for the task. In addition, the establishment of a 24-hour telephone service with a competent professional at the receiving end is an absolute essential to determine the degree of hazard involved in the case. Experience with this has been good in Los Angeles, in Miami, in the more recently established service at the Kings County Hospital Center in Brooklyn, and wherever this device for immediate contact between the suicidal person and professional help has been provided. The Samaritans in London have shown the value of the intelligent and well-trained volunteer to whom the patient, under care, is assigned. He acts as a devoted friend in time of need. He relates his charge to the professional psychiatric and social services as they are needed. Fortunately, our communities are full of warm-hearted people who would be happy to play a constructive role in such a program. We can already see a group of trained volunteers beginning their work in Los Angeles, serving with the professionals of the Suicide Prevention Center there. The Friends of Miami are likewise demonstrating the value of such devoted volunteers. It is vital, however, that these volunteers be carefully chosen and then adequately instructed and trained in the part they can perform.

I am keenly interested in the plan which Dr. George James, the Health Commissioner of New York City, and his psychiatric colleague, Dr. Samuel Oast, are developing. They have made a survey of the field to discover ways of reaching high-risk cases and to learn what services for them are already available in the Health Department and what other services can be brought to bear favorably on these cases. During an initial six-month period they plan to maintain close contact with one or more municipal hospitals where emergency services are now available and determine what new services, if any, will be needed. In the end, we can be sure that the plan of office and staff organization resulting from these initial steps will be valuable for study by health officers generally. This should provide a blueprint showing the main lines of the organization finally evolved in this exceedingly well-organized health department. Most important will be the line of contact which the department will make with the practising physicians of the city, the various municipal departments, including hospital, fire, and police departments (which very often see the attempted suicide first) and how the stream of information which will come into the center from these various contacts will be utilized to serve the attempted suicide best.

There is, of course, much room for variation of organization from place to place, depending on the size of the city, the possible number of cases to be handled, the part the public health nurses will play in the program, the use of volunteers, etc. Of one thing we should be certain, and that is the importance of the central record office through which the continuous history of the cases can be traced to the point of termination by either recovery, death, or removal to other jurisdictions. Only in this way will it be possible over a period of years to assess the size of the problem, the extent to which it is coming under control, and what additional facilities are needed.

In some large cities we now have mental health authorities operating independently of our traditional public health departments, and their number will increase with time. Their directors may reasonably feel that leadership in dealing with the local suicide problem belongs with them. I would not quarrel with such a view of jurisdiction if the mental health workers were equipped to handle the problem effectively. There is plenty of room for both groups. The important consideration is that the working plan be developed through study and conference to meet local conditions. Whatever the plan is, it must provide for a center of local interest in and responsibility for the prevention of suicide, where the cases will be registered and the necessary services made quickly available and followed up. Coordination of all agencies, both official and voluntary, is of the very essence. A basic outline of a plan can then be designed which will make a good beginning in most places.

I suggest, therefore, that a number of demonstration centers for the prevention of suicide be set up in our larger metropolitan areas under the auspices of the local health officer or his equivalent, the local director of mental health. We know in broad terms the dimension of this problem, some of its causes, and some evidence of its preventability. There is already a number of local agencies which could play an important part in such an effort at prevention. What is needed above all else is leadership and direction. This the health officer can give. Where a mental health authority is already effectively at work, the director may wish to take this responsibility. I am confident that neither the one nor the other will have any great difficulty in calling a conference of all the interested groups in his area who, in one way or another, serve those who are suicide prone.

Most important, of course, will be the wholehearted cooperation of the local medical society, the psychiatrists and psychologists, the directors of poison control centers, the social workers, and the leaders in mental health. Such a conference should produce a good working plan, including a 24-hour telephone service, around-the-clock availability of a psychiatrist, and a small staff of public health nurses, psychologists, social workers, and friendly and well-trained volunteers, all reporting to the central office where records are kept and a followup service is directed. Behind all this is the good will and intelligent interest of, and assumption of responsibility by, the public health officer or mental health director. In this way, the problem of suicide prevention will become a continuous municipal health department function, supported by public funds, and thus be assured of centralized responsibility for its ultimate control.

There are other good reasons why the health officers and the mental health authorities of the country should participate actively in programs of suicide prevention at this time. Experience has shown that the most effective preventive of this unfortunate condition is a state of sound mental and emotional health, and it is high time that the health profession in its broadest sense assumed greater activity and responsibility in this field. The charter of the World Health Organization struck the right note when it emphasized the importance of sound mental health as a precondition of general community health. Unfortunately, this injunction has been heeded all too little by the rank and file of the health profession. The development of a strong interest in suicide prevention may be an excellent first step into the larger field of sound mental health in our increasingly complex and bewildering society.

## REFERENCES

1. "Suicide and Public Health: An Attempt at Reconceptualization," *American Journal of Public Health,* 49:881–887, 1959.
2. This paper is an elaboration of one originally presented at the Annual Meeting of the American Public Health Association, Kansas City, November, 1963.

Part III

# PSYCHOLOGICAL AND PSYCHIATRIC ESSAYS

That the psychology and psychiatry of self-destruction are manifested by a wide variety of types of activities is perhaps nowhere more evident than in this section, containing as it does chapters representing a number of genres: discursive essays, focussed biography, empirical surveys, experimental studies, discussions of remediation and therapy, and programs for community action. Much of the praxis of this volume is contained within this section.

Avery Weisman investigates the relation between self-destruction and sexual perversion. He believes that there are many intermediate forms of self-destruction short of suicide, and that there are psychodynamic similarities between self-destruction and sexual perversion. He has found that, in some cases, one may substitute for the other as a method of resolving conflict, whereas in other cases, one may be either the equivalent or the precondition for the other. He illustrates his thesis with reports of three patients who were in psychoanalytic therapy over long periods of time, and correlates, in this way, clinical description with both psychodynamic formulation and existential appraisal.

James Diggory concerns himself, in his chapter, first with the problem of defining depression—including an examination of the several methodological issues involved in attempting to establish the relationships between depression and suicide, and then—after a sharply critical indictment of the Existentialists, as steeped in gloom because they address themselves to goals impossible to achieve—with an examination of the components of personal despair. Dr. Diggory believes that these components include, especially, hopelessness, defined as the improbabilty of achieving a goal or the improbability of having a desired goal to achieve. In discussing this concept, he gives examples from the work of Kurt Lewin and a number of other studies, including several of his own.

Robert Litman's chapter answers the question: What did Freud say about suicide? One surprising finding is that Freud wrote quite a bit about this topic. Dr. Litman, restricting himself solely to Freud's writings and to Jones' biography of Freud, has divided his presentation into "Early Experiences" (1881–1910) and "Theories and Speculations" (1911–1939). He concludes with a synthesis and evaluation dealing with certain general features of the human condition, discernible suicidal mechanisms in individual cases, and specific predisposing conditions. Among the contributions in this chapter is Dr. Litman's focussing our attention on the importance of helplessness and (frustrated) dependency needs in self-destruction, above and beyond the traditional psychoanalytic emphasis on hostility.

Neil Kessel presents a detailed study of 465 self-poisoned persons admitted to an Edinburgh hospital during a recent one-year period. Dr. Kessel makes two major additional points: A practical one, in which he decries the unnecessary ease with which anyone can purchase and retain poisonous substances (including salicylates), and a theoretical one, in which he distinguishes sharply between "attempted suicide" and "self-poisoning," pointing out that the former term is clinically inappropriate and misleading, often serving, paradoxically, to prevent a necessary psychiatric examination for the self-poisoner.

Norman Farberow discusses the problem of the therapy of suicidal persons, noting the special features arising from the fact that they are in what is for them a crisis situation. Dr. Farberow draws some parallels to the reactions of persons who have undergone natural catastrophes, to indicate the emotional states to which the suicidal person is sometimes reduced. Some differences are also pointed out; especially that the victim of a natural catastrophe feels that he is not alone and that what has happened to him is not a result of his own personal inadequacies, whereas the suicidal person feels dreadfully alone, often as a result of his own feeling of unworthiness.

Norman Tabachnick permits us to share the intellectual

history of the development of his own thoughts in relation to the psychology of accident. Dr. Tabachnick started with a rather orthodox psychoanalytic position involving the belief in unconscious impulses and the possible operation of a death instinct, but as he and his group of investigators began to interpret their own data—obtained from thirty-five sets of interviews either with survivors of fatal accidents or individuals who themselves had had severe accidents—they came to understand serious accidents primarily as the unplanned side effects in persons with a special penchant for "action," who were transiently involved in situations of overwhelming anxiety-filled responsibility. All these points, and more, are illustrated in a detailed case, "The Accident of Ernest."

Dr. Friedman's chapter is an historical find. This study of 93 suicides among New York City policemen from 1934 to 1940 was initiated by a committee headed by Dr. Gregory Zilboorg and supported under the aegis of a direct grant from Marshall Field. The entire project was actively endorsed by Mayor Fiorello La Guardia. The chapter which appears in this book (except for the contemporary postscript) was completed in essentially its present form over a quarter-century ago. Even so, this paper is far more timely than it is anachronistic; it represents both an historic document and an essay which provides us with cogent insights which have great contemporary usefulness.

# 13. Self-Destruction and Sexual Perversion

Avery D. Weisman

Wanting to die, crying for help, or seeking oblivion are only a few of the many motives for suicide. Just as a religious person ponders the promise of immortality, so is a suicidal person lured by the prospect of a special kind of death which only an act of self-destruction will achieve. Motives for self-destruction are certainly not less complicated than motives for wanting to survive. Suicidal patients may be depressed, and depressed people are often suicidal, but there are many people afflicted with chronic depression, recurrent disappointment, or intractable despair who seemingly consider deliberate self-destruction unthinkable. In contrast, there are others for whom the ready accessibility of suicide is one of the conditions that makes life tolerable.

Suicide is only an extreme form of self-destructive behavior in which the wish to obliterate oneself happens to coincide with the wish to discover oneself through death. Suicide is a product of a mood, a time, and a season, but self-destructive acts assume many guises and may often endure throughout an entire lifetime. Authorities agree that the number of reported suicides is only a fraction of the total number of suicide attempts, and it is probable that each year there are fewer people who attempt suicide, or otherwise put their life in jeopardy, than there are those who, knowingly or not, *practice* self-destructive acts.

Suicide statistics resemble those of the population explosion—impressive, incredible, regrettable, and difficult to control. Perhaps reckless self-destruction and unbridled propagation have something more in common, in that each may serve an opposite purpose. For example, like an epidemic, suicide thins the population and makes it easier for others to survive. Analogously, a relentless drive to propagate may drive entire societies deeper into poverty, unemployment, demoralization, and hopelessness and bring about a form of self-destruction. As in the life cycle of the lemming, sometimes the drive to survive is linked to extinction. For others, self-destruction is a passport to a new order of idealized survival.

Disposition toward suicide is, at times, like sexual desire, because both are preemptory, primitive forces that are difficult to deny. Although suicide prevention is a magnificent objective, suicide has a refreshing appeal for some patients, exceeding what life manages to offer them, and to try to prevent these people from destroying themselves is a little like preventing them from dreaming. Patients like this do not merely hint about suicide; they fly banners. Trying to save these lives is like preventing death and destruction during a hurricane; we nail down the furniture, tape up the windows, and hang on until the crisis is over. However, it is still mandatory that we search for ways to prevent suicide, just as we seek out new and effective ways to prevent murder.

The human organism is constantly in a state of change. We come to be and pass away; we come apart and cease to be. In his unending oscillation between hope and despair, man's nature seeks to change the unchangeable and preserve the transitory. At times he will not only hasten change but, in order to mitigate his helplessness, will destroy valuable parts for the sake of the whole and discard the whole in order to improve a defective part.

Menninger believes that it is the energy derived from destructiveness that does the world's work, but he also maintains that this same force may revert and destroy those who use it.[1] His viewpoint resembles de Sade's scorn of those who believe man is other than self-seeking and destructive.[2] Even though destructiveness may permeate every aspect of our lives, it does not follow that there is a so-called death instinct at work. Actually, patients who are near death are singularly placid and undestructive. Nor do they frequently complain about their fate or of the destructiveness of the disease that has brought them to the brink of death.

If destructiveness and natural death are so little alike, we must look upon self-induced death as a vehicle of destruction that resembles murder, not death. In discussing the psychoanalytic theory of melancholia, for example, Nunberg indicates that suicide offers both masochistic gratification and atonement for homicidal wishes.[3] Although suicide may relieve guilt and hatred, the victim is also free to destroy others by his act. Suicidal patients may inflict a lifelong burden upon their survivors, and, however painful their own existence has been, it is often matched by the cruelty that their self-destructive act imposes upon others. Under certain circumstances, therefore, suicide may not be too high a price to pay for destroying one's enemies.

## Self-Destruction and Psychoanalysis

People enter psychoanalytic therapy to seek relief from their suffering and to understand why they feel as they do. They may recognize irrational, painful, and disabling limitations within themselves, but their suffering is apt to be ascribed mostly to an intolerable discrepance between how they see themselves and the way they would like to be. For example, a man may yearn for unequivocal appetites but find only aversions toward everything. He feels apathy when he wants enthusiasm. He fails when he needs success. He finds himself isolated from others and also discovers strange alliances and divisions of wishes and fears within himself. He may be baffled, anxious, depressed, but, above all, he is *compelled* to realize that he has become a victim instead of a master.

It is rarely made explicit, but many people enter therapy with the tacit proviso that they are not to be influenced or changed unless they so choose. Despite intense suffering, they may cling tenaciously to a way of life that has brought only defeat. The implicit goal of some patients is to be able, somehow, to coerce the world into an apology for its past offenses. Without modifying their unrealistic demands, these patients turn psychoanalysis into an epic of passionate self-justification within a hostile world.

Other patients are eager to change but want to change so radically that only failure can result. For example, timid people want to become bold; compliant people want to learn how to bend others to their will. Some patients crave omniscience instead of understanding. Others seek ways to ignore conflict and deplore any objective that does not guarantee superlative achievement. These antithetical aims are as pathological as the original suffering. They suggest that there are many people who truly want to stop being the victim and become the master—but master of whom? In fantasy, their purpose is not just to find necessarily circumscribed benefits or merely to enhance the range of responsibility and available choice but to bring the world to its knees and thus *turn the tables on reality*. In short, some people may be willing to undergo almost any hardship, pain, sacrifice, suffering, or martyrdom if they can be assured a final rebirth into glory.

Fortunately, such self-defeating stipulations, plus an eagerness to suffer, do not always add up to a wish for self-destruction or death. Many patients court disaster without feeling that death is at all desirable. Furthermore, although depression, guilt, anxiety, or hostility may lead to conjuring up some image of self-destruction, they rarely induce actual suicide. Indeed, to experience emotional extremes is often part of everyday life and is not at all pathological.

Fantasies may be better or worse than reality, but they are never identical with it. Some people compound their suffering in order to bring the world closer to their fantasies, and others fall victim to these fantasies. They take pleasure in torment, find success a bitter pill to swallow, and, by their behavior, actually bring about the opposite of what they profess to want.

Although death is an inescapable fact of life, preoccupation with death is singularly lacking among psychoanalytic patients. There are grief, poignant recollections of the dead, and anxiety about fatal illness, but these are just problems and obstacles encountered in the course of an unswerving drive to survive. As a rule, the significance of death as a human institution, or of total extinction as an imminent possibility, is of surprisingly little concern to most psychoanalytic patients.

Of course, there are exceptions to this rule. Some of the most dramatic exceptions are people with sexual perversions. These patients are not only concerned about death but also indirectly oppose change in themselves and cling to the very symptoms that cause suffering. Nacht and his associates have pointed out that few people seek psychiatric treatment because of sexual perversions.[4] Despite what is often a hazardous, restrictive way of life, perversions provide gratification, albeit short-lived, that seem to compensate for whatever else must be sacrificed.

Patients with preemptive perversions who do seek psychiatric treatment are motivated more by their neuroses than by sexual deviations. Among the neurotic symptoms which they would be most eager to give up is an excessive concern with fantasies of killing, being killed, and dying. Some of these patients may have committed unmistakably self-destructive acts, including suicide attempts. Others have at least been strongly preoccupied with thoughts of extinction, although suicide may not have been seriously contemplated. In short, patients with self-destructive inclinations and sexual deviations may actually live in the shadow of death while struggling with the problems of life.

## Literature

Studies of destructive urges and sexual deviations have been traditional topics of psychoanalysis ever since Freud. Yet there still remains a wide gulf between theoretical conjectures and clinical practice. For example, clinical psychoanalysis tells us surprisingly little about suicidal patients, except as extrapolations from work with depressed or sadistic patients. There are few detailed reports of patients who commit suicide during or after analysis.

Because patients with sexual perversion who are unfettered by more pressing neurotic problems rarely are studied by psychoanalysts, we are obliged to look upon sexual perversion, in Freud's terms, as the "negative" of neurosis.[5] Briefly, this means that (1) whenever there is neurosis there is also sexual impairment of one kind or another, (2) neurotic symptoms present themselves in place of a manifest sexual perversion, and (3) both perversions and psychoneuroses are complementary ways of containing conflict. It is significant that, despite extensive work in the field, alternative hypotheses[6] have not led modern writers drastically to alter Freud's original formulations. Karpman's monumental text, Gillespie's review of contemporary theory, and Rosen's recent symposium are notable instances.[7]

Gillespie emphasized that so-called partial instincts and polymorphous models may provide the raw material for perversions that persist into adult life but that perversions themselves are not direct derivatives of infantile sexuality. Glover,[8] as well as many other modern investigators,[9] concurs with Gillespie's viewpoint. The contemporary consensus is that sexual perversions serve *defensive* purposes; they do not merely carry out instinctual aims.

It is difficult to discover clinical defenses which are uniquely characteristic of patients with sexual perversions. On the whole, these patients demonstrate a wide variety of defenses. Nevertheless, if the defensive operations reported by various authors are carefully examined, there seem to be three outstanding defensive processes. These are: (1) *libidinization of anxiety, guilt, and pain,* (2) *identification with a narcissistic object choice,* and (3) *bipolar emotional attitudes.* Although a full discussion of these defensive operations lies outside the scope of this chapter, they may be briefly described as follows.

*Libidinization of anxiety, guilt, and pain* means that an emotion which is ordinarily painful, humiliating, or frightening becomes a necessary component of a patient's established behavior. The emotion itself need not be pleasurable, nor need the pursuit of these distressing emotions be specifically intended. Nevertheless, to experience such emotions is a necessary condition that makes a forbidden act permissible. Libidinization, therefore, participates in the different ways by which a patient overcomes conflict and defines his sense of reality.

*Identification with a narcissistic object choice* has two forms: (1) The patient sees his sexual object as an idealized image or extension of himself, or (2) the object is a restoration and fulfillment of idealized early relationships. Both forms of identification are intended to enhance the patient's self-esteem. Sometimes, only a partial identification is required, and this frequently includes transsexual characteristics. Men may take on idealized female characteristics, and women may adopt traits of a masculine ideal.

*Bipolar emotional attitudes* refers to the way in which patients with sexual perversions may oscillate between emotional extremes in their relations with people. Profound distortions of perception may exist side-by-side with intact reality testing. Patients may swing from total absorption with an idealized love object—animate or inanimate—to utter disgust and contempt for the same object. People, as human beings, have little sense of reality for these patients, who find it difficult to adopt a modulated relation. Except for a libidinal association, other people are mere phantoms. Within these libidinal associations, however, one emotional extreme may be a militant reaction formation, while at the other extreme, attraction toward an object may be tantamount to a fetish.

Other types of defenses which have been described in perversions are more familiar: isolation, denial, dissociation, reversal of affect, reversal of aim, and so forth. Although a forbidden sexual act may not ordinarily be considered a desirable defensive measure, it may be more effective than less conspicuous defenses. According to prevailing psychoanalytic theory, perversion shares its psychodynamic roots with neuroses, dream-work, and other manifestations of psychic conflict. The predominant conflict in perversions need not be primarily a sexual conflict. Destructive or sadistic phantasies, in particular, may be expressed in somewhat truncated form. Psychoanalytic theory contends that as a result of expressing a partial or modified version of a conflict, the repression of remaining fantasies is fortified. This may be termed the *theory of partial residues*. It is comparable to the belief that neurotic symptoms help to repress, as well as to represent, primary conflict. For example, Sachs postulated a theory of partial residues to account for cases of fetishism.[10] By allowing the expression of a relatively harmless fragment, the defensive apparatus is able to repress a far more dangerous residue. Sachs also extended this concept to demonstrate how various neurotic symptoms contribute to the creative process. The theory of partial residues is not only applicable to other kinds of perversions but may also explain why some patients are reluctant to enter therapy. Not only are they content with a more or less effective defense; they are afraid to disturb their psychic equilibrium.

Although psychoanalytic hypotheses imply that there is almost a complementary relationship between destructiveness, suicide, and perversion, the ways in which one is transformed into the other are fully as conjectural as are the internal and external events that determine the final form of expression. Despite this uncertainty, however, strong overtones of the suicide theme often accompany reports of patients with sexual perversions. Reik discussed the relation of suicide to sexual masochism, and Menninger's statements about the wish to kill, to be killed, and to die lead us to expect an even more inclusive correlation between self-destruction and deviant sexuality.[11]

Boss has challenged the almost complacent tendencies of psychoanalytic writers to emphasize the destructive component of sexual perversion and to slight more constructive factors.[12] He finds the element of destructiveness to be similar to attitudes of activity and passivity in sexual relations: they are not primary sources of gratification but secondary methods which enable people to break through emotional barriers into a wider reality. According to Boss, sexual perversion is a concrete characteristic of many states of being. These patients are seeking a version of reality that will bring harmony to the dialectic between love and the world.

Despite the obvious disparity between terminologies, or the imbalance of emphasis, these different viewpoints have common themes. Patients who have sexual perversions and self-destructive inclinations contend with conflicts that are polarized, in some cases, according to sexual appetites, and in others, according to destructive fantasies. Both forms of expression are exceedingly restrictive. Conflicts are neither harmlessly contained nor satisfactorily resolved—the price of relief is paid for with briefer periods of quiescence and more restricted avenues of expression.

The balance between hope and despair is influenced by the proportion of fulfillment and destruction. Although sexual perversion supplies varying amounts of gratification and fulfillment, progressively narrowed channels of expression demand more self-extinction. Naturally, self-destructive behavior contains a high degree of self-extinction, but even in its ultimate form—suicide—the self-destructive act is not all negative. Because it is a way out of conflict and fear, an act of annihilation still has a residue of fulfillment and gratification.[13]

## Sexual Perversions

In general, we may make a distinction between two kinds of deviant sexual behavior: (1) impulsive acts of sexual perversion which are relatively infrequent and which tend to be symptomatic responses to unusual stress, and (2) constitutive acts, in which perverse components are obligatory, preferential, regular, or exclusive forms of sexual response.

Although the term "perversion" has pejorative implications that are objectionable, suggested synonyms such as "paraphilia" lack the advantage of common usage. In this chapter, therefore, I have used the term to designate the kind of stereotyped, preemptive, and motivated deviant sexual behavior which is regularly preceded by sexual fantasies or, less conspicuously, by heightened conflict. By this qualification, the meaning of perversion includes both sexual and nonsexual aims, just as so-called normal sexuality contains both.

We know that sexual perversions differ, even within subgroups, and that psychoanalytic psychiatrists are likely to have only a skewed sample to study. As a rule, perversions are defined within the framework of the circumstances and characteristics by which they are recognized as deviations from the established norm of acceptable behavior. *By necessity*, perversions are overt acts which violate a social prohibition, but in some patients, perversions can also be inhibited acts which depict ways in which the person shrinks from fulfilling a social directive. Perversions express fears as well as wishes, and the overt act which receives so much attention may be secondary to a primary conflict. Many so-called perversions are only efforts to maintain a semblance of "normality," and their inner rationale may be best understood by discovering within the act the *missing* factor that would bring patients closer to this normality.

Perversion, like any defensive operation or method of gaining relief from suffering and conflict, may be constructive as well as destructive in purpose. Even though so-called normal sexual attitudes cannot be precisely defined, patients with sexual perversions seem to want what repels many other people and avoid what most people want. Presumably, appetites and aversions have exchanged positions; destructive acts offer constructive possibilities, and conventional values or directives become potentially devastating. Psychodynamic psychology is not designed to encompass the full scope of what it means to be a human being, and the meaning of total human behavior cannot be inferred from isolated acts or intentions. Perverse acts, like any other variety of behavior, are only as "representative" as we choose to make them.

## Self-Destruction

Sublethal self-destruction is even more difficult to define[14] than is sexual perversion. Although we may question whether suicidal patients always intend to kill themselves, the completed act is, at least, an unambiguous event. In milder forms of self-destruction, the blending of intent and inference within "representative" acts resists analysis, and even a qualified judgment that some acts are primarily "self-destructive" may be open to dispute.

To restrict the concept of self-destruction without limiting it to suicide, and also to prevent its loose application, I have tried to exclude patients in whom self-destruction is secondary, subintentioned, or highly inferential. For example, while a self-destructive component is almost certainly present, a transvestite who insists upon crossing streets against the traffic flow and a homosexual who consistently seeks partners in places where he can be recognized *may* be indifferent to misfortunes or may merely intend to defy fate. A woman patient who regularly performs fellatio upon casual dates can scarcely be surprised when these men do not subsequently propose marriage. Because she ostensibly wants to be married, it is reasonable to interpret her promiscuity as self-destructive. Nevertheless, however clear the self-destructive component seems to be in these examples, the mode of sexual perversion cannot be as readily articulated with the manner of self-destruction, nor can the psychodynamic linkage be firmly established. Accordingly, I have distinguished three major types of self-destructive behavior: (1) *suicide attempts*; (2) *sadomasochistic acts*, and (3) *self-extinction*. These are called primary forms of self-destruction largely because their conjunction with sexual perversion is clinically apparent and psychodynamically intelligible, as in the following cases.

## Case Reports

I shall present, in condensed version, three patients who combined unequivocal sexual perversions with primary forms of self-destruction.

Because these communications were necessarily confidential, it will not be possible to present the full range and details of the clinical material, nor can I, for reasons of space, offer more comprehensive documentation for my conclusions. Therefore, the case summaries will be limited to a description and brief discussion of each patient's background, sexual orientation, and self-destructive trends.

*Case 1. Suicide attempts*

A male patient with a problem of homosexuality committed suicide when he was confronted with growing heterosexual desire and no longer was able to fulfill the preconditions of his homosexual perversion.

A thirty-two-year-old business executive sought psychoanalysis because of severe anxiety, suicidal inclinations, depressive episodes, and homosexuality. The immediate reason for wanting treatment was that he had failed to make his roommate totally dependent upon him and had become agitated and depressed shortly after the roommate announced his forthcoming marriage.

The patient's father had lost his job in middle life, largely as a result of shady business practices and alcoholism. The family then moved to a rural community several hundred miles from the original home. The father earned meager wages as a night watchman, while his mother took in boarders; and other members of the mother's family had to contribute as well.

In addition to poverty, loss of status, and chronic alcoholism in both parents, the patient was burdened with the knowledge that his mother had been intimate with several of her roomers. Nevertheless, he chose to ally himself with her and did, in fact, become her favorite, as well as the pride of the community. He was always an honor student, was captain of the debating team, sang in the church choir, and for a long time it was expected that he would become a clergyman. However, he had had enough of poverty and rural towns, so after graduating from college he joined a large company and, within a short time, became one of its most promising young executives.

To the outside observer, the patient was generous, dedicated, and considerate. He was a young man of unusual ability who had raised himself to astonishing heights. Although he did not live with his family, he was able to support them in comparative comfort. He moved in fashionable and sophisticated circles, but he also had other friends. Some of his friends were impoverished young men who needed his help, advice, and encouragement. In addition, he often helped his younger brother, who was not only chronically unemployed but was frequently arrested for brawling, drunkenness, and occasionally on paternity charges.

To the observer who penetrated his façade of urbane charm, the patient was a militant snob who despised his parents, ruthlessly outmaneuvered his colleagues, cynically cultivated people who had inherited their wealth, and, although willing to help impoverished young men with money and support, also sought to bind them to him.

In order to be his friend, these young men had to satisfy several requirements. First, they had to be smaller than he was, somewhat muscular, quite handsome, and practically penniless. Also, they had to be his inferior in every respect but one—they not only must they be unusually adept in making sexual conquests, but they must be sought by girls and women. In return for his help, the patient exacted one further requirement: in the same way that women were utterly compliant and submissive to these men, they, in turn, were to be controlled by him. In exchange for the gratification of being their mentor, friend, and patron, he subsidized their education, sponsored them in various jobs, and lent them money. He dominated them by force of his intellect, by his persuasive powers of speech, by his worldly ways, and by his pocketbook.

At various times during his relationship with each of these young men, he managed to share a bed with the young man, particularly when he believed that his friend had recently been in bed with a woman. There was never anything explicit about this requirement, and he would reject any hints from the analyst that this was the principal factor behind his interest in his friend's welfare. Nevertheless, while both pretended to be asleep, the patient would fondle the other man's penis or have femoral intercourse with him.

This representative perversion was not merely genital-femoral. It required an emotional and social setting in which he became an aloof, immaculate, aristocratic tyrant. He had even more expansive fantasies in which hordes of men became his subjects as well as the beneficiaries of his gold. They would come to him in awe and kneel and touch his penis as pilgrims might kiss a prelate's ring.

On the reverse side of this fantasy of riches, power, and nobility, were fears of poverty, helplessness, and insignificance. Most of all, he hated and feared women. In his nightmares, women compelled dirty brutes of men to tie him up and then violate him sexually. He would often wake at night in terror, because he believed a thug was hiding in his bathroom.

His fear of women was accompanied by strong self-disgust at his sense of weakness. It eventually became clear that he derived more satisfaction from dominating men, as women seemed to do, than from actual homosexual acts. He would not under any circumstances allow himself to be seduced by another man, and obvious homosexuals disgusted him.

Although he hated and feared women, he also envied them. "With a man's penis to hold, women can control everything!" "Suicide is better than being manhandled by a woman!" Although suicidal thoughts frequently occurred to him when he felt subservient, a specific kind of fantasy prompted both panic and ideas of suicide. In this fantasy, overpowering women bit off men's penises and left the man to die in blood and pain. His anxiety awakened at a point when he found himself enjoying the fantasy and simultaneously feeling sensations of tightness around his mouth and anus. In apparent contradiction, he often announced that if he could never marry and raise a family, he would commit suicide. Indeed, he carried a bottle of pills for the purpose of killing himself whenever he chose.

He was in analysis for several years before still another promotion forced him to leave the city. His anxiety had abated, and he had even begun to date girls. However, he really looked upon their company as a social requirement and not particularly desirable. He had acquired no other protégés, primarily because most of his bachelor associates were just as successful as he was.

Three years after interruption of analysis he again became extremely anxious. He had recently experienced a resurgence of homosexual desire for his current roommate, who was, not unexpectedly, highly adept at seducing women. More pressing, however, was his concern about a young woman he had been dating. He had discovered that his interest was more than mere pretense, and he had even become sexually aroused while caressing her. So far he had managed to avoid sexual relations with her, but he thoroughly expected that this could not be postponed much longer. He still retained his bottle of pills and his suicide plan in case his professed dream of a home, wife, and family did not materialize.

At this point it seemed reasonable to believe that his growing heterosexual appetite had stirred up anxiety about women and reawakened homosexual fantasies about his roommate. We arranged to resume therapy on a weekly basis, but several days later, because he was feeling considerably calmer, he cancelled the appointment.

Two weeks later, after a double date with his roommate, he went to his girl friend's apartment. Once again, despite her obvious attempts to seduce him, he was able to avoid sexual intercourse. Feeling dejected and disgusted with himself, he went home to find that his roommate had already returned, after another conquest. The patient noted that his roommate's genitals could "make four of his."

He was particularly unhappy on the following day when he discovered that his girl friend was not at home. He had wanted to arrange another date to celebrate his birthday. Naturally, the date would also include his roommate. However, he began to conclude not only that his girl friend was disgusted with him but that she and his roommate had been having an affair. As a replacement, he telephoned another girl, made a date for that evening, and then telephoned his roommate to tell him about the plans. Later in the afternoon, he went home to prepare for the evening's entertainment. He bathed, shaved, put on clean shorts, stretched out on his roommate's bed, and took 38 sleeping pills.

It was no surprise that his roommate returned home in time to discover the patient's plight and to call a physician. After recovering, however, the patient insisted that nothing really serious had happened except that the bottle of pills had lost its power. Because he had tried suicide and failed, he now believed that he was spared for a reason. The lucky star that had seen him through poverty to a successful career must still be guiding him. His life must have another purpose besides having intercourse with girls. He felt indebted to his roommate and now hoped for a closer friendship with him.

The patient's mood was that of quiet yet amiable resignation. There was no indication of apathy, bafflement, depression, or anxiety. Yet one week later he was dead—this time the suicide was successful.

What brought this man to destroy himself? Suicide had been thought of for many years, but only as a last resort when all else had failed. The psychodynamic factors were approximately the same on several other occasions, and the events were essentially the same as those that originally led him to seek psychiatric treatment. One significant difference, however, was that he now found it difficult to repudiate his heterosexual desire and disappointment and he still could not establish a dominant position over a dependent young man, while using him as an intermediary. In short, he was not able to contend with his heterosexual conflicts by homosexual means. His identifications had always been divided between women who controlled men and dependent men who were specialists in seducing and controlling women. Neither type of identification afforded him enough protection from suicide. After the first suicide attempt he tried to minimize his heterosexual urges and to fortify his relation with his roommate. By pretending that he led a charmed life, he reasserted his belief that he could not be annihilated.

*Case 2. Sadomasochistic acts*

In her youth a woman patient attempted suicide by hanging. Later on, subjugation and suffocation became essential parts of her sadomasochistic sexual pattern. She also regularly practiced many other kinds of sublethal self-destructive acts.

A forty-two-year-old woman had been in and out of psychiatric treatment since she had been confined to a sanatorium for four months at the age of twenty, following a suicide attempt by hanging. Despite many years of psychotherapy, her complaints remained essentially the same: obesity, periodic overeating, constipation, hypochondriasis, and recurrent depression.

Her depressive episodes usually started with an inordinate rage about being unappreciated by her family and being overburdened at her job. Actually, she volunteered to take on unpleasant, unrewarding, or particularly menial tasks, until their accumulation became intolerable. Then, in great paroxysms of self-pity, she would weep and grow angry. After denouncing people from whom she had sought approval, she would often devour a whole loaf of bread, consume a pound of candy, masturbate compulsively, and finally, with her abdomen distended to the point of pain, she would induce vomiting. On the following day, filled with self-loathing, she would become more despondent and want to kill herself. She could often abort suicidal inclinations by writing long letters of explanation, in which she would go to great lengths to rebuke and then exculpate the people who had angered her.

All of the patient's early memories were of being punished for having been unintentionally destructive or blamed for circumstances beyond her control. For example, she recalled that when her mother told her she was not old enough to go to school with her brothers she felt at fault for being so young. Another time, she failed to heed a nursemaid's warning, fell backward from a porch chair, and again felt that she had perpetrated an unintentional crime. Her envy of her older brothers was limitless, even in later years when both of them became alcoholics.

As she was growing up, her mother punished her for a variety of misdeeds, few of which she understood; she knew only that in some fashion she had been bad. The form of punishment, however, was quite explicit.

She would be instructed to bend over a table or bed or to kneel and expose her buttocks. Her mother would then beat her with a small switch or whip.

Gradually the patient grew to anticipate this punishment. Not only did it make her feel close to mother, but it convinced her that by such absolute submission she could avoid blame for unintentional offenses and, moreover, win her mother's approval. She believed and practiced this formula throughout her life; if you do everything that people want, even more if possible, you can never be blamed, and they will be *forced* to love you! Consequently, she sought situations in which she did other people's bidding or, as a token of submission, did their dirty work.

Like her daughter, the mother was also obese and unhappy. She had married a much older man after being rejected in an earlier love affair; and she warned the patient about the hazards of marriage and the duplicity of men. Despite these admonitions, the patient was popular with young men but was frightened by her sexual intensity. On one occasion, during a riotous fraternity party, she fell down a flight of stairs, sustaining a concussion and fracturing her arm. She interpreted the accident as punishment for being an incorrigible sinner and a disobedient daughter.

After this episode, in an effort to "reform," she became more depressed, fought against masturbation, and was tormented by homosexual fantasies about her roommates. While trying to control her anguish one night, in sheer despair she covered her face with a pillow, helping to bring about suffocation and relief. Instead, she found this to be sexually exciting. After this, she often used self-asphyxiation as a means either of bringing about an orgasm or of inducing a state of mind in which masturbation was permissible.

Her depressions became more frequent and more severe. Finally, she attempted to commit suicide by hanging herself. While feeling the noose tighten and sinking into oblivion, she was startled by an overwhelming orgasm. After this, "partial hanging" replaced the pillow as a way to exculpate herself from the shameful orgasm she so desired. "Suicide" allowed her to experience a gratification and, at the same time, to be punished for it. She could bring about pleasure while pretending to be a passive victim. It was during one of these episodes, when she was twenty, that she was unable to release the rope. She was discovered by her roommate and was sent to a hospital for treatment of depression. She had been failing in school, and this was presumed to be the cause of her despondency.

After discharge from the hospital, she was sent to Europe by her family in order to complete her education and to regain her health. Her emotional conflicts continued, of course. For example, she became unusually stirred by erotic frescoes in Italy and wondered what it would feel like to be filled with plaster, to have every orifice stuffed, to be cut into pieces, or to be broken into bits, like a fragment of statuary. By these fantasies she imagined that she could destroy both desire and the source of desire but was aware that the fantasies also had sexual appeal of their own.

With a group of older tourists, she visited a brothel where pornographic films were shown and was particularly intrigued by scenes in which women either volunteered or, subserviently, were forced to undergo anal and oral perversions. At the end of the evening, the guide invited her to his room. She complied eagerly, but was disappointed when, without preliminaries, he had anal intercourse with her twice and then sent her away. The memory of this episode and recollection of the films became models of compliance, subservience, and humiliation, and were the preconditional fantasies of her subsequent perversions.

In later years, she withdrew more and more from social life until, like her mother, she became a hypochondriacal recluse. Nevertheless, she continued to have fantasies in which brutal or imperious men killed or raped her. Often she introduced foreign objects into her vagina and gave herself copious enemas of intolerably hot water.

While traveling in foreign countries, as she did from time to time, she could usually find a man who would perform anal intercourse, for a fee. Payment was necessary in order to preclude "involvement." In fact, she refused the attentions of several men on her own cultural and social level because she preferred men who would threaten and degrade her. When the man forced her into an act which involved suffocation as well as danger and humiliation, her excitement almost caused her to lose consciousness. However, if any of her partners showed concern for her, she lost interest. She wanted them to be dispassionately cruel or imperious and not to display overt sexual excitement. It is significant that she referred to orgasms as "contractions" and to her partner's emissions as "urination."

Although the patient was unsuitable for a more ambitious type of psychotherapy, it was possible to investigate in considerable detail the inner relationships between personality traits, sexual perversions, and fantasy life. This resulted in finding still other unexpressed and even unrecognized ideas and images within her fantasies. For example, she remembered that during the periods when she was subjugated by a man she would imagine that there was an older woman standing silently in a corner of the room. This woman acted as a "chaperon," to give approval by her inconspicuous presence, but also to intervene if the patient were ever in danger.

In later phases of psychotherapy, after the beating fantasies receded, the image of the silent and supportive older woman remained. Then she began to yearn for a large, ample-bosomed Negro woman who would feed her, even suckle her. Instead of beating, the patient wanted her substitute mother to massage her buttocks and to give her enemas. Most of all, she wanted to be held so closely that she could no longer breathe. Suffocation and death in Mother's arms brought about fulfillment that proved Mother's single-minded love for her. That was the nuclear wish: if she could be compliant the way a nursing child is compliant, she would not need to be as compliant as a slave—and would not be punished for having too much appetite.

### *Case 3. Self-Extinction*

A male patient developed symptoms of narcolepsy and depression. Several of his sensations, conflicts, fears, and perceptions were reminiscent of those he had experienced during sexual perversions in earlier life. His life pattern was characterized by self-destructive neutrality, concealment of emotion, and anonymity.

A thirty-five-year-old machinist had complained of intervals of drowsiness for three years. Despite treatment with large doses of amphetamine these episodes became more frequent, and he also became markedly depressed. In addition to feeling unusually heavy, apathetic, and emotionally empty during depressed periods, he complained of an impaired sense of reality with blunted sensations of all kinds. He reported that sometimes he felt "as if a shroud came over me." This feeling did not frighten him. He even welcomed it as an interruption of the deadness of his existence.

Six months before he sought psychiatric aid he had become convinced that he was turning into a "Lesbian." He chose this way to convey his feelings because he was certain that men who were attracted to other men would not have feelings like this. Although he candidly reported that he was not a stranger to homosexual experiences, he insisted that he preferred women exclusively. From time to time, he had found himself believing that he had an erection, when in fact he had not. These "phantom" erections turned out to be related to the conviction that he was becoming a Lesbian. Both types of unfounded convictions were frequently followed by waves of drowsiness or sexual excitement.

The patient was poised and articulate and gave the impression of being more capable than his blue-collar job indicated. In some areas he was excessively candid but was inclined to be cautious and reticent in others. For example, he was in psychotherapy for several months before confiding that he had graduated from college and that he wanted no one else to know. He had deliberately avoided promotions because he regarded them as failures. He was prone to telling long-winded stories to illustrate the incompetence of his superiors, however, and enjoyed being contemptuous of others, not hesitating to expose their faults. As a bachelor, he moved about comfortably in lower-middle-class circles without close attachments. He did not intend ever to marry.

He had been adopted from an orphanage at an early age, but his adoptive father died when the patient was twelve. His foster mother and he then moved to a distant city where they lived with her widowed mother and an unmarried older sister, who became his "aunt." He was aware of being a welcome male in a household of females, but sometimes he felt that he was also regarded as a nobody who had intruded. When he was fourteen his mother died, and his grandmother died two years later.

He recalled very little grief after any of these losses. Although he occasionally wondered where his real parents lived, all in all his home life with his aunt was tranquil. She worked to support him, with the help of a small legacy from her mother, but he readily assumed more adult responsibilities in addition to his school work. He was bright and sociable, somewhat athletic, and popular with his classmates. He supplemented the household income by working after school, and he often escorted his aunt to the theater and social engagements. There would be conflict between them, however, when he could not take her to these functions, particularly if he had a date with a girl. They argued; she threatened him with expulsion from their home and he, in fact, would actually disappear for a few days. Although he had merely gone to stay with a friend, he enjoyed exposing his aunt's concern by ostensibly complying with her threats.

Shortly before he graduated from high school he and his aunt began to quarrel more frequently. Although they always became reconciled, particularly after he had left home for a day or two, tension gradually increased. It was at this time that she became ill and went to the hospital for a minor operation. He felt both angry and guilty during her absence, and when she returned he spent most of his time waiting upon her. Then, without a precipitant, they began to share the same bed. There was no overt sexual contact, and neither one discussed their sleeping arrangements. However, he was often unable to sleep until he had masturbated.

The patient had had infrequent heterosexual relations since the age of 14, but now began to shun girls of his own age. On weekends he drank quite heavily and realized that he wanted to have intercourse with his aunt. Finally, at the suggestion of a friend, he allowed himself to be picked up in a bar that catered to homosexuals. He discovered that instead of feeling guilty, he was angry at his aunt, blamed her for a nonspecific offense, and enjoyed the ensuing sense of revenge.

Soon after this he was seduced by an elderly female physician for whom he had worked afternoons. It was no coincidence that she was also his aunt's physician, nor was his seduction unilateral. As he had with male homosexuals, he arranged to be seduced by seeming to be just a passive and compliant partner. He had been enormously attracted by the doctor and had anticipated being her first and only love. Instead, he discovered that, unlike his spinster aunt, she had been married at least twice and had had considerable sexual experience with both men and women. He told her about his homosexual encounters, and in response she introduced him to other anal and oral sexual practices. His predominant emotions were feelings of triumphant resentment toward and revenge upon his aunt.

His first year at college was a disaster. He drank excessively, cut classes, and visited houses of prostitution, where he discovered that he envied the women. He became progressively despondent and, after obtaining a leave of absence, returned home to resume his affair with the doctor. Whenever necessary, he made money by letting himself be seduced by a homosexual.

Then, through an involved series of events, he became the paid sexual partner of several older women. In contrast to his feelings about homosexual encounters, he found this phase of his life extremely gratifying; he was reassured about his heterosexuality, found that he was worth being paid for, and, most of all, felt an immense sense of elation, not unlike what he had first experienced with the woman doctor. He also knew that unless these women were so desperate and lonely that they wanted the physical presence of any man they would not have wanted him. This realization heightened his gratification by making him feel prized for being an anonymous nobody. His sense of triumph increased with the degree of perversity of the situations in which he participated. By exerting power passively he could debase women and thereby elevate himself.

Further instances of specific perversions and episodes cannot be reported here, but it was apparent that participation for pay in a variety of sexual practices was itself a complicated perversion. However, as the rewarding and exalted responses gradually waned, his quest for anonymity and neutrality became sated and then replaced by tedium. His depression returned, and he thought about drowning himself. His fantasies were concerned with different ways in which he could experiment with dirt and depravity. He visited prostitutes and, in a sense of kinship, called them his "sisters." In fact, his ideal status was that of a highly coveted, but anonymous, prostitute who could rouse desire while being shut off from every desire herself. He could feel a semblance of importance through acquiescence, followed by an awareness of feeling like a woman—sometimes like a dead woman. Finally he became so indifferent that even suicide held no further promise.

To tell how the patient finally emerged from this ordeal would require a far more extensive essay. Although he was able eventually to salvage a portion of his talent, he had already decided that anonymity was his fate. Starting as a nameless orphan and going on to bisexual prostitution, he ended up in a job that offered him nothing but an opportunity to conceal himself. His renunciation of success and promotion in his work belonged in a category with his earlier wish to be a female prostitute, or Lesbian, who was desired but did not desire in return—a woman who could submit with amiable scorn to either sex and whose only satisfaction came from passive domination.

## Discussion

Our task in this chapter is not completely to chart the pathways and bypaths these patients followed on their way to sexual perversion and self-destruction. We can, however, examine some of the characteristics they shared.

### *Relation to Mother*

Their attitudes toward Mother covered a wide span. They ranged from wishes to protect and please her to fantasies that sought to betray, degrade, and punish her. The wish to be the sole recipient of her limitless affection was expressed in numerous fantasies of rediscovery of Mother, realliance with her, and reaffirmation of her love, even though the circumstances in which this was to occur were distorted or dangerous. Case 1 feared domineering women, but pitied his own alcoholic, promiscuous mother. The demonstrative sadomasochism of case 2 was centered upon winning Mother's silent approval and the tangible gift of her breast to suckle. Case 3 not only had not known his real mother but had lost his adoptive mother. He turned to his aunt, and to the woman doctor, hoping to gain fulfillment as well as revenge for what he had sought and did not find. Later, he tried to destroy his desire for an idealized mother by degrading other older women.

### *Anal and Oral Perversions*

None of these patients derived satisfaction from heterosexual intercourse, either in fact or in anticipation. Case 1 had managed to avoid coitus to the end of his life, but cases 2 and 3 had had intercourse frequently. Ordinary coitus failed to satisfy the conditions of domination and submission, coercion and control, that they required. A powerful incentive to perversion was the anticipation of defying a social taboo, with a further hope of "breaking through" an emotional barrier as well. Anal and oral perversions absolved these patients from any obligation to think of their partners as separate human beings; there was complete self-fulfillment and a sense of confluence in which only orifices and fluids were real.

### *Polarization between Victim and Master*

Vacillation between the victim or the master permeated these patients' lives. Case 1 made a career of being a King Midas who could generate gold by his powerful touch. Yet, like Midas, he became his own victim. In contrast, case 2 sought ways in which she could be victimized, but this was a transparent device which only betrayed its opposite intent. Case 3 also tried to become a victim and a passive partner, but in his fantasy world he achieved triumphant revenge.

In these patients the wish to overpower and the fear of being overpowered lacked the modulations usually found in other people. Relations with others tended always to be in extremes; they were master, slave, or totally neutral. They felt either absolute dedication or utter disgust toward their love objects, with few intermediate states of compromise. This state of fluctuation between extremes of desire and despair, when combined with complexities of denial and concealment, made it exceedingly difficult to recognize when they were the master or when they were the slave. This ambiguity of aim, coupled with a wish to be confluent with the other person, sometimes seemed to produce states of depersonalization or feelings of unreality.

### *Defensive Patterns*

Many patients with sexual perversion will avoid, or be repelled by, situations in ordinary life that, in the sexual sphere, will evoke powerful appetites. Still other patients with pronounced sexual deviations may lead staunchly conventional lives and even participate in conventional forms of sexual expression. The first group shows, in effect, reversal of affect, while the second group tends to *isolation*. These two qualities do not exhaust the differences between the ego functions of one group and those of the other. However, in the first group, deviant sexuality is *complementary* to the rest of the personality. In the second group, it is *idiosyncratic* and is more difficult to coordinate with the mainstream of motivation.

In contrast, the life styles of these three patients corresponded exactly with sexual patterns. Everyday life was totally involved with images, impulses, the idioms that originated in deviant sexuality. The relation between their sexual perversion and life behavior was neither complementary nor idiosyncratic but *symmetrical*. As a result, their defensive patterns differed in two important respects from other groups of patients with sexual perversion. First, their range of motivation was narrower, and the number of available ways to act upon motivation was more restricted. Second, what they did and how they did it, in *any* sphere of life, was highly libidinized. The defensive measures used to conceal more flagrant fantasies not only were surprisingly transparent but even offered significant gratification in themselves. For example, cases 2 and 3 used passivity as a technique to dominate their sexual partners; they also used submission and abnegation as a technique in their social and business transactions. In brief, the defensive measure of abdication and pseudosurrender not only relieved conflict but was, in itself, gratifying. Despite their renunciation of genital sexuality, life was highly sexualized for all three patients. Problems within one area were readily translated into practices in other areas.

For these three patients, other people had little independent reality; they were only playing roles determined by the script of an inner drama. Instead of developing a comparatively healthy ambivalence toward any one person, these patients used *dissociation*. They usually felt only one way toward any one person and quite an opposite way to another. For example, case 1 feared and despised all womankind, while feeling only pity, if no tenderness, for his mother. In all three patients, homosexual inclinations were strong in both the sexual and nonsexual spheres. Together with self-pity and paranoid views of other people, their defensive trends included *isolation*, *idealization*, *externalization*, and *displacement*. Their dominant wish was to be cared for by an unlimited source of nutriment and strength. Even though these patients blamed others for not being this source of unlimited care, everyone was kept at such distance that it was apparently not a realistically feasible relationship they were seeking.

## *Fantasies of Suicide*

Few workers in the field of suicide believe that the mode of self-destruction is a purely fortuitous choice. People who slash their wrists and others who swallow pills are likely to do so for quite different reasons.[15] In many instances, the *form* of the act is no less appropriate than is the *time* that suicide is attempted. Sometimes the form is an ironic affirmation of the problem that brought the patient to the brink. For example, an elderly woman patient slashed her wrists while feeling hopeless and depressed about her loneliness and self-defeating aloofness. She seemed to be declaring, "These arms are never going to embrace anyone, and I have pushed away everything else that mattered!"

Although analogies between the mode of suicide and the inner conflict are often graphic, even highly dramatic, in many instances the relation between the two cannot be found at all. However, we may often learn more from the mode of the suicide attempt than from the suicide note or the communicated intent. The reason for this is not difficult to find. What people say and what they do are, of course, quite different. What people who attempt suicide say or write—case 2, for example—is apt to be self-justifying or conciliatory, whereas what they do, even if it is not intended to bring about death, may have a direct honesty or relevance about it. Case 2 made repeated suicide attempts and pursued self-destructive aims by strangling, suffocating, and stuffing herself with food, drink, foreign objects, and hot water enemas. By filling every orifice, emptiness would disappear. Her fantasy of being an infant held tightly between her mother's breasts combined her wish to be subjugated with the wish to be suffocated. This was the link between the mode of sexual perversion and the mode of suicidal attempts. That the connection between her perversion and her suicidal fantasy emerged after so many years suggests that a specific psychodynamic correlation between the mode of suicide and the type of conflict may be more prevalent than can be documented. Failure to find a relation may be the result of a relatively casual method of investigation. After all, without investigation on a deeper level, it would require considerable tour de force to surmise, on the basis of the sexual sadomasochism of case 2, that her central wish was for a rewarding reunion with her mother.

The suicidal fantasies of case 1 centered on the bottle of pills, with its implicit promise of bringing about a version of triumph in the guise of sleep. Preparation for his next-to-last suicide attempt could hardly be distinguished from the behavior of a man who was about to meet his lover. The oblivion of sleep might also be compared with the serenity of surrender, except that the patient intended to use suicide as a way to make his roommate more dependent on him. Although the patient expressed indebtedness to his rescuer, we wonder if someone who rescues another does not also assume responsibility for him and share in his subsequent life. True or not, this is what the patient sought. He also believed that "a guiding star" watched over him and would not let him die unless death could lead him into a greater glory.

Because he did not actually attempt suicide, the suicidal fantasies of case 3 were less apparent. After all, his life style was of self-extinction and passionate neutrality. Had he been more dependent upon others he might have had more explicit suicidal fantasies. Another patient, in the midst of confusion and incipient psychosis, declared that if he were not so depressed he would commit suicide! As it was, he was paralyzed with self-doubt and, therefore, could not make such an important decision. In other words, case 3 did not want oblivion, nor did he seek an unequivocal act of either self-destruction or fulfillment. He wanted the indifferent equilibrium of a man who has reached bottom. He had nothing more to lose or to gain; suicide had nothing to offer him.

Psychodynamic parallels between the mode of self-destruction and the predominant conflict, on the one hand, and, on the other hand, between the predominant conflict and the mode of sexual perversion, suggest that the link between sexual perversion and suicide may have far-reaching significance. Suicide attempts may be shown to have constructive components and not to be wholly destructive. The fantasies of suicide and the preferred method of annihilation may be disguised sexual perversions. In a similar sense, fantasies associated with sexual perversions may not be exclusively sexual; they may refer to the patient's predicament, to the way he has chosen to define himself, and to what is needed to re-establish his link with the world. Perversion and suicide may be related efforts to *protect* as well as to *protest*.

### *Libidinization of Death*

Perhaps the most pervasive, yet elusive, quality of any patient is to be found in his relation to reality. We learn more about who and what people are by watching how they behave in the world and by listening to what they say about others than we do by accepting their self-conscious appraisal of themselves. Relation to reality includes more than representative acts and attitudes; it includes the key events which typify the kind of working relations people have formed with life. To be sure, for these three patients, sexual perversion became an eroticized way of transforming vulnerability into strength. Although their intent was often concealed, frequently even from themselves, perversion and self-destruction became a *fulcrum* with which to move and manipulate others as well as a *formula* to apply in contending with conflict. Their relation to reality, in short, became a means of reaching beyond an impasse, or even defeat, to an idealized reality.

In the course of living and dying amid extremes of emotions and shadows of master-victim relationships, sexual perversion became a type of self-destruction, while self-destruction became a perverse form of self-idealization. Patients with sexual perversion will characteristically libidinize their defenses[16] and thereby impose strong restrictions upon their view of the world. These patients went beyond this truism by *choosing* self-extinction, along with abrogation of genital relations, in order to become reinstated in a more or less idealized world. In other words, they attempted to defend themselves against overwhelming forces by using defeat as an instrument of victory. In this respect they are like defeated nations that use poverty, hunger, and need as diplomatic weapons and strategic implements.

### *Disease, Defeat, and Depravity*

If we could possibly accept the reality of possession by devils, it would be comparatively easy to understand the affinity between self-destruction and sexual perversion. In fact, the only remaining problem would be to decide which was which and in what way one was a cure for the other! As Huxley depicted their predicament, the unfortunate nuns of Loudun were enthralled in both senses of the word—by the unmitigated evil of the devils that enslaved them and by the sexual ecstasy which they could receive only from minions of the netherworld.[17]

According to the reigning moral and religious fiats of society, self-destruction and sexual perversions are products of disease, defeat, and depravity. Conventional judgment decrees that any disorder which violates society's established values, motives, and institutions is a *moral* defect. Consequently, with an easy hypocrisy, society banishes the victims of these disorders; it imposes moral judgments that merely rationalize drastic measures of retaliation, such as death, disgrace, exile, and dehumanization. In earlier times, the bearer of bad tidings was often punished, and the sword that killed a man was destroyed. We are not yet entirely free of this inclination. For example, mental disorder has been partially sanctioned by society by calling it "illness." This euphemism exempts patients from social condemnation by defining their incapacity in such a way that it does not challenge, expose, or undermine the pseudoperfection required by conventional morality.

In the past few decades, we have seen indications of a more reasonable attitude toward many social facts of life that once were condemned or ignored. For example, nowadays anyone who has attempted suicide is not automatically scorned as a weakling, a psychotic, or a sinner. There are even influential opinions that homosexuality between consenting adults need not be a criminal matter. Nevertheless, even among so-called enlightened people, suicide and perversion, along with drug addiction, venereal disease, pornography, prostitution, poverty, unemployment, and psychosis, still retain stigmatic residues of the moral judgments of their forebears. According to the moralistic residue, disease, defeat, and depravity are all one.

Not until recent times has medicine fully appreciated the adaptive significance of disease.[18] Illnesses and symptoms are no longer considered to be mere end-products of deranged bodily processes. Instead, they are indications of the ways in which the body goes about healing itself. As a result, medicine's treatment of sick people has changed; we now try to treat people instead of diseased organs or social rejects. For example, the drunks and inebriates of a generation or two ago have become people with a "problem" of alcoholism.[19] This is more than a semantic nicety. Part of this change in viewpoint depends upon the necessity for recognizing that some people are trying to be sober when they drink, just as a man who stumbles is trying to walk straight. Some people can adapt to inner problems and impairments only by calling upon methods that actually prevent wholly successful adaptation. One such example is sexual perversion and self-destruction. For these patients, death may be both a measure and a method of adaptation.

### *Death as Measure and Method*

Society attempts to maintain itself by getting rid of those who expose its defects. One way of doing this is to regard disease, defeat, and depravity as identical evils. Patients with sexual perversions or self-destructive trends are also members of society and, to some extent, must share in its values and decisions. Therefore, we have two problems: what are the forces within some people that bring about sexual perversion or self-destruction as adaptive measures and how do these people go about "normalizing" themselves?

From a psychoanalytic viewpoint, sexual perversions and self-destructive acts may be interpreted as manifestations of *id, ego,* and *superego.* From the id viewpoint, they are vicissitudes of instincts. From the ego viewpoint, the search for instinctual fulfillment must be joined to the practical problem of bringing it about with a minimum of risk. From the perspective of the superego, sexual perversion and self-destruction are vehicles by which instinctual gratification and practical performance become reconciled with the dominant directives and prohibitions of the world. For some patients, self-destruction and sexual perversion are ways to "normalize" themselves; to feel in control, not enslaved; to attain consummation not extinction; and, in effect, to be wholly responsible. Although deviant sexual behavior or self-destructive acts are dubious methods of social adaptation, by engaging in such acts, these patients may endure threatening crises, neutralize overwhelming forces, and, in some cases, reaffirm themselves. In order to do so, however, two unique processes are required: *transposition of opposites* and *transmutation of objectives.* Activity becomes passivity, passivity becomes activity; appetites change into aversions, disgust into fascination; destruction promises both relief and fulfillment, whereas reality demands despair. In brief, patients discover their affinity with death.

As a rule, patients with sexual perversion tend to avoid conflict by shunning genital intercourse; other patients neutralize their helplessness by destroying themselves or by making death exciting. In this way, they may reverse their conflicts and thereby cease to be victims. If conflicts can be transposed into external acts and transmuted into desirable events, then these patients can eliminate unloved, enfeebled, victimized, or unreal parts of themselves by a simple act of self-destruction.

Even without considering the many other factors which contribute to pathological adaptation, it seems evident that some patients with sexual perversion and self-destruction are *driven* by a desire to create their own version of death. People who are in constant danger of death will sometimes seek to force the issue in one way or another. Analogously, other people who find themselves close to being overwhelmed may wish to die in triumph rather than in defeat. They seek to discover death and to disarm it.

## *Conflict*

To be comprehensible, the psychodynamic theory of conflict requires a concept of the unconscious. By providing for a common source of meaning, being, and motivation, it is the psychological basis for a coherent theory of the world. From the metaphysical standpoint, the dynamic unconscious offers an ultimate justification for our sense of being here and making sense. Sometimes, however, it is deceptively easy to accept a generalization because there is no good reason to challenge it. Once this is done, it is just as easy to accept ancillary ideas and secondary inferences as if they were undisputed facts. A typical example of this is the concept of psychodynamic processes, which are often misunderstood to mean fixed and formal mental structures.

We cannot deny the reality of psychological processes that determine how we understand meaning, being, and motivation. The problem is to describe and define these processes with minimal ambiguity, reification, and misplaced concreteness. If the elaborate hierarchy and catalogue of ego structures and functions were reduced to simplest terms, we would readily see that psychodynamic processes are actually hypotheses. Their purpose is to account for the way in which one motivated act or attitude is transformed into another.

In simplest terms, conflict arises when incompatible motivated acts seek simultaneous fulfillment. These acts and attitudes may be called by a variety of terms—appetites and aversions, wishes and fears, attractions and repulsions, directives and prohibitions, and so forth. The psychiatrist's problem, however, is not so much to define conflict as it is to detect conflict. He must be able to tell the difference between the *composition* of a conflict, the methods used for *resolution* of a conflict, and the inner *experience* of conflict. Psychodynamic formulations, as a rule, emphasize the composition of a conflict and the defenses against conflict.[20] The inner emotional experience slips through the formulation, often because we do not have an adequate language to describe it. If, however, it were possible to creep *within* the conflicts of the three patients described in this chapter, we would discover the kind of reality and image of death found only in the stern eschatology of medieval times—that man is totally depraved, the world is evil, and salvation is found only by departing into another world. Present-day society tends to dismiss certain groups of people because they epitomize the unity of disease, defeat, and depravity. Among these people are those who practice self-destruction or sexual perversion. Ironically, it is just these properties in themselves and in the world that patients with sexual perversion and self-destruction want to change. Patients with sexual perversion often eroticize pain, anxiety, or guilt, and sometimes look to suicide as an ultimate form of resolution of conflict. In other words, threatened with annihilation or depravity, they may try to resolve conflict and to validate group judgments by changing an intolerable reality into an idealized and libidinized existence. If this is not possible, then an idealized existence may be anticipated in death.

These patients were not conscienceless psychopaths; they were seeking highly conventional states of fulfillment by destroying themselves. We do not hesitate to recognize "loss of self-esteem" in cases of depression or "loss of control" in anxiety. In patients who combine perversion with self-destruction, loss of self-esteem and control are only part of the greater problem—to revamp reality according to an idealized version.

There are some conflicts so deeply imbedded in incompatible urges and repulsions, and compounded of so much desire and despair, that hope, as we understand it, is utterly meaningless, and survival is feasible only by complete capitulation. Frankl[21] has described his concentration camp experiences in terms that parallel this hypothesis. What happens to people when submission is used as a strategy for regaining mastery? We concede that some men are willing to die for a cause. In suicide and sublethal self-destruction men may sacrifice themselves, but without an ennobling justification. Death and life have become so ambiguous for these patients that they have libidinized reality and have turned death into an idealized extension of themselves, the way a man who dies for a cause sees in death a glamorized justification of his own values.

The idea of death as an extension of one's own libidinal field is unfamiliar only because of our contemporary vocabulary. We do not often talk about salvation, sin, and depravity in modern psychology. Yet this is how many patients see themselves. The age-old question, "What shall we do to be saved?" differs from its modern version, "How shall we prevent disaster?" only because now our ideas of damnation, disaster, and what we ought to be saved from have different meanings. Every domain has its private libidinizations of death. There is a long but strong thread which connects humanity and its heroes with themes of life-in-death and death-in-life. Tristan, Oedipus, Abelard, and Faust are among the most prominent examples. Triumphant death and idealized self-destruction permeate many legends and myths. After all, martyrdom is a strategy as well as a sacrifice.

Sacrifice is the strategy of suffering whereby death is courted in order to sustain hope, even when the nature of this hope is uncertain and the remote reward is suspiciously similar to what we may have avoided all along. This viewpoint has brought about unmeasured agony and anxiety, guilt and pain. Yet, the formula is deceptively simple: *Suffering→death→resurrection.* We become bogged down, however, when we try to discover what meanings can be assigned to parts of the formula and what applications of it are relevant to our own lives.

For the purposes of this chapter, let us try to strip away the film of morality and reaction formation that obscures our psychological vision. Let us then assume the viewpoint of a man—any man—who wants to believe that his life is not altogether meaningless; if there were only someone, something, some way, or even some state of mind in which he could believe, then reality would seem to care about him. Just as he believes that somehow the world is concerned with him, he will also hope that all his misdeeds, mistakes, failures, and disappointments can be justified, even rectified. This state of mind may be called "heightened narcissism." If the libidinal field of his self-image happens to coincide with how he sees the world, his hopes will not be restricted by reality. We can now appreciate that for this man feasible reality has changed places with idealized fantasies. If the connotation of dread, decay, and destruction can be removed from his conventional view of death, then death itself may be idealized, and he will seek ways to attain it.

### *Self-Destruction and Perversions as Strategies*

Suicide is a strategy of death in which the victim is able to choose his own fate. Although we usually interpret suicide as a drastic means of ridding oneself of an objectionable element—comparable, perhaps, to burning the house down to get rid of an offensive odor—the suicidal act also has its manipulative aspects. Like illness, suicide and self-destruction may be attempts to heal themselves. In other words, self-destruction may have more ambitious aims than merely to manipulate and coerce others; it can also be a technique for controlling nature and preventing change.

Analogously, sexual perversions are eccentric forms of behavior which use parts of the self—namely, objectionable sexual appetites and apparatuses—in order to bring about another kind of mastery. Insofar as patients with sexual perversion eroticize their depression, guilt, or anxiety, they are able to fortify themselves against disaster and reaffirm their control over nature. Libidinization of death, identification with narcissistic object choices, and readily reversible, bipolar emotional attitudes may even create conditions in which guilt, anxiety, and depression are actively sought.

To a lesser degree, similar transformations may be found in the strategy of *self-pity*. Patients with a strong sense of self-pity seem to believe that under some conditions it is more desirable to be the passive victim of heedless or hostile forces than to admit to having even partial control over their fate. In this way, even if they undergo humiliation, betrayal, failure, or abuse, their self-esteem is intact. There are several reasons for preferring to be the victim; they are absolved from censure and are even free to censure others for having failed them. Furthermore, despite humiliation, betrayal, failure, or abuse, they have still survived. In a sense, they have chosen to be the victim in a highly circumscribed context and, as a rule, to acknowledge being a victim in one context makes it permissible to triumph in another. Patients who combine sexual perversion and self-destruction frequently use this strategy as part of their surge toward a lost, inaccessible, or idealized reality.

### *Distinction Between Neurosis and Perversion*

The coincidence of neurotic symptoms and perverse behavior in the same patient is neither accidental nor obligatory. The boundaries of both syndromes are usually so flexible that it is not uncommon to find patients with neurotic disorders who also report sexual perversions. However, the psychodynamic relation between neuroses and perversions is not at all clear. Freud's dictum about one being the negative of the other is almost diagrammatic in its simplicity. To have a preponderance of one certainly does not automatically "protect" the patient from the other, although this inference has often been drawn.

We must also recognize that the imputed relationship between neuroses and perversions may be determined in part by the psychiatric perspective. Psychiatrists are oriented to a psychopathological, psychodynamic viewpoint and often use terms and categories that bespeak illness, disordered function, and deranged motivation. For example, philanthropy may be ascribed solely to a wish to be rid of guilt, but, correct or not, this is a highly polarized viewpoint. Inescapably, we can only examine events from our own perspective, in our own terms, and within the boundaries of our own dimensions.

For these and other reasons, I recognize that psychoanalysts usually find sexual perversion to be a clinical counterpart of psychoneuroses. Other people will, naturally, have other types of antithetical alternatives, based upon their special orientation. Forensic psychiatrists, for example, will acquire their special viewpoint by repeatedly comparing sexual perversions with criminal offenses. State hospital psychiatrists are apt to interpret sexual aberrations against a background of severe psychopathology. For psychodynamic psychiatrists, however, the meaning of sexual perversion is more succinctly understood by contrasting it with psychoneurosis.

From a psychoanalyst's viewpoint, therefore, neuroses and perversions are both efforts to resolve inner conflict. In neither case is the patient satisfied to be a victim unless he has worked out an arrangement whereby victimization, or passivity, can be used as a means of exerting control.

Opportunities to dissimulate are available to everyone, and the wish to be master, not victim, is not limited to patients with sexual perversion or self-destruction. However, the psychoanalyst finds significant differences between patients with sexual perversions and those with psychoneuroses.

Patients with perversions fluctuate between extremes in their emotions and interrelationships. They use other people simply to bring about one-sided fulfillment of fantasies. Patients with psychoneuroses are more adept in achieving compromise and conciliation between opposing impulses. They are able to develop a healthy ambivalence and look upon people as people, not as mere unilateral instruments and objects. Patients with neuroses are able to maintain a level of tension not often possible for those with perversions. Psychoneurotic patients accomplish this by repressing affect, inhibiting action, and temporizing wishes. Patients with perversions frequently control their fantasies by splitting their emotional attachments according to action and counteraction and become all one way or another toward anyone who means anything to them. Consequently, other people are always as they are perceived at any moment, and responses to them are singularly exaggerated. People with psychoneuroses do impose their fantasies and expectations upon reality, but people with perversions use different kinds of reality to conform with their fantasies. The inner rationality of psychoneuroses is like the distortions and corrections built into lenses. If, indeed, there is an inner rationality in perversions, it is like the crystals that reconstitute themselves by being broken along some established line of cleavage.

## Summary

Physicians are required to face death and to devise ways to circumvent it. On the whole, however, the medical profession is involved only with impersonal death. Yet, no less than anyone else and perhaps even more, doctors must be concerned with how people contend with death in all its dimensions.

There is no way to know how often people think about death or what they do about it. Considering the inevitability of death, it is strange that people talk and act as if they were going to live forever, while at the same time they look upon death as a necessary evil. Even when threatened by illness or injury, some people deny that they are concerned about death; others, during severe anxiety or profound depression, are certain that death is imminent. Among the troubled people who consult psychiatrists death is seldom in the foreground. The drive to survive at any cost usually blocks out thoughts of personal extinction. In seeking to clarify specific emotional conflicts, however, we may also wonder how people in general are able to resolve pervasive conflicts about living and dying. Since it is unlikely that thoughts of death seldom trouble people, or that troubled people rarely think about death, death evidently wears different disguises. How shall we then recognize it?

That death does, in fact, wear disguises seems apparent from the variety of ways in which people face it. They may deny it or challenge it; they may glorify it in social and religious practices; others may court it; and a few may even try to defeat it. From the psychiatrist's viewpoint, patients who demonstrate patterns of life in which thoughts of death are expressed by self-destructive fantasies, fears of killing and being killed, seem to reveal most clearly how death acquires psychodynamic significance. Yet, it is difficult to learn about any patient's genuine attitude toward death by ordinary interview techniques. Although self-destructive and self-defeating tendencies are common among psychiatric patients, they are only indirectly expressed. Highly narcissistic patients, for example, usually do not conceal their inordinate wish to be loved or to be emotionally fed. They are less explicit about their contrapuntal fear of being hated, or destroyed, or emotionally starved. Patients with sexual perversion, however, will often demonstrate intense fears of death and destruction that require little inference. I chose to limit this study to three patients whose psychodynamic patterns linked sexual perversion with self-destructive behavior. These patterns of eroticized self-destruction, or self-destructive eroticism, may be divided into three groups: *suicidal attempts, sadomasochistic acts,* and *self-extinction.*

Psychodynamic propositions must be constantly revised, just as generalizations of all kinds must allow for invalidating cases.[22] Psychodynamic explanations appeal to established beliefs and conventional concepts as the basis for their credibility, but this may result only in redundancies and acceptable banalities. In addition, psychodynamic explanations sometimes need a touch of the preposterous to clarify meaning, to prevent premature conclusions, and to introduce novelty. I have not intended to reach comprehensive conclusions here, but have tried to point out further dimensions in which problems of suicide, self-destruction, and sexual perversion may be studied. To deny that death is an essential part of the process of living would be as absurd as to deny that the skull is part of the head. Yet psychiatrists frequently study emotional conflicts by emphasizing only issues of life, as if the dilemmas that death imposes could be strategically ignored.

To summarize then, let me offer several preposterous propositions.

Let us deny that all suicidal patients want to kill themselves or expect to die. Instead, let us recognize that there are some patients who are self-destructive in order to *preserve* themselves and to *triumph* over death. This means that the hostile side of self-destruction is secondary and that death—so universally deplored—becomes idealized.

Let us also claim that some patients with sexual perversions are not primarily concerned with sexual gratification and that their hedonistic, appetitive behavior may be instigated by nonsexual motives. In a sense, these patients are *virginal romantics* who are poignantly aware of the difference between impersonal male-female coitus, full interpersonal love, and the use of body surfaces and orifices for nonsexual aims. As a result, out of fragments of acts, sensations, organs, meanings, and fantasies, they put together a way of life which condenses conflict into deviant sexual behavior. The distinctive quality of their deviant sexuality is that they simulate what is shunned and idealize what is inaccessible. Indeed, their jaded sensuality may conceal a romanticism, and what is commonly thought of as degradation or depravity may be for them an inverted image of a fulfilling reality. The perversion calls attention to what is *not* there, to what is lost, or sought, or cannot be found. Under these circumstances, death may be romanticized.

There are some types of masochism in which defeat, pain, and submission are simulated pretexts for ultimate victory, pleasure, and dominance. Similarly, self-destruction combined with sexual perversion may be a state of being in which one is *almost* overcome by death. Is it possible to play a game skillfully and, at the same time, court defeat? This is a dilemma for these patients. Although death may well be a calamity fringed with failure and defeat, it may also be a fulfilling kind of reality.

## REFERENCES

1. K. Menninger, *Man Against Himself* (New York: Harcourt, Brace and Company, Inc., 1938).
2. D. de Sade, *The Marquis de Sade: The Complete Justine, Philosophy in the Bedroom and Other Writings,* comp. and trans. R. Seaver and A. Wainhouse (New York: Grove Press, Inc., 1965).
3. H. Nunberg, *Principles of Psychoanalysis: Their Application to the Neurosis,* trans. M. and S. Kahr (New York: International Universities Press, Inc., 1955).
4. S. Nacht, R. Diatkine, and J. Favreau, "The Ego in Perverse Relationships," *International Journal of Psychoanalysis,* 37:404–413, 1956.

5. S. Freud, *Three Essays on the Theory of Sexuality* (1905), *Standard Edition of the Complete Psychological Works of Sigmund Freud*, trans. J. Strachey (London: The Hogarth Press, Ltd., and Institute for Psychoanalysis, 1953), vol. VII, pp. 125–245.
6. W. Gantt, *Experimental Basis for Neurotic Behavior: Origin and Development of Artificially Produced Disturbances of Behavior in Dogs* (New York: Paul B. Hoeber, Inc., 1944).
7. B. Karpman, *The Sexual Offender and His Offenses: Etiology, Pathology, Psychodynamics and Treatment* (New York: Julian Press, 1954); W. Gillespie, "General Theory of Sexual Perversion," *International Journal of Psychoanalysis*, **37**:396–403, 1956; I. Rosen (ed.), *The Pathology and Treatment of Sexual Deviation* (Fair Lawn, N. J.: Oxford University Press, 1964).
8. E. Glover, "The Relation of Perversion-Formation to the Development of Reality Sense," in *On the Early Development of Mind* (New York: International Universities Press, Inc., 1956), pp. 216–234.
9. Rosen, *op. cit.*
10. H. Sachs, "Creativeness in the Obsessional Ritual," in *The Creative Unconscious: Studies in the Psychoanalysis of Art* (Cambridge, Mass.: Sci-Art Publishers, 1942), pp. 344–358.
11. T. Reik, *Masochism in Modern Man*, trans. M. Beigel and G. Kurth (New York: Farrar, Straus & Giroux, 1941); Menninger, *op. cit.*
12. M. Boss, *Meaning and Content of Sexual Perversions: A Daseins-analytic Approach to the Psychopathology of the Phenomenon of Love*, trans. L. Abell (New York: Grune & Stratton, Inc., 1949).
13. P. Landsberg, *The Experience of Death. The Moral Problem of Suicide*, trans. C. Rowland (New York: Philosophical Library, Inc., 1953).
14. E. Shneidman, "Suicide: Some Classificatory Considerations," *Special Treatment Situations*, Forest Hospital Publications, **1**:4–8, 1962.
15. P. Sifneos, and W. McCourt, "Wishes for Life and Death of Some Patients Who Attempted Suicide," *Mental Hygiene*, **46**:543–552, 1962.
16. O. Fenichel, "Organ Libidinization Accompanying the Defense Against Drives," in *Collected Papers, First Series* (New York: W. W. Norton & Company, Inc., 1953), pp. 128–146.
17. A. Huxley, *The Devils of Loudun* (New York: Harper & Row, 1953).
18. H. Selye, *The Stress of Life* (New York: McGraw-Hill Book Company, 1956).
19. M. Chafetz, and H. Demone, *Alcoholism and Society* (Fair Lawn, N. J.: Oxford University Press, 1962).
20. A Weisman, "Psychodynamic Formulation of Conflict," *Archives of General Psychiatry*, **1**:288–309, 1959.
21. V. Frankl, *Man's Search for Meaning: An Introduction to Logotherapy*, trans. I. Lasch (New York: Washington Square Press, Pocket Books, Inc., 1963).
22. A. Weisman, *The Existential Core of Psychoanalysis: Reality Sense and Responsibility* (Boston: Little, Brown and Company, 1965).

# 14. The Components of Personal Despair

JAMES C. DIGGORY

## Apologia for the Attempt

To anyone who has examined the life situation of a person who has committed suicide or of one who was passively resigned to his own impending death, there is likely to occur the notion that these people were in hopeless or desperate situations. The literature on suicide and attitudes toward death indicate that similar thoughts have occurred to psychologists and psychiatrists who write about depression. The category of depression includes many "indicators" such as sagging posture, drooping countenance, slowing of thought and action, and a general disinclination to seek any experiences or activities, even those which previously were most rewarding. Also prominently mentioned are "feelings" or negative affects of gloominess, sadness, hopelessness, emptiness, worthlessness, and despair. Discussions of depression, more often than not, include references to suicide; and discussions of suicide almost invariably contain allusions to depression.

Indeed, for some people the relation between depression and suicide is axiomatic, and there are case files of hospitalized mental patients in which the entry "depressed" was added to the diagnosis *after* the patient had surprised everyone by killing himself. Now, regardless of whether a person's view of the world depends on common sense or on more refined categories, such an event might result in his issuing a show-cause order to the experts: "Why should you not cease and desist from trying to persuade me that there is a connection between what you call 'depression' and the act of suicide?"

In a preliminary hearing before a Court of Cognitive Responsibility, the complainant might present his grounds for believing that the alleged connection between depression and suicide is not something that he could observe in nature, not a verifiable connection between two things independently defined, but simply an unfounded assertion by the experts. In reply, experts can (and have) used one, or a combination, of the following statements:

First, the alleged connection between depression and suicide is found in the writings of the founder of the system to which the expert and his colleagues subscribe. If they talked to each other in any different manner they would be outside the system and possibly unable to communicate with each other at all. The system is good for many things, including its service as a basis for affiliation with colleagues, and out of deference to the general value of the system its possible cognitive shortcomings in this and a few other cases are customarily overlooked.

A second type of defense, not much different from the first, is that the required evidence cannot be presented publicly and at large. It is based on the private intuition of the expert. He and his colleagues agree that such intuitive interpretations, the principles of which cannot be described except to a colleague trained in the same way they are trained, are useful and trustworthy bases for the assertions they make. The truth of their assertions consists in their being agreed to by most experts with similar training.

Or, the expert might say that his sole business is to prevent other people from killing themselves. He will attempt such prevention by every means he can devise. But if his efforts are to be directed efficiently he must be able to identify persons to whom he can attach a high risk of suicide. He makes this identification by a straightforward empirical process. For example, data from a number of nations show that the proportion of suicides among men is consistently higher than it is among women; so being a male entails a relatively high empirical risk of suicide. By the same principle, the suicide risk is higher for white people than for Negroes; it generally increases with age; and from 1929 to 1959, the suicide rate among white men between 45 and 54 years of age shows a very close correspondence with the percent of the labor force unemployed. This correspondence is so close that when the expert displays the unemployment curve and the suicide-rate curve separately, nobody in court can tell which is which.[1]

"I see that you have something very interesting and important here," says the complainant. "That last demonstration with the two curves was most dramatic. But you haven't convinced me that because a person is male, white, unemployed, and older than 45, he will commit suicide. I suppose, in fact, that most of those people will not." The expert agrees with this; he may even add that the highest recorded suicide rate that he knows of among white males 45 to 54 years old in the United States was a little short of 70 per 100,000. That happened in 1933. "Isn't that a phenomenon of very low incidence?" the complainant asks.

But the Court intervenes and rules that the last question is irrelevant to the immediate purpose of the line of questioning. Court opines that the accused has been merely illustrating what he means by the identification of relatively high suicidal risk. Court demands direct testimony on the substance of the cease-and-desist order, the alleged connection between depression and suicide. Expert produces tables to show that in a series of mental patients a "significantly" higher proportion of those with a diagnosis of depression committed suicide than of those, otherwise similar patients, who had not been diagnosed as depressed. He urges that a diagnosis of depression thus increases the risk of suicide. On similar grounds the expert argues that the objective risk of suicide is higher among people who have thought about committing suicide, or threatened to do it, or actually attempted it, than among people who have done none of these things. The expert wants to reduce wastage of human resources. He wants to save lives. Thus, he argues, he should take seriously anything which signals an increase in the probability that a person will take his own life.

The complainant admits that this is exactly the way he himself would act. But the expert has only described *prudent* behavior, not given evidence for a close material connection between depression and suicide. The expert tries to specify more narrowly the extent to which the presence of depression increases the risk of suicide. The expert admits that depression is a form of mental illness, but not the only form. There are some people who are mentally ill, but never diagnosed as depressed. The complainant then introduces some facts on his own account: Fisch[2] compiled data on 114 American military men who had attempted suicide and found that only 28 percent were diagnosed as psychotic; records of 114 people who had actually committed suicide in Seattle showed that only 29 percent had been previously diagnosed as psychotic;[3] in Massachusetts only 28 percent of 115 people who attempted suicide were diagnosed as psychotic;[4] and of 200 consecutive admissions in England to a general hospital for attempted suicide, only 24 percent were discharged to mental hospitals;[5] and many investigators found that the average incidence of psychotics among cases of actual suicide is about 25 percent.[6]

Again, although the incidence of "depressive illness" in both members of monozygotic twins may be as high as 90 percent, the incidence of suicide in both is only about 5 percent, even when both were depressed.[7]

Futhermore, the meaning of depression does not seem very clear. For instance, what is to be made of these statements: "depression seemed to be at work" in 55 percent of a group of mental hospital patients who killed themselves, but only 10 percent had "a diagnosis of depression";[8] and whereas 100 percent of another group of suicides "showed evidence of depression," only 19 percent "had a diagnosis of psychotic depression."[9] "Now," says the complainant, "I see that the situation is worse than I thought it was when I started this action. I grant that the expert should be encouraged to use all possible clues that might identify people who are likely to put their own lives in danger. But in terms of systematic knowledge, to say that there is a close correlation between depression and suicide, or to act as though such a correlation exists, is at least to go beyond the evidence and possibly even to perpetuate a falsehood. But now I see that we aren't even sure of what we mean by one of the terms in the alleged connection—depression. Tell me what you mean by depression."

It seems that depression refers most generally to a mood or affective state which is described as gloomy, sad, blue, or melancholy. Such sufferers sometimes say that they feel hopeless, despairing, empty, or helpless; and they act without spontaneity and neglect their usual activities, even routine maintenance of their own house or person. Neither threats nor enticements can rouse them to action. Nothing, whatever its aim, seems worth doing. Some are overwhelmed by regret, or guilt, or self-blame by things they have done or left undone in the past. In some cases it seems that these omissions or commissions are only imaginary. And often, even when they were real, they were not so bad as they *now* seem to the person who is depressed. Now, nothing is worth anything—not love, laughter, thinking, talking, music, games, or work; not even the sufferer himself. Why bother to do anything? Most things only have to be done over again sooner or later. And even if the person can see that there is some ultimate utility to an action, he simply does not feel like doing it. This is, perhaps, a description of an unusually severe or extreme degree of depression. Not all episodes of depression are so profound or so pervasive. Furthermore, some of these episodes last for only a few hours and others may last for years. Some individuals may experience a depressed mood almost every day, and others may have the experience only once or twice in their lives.

The most safe prediction to make about a depressed mood is that it will terminate, whether or not the individual is subjected to psychotherapeutic treatment. Electric shock therapy seems to shorten the period of depression; but people so treated have a higher likelihood of going through another period of depression than are those who were allowed to recover "spontaneously." Apart from differences in the severity, duration, and frequency of periods of depression some of them begin without the presence of any events or conditions in the person's life which could be thought of as in the least discouraging or frustrating, or in any way assignable as "causes" of depression. Furthermore, some people are more likely than others to have recurring intervals of depression without reasonably assignable causes. People with this kind of life history are likely to have ancestors with similar histories; and in monozygotic twins, if one suffers depressions, then the other will also—in nine out of ten pairs. These facts suggest that some depressions result chiefly from characteristics of the individual and are relatively independent of environmental events which impinge on him. They appear to be of "interior origin," and are called "endogenous."

On the other hand, some people have periods of depression when they seem to have objective cause to be discouraged: A loved one has died, he has suffered financial reverses, he cannot keep a promise he made, he has witnessed something unpleasant, he was betrayed by people he trusted or he himself betrayed a trust, or his abilities have been overtaxed and his undertakings have failed. In many cases it appears that some one or a combination of these situations is the precipitating "cause" of the depression. The depression is the reaction to the situation, and would be called "exogenous" or "reactive."[10]

This recital causes the complainant to reflect that it is small wonder that the expert believes there is some connection between depression and suicide. Indeed, the problem seems to be: Why should a man in such a state as the expert has just described want to go on living at all? But then, why isn't the connection between depression and suicide stronger, easier to see? Further testimony from the expert elicits the information that "depressive" patients do not often commit suicide when they are in the depths of the depression. They are most likely to do it when they are getting better, when the gloom of their mood is dissipating, at a time when people inexperienced in these matters are likely to be surprised by the suicide. But now the complainant is surprised. How can these things be? First they describe a situation that would make any reasonable man want to end it all and then they tell you that the risk of suicide seems to go up exactly when the reasonable cause of it appears to be abating. The complainant is so stunned that he cannot continue. The Court grants his request for an indefinite recess; he needs much time to think.

The complainant muses as follows: In his description of depression the expert focussed on the conscious mood of sadness or gloom, on "feelings" of helplessness, hopelessness, and despair. Probably not all depressed people describe their moods in exactly the same way, except possibly for what we might loosely call sadness. Further, psychology has made great strides in the past fifty years precisely when most psychologists were paying little attention to any aspect of consciousness. If William James had not been so "literary," if he had used words more precisely, like his brother Henry, he might have hastened the revolution against defining psychology exclusively in terms of consciousness. He might even have guided us into the broader view that we now enjoy without our having had to suffer the sloganeering atrocities of the Watsonian revolution.

But James wrote of the "stream of consciousness," implying that consciousness is continuous and thus coined a battle slogan for those who thought psychology would perish with Titchener. In the heat of battle, and flushed with their early successes, the behaviorist absolutists overlooked the significance of James's almost offhanded remark that "ordinarily, we have *sciousness* rather than *con*sciousness." Thus, some of us believe that the enduring values of the Watsonian movement were its emphasis on objectivity and its broadening the scope of psychology to include children and all animals as proper objects of study. The emphatic and absolute exclusion of consciousness was perhaps necessary, in a sense, for the realization of the positive values; but its long-range effects were just as bad for science as the exclusion of everything *but* consciousness had been. Our current broader perspective is this: we have no reason at all to believe that there is any important human problem which cannot be dealt with, in principle, by the most objective methods we can devise; and there is no reason to believe that, in devoting ourselves to studying behavior by objective methods, we will thereby automatically leave anything of importance out of consideration, including consciousness.

Now, the musing continues, since it appears that the specific consciousness of sadness is not strongly related to the fact of suicide and probably bears no simple relation to it at all, I can suppose that it may have a minor correlation with siucide and yet never clearly enter into the causation of suicide. That might happen if there were situations which caused suicide and also *sometimes* caused sadness. Thus if a person were going about his ordinary daily web of purposive activities, he might, without having consciously planned it, work himself into a situation that he then discovers offers suicide as the only remaining alternative action. This discovery might shock him, or make him angry, or frightened, or sad. Or his initial response to the situation might be to become sad, and the idea of suicide might occur to him only later. Or the situation might produce suicide without any previous condition of mood, posture, or action that a psychiatrist would notice as "depression." In fact, *I* remember wondering while the expert was defining depression why any man would want to go on living at all if he were really in such a situation of despair and hopelessness as some of the patients seem to describe. Would it help us to understand suicide, and perhaps increase the expert's precision in identifying high-risk cases, if we could describe more precisely what we mean by despair? It certainly seems worth a try.

## Apologia for Henceforth Ignoring the Existentialists

No one who inquires about despair today can avoid some confrontation with the European philosophical movement called *existentialism*. It has been criticized as a "philosophy of despair."[11] Because of its widespread influence on recent literature it pushes despair before us and forces us to consider it.

Recently, in a number of books and articles and at least one new journal, existentialism has been thrust specifically at psychiatrists and psychologists. According to the most active American spokeman for this "new dimension," the aim of the existential psychotherapists is, with the help of Freud's ideas, to understand man as the being who is human, and so to unite science and ontology.[12]

The existentialist psychotherapists do not advocate or use a particular method; rather, they adopt a special set of attitudes. Dissatisfied with the gaps in their understanding of human beings, the fear that they may not be seeing the patient "as he really is, knowing him in his own reality," they believe that a more satisfying view of man may be constructed on the basis of the philosophical writings of Martin Heidegger. It appears that Heidegger's analysis of existence "opens up the vast provinces of inner, subjective reality and indicates that such reality may be true even though it contradicts objective fact."[13] Laboratory experiments will not get us to the bottom of a person's problems; to know another person, we must, in a broad sense, love him.[14] "The fundamental drive of organisms . . ., the blocking of which leads to neurosis . . . is to live out one's potentia."[15] In other words, the full meaning of being human lies in emerging or becoming; man is future-oriented and not given once for all. To become himself he must be aware of himself because that is the only way to be responsible for himself. But man's being is always in dialectical relation with nonbeing, or death, and he can choose nonbeing. This choice does not appear only when a man considers suicide; it is, in "some degree a choice made at every instant." That man is *aware* of the fact that he will die is the basis for his asserting his absolutely supreme value incommensurate and distinct from the rest of the universe, although the universe can, by any tiny event, destroy him. What May calls the "I-am" experience is a *precondition* of ego development, independent of achievement or status, inexplicable in terms of transference, beyond ethical and moral norms, and by no means to be identified with the functioning of the weak, passive, shadowy ego. Man's uniqueness *qua* man is conditioned on the knowledge that he is going to die.

Though humans are distinct from nonhuman things, "the person and his world are a unitary, structural whole; the hyphenation of the phrase being-in-the-world expresses precisely that. . . . Self implies world and world self; . . . *World is the structure of meaningful relationships in which a person exists and in the design of which he participates.*"[16] The world has three modes: the world of objects into which the individual is "thrown," like an object; the world of social relationships; and the individual's own world, private, unique, least understood of the three, in which the chief issue is the relation of self to itself. All three of these modes of world constantly interact and condition one another. To emphasize one at the expense of the others is to lose the meaning of the human being.

In this world, the individual experiences the imminent threat of nonbeing, an experience which May calls ontological anxiety. If anxiety can lead to the blocking of potential, for oneself or others, then it produces guilt. But ontological guilt is not the same as morbid or neurotic guilt, for everyone participates in it. None of us fails to distort the reality of his fellow man, and none of us fully realizes his own potentialities. "Just as neurotic anxiety is the end-product of unfaced normal ontological guilt."[17] If ontological guilt is properly faced, or "confronted," it does not lead to symptom formation, "but has constructive effects in the personality. Specifically, it can and should lead to humility, . . . sharpened sensitivity in relationships with fellow men, and increased creativity in the use of one's own potentialities."[18]

These are brave words, and not at all the dismal, despairing stuff that the existentialist "litterateurs" may have led us to expect. But though some of the vocabulary looks new, I have often heard these sentiments, in one form or another, before I ever heard of existentialism. Can it be that the philosophers Heidegger and Sartre have provided sound reasons for our believing these things? Is it possible that they have developed a praxis by which we can realize them? Since none of the existentialist psychologists has done the homework for us, we must do it for ourselves.

It does not take a very careful reading of the lengthy and unsystematic writings of the existentialist philosophers to discover their operating premises. They regard man, generically or individually, as being so radically different from other entities that separate vocabularies are required to discuss man and the world. Heidegger's special word for human reality is *Dasein*, which in German colloquial and literary usage simply means "being," as in "a happy being," "a beautiful *creature*;" but he often writes *Da-sein* to emphasize what he regards as a fundamental "structure" of human reality—"being-there" (*Da* [there] plus *sein* [to be]). Sartre says that human reality is "for-itself" as against being "in-itself" the way nonhuman things are.[19] There is no middle ground. So great is the gulf between the being of man and the being of the world that the differentiation of the nonhuman world into organic and inorganic goes *totally unrecognized*. To speak of "organisms" in this connection, as May does, is to suggest that the existentialist philosophers have said something which they have emphatically *not* said. The basis of this division is what the existentialists want to believe about human cognition. Man has what Heidegger calls a vague, average, everyday understanding of Being, which Sartre calls a "pre-reflective *cogito*." This cognition is a fundamental aspect of the nature of man and is temporarily prior to and the foundation of all systematic, critical, conceptually differentiated knowledge. Since man is the questioner, his being is such that his very being is in question (Heidegger); or, since a question implies the possibility of a negative answer, man's essence is *negativity*, and as such it is the basis of all negation, logical or otherwise (Sartre).

Their method is that of phenomenological analysis, and they take the word phenomenon to mean "that which appears." For Heidegger, to say that something exists is equivalent to saying that it appears, or is "given" or "apprehended," whether in the relative immediacy of perception and memory or in the complex symbolic codes of discursive language. And Heidegger employs one of his oft-invoked etymological exercises to argue that the ancient Greek word which we usually translate as "truth" actually referred to what is unconcealed or *dis*-covered. But this is exactly the nature of existence as phenomena, so the apprehension of a phenomenon is *true*. Hence, truth is not agreement with the various mensurational or calculative criteria used in the sciences, which are variously characterized as "false,"[20] "atrophied [at] the root . . . in their essential ground"[21] and therefore inadequate to a degree, especially for "understanding" man.[22] So also logic, "the logical degeneration of which can be seen in 'logistics,'" has nothing to do with "the experience of the truth of Being."[23] But even this criterion of truth as appearance will not work for human reality, which is not apprehendable in phenomena. Corresponding to the radical difference between human beings and nonhuman entities, there are radically different modes of cognition: *understanding* and knowing, respectively. Heidegger's explicit reference to the origin of this notion in the work of Wilhelm Dilthey[24] indicates that it is no new invention of the contemporary existentialists. *Knowing* is the cognitive province of the natural sciences and depends on logical analysis, measurement, calculation, and experiment. But we cannot know man, we can only *understand* him, and to do so we must query phenomena so as to arrive at "Interpretations" (Heidegger's term) and so elucidate their meaning. These Interpretations are not products of analysis or syntheses of facts; rather they are apprehensions of the symbolic meanings of complete (whole) experiences. Heidegger's earliest reference to this cognition of wholes (*Gestalten*) is to Dilthey; Sartre's is, without specific citation, to "the experiments of the Gestalt school," which clearly means the modern psychological movement associated with the work of Wertheimer, Koffka, and Köhler.

Perhaps it is an innovation of the existentialists that they assert the direct cognitive efficacy of affective states; not in the sense that these states are objects of knowledge or understanding, but that in a way they constitute understanding, they reveal things to us. This is especially true of the negative states—fear, anxiety, dread, despair, anguish, and nausea. Sartre simply names these, more or less conventionally, and describes them as seems suitable to himself. Heidegger calls them *Stimmungen*, a word which admits of translation either as "moods" or "attunements," and by which he intends to convey that in the affective states we directly apprehend some "mode" of Being, or some aspect of ultimate reality. I suggest, though perhaps it is temerarious to do so, that the existentialists' preoccupation with negative affects is one of the reasons that some psychotherapists have been attracted to their writings. I disagree with Maslow's suggestion that we do not need to "take too seriously the European existentialists' harping on dread, on anguish, on despair, and the like. . . .[25] This harping is both the warp and the woof of their philosophies, in the sense that the gloomy, depressed atmosphere is introduced in two distinguishable ways.

First, both Sartre and Heidegger introduce negative affects arbitrarily, without prior preparation. They drag them in by the neck, so to speak. Whatever we are immediately afraid *of*, we are always basically afraid *for* ourselves, either directly or indirectly. Fear, in any of its modifications, points to man's being—primordially, basically, ontologically fearful.[26] Also, man's behavior is often "nihilating," as is seen not only in rational negation, but also in opposition, loathing, refusal, interdiction, and renunciation. "The permeation of Da-sein by nihilating modes of behavior points to the perpetual, ever-dissimulated manifestness of Nothing, which only dread reveals in all its originality. Here, of course, we have the reason why original dread is generally repressed in Da-sein. Dread is there, but sleeping."[27] Likewise, "error is part of the inner structure of Da-sein," and since the total essence of truth contains at the same time its own "dis-essence," man is "ever turning this way and that but always into misery."[28] "It is in anguish that man gets the consciousness of his freedom, or if you prefer, anguish is the mode of being of freedom as consciousness of being. . . ."[29] Our basic response to anguish, Sartre says, is to flee it. But none of our maneuvers can hide our anguish, for we *are* anguish. Since we cannot flee what we do not know, when we flee anguish we *are* anguish in the mode of not being it. To be sure, both Heidegger and Sartre mention joy. But they devote one line to joy for every two hundred pages they devote to sorrow.

Surely we could dismiss all this as flummery, or as gratuitous and unfounded assertion. But we would still have to consider the second way in which the existentialists generate a pervading sense of despair and hopelessness. This way is embedded in their discussion of human reality as essentially striving, or "projecting." It appeared to Maslow that "the core of European existentialism is that it deals radically with that human predicament presented by the gap between human aspirations and human limitations (between what the human being *is*, what he would *like* to be, and what he *could* be)."[30] Certainly the existentialists discuss at length a great many aspects of human purposive activity. Some of their best writing is to be found in their discussion of human involvement with concrete purposes, instrumentalities, and means-end relations. Their descriptions are sensitive and insightful. But for all this they are no better than their predecessors—Hobbes, Locke, Hume, Bentham, Peirce, James, Höffding, Freud, von Ehrenfels, Dewey, or Woodworth; nor better than their contemporaries—Hull, Tolman, Lewin, Henry Murray, Bertrand

Russell, E. S. Russell, or Stephen Pepper, who contributed enormously to our knowledge of purposive behavior and have opened vistas which we can explore to increase our knowledge. Such knowledge is quite evidently needed today. We need all the help we can get to contribute to the enterprise. Are the existentialists helping?

In what follows I hope to show that they are not helping, and that they never intended to help. All their skill in discussing concrete human purposive action and all their persuasive exposition of its general objective structure are applied to *ends* or, more precisely, to a *single end* which is inherently impossible to achieve. *Of course* we must fail if we choose such goals. And if we cannot choose our goals, if we are constrained and essentially without choice at some crucially pivotal moment, then our failure is ineluctable and our despair and hopelessness are unconditional. In this sense we can be said to *be* failure and hopelessness and despair. The "argument" which designates an impossibility as our only "authentic" goal (Heidegger), or the only goal to which all our concrete strivings can possibly refer (Sartre), is not capable of either substantiation or correction by any canons of evidence whatever. It is vain for anyone to attempt to unite science and ontology. It is impossible on the premises of the existential ontologists. That this can so easily be discovered strengthens my suspicion that the existential psychotherapists are inviting us to something the foundations and implications of which they are ignorant.

In Heidegger's view a basic "mode" of being-human, "equiprimordial" with other modes, is Being-in-the-world. This means being absorbed in the painful, prudent, circumspective execution of our purposes (projects). This absorption is relatively unanalytic, uncritical, and unselfconscious. This is how we are, "proximally and for the most part," whether we deal with things or with other people. If we become the least bit thoughtful about what we are doing or what we are concerned with, we see that the instrumental things immediately ready-at-hand imply references to an infinity of other instruments and we are confronted with the phenomenon of the world as a whole, but we will have missed our "authentic" Being-ourselves, that is, "Dasein's ownmost Being—a being which essentially can have no involvement, but which is rather that Being *for the sake of which* Dasein is as it is."[31] That is, we have not only missed our own unique individual being, we have even forgotten Being as such. In our everyday concerns we have "fallen into the world" and become subject to public standards of discourse ("idle talk" and "scribbling"), esthetics and entertainment ("curiosity"), and evidence ("ambiguity"). But the fall gets interpreted as a way of ascending, a way of living concretely, and we are tranquilized into the belief that we understand or could understand everything. But this is sham authenticity, in which all our purposive strivings must end unless they aim at the ultimate cognitive purpose of our "*authentic* potentiality-for-being-a-whole."[32] This is only one aspect of the potentiality-for-Being which man is, and wholeness in the sense of completedness—of being finished—points to the possibility of no longer realizing any possibilities, that is, points to death. Thus, Heidegger argues, "because Death is a possibility not to be outstripped," then in an individual who resolutely confronts the possibility of his own death (i.e., "has a resolute Being-toward-Death"), "*Dasein's* authentic existence cannot be outstripped by anything, and in this sense it is *true* and has *certainty*."[33] More narrowly, *Dasein's* authentic project is to be its own foundation, its own understanding. This is a metaphysical concern and has nothing to do with practicality. It is not to make things easier but only more difficult, and it is to be accomplished solely by thinking the only thing worthy of thought—the thought of Being. But an existence which thus founds itself is the *First Cause*.[34] This is as close as Heidegger has come to saying what Sartre had blatantly declared earlier: "man fundamentally is the desire to be God."[35]

The thirst for absolutes, which plagued nineteenth-century German philosophy, clearly drives the modern existentialists. But while Heidegger seeks his absolutes doggedly, soberly, and quietly, Sartre, already awash with absolutes, cries in a frenzy for more. Consciousness is absolutely nothing, absolutely pure, absolutely whole, absolutely unknowable, absolutely for itself, absolutely free. The structure of all our motives is lack or deficiency, which our purposes aim at filling. Since the aim of any purpose is to provide what is lacked, it aims at nothingness, at something which does not exist, which is not present. But these are only the superficial phenomena of motivation. They can be interpreted as pointing to basic ontological structures. If consciousness is purposive and aims at the nonexistent, then it has the peculiar necessity that "in its most immediate being, in the intrastructure of the pre-reflective *cogito,* [it] must be what it is not and not be what it is."[36] Human reality is *possibilities* and it recognizes this aspect of itself most clearly in anguish. In anguish we are aware of the ineffectiveness of our motives to produce action and of the inefficiency of our acts to achieve their ends. Our absolute subjectivity is threatened, we are endangered, in the mere fact of recognizing the Other. Transfixed by the "look" of the Other we are instantly in shame *because* in the very fact of that look we are degraded from our pure subjectivity to the status of objects. Thus all of our dealings with others are aimed at capturing the Other's freedom, so that we will never be in danger of losing our own freedom by being made objects for the Other. But the Other's freedom is as absolute as our own, and his subjectivity is just as incomprehensible to us as ours is to him, so all our hostile or self-interested dealings with the Other automatically fail. Indeed, our fundamental project to be the basis of our own objective being—to become in-itself-for-itself—is doomed to failure. "Every human reality is a passion in that it projects a losing itself so as to found being and by the same stroke to constitute the In-itself which escapes contingency by being its own foundation, the *Ens causa sui,* which religions call God. . . . But the idea of God is contradictory and we lose ourselves in vain. Man is a useless passion."[37]

By now the answer to the question must be clear. The existentialists are not helping us, nor are they likely to. They have added nothing of systematic importance to our descriptions of purposive activity. Specifically, they have not helped us with despair, for they have used their all-too-poignant sensitivity to despair to insert an impossible ultimate human goal into their system of axioms. Thus prepared they can make it appear that we *must* fail before we start. Heidegger invites us to retire with him into the mystical contemplation of Being-in-itself, and Sartre simply leaves us in despair. On the other hand, the existentialists have not convinced us that we must despair utterly of all our projects, only of the one that they insist upon. There is still hope that we can get ourselves a little clearer about despair, even if only in the "factical," or everyday sense which the existentialists despise. That is the hope which will lead us from now on.

## The Components of Personal Despair

To begin with, the words "despair" and "hopelessness" point to situations in which a person is attempting or planning some purposive act: either an appetitive one, to get some positive good such as persuading a certain woman to marry him, building a house, finishing a work of art, teaching something to another person, or formulating the structural description of a complex organic molecule; or an aversive one, avoiding something he does not want, such as freezing to death in a blizzard, getting involved in an automobile accident, attending a boring party, or going to Hell after he dies. If the person conceives that there is a fairly high probability that he will achieve his aim, then the situation is "hopeful."

But if the probability of achieving his aim remains low no matter what he does, then the situation is hopeless or desperate. This is essentially the way in which the late Kurt Lewin defined hope and hopelessness.[38] Despair of achieving a given goal is independent of the value or importance of the goal. The ability to conceive and manipulate probability of success and value of a goal independently of each other has enabled us to demonstrate that the effects of actual or anticipated failure depend on the value of the goal being pursued.

Lewin gave two illustrations of concrete situations of hope and hopelessness in which important outcomes were at issue. In one illustration he described something of the plight of the Jewish community in Germany during the early days of the Hitler regime. He distinguished the reactions and attitudes of Jews who were Zionists from those who were not. The Zionist community exhibited a great deal of social solidarity and engaged in fairly effective resistance to Hitler's initial moves against the Jews. They communicated with each other, consulted with each other, collected money, arranged passports, and did other things necessary to get their most threatened brethren out of the country. Perhaps conditioned by their group solidarity was their strong respect for Jewish history, including many previous persecutions which, as a group, they had survived. Their attitude toward the future was that as a group they would survive this latest attack even though many individuals would not. The non-Zionists, on the other hand, had no such identification with Jewish history and very little group solidarity so that, although many individuals among them tried to help their fellow Jews, they were less effective than the less numerous Zionists. As individuals they more quickly gave way to hopelessness, apathy, and passive or nonadaptive submission to the annoyances and atrocities to which they were subjected. The point is that where group solidarity—interest for the group rather than for any particular individual—is the instrument of group survival, then the individuals, whatever their ultimate fate, have a goal and a means for achieving it which renders their situation hopeful or at least less desperate than the situation of those who lack such an instrument or who do not accept the goal. Kobler and Stotland[39] argue that when someone is having difficulty solving life's problems he may appeal to other people for concrete help, and if the people he appealed to appear interested and willing to help, then the minimum condition for the revival of hope, or for halting the plunge into despair, is met. Thus, in the first expression of interest and willingness, another person offers himself as a possible instrument for solving the problems. But the effectiveness of this or any other instrument can be tested only by the results of using it. If subsequent developments reveal that the interest was only perfunctory, then the means for solving the problem are not genuinely available. Or, if the most diligent efforts of the "helper" are ineffective, then those means simply do not exist. Thus the last shred of the sufferer's hope may vanish and self-destruction or some equivalent behavior remain as his only alternatives.

Lewin's other example comes from data that were gathered by his student Maurice Farber in a prison in one of our midwestern states.[40] Lewin and Farber noted a fact well known to penologists: that some prisoners with long sentences "do hard time," that is, they suffer psychologically. They speak and act hopelessly. They run through their daily routines in dull apathy, and the atmosphere which they communicate is one of gloom and depression. But other prisoners with equally long sentences "do good time." They go through their days with a certain amount of sprightliness. They produce and appreciate humor. They are alert and interested in a variety of things. Lewin and Farber found that the occurrence of these attitudes was independent of length of sentence, kind or harsh treatment by guards, or the difficulty, dirtiness, or social status of the prison jobs which the men held. But the hardness or goodness of a man's time was correlated with certain attitudes toward the past and future. The men who suffered thought that their sentences were unjust or unreasonably long; the nonsufferers admitted that their sentences were just, in most respects. As for the future, those who suffered generally had no families or friends to whom they could turn outside the prison; they had no prospects of jobs or other useful activities awaiting them; they distrusted the parole machinery and did not believe that their sentences would be reduced for good behavior. The nonsufferers faced a different prospect: they had wives, relatives, or friends with whom they were in communication; they expected to get time off for good behavior; and they expected to find jobs. Now since these data are only correlational, we cannot hope to discern anything about cause in them. But they do point to some aspects of situations which define them as hopeful or hopeless. They can be summarized, without undue causal misinterpretation, by saying that those who suffered most conceived that they were in a bad situation through no fault of their own and they had neither goals to look forward to nor means for improving their condition. On the other hand, those who suffered least were making the best of a bad situation for which they accepted some responsibility; and they thought they would have a part in terminating the situation and would move on to something better.

In the pioneer laboratory investigations of success and failure, Hoppe[41] found two conditions under which most of his subjects would spontaneously quit working at a particular task. One was the experience of profound or repeated failure to do what they wanted with the materials of the task. The other was that the subject had mastered the manipulation of the task materials so completely that the physical nature of the task provided no opportunity for further improvements in performance. In either case the probability of success is zero or nearly zero. The person who has never experienced success has probably convinced himself that his abilities are simply inadequate for achieving the goals he attempted to reach. But the person who has exhausted the possibilities of the task has no reason to distrust his abilities. If *he* suffers it is from lack of opportunity to use his abilities. In either case the persons quit but did not lapse into total inactivity. They merely stopped those particular endeavors: the one, the vain pursuit of any success at all; the other, the equally vain pursuit of any additional success.

In examining the limits suggested by these situations, we can imagine first a man who has never succeeded in achieving a single goal that he has attempted, although he has seen other men achieve the same or similar goals every day. This man is in a profound state of despair because his experience has given him nothing but the information that as an instrument for achieving ordinary human aims he is totally inadequate. At the other extreme, we can imagine a man with a past history of a fair share of successes achieved by various amounts of self-stressing and with a sufficient sprinkling of failures to add the spice of anxiety to his strivings. And now he stands, with his abilities unimpaired but convinced as far as conviction is possible that there are no more opportunities to pursue the goals for which his abilities are suited, that every path is a blind alley, that every door is firmly bolted, that all avenues of achievement are closed to him. Is he not also in profoundest despair? Are not his abilities analogous in value to that of a pocketful of money when there is nothing to buy? In such an environment he is just as worthless as the man who can achieve nothing in a rich field of opportunities.

Now suppose that we are talking not about men but about machines; tractors, for example. Here is a tractor which appears just as well constructed as any other, but every time we try to use it it does not have sufficient power, or some part breaks, and after many efforts we have not remedied its defects. As a tractor it is useless, a perpetual failure. On the other hand, here is a fully capable tractor, powerful and durable, that has satisfied every demand made upon it. But now, because its owner has permanently abandoned all activities in which tractors are useful, it sits idle and slowly rusting. As a tractor, it is useless, because it is not needed. Surely the behavior of the owners toward these two machines would be either completely indifferent or actively destructive. Would the two men in the previous illustration fare any better at their own hands? I think not. In the situations of extreme hopelessness or despair as we have described them it is likely that the men would become care*less* about themselves, about their continued existence. They might actively seek to destroy themselves, readily accept death if it came, or be utterly apathetic and indifferent to it.

But these limiting cases in which probability of success is zero because of ineptitude or lack of opportunity are infrequent. Most often failure is not a *fait accompli* but only a possibility. Then, our modal behavior is to investigate alternatives, exploring for substitute means or substitute goals. More often than not we find some kind of substitute.

The experiences of chronically unemployed heads of families provide illustrations on this point.[42] The loss of gainful employment deprived these men of activities which were directly rewarding to most of them in terms of the exercise of skill, association with fellow-workers, status, and reputation. Furthermore, many of the skills needed to be practiced daily or they would deteriorate. But beyond these losses, the cessation of income forced the curtailment of purposes in a wider field: diets became scantier and less interesting; family relations went from affection to antagonism; religious and community involvements had to be abandoned; children's educations were interrupted or completely terminated. Some men in this situation gave way completely to apathy and some to suicide, but none of them did so immediately and only a relatively small proportion ever did so at all. The outstanding characteristic of the unemployed was their resourcefulness in curtailing expenditures, finding odd jobs, keeping their names on lists at employment offices, and conserving their savings or the proceeds from sales of their property. Some laboratory experiments have shown that individuals faced with the prospect of almost certain failure will not change even to an available substitute activity before they have explored alternate ways of succeeding at the one they have already started.[43] Thus a person is not likely to descend into the abyss of despair on the occasion of his first experience of failure or his first recognition that failure is a possibility. Complete despair probably results from the fact that alternatives have already been explored and found useless. Individuals probably differ widely from one another in the ingenuity they bring to this kind of exploring and also in the range of alternatives which will satisfy them. Even a long series of failures will not make a person view his probability of success as zero if there remain some possible means which he has not yet tested.[44]

I suggest that we can and should use increasingly objective methods to collect data which relate to the loose hypotheses about despair which I have already outlined. I do not suggest that we abandon forthwith any but the most rigorous laboratory investigations. We should be ready to use "soft data," especially when we are trying to survey a field of phenomena rapidly to find out whether there is anything worth investigating. Ultimately we should aim at using whatever ingenuity we can summon to devise laboratory tests of our hypotheses by increasing refined experiments.

First, can we get any evidence that people think about death in connection with the actual or anticipated demonstration that their capacities are inadequate to achieve their goals? From some rather soft data I think it is fair to conclude that some people, perhaps a large proportion, do think this way. I asked about 600 people of both sexes, ranging in age from 15 to more than 65 years and from a variety of religious and socioeconomic backgrounds, to answer the question, "Under what circumstances, if any, would you be relatively indifferent to the idea of your own death?" Some said there were no such conditions; others gave no answer or at best an irrelevant answer. But two cataloguers reliably placed 57 percent of the answers in one of the following categories: (1) loss or decline in capacity from disease, accident, or senility; (2) high achievement so that (*a*) capacity was at its limit, or (*b*) desire for further achievement was exhausted; and (3) an environment where desired goals were absent and would probably never exist. Then, in our laboratory, Dr. Doreen Rothman demonstrated that college students who failed to qualify for admission to an activity for which they had volunteered markedly reduced their evaluation of their abilities which had been tested *and* spontaneously increased the amount of death-imagery in stories they wrote after the failure as compared with stories they wrote before. She later confirmed this observation on a group of public-secondary-school students.[45]

Another point about the effects of success and failure is that sometimes a single success so elates a person that he talks and acts thereafter as though nothing were impossible to him. Conversely, some people are crushed by a single failure to the point where they say that they are good for nothing and act that way too. Most often, single failures or successes are reacted to more moderately. The person who has failed looks to see what went wrong, picks up the pieces, and ultimately gets the job done or abandons it for something more promising. The person who succeeds most often expresses his gratification even while he is getting on with the next thing or deciding what he will do next. On the basis of such observations we *guessed* that the stronger reactions would be conditioned by the fact that capacities important to the person were involved or that very important goals were at stake.[46] In a laboratory experiment we "tested" thirty college freshmen to see whether they were qualified for membership in a group which all of them said they wanted to join. Although they were told that they would have to pass five tests, each representing a different ability, they actually got only the first test, which all of them were made to fail. Half of them failed on a test of the ability which they had previously rated as their best among the five; and the other half failed on what they called the weakest among the five abilities. By comparing their evaluations of *all five* abilities before the test with those made afterwards, we found that the experience of failure with the initially important ability produced the greatest amount of generalization about the other abilities in the set. On the average, the fifteen subjects who had failed in the use of their highest-rated ability reduced their ratings of 3.1 of the five abilities; while those who failed in the exercise of their lowest-rated ability reduced the ratings of only 1.4 of the five abilities. Moreover, the average *amount* of change in the two groups corresponded with the average direction of change.[47]

In a later experiment we confirmed these findings, but we added a condition of success which produced the following results. After success with the subjects' highest-rated abilities they showed little tendency to increase the evaluation of the *tested* abilities, but the average rating of the untested abilities increased by fairly large amounts. But when the subjects succeeded in a test of the lowest-rated abilities, then the *tested* ability was rated much higher, and ratings of the untested abilities hardly changed at all. Another feature of this later experiment was the introduction of a condition where the tests given were presented only as practice tests the results of which would be irrelevant to whether or not the student qualified for group membership. Nevertheless, as part of the practice, the scoring procedure was explained, and scores were announced relative to the pass-fail criterion. Generally, we found what we expected in the irrelevant-test conditions—no generalization effects of any kind, a point which Rothman also confirmed. But the reactions of some of our individual subjects in the irrelevant condition were interesting and potentially instructive. In one condition the subjects were given a test of their highest-rated ability, a test which, being only for practice, had nothing to do with their getting into the group. By implication, the ability itself was declared of no value or interest to the group. In this condition some of the subjects who got a passing score on the test of their highest-rated ability followed this with a profound *decrease* in their ratings of the untested abilities. This observation is important because of its obvious relevance to the idea that loss of value in abilities can occur not only through deterioration of the abilities but through denial of opportunities to use them. However, the observation is ambiguous as it stands. Nothing more can be made of it except the fact that we know that we can do experiments to find out more about it in detail.

Another interesting fact is that some subjects in the irrelevant test conditions changed their second ratings exactly as though the test had meant something for their qualifications as group members. When asked about this after the experiment they replied, in effect, that they never regarded *any test* as irrelevant. If these people are as completely lacking in the defensive capacity to rationalize as their response seems to suggest, then they are peculiarly open to despair. This point, too, awaits further study, but that investigation does not seem to be beyond our reach.

To summarize the hypothesis: The components of personal despair are precisely those conditions under which an individual's special *raisons d'être* are rendered nonexistent. Either no goals which he is equipped to pursue are permitted to him; or else he has not sufficient ability to achieve any goals at all. In either of these conditions a man is good for nothing, and some men recognize this and say it of themselves. Most people take a lot of convincing before they recognize their own situations as hopeless. Sometimes they are ready to give up the struggle completely before they have explored all the alternatives. If so, they have simply made a mistake in judging the situation and themselves. They are still within reach of human help. But probably the only aid that will work is the outline of methods for searching and testing alternatives and the arousal of the person's interest in the possibility that he can find something to do which will satisfy him. Very likely he will not be satisfied with a goal unless he finds it and chooses it for himself. Selection from a grab bag of goals presented by a helper may only further reduce the sufferer's self-evaluation: he was not even good enough to do that for himself. Likewise, kindliness and attempts to increase the sufferer's "narcissistic" gratifications may only emphasize his despair if presented alone. Or this maneuver may increase his guilt that anyone should waste time with so worthless a creature as he.

We may make a fundamental error if we insist on defining despair or happiness in terms of affect alone. Our consciousness of our affects is evanescent and unreliable. Frequently we discover happiness or despair only by retrospective detective work on our own history. We were, or have been, happy or despairing. Our most certain knowledge of these states relates to the objective conditions under which they have occurred. The evidence is by no means complete, but what there is of it points clearly to the area of our purposive activities as the residence of our happiness and worth as well as of our worthlessness and despair. When we are attempting "to be a cause," as Cooley put it,[48] whether we are modifying ourselves by increasing our knowledge and practicing our skills or modifying our environments, only then are we testing our evaluation of ourselves, and only in such testing lies the knowledge of how to confirm our estimates or how to increase them. The kind of data alluded to above is meager and incomplete and shadowy in their reference. We need more information if only to see that which we have more clearly. From what has been done so far it is reasonable to project that with moderate ingenuity and diligence we can get more. That and the problem of despair itself are sufficient justification for the attempt.

## REFERENCES

1. The facts about suicide cited in this paragraph are summarized from B. MacMahon, S. Johnson, and T. F. Pugh, "Relation of Suicide Rates to Social Conditions: Evidence from U. S. Vital Statistics," *Public Health Reports*, 78:285–293, 1963.
2. M. Fisch, "The Suicidal Gesture; a Study of 114 Military Patients Hospitalized Because of Abortive Suicide Attempts," *American Journal of Psychiatry*, **111**:33–36, 1954.
3. T. L. Dorpat and H. S. Ripley, "A Study of Suicide in the Seattle Area," *Comprehensive Psychiatry*, **1**:349–359, 1960.
4. P. E. Sifneos, C. Gore, and A. C. Sifneos, "A Preliminary Psychiatric Study of Attempted Suicide as Seen in a General Hospital," *American Journal of Psychiatry*, **112**:883–888, 1956.
5. I. R. C. Batchelor and M. B. Napier, "The Sequelae and Short-Term Prognosis of Attempted Suicide," *Journal of Neurology, Neurosurgery and Psychiatry*, **17**:261–266, 1954.
6. K. G. Dahlgren, *On Suicide and Attempted Suicide* (Lund, Sweden: A. B. Ph. Lindstedts University-Bokhandel, 1945).
7. F. J. Kallman and M. M. Anastasio, "Twin Studies on the Psychopathology of Suicide," *Journal of Nervous and Mental Diseases*, **105**:40–55, 1947.
8. S. Levy and R. Southcombe, "Suicide in a State Hospital for the Mentally Ill," *Journal of Nervous and Mental Diseases*, **117**:504–514, 1953.
9. Dorpat and Ripley, *op. cit.*

10. E. W. Busse, "Psychopathology," in J. E. Birren (ed.), *Handbook of Aging and the Individual* (Chicago: University of Chicago Press, 1959), pp. 364–398; S. H. Kraines, *Mental Depressions and Their Treatment* (New York: The Macmillan Company, 1957); E. A. Strecker and F. G. Ebaugh, *Practical Clinical Psychiatry* (5th ed.; Philadelphia: The Blakiston Company, 1940); R. W. White, *The Abnormal Personality* (2d ed.; New York: The Ronald Press Company, 1956).
11. M. Heidegger, "What Is Metaphysics?," trans. R. F. C. Hull and A. Crick. (From *Was ist Metaphysik?*, 1929). In W. Brock (ed.), *Existence and Being* (Chicago: Henry Regnery Company [Gateway Editions], 1949), p. 353.
12. R. May, "The Origins and Significance of the Existential Movement in Psychology," in R. May, E. Angel, and H. F. Ellenberger (eds.), *Existence: A New Dimension in Psychiatry and Psychology* (New York: Basic Books Inc., Publishers, 1958), pp. 3–36.
13. May, *ibid.*
14. R. May, "Contributions of Existential Psychotherapy," in May, Angel, and Ellenberg, *op. cit.*, pp. 37–91.
15. May, "The Origins and Significance of the Existential Movement in Psychology," *op. cit.*
16. May, "Contributions of Existential Psychotherapy," *op. cit.*, p. 59.
17. *Ibid*, p. 55.
18. *Ibid.*
19. The existentialists say that they are primarily interested in ontology (Greek *ontos*, "of being"); hence a peculiarity of their writing is that they limit themselves as far as possible to derivatives of the verb "to be" or its equivalents.
20. M. Heidegger, *An Introduction to Metaphysics*, trans. R. Manheim. (From German edition [1953] of a lecture originally given in 1935.) (New Haven, Conn.: Yale University Press, 1959).
21. Heidegger, "What Is Metaphysics?," *op. cit.*, p. 326.
22. M. Heidegger, *Being and Time*, trans. J. Macquarrie and E. Robinson. (From *Sein und Zeit* [3rd ed., 1931 and 7th ed., 1957].) (New York: Harper & Row, 1962).
23. Heidegger, "What Is Metaphysics?" *op. cit.* pp. 355–356.
24. *Der Aufbau der geschichtlichen Welt in den Geisteswissenschaften. Abhandlungen der Köngiglichen Preussischen Akademie der Wissenschaft; Philosophische-Historische Klasse*, 1910.
25. A. H. Maslow, "Existential Psychology—What's In It For Us?" in R. May (ed.) *Existential Psychology* (New York: Random House, Inc., 1961), p. 60.
26. Heidegger, *Being and Time*, *op. cit.*, pp. 180–182.
27. Heidegger, "What Is Metaphysics?," *op. cit.*, p. 343.
28. M. Heidegger, "On the Essence of Truth," trans. R. F. C. Hull and A. Crick. (From *Über die Wesen der Wahrheit* [1943]). In W. Brocke (ed.), *Existence and Being* (Chicago: Henry Regnery Company, [Gateway Editions], 1949), pp. 313–321.

29. Jean-Paul Sartre, *Being and Nothingness,* trans. H. E. Barnes. (From *L'Etre et La Neant,* 1943.) (New York: Philosophical Library, Inc., 1956), p. lxii.
30. *Op. cit.,* p. 54. In fairness to Maslow it should be stated that, in the essay cited, he says that he is not an existentialist nor a careful student of existentialism and that he finds much in the existentialists' writings that is difficult or impossible to understand. But in the passage quoted he puts his finger on an important feature of their writings, if only in the sense that they devote the bulk of their pages to it.
31. *Being and Time, op. cit.,* p. 160.
32. *Ibid,* p. 348.
33. *Ibid.,* p. 370.
34. M. Heidegger, *Essays in Metaphysics,* trans. K. F. Leidecker. (From *Identität und Differenz,* 1957.) (New York: Philosophical Library, Inc., 1960).
35. Sartre, *op. cit.,* p. 566.
36. *Ibid,* p. 68.
37. *Ibid,* p. 615.
38. "Time Perspective and Morale," in G. Watson (ed.) *Civilian Morale* (New York: Reynal & Hitchcock, Inc., 1942), pp. 48–70.
39. A. L. Kobler and E. Stotland, *The End of Hope: A Social-Clinical Theory of Suicide* (New York: The Free Press, 1954).
40. "Imprisonment as a Psychological Situation," *University of Iowa Studies: Studies in Child Welfare,* 20:153–228, 1944.
41. F. Hoppe, "Erfolg und Misserfolg," *Psychologische Forschung,* 14:1–62, 1930.
42. E. W. Bakke, *Citizens Without Work* (New Haven, Conn.: Yale University Press, 1940); M. Elderton (ed.), *Case Studies of Unemployment* (Philadelphia: University of Pennsylvania Press, 1931); E. Ginzberg, E. L. Ginsburg, and D. L. Lynn, *The Unemployed* (New York: Harper & Row, 1943).
43. I. G. Cetlin, *Persistence, Defensive Behavior and Self-evaluation as a Function of Early and Late Anticipation of Failure,* doctoral dissertation, University of Pennsylvania, Philadelphia, 1964.
44. R. E. Cetlin, *Estimated Probability of Success as a Function of Number of Abilities Available for Goal Achievement,* doctoral dissertation, University of Pennsylvania, Philadelphia, 1964.
45. *The Effects of Success and Failure Experiences in Normal, "Neurotic," and Schizophrenic Populations,* doctoral dissertation, University of Pennsylvania, Philadelphia, 1963.
46. J. C. Diggory and D. E. Magaziner, "Self-Evaluation as a Function of Instrumentally Relevant Capacities," *Bulletin de L'Association Internationale de Psychologie Appliquée,* 8:1–19, 1959.
47. *Op. cit.*
48. C. H. Cooley, *Human Nature and the Social Order* (rev. ed., New York: Charles Scribner's Sons, 1922), p. 177.

# 15. Sigmund Freud on Suicide

ROBERT E. LITMAN

*"The fateful question for the human species seems to me to be whether and to what extent their cultural development will succeed in mastering the disturbance of their communal life by the human instinct of aggression and self-destruction."*[1]

Sigmund Freud

According to Sigmund Freud, commenting on man's fate in 1930 toward the end of his own long career, suicide and war are different aspects of a unitary problem. They are expressions in human beings of instinctual aggression and instinctual destruction which in turn are interchangeable elements of the death instinct. Furthermore, the process of civilization, which offers the only possibility of deferring the end of mankind by group violence, undermines the psychic health of the individual members of the group and threatens each of them with suicide.[2]

In this essay I shall review the clinical experience and theoretical steps that led Freud to his various conclusions about suicide. My purpose is to abstract from the totality of Freud's writings his pertinent observations and to evaluate the contribution they make to an understanding of suicide and of suicide prevention in our own time, a full generation after Freud's death. The reader who follows me in this task will, I am afraid, encounter difficulties in his path from time to time, although I will try to mark the way as clearly as I can. Unfortunately, Freud never synthesized his views on suicide into an organized presentation. There is no paper on suicide comparable to Freud's dissertations on war.[3] His many clinical observations, inferences, and speculations, which illuminate multiple aspects of suicide, are scattered through numerous papers concerned primarily with other issues and other goals.

In its general outline this review will trace the theme of suicide in Freud's writings from 1881 to 1939, at points deviating from a strictly temporal progression for special topical development. The first section deals with Freud's earlier observations, mostly personal and clinical. The second section is concerned with Freud's later contributions, mostly theoretical and speculative. The third section includes my attempt at synthesis and evaluation. To avoid unnecessary complications, the source material will be limited to Freud's writings and Ernest Jones' biography of Freud.

## Early Experiences: 1881–1910

It would be a mistake to assume that Freud's experience with suicide was only theoretical or philosophical. On the contrary, Freud had considerable clinical experience with suicidal patients. There are, for example, references to suicidal symptomatology in all of the case histories that Freud published except that of Little Hans, a five-year-old child.

Suicidal behavior was an important aspect of the symptoms of Josef Breuer's patient, Fraulein Anna O. Breuer discovered the cathartic method of treatment which constituted the beginning stage of the treatment approach that Freud later developed into psychoanalysis. Anna O. at times displayed complete psychic dissociation with two entirely distinct states of consciousness and for awhile spoke only in English. She became suicidal after the death of her father. On the doctor's recommendation and against her will, she was transferred (in June, 1881) to a country house in the neighborhood of Vienna, because of the danger of suicide. The move was followed by three days and nights completely without sleep or nourishment and by numerous attempts at suicide, by smashing windows and by other methods. After this she grew quieter and even took chloral at night for sedation.[4]

Although Freud described this case several times, he did not refer particularly to the suicidal elements. Very early in his career as a psychoanalyst, however, Freud was aware of the importance of guilt over hostile impulses against parents causing symptoms, especially after the parents' death. In May, 1897, in a letter to Wilhelm Fleiss, Freud wrote: "Hostile impulses against parents (a wish that they should die) are also an integral part of neuroses. . . . They are repressed at periods in which pity for one's parents is active—at times of their illness or death. One of the manifestations of grief is then to reproach oneself for their death. . . ."[5]

Possibly Freud's most intense personal experience with suicide occurred in August, 1898. "A patient over whom I had taken a great deal of trouble had put an end to his life on account of an incurable sexual disorder." The suicide of the patient, according to Freud, stirred up in Freud certain painful fantasies connected with death and sexuality, which he more or less successfully repressed. Several weeks later, still under the influence of these unconscious fantasies, Freud was unable to recall the name of Signorelli, creator of magnificent frescoes about the "Four Last Things"—Death, Judgment, Hell, and Heaven. Freud tried to visualize the frescoes and the artist and felt the inadequacy of his associations as a source of inner torment. With great effort he reconstructed his conversation with a traveling companion immediately before the forgetting. The topic was foreign customs, the Turks, their confidence in doctors, their resignation to fate, even death. Freud had thought of telling an anecdote. "These Turks place a higher value on sexual enjoyment than on anything else, and in the event of sexual disorders, they are plunged in a despair which contrasts strangely with their resignation toward the threat of death." A patient (Freud's?) once said, "Herr (Signor), you must know that if *that* comes to an end, then life is of no value." Feeling suddenly uncomfortable, Freud suppressed the anecdote, deliberately diverted his own thoughts from death and sexuality, and changed the subject to the famous frescoes. But in his unconscious effort to continue to forget the suicide, Freud now forgot the painter's name, which joined the memory of the suicide in Freud's repressed unconscious, until someone else suggested the correct name. Freud recognized it instantly and used it to recall the repressed fantasies and reconstruct the mechanism of forgetting. Freud reported the episode immediately to his friend, Fliess,[6] and published an account of it several months later,[7] omitting in these first two reports, however, the fact that the specific unpleasant news which precipitated the forgetting was a patient's suicide. Later, when Freud rewrote the material as the first example in his book *The Psychopathology of Everyday Life* (1901) he included the fact of the suicide.[8]

Ernest Jones says of this incident, "As I hope to expound in a revised edition of Volume I of this biography, it was connected with a significant episode which must have played an important part in the inception of Freud's self-analysis."[9] Unfortunately, Jones died before revising the biography. We are left with an intriguing biographical mystery and an important scientific problem. We ask, Who was this patient? What happened in the analysis? Did Freud describe fragments of the case, even heavily disguised, somewhere in his writings? Or was the history of the patient totally repressed from the memory of science? Why did Jones, who has so much to report about Freud's work and his patients, choose to postpone the illumination of the suicide incident? The important scientific problem is this: Is the taboo on suicide so intense that even psychoanalysts are reluctant to expose their case materials and personal experiences in this area? But here, and many times hereafter, I must restrict digressions or this essay will be a book.

Hopefully, other biographers will supply the missing episode that Jones omitted. My guess is that it related to Wilhelm Fliess, Freud's close friend during the 1890s. Freud began his self-analysis as a systematic project in July, 1897. Why exactly then? For approximately ten years he had been listening to patients, developing and improving his ability to interpret dreams and free associations, including his own. From this material he was being forced to draw some strange and disturbing inferences. Repeatedly and consistently, the stories from his patients forced him to conclude that sexual abuse by the fathers was responsible for the patients' illnesses. He was becoming convinced of the disagreeable reality of rivalries, death wishes, and incest in families. The death of his aged father (October 23, 1896) affected Freud deeply. "At a death the whole past stirs within one. I now feel as if I had been torn up by the roots."[10] Freud's dreams revealed hostility to and guilt feelings about, as well as admiration for, his father. Apparently, some of Freud's unconscious reactions toward his father were transferred to Fliess. Freud found himself becoming irritable with his friend. Freud's dreams and associations connected Fliess with Italy, travel, and Italian art.[11]

Freud was moody, anxious, and depressed for several years after the death of his father. He worked his way back to health through his self-analysis and his writing. There is no evidence that Freud was suicidal during this period, although a possible guiding fantasy was that of death and rebirth. In a letter dated June 12, 1897, he wrote, "I have been through some kind of neurotic experience, with odd states of mind not intelligible to consciousness—cloudy thoughts and veiled doubts, with barely here and there a ray of light. . . ." Freud continued the letter with a paragraph describing a new case, a 19-year-old girl whose two older brothers shot themselves, and then concluded, "Otherwise I am empty and ask your indulgence. I believe I am in a cocoon, and heaven knows what sort of creature will emerge from it."[12] During this whole period, Freud was struggling most particularly with painful feelings of guilty rivalry with his father and with Fliess.

As far as I know, Freud's only overt suicide threats occurred during his long, passionate, and stormy engagement. In 1885, he wrote to his fiancée Martha, whom he eventually married, his decision to commit suicide should he lose her. A friend was dying, and in this connection Freud wrote, "I have long since resolved on a decision (suicide), the thought of which is in no way painful, in the event of my losing you. That we should lose each other by parting is quite out of the question. . . . You have no idea how fond I am of you, and I hope I shall never have to show it."[13] So Freud could understand how someone, like the Turks of the censored anecdote, or his deceased patient, could turn to death when frustrated sexually. "One is very crazy when one is in love."[14] Many years later, Freud was to comment that the two situations of being most intensely in love and of suicide are similar, in that the ego is overwhelmed by the object.[15] In his early theory the claims of love (libido) and self-preservation were opposed, and he consistently maintained that to love is dangerous (acknowledging always that not to love poses an even greater peril). "We behave as if we were a kind of Asra who die when those they love die."[16] (The Asra were a fictitious tribe of Arabs who "die when they love.")

The histories reported by Freud's psychoanalytic patients contain numerous accounts of suicidal behavior. For example, the only sister of Freud's most celebrated patient, the Wolf Man (so called because of his childhood phobia of wolves), committed suicide by poisoning herself. The patient's strange lack of grief over the sister's death aroused Freud's special interest until the psychoanalysis clarified the complicated processes of displacement of the mourning reaction in this patient.[17] The dramatic case of Dr. Schreber's paranoia (1911) included descriptions of Schreber's longing for death. "He made repeated attempts at drowning himself in his bath and asked to be given the 'cyanide that was intended for him.' "[18]

The first of Freud's longer case reports (1905) described fragments of the analysis of an 18-year-old female hysteric whom he called Dora. She pressured her parents into obtaining treatment for her by writing a letter in which she took leave of them because she could no longer endure her life and leaving the letter in a place where they would be sure to find it. Just when Freud's hopes for a successful treatment were highest, she unexpectedly broke it off. Dora was not the first person in the family to talk of suicide. Her father once told the story that he had been so unhappy at a certain time that he made up his mind to go into the woods and kill himself, but Frau K., a friend, recognizing his state, had gone after him and persuaded him by her entreaties to preserve his life for the sake of his family. Dora did not believe the story. No doubt, she said, the two of them had been seen together in the woods having an affair, and so her father had invented this fairy tale of the suicide to account for the rendezvous.

From this case we learn about suicide as a communication, attention getter, cry for help, method of revenge, and as a partial identification, in this case with the father. Also, obscurely, there is in Dora's behavior a deep theme of sadism and aggression; possibly she is doing to others, including Freud, what she believes others have done to her (stirred up false hopes, lied to her, abandoned her cruelly).[19]

Additional insights appear in Freud's 1909 case history of a man with severe obsessional neurosis, whom Freud sometimes called "the man with the rats" because of one dramatic feature of the neurosis, a special fantasy about rats. The patient's many obsessions and compulsions included suicidal impulses and commands. In the analysis, numerous examples of these suicidal commands were identified as punishments for rage and jealousy toward rivals. Freud said, "We find that impulses to suicide in a neurotic turn out regularly to be self-punishment for wishes for someone else's death."[20] Freud was well aware that suicide is not a great danger in obsessive neurotics. The patient said that he might actually have killed himself on several occasions were it not for his consideration for the feelings of his mother and sister. The same sister, incidentally, had told him once when they were very young that if he died she would kill herself. He knew that his own death would pain his mother terribly because a cousin had killed himself eighteen months before, because of an unhappy love affair, it was said, and the man's mother, the patient's aunt, was still miserable.[21]

In *The Psychopathology of Everyday Life* (1901), Freud cited numerous clinical observations that convinced him of the important part played in mental life by an instinct for self-destruction.

There is no need to think such self-destruction rare, for the trend to self-destruction is present to a certain degree in very many more human beings than those in whom it is carried out. Self-injuries are, as a rule, a compromise between this instinct and the forces that are still working against it, and even when suicide actually results the inclination to suicide will have been present for a long time before in less strength, or in the form of an unconscious and suppressed trend. . . . Even a *conscious* intention of committing suicide chooses its times, means, and opportunity; and it is quite in keeping with this that an *unconscious* intention should wait for a precipitating occasion, which can take over a part of the causation and by engaging the subject's defensive forces, can liberate the intention from their pressure.[22]

The clinical examples include an officer who had been deeply depressed by the death of his beloved mother. When forced to take part in a cavalry race, he fell and was severely injured. A man shot himself in the head "accidentally" after being humiliated by rejection from the army and being jilted by his girl friend. A woman injured herself out of guilt for an abortion. After the injury she felt sufficiently punished.[23]

Despite his many clinical observations concerning suicide, Freud was unable to organize them systematically into his psychoanalytic theory of instincts. On April 20 and 27, 1910, there was a discussion of the Vienna Psychoanalytical Society on the subject of suicide. On this occasion, Adler and Steckel talked at great length and in great detail, emphasizing the aggressive aspects of suicide. Freud, by contrast, said very little, contenting himself with these concluding remarks:

I have an impression that in spite of all the valuable material that has been brought before us in this discussion, we have not reached a decision on the problem that interests us. We are anxious, above all, to know how it becomes possible for the extraordinarily powerful life instinct to be overcome; whether this can only come about with the help of a disappointed libido or whether the ego can renounce its self-preservation for its own egoistic motives. It may be that we have failed to answer this psychological question because we have no adequate means of approaching it. We can, I think, only take as our starting point the condition of melancholia which is so familiar to us clinically and a comparison between it and the affect of mourning. The affective processes in melancholia, however, and the vicissitudes undergone by the libido in that condition are totally unknown to us. Nor have we arrived at a psychoanalytic understanding of the chronic affect of mourning. Let us suspend our judgment until experience has solved this problem.[24]

Actually, in 1910, Freud knew a great deal about suicide. He had identified many important clinical features: (1) Guilt over death wishes toward others, especially parents; (2) identification with a suicidal parent; (3) loss of libidinal gratification, or more accurately, refusal to accept loss of libidinal gratification; (4) an act of revenge, especially for loss of gratification; (5) escape from humiliation; (6) a communication, a cry for help; and finally (7) Freud recognized the intimate connection between death and sexuality. Sadism and masochism were obviously the deepest roots of suicide. Freud could not decide, however, where to assign such overwhelming sadism and masochism in his theoretical framework. According to Freud, human behaviors are derived ultimately from needs to satisfy instinctual drives. In his early theory the basic, conflicting instinctual drives were thought to be libido (sensuality, sexuality) and self-preservation (hunger, aggressive mastery). How could suicide satisfy the needs either of sexuality or self-preservation?

## Theories and Speculations: 1911–1939

Eventually, Freud revised his theory of the instincts in order to provide appropriate recognition of the importance of self-destructiveness. In 1932, reviewing his life's work, Freud commented, "Sadism and masochism alike, but masochism quite especially, present a truly puzzling problem to the libido theory; and it is only proper if what was a stumbling block for one theory should become the cornerstone of the theory replacing it."[25] More accurately, the new concept of a death instinct supplemented rather than replaced libido theory.

In considering the totality of Freud's writings, one must view his various contributions against the background of the time in which the writing was done. Up until 1910, the formulations on suicide were in the framework of the libido theory. After 1920, they were in the framework of the death-instinct theory. The articles written in 1914 and 1915 form a transition chapter.

In "Mourning and Melancholia" (written in 1915, published in 1917), Freud followed his own suggestion and took as his starting point a special type of patient, melancholics who express great guilt and self-reproach:

> We see how in him one part of the ego sets itself over and against the other, judges it critically and in a word takes it as its object. Our suspicion that the critical agency which is here split off from the ego might also show its independence in other circumstances will be confirmed by every other observation.[26]

How does this splitting-off occur? The explanation in terms of psychic energy (libido) is quite complicated. Energy withdrawn from a lost object of love is relocated in the ego and used to recreate the loved one as a permanent feature of the self, an *identification* of the ego with the abandoned object. "Thus, the shadow of the object fell upon the ego, and the latter could henceforth be judged by a special agency as though it were an object, the forsaken object."[27] "Shadow" objects existing as structures in the ego (identifications) obviously are not fully integrated into the total personality. A demarcation zone, or fault line remains, along which ego splitting occurs.

Also significant was Freud's speculation that certain ways of loving are less stable than others. Narcissistic love of another, for example, is especially vulnerable to disorganization and regression toward immature and primitive stages of the libido, especially sadism.

It is this sadism alone that solves the riddle of the tendency to suicide which makes melancholia so interesting and so dangerous. So immense is the ego's self love, which we have come to recognize as the primal state from which instinctual life proceeds, and so vast is the amount of narcissistic libido, which we see liberated in the fear that emerges at a threat to life, that we cannot conceive how that ego can consent to its own destruction. We have long known it is true that no neurotic harbors thoughts of suicide which he has not turned back upon himself from murderous impulses against others, but we have never been able to explain what interplay of forces can carry such a purpose through to execution. The analysis of melancholia now shows that the ego can kill itself only if, owing to the return of the object-cathexis, it can treat itself as an object—if it is able to direct against itself the hostility which relates to an object and which represents the ego's original reaction to objects in the external world. Thus, in regression from narcissistic object-choice, the object has, it is true, been gotten rid of, but it has nevertheless proved more powerful than the ego itself. In the two opposed situations of being most intensely in love, and of suicide, the ego is overwhelmed by the object, though in totally different ways.[28]

The above excerpt is quoted frequently in the literature concerned with suicide, most often with misplaced emphasis on the aspect of the original hostility and murderous impulses. In my opinion, the more important creative concepts are those of regression, disorganization, and ego-splitting, pathologic processes which allow a portion of the ego to initiate action while disregarding the interests of the remainder. Moreover, the positive, didactic quality of the isolated paragraph quoted is misleading in that the impression is created that Freud was making assertions about all suicides, which was not his intention. The tenor of the article as a whole is modest and tentative; and in the first paragraph Freud specifically disclaims general validity for findings based on the analysis of a few specially selected melancholics.

Within a few years Freud had discovered that the process of establishing objects as identifications in the ego was very common. In fact, the ego is made up in large part of identifications. Freud did not carry the theory of identifications much further, but a consistent development of his concept has led to our modern notion that the original representation of most loved objects is split into several parts, good and bad, in both the ego and the superego. These multiple object-identifications, plus the need for establishing defenses and maintaining repressions, result in splits and fissures in every ego. In the 1920s, Freud developed a structural model of mental activity (id, ego, superego) and assigned various functions to the different parts of the model.[29] He stated that the very earliest identifications play a special role in the total self, in that they are more completely split off from the rest of the ego and become the superego, which includes conscience and ideals, has the functions of loving, supporting, judging, and punishing the ego, and may become diseased on its own account. Concepts or images of suicide appear only in the ego and superego, for the id knows nothing of its own death. "In the unconscious everyone of us is convinced of his own immortality."[30] Indeed, even consciously, it is impossible to imagine our own death. "Whenever we attempt to do so we can perceive that we are in fact still present as spectators."[31]

Freud paid little attention to the role (spectator, participant, rescuer, or betrayer) of others in a suicide. He recorded the observations but had no room for them in his theory. For example, he wrote briefly in 1921 about a young man who was tormenting his mistress. He was trying unconsciously to drive her to suicide in order to revenge himself on her for his own suicide attempt several years before in connection with a different woman.[32] In 1916, Freud discussed the characters of the play *Rosmersholm*. In this drama a poor wife, Beata Rosmer, is psychologically poisoned by her rival, Rebecca Gamvik. The wife commits suicide as a reaction to abandonment by her husband and her own sense of worthlessness.[33] Suicide is not a direct theme of either of the papers, which are concerned respectively with telepathy and with guilt over success. Another literary analysis (1928) concerns the story of a mother who tries unsuccessfully to rescue a young gambler from suicide.[34]

The last of Freud's longer case reports, "The Psychogenesis of a Case of Homosexuality in a Woman," was published in 1920. Freud used it to develop further his views on homosexuality, female sexuality, and some technical aspects of psychoanalytic therapy. The patient was an 18-year-old girl, who was brought to Freud by her father about six months after she made a suicide attempt. What disturbed the family was not so much the suicide attempt as the girl's homosexual attachment to a woman about ten years her senior. The woman had not greatly encouraged the girl, and when they were walking together one day and met the father, who gave them a furious look, the woman told the girl they must now certainly separate. Immediately the girl rushed off and flung herself over a wall down the side of an embankment onto the suburban railway line which ran close by. Although fortunately little permanent damage was done, the girl was in bed for some time, and Freud felt that the attempt was undoubtedly serious.

After her recovery she found it easier to get her own way than before; the parents did not dare to oppose her with so much determination, and the lady, who up until then had received her advances coldly, was moved by such an unmistakable proof of serious passion and began to treat her in a more friendly way.[35]

It seemed to Freud that much of the girl's behavior was a reaction to the birth of her third brother three years previously. It was after that event that she turned her love away from children toward older women. Concerning the suicide attempt, Freud said,

The analysis was able to disclose a deeper interpretation beyond the one she gave (despair over loss of the lady). The attempted suicide was, as might have been expected, determined by two other motives besides the one she gave: It was the fulfillment of a punishment (self-punishment), and the fulfillment of a wish. As the latter it meant the attainment of the very wish which, when frustrated, had driven her into homosexuality—namely the wish to have a child by her father, for now she fell through her father's fault. From the point of view of self-punishment the girl's action shows us that she had developed in her unconscious strong death wishes against one or the other of her parents—perhaps against her father out of revenge for impeding her love, but more probably against her mother, too, when she was pregnant with the little brother. Analysis has explained the enigma of suicide in the following way: Probably no one finds the mental energy required to kill himself unless, in the first place, in doing so, he is at the same time killing an object with whom he has identified himself and, in the second place, is turning against himself a death wish which had been directed against someone else. Nor need the regular discovery of these unconscious death wishes in those who have attempted suicide surprise us (any more than it ought to make us think that it confirms our deductions), since the unconscious of all human beings is full enough of such death wishes against even those they love. Since the girl identified herself with her mother, who should have died at the birth of the child denied to herself, this punishment-fulfillment itself was once again a wish fulfillment. Finally, the discovery that several quite different motives, all of great strength, must have cooperated to make such a deed possible is only in accordance with what we should expect.[36]

In a footnote Freud noted "that the various methods of suicide can represent sexual wish fulfillments has long been known to all analysts. (To poison oneself=to become pregnant; to drown=to bear a child; to throw oneself from a height=to be delivered of a child.)"

The most significant of the ideas expressed above is the discovery that suicide is multiply determined by the interaction of several motives. The emphasis is on ego-splitting and identifications. The suicidal act is explained as a reenactment, by a split-off ego identification with mother, of the delivery of the brother. The murderous look the father gave the girl is mentioned. Allusion is made indirectly to the theme of death and rebirth (rescue). The effect of a suicidal act as a communication that changes the environment is recorded. Erotic and masochistic elements of the suicide attempt are specially noted. Death wishes are described as the source of the energy required for suicide, yet death wishes are not limited to suicides but are typical of all human beings.

Evidently, from Freud's later writings, the announcement of a solution of the enigma of suicide was premature. Many questions and uncertainties remained. For example: Was it true that in most suicides the ego murdered the object? Or, more often, did the incorporated object murder the ego? Freud continued to feel that his theorectical explanations were incomplete for several major clinical phenomena associated with self-destructiveness.

The most important of these for psychoanalysis is the "negative therapeutic reaction."[37] Some neurotics inevitably respond to good news, congratulations, or progress in analysis, by increased anxiety, depression, or self-injury.

Judged by all their actions the instinct of self-preservation has been reversed. They seem to aim at nothing other than self-injury and self-destruction. It is possible, too, that the people who in fact do, in the end, commit suicide, belong to this group. It is to be assumed that in such people far-reaching diffusions of instinct have taken place, as a result of which there has been a liberation of excessive quantities of the destructive instincts directed inward. Patients of this kind are not able to tolerate recovery toward treatment and fight against it with all their strength. But we must confess that this is a case which we have not yet succeeded completely in explaining.[38]

Also unexplained was the problem of masochism. Why should many people require pain, punishment, humiliation, and degradation as prerequisites for sexual pleasure? In 1920 Freud proposed for speculative consideration that there might be an instinctual drive toward death.[39] His arguments were partly on clinical grounds (traumatic neuroses, repetitive actions) and partly biological and philosophical. Although at first the new ideas were advanced tentatively and cautiously, Freud soon came to accept them fully and with increasingly complete conviction.[40]

After long hesitancies and vacillations we have decided to assume the existence of only two basic instincts, *Eros* and *the destructive instinct.* The aim of the first of these basic instincts is to establish even greater unities and to preserve them thus—in short, to bind together; the aim of the second is, on the contrary, to undo connections and so to destroy things. In the case of the destructive instinct, we may suppose that its final aim is to lead what is living into an inorganic state. For this reason we call it the *death instinct* . . . In biological functions the two basic instincts operate against each other or combine with each other. Thus, the act of eating is a destruction of the object with the final aim of incorporating it, and the sexual act is an act of aggression with the purpose of the most intimate union. This concurrent and mutually opposing action of the two basic instincts gives rise to the whole variegation of the phenomena of life . . .[41]

The dangerous death instincts are dealt with in individuals in various ways; in part they are rendered harmless by being fused with erotic components; in part they are diverted toward the external world in the form of aggression and, to a large extent, they continue their internal work unhindered.

When the superego is established, considerable amounts of the aggressive instincts are fixated in the interior of the ego and operate there self-destructively. This is one of the dangers to health by which human beings are faced on their path to cultural development. Holding back aggressiveness is, in general, unhealthy and leads to illness . . .[42]

The death-instinct concept was a major theoretical construction. It has, however, received relatively little acceptance among psychoanalysts. Why was Freud so convinced of its usefulness? Ernest Jones suggests that there were subjective motives and reports insightfully on Freud's intense, complicated, personal, daily fantasies about death.[43] However, Freud's own explanation is logically consistent. Freud said he accepted the death-instinct theory because he needed it to explain masochism (and suicide). How then do suicide and masochism appear from this viewpoint?

> If we turn to melancholia first, we find that the excessively strong superego which has obtained a hold upon consciousness rages against the ego with merciless violence . . . What is now holding sway in the superego is, as it were, a pure culture of the death instinct and in fact it often enough succeeds in driving the ego into death . . .[44]

In melancholia the ego gives itself up because it feels itself hated and persecuted by the superego instead of loved. To the ego, therefore, living means the same as being loved by the superego, so that the death by suicide symbolizes or reenacts a sort of abandonment of the ego by the superego. It is a situation similar to separation from the protecting mother.[45]

The original quantity of internalized death instinct is identical with masochism. The individual tries to externalize this energy as aggressiveness or sadism. Where there is a cultural suppression of the instincts, the destructive instinctual components are turned back into his superego. Now we see a helpless, masochistic ego in relationship with a sadistic superego. The modality of the relationship is punishment. In order to provoke punishment the masochist must do what is inexpedient, must act against his own interests, must ruin his prospects, and perhaps destroy himself. But since there is always some fusion of the erotic and destructive instincts; there is always an obvious erotic component in masochism, so that even the subject's destruction of himself cannot take place without libidinal satisfaction.[46]

Due to the prolonged, extreme biological and social helplessness of the human infant, who cannot unaided satisfy his vital needs or regulate his own destructive instincts, each individual must incorporate controlling, coercing, and punishment components into his superego.[47] By this process the instincts are tamed, and the child can participate in family life and education. By an anthropological analogy, Freud viewed civilization as a group superego development. In civilized man, extra aggression is channeled into the superego and turned against the ego. It is now felt as unconscious guilt, masochism, a need to be punished, or an obscure *malaise* and discontent. The price we pay for our own advance in civilization is a loss, to some degree, of the possibilities of happiness.[48] "We owe to that process (civilization) the best of what we have become, as well as a good part of what we suffer from."[49]

To Freud, suicide represented a symptom of what we suffer from, a product of man and his civilization, a consequence of mental trends which can be found to some degree in every human being.

## Synthesis and Evaluation

Experience has confirmed Freud's statement that each suicide is multiply determined by the interaction of several motives. Suicide is by no means a homogeneous or unitary piece of human behavior. On the contrary, suicide comprises a variety of behaviors with many important aspects—historical, legal, social, and philosophical, as well as medical and psychological. The psychoanalytic explanations of the psychopathology of suicide are complex, multidimensional and, at some points, ambiguous and redundant.

There are, according to Freud, *general features* of the human condition, at least in Western civilization, which make each individual person somewhat vulnerable to suicide. These general features include: (1) The death instinct, with its clinical derivatives, the aggressive instinct directed outward and the destructive instinct directed inward; (2) The splitting of the ego; this is inevitable because of the extreme helplessness of the human ego in infancy when it is unable to master its own instincts and must conform to the parents or perish; and (3) The group institutions, family and civilization, which require guilty compliance from every member of the group.

The above general features only begin to account for any individual suicide. Individual suicides involve certain *specific suicide mechanisms*. All of them involve a breaking down of ego defenses and the release of increased destructive, instinctual energy. Examples are: (1) loss of love objects, especially those who have been loved in certain dangerous ways; (2) narcissistic injury, symbolically through failure or by direct physiological injury through fatigue or toxins; (3) overwhelming affect: rage, guilt, anxiety, or combinations; (4) extreme splitting of the ego with decathexis of most elements and a setting of one part against the rest; and (5) a special suicidal attitude and plan, often based on an identification with someone who was suicidal.

Finally, there are a great number of *specific predisposing conditions* that more or less favor suicide, although they are not precipitating mechanisms of suicide. These include: (1) a disorganized or disharmonious ego structure which splits up under relatively low conditions of stress; (2) a tendency of the libido to be fixated at preoedipal positions, especially strong tendencies toward sadism and masochism; (3) disease of the superego due to cruel parents, dead parents, parents that wished the person dead, or some constitutional inherited superego trait of excessive destructiveness; (4) strong attachment of the libido to death, dead loved ones, or a fantasy of being dead; (5) vivid erotic fantasies which symbolize and cover up death wishes; for example, the fantasy of bearing a child by father, symbolically actualized as a fall from a height; and (6) a chronically self-destructive living pattern, expressed, for example, as gambling addiction or homosexuality.

The following evaluative comments are based on my several years' experience as chief psychiatrist in a multidisciplinary project of research, training, and clinical service for suicide prevention. My experience is in agreement with Freud's general schematic view. Deep down, there is a suicidal trend in all of us. This self-destructiveness is tamed, controlled, and overcome through our healthy identifications, ego defenses, and constructive habits of living and loving. When the ordinary defenses, controls, and ways of living and loving break down, the individual may easily be forced into a suicidal crisis. At such times he feels helpless, hopeless, and abandoned and may or may not be aware of a great deal of unexpressible, aggressive tension.

However verbalized, most of the therapeutic actions of therapists at the Suicide Prevention Center are aimed at reinforcing the ego defenses, renewing the feeling of hope, love, and trust, and providing emergency scaffolding to aid in the eventual repair and healing of the splits in the patient's ego. Direct psychological techniques for turning the aggression outward have not been particularly successful in our experience. Frequently, we try to deal with the emotional turmoil directly with drugs. Hopefully, we may eventually move into the future predicted by Freud: "The future may teach us to exercise a direct influence by means of peculiar, particular chemical substances on the amounts of energy and their distribution in the mental apparatus." He added, "It may be that there are other still undreamed-of possibilities of therapy, but for the moment we have nothing better at our disposal than the technique of psychoanalysis. For that reason, despite its limitations, it should not be despised."[50]

In my opinion, we still have nothing better at our disposal than psychoanalysis or psychoanalytic psychotherapy as remedies for many of the chronic neurotic reactions and weaknesses which, if uncorrected, may eventually lead toward suicide but are not in themselves precipitating mechanisms of suicidal crises. The years have brought innovations based directly or indirectly on psychoanalytic principles that greatly expand our therapeutic range. These include various brief psychotherapy techniques, psychotherapy in groups, and environmental therapy in hospitals and clinics. All of these approaches, and others, are effective when they are employed at the suitable moment in the appropriate case.

Many of Freud's perceptive inferences have been explored and consolidated by later workers. For example, Freud often referred to certain dangerous ways of loving, in which the ego is "overwhelmed" by the object. Typically, the psychic representations of the self and other are fused, and the other is experienced as essential for survival. Modern writers have termed these attachments "symbiotic," making explicit the analogy to the primitive dependent relationship between a baby (or fetus) and its mother. Freud's observation that symbiotic love is a potential precursor of suicide still holds true.

Freud's dictum that suicide starts with a death wish against others, which is then redirected toward an identification within the self, has been overly accentuated among some psychotherapists, in my opinion, and has become a cliché. Freud is quoted as support of a relative overemphasis on aggression and guilt as components of suicide, with underemphasis of the helplessness, dependency, and erotic elements. Often, however, the suicidal drama reproduces not so much guilt for the unconscious wish of the child to murder the parent but rather a reaction of abandonment on the part of the child to the parent's unconscious wish for the child's death. The mechanism of regression and the themes in suicide of helplessness, constriction, and paranoid distrust have made the deepest impression on me.

Freud pointed out that infantile helplessness is the essential circumstance which creates masochism, but Freud was accustomed to using his concept of the oedipal complex as his reference point for psychopathology. From that viewpoint, guilt over rivalry with parents, especially the father, looms large. At the Suicide Prevention Center, I am more accustomed to using the mother-child preoedipal relationship as a reference concept. Further research, hopefully, will clarify this issue.

It is remarkable that Freud said so little about the all-important attitude of the mother in instilling into a child the desire for life. It is remarkable because Freud was well aware of the influence of his own mother in instilling in him a feeling of confidence and zest for living.[51] Moreover, he had found in his patients and in himself, as a reason for continuing to live, the idea that his premature death would be painful to his mother. When his mother died in 1930, aged 95, Freud noticed in himself a feeling of liberation. "I was not allowed to die as long as she was alive and now I may."[52]

Freud's personal attitude toward death, according to the sharp eye of his biographer Jones, was altogether a rich and complex one with many aspects. "In the world of reality he was an unusually courageous man who faced misfortune, suffering, danger, and ultimately death itself with unflinching fortitude. But in fantasy there were other elements." There was at times a curious longing for death. "He once said he thought of it every day of his life, which is certainly unusual."[53]

In three essays on war and death, Freud expressed himself as a cautiously hopeful realist. Horrified and depressed by the cruelty, fraud, treachery, and barbarity of World War I, he tried to extract some value out of discarding his illusions about civilization and facing disagreeable truths (1915). "To tolerate life remains, after all, the first duty of all living beings. Illusion becomes valueless if it makes this harder for us." And, characteristically, he added, "If you want to endure life prepare yourself for death."[54] Freud described himself as a pacifist (1933). "We pacifists have a constitutional intolerance of war . . . whatever fosters the growth of civilization works at the same time against war."[55] Perhaps some of the psychotherapists whose work exposes them continuously to affects of violence, sadism, and death gain in confidence and flexibility by partially identifying with the complex personality of Freud.

Freud had a few recommendations for society. Possibly, he thought, there would be less suicide if society permitted more sexual and aggressive freedom to its members, though one could not be sure. He thought there was an advantage in providing at intervals opportunities for mass release from inhibitions as, for instance, in carnivals or the ancient Saturnalia. Certainly, Freud saw in our present civilization and its future extensions the only hope for mankind.

Civilization is a process in the service of Eros, whose purpose is to combine single human individuals and after that families, then races, peoples and nations into one great unity, the unity of mankind. Why this has to happen, we do not know. The work of Eros is precisely this: These collections of men are to be libidinally bound to one another. Necessity alone, the advantages of work in common, will not hold them together, because man's natural aggressive instinct, the hostility of each against all and all against each, opposes this program of civilization. Now I think the meaning of the evolution of civilization is no longer obscure to us. It must present the struggle between Eros and death, between the instinct of life and the instinct of destruction as it works itself out in the human species. This struggle is what all life essentially consists of, and the evolution of civilization may therefore be simply described as the struggle for life of the human species.[56]

This philosophy of joining together and of enjoying each other has, I believe, played a large part in the forming of the spirit of the Suicide Prevention Center. The group spirit has in turn supplied a great deal of the constructive energy required to continue effective work in an area so full of destructive attitudes and hazardous outcomes. The injurious effect on the suicidal person of separation and alienation from the other persons who have loved him was indicated but not emphasized by Freud. We find that in helping a suicidal individual through a crisis, therapists often enlist the cooperation of many people. The goal is to reduce the patient's withdrawal and self-preoccupation and involve him once again in the common interactions of the living.

In our day-to-day therapy of suicidal crises we pay little attention to theory, particularly such deep abstractions as the death instinct. In speculative moments, however, we wonder if perhaps Freud's ominous correlation of suicide and war may not have been a fateful forecast. What if nuclear war were to be precipitated not by accident or policy but by a suicidal individual willing to kill "the others" with him? We encounter potential destroyers of their worlds at our Center fairly often. We take care to leave a door open and not to box them in. In such emergencies, of course, we work not from theory but with intuition and judgment, seeking words, gestures, or actions that will relieve tension and establish communication. The key might be an understanding look, a shared feeling, or a cup of coffee.

Freud was well aware of the difference between philosophic speculations about the general causes of man's misery and the requirements of practical life to do something about it. In a letter to Einstein (1933) on the problem of preventing war, he commented, "The result, as you see, is not very fruitful when an unworldly theoretician is called in to advise on an urgent practical problem. It is a better plan to devote oneself in every particular case to meeting the danger with whatever means lie at hand."[57] Freud applied the same advice to his own clinical endeavors. In 1926, discussing a young patient, Freud wrote, "What weighs on me in his case is my belief that unless the outcome is very good it will be very bad indeed; what I mean is that he would commit suicide without any hesitation. I shall therefore do all in my power to avert that eventuality."[58] That last could well be the motto of the Suicide Prevention Center.

## REFERENCES

1. With the exception of the last reference, all the citations in this chapter refer to one of three works: S. Freud, *The Origins of Psycho-Analysis* (New York: Basic Books, Inc., Publishers, 1954); S. Freud, *Standard Edition of the Complete Psychological Works* (London: The Hogarth Press, Ltd., 1953–1965); and E. Jones, *The Life and Work of Sigmund*

*Freud.* (New York: Basic Books, Inc., Publishers, 1953–1957). They will be cited as *Origins, Works,* and *Life,* respectively. The sentence quoted is from *Civilization and Its Discontents* (1930), *Works,* vol. 21, p. 145.

2. *New Introductory Lectures on Psycho-Analysis* (1933), *Works,* vol. 22, pp. 110–111; and *An Outline of Psycho-analysis* (1940), *Works,* vol. 23, pp. 148–150.
3. "Thoughts for the Times on War and Death" (1915), *Works,* vol. 14, pp. 289–300; and *Why War?* (1933), *Works,* vol. 22, pp. 213–215.
4. *Studies on Hysteria* (1893–95), *Works,* vol. 2, p. 28.
5. *Origins,* May 31, 1897, p. 207.
6. *Origins,* Sept. 22, 1898, pp. 264–265.
7. "The Psychical Mechanism of Forgetfulness" (1898), *Works,* vol. 3, pp. 290–296.
8. *Works,* vol. 6, pp. 1–6.
9. *Life,* vol. 2, pp. 333–334.
10. *Origins,* Nov. 2, 1896, pp. 170–171.
11. *Origins,* Apr. 28, 1897, pp. 193–195.
12. *Origins,* p. 211.
13. *Life,* vol. 1, p. 122.
14. *Life,* vol. 1, p. 122.
15. "Mourning and Melancholia" (1917), *Works,* vol. 14, pp. 247–252.
16. "Thoughts for the Times on War and Death" (1915), *Works,* vol. 14, pp. 289–300.
17. "From the History of an Infantile Neurosis" (1918), *Works,* vol. 17, pp. 21–23.
18. "Psycho-Analytic Notes upon an Autobiographical Account of a Case of Paranoia" (1911), *Works,* vol. 12, p. 14.
19. "Fragment of an Analysis of Hysteria" (1905), *Works,* vol. 7, pp. 3–122.
20. "Notes upon a Case of Obsessional Neurosis" (1909), *Works,* vol. 10, pp. 153–318; and *Totem and Taboo* (1913), *Works,* vol. 13, p. 154.
21. "Notes upon a Case of Obsessional Neurosis" (1909), *Works,* vol. 10, pp. 153–318.
22. *Works,* vol. 6, pp. 178–185.
23. *Ibid.*
24. "Contributions to a Discussion on Suicide," *Works,* vol. 11, p. 232.
25. *New Introductory Lectures on Psycho-Analysis* (1933), *Works,* vol. 22, p. 104.
26. *Works,* vol. 14, pp. 247–252.
27. *Ibid.*
28. *Ibid.*
29. *The Ego and The Id* (1923), *Works,* vol. 19, pp. 3–66.
30. "Thoughts for the Times on War and Death" (1915), *Works,* vol. 14, pp. 289–300.
31. *Ibid.*
32. "Psycho-Analysis and Telepathy" (1941), *Works,* vol. 18, pp. 191–192; and *New Introductory Lectures on Psycho-Analysis* (1933), *Works,* vol. 22, pp. 45–46.

33. "Some Character-Types Met with in Psycho-Analytic Work" (1916), *Works,* vol. 14, p. 325.
34. "Dostoevsky and Parricide," *Works,* vol. 21, pp. 191–194.
35. *Works,* vol. 18, pp. 147–172.
36. *Ibid.*
37. *The Ego and the Id* (1923), *Works,* vol. 19, p. 49.
38. *An Outline of Psycho-Analysis* (1940), *Works,* vol. 23, pp. 180–182.
39. *Beyond the Pleasure Principle, Works,* vol. 18, pp. 3–64.
40. *Life,* vol. 3, pp. 275–280.
41. *An Outline of Psycho-Analysis* (1940), *Works,* vol. 23, pp. 148–150.
42. *Ibid.*
43. *Life,* vol. 3, pp. 275–280.
44. *The Ego and the Id* (1923), *Works,* vol. 19, pp. 53–58.
45. *Ibid.*
46. "The Economic Problem of Masochism" (1924), *Works,* vol. 19, pp. 169–170.
47. "Inhibitions, Symptoms and Anxiety" (1926), *Works,* vol. 20, pp. 154–155; and *Civilization and Its Discontents* (1930), *Works,* vol. 21, pp. 134–135.
49. *Why War?* (1933), *Works,* vol. 22, pp. 213–215.
50. *An Outline of Psycho-Analysis* (1940), *Works,* vol. 23, pp. 180–182.
51. *Life,* vol 1, p. 5.
52. *Ibid.,* p. 153.
53. *Ibid.,* pp. 275–280.
54. "Thoughts for the Times on War and Death," *Works,* vol. 14, pp. 289–300.
55. *Why War? Works,* vol. 22, pp. 213–215.
56. *Civilization and Its Discontents* (1930), *Works,* vol. 22, pp. 213–215.
57. *Why War?* (1933), *Works,* vol. 22, pp. 213–215.
58. S. Freud, *Psychoanalysis and Faith* (New York: Basic Books, Inc., Publishers, 1963), pp. 101–102 (letter to Rev. Oskar Pfister).

# 16. Self-Poisoning*

Neil Kessel

As recently as a century ago the problem of self-poisoning scarcely existed. People poisoned themselves then as now, of course, but of those who did, even of those who were brought to the hospital, few survived. Those who did were, like suicides everywhere, generally either lonely old people, often sick or ailing, whose going could hardly be considered grievous, or else they were insane and their management, therefore, a simple problem. In any case they were not numerous.

The picture is different today. Self-poisoning has become a frequent practice. More than one in every thousand of the adult population of Edinburgh is admitted to hospital each year following such an act. The fashion has so developed over the last twenty years that today we regard it as almost commonplace. Yet these individual instances, summed, constitute an important medical problem; it is no longer only academic. It presents toxicologists, psychiatrists, and public health doctors with practical problems which must be answered. For now the great majority of those who poison themselves survive and this fact goes far toward explaining why the practice has spread.

Poisoning used to be regarded as fatal. Instances of recovery there might have been, but it was still clearly understood that poisons were lethal. Theriac, terra sigillata, bezoar stones, from a long line of alexipharmics, each had its vogue as an antidote, but people really knew that they

* This chapter is a condensation of the Milroy Lectures delivered at the Royal College of Physicians of London on February, 1965, and is printed with the permission of the *British Medical Journal*, wherein these lectures appeared under the title "Self-Poisoning", Issue **5473**:1265–1270, 1965, and Issue **5474**:1336–1348, 1965.

were of little effect. The history books do not disclose many examples of recovery. Mithridates, fearful of being poisoned by his enemies, had over the years repeatedly taken small doses to make himself immune. When he eventually tried to kill himself with poison he failed. There are still tribesmen who so season themselves against the ill effects of eating the flesh of the prey which they poison. Yet even these are examples of poison being taken for beneficial not for hurtful purposes. Instances of someone taking poison deliberately to harm himself, but with the intention of surviving, are hard to find. Juliet did so, but Romeo had so little thought that she might not be dead that he killed himself in despair. He knew, as everyone knew, that if you took poison you died. Conversely, you did not poison yourself unless you wanted to die. This is not so today.

The growth of pharmaceutical products has brought about the change. In every century before our own, poisons and drugs were dissimilar. Poisons were substances which should not be taken at all, the province not of physicians but of wizards. Their properties verged upon the magical. They were, indeed, "unctions bought of mountebanks." By the second half of the nineteenth century, science had displaced sorcery and poisons were purchased from the chemist, not the alchemist. But they still differed from drugs. Drugs, with few exceptions, though recognized to produce undesirable actions if taken in excess, were not considered lethal agents and were not used to kill. The growth of self-poisoning has come about in the train of a rapid rise in the number of highly dangerous preparations employed therapeutically, together with a great contemporaneous increase in prescribing.

The effect of this medical revolution has been to make poisons both readily available and relatively safe. The way has thus been opened for self-poisoning to flourish, since few who practice it have their minds set on dying. Facilities for self-poisoning have been placed within the reach of everyone.

There are auspicious circumstances for studying the subject in Edinburgh. For many decades the Royal Infirmary has had an "incidental delirium" ward for patients who require overlapping general medical and psychiatric care.[1] Today, three-quarters of the patients admitted to the ward are cases of self-poisoning. Its principal function has come to be that of a poisoning treatment center that serves the city of Edinburgh and the surrounding region. A general medical team and a psychiatric team work alongside each other. Adult poisoning cases from the whole of the city come or are sent there. If they first arrive at another hospital it is common for them to be transferred, but the great majority of patients are brought directly to the infirmary, where it is the practice in the out-patient or casualty department to send to the ward *all* patients who have taken an overdose. The casualty officer does not have to make a hurried judgment about whom to send in; nor need he exercise a disliked discretion about whether a case is "serious" enough to be admitted. Whether a patient has taken a hundred amytal tablets or a dozen aspirins makes no difference. Every case of poisoning is accepted.

This study, therefore, embraced the full range of survivors of deliberate self-poisoning acts. Some patients were deeply unconscious and required sophisticated techniques of resuscitation to save their lives; others had been scarcely physically harmed by their experience. Consequently, the case material is varied because it is complete.

We investigated one year's admissions to the unit from June, 1962, onward, the research team being responsible for the psychiatric service. Social, demographic, and clinical data were obtained on every patient while he was still in the hospital, excepting only the handful who died without recovering consciousness. It is most important that the situation is assessed by inquiry of both the patient and an independent informant at the time of crisis and before the family enters into a collusion, as it readily does once the immediate danger is over, to present an identical, idealized, and false picture. This is what commonly happens if the patient is not seen by a psychiatrist until some days or weeks later at an out-patient clinic.

Specially prepared schedules were used to expand and systematize the customary clinical records. For a small number of patients who discharged themselves precipitately we lack some items. Every patient was followed by home visiting for one year after his admission.

The patients in the ward made up more than 90 percent of all adult cases of self-poisoning who arrived at any hospital in Edinburgh. In a separate study[2] we sought the remainder and obtained essential details so that they might be included whenever we compiled rates for the city. Our rates, therefore, refer to all self-poisoned patients resident in the city of Edinburgh, who were seen at any hospital, whether or not they were admitted. Our other information applies to the 151 men and 314 women who were admitted to the ward during the year, whether they came from within or outside the city. These 465 people made between them 522 admissions, for some repeated their acts.

Self-poisoning refers to the intentional taking of too much of a poisonous substance believing that it will be noxious. These are the three essential components of the act: that it must be deliberate and not accidental; that the quantity must be known to be excessive; and that it is realized that this may be harmful. Poisoned patients who did not satisfy these criteria were excluded.

It is hard to describe how "severe" a case of self-poisoning is, to assess the degree of the danger to life to which the patient, from his standpoint, exposed himself. The quantity of poison ingested is certainly relevant, although patients often have wildly wrong notions about the toxic effects of what they have done. Of equal importance is the extent to which the action is concealed or disclosed. To take tablets knowing that this will remain undiscovered for many hours is a very different matter from promptly entering the living room and brandishing the offending bottle before the assembled family's startled gaze. These two factors were combined to produce an "index of endangering life." The untreated consequence of the amount of substance ingested forms one axis; the other comprised the steps taken by the patient to avoid or alternatively to ensure discovery. From this we have derived four categories of *predictable outcome* of the act; death, death probable, death unlikely, and certain to survive. Where a quantity of drug was taken which would have been fatal were no treatment administered, and if the patient took steps to avoid discovery or else took no particular action in this respect, then the predictable outcome is "death." Under the same circumstances a probably fatal dose puts the outcome into the "death probable" category. A smaller dose, but one which still carries some risk, scores in the "death unlikely" class, and so does a fatal dose if the patient took steps that he considered would ensure that he was soon discovered. In all other circumstances where he took such steps, or where the quantity of poison taken could not possibly have killed, the outcome is "certain to survive."

This index is not perfect; we do not always know how much a patient has taken of which substance; nor is it possible to decide precisely what amounts of barbiturate or of aspirin would be fatal or to gauge the effects of overdoses of uncommon drugs. We have had to say that every case of coal-gas poisoning would have proved fatal if not discovered, even though patients often have a shrewd idea that there is little money in the meter. In spite of these difficulties, the index is usually easy to apply. Such a categorization of cases is necessary in order to appreciate the sort of acts we have been studying and to be able to compare the work of different centers.

The predictable outcome for a fifth of our patients was death. For 35 percent, some risk was involved. Almost half the patients did not jeopardize their lives. But this, as we shall see, does not justify regarding such cases as trivial and not serious. The exact percentages, for males and females respectively, were as follows: death, 19, 19; death probable, 11, 11; death unlikely, 29, 21; and certain to survive, 41, 49.

## Social and Demographic Findings

The city of Edinburgh is divided into twenty-three wards and the annual self-poisoning rate was calculated for each of them. Individuals, not episodes, supplied the numerator values. The wards were ranked in order and divided into four groups, the six with the highest rates, the next six, the next five, and the six with the lowest rates. The wards with the high rates lie in the old, central areas where the overcrowded tenements, the city's slums, are to be found. The only other section with high rates is an apartment area (Craigmillar) developed in the late 1930's to rehouse those living in the worst of the central districts. Groups of families were moved there *en bloc*, and they took many of their problems with them.

The next highest rates occurred principally in the factory suburbs which grew up during the industrial revolution. These are between Princes Street and the shores of the Forth. They are mean districts, where employment is often precarious and life far from easy. In the same group, however, is one of the wards on the southern perimeter, Liberton, where postwar housing estates are now rapidly proliferating. Moderate rates characterized an inner band of suburbs chiefly to the south, while the lowest rates were found in the solid, respectable, predominantly middle-class wards on the city's west side. This distribution is no artifact resulting from practitioners managing patients from better districts at home. The same pattern was observed when only patients admitted unconscious were considered, and few doctors fail to send in such patients. Well-planned house estates need not produce high rates; one of these low-rate western wards is Sighthill, where a prosperous and secure working population live in new housing areas close to, and developed in conjunction with, new industrial and office enterprises.

At the heart of the bad areas lies the ward of St. Giles, where the majority of the hostels and the lodging houses of the city are to be found. This ward has the highest rates of all, and the hostel and lodging-house populations contribute excessively. The self-poisoning rate for people living under such circumstances is twice that for those in more sound circumstances.

We correlated the self-poisoning ranking of the city wards with similar rankings for other characteristics reported in the census (Table 1).

Table 1

Correlations of City Ward Rankings for
Self-Poisoning and Other Social Indices
Edinburgh, 1962–1963

| Self-poisoning with: | Kendall's tau | P |
|---|---|---|
| *Indices of social disorganisation* | | |
| Overcrowding (proportion > 1.5 per room) | 0.526 | 0.0034 |
| Family dislocation (proportion in lodging houses, hostels, and institutions) | 0.411 | 0.0032 |
| Where criminals live | 0.356 | 0.0048 |
| *Indices of social isolation* | | |
| Living alone (proportion of single-person households) | 0.249 | Not significant |
| Living in hotels (proportion of people) | 0.134 | Not significant |

The results amply confirm the relation between high self-poisoning rates and indices of social disorganization. Very significant associations were found with overcrowding, which is itself a sensitive measure of poor social circumstances; with the proportion of people living out of a normal family setting, that is, in hostels or lodging houses and where criminals live; for this we obtained, from a reliable source, an estimate of which wards housed most felons and which least. But with indices of social isolation, for example, the proportion of single-person households and the number of hotel rooms, there were no significant correlations. These, as we know, are the factors which Sainsbury[3] found to be associated with suicide, but self-poisoning is generated by different forces. The ecology of self-poisoning can be summed up simply: high rates are associated with living in overcrowded, poor surroundings, living in bad social conditions.

## Age

Age-specific rates differ between the sexes (Fig. 1). Male rates, between the ages of 20 and 65 remain fairly constant at between 80 and 100 per 100,000 per annum. The male teenage rate is only half as great, and for males over 65 the rate is very low indeed. For females between 20 and 25 years old the rate is 280 per 100,000. With increasing years there is a progressive, regular, and steep fall until over the age of 45 there is no

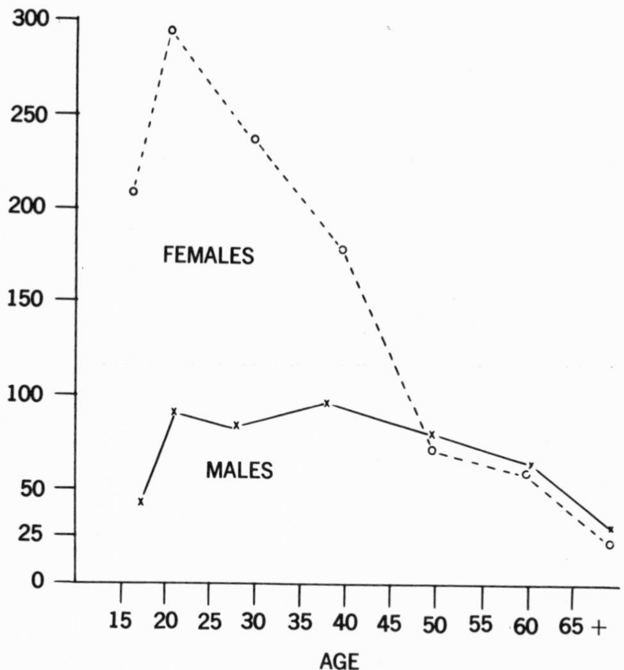


Fig. 1. Self-Poisoning
One-year admission rates per 100,000
By age and sex. Edinburgh adults only.

longer any difference between the sexes. The female teenage rate is very disquieting. In a single year more than 1 out of every 500 Edinburgh girls between the ages of 15 and 19 poisoned herself.

There is no simple explanation for the high rate of self-poisoning among young women in their early twenties. It may be perhaps that this is the female counterpart of delinquency in young men. Such a hypothesis would suggest that women turn their aggression against themselves, whereas men act against society. Clinical study suggests a different formulation. These women, although fully engaged in their normal social setting, mothering and running a home, are emotionally isolated. Until recently they were experiencing an active social life; they have not yet had time to adjust to the confines of domesticity. Often they have no one with whom to share their feelings or give expression to and explain their dissatisfactions. Unhappiness mounts and then suddenly explodes at a moment of special crisis.

## Social Class

Because the 1961 census findings for Edinburgh were not available, only the percentage distributions of the classes among our patients were examined. For males, but not for females, there is a seeming excess in the lower social classes. This suggests that the personal characteristics which lead to self-poisoning may drag men down socially, whereas women, whose social class is determined by their husbands' occupation, do not suffer this effect.

## Marital Status

The distribution of marital status is noteworthy only for the high figure for divorced men: 12 percent. Because of this, we analyzed the current state of the marriage of the 91 men and 161 women between the ages of 20 and 64 who had ever been married. A very high proportion of the marriages, 30 percent for male patients and 26 percent for females, had been unnaturally interrupted by separation or divorce. In a sixth of these cases the break had been recent, within a month, and it probably played a part in causing the self-poisoning act. But generally the separation was of long duration. Nearly half the broken marriages had ended five or more years before the act took place.

For the marriages that subsist, the going is not good either. Whichever was the patient, husband and wife always concurred in telling us about their marital relations, and nearly always they agreed that they were bad. Frequent hostility, admitted by both spouses, characterized 85 percent of the marriages of male patients and 68 percent of females. Frequent hostility does not invariably mean that a marriage is unsound. The psychiatric social worker who had seen both partners graded only half the marriages as poor or bad, and more of male patients than of female. Perhaps, however, one has to be inside a marriage really to assess its satisfactions and its failures. Despite the hostility not many patients or their spouses desired that their marriages terminate. More often it was the wife that did, no matter which one was the patient. We found, when we followed our cases subsequently, that where either partner had expressed such a wish to end the marriage there was rarely any reconciliation later.

It may be the patient or the spouse who is responsible for these unfortunate marriages, or it may be both. Certainly the other partner is not blameless. Unfaithfulness and, for the husbands of our women patients, jealousy, gambling, and above all excessive drinking were frequently encountered. We accepted the attribute only if the spouses of our patients themselves revealed it. Only half of them impressed the psychiatric social worker who interviewed them as normal. The others mostly exhibited character disorders, although a proportion of the wives of male patients were psychiatrically ill.

Other personal relationships did not fare better. Seventy percent of the men and fifty-nine percent of the women who were single, or whose marriages had ceased, got on badly with whoever was the principal figure in their life situation. This bad relationship with the key individual, spouse, other relative, or friend was the dominant theme in the story of nearly every patient, whether narrated by himself or by an informant. More than any other factor it provided the setting for the self-poisoning act. Yet, in many cases, it only set the seal on a life pattern characterized by adverse circumstances: a bad work record, chronic debt, and constant changes of home, often the product of separations. Moreover, the life story seemed to repeat a similar story in the parents. There had been a great amount of parental absence during the patient's childhood. By the age of five there had been abnormal absences due to death, hospitalization, or separations arising from marital disharmony, but excluding those due to war service or employment, of 13 percent of the mothers and 25 percent of the fathers. Most of these were due to the parents' separating because their marriage had broken down. We took a minimum period of six months as the criterion of absence, but in practice a much longer time than this was usually involved. The greater amount of paternal rather than maternal absence is because, when a marriage breaks, the child tends to stay with his mother. But for 10 percent there had been separation from both parents. Exactly half the patients had lacked one or another parent by the age of 15 and a fifth lacked both. These are very high figures indeed. Whether the broken parental home is the root from which stems the disorganized life pattern, the disorganized marriage, the dwelling in disorganized districts, must remain a matter for speculation; but certainly, all these four circumstances are found very frequently in the stories of people who poison themselves.

This is the background upon which precipitating factors are superimposed. Table 2 shows the frequency with which certain items occurred and were important in the stories we obtained. Excessive drinking is prominent. Unemployment plays its part with men. Money worries were often mentioned, housing problems less commonly. Girls, in particular,

Table 2

Major Precipitating Factors of Self-Poisoners, in Percentages (Edinburgh, 1962–1963)

| | Males | Females |
|---|---|---|
| Marital disharmony | 68 | 60 |
| Drinking a problem | 51 | 16 |
| Financial difficulties | 44 | 31 |
| Unemployment | 34 | 18 |
| Kin disharmony | 28 | 30 |
| Isolation | 15 | |
| Crime | 15 | |
| Housing difficulties | 14 | 19 |
| Difficulties at work | 14 | |
| Love affairs going badly | | 16 |
| Forced separation | 12 | |

Percentages of 165 males and 350 females, except for marital disharmony and forced separation, which are based on 68 married males and 147 married females. More than one factor might be present. Bereavement, gambling, and sexual problems occurred in less than 10 percent of cases and have been omitted.

were sometimes driven to the extremity of poisoning themselves by a broken or a breaking love affair.

## The Means Adopted

Just over half (55 percent) the acts involved barbiturates. Almost all the barbiturates had been obtained legally by prescription, although these were not always written for the patients themselves; not uncommonly the tablets were intended for someone else. Nor was the illness for which they had been prescribed always current; often they had remained in the house for some time. One patient in eight (12 percent) took aspirin or a related compound. The second largest group, accounting for nearly a quarter of all admissions (23 percent) were "other drugs." These were generally the newer medicines, sedatives, stimulants, tranquilizers, and antidepressants designed to treat symptomatically some abnormal mental state. Only 1 percent employed a substance which was not meant to be taken at all and 9 percent used coal-gas. There were no differences between the sexes; the distribution of methods was the same for men as for women.

This pattern has been established only recently. The ward admission books from 1928 onwards have yielded an interesting picture of how fashions have altered since that time. Thirty-five years ago, nondrug poisons, chiefly lysol and other corrosive agents, were responsible for the majority of admissions and, together with coal-gas, accounted for nearly all the cases. Over the years nondrug poisons have been almost entirely given up, and the few cases that still do occur generally involve a fairly mild substance. Coal-gas (domestic-gas) poisoning remained at about the same level until the mid-1950s; since then it has slowly risen. This may very well be owing to a changing admission policy; nowadays every case is admitted whether or not the physical condition of the patient necessitates it.

It is not likely, however, that we can ascribe the rise in salicylate poisoning to administrative adjustments, because similar findings have been reported nationally. Cases began to occur to a somewhat important extent shortly after the war, and numbers are still rising.

The first patient suffering from barbiturate poisoning was admitted to the ward in 1932. About half a dozen cases a year came in regularly until the end of the war. Then began a spectacular increase. Barbiturate poisoning is now an outstanding problem. Sleeping tablets—and they are mostly barbiturates—are the accepted mid-twentieth century passport to oblivion, and doctors seem only too ready to issue the necessary visa.

Yet perhaps the most important rise to comment on is that of the "other drug" poisons, chiefly psychotropic preparations. Chlorpromazine was introduced into psychiatry in the early 1950s. A growing panoply of drugs has come into use since then, and we are having to deal increasingly with the results of their deliberate misuse. Those who are currently under treatment by a psychiatrist adopt this method of poisoning more often than do others—35 percent as against 23 percent. Their growing use seems to be as well as, not instead of, other means. In the matter of method, the physician leads, the layman follows. On the whole, such drugs are not as dangerous as are barbiturates. Yet because the lifespan of both may be short—even their principal constituents enjoy a relatively brief vogue—it is hard to develop the routine of correct toxicological management that is so important for successful resuscitation. The mounting use of these drugs for self-poisoning requires that they be carefully watched.

People of different ages employ different methods (Fig. 2). Both the percentage using barbiturates and the percentage using coal-gas rise with age. On the other hand, the proportion using salicylates falls. "Other drugs" show little variation with age except that they are not employed

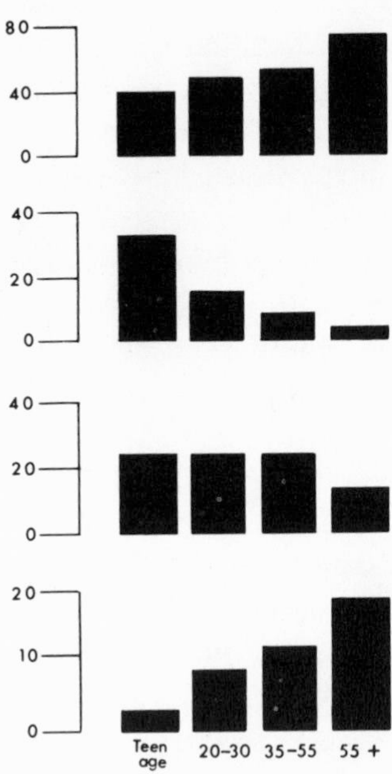


Fig. 2. Method used at different ages;
Percentages of all in each age group

by patients over the age of 55. This is strange since one would think that these drugs would have been optimally prescribed for the symptomatic management of elderly patients.

The other age trends are easy to explain. Insomnia is increasingly complained of as age advances, hence the extra prescribing of barbiturates. Young people presumably employ salicylates because it is less easy for them to get sleeping pills. Elderly people use coal-gas because they are often alone in the home for long enough to do it and they do not have, as do younger women, children in the house whose lives would be endangered. Cultural factors may also be important; when they were younger it was one of the traditional methods of self-poisoning, and they have carried this accepted pattern with them into old age. The young people of today probably will not employ gassing when they get old. A word of warning is appropriate here. Some instances when an elderly person is overcome by carbon monoxide are certainly accidents, but sympathetic physicians, to spare patients or their relatives unnecessary distress, often feel disposed to fall in with this explanation whenever it is proffered. Such stories should not be accepted without thorough enquiries. In our experience coal-gas poisoning does not very often turn out to be accidental. It is not a kindness to a patient to discharge him to his home with his depression undisclosed and untreated and the circumstances all too ripe for a repeat performance.

In most cases the patient did not use all the tablets that were available. Even when they were taken impulsively there was generally some calculation, which the patient would express like this: "I don't know exactly how many I took. I took what I thought was enough." Enough, but enough for what? The answer is far from simple.

## Diagnosis

The appropriate terms of conventional psychiatric nomenclature, depression, neurosis, personality abnormality, and the like, are ill suited to describing, differentiating, and categorizing the patients. We have been forced into unreal decisions about whether a patient's manifest unhappiness should be attributed to a depressive illness or regarded as understandable distress at intolerable living circumstances. We have had to distinguish, with what success I cannot judge, between normality and personality disorder. Very few of the patients were schizophrenic or organically ill (Table 3). Depressive illness, the commonest condition, was hardly ever accompanied by psychotic phenomena and was preponderantly mild. Women were more often diagnosed as depressive, whereas men suffered more from personality abnormality. It is of particular importance that 26 percent of the men and 20 percent of the women had no psychiatric illness. It has often been argued that to poison oneself is such an abnormal act that everyone who does so must be psychiatrically ill. We have not fallen into that tautological trap, for to contend thus is to make the recognition of psychiatric illness no more than a dependent phenomenon. Instead, we reasoned as follows: The diagnosis of a psychiatric condition must be made from positive features. These are detected either from the history or on clinical examination. If all the information about the patient's mental state at the time of his act, obtained from both him and an informant, does not indicate any departure from normal, and if clinical examination after physical recovery fails to reveal any significant disorder, then there are no grounds for concluding that the patient is psychiatrically ill. This view will not be acceptable to everyone. There are psychiatrists who assign the sobriquet of abnormality of personality very readily. But even if they would have labelled as suffering from a character disorder some of those whom we have judged to be normal, that disorder was certainly not marked. It was not enough by itself to explain their self-poisoning acts. Nor is this unexpected. Distress drives people to self-poisoning acts, and distress is not the exclusive province of the mentally ill. The significance of the finding that so many patients had no psychiatric disorder is that it focuses attention on the purposes of the act and makes us concentrate on personal relationships in their social setting. It is a finding that we were able to make because we dealt with the total picture of self-poisoning coming to the hospital and not just with those cases somehow selected for psychiatric investigation.

Table 3

Diagnoses of Self-Poisoners, in Percentages
(Edinburgh, 1962–1963)

| | Males (165) | Females (350) |
|---|---|---|
| Organic psychiatric illness | 5 | 4 |
| Depression | 26 | 43 |
| Other psychoses | 5 | 5 |
| Other neuroses | 5 | 12 |
| Personality disorder only | 32 | 16 |
| No psychiatric illness* | 26 | 20 |
| Total | 100 | 100 |

NOTE: 7 patients left before any diagnosis could be made.

* In the terminology of the American Psychiatric Association Manual most of these could be classified as 000 × 82, Adult Situational Reaction, or 000 × 85, Adjustment Reaction of Adolescence. Neither of these is, of course, a psychiatric diagnosis.

Those with no psychiatric illness tended to be younger; those with organic illnesses were generally old. Apart from this, the relationship between diagnosis and age was not close.

The principal diagnosis was related to the index of endangering life (Table 4). The acts of those with a formal psychiatric illness (excluding character disorder) were more life-endangering than were those with personality abnormality or without a psychiatric illness. Yet the majority of acts of even the people who were more ill were clearly pointed toward survival.

Table 4

Diagnosis and Index of Endangering Life, in Percentages (Edinburgh, 1962–1963)

| Predictable Outcome | All psychiatric illnesses (292) | Personality disorder only (108) | No psychiatric diagnosis (113) |
|---|---|---|---|
| Death | 25 | 12 | 12 |
| Death probable | 11 | 11 | 10 |
| Death unlikely | 20 | 26 | 30 |
| Certain to survive | 43 | 51 | 49 |
| Total | 100 | 100 | 100 |

Chi-square = 18.99; 3 degrees of freedom; $P < 0.001$. The chi square was calculated by comparing all psychiatric illnesses against the two other categories combined.

The different diagnostic groups do not vary much in the methods they choose. The only features of note are that those without a psychiatric illness use aspirin rather more often than do the others and that people with an organic illness more often use coal-gas. Those findings are probably attributable to the ages of those involved.

Quite commonly patients who were suffering from depression had an underlying character disorder. The combination of depression and psychopathy occurred frequently. This conjunction seems especially prone to manifest in self-poisoning acts. Personality disorder either as a principal or as an accessory diagnosis was recognized in 41 percent of men and 27 percent of women patients, and about half of these were classed as psychopaths. A smaller proportion appeared to us to be abnormally immature in their outlook. No other sort of personality abnormality occurred frequently.

Associated diagnostic factors included alcoholism, drug addiction, epilepsy, and subnormality. Fifty-two percent of the men had one or more of these conditions, and the dominant factor is alcoholism; thirty-nine percent of the men and eight percent of the women were alcoholics, seasoned drinkers, or unquestionably addicted, many of whom bore physical signs of chronic alcoholism. Alcoholism is a major factor in predisposing to self-poisoning. So is alcohol itself. Fifty-six percent of the men and twenty-three percent of the women had been drinking just before the act took place—a deliberate act in every case. The methods adopted by alcoholics did not differ from those employed by the nonalcoholic patients; and the acts which led to their admission and to the admission of those inebriated at the time were neither more nor less serious than those of other people. But of the six patients, four men and two women, who killed themselves within a year of discharge, five were alcoholics.

### Recommended Disposition

Twenty-six percent of the patients were sent for further in-patient psychiatric treatment; thirty-eight percent were recommended for out-patient treatment, which, unless they had previously been under the care of another Edinburgh psychiatrist, was carried out by our own service. For 36 percent, no further psychiatric treatment was arranged (Table 5).

Table 5

Diagnosis and Disposal, in Percentages

| | | Patients with a psychiatric illness (286) | | Patients with personality disorder only (103) | | Patients with *no* psychiatric diagnosis (112) | | All patients* (501) | |
|---|---|---|---|---|---|---|---|---|---|
| Further psychiatric treatment: | In-patient | 37 | 77 | 17 | 51 | 8 | 45 | 26 | 64 |
| | Out-patient | 40 | | 34 | | 37 | | 38 | |
| No further psychiatric treatment | | | 23 | | 49 | | 55 | | 36 |

* This is excluding 21 patients who discharged themselves before disposal was arranged.

Sometimes this was because the patient refused our suggestion, but in most cases we did not think that further treatment was called for. This was either because there was not a condition present to treat, and the tangled precipitating social web had been unravelled while the patient was still in our care, or because the personality disorder from which they suffered was so ingrained that treatment would not avail. Diagnosis is correlated with disposal, but this was not primarily decided on the basis of the diagnosis made. The proportion recommended for in-patient care must inevitably depend on availability of psychiatric beds. Similarly the extent of out-patient care depends on the amount of psychiatric time allotted for this.

It does not follow that one can only benefit from treatment if one have a psychiatric illness. Nearly half of those without such illness were judged to be helpable by further care, a term which embraces social work as well as psychiatric therapy. Generally this was on an out-patient basis, but 8 percent of them were required to be in-patients so that they might properly be helped over the acute crisis situations which had caused their acts.

## Distress

Is there a unifying basis to self-poisoning acts? Is there some feature that informs them all? The answer has already been hinted at. Distress drives people to self-poisoning acts. Distress and despair, unhappiness and desperation. It may arise from within, from a morbid appreciation that the patient has of himself in the world; such is the person with a depressive illness. Often it is generated from outside, from the intolerable yet insoluble social situation in which he is caught; that is why so many patients cannot be classed as ill. Sometimes it springs from both sources. Nobody takes poison, a little or a lot, to live or to die, unless at that moment he is distressed beyond what he can bear and so desperate that he cannot see a more rational solution. He thinks that a solution exists, but he cannot find it himself. The suicide says, in effect, "There is no way out," but people who poison themselves are saying "I cannot see a way out." They find themselves trapped. They are desperate. And their distress drives them to an action that is both stupid and, at the same time, a blow for liberation, an action that is both senseless and purposeful. We must respect the conjunction of these epithets. The patients almost always can. Many of them did so even as they were taking the tablets.

Example: A married woman of twenty-seven, whose husband was threatening to leave her, took fifty aspirins: "I didn't think they'd kill me. I thought they might. I hoped they wouldn't. I thought of my mother and father. I couldn't let them be hurt. I hoped really it would bring John back. If it didn't I might as well die." Senseless and purposeful. It is a paradox that we have to accept.

## Motives

The sorts of predicaments which cause people such distress are legion. "Every unhappy family is unhappy in its own particular way." Yet some generalizations can be made. Some patients referred the drama to something wrong within themselves (Table 6). They considered their feelings about the world faulty; however, such notions were by no means always accompanied by self-blame. Others explicitly incriminated bad relations with someone else—generally, if they were married, the spouse. Although they recognized that it takes two to quarrel they inclined to reproach the other more than themselves. Very often they were right. Not many mentioned material circumstances, debt or unemployment, for instance, and very few indeed held them to be the only factors at work. Broadly speaking, our assessment of these factors corresponded with the patients' views.

Table 6

"I Did It Because . . ."

| | Males (163) percent | | Females (348) percent | |
|---|---|---|---|---|
| Troubled relations with other people | 39 | (51) | 59 | (65) |
| Distress arising from within | 45 | (66) | 37 | (49) |
| Material problems (money, housing, etc.) | 15 | (18) | 14 | (16) |
| "No reason" or "don't know" | 23 | | 16 | |

These factors are not exclusive of each other. Figures in parentheses are the clinical assessments based on interviews with relatives as well as parents.

We noted one phenomenon over and over again. An insensitive spouse, generally the husband, although he cared for his wife, had failed to sense either her need for emotional support and encouragement or the growing sense of isolation, within the home, that stemmed from their lack. The desperate action she took and the consequential action we took at the time of crisis to get this across to the husband were both important in ameliorating an unhappy state of affairs that need never have arisen. In our follow-up study we found the outcome of such cases to have been the most satisfactory.

Ill health, rather surprisingly, was rarely mentioned by patients, although frequently present both as acute illness and as chronic disability. Many of the conditions we counted were not severe, but none was negligible. Almost always the patient was aware of his illness and complained of it, yet he did not relate it to his having poisoned himself. Nevertheless, the debilitating effect, or the handicap, probably contributed materially to the patient's state of mind.

The immediate spark to many acts was a quarrel. Where a good relationship exists between two people a quarrel, however bitter or violent, does not provoke either party to take poison; but where the relationship is bad this is often the impetuous result.

## Impulsiveness

Two-thirds of all acts were impulsive (Table 7). This astonishing finding is of the utmost importance. Five minutes before the act took place, sometimes one minute before, the idea of taking poison was not in the person's mind. He may have, he frequently had, thought about doing it in the past. Hours of rumination may have preceded the determination which was formed in a single moment. But in the event and at the time of the event, a feeling of despair arose, often suddenly, from a trivial cause and was as suddenly acted upon. It was no culmination of a gathering plan. There was no plan. "Why did you do it?" one asks such patients. "I don't know; it just came over me." And they do not know.

Table 7

Impulsiveness and Age

| | Teenage (65) | 20–34 (196) | 35–54 (172) | 55+ (69) |
|---|---|---|---|---|
| Percentage of acts that were impulsive | 71 | 71 | 63 | 58 |

It is not that they have forgotten. They are not prevaricating. They never worked it out. They never had a period when they were intending to do it. It just came over them.

Example: A thirty-year-old woman, who had long endured an unhappy marriage to an aggressive ne'er-do-well, related how one day they had a protracted quarrel. There was violence and she collapsed, crying, in an armchair. What was she to do? While she was weeping she remembered that a little while earlier a bottle of sleeping tables had slipped down the back of the chair and she had never retrieved it. She reached down her hand, found the bottle, and took twenty Seconal capsules.

We could multiply that example over three hundred times with equally impulsive instances. Men and women acted impulsively in similar proportions. Impulsive acts were not related to alcoholism; also, they were no more common among the inebriated than among the others. They had little bearing on the method adopted. Impulsiveness was more common than premeditation at all ages, although its incidence was rather less in women over the age of fifty-five because of an increase in depressive illness in this group. Patients with formal psychiatric illnesses, more often than others, premeditated self-poisoning but even among them, impulsiveness characterized just over half the acts. Impulsive acts were less life-endangering than were premeditated ones (Table 8). Still, 16 percent of them had a predictable outcome of death.

Table 8

Impulsiveness and Index of Endangering Life
(Edinburgh, 1962–1963)

| Predictable outcome | Impulsive acts (333) percent | Premeditated acts (169) percent |
|---|---|---|
| Death | 16 | 27 |
| Death probable | 10 | 14 |
| Death unlikely | 23 | 24 |
| Certain to survive | 52 | 35 |
| Total | 100 | 100 |

Chi-square = 16.27; 3 degrees of freedom; $P>0.01$; there were no differences between the sexes.

People who act impulsively have a chance to seek aid immediately afterwards. Premeditation on the other hand carries with it the opportunity to warn someone in advance. Nearly everybody who had premeditated the act had done so for the most part very recently. The young girl who took the aspirins told her husband that she was thinking of taking her life. He did not take her seriously. Unfortunately, that is commonly the case.

Such warnings are part of the "appeal" quality of self-poisoning acts. Stengel,[4] who more than anyone else has been responsible for focussing attention on this important aspect, has urged that the appeal is usually unconscious. Among our patients, however, it was common to find that it was quite conscious.

Example: A rigid, respectable, intolerant, middle-aged man whose wife had left him suddenly a month earlier took about 25 aspirin tablets.

"To tell you the truth, it was exhibitionism, really. I thought it might arouse her sympathy. I'd tried everything, letters, flowers, nylons, the minister, a lawyer—so I thought I'd try this. To be very truthful, I made enquiries as to the fatal dose. Of course I didn't do so directly. I went to the chemist and said, 'We've been arguing in the canteen about the number of aspirin you'd need.' He said that about 40 would probably be fatal. So I took between 25 and 30." I asked him why he had not taken 40 and the answer was immediate: "Self-preservation. Life's too sweet."

Such patients are often condemned as frankly manipulative and therefore somehow undeserving. When the purpose is so apparent the distress and the despair are less obvious. But they are there. This man was so disturbed that he had to be legally restrained a month later from continually molesting his wife to secure her return.

Others achieve their purpose. Admission to the ward for having poisoned oneself can be, for instance, a powerful weapon in bringing back errant boyfriends. Girls who resort to it are, all the same, very much distressed; in their despair they do something stupid and senseless and it works. Should we judge them harshly on that score? Perhaps what we most resent is that although there was probably a negligible risk to life, they are held by their circle of friends to have narrowly escaped death. They have had their drama; to us it only means work. But we can hardly expect our patients to have borne that in mind.

## Statement of Intention

Sixty percent of the patients claimed, once they had recovered, that they were intending to die, whereas a quarter said categorically that this was not their purpose. The rest either did not know or were evasive. Little credence can be placed on their statements. The patients did not express them with conviction. They were not true recollections. The intention is not usually worked out at all, let alone with such precision in terms of living and dying. Between those who said that they had intended to die and those who said they had not, there was some, although little, difference in the degree to which they had endangered their lives. We find it more profitable to emphasize with the patient any constructive purpose there may have been in his act than to stress the destructive element, which, in any case, is evanescent. Very few patients—and they were almost all severely depressed—said after physical recovery that they still wished to take their lives.

## Prevention and Management

Since the outcome of self-poisoning acts is often beneficial ought we to try to prevent them? Such an argument cannot be countenanced. It is not the result of the self-poisoning which produces the benefit but the disclosure and solution of the underlying problem, and there are certainly better and safer ways to bring these problems to light. Self-poisoning is a dangerous practice. Some people kill themselves by it, by accident or, perhaps, by design. Resuscitation is difficult and time-consuming. It should be possible for people to secure at a smaller price the psychiatric and social help required.

We have looked so far at the face that self-poisoning presents to the patient. The professional worker views it differently. To the general physician it is a medical nuisance: he knows that it involves his staff and himself in considerable work and worry in dealing with the effects of what does not seem to be illness at all. To the psychiatrist it presents a perplexing problem chiefly because of the disparity between the gravity of the situation and the paucity of the clinical findings. To the social strategist it is a setback and a challenge, one more piece of evidence of the malaise generated by bad social conditions. Everyone would like to see self-poisoning prevented.

We cannot alter the disturbed backgrounds from which the patients come. We do not have the means to lessen parental separation or reduce adverse life experiences and the bad social circumstances in which so many of these patients live. There are many pressing reasons for doing all these things, but the action required is political and not medical. All we may do is to add the knowledge that they generate self-poisoning to the weight of the indictment against such conditions and our voices to the swell of protest against their continued existence.

In the narrower context of the family setting, however, we may be less impotent. The majority of self-poisoning acts arise from strains within that setting; hence the importance of the fact that so many of the patients, and their spouses, relate the act to interpersonal difficulties, and hence the importance of the finding that so many patients had no psychiatric illness. If the act has a constructive component in drawing the attention of an insensitive spouse to the emotional needs of the other, then surely it is possible to find less painful ways of bringing this about. And if this is accepted as a medical problem and a medical responsibility—it need not be, but if it is so accepted—then the person to shoulder it is the general practitioner in his chosen role of family doctor. For this, as nothing else, is doctoring the family.

Certain preventive measures are suggested by our study of the means adopted, bearing in mind that two-thirds of the acts were carried out impulsively. Consider first the sale of salicylates. No one would wish to see aspirin available only by prescription, but it is not necessary for it to be sold in lethal quantities, without any check on the reason why it is being purchased. Aspirin in large amounts is a dangerous preparation with a measurable mortality rate from overdosage. Untrained and unlicensed people should be stopped from selling it in such quantities. Its sale outside of pharmacies, in grocer's shops and public houses, for instance, should be restricted to packets of half a dozen tablets for emergency use. Only pharmacists should be allowed to sell more than that, and they should be advised to exercise some discretion over its sale, particularly to young people. At present they do not do so. It is commonly sold by junior assistants and the pharmacist himself without any regard to its dangers. We sent a young girl, sobbing, into six pharmacies within a mile of each other in Edinburgh. In each she said: "May I buy 200 aspirins please?" There could have been no economic motive for purchasing such a quantity, for the largest bottle contained only 100 tablets. Nowhere was she refused, whether served by an assistant or by the manager. Only once was any concern expressed— "Two hundred? Are you all right? You ought to go and have a cup of tea"—although she received several curious glances and was watched through the window as she left more than one shop. A distraught-looking girl, 200 aspirins asked for—curiosity and interest, but no hesitation about the sale. This is irresponsible. The pharmacist, who knows of the dangers of salicylates, should personally supervise their sale and should discourage purchases of more than twenty-five at a time. Indeed, there is no good reason why bottles of more than fifty tablets should be available at all. Anyone could, of course, go from shop to shop, but doing this would allow time for the impulse to wear off.

Control of the sale of aspirins, by pharmacists and others, could be achieved very simply. But it is only a small part of the problem. The majority of the poisons taken were obtained by prescription. The changing pattern over the years reveals that an increase in admissions of poisoned patients in the 1940s continued at an accelerating pace in the 50s and 60s.

To anyone who works in a poisoning treatment center the conclusion is inescapable that dangerous substances are prescribed unnecessarily often and in excessive quantities. To afford a patient sleep is praiseworthy, but unfortunately it is not possible to do this without at the same time giving him the means to produce unconsciousness and even death. If the insomnia is a symptom of depressive illness, the gloom-ridden patient may interpret the piece of prescription paper as a license to poison himself. Several of our patients recounted their surprise that sleeping tablets were prescribed so readily. The growing frequency of self-poisoning acts makes it imperative to use the utmost circumspection in the prescription of barbiturates. The average number of tablets ordered on a single prescription in 1959 were, according to a survey reported by Brooke and Glatt,[5] phenobarbitone, 60; soneryl, 44; amytal, 49; nembutal, 40; drinamyl, 48. These were the average quantities; some prescriptions were for amounts greatly in excess of these. It is difficult to concede that all this barbiturate was really necessary.

There is, too, a growing popularity of drugs for the mental state. The practitioner, with the assistance sometimes of the psychiatrist, has a double encouragement to prescribe considerable quantities to just those patients who are most likely to indulge in overdosage. For if the tablets work, then he continues to order them; and if they do not, and the patient's symptoms continue, the doctor perseveres, if not with the same drug, then with a similar one. Often it is the patient who first decides to desist. Finding he is not being helped he gives up taking the tablets, and so they accumulate in his home, waiting. After an episode of illness is over, supplies of every kind of tablet customarily remain in the house; in a moment of crisis they are there as an irresistible temptation. The greatest single public health measure that could be taken to reduce the extent of self-poisoning would cost nothing at all: It would be that every doctor during the next few months whenever he visits a patient's house empty the excess stocks of drugs that he finds there. He would meet little opposition from his patients. Often they are ignorant of the fact that they hold such a lethal supply. It is only at a time of sudden despair that a search is made and the bottle is found and the tablets are taken.

Would patients cut off from a supply of drugs resort to more dangerous or more violent action—gassing themselves, swallowing corrosives, slashing their wrists, or jumping from heights? I do not think this likely. Few self-poisoning patients want to damage themselves irreparably. They would probably seek another way of getting the help they desperately claim they need. Almost certainly it would be a healthier way.

Fifteen percent of our series of patients were admitted again within a twelve-month period. The problem of repeated self-poisoning is closely bound up with the presence of personality disorder. Such patients are likely to adopt this pattern of behavior over and over again when they become depressed and have no other outlet. In our service we try to cope with this situation by offering them the opportunity to call on our help when they need it without feeling that they have to take an overdose in order to secure attention. Sometimes this necessitates the immediate admission of a patient who is only threatening to take tablets. This is a duty which the psychiatric services should accept. If they were to do so, I am convinced that the number of repeated self-poisoning acts would decline. At present it can often be difficult to secure emergency admission to a psychiatric hospital of patients with personality abnormalities who become suddenly, but not severely, depressed. They consequently obtain their necessary removal from the acute situation by taking an overdose and getting a hospital bed in this way. An emergency psychiatric admission is safer and cheaper than an emergency admission to a poisoning treatment center.

Prevention is best. But cases will continue to arrive in large numbers at our present hospitals, and we will have to deal with them. The patients we have been considering were all brought to the hospital, but we know that there are many other cases which are handled without this recourse. Our rates, high as they are, are necessarily underestimates of the total problem of self-poisoning. They are available in Edinburgh because we studied every case coming to the hospital. There is little reason to believe that similar rates would not be found elsewhere. Both alcoholism and unemployment are more rife in Scotland than in England, and they will have swelled in the incidence; but figures of comparable order would almost certainly be revealed in other places if the procedure of automatic admission of every case of self-poisoning arriving at hospital were followed. Admission does not invariably require that the patient spend even one night in the hospital. The routine of necessary medical care and prompt and thorough psychiatric assessment can be performed quickly, but first it must be firmly established. At present it still goes by default in many hospitals.

It is the correct medical approach, because it makes sure that the proper treatment is applied at the point when it is most effective. By striking while the iron is hot the psychiatrist makes sure that the principal figures are most malleable. This is the time when skillful intervention can do the most. While the patient is in the ward under our care, generally for one, two, or three days only, he and his relatives receive a lot of attention. We practice, whenever we think it necessary, what I term stösspsychotherapy—management of patients by quickly administering a massive dose of psychiatric treatment. Such a service, described in detail elsewhere,[6] should form an integral part of every poisoning treatment unit, for there is considerable advantage in conducting resuscitation and psychiatric management in the same clinical setting. The time is past when patients should be discharged from in-patient care—or worse, after a brief unpleasant sojourn in the casualty department without psychiatric assessment. Physicians still handle the situation this way because of a misconception of, and nurtured by, the term "attempted suicide."

I have throughout this chapter used the term "self-poisoning" rather than "attempted suicide" because I consider that second term both clinically inappropriate and misleading. It is true that in the popular mind deliberate self-poisoning is linked, indeed romantically, with the idea of suicide. It is true that some of our patients did all they could to encompass their deaths; this minority can be said to have failed at suicide. But for four-fifths of the patients the concept of attempting suicide is wide of the mark. They performed their acts in the belief that they were comparatively safe, aware, even in the heat of the moment, that they would survive their overdosage and able to disclose what they had done in good time to ensure their rescue. What they were attempting was not suicide. Moreover, what they were attempting they commonly achieved. To that end the simulation of death, the hint of suicide, heightened its effectiveness. But the act was not attempted suicide. Doctors do not have to be deceived by simulation; the drama was enacted for their own circle only.

If the term "attempted suicide" were merely meaningless it could be tolerated, but it is positively wrong and should be discarded. The motives of our patients clearly proclaim this. In the first place, the majority of acts were impulsive. Then, too, they were stupid and senseless, and the patients themselves acknowledge this. Not thus does a man drive himself to suicide. Also, they demonstrated some purposefulness; but the purpose was to alter their life situation, not to die.

These patients were not attempting suicide. That term leads to errors of judgment. The chief of these is measuring the need for psychiatric treatment by the yardstick of the physical state of the patient. If he has taken only a small quantity of drugs then he was not really attempting suicide, so runs the argument time and again; he was just making a suicidal gesture, which need not be taken seriously. Whether or not the patient receives psychiatric help must not depend upon whether the doctor in the out-patient department thinks the patient is *physically* ill enough to need admission. This doctor will be more impressed by the dozen tablets that the patient has taken than by the threescore that he was prevented from swallowing. The extent of physical damage is no criterion either of the seriousness of psychiatric illness or of the need for psychiatric care (Table 9). The index of endangering life—our measure of the seriousness of the act—was not correlated with the need for psychiatric treatment.

Table 9

Index of Endangering Life and Disposal, in Percentages

| | Predictable outcome | | | |
|---|---|---|---|---|
| | Death | Death probable | Death unlikely | Certain to survive |
| In-patient psychiatric care (131) | 40 | 23 | 22 | 23 |
| Out-patient psychiatric care (190) | 30 | 45 | 40 | 39 |
| No further psychiatric care (179) | 30 | 32 | 38 | 38 |

Chi-square = 12.05; 6 degrees of freedom $P > 0.05$.

Mistakes occur, and result in many tragedies, because doctors cling to the notion of attempted suicide. Attempted suicide is not a diagnosis. It is not even a description of behavior. It is an interpretation of the motives for the act of self-poisoning—an unnecessary and usually wrong interpretation. The alternative is simple: Everybody who has poisoned himself warrants psychiatric examination. The fact of self-poisoning should be a sufficient criterion for the doctor who sees the patient to decide to obtain a psychiatric assessment. This is much easier for him than to have to try to estimate whether or not the patient positively meant to die. It is easier and more correct—better medicine and simpler. We should discard the specious concept of attempted suicide. Clinical practice will then be to ascertain whether self-poisoning has taken place, and if it has, to arrange, irrespective of the physical state of the patient, a psychiatric examination to be performed before the patient is discharged.

The fashion of self-poisoning will be with us, almost certainly, and will continue to grow, for years to come. We cannot afford to miss the point of it by calling it something else.

## Conclusion

Deliberate self-poisoning is becoming more and more common and a matter of public health concern. Its management, other than resuscitation, is best achieved by psychiatric methods. The means of self-poisoning are usually provided by physicians, and it is as a general medical problem that the poisoned patient first presents.

I have attempted to illuminate each of these aspects by a clinical and epidemiological study of 465 cases for one year (1962–1963) in Edinburgh. This has led to an explanation of the recent rapid rise in incidence and to suggestions for prevention and for management. An understanding of all aspects is necessary for proper appreciation both of individual patients and, collectively, of an important medical problem.

## REFERENCES


1. I would like to thank Dr. J. K. Slater who was, until his retirement, physician-in-charge of ward 3 of the Royal Infirmary of Edinburgh, for his encouragement. Dr. Henry Matthew, his successor, has given me a great deal of advice and help as we have thought through problems together. This paper would be the poorer without the stimulus of his ideas, and I am deeply grateful. I must also thank the medical and nursing staff of the ward for all their assistance.

   To Mr. J. W. McCulloch, my psychiatric social worker colleague in the Medical Research Council Unit for Research on the Epidemiology of Psychiatric Illness, I owe more than thanks. He has partnered me in this work.
2. N. Kessel, W. McCulloch, J. Hendry, D. Leslie, I. Wallace, and R. Webster, "Hospital Management of Attempted Suicide in Edinburgh," *Scottish Medical Journal,* **9**:333–334, 1964.
3. P. Sainsbury, *Suicide in London* (London: Chapman & Hall, Ltd., 1955).
4. E. Stengel and N. C. Cook, *Attempted Suicide* (London: Oxford University Press, 1958).
5. E. M. Brooke and M. M. Glatt, "More and More Barbiturates," *Medicine, Science and the Law,* **4**:277–282, 1964.
6. N. Kessel, W. McCulloch, and E. Simpson, "Psychiatric Service in a Centre for the Treatment of Poisoning," *British Medical Journal,* **ii**:985–988, 1963.

# 17. Crisis, Disaster, and Suicide: Theory and Therapy

Norman L. Farberow

The theory and therapy of crisis, disaster, and suicide have much in common. They all refer to more or less violent disruptions of the functioning of individuals, significant others, and society as the result of the impact of an internal and external critical event. There are, of course, distinguishing differences as well. This chapter, while it focuses primarily on the suicidal crisis, will examine the essential differences and similarities of crisis and disaster theory for the possibility of increasing understanding and improving effective prevention of suicide. The first section examines crisis theory and therapy; the second notes disaster studies and its body of research; and the third describes the suicidal situation and details, especially the handling of suicidal crises.

Crisis theory has considerable currency in the mental health field today. It is difficult at this time to find an article dealing with mental health and emotional problems that does not make at least some reference to it if not an attempt to relate it. The development of crisis theory has emerged since the late forties and early fifties from several trends—an increasing sophistication and awareness of mental health by the public, an increasing demand for services, a growth of information about brief psychotherapy and its feasibility, the development of social psychology and psychiatry, and the growth of the concept of community mental health. The area was pioneered by Lindemann with his classic study of the bereavement experiences of families who lost someone in the Boston Cocoanut Grove nightclub fire.[1] It was as early as 1948 that Lindemann and Caplan initiated the Wellesley Human Relations Service to study and test ideas about crises and crisis intervention.

## Crisis

Crisis has been defined in many ways. Webster indicates that the word crisis comes from the Greek *krisis,* from *krinein,* which is akin to the Latin *cernere,* both of which mean to separate. Crisis is defined as a turning point in the course of anything; as a decisive or a crucial time, stage, or event; a crucial situation whose outcome decides whether or not bad consequences will follow. A crisis in medicine is a point at which it becomes clear whether the patient will recover or die. Caplan defines crisis broadly as "an upset in a steady state or disturbance of homeostasis."[2] He differentiates between crisis and stress, with crisis being time-limited whereas stress need not be. Caplan had defined crisis earlier as a time when a person faces an obstacle to important life goals that is for a time insurmountable through the use of customary methods of problem-solving.[3] He stated that it is a period of disorganization followed by a period of upset during which many different abortive attempts at solution may be made. Eventually, some kind of adaptation is achieved which may or may not be in the best interest of that person and his fellows.

Morley, referring to Lindemann and Caplan, distinguishes between an emotionally hazardous situation, a crisis, and an emotional predicament.[4] An emotionally hazardous situation is one in which any sudden alteration in the field of social forces causes the individual's expectation of himself and his relations with others to undergo change. Such alterations could involve actual loss or a threatened loss of a significant relationship, introduction of one or more significant new individuals into the social orbit, or transition in social status and role relationship as a consequence of such factors. Crisis is a term reserved for the acute and often prolonged disturbance that may occur to an individual or a social orbit as a result of emotional hazard. Emotional predicament is a generic term that encompasses the distressed individuals, the crisis situation, and the emotional hazard, all of which must be appraised and assessed. Bloom analyzed the elements that went into the definition of the crisis concept.[5] The most important element seemed to be a known precipitating event. Secondarily, there seemed to be either no reaction or a slow resolution requiring a month or more. Bloom's judges suggested that situations in which the resolution was rapid illustrated appropriate responses applied to reality situations. When there was no known precipitating event, the situation was likely to be considered a psychiatric disorder rather than a crisis. Elements of internal tension, behavioral disorganization, and rapidity of onset were not considered so important in the definition of a crisis. Most theorists, however, continue to make the definition of crisis broader than did Bloom's judges.

Precipitating stresses produce varied threats. These threats may occur in terms of loss of social self, threat to family integrity, changes in social roles, sudden illnesses, hospitalizations, or loss of a loved one through death, separation or divorce. Erikson refers to "developmental" and "accidental" crises.[6] Caplan differentiates between "individual" and "situational" precipitating events.[7] These seem similar to Erikson's concepts and are allied to intra- and interpersonal aspects of situations. Rapoport states that the threat may be to fundamental instinctual needs or to a person's sense of integrity, whereas the loss may be actual or a feeling of acute deprivation.[8] She enumerates three sets of interrelated factors which may produce crisis: (1) A hazardous event which poses a threat; (2) a threat to instinctual needs symbolically linked to earlier threats that results in vulnerability and conflict; and (3) an inability to respond with formerly adequate coping mechanisms. Parad and Caplan and Harris and others also refer to "conflict derivatives" in which the precipitants are current threats to instinctual needs symbolically linked to earlier conflicts.[9] Forer, using an internal structural point of view, describes crises from three levels: situational crises, crises of secondary narcissism, and crises of primary narcissism.[10] Psychotherapy is the resolution of a series of crises in which rigid defenses are replaced by adaptive ones. Reusch classifies individual crises from a communication viewpoint as input crises, anticipation and recollection crises, decision-making crises, and output crises.[11]

A crisis may also be viewed in terms of its temporal elements. Rapoport emphasizes that crisis is usually self-limiting in a temporal sense. Caplan divides the crisis period into four phases: (1) a rise of tension, unpleasant affect, and disorganization of behavior stemming from the impact of the stimulus—all of which call forth habitual problem-solving techniques; (2) a lack of success in resolution along with the continuation of the stimulus impact exacerbates the state of tension; (3) tension-reducing activities mobilizing additional internal and external resources may result in the problem abating in intensity, the use of emergency problem-solving mechanisms defining the problem in a new way, or giving up goals that are unobtainable; and (4) if the problem continues and cannot be solved by need satisfaction, avoidance, giving up goals, or perceptual distortion, major disorganization of the individual occurs.[12] In general, investigators describe a rise in tension toward a pervasive feeling of helplessness; cognitive confusion in which the individual does not know how to think of the problem or how to evaluate reality; difficulty in formulating possibilities for problem-solving; perceptual confusion, in extreme states, in temporal and spatial senses; and feelings of anxiety, somatic symptoms, or extensive use of denial or repression.[13]

Affective reactions to crisis situations may range through all levels. There may be all kinds of emotional reactions, including anxiety, tension, panic, sense of loss, personal and social feelings of confusion and chaos, helplessness, hopelessness, and disorganization. In addition, magical thinking, excessive fantasy, regressive forms of behaviors, somatization, and withdrawal from reality may occur in some of the more severe forms.

Some activities, however, may be adaptive in nature, especially if the behavior is task-oriented. Tyhurst suggests that crisis may not be an illness but an opportunity for growth, however severe the impact may be.[14] Rapoport also indicates that crises may be differentiated between potentially pathogenic stress and potentially growth-stimulating stress. Morley[15] and Forer also state that individuals in crises are ready for great change and can be maximally influenced by another person. Mental work may be directed toward correcting the cognitive perception, which means predicting and anticipating the outcome through a cognitive restructuring. Thus, there may be a correct cognitive perception of the situation, management of affect through awareness of feelings, appropriate verbalization leading to tension discharge and mastery, and development of patterns of seeking and using help from institutional and interpersonal resources.

The principles and techniques of handling crisis situations have been outlined by a number of persons. Rapoport outlines several steps: (1) Clarify the problem that led to the call for help; (2) indicate explicit acceptance of the disordered affect, irrational attitudes and negative responses: (3) use interpersonal and institutional resources to provide support and to mobilize energy for reaching out to others; and (4) recognize that you are intervening as one part of a network of resources and that you are not the single available resource. She describes four broad principles for treatment: (1) Keep an explicit focus on the crisis; (2) help with cognitive mastery; (3) offer basic information and education; and (4) create a bridge to other community resources.[16] As explicated in a later section, these principles are similar to those operating in the treatment of the suicidal crisis. Morley specifies four important points of view that the helping person must have: (1) that brief therapy is the most effective; (2) that short-term therapy is parallel; (3) that thorough assessment is not needed and that diagnosis or assessment is carried out only insofar as it leads to an identification and explanation of the crisis; and (4) that the consultant must be willing to take an active role and make full use of many diverse techniques. The steps in the handling of the crisis situation are listed as: (1) assessment of the problem, including evaluation; (2) planning the nature of the therapeutic intervention, including an assessment of the resources of the individual; (3) intervention with techniques, including focusing on the problem, integrating the crisis into the life-pattern, assisting with a cognitive grasp of issues, exploring alternative mechanisms of coping, redistributing the role of relationships within his group, and clarifying and reemphasizing the individual's responsibility for his own behavior, decisions, and way of life; and (4) resolution of the crisis with anticipatory planning for the next step.[17] Jacobson states that the factors which help in the crisis situation are (1) increasing hope, which results from the offer of help; (2) encouraging the patient to find adaptive solutions to a current life problem; and (3) limiting the regressive exacerbation of the infantile, neurotic conflicts. He, too, stresses the positive potential from crisis situations at a time when significant insights might be more easily obtained because the defensive system is at a disequilibrium. He formulates the steps in handling the crises as (1) evaluation of the dynamics of the case, including unconscious and genetic aspects; (2) telling the patient about these conclusions, but in the patient's terms; (3) showing the patient where his coping mechanisms have failed; (4) avoiding discussion of chronic problems, avoiding direct advice, and discouraging dependency; and (5) beginning planning discharge at the first interview.[18] As may be noted, these writers feel that the therapist should not attempt at this time to resolve the basic conflicts of the patient. As Gill states, the patient works through the "derivative conflicts" without working through basic conflicts.[19]

Bellak and Small explicate in great detail the principles and procedures of emergency psychotherapy and brief psychotherapy.[20] While they do not start from the same point of viewing the situation as a crisis and outlining the principles in terms of handling a crisis situation, many of their suggestions directly overlap the principles of the fields of general crisis and suicidal crisis intervention. Most of their formulations take the principles of long-term psychoanalytically oriented therapy and adapt them, with some modification, to brief psychotherapy, which is to be accomplished in anywhere from one to six therapy sessions. They indicate that the therapist must be alert to every meaningful communication, rapidly forming the common denominators, filling in omitted parts from the vantage point of uncommon sense, and simultaneously deciding on the most fruitful intervention. All the while, he is to assess the patient's ego strength and real-life circumstances and conditions. Since there is not enough time for insight to develop, it must be stimulated. Working through cannot be waited upon so it must be stimulated with invented alternatives. Emergency psychotherapy is seen as brief psychotherapy applied in special situations of crisis and exigency. Emergency psychotherapy is viewed as a treatment for symptoms and maladaptations without an attempt to restructure the personality. The goal is to improve the individual's psychodynamics of the situation sufficiently to permit him to continue functioning, to "allow nature" to continue the healing process, and to increase his self-supporting ability sufficiently so that he may be able to continue with more extensive psychotherapy.

In brief psychotherapy, positive transference is sought and maintained. The basic processes are actually common to all dynamic psychotherapy: communication, insight, and working through. Bellak and Small stress the importance of the diagnostic formulation in order better to understand the relationship between the patient's complaints, the dynamics of the precipitating situation, and the historical factors. They then talk about an assessment of ego functions to indicate those disrupted or weakened and those unaffected. The amount of activity of the therapist will depend upon the assessment of the patient's regulation and control of the drives and the ego's ability still to mediate between instinctual drives and counterdemands of the superego. In the process of intervention the procedures followed may include imparting insight, increasing self-esteem, catharsis, drive-repression and restraint, reality testing, sensitization to signals, intellectualization, reassurance and support, counseling and guidance, conjoint consultation, and group therapy. They consider adjuncts to brief psychotherapy important but insist that all such adjuncts must be based in their application upon carefully determined psychodynamic indications. The adjuncts may include the administration of drugs, electro-convulsive therapy, and the manipulation of personal, social, familial, or occupational environments.

## Disaster

Another model for crises and their treatment exists in the study of disasters. Some of the characteristics are useful for an understanding of the suicidal crisis, which may be likened to the extreme state of destruction described as one stage in the natural catastrophe. In many instances, the reactions of the suicidal person, especially in the acute suicidal state, are markedly similar to those of disaster victims.

Some of the similarities and differences between disaster and suicide may be noted. Baker and Chapman have brought together most of the important studies of disaster, including theoretical analysis of the events.[21] The definition of disaster—from Cisin to Clark—is an event or series of events which seriously disrupt normal activities.[22] The events are natural or man-made catastrophes imposed externally upon individuals or groups. In contrast, the suicidal person generally becomes so because of events which seem imposed—such as death, separation, loss, or threat of loss of prestige or status. Like disasters, these events occur with sufficient impact to disrupt normal relations and activities. The special feature of suicide is the added feelings of self-doubt and loss of self-esteem which turns the thoughts to self-destruction.

The temporal sequence of disasters has been noted by Powell and Rayner,[23] and it is not unlike the development of the suicidal situation: warning, threat, impact, inventory, rescue, remedy, and recovery. Baker and Chapman summarize the characteristics of these sequential phases in disasters.[24] The periods of warning and threat have been examined especially in terms of the manner of handling anxiety, with marked repression exhibited by some and patent overreactivity by others. The quality of threat to normal functioning is also essential to the development of a suicidal crisis, with the handling of the accompanying anxiety essentially an over- or underreaction. In either case, the result is exhaustion of inner resources and a feeling of dread and helplessness.

Studies of the results of separation and attempts at evacuation in disasters—by Bowlby and A. Freud and Burlingham—have indicated the intensity of the bond established with the familiar and the known.[25] The resistance to the disruption of these bonds by simple physical separation for a temporary period, despite elaborate preparations, was marked. In suicide, when the separation is complicated by feelings of rejection, stirring feelings of being unloved and unworthy, the reaction with self-destructive feelings becomes very understandable.

The period of panic in catastrophes is pointed out as one of the self-perpetuating myths. Interestingly, personal panic occurs rarely and then often only as a restricted individual occurrence without much group significance. One notable, and rare, exception, in which panic spread through the group, was the Cocoanut Grove fire in Boston. Otherwise, the notion of panic seems to be more of a journalistic belief perpetuated for the drama it adds. In suicide, however, panic is not an infrequent state. Panic reactions occur with the dissolution of the accustomed coping mechanisms, the continuing threat to all that is familiar and desired. These are seen in the wild impulse of self-destructive behavior, in distinct contrast to the relatively infrequent, thoughtful, well-planned, carefully designed suicide.

Another effect of the impact of the catastrophe is the fragmentation of the social scene for isolated individuals. This is the period when he feels most separate and alone. This is generally followed by a rush of warm feelings for other survivors and a strong impression of the sympathy, helpfulness, and emotional accessibility of others. The suicidal person, in marked contrast, does not experience any feeling of camaraderie and sense of sharing. He remains left out in the cold and feels that there is no understanding or concern for his condition. These feelings occur especially in situations where the communication processes have broken down and no rescue possibility appears. If rescue should occur, however, the suicidal person may swing to an excess of gratitude, just as does the disaster victim. Generally, he continues to feel isolated and alone unless he accepts the changed situation or is successful in maneuvering the environment to meet his demands.

In disasters, "convergence behavior" has been described by Fritz and Mathewson as the pouring in of persons eager to help and anxious for their loved ones or simply curious.[26] Unhappily, this same convergence behavior does not typically occur for the suicidal person. It is, however, what the patient is unconsciously asking for and what the therapist tries to bring about. He must enlist everyone he can to meet the patient's need for reassurance that he has not been abandoned and doomed to be alone.

There is interesting conjecture about the long-term effects of disaster on a community. Some interview material suggests that a recovered community always retains a heightened sensitivity to the life-and-death issues that it confronted at the time of the disaster. There is informal working-out of allocation of blame and innocence, which subsequently affects the status of some individuals and organizations. These are familiar stages in the gradual recovery and reconstruction processes for the suicidal individual and the important relationships. Of most interest is the occasional noting of a positive result for the community that has suffered a disaster. Udall, Kansas, after a destructive tornado, grew to a much larger population than before because a lower rate of interest offered to builders attracted not only industry but also potential home builders from nearby towns. We have seen suicidal persons experience the same thing; the crisis forced discussion of issues and clarification and consolidation not available before. The potential benefit from the experience of crises other than suicidal described by other researchers (Morley and others, Rapoport, and Forer) has already been referred to.

Much has been written about the affective reactions to disaster. It is interesting to note how often these descriptions parallel the emotional states ascribed to the suicidal situation. Friedman and Lum, referring to the sinking of the *Andrea Doria*, and Wallace, speaking of a tornado in Worcester, Massachusetts, describe the initial psychic shock followed quickly by psychomotor retardation, flattening of affect, somnolence, amnesia, suggestibility, and "affective anesthesia."[27] Two stages emphasized by the authors are the marked increase in dependency needs characterized by regressive behavior and a traumatic loss of feelings of identity. These feelings are also similar to those of the suicidal patient, whose dependent, regressive behavior often makes sharp demands on those around him and who frequently display excessive preoccupation with self-identity.

Probably the most extensive analysis of the affective relations to disasters has been presented by Martha Wolfenstein in *Disaster: A Psychological Essay*.[28] Approaching the event from a psychoanalytic viewpoint, she has reconstructed the dynamics of the "disaster syndrome" in which there is an absence of emotion, a lack of response to stimuli, inhibition of outward activity, docility, undemandingness, etc. There is first a tendency to deny what has happened, accompanied by a fear of being overwhelmed by painful feelings once a reaction is allowed. All energies are engrossed in mastering the terrible experience with subsequent resistance to taking in any more stimuli. This accounts for the apparent insensitivity of the victim to what is going on around him. The similarity of this description to what occurs in suicidal situations is underlined by the following statements of Wolfenstein:

> If we consider the combination of emotional dullness, unresponsiveness to outer stimulation and inhibition of activity, and ask what familiar clinical syndrome it suggests, I think the answer would be that it most resembles what is observed in depression. There are several factors conducive to a depressive reaction in disaster. The individual's assumption of his own omnipotence is brusquely thrust aside by the occurrence of the disastrous event. The expectation of beneficent supplies from a loving environment is frustrated; the powers that rule the world seem to have abandoned the disaster victim. Further, there may be the feeling that what has happened is a punishment, that the individual must have de-

served it. The individual who has just undergone disaster is thus apt to suffer from at least a transitory sense of worthlessness; his usual capacity for self-love becomes impaired. (p. 80)

Some individuals will be more and others less susceptible to post-disaster depression. When shock or loss occurs for the more or less "normal" person, the depression is transitory. When the person requires insatiable and incessant manifestation of love from the environment, frustration and despair are unavoidable. It is a situation of "unusual" deprivation with a much greater need for outside support because of great feelings of helplessness. Because in the disaster situation the emergency is temporary, the depression is also likely to be short-lived. For the suicidal person, the depression will be long or short depending upon the extent of loss and recovery of objects and the amount of outside support. Wolfenstein contrasts disaster and accident victims (p. 83), but her description of the reactions of the accident victim is remarkably similar to that of suicidal individuals. She points out that disaster victims are frequently docile and subdued; they act like severely beaten children or become extraordinarily good and make few demands. The accident (suicide) victim is more apt to be demanding, complaining, excited, and clamorous. The big difference may lie in his feeling of being one of many similarly affected as compared with a feeling of isolated damage and attack. The disaster victim experiences destruction and restoration of his world in the actions of the rescuer. There is reaffirmation of his existence. The (accident) suicide victim does not receive this impression. His suffering is aggravated by the feeling that it is undergone alone. The complaints are in part related to resentment against the rest of the world for being untouched.

There are also differences in the sense of conscious responsibility. The suicide victim is apt to have some manifest ground for blaming himself. Some of this he may project onto others. In a disaster there are no feelings of direct responsibility for the event, although there may be some deep-lying and irrational feelings of culpability.

Wolfenstein also discusses panic reactions to disasters in ways which emphasize similar reactions in suicidal situations. In panic there seems to be no way out, no escape, even though the way to safety is close at hand. This feeling arouses terror and oftentimes chaotic, disorganized behavior along with impaired judgment. Sometimes it seems that panic is part of the wish that the other should die rather than himself. The suicide victim has the same feelings of being trapped, feeling helpless and with no solution, despite the fact that the resolution by the significant-other seems so feasible. Projection of death wishes is also frequently noted.

There are also some relevant comments about the wish to be a rescuer. Some workers have the ambition to undo all of the damage and make it "good" again—a sense of omnipotence which is remarkably similar to that which occurs in some suicidal rescuers and against which much effort must be directed. The Jehovah complex may lead the rescuer to feel he is the only one who can accomplish this, or the "good mother" identity may cause the rescuer to assume the complete responsibility for meeting all demands. In some disaster rescuers, there may be a strong motive that stems from the feeling of gratitude that it was not they who had been in the disaster and suffered the terrible catastrophe. Among some suicide rescuers, an impelling motive may be the counterphobic reaction against the fear that the same thing could happen to them.

In summary, we have seen from the examination of some of the formulations about disasters that it is possible to observe a great many similarities and some important differences with suicide. Preparation and anticipation of disasters in some terms of reactions to warnings and threats arouse great anxiety in some people and denial in others. The impact brings affective reactions labeled the "disaster syndrome," eliciting over- and underreactions, docility, desire to be good, etc. The affective reactions most characteristic of the "suicidal syndrome," on the other hand, are heightened, continued anxiety, depression, and agitation. Of most significance is the effect on the victim of the activity of the rescuers. In disasters it amounts to a reaffirmation of the possibility of existence. In suicide, the intervention of rescuers reassures the person, indicates he is not alone, and reasserts his identity and worthwhileness.

## Suicide

The suicidal crisis, best seen as a particular event within the general area of crisis, is especially characterized by the potentiality of an abrupt, irreversible, and final end and the heightened tragedy-laden impact of death. It is thus the epitome of crisis, but it has, in addition, the unique quality of the individual's own rejection of society and self. The threat of death carries special impact for all concerned—the patient, the significant-other, the family, relatives, therapist, friends, neighborhood, employer, society, etc. Touching as it does all the fundamental ethics of life and living, it is a vital area for community concern.

The time involved in the suicidal crisis may be short or long. Most crises are resolved within two months. On the other hand, some suicidal situations remain chronic for many months, accompanied by minor exacerbations at irregular, relatively nonspecific times. The precipitating situations for the suicidal reactions are both inter- and intrapersonal; they are usually a mixture that varies for different age groups. Thus, the young girl may feel unlovable because her boyfriend has jilted her, or the older man may feel worthless when he loses his long-time position.

The stages through which the suicidal person goes are very similar to those outlined by Caplan and Rapoport for crises in general, i.e., a rise in tension, unpleasant affect and disorganization of behavior, cognitive confusion, a lack of success in resolving the conflict, further use of problem-solving techniques now verging on emergency procedures, and perceptual distortion, confusion, and disorganization. When feelings of agitation, denial, great anxiety, hostility, worthlessness, and inadequacy develop, the person may turn to suicide and consideration of self-destruction. We often then see magical thinking and fantasy accompanied by cognitive constriction, especially loss of alternatives. Why the person turns to self-destruction as a form of resolution rather than to other major resolutions, such as psychosis, illness, withdrawal, etc., is not clear. What must play a large role are social and cultural factors, especially attitudes within the ethics of the society and religion about self-destruction. Within the Anglo-Saxon ethos as a weapon for influencing, forcing, shaping, and manipulating the attitudes and behaviors of others, the threat of suicide has no peer.

There are several unique aspects of the suicidal crisis which should be noted:

*Feelings about death.* The introduction of death as a possible result of the behavior of the individual lends special significance to the suicidal crisis. In the Anglo-Saxon culture, death is not easily accepted as an inevitable part of life and living. It is instead influenced by powerful taboos and is accompanied by strong feelings of rejection and denial. Feelings about death evolve within the framework of the culture in which the individual is reared as well as within the individual's own experience and personal background. Feelings about death are especially important for the worker in a suicide prevention facility where his own reactions might influence his handling of the suicidal patient.

*Communication.* Suicidal behavior can often be best understood as a form of communication in which the person is expressing in a desperate and dangerous way his feelings about himself, the situation in which he feels enmeshed, and his need for some kind of attention and help. Suicidal people are reduced to this method because of feelings of helplessness, a hopeless sense of inability to cope with their problems, and the unhappy conclusion that others do not care or are no longer listening. A communication may be either verbally expressed, through a direct statement such as "I am going to kill myself" or an indirect hint that one feels inadequate and worthless; or it may be behaviorially expressed with direct activity in the form of overt injury to oneself or the preparation for an attack, such as the procuring of pills or guns. It may also be indirect behaviorally, as in the preparation for permanent absence by giving away treasured possessions or physical depression symptoms, such as insomnia, anorexia, apathy, withdrawal, or agitation. The communication may be either to a specific person or to the world in general.

The communication can also be seen in terms of the motivations of the suicidal person, the content of the communication, and the effect upon the recipient of the communication. The motivations may be to explain, blame, or expiate and absolve. It may be specifically designed to arouse particular feelings within the listener. These feelings can be reactions of sympathy, anxiety, anger, hostility, guilt, and others. The content of the communications may contain material designed to arouse these various feelings or instructions for survivors. Often the notes indicate the extremes of ambivalence along with marked confusion and disorganization strong enough to approach psychotic bounds.

*Ambivalence.* This is one of the most prominent features characterizing the suicidal person; that is, feelings of wanting both to live and to die which are present at the same time. The feeling is exemplified by the person who ingests a lethal dose of barbiturates and then calls someone to rescue him before he loses consciousness. Ambivalence is seen in the notes in which the person expresses feelings of regret about the fact that he must leave yet cannot stop himself. Strong feelings of both hate and love will be expressed toward the same person. In the normal person, it is assumed that there are opposing impulses to live and to die but that these are generally kept in appropriate balance.[29]

## Treatment and Handling of the Suicidal Crisis

Three main features characterize suicidal crisis therapy: (1) activity, (2) authority, and (3) involvement of others. These characteristics entail an attitude and behavior on the part of the therapist that is generally in marked contrast to the kind of role he plays in more familiar therapeutic situations. In the more traditional office psychotherapy, the therapist generally is not concerned with time pressures. He is able to view his work with his patient as it develops over a long period of time and can plan leisurely for the intensive analysis of various behaviors. The therapist in the suicidal crisis, however, does not have the luxury of time. He must work quickly, incisively, and often with a minimum of information. The situation is frequently presented to him at the height of its emotional efflorescence and is marked by chaos, disorganization, and distress. A cardinal aim is to restore some semblance of order, to help the patient and his "others" regain control, in effect, to reconstitute the situation so that it can be seen more clearly and appropriate action can be taken. For some persons reconstitution of the previous *status quo* could be all that would be sought. For others, especially for those for whom it was felt that the crisis might lead to further, positive development, reconstitution would be only the first, albeit necessary, step. Activity, authority, and involvement of others are essential in reconstitution therapy. They may, but more likely will not, be found in long term, rehabilitative therapy.

In the suicidal crisis the therapist must be active, because the patient is in real need of a feeling that something is being *done*. The more varied and the greater number of actions that can be initiated at this time of severe emotional stress, the more possible it is to reestablish in the patient the feeling that he is important and that everything possible is being done in the one focal task of helping him through his difficult situation. The patient's need is for some indication of meaning to his life and some affirmations of self-esteem; the activity of the therapist plays an essential role in supplying this.

The second feature which characterizes therapy of the suicidal patient is authority. The therapist deliberately assumes authority, takes charge, and directs the patient—temporarily. The patient's state of mind at the time of a suicidal crisis makes this necessary. He is experiencing overwhelming feelings of hopelessness and helplessness, and he feels incapable of working out any solutions. In addition, he feels unable to make any decisions or to use customary judgment and reason. The patient is both "dilated" and "constricted," to use Kelly's terms.[30] On the one hand, there is chaos, disorganization, and confusion, a state in which all possibilities become vague; and, on the other hand, there is an over-focus in which the patient's preoccupation with his problems narrows the arena to such an extent that he is unable to see other alternatives besides death. Fortunately, this state of mind is temporary, and the presence of an authoritative figure seen as strong, stable, and supportive allows reconstitution to take place quickly. In addition, it is important for the patient to feel that this authoritative figure knows exactly what is going on, knows the distress and disturbance that is being felt, and through his experience can help.

The activity and authority features are closely related to the third characteristic—involvement of others in the therapy of suicidal people. At this point in their lives, suicidal people feel lonely, deserted, and rejected. Other people, and especially the significant-others in the situation, help to build up his feeling of self-esteem and self-confidence as well as to reestablish the bonds between himself and others which he feels have been broken or blocked. The character of the interaction within these relationships often holds the key to understanding the suicidal behavior. It also is not too infrequent that suicidal behavior in one member of a dyad signals the potentiality of suicidal acting out in the other member.

A word might be added about the feelings of the therapist. Although anxiety in therapists beginning in suicide prevention is usually great, a swing to the other extreme might also be anticipated. As successes accrue, the Jehovah complex readily appears, especially with the demand upon the therapist to assume the authoritative, directing, controlling role in the treatment of suicidal people. He feels that he and only he can save the patient. It stems in part from the desire to deny the imminence of death. Weisman and Hackett talk about the physician's feelings in the medical treatment of a terminally ill patient.[31] One of their remarks is equally appropriate here: "If a doctor can accept death as a fact of life and not as a failure of treatment he can accept the reality of a patient dying." On the other hand, one cannot deny that treatment of a suicidal patient incurs considerable emotional stress and strain for the therapist. The possibility of an impulsive, lethal acting out is ever present, and the therapist must be able to bear the consequence of an honest-but-tragic error, as well as be prepared for complete and sudden dissolution of the cherished therapeutic program. Another reaction sometimes appears in the therapist, perhaps more often in nonprofessional volunteer workers. The "maternal complex" may impel them to assume the responsibility of meeting all the needs and demands of the suicidal patient, an all too often impossible task.

One aspect of work with suicidal patients, the telephone, has developed as specific, unique, and important. In over 95 percent of the caseload of the Suicide Prevention Center in Los Angeles, initial contact is made over the telephone. In 50 percent of the calls, the first contact is made by the patient himself; the rest are made by someone else, such as family, friend, agency, or others. The patient is not seen in 85 percent of these contacts. Handling the suicidal emergency by telephone requires particular techniques and specific procedures, especially with regard to the feelings of the therapist.

Generally in the past, the telephone was avoided in rehabilitative therapy. It was primarily used to make or break appointments and often aroused feelings in the therapist of resistance to the intrusion when insisted upon by the patient. The telephone, of course, imposes obvious difficulties in the therapeutic situation. It is apparent, for example, that the patient now has much more control and can direct the therapeutic process as he wishes. He obviously has the capability of terminating the interview at any moment in reaction to any whim or impulse. The therapist must be willing to accept and work with these conditions, to relinquish the need for complete control, and to accept the relationship in which the terms are not his own.

Sometimes the aspect of anonymity is embellished by the patient and used as a deliberate exercise of power. A standard procedure at the Suicide Prevention Center is to request identification and the telephone number from the patient, but it is not too unusual for the patient to reserve this essential bit of information until the very end of the conversation. A study by Tabachnick and Klugman of persons who have refused to identify themselves when calling the Suicide Prevention Center indicates a quality different from the calls usually received at the Center.[32] There are more intensive aspects of ambivalence, sadomasochism, and the need to control, which defeat the very purpose of the call. The therapist has to remember that the person has called—the important signal in the situation. Most of all, in the use of the telephone one misses cues obtained from observation of nonverbal behavior—facial changes, mannerisms, posture, and stance. The therapist must be prepared to make decisions and be willing to take responsibilty despite the greatly reduced number of cues.

*Procedures in the treatment of the suicidal patient:* At least five steps occur in the treatment of the suicidal patient who calls or comes to the Suicide Prevention Center. These apply particularly to the handling of the telephone call, although the same steps occur if the first contact is face-to-face. Sometimes the therapist will react to the telephone call by having the patient come in, usually to obtain more information or to establish a personal contact. The five steps may or may not occur concomitantly and are as follows: (1) Establishment of a relationship—maintain contact and obtain information; (2) identification of and focus on the central problem; (3) evaluation of suicidal potential; (4) assessment of resources and mobilization of outside resources; and (5) formulation and initiation of therapeutic plans. Each step is outlined in more detail below:

1. *Establishment of a relationship—maintain contact and obtain information.* The worker offers hope and help. He provides complete acceptance of the patient and his problems, indicating by his attitude both experience and authority. In this way he lets the person know that right action was taken in calling and that help will be forthcoming. Identifying information should be obtained, indicating that it might be necessary to reestablish contact if the connection is broken. Names and phone numbers of significant-other persons in the environment, such as family, physician, and friends, are also obtained as possible resources for the patient. The worker's task is to obtain sufficient information to identify the focal problem and to evaluate the suicidal potentiality.

2. *Identification of and focus on the central problem.* Many callers indicate a pervasive sense of anxiety which produces disorganized, oftentimes chaotic, thinking. The anxiety permits a number of situations ordinarily manageable to become threats. The patient frequently feels overwhelmed and unable to move in any direction without catastrophe. The worker selects the problem that seems central to him and formulates it specifically to the caller. This provides the patient with purpose and direction. In some instances, the caller may have little difficulty focusing on his central problem but insists instead that he knows no further way to turn. The worker, as an objective expert, may suggest a number of additional alternatives.

3. *Evaluation of suicidal potential.* The worker's main purpose is to keep the caller alive. He must be able to evaluate the probability that the patient will act out with self-destructive behavior in the immediate or near future. A number of criteria to evaluate suicidal potential have been developed out of research and experience at the Suicide Prevention Center. Suicide potential can, of course, vary on a continuum from none, in which there is no danger that the patient will kill himself, to high, in which the possibility that the patient may kill himself is both high and intense. The criteria are as follows:

*a. Age and sex.* Within the Anglo-Saxon culture, both statistics and experiences have indicated that the suicide rate for committed suicide rises with increasing age, especially among men. A suicidal communication from an older male tends to be most dangerous; from a younger female, least dangerous. It is rare that a suicidal communication from an older male is not serious. On the other hand, a suicide communication from a younger male or female may or may not be dangerous. Age and sex thus offer only a general framework for evaluation of lethal potentiality. Each case requires further individual appraisal.

*b. Suicide plan.* Three main elements are considered in appraising the suicide plan: (1) Specificity of details; (2) lethality of proposed method; and (3) availability of means. When a person specifies a method of suicide with great detail, he indicates that he has spent much time and effort in planning and is attracted to the suicidal acting out. If the person's choice of method includes procedures of higher lethality, such as using a gun, jumping or hanging, the situation is more serious than one in which pills or gas may be considered. In addition, if the means are available, that is, if the gun or the high building are at hand, the situation is more serious. Sometimes the details of the plan are so bizarre that they indicate possible psychosis. Psychotic people with ideas of suicide are high risks, regardless of the three elements listed above.

*c. Stress.* Precipitating stresses may be either inter- or intrapersonal or both. The caller will refer to such events as loss of a loved person by death, divorce, or separation; loss of a job, money, prestige, or status; physical illness, sickness, surgery, accident, or loss of limb; threat of prosecution, criminal involvement, or exposure; etc. Stress must be evaluated from the patient's point of view and not from the point of view of the worker or society. The patient's reaction to the stress is helpful in diagnostic formulations.

*d. Symptoms.* Suicidal symptoms are not limited to any one psychological state. The most common symptom is depression, which may be evidenced in both physical and psychological manifestations of sleep disorder, weight loss, anorexia, withdrawal, apathy, loss of interest, despondency, severe feelings of hopelessness and helplessness, and feelings of psychological exhaustion. Agitation complicates the picture and heightens the suicidal potentiality. Feelings of tension, anxiety, guilt, shame, rage, anger, hostility, and revenge, along with poor impulse control, may bring about intolerable internal pressure. These may be exhibited through marked tension, fearfulness, restlessness, and pressure of speech. Psychosis complicates the picture by adding the possibility of unpredictable reaction to unexpressed impulses within a framework of poor ego controls. Alcoholics, homosexuals, and drug addicts also tend to be high suicidal risks.

*e. Resources.* External resources useful in supporting the patient may be present from many different levels, separately or at the same time. At one level may be family, relatives, or close friends. At another level may be physicians or clergymen; and at still another level may be a therapeutic agency or professional therapist. If the patient is already in contact with the latter, he usually should be referred back to the therapist or agency. The patient's occupation and place of work may be an important resource, especially when it provides him with some self-esteem and gratifying relationships. Financial status can be important in determining the feasibility of immediate physical and psychological care. The psychological feeling that there are persons yet interested and concerned is probably most important for the suicidal person.

If both physical and psychological resources have been exhausted, the situation becomes more ominous. Long-term, chronic patients have frequently become known to most therapeutic resources within the community who are no longer able to offer continuing support. When family and friends have turned away too, the potentiality is increased. At such times, a brief period of hospitalization is usually necessary. Any attempts by either patient or family to keep the suicidal situation a secret, or to deny its existence, must be vigorously counteracted. The suicidal situation must be vigorously and openly dealt with.

*f. Characteristic functioning.* This characteristic refers to a stable versus an unstable existence in the caller and includes an evaluation of the suicidal behavior as acute or chronic. A stable person will indicate a consistent work history, consistent marital and family relationships, and no history of prior suicidal behavior. The unstable person will report repeated difficulties in the main areas of life, such as interpersonal relationships, employment, frequent hospitalizations, etc. Acute suicidal behavior will be found in either a stable or an unstable personality; chronic suicidal behavior is found only in the unstable person. Acute versus chronic refers primarily to the temporal aspects of the behavior rather than intensity of it. The precipitating stress for the suicidal reaction in the unstable person will frequently be difficult to see.

*g. Communication.* An alarming signal is when communication between the suicidal person and other important persons has become blocked. This usually indicates that the suicidal person has reached the limits of his external resources and implies that the possibility of rescue is considerably lessened. As indicated previously, the communication by the suicidal person may be either verbal or nonverbal and either direct or indirect. The highest potentiality for suicide occurs when the person engages in nonverbal and indirect suicidal behavior. These "action communications" are difficult to interpret and easy to deny.

*h. Reactions of significant-other.* The worker may evaluate the significant-other as either a rescue resource or as nonhelpful. The significant-other who has already withdrawn, or has rejected or denied the suicidal patient and resents the increased demands or insistence on gratification of dependency needs, may even be injurious to the person. If he feels helpless in addition, this may communicate itself to the suicidal patient and heighten the patient's feeling of hopelessness. The helpful significant-other is one who recognizes the communication, is aware of the problem, and seeks help for the patient. The patient feels from this that his communications are understood and that something is being done to help him.

*i. Medical status.* Persons with chronic illness may be subjected to situations which involve great change in self-image and self-concept. Relations with the medical profession, including their family physician, hospital personnel, or rehabilitation therapist, are of great importance. When the patient sees such resources as uninterested and unconcerned, he may feel abandoned. Patients frequently suffer from ungrounded fears of a fatal illness, such as cancer or brain tumor, indicating their preoccupation with death and dying. The history of many repeated, unsuccessful experiences with doctors, or a pattern of failure in previous therapy, is a negative sign.

*j. Prior suicidal behavior.* Studies have shown that where there has been previous suicidal behavior, the possibility of future suicidal acting out is increased. This is especially indicated by multiple attempts, that is, a history of two or more prior attempts.

In general, no single criterion need be alarming in and of itself. The one exception is the prediction of a lethal and specific plan for suicide, the criterion which best expresses the status of the self-destructive behavior. Otherwise, the evaluation of the suicidal potential should be based upon the general pattern of all the other criteria within the individual case.

4. *Assessment and mobilization of resources.* The primary goal at this time is to get the patient through the difficult emergency situation. Information should be sought about the resources available to him. The evaluation of the suicidal potential, and the resources which are available, will determine the formulation of the management plan.

The resources will generally fall into three main areas which are nonprofessional, professional but nonmental health, and professional mental health. Nonprofessional resources will generally be family, relatives, friends, neighbors, employer, and police. These are the usual possibilities in the immediate environment of the person, and these frequently can be used to great advantage, especially in a difficult emergency period. A member of the family or a friend can be asked to stay during the night with a disturbed person, for example. Nonmedical health professional would be family physician or clergyman. They are especially useful as strong sources of authoritative support. The professional resources may be both private and public community agencies or the professional community. If the worker is at an agency which treats patients, the patient might be called in. Agencies in the community, such as social work and family agencies or mental health community centers, will be useful. If the patient has money, he may be referred to a private therapist; if not, to a psychiatric clinic. Probably the most important liaison with any professional agency is a psychiatric hospital. It will be necessary at times to have a resource in which a seriously disturbed and acting-out suicidal person can be placed for a short period. The psychiatric hospital, or the psychiatric ward of a general hospital, is almost a requisite for successful functioning of a suicide prevention center.

5. *Formulation and initiation of therapeutic plans.* The evaluation of the suicidal potentiality and the information about the patient's resources will determine what will be done for the patient. The responsibility for the patient rests with the worker until the situation is handled by some other resource. To this extent, the patient is transferred rather than referred. The worker remains active in the case until the patient has actually carried out the plan or has definitely indicated that he no longer wishes any help. This is yet another way in which therapy in the suicidal crisis differs from the usual long-term therapy in that the therapist must be ready to assume an active role and maintain it throughout the contact.

Another comment about therapy in the suicidal situation: As previously emphasized, the therapist is both active and authoritative. To be effective, he must be ready to enter readily into the situation and provide the patient with a virtually unlimited, albeit temporary, source of dependency gratification. Often, he must invite it. Afterward, disengagement must occur, and this is frequently difficult. To this extent, the procedure of frequent consultation on his cases with colleagues or a supervisor is important in allowing the therapist to maintain an objective and practical approach to the situation and to relinquish his own ego involvement when referral to another resource, or a change of therapeutic approach, is the next appropriate step. The consultant also helps open channels of communication between patient and therapist that may become blocked within the handling of the crisis situation.

## Concluding Remarks

Some brief concluding comments may be made about suicide prevention and the handling of the suicide crisis. It is apparent that efforts in suicide prevention have been on the crisis and the development of procedures for effective intervention in the emergency. The focus of future efforts must shift to earlier intervention and, possibly, primary prevention. The history of the Suicide Prevention Center provides the analogy for the past, present, and future of suicide prevention. The Center was preceded by a comprehensive study of suicidal deaths in Los Angeles County.[33] When the Center was started, its caseload was made up entirely of persons who had attempted suicide. As it developed and the Center became better known in the community, more of its caseload shifted to persons with suicide threats, thoughts, ruminations, depression, etc. In other words, intervention gradually moved to an earlier point along the continuum of the development of the suicidal crisis and the appearance of suicidal behavior. The advantage of this requires no discussion, but emphasizes that the point of intervention must be pushed to an even earlier status.

The parallel to other levels of prevention is immediately apparent. Limiting the disability and making efforts at rehabilitation are appropriate goals in working with persons who have already acted on their self-destructive impulses and need to be helped to rebuild their lives. At this stage of our knowledge, effective primary prevention, that is, the fostering of conditions for optimal mental health for all members of the community, is probably still not possible. But an intermediate step seems feasible, or at least should be the next focus for a continuing program in suicide prevention. This might be development of procedures for very early intervention, based upon refined case-finding techniques and initiated before the problem is permitted to develop to a more dangerous state. It would attempt to anticipate a potential crisis and apply interventive procedures as prevention rather than as remediation.

A program of anticipatory crisis intervention does not, on early thought, seem too difficult to outline. Suicide has its sources in two main areas, i.e. psychological and social. It would require the identification of population groups at large who are greater suicidal risks and the categorization of the kinds of crisis situations which rank high as precipitating events for self-destruction. Many of these populations of high risk and situations of high potential have already been identified. Some examples are: The older, Caucasian male, physically ill, widowed, retired, children married and out of the home, alone, etc.;[34] the population of neuropsychiatric hospitals and their alumni; known groups of alcoholics or homosexuals; older persons with terminal illness;[35] and persons with prior suicidal behavior.[36] Precipitating events known to be emotionally stressful and depression-producing include: physical illnesses, such as loss of limb or sense; discovery of a chronic or fatal disease; surgery; first heart attack;[37] inter- and intrapersonal events, such as separation, divorce, loss of loved one by death, loss of fortune, or loss of or retirement from a job.[38]

A considerable body of literature already exists around the problem of early prevention in mental health and the task of implementation. Parad reports on the effects of preventive casework in the area of traditional family casework and child welfare.[39] Irvine emphasizes the need to identify children at risk in the community for early application of preventive mental health programs.[40] Vernick is concerned with children and adolescents faced with hospitalization.[41] Klein and Ross consider kindergarten entry as a crisis in role transition, both for parents and children, and Klein and Lindemann held discussions with groups of parents of children entering school.[42] Le Masters, Dyer, Cyr, and Caplan, Mason, and Kaplan discuss aspects of pregnancy, parenthood, and premature birth as crises.[43] Much can be learned from the experiences of these authors.

Liaison with community agencies and groups and early indentification and intervention might be avenues for the most effectively accomplished goals. Groups which come into direct contact with individuals and families in their homes and neighborhoods, such as physicians, police, public health nurses, educators, and teachers, would be primary target groups for education and early case-finding. The use of the community's own resources in a considered fashion for its own mental health seems most appropriate as a means for reducing the unnecessary and premature loss of its valued members.

## REFERENCES


1. E. Lindemann, "Symptomotology and Management of Acute Grief," *American Journal of Psychiatry*, **101**:141–148, 1944.
2. G. Caplan, *Principles of Preventive Psychiatry* (New York: Basic Books Inc., 1964).
3. G. Caplan, *An Approach To Community Mental Health* (New York: Grune & Stratton, Inc., 1961).

4. W. E. Morley, "Treatment of The Patient in Crisis," *Western Medicine*, **3**:77, 1965.
5. B. C. Bloom, "Definitional Aspects of The Crisis Concept," *Journal of Consulting Psychology*, **27**(6):498–502, 1963.
6. E. Erikson, "Growth and Crisis of The 'Healthy Personality,'" in C. Kluckhohn, H. A. Murray, and D. M. Schneider (eds.), *Personality in Nature, Society and Culture* (2nd ed.; New York: Alfred A. Knopf, Inc., 1953).
7. G. Caplan, "Emotional Crises," *The Encyclopedia of Mental Health*, **3**:521–532, 1963.
8. Lydia Rapoport, "The State of Crisis: Some Theoretical Considerations," *Social Service Review*, **36**:211–217, 1962.
9. H. J. Parad and G. Caplan, "A Framework for Studying Families in Crisis," *Social Work*, **5**(3):3–15, 1960; M. R. Harris, Betty Kalis, and Edith Freeman, "Precipitating Stress: An Approach to Brief Therapy," *American Journal of Psychotherapy*, **17**:465–471, 1963.
10. B. Forer, "The Therapeutic Value of Crisis," *Psychological Reports*, **13**:275–281, 1963.
11. J. Reusch, *Therapeutic Communication* (New York: W. W. Norton & Company, Inc., 1961).
12. G. Caplan, "Patterns of Parental Response to the Crisis of Premature Birth," *Psychiatry*, 23:365–374, 1960; and "Emotional Crises," *The Encyclopedia of Mental Health*, **3**:521–532, 1963.
13. Rapoport, *op. cit.*
14. J. S. Tyhurst, "The Role of Transition States—Including Disasters—in Mental Illness," in *Symposium on Preventive and Social Psychiatry* (Washington, D. C.: Walter Reed Army Institute of Research, 1957).
15. Morley, *op. cit., ibid.*
16. Rapoport, *op. cit.*
17. Morley, *op. cit.*
18. G. F. Jacobson, D. M. Wilner, W. E. Morley, S. Schneider, M. Strickler, and G. Sommer, "The Scope and Practice of An Early-Access Brief-Treatment Psychiatric Center," *American Journal of Psychiatry*, **121**:1176–1182, 1965.
19. M. Gill, "Psychoanalysis and Exploratory Psychotherapy," *Journal of American Psychoanalytic Association*, **2**:771–797, 1954.
20. L. Bellak, and L. Small, *Emergency Psychotherapy and Brief Psychotherapy* (New York: Grune & Stratton, Inc., 1965).
21. G. W. Baker, and D. W. Chapman, *Man and Society in Disaster* (New York: Basic Books, Inc., 1962).
22. I. H. Cisin, and W. B. Clark, "The Methodological Challenge of Disaster Research," in G. W. Baker and D. W. Chapman (eds.), *Man and Society in Disaster* (New York: Basic Books, Inc., 1962).
23. J. W. Powell, and Jeannette Rayner, *Progress Notes: Disaster Investigation, July* 1, 1951–*June* 30, 1952 (Edgewood, Md.: Army Chemical Center, Chemical Corps Medical Laboratories, 1952).
24. *Op. cit.*

25. J. Bowlby, *Maternal Care and Mental Health* (Geneva: World Health Organization, 1952); Anna Freud and D. Burlingham, *War and Children* (New York: Medical War Books, 1943).
26. C. E. Fritz, and J. A. Mathewson, "Convergence Behavior in Disasters," *National Academy of Sciences Publication* 476 (Washington, D. C.: National Research Council, 1957).
27. P. Friedman and L. Lum, "Some Psychiatric Notes on the *Andria Doria* Disaster," *American Journal of Psychiatry,* **114**:426–432, 1957–58; A. F. C. Wallace, "Tornado in Worcester: An Exploratory Study of Individual and Community Behavior in an Extreme Situation," *National Academy of Sciences Disaster Study Number* 3 (Washington, D.C.: National Research Council, 1956).
28. New York: The Free Press, 1957.
29. K. Menninger, *Man Against Himself* (New York: Harcourt, Brace & World, Inc., 1938).
30. G. A. Kelly, "Suicide: The Personal Construct Point of View," in N. L. Farberow and E. S. Shneidman (eds.), *The Cry for Help* (New York: McGraw-Hill Book Company, 1961).
31. A. D. Weisman, and T. P. Hackett, "Predilections to Death," *Psychosomatic Medicine,* **23**:232–256, 1961.
32. N. Tabachnick, and D. J. Klugman, No Name—A Study of Anonymous Suicidal Telephone Calls," *Psychiatry,* **28**:79–87, 1965.
33. E. S. Shneidman, and N. L. Farberow, "A Socio-Psychological Investigation of Suicide," in Henry P. David and J. C. Brengelmann (eds.), *Perspectives in Personality Research* (New York: Springer Publishing Co., 1960).
34. Farberow and Shneidman, *The Cry for Help, op. cit.*
35. A. Temoche, T. F. Pugh, and B. McMahon, "Suicide Rates among Current and Former Mental Institution Patients, *Journal of Nervous and Mental Disease.* **138**(2):124–130, 1964; R. E. Litman, "Emergency Response to Potential Suicide," *Journal of The Michigan State Medical Society,* **62**:68–72, 1963; N. L. Farberow, E. S. Shneidman, and Calista Leonard, "Suicide among General Medical and Surgical Hospital Patients with Malignant Neoplasms," *Medical Bulletin 9* (Washington, D.C.: Veterans Administration, 1963).
36. S. Eisenthal, N. L. Farberow, and E. S. Shneidman, "Follow-up of Neuropsychiatric Hospital Patients Placed on Suicide Observation Status," unpublished report, 1965.
37. N. L. Farberow, S. Cohen, J. W. McKelligott, and A. S. Darbonne, "Suicide Among Patients With Cardiorespiratory Illnesses," *Journal of The American Medical Association,* **195**:422–428, Feb. 7, 1966.
38. Farberow and Shneidman, *op. cit.*
39. H. J. Parad, "Preventive Casework: Problems and Implications," in *National Conference on Social Welfare* (New York: Columbia University Press, 1961).
40. Elizabeth E. Irvine, "Children at Risk," *Case Conference,* **10**:293–296, 1964.

41. J. Vernick, "The Use of the Life Space Interview on a Medical Ward," *Social Casework*, **44**:465–469, 1963.
42. D. C. Klein, and Ann Ross, "Kindergarten Entry: A Study of Role Transition," in Morris Krugman (ed.), *Orthopsychiatry and the School* (New York: American Orthopsychiatric Association, 1958); D. C. Klein, and E. Lindemann, "Preventive Intervention in Individual and Family Crisis Situations," in G. Caplan (ed.) *Prevention of Mental Disorders In Children: Initial Explorations* (New York: Basic Books, Inc., 1961).
43. E. E. Le Masters, "Parenthood As Crisis," *Marriage and Family Living*, **19**:352–355, 1957; E. D. Dyer, Parenthood As Crisis: A Re-study," *Marriage and Family Living*, **25**:196–201, 1963; Florence E. Cyr and Shirley H. Wattenburg, "Social Work in a Preventive Program of Maternal and Child Health," *Social Work*, **2**:32–39, 1957; G. Caplan, E. Mason, D. Kaplan, "Four Studies of Crisis in Parents of Prematures," *Community Mental Health Journal*, 1:149–161, 1965.

# 18. The Psychology of Fatal Accident

Norman Tabachnick

Man's life moves along two paths: One consists of his usual patterns of behavior, proceeding in interaction with predictable aspects of his environment. It is relatively comfortable, usually steady, sometimes monotonous, and often so routine that the energy and processes connected with it go unnoticed. Then, at certain times in each person's history, more dramatic events occur. Precipitated by something radical in what the world offers, or by some disequilibrium in his inner balance (and often by a combination of both), there is sudden change in a person's life. At such times the microscopic study of his life situation and the intimate details of his hopes, fears, and conflicts compel attention.

Often such changes, although partaking of the nature of crisis, have beneficial or, at the least, nonharmful sequelae. For example, falling in love or reacting to the sudden loss of a dear person or prized possession may enhance the development of character. However, certain life crises, such as the overthrow of one's external world (by revolution, let us say) or the overthrow of one's inner world (by psychosis, let us say), may not bring about enhancement of character but rather disintegration or destruction of it.

Fatal and near-fatal accidents are often instances of such morbid life crises, and it is in the interests of understanding these tragic situations that this essay is written.

First, let me acknowledge my debt of gratitude to a group of southern California psychoanalysts (of the Southern California Psychoanalytic Institute) who have been my colleagues in the study of accident. We have been collaborating closely for several years in our study, and it is difficult now to tell from whom each creative idea first emanated. Let this essay then stand as a contribution of the entire group.[1]

## Previous Theories of Accidents

Before describing our understanding of accident victims, it would be informative to review the thinking of some of our predecessors. The literature on accident seems to fall into three main categories. One group describes the conditions under which accidents are statistically most likely to occur—automobile accidents at twilight, defective machinery, etc. A second focus is on specific, contributing factors—alcohol ingestion, physical disabilities, careless or faulty labeling of potentially lethal substances. These categories are significant ones. However, although they have an important relation to psychological factors, they do not stress such factors. Let us, therefore, consider the third category, namely, the specifically psychological features of accidents.

In *The Psychopathology of Everyday Life*,[2] Sigmund Freud gave a number of explanations for ordinary, bungled action. (1) Self-punishment, which may result from guilt over some recent action, as, for instance, an abortion, or for some long-past thought, such as a wish that one's father may die. Nearly everyone has self-punishing attitudes present to some degree, lying in wait and ready to seize upon a suitable opportunity to gain expression. (2) Self-injury as a sacrifice: injury may have the purpose of warding off greater disaster, such as loss of a loved one, or of magically protecting against castration. (3) An accident may result from an unconscious desire to get rid of something that has depreciated. Freud's example was of an old inkstand, which he broke with a clumsy movement. A present-day example might be an old car. The temptation might be especially strong when there is a possibility of getting something better if the depreciated possession is destroyed. (4) The purpose of an accident may be erotic. Freud quoted a folk saying: "When a girl falls, she falls on her back." Certain accidents rather skillfully place the victim in close connection with actual or symbolic love objects. Some people equate a violent collision with sexual orgasm. (5) An accident may be a means of escaping or avoiding something unpleasant. Forgetting an appointment or making a wrong turn in traffic may have such a motive.

Previous formulations dealt with ordinary, nonfatal accidents, those that are a part of the "psychopathology of everyday life." However, something additional was required to explain serious and fatal accidents. Freud's thoughts in this connection turned to a similarity between accident and suicide. This thinking proceeded from the assumption that human beings possess a death instinct which in certain individuals overpowers the instincts that further the preservation of life. Suicide was seen as an outstanding example of the workings of the death instinct. Accident was conceived of as an additional manifestation. In Freud's words,

anyone who believes in the occurrence of half-intentional self injuries will be prepared also to understand that in addition to consciously-intentional suicide, there is such a thing as half-intentional self-destruction—self-destruction with an unconscious intention, capable of making skillful use of the stress of life and disguising it as a chance mishap.

These ideas were also later elaborated by Karl Menninger.[3]

An additional landmark of psychological thinking with regard to accidents was the concept of the accident-prone individual. This was popularized in the early 1940s by Dunbar and Alexander,[4] as well as others. These investigators studied individuals who had multiple accidents, ranging from slightly to moderately serious. The victims were described as quick, decisive, active, independent, and adventurous. Immediately prior to the accident, there had been some situation that threatened the victim's complete independence. These investigators challenged the concept of accident as a manifestation of death instinct. They felt that the victim's total personality in his life situation was significant. The formulation was that the accident-prone personality, under certain conditions of stress, in situations that were potentially dangerous, would tend to have accidents.

Reevaluation of the accident-prone hypothesis became necessary, however, because of two sets of critical findings. First, the accident-prone hypothesis was severely questioned by statisticians. They commented that the samples demonstrating accident proneness showed a distribution of accidents not significantly different from what could be expected by the laws of random distribution. Second, follow-up studies demonstrated that the population of accident repeaters is constantly changing. Individuals who are accident repeaters at one time drop out of the group and new ones join it. Thus, the hypothesis that certain individuals have characteristics which make them accident-prone must be questioned, *at least to the degree that these characteristics are conceived of as relatively permanent.*

It is possible, however, that those characteristics or life styles which accompany the likelihood of accident may be transiently entered under certain conditions. This possibility makes the psychological study of human lives in which accidents have occurred a useful research endeavor. A contribution along this line was made by Hirschfeld and Behan.[5] They postulated that many industrial accidents took place as part of an ongoing, dynamic situation, which they called the accident process. They believed that as a result of certain stresses in the accident victim's life he unconsciously moved towards the situation of having an accident. The stresses enumerated by these authors were loss of income, loss of peer-group status, and loss of opportunity for social interaction.

In summary, the important ideas of earlier researchers on accidents have been: (1) An accident may be the expression of a relatively unconscious impulse; for example, a death instinct or death wish; and (2) accidents may occur in individuals whose characters, perhaps transiently, are organized along lines which make the possibility of accident more likely.

## A Case of Near-Fatal Accident

In our current research, we have been observing a number of men, both living and dead, who have been involved in severe accidents. Those who survived were seen soon after their accident in the hospitals in which physicians were struggling to keep them from death and to return them to productive life. Often they were seen for weeks and months afterwards, since it was the shared opinion of victim and psychoanalyst that there was good reason for therapeutic collaboration. We observed the deceased through the eyes of the friends, relatives, and physicians who knew them when they were alive. In this way, we attempted to understand what might have led to their untimely deaths.

Here now are some of the details of the accident and life situations of one of our subjects. In the study of Ernest, as with our other accident subjects, careful efforts were made to discount the possibility of such accident-producing factors as impaired personal health, defective machinery, and bad road conditions; further, most of our accident studies were of men who were the drivers in single-car accidents, that is, they drove a car that went over a cliff, struck a stationary object, or encountered some analogous mishap.

*The Accident of Ernest*

Ernest, a twenty-three-year-old man, leaves the home of friends where, after his day's work, he has had dinner and a few beers. He is anxious to pick up his wife and new son—they had been staying at her mother's house—and return to his own home. He is driving a familiar route, along which is an intersection that is potentially dangerous for two reasons. On his right is a tall, concrete wall, which extends to the corner. Across the intersecting street the road he is traveling begins to decline sharply. Usually, on approaching this corner, he proceeds slowly up to and across the intersection, keeping his eye on cars possibly approaching from the right. Tonight, he drives differently. On approaching the intersection, he accelerates the car instead of slowing down. As he goes through the intersection, he has the impression that another automobile is approaching on the right. He further accelerates his car and twists the steering wheel sharply to the left. The car shoots over the intersecting street and goes into the air much as a skier would leave a slope if his forward speed were increased. It then lands with the wheels in the gravel of the road's shoulder, skids out of control, and with great impact hits a tree. The car is demolished, and the young man is critically injured. He barely survives. Later, he is not sure that he had seen another car approaching the intersection.

Ernest's accident brings to mind a series of questions. Why was Ernest's wife not home that evening? Was he upset about that or anything else? Was beer drinking usual for him before driving, or was it linked to some upsetting situation? Why did he speed his car as he approached the blind intersection? What is the meaning of his unsure impression of the approaching car?

Let us now look into Ernest's life situation at the time of his accident and also into significant events in his past.

From the onset, Ernest was noted as affable and sociable. The hospital staff admired him and were interested in him. He seemed to strike up a close relation with his interviewer, but this had certain peculiar aspects. Although he claimed interest in a psychological investigation of his life and declared that it might save him from a future fatal accident, he was in some ways evasive with his doctor.

This evasion was particularly evident with regard to certain aspects of his personal life. Ernest at first represented himself as unmarried. Months later it was learned that he had been married for several years and had two children, including a recently arrived son. In the hospital

Ernest had maintained that he was a rather gay bachelor type who had many girl friends but was not serious about any of them.

Ernest's evasiveness became dramatically apparent when he left the hospital. Even though he had agreed to continue contact with his doctor, he left the hospital without notifying our colleague of his departure. When he was followed to his given address, it was found to be a false one. However, we did manage to find Ernest and establish a long-lasting relationship with him. During the course of many sessions, a picture of his life developed.

Ernest was born in Texas of Mexican parents. He was one of the middle children in a family of seven. His father is an unskilled workman who has not made a comfortable adjustment in this country. He has been able to work only sporadically and has never become a citizen. His main position in the family has been passive, although he had given Ernest some support in the latter's study of music. The family was mainly supported and integrated by Ernest's mother, who was assisted by the children as they grew older.

Ernest's mother is an energetic, controlling person, who is driven by concern about destruction. She sees herself as a member of a disliked minority in a country full of dangers. Surrounded by potential enemies and on unfamiliar terrain, she is constantly vigilant and engaged in maneuvers calculated to increase her security. From her viewpoint, it is inappropriate—in fact, self-destructive—to expend energy on pleasure or enjoyment. These are constantly deferred to the future.

His mother's life orientations made a lasting impression on Ernest. Let us examine them in regard to two areas of his life—attitudes toward work and attitudes toward driving.

Ernest was interested in music. Learning what he could at school and on his own, he had become proficient as a trumpeter. He had played in dance bands and was thinking of becoming a professional musician. His mother dissuaded him from this course, indicating that the rewards were meager and uncertain. Music might not always be in demand; if a time should come when people would have little money, they would not support musicians. In addition, as a Mexican, racial prejudices might work against his employment.

In his mother's opinion, what was better was a career in some more essential service or business. Ernest listened to his mother and retired his trumpet and musical career—they were retired, one might add, like the father who had encouraged them. Ernest turned to commerce and became associated with a growing, local company. He had many potentialities for success and began to move upward in his firm. It was his ambition to become a salesman—a position which he saw as prestigious and lucrative.

However, his mother had negative judgments about this job also. Although safer than the career of a musician, there were still pitfalls. Personalities could work against a Mexican, success could be prevented, and one could even be turned out after many years of labor. Mother's ideal was government civil service. Although the immediate rewards were less, one could have security. Ernest, at first, had decided to oppose his mother and stay with his firm. However, in recent months he had encountered a difficult situation. He worked in a branch of the company in which further progress was slow. In addition, he had a supervisor who disliked him. For these reasons he was reconsidering a civil service career.

Another instructive view of Ernest's relation with his mother and how it influenced his feelings and modes of living can be obtained from a consideration of his attitudes about driving.

Ernest loved to drive. At home there were many restrictions, rules, inhibitions—all emanating from his mother in her search for the most secure way of doing things. Pleasure there had to be subordinated to purposeful, productive—and monotonous—work. These attitudes were internalized by Ernest and used to guide many of the activities he himself initiated. But, alongside this trend, there was a tendency toward free, relatively impulsive and pleasurable activity. His musical avocation was one area in which this tendency was expressed—but driving was even more important.

Ernest remembered being taught to drive by a beloved older sister. She encouraged his activity—brought out the man in him. Even the setting of the lessons had been idyllic—down orchard roads between rows of trees. Ever since, driving had been a solace for him, a relief from the oppressive restraint of everyday life—a situation in which one could be active and free.

However, the pleasurable, free feelings about driving were often reversed when he was with someone else. Such a situation brought to mind his mother's many years of backseat driving. During those years she would constantly warn him to go more slowly and to drive carefully, while she obsessively recalled an auto accident in which she had been injured. After Ernest had married, his wife, with her warnings against unsafe driving, seemed to take a place on the backseat next to Mother.

There was an additional situation which added tension to Ernest's life. He married at twenty-one, which was too early for him. Marriage was another restriction, a feeling which was emphasized when his first child was born. Shortly before the accident, a second child, again only ambivalently desired by Ernest, arrived. He and his wife were having frequent quarrels—that is why she was with her mother on the evening of the accident. He was not interested in giving up his family, yet he was indeed sorely tried by the responsibility they represented.

The above, then, is a description of the character and life situation of a rather typical accident victim. Next we would like to detail the theoretical conceptions which we have used to understand certain aspects of the life styles of such people.

## Life Styles of Accident Victims

What, then, is the character picture of a man who may be about to have a severe accident? We must state that our findings may be representative of only one or a few types of severe or fatal accident, since our contacts were with only thirty-five people. Yet, within this group certain findings occurred so frequently that we felt we could begin to understand at least one kind of accident situation.

The people we began to know as accident victims were at first somewhat strange to us. They did not share the character pattern and philosophical values of most psychiatric and psychoanalytic patients. The latter are, for the most part, serious and introspective individuals. Although they do not always hold severely negative ideas about themselves, they are inclined to be moderately dissatisfied with some aspects of their lives. They often feel that they have not come up to their own expectations and that they have been, and will continue to be, losers in the game of life.

The severe accident victims do not at all fit this picture. First of all, they appear to have a fairly high regard for themselves. Performance and appearance are important dimensions for measuring their competence, and usually they feel that they are doing well in these spheres. When this is not so, they tend to swing into action. This often consists of immediate, impulsive verbal or motor activity. For example, a metal worker is criticized for an imperfect product by his foreman. He slams his tools down with a curse and walks indignantly off the job. A young man may be unsuccessful in dating an attractive girl. He leaves his room, jumps into his car, and goes on an aimless but speedy drive. What is emphasized here is that impulsive action, unaccompanied by deliberate thought, is one important way of life for many accident victims.

This is particularly true when one is considering their response to stressful situations. They seem to be focused on their appearance and performance, so that if something does not go well for them, they choose to make themselves feel better by performing some action which makes them "look better" to themselves and to others. Having performed the actions that make them look better, they feel pleased—indeed, often proud. They have made some impact on the world, shown that they dared, and thus added to their stature. They also have restored their feeling of functioning well and of being winners. This is a state that they consider necessary.

It seems that in the "accident" people, the action that is taken to make themselves feel better often has what is known psychologically as "regressive" qualities. That is not to imply that these people are not quite accurate in anticipating that their action will make them feel better. It frequently does this, but a regressive mode—such as swinging into impulsive action—is the one that is chosen because it allows individuals to relive (often unconsciously) a previous developmental period. Such a time is felt to have been more gratifying and freer of problems than the present one.

At this point it may help to review the usual fate and utilization of action in a human being's development. In a very young infant, action occurs in a relative impulsive, haphazard, and unintegrated fashion; that is, it is often not used in the service of a planned out goal. Action is, first of all, a pleasure or gratification for the infant. Later, this primary pleasure has a number of secondary ones added to it. Parents and others give approval for particular kinds of action. (The image of a toddler making his first steps with the prideful encouragement of his family illustrates this kind of social reinforcement.) In addition, the developing child learns that he can accomplish important tasks, such as bringing cherished toys near to him. This is pleasant, not only because he gains new gratifications but also because he feels that he is mastering and developing his own potentialities. He may also feel that he is dealing successfully with various aspects of the external world.

This good feeling of adding to one's accomplishments and pleasures through action does not exist without its risks. When one learns to walk, one may fall. The ability to reach out and grasp something carries with it the possibility of overturning a kettle of boiling water. The risks, however, are greatly neutralized in the presence of concerned and guarding parents. As the child grows older, his knowledge of the dangers of the world and his development of ways of dealing with it, which takes cognizance of the possibility of risk, allow him to utilize his tendencies for action in a safer way. As this occurs, the adults who have normally guarded him withdraw their vigilant observation.

Of course, we are here describing only one of the ways in which a growing child is given more independence and responsibility. Now we need to consider the specifically regressive kind of activity that occurs in the accident victims. It seems that they have remembered, in some especially meaningful way, all the pleasures that were present with regard to action during their early days. What is especially important is the way their pride and self-esteem were enhanced by the daring use of action. (An adult may not believe that learning to walk is much of an accomplishment, but think of its meaning to the infant.)

Under certain conditions (when they are feeling depressed or insignificant, for example), it becomes very important for accident-prone people to do something that is brave and daring. They rush into activity—sometimes many kinds of activity—in order to create this feeling, and they are usually successful in accomplishing their end. However, in this sequence of events, the possibility of accident makes its appearance. This is because there is not sufficient vigilance against it. When one is an infant, one's parents protect him, but these people are no longer children. When one is an adult, one's own experience, skill, and the presence of certain vigilant and integrating qualities serve as a guard. But accident-prone persons have thrown off these safeguards. They are in that peculiar state—not completely children and yet not sufficiently adult—that is called regression. This is when an accident can—and sometimes does—occur.

Why are their safeguarding qualities not working for accident-prone people at this time? We think that action as a method of making them feel better is so important that it has become an all-consuming passion. Relatively speaking, they lose those observing and protecting qualities which would protect them from mischance. In a sense, they are like drug addicts who will take any risk to indulge their habit. In the case of our victims, the habit is action.

There is a further issue with regard to action and activity in the personalities of accident people. This is the unresolved struggle between active and passive orientations in their natures. Passive wishes—desires to be taken care of and to give up one's autonomy to others—are opposed by active desires to be master of one's own fate, to be a leader in life's enterprises. Yet the latter impulses often carry with them fears; for example, hostile retaliation by one's competitors. Such fears may again move individuals into more passive states.

Ernest's conflict between freedom and "manliness" (activity) and "security" (passivity) is an example of this struggle. We believe that the alternating nature of such conflicts, passing rapidly from one phase into another, might prove to be a significant explanatory concept for the lack of critical control, which is, to some degree, responsible for accidents.

## Life Crises in Accident Victims

Having sketched a picture of the character of accident victims and the significant place that action plays in their lives, we would next like to explore the life situations—shall we say the precipitating events—which surround serious accidental occurrences.

At the time we started our researches, we believed that we might find certain traumatic situations which would more or less regularly precede accidents. We recalled that individuals who attempted or completed suicide had rather often suffered the loss of some important person or relationship. We were thinking of accident as an analogue of suicide, and we wondered what the analogous, traumatic situation would be.

As we began to understand the exhibitionistic, prideful nature of accident victims, we wondered whether some embarrassment or humiliation would be found to be "the cause" of accidents. As time went on, however, these anticipations were not supported by our observations. Although slights and humiliations were significant in the lives of accident victims, in the period immediately preceding the accident, we could not find evidence of pronounced humiliation or disappointment. Actually, there was little or nothing that would indicate cause for lowered self-esteem or a feeling of external loss. As a matter of fact, most of the people we studied seemed to be living in anticipation of probable changes for the better. Some of the young people were about to enter college; a number of the men were conducting successful courtships and contemplating or planning marriage; some people had recently received promotions at work.

These observations, which were refutations of our preconceived ideas, began to suggest a somewhat different type of precipitating stress. We wondered if the anxieties and uncertainties which attend the assumption of new responsibilities would have something to do with accident. We have come to believe that such new responsibilities do carry with them specific threats for accident-prone people.

How can new responsibilities—transitions to importantly different living situations—act as stresses to the human being? Such stresses can and have been discussed from many viewpoints. We would suggest that an important overview might start with the conception that such transitions importantly disturb a person's sense of coherent identity.

The need of individuals for a strong sense of identity has become increasingly apparent in the understanding of human behavior. A sense of identity may be defined as a feeling that one's life goals, and the means which are utilized to achieve them, have a certain pattern of consistency that has significance both for the individual and the society in which he lives. From this definition it is apparent that an individual's sense of personal identity can usefully be observed and described from two usually related points of view. One deals with the various expectations and demands which society makes upon an individual. In another place, I have called this root of identity "social definition."[6] To the degree that an individual occupies one of the recognized roles which society offers, his societally defined identity is maintained and enhanced.

The other root of identity may be called "self-realization." It refers to a feeling of self-sameness and continuity that emerges from a person's sense that he is following goals and using methods that are, in an important sense, his own. It is evident that as new responsibilities, which may be assigned by society or the individual himself, are undertaken, various identity crises may occur. This is because the individual has doubts at the assumption of responsibility about the adequacy of his subsequent performance. If he could know at the onset that the responsibility would be well discharged, there would be no anxiety. However, this happy state of affairs does not often exist. Indeed, it often cannot exist, because man's ambition typically runs ahead of his definitely established capabilities. The result is what may be called "identity anxiety," since it is related to the individual's concern that neither he himself nor his society are convinced that he will do his duty in a way that is acceptable to both.

This exposition of various identity concepts can usefully be applied to some of the findings in severe-accident situations. A great number of our subjects were, at the time of their accident, assuming important, new responsibilities. Many were young adults, actually older adolescents, facing a number of situations characteristic of that time of life. Such situations simultaneously present possibility of intriguing gratification and threatening challenge. The excitement and anticipation of an impending marriage or first child, or the feeling of worldliness and importance that accompanies the first promotion at work, are often accompanied by a persistent and not quite recognized fear that one will not succeed.

These problems, although abundantly present in adolescence, are not exclusive to that time of life. A widower of fifty, whose son has been his living companion since the death of the wife and mother, faces an equivalent important change in life conditions when, within the period of a month, his son leaves for the Army and he marries a second wife. An elderly person whose job has ended may encounter much anxiety as he considers the opportunities and limitations of retirement.

Thus, at any point in the span of life the urge that comes from within, or the demand that is made from without, can thrust one into a desired but frightening situation which challenges a person's sense of steadiness and oneness. At such a time individuals may lose whatever qualities of soberness and deliberateness that have attended their previous conduct of life and fall back on more primitive, urgent, and immediate methods of dealing with life situations. (These methods are often chosen because in a particular person's life they had once been effective in dealing with difficulties). What we emphasize here are modes of problem-solving that, inept though they may turn out to be, have the purpose of coping with new situations and maintaining a feeling of steady identity.

For the accident victims these modes include movement into direct, impulsive, and relatively unconsidered action. We have already described how action is an important issue in such people's lives and can understand how they are drawn to its comforting use. Let us now investigate some of the more specific meanings of this behavior in solving problems of identity.

First, we will focus on the issue of moving backward or regressing. Let us suggest that the regression occurs because the individual wishes to find a new beginning. Our subjects were faced with life situations that were quite confusing. For a while they could not decide whether to move forward to their new goal or backward away from it. They wished to obtain the tantalizing reward but were not sure they could succeed. They feared that to attempt at all might bring not only lack of success but two consequences even more shattering—self-reproach and humiliation in the eyes of others. We have noted that from this dilemma there was a regression, a movement backward to the mode of impulsive, urgent action, which is a stage in the early lives of all people. We suggest that one important meaning of this regression is that it is an attempt to regain an early developmental stage in order to learn a new, more effective method of coping with life problems.

Erikson has described this type of regressive experience in adolescence.[7] He indicates that adolescents in an attempt to solve problems often move into negative and regressive modes of living because sometimes rock bottom may be "the only firm foundation for a renewed progression."

In addition to longing for a new, more effective method of coping with newly challenging problems, there is also a need for more time. Erikson has written of the "psycho-social moratoria" that societies and individuals designate at uncertain periods of life—such as adolescence. Thus, an adolescent may declare himself emotionally ill, and society may concur in this decision. Other psychosocial moratoria may be a temporary interruption of school or a hitch in the Navy. All of these give the person some breathing space, a period of time in which to sort out desires and ambitions and learn to fit his capabilities to them.

The regressive mode of impulse activity which precedes many accidents may be an entryway into a psychosocial moratorium—and this in two possible ways. First, the bizarreness, inappropriateness, and accompanying anxiety of this mode of behavior may signal that something is wrong. Friends and relatives begin to whisper to each other—"anyone who acts that way must have something wrong with him." Second, if the activities result in a serious accident, a psychosocial moratorium is declared—in fact, it must be declared. The victim is physically unable to take new responsibilities for a period of time. He does withdraw and, hopefully, has time to consider how he may deal with the problem in a more effective way. Perhaps he will change the focus of his efforts to a different area or decide to give himself more time to accomplish his ends.

There is a final method by which regressive action can help solve identity problems. This, of course, is death. He who is dead no longer needs to cope with handling new responsibility or any other issues. At this point we return to the question, "Do these people intend to die?"

Our tentative impression is that our subjects are and were people who not only want to live but are desperate to find a better way to live. The road that their destiny forces them to traverse is fraught with anxiety. On this road there is fear, a feeling of impending loss of self, and a desperate urgency to reconstitute themselves. As with other urgencies, there is often a lack of attention to detail. Tragically, the detail to which they do not attend is preserving their life. The essence of the tragedy, however, is not that these people *wish* to die, but that the very efforts that are designed to enhance their lives misfire and, in fact, carry them to their deaths.

In summary, we can state that our recent research into fatal accident took as its starting point Freud's exposition of accident as the manifestation of unconscious impulse. We were challenged by his assertion that in such situations it would be possible to discern evidences of the death instinct.

However, as we interpreted our data, we found ourselves moving into a different theoretical pathway. Our impression was that (some, at any rate) serious accidents may be understood as the unplanned side effects of certain patterns of behavior. These are transiently entered when persons with a potentiality for "action" ways of life encounter anxiety-filled and temporarily overwhelming responsibilities.

## REFERENCES


1. This group includes Drs. Jay Cohn, Warren Jones, August Kasper, Robert Litman, John Moffat, and Marvin Osman.
2. *Complete Psychological Works* (London: The Hogarth Press, Ltd., 1960), vol. VI.
3. "Purposive Accidents as an Expression of Self-Destructive Tendencies," *International Journal of Psychoanalysis*, **17**:6–16, 1936.
4. H. F. Dunbar, *Psychosomatic Diagnosis* (New York: Paul B. Hoeber, Inc., 1943); F. Alexander, "The Accident-Prone Individual," *Public Health Reports*, **64**:357–362, 1949.
5. A. H. Hirschfeld, and R. C. Behan, "The Accident Process," *Journal of The American Medical Association*, **186**:300–306, 1963.
6. "Three Psychoanalytic Views of Identity," *International Journal of Psychoanalysis*, **46**:467–473, 1965.
7. E. H. Erikson, "The Problem of Ego Identity in Identity and The Life Cycle," *Psychological Issues*, (New York: International Universities Press, Inc., 1959), vol. I, no. 1.

# 19. Suicide Among Police: A Study of Ninety-three Suicides Among New York City Policemen, 1934-1940

Paul Friedman*

In the six-year period from January 1, 1934 to January 1, 1940, ninety-three New York City policemen committed suicide—almost twice the number who had killed themselves in the previous six years. A primary aim of this paper is to delineate some of the more important characteristics of these ninety-three men, recognizing that suicides among policemen have unique factors that differentiate them from suicides within the general population, and, on the other hand, recognizing that such suicides possess many features that are not unlike those of the average man. The uniqueness comes from the fact that we are dealing with a select group of men of a type who would be attracted to the career of making their livelihood through police work. Although the individuals are a cross-

* Editor's Note: I was introduced to Dr. Friedman by my good friend Jacques Choron in April, 1967. I knew of Dr. Friedman's long devotion to the study of suicide and particularly of his collaboration with the late Dr. Zilboorg. In one weekend of concentrated work together I grew quickly to admire and respect him. We mutually decided that the material included in this volume is of extraordinary importance and must no longer remain inaccessible to the scientific community.

We have since talked many times. In a letter that Dr. Friedman sent me (permission for reproduction granted) he wrote as follows: "I hesitated to interject myself into this study of the police cases because I joined the staff only at the end of 1939. [The other staff members at that time were: Dr. Nathaniel Ross, Dr. Herbert Wiggers, and Elizabeth Wadleigh, executive assistant.] However, I had the good fortune to acquaint myself with the bulk of the material, making it my labor of love for the next few years. I continued to work closely with Dr. Zilboorg on these data subsequent to the dissolution of the Committee with a view toward their ultimate publication. The files were turned over to my exclusive custody by Howard A. Seitz, legal representative

section of the types attracted to the force, they are not exemplary of policemen as a group; because they committed suicide they are more representative of those who could not, because of varying degrees of psychological instability, contend with the strains and stresses of their life and work. Their maladjustment within the scope of their total life was even more evident than within their work as policemen.

In this paper, special emphasis will be given to those aspects of the lives of these ninety-three individuals as policemen as well as to those aspects of their lives before their acceptance by the police department that might furnish significant clues to the understanding of the suicidal act.

## Historical Background

At the outset, two historical items need to be mentioned in order to put these data in their proper perspective:

1. The psychological atmosphere that existed in New York in the 1920s, especially during the years 1925–1927, was a period of Tammany control. It was a time of protection by a political boss, the so-called "rabbi," who not only got a man placed on the police force, but acted as the source through which the patrolman once on the force obtained special assignments and became part of a system of accepting and dispensing graft and gratuities. One obvious implication of this historical fact is that the standards of competence or stability were obviously not always the criteria for selection to a police department.

2. The second relevant historical fact concerns the impact of the changes in the psychological atmosphere within the New York Police Department that followed the election (in 1933) of Fiorello La Guardia as mayor. These changes affected particularly the status of the police officer who was overly aggressive, alcoholic, or profligate—many of whom had been

---

for the Committee, in September of 1960, following the death of Dr. Zilboorg. (The first legal adviser to the Committee was the late Lewis S. Weiss.) I am really grateful to fate and to Jacques Choron that we got together and released this material from its dormant state. It is an inexhaustible mine of valuable data. Special tribute is due Dr. Zilboorg for this rich scientific legacy, a source of great inspiration to other investigators. Equal tribute is due Marshall Field, whose generosity and social concern provided the means for this pioneering project. I shall always recall with admiration the devotion and enthusiasm that Michael Dunn brought to his work. I know a Latin motto which so aptly befits this study of the police. It used to be affixed at the Second Anatomic Institute in Vienna: 'Hic locus est ubi mors gaudet succurrere vitae'. The last two lines of the inscription to be found in the Offices of the Chief Medical Examiner of New York City is an excellent translation of this pithy wisdom: 'Let conversation cease; / Let laughter flee. / This is the place where death / Delights in helping the living.' "

tolerated (or even unconsciously encouraged) in the police department during the pre-La Guardia era.

The information given here on suicide among policemen in New York City was an outgrowth of research undertaken by the Committee for the Study of Suicide at the special request of the late Mayor Fiorello La Guardia. It was carried out between 1939 and 1940 by the late Michael Dunn, Ph.D., psychologist, under the supervision of the late Gregory Zilboorg, M.D., and Bettina Warburg, M.D.

Under a grant given by Marshall Field, an organization called the Committee for the Study of Suicide was incorporated in December, 1935, and began its activities in January, 1936. The Board of Directors were: Dr. Gerald R. Jameison, Mr. Marshall Field, Dr. Henry Alsop Riley, Dr. Gregory Zilboorg, Miss Elizabeth G. Brockett, Dr. Franklin G. Ebaugh, Dr. Herman Nunberg, Dr. Dudley D. Shoenfeld, and Dr. Bettina Warburg. The committee was organized under the guidance of its first chairman, the late Dr. Mortimer Williams Raynor, medical director of Bloomingdale Hospital. Dr. Henry E. Sigerist, professor of the history of medicine at The Johns Hopkins University, and Dr. Edward Sapir, professor of anthropology at Yale University, were consultant members of the committee.

The committee planned to undertake a comprehensive study of suicide as a social and psychological phenomenon. To achieve this the following general outline was adopted: (1) *Intramural studies* of individuals inclined to suicide in selected hospitals for mental diseases, to include constitutional, neurological, psychiatric, and psychoanalytic investigations of the phenomenon with special reference to therapy and prevention; (2) *extramural studies* of ambulatory cases afflicted with suicidal trends or with obsessional wishes for their own death; these studies were to be primarily therapeutic in nature, the cases to be treated in especially selected out-patient clinics and by qualified psychiatrists and psychoanalysts; (3) *social studies* of suicide along the following general lines: Various attempts at suicide were to be followed up by experienced psychiatric social workers; all cases were to be studied from the standpoint of social background and history, and those who failed in their attempts or had recovered from injuries following a partially successful attempt (prolonged unconsciousness or physical illness) were to be urged to submit to psychiatric and psychoanalytic treatment; (4) *ethnological studies,* i.e., comprehensive investigation of suicide among primitive cultures in the belief that suicide is a rather frequent occurrence among many primitive peoples still extant and when studied may throw some light on suicide as a psychobiological phenomenon; and (5) *historical studies* of suicide, in order to make available a scientific history of the phenomenon as a social and medicopsychological problem.

The research activities of the committee ceased in 1941 with the advent of World War II. Up to that point, the committee had collected data on more than 1,500 cases—including 123 adolescents and 93 policemen—mostly from hospitals located in New York City (Bellevue), Denver (Psychopathic Hospital), Boston (McLean), and at the Chicago Institute of Psychoanalysis, where, under the auspices of Dr. Franz Alexander and Dr. Thomas French, a number of patients had been psychoanalyzed. By that time also, Dr. George Devereux had published his field work on suicide among the Mohave Indians.†

There were approximately 4,000 triple-spaced typewritten pages summarizing the case histories by the time the committee ceased its official functioning.

The intervening war years and the protracted illness of Dr. Zilboorg precluded publication of the material, which was originally to be published in three volumes: (1) history, anthropology, and sociology of suicide; (2) case histories, phenomenology and dynamics of suicide; and (3) suicide among policemen.

The historical background of the police study may be summarized as follows: The suicide rate among policemen had reached alarming proportions at that time, and what particularly triggered public interest was the suicide of a police inspector who had been on the force for thirty years.‡ He shot and killed himself with his own gun after a series of disturbing personal and departmental events.

The police study was initiated at the special request of Mayor Fiorello La Guardia. (It was the committee's plan to organize similar studies in various cities all over the United States.) The following memorandum was sent to the Mayor on June 8, 1939, by Dr. Zilboorg:

As it was pointed out in our conversation of recent date, the rate of suicide in the Police Force of New York City for the last few years is approximately six and one half times higher than the maximum rate per 100,000 population shown by modern statistics.

† George Devereux, "Primitive Psychiatry; Funeral Suicide and Mohave Social Structure," *Bulletin of the History of Medicine*, 1942, vol. 11, 522–542; and more recently: *Mohave Ethnopsychiatry and Suicide: The Psychiatric Knowledge and the Psychic Disturbances of an Indian Tribe* (Washington, D. C.: Bureau of American Ethnology, Smithsonian Institution, No. 175, 1961).

‡ In his book, *The Trouble with Cops* (New York: Crown Publishers, Inc., 1954), the late Albert Deutsch reported that "In the 1930's, a wave of suicides struck the New York City Police force; about a hundred members killed themselves within a little more than six years." He also cited the impression of some observers that "there are more crimes of violence among policemen in proportion to their numbers than among any other occupational group this side of the criminal line."

The Committee for the Study of Suicide will be glad to undertake the study of all available case histories of policemen who have committed suicide in the course of the last five or six years. These histories are to be made available to the Committee. It is hoped that in addition to the purely scientific psychological data that may be obtained from the study of the cases, some practical conclusions may be derived as to methods of prevention. To this end the study will not be confined to purely psychological aspects of the problem—a detailed sociological study will be made wherever possible.

It is understood that the material obtained by this study may be embodied in part or in whole in the scientific report which the Committee for the Study of Suicide intends to publish (3 or 4 volumes). The study will probably take from nine months to a year. The Committee will undertake all the expenses involved in this study. No financing on the part of the City of New York will be required. Upon the completion of the study a detailed report will be submitted to the Mayor.

The following is the full text of the Mayor's reply:

Thank you so much for your letter of June 8th. I have communicated with Commissioner Valentine. I would suggest that you call the Commissioner at Canal 6–2000 or write him. Every cooperation and aid will be afforded. I want to take this opportunity to sincerely thank you and the committee for making this investigation for us, which I think will serve a very useful purpose.

No sooner had this study begun when criticism and protest were leveled against the committee for undertaking this research of what would now be called "psychological autopsies." It was believed that the committee should concern itself only with attempted suicide and not with "dead policemen." It became a matter of public concern. Clarification was necessary, as shown by the following letter that was not only an apologia but also an accurate reflection of the psychological atmosphere in which this whole study took place:

July 13, 1938

The Editor
The *New York Post*
75 West Street
New York City

Dear Sir:

Upon my return from California I noted your editorial "Why So Many Police Suicides" and I want to tell you that in keeping with your tradition this editorial, like all the others, is timely, intelligent, and provided with a keen social sense.

I should like to correct one point and to presume to make suggestions about another point.

The statement that the Committee for the Study of Suicide is concerned only with attempted suicide is not accurate. Our study extends into all the fields into which the problem leads, and a number of "post-mortem" studies are already being made. It has been proven that it is quite irrelevant psychologically whether a person does or does not succeed in dying after an attempt to commit suicide. There are many circumstances purely fortuitous which lead to the saving of a person after a serious attempt to commit suicide and to us all cases in which people make an attempt to do away with their lives are suicides. The distinction between those who succeed and those who do not succeed, that is, between attempted and actual suicides, is an old distinction, made in the days when the law, and not psychiatrists, dealt with the problem and it was important for the law to know whether the "criminal" (the suicidal individual) just committed a minor crime through surviving his attempt or a felony upon himself by actually dying. As a matter of fact there was a time when the law demanded that a dead body of a dead felon be produced in court, tried, convicted, and sentenced, and then legally executed before one could feel that justice had been done. From the historical point of view, the distinction between attempted suicide and suicide, being of legal origin, is approximately the same as first degree manslaughter (if the person shot did not die) and first degree murder.

The second point concerns the specific case of Inspector Neidig [age 52, had been in command of one of the most important divisions in the city for four years] which you are discussing. Generalizations on reasons for suicide prove as a rule as inadequate as generalizations for such predilections as liking strawberries. Each individual case presents its own story and its own reasons. While the story of Inspector Neidig is not fully known, it appears more than significant that only recently his brother and mother were carried away by a serious illness. People symbolically joining their dead by means of suicide are more frequent than one would be inclined to suspect. Seemingly unmotivated suicides on the anniversaries of relatives' deaths or on some other occasions which revive the memory of a departed close relative are not infrequent. One single motivation almost never leads to a suicidal act. Usually it is a combination of motivations which we, in our technical language, call constellations of motives. The fact that of recent years there have been a number of suicides among policemen is undoubtedly of great sociological importance; also, the fact that this "suicidal period" appears roughly to coincide with the anti-racketeering crusade is suggestive. The law and crime have marginal connections. The fringes of both margins intermingle. The law officer, even the most serene and conscientious, carries within him a complicated psychological structure: while defending the integrity of society and the safety of its citizens, he, like a soldier, must do it through extreme mobilization of his inner powers of aggression which he always keeps available to work. In time he gets disciplined or otherwise faces a situation in which he must submit instead of pushing others into submission; his aggression becomes dammed up and turns upon the individual himself. That is the reason why, perhaps, there are more suicides during peace time than during wars and revolutions, for in peace time the individual has much fewer direct outlets for his inner aggressions. That is why, incidentally, such a country as Germany has always showed a greater number of suicides than any other nation in the world and a smaller number of murders in proportion; for the Germans have been preeminently living in a psychological state of passive submission. On the other hand, when the would-be suicide succeeds in finding an outlet for his aggression he presents to us a picture of running a Hitlerian amok. It is not therefore impossible that Inspector Neidig, like many of his colleagues, fell victim to this internalized aggression; that is, he shot himself when he couldn't shoot his boss.

Your remark that most police suicides are by shooting touches upon one of the most vital points in the problem of suicide. The method of suicide has an important meaning. The fact that policemen carry guns, I suspect, plays only a very minor part. Shooting is as a rule a so-called masculine way of doing away with oneself. The American Indians used to hang themselves until white men taught them to shoot. The available means of killing himself is not always used by the suicide.

As noted at the beginning of this letter, I shall greatly appreciate it if you do not publish this letter on your special page of letters to the editor. I wrote this purely because I felt prompted to tell you some of our views in response to a serious and intelligent editorial.

Yours very sincerely,
Gregory Zilboorg, M.D.
Director of Research.

## Description of the Ninety-three Suicidal Policemen

Some of the generalizations which can be made about the ninety-three New York City policemen who committed suicide from 1934 to 1940, are as follows:

*Age:* These 93 policemen ranged in age from 24 to 50. The distribution of ages indicated that approximately 10 percent were in their 20s; 45 percent were from 30 to 39; 30 percent were in their 40s, and 15 percent were in their 50s. Most of the individuals were in their 30s and mid-40s. There seemed to be two peaks of ages at the time of suicide—one from 30 to 35 and the other from 39 to 45. Eighty-three percent of the ninety-three suicides occurred within these two age groups.

*Marital status:* Three-fourths (75 percent) of the group were married, 24 percent were single, and, surprisingly, only 2 individuals were widowers.

*Rank:* Of the 93, two-thirds (64 percent) were patrolmen when they committed suicide, although all ranks (sergeant, lieutenant, captain, inspector, and deputy inspector) are represented in the total list of suicides. It is of more than passing interest that only one of the 93 suicides was from the motorcycle squad, and only 3 of the 93 were plainclothesmen.

*Health:* The study reveals that of this group of police officers, 20 were probably alcoholic, 32 had a "significant sick record," 5 had previous recorded suicide attempts, 26 had seen the police surgeon for gastric ailments (usually gastritis, probably connected with drinking), 26 had some chronic disability, and 27 had medical records in which a psychiatric diagnosis had been made by a police surgeon. They were reported as follows: 20 cases of psychoneurosis (including 5 neurasthenia), 3 cases of psychosis, 2 cases of psychopathic personality, and 2 needed psychiatric hospitalization for observation.

*Method of suicide:* Nine out of every ten individuals in this group killed themselves with revolvers. Of this group of gunshot deaths, 82 percent were gunshot wounds in the head. Other methods of suicide—involving from 1 to 4 individuals each—included carbon monoxide, jumping from high places, poisoning, hanging, and throat-cutting. Five of the 93 cases involved homicide-suicide combinations in which the officer first shot another person (usually his wife or girl friend) and then himself.

*Year of joining the Department; and some implications:* The individuals who committed suicide in the years 1934 to 1940, joined the New York Police Department from the years 1904 to 1938. Seventy-one of the 93 (76 percent) came into the Department during the heyday of Tammany, from 1918 to 1934; 37 of the 93 (40 percent) joined the Department in the three-year period 1925–1927. In the course of the study, many policemen and a few superior officers claimed that during the years 1925 to 1927, admission to the force was easily possible through illegal and improper means, independent of examinations and personal qualifications. It was a period of the political boss, or protector.

Because the number of individuals joining the force varies substantially from year to year, the question thus arose about whether the high proportion of 1925–1927 recruits among those who committed suicide in the period under study might not be merely a reflection of high recruitment during that three-year period. The Police Department's recruitment figures (these figures were given to me recently by Chief Inspector Sanford Garelik) indicate that the number of new recruits during the 1925–1927 period was indeed higher than for either the immediately preceding or the immediately following three-year periods and that 1925 was a peak year with respect to the number of new recruits (see Table 1). However, the annual differences in the number of recruits are definitely not sufficient to explain the high proportion of the 1925–1927 recruits among the police-suicide cases in the period under study. It may also be noted in this connection that the recruitment rate was also quite high in 1924 but that there are only three 1924 recruits among the ninety-three suicide cases. Of course, too much weight should not be given to the relatively small proportion among the ninety-three cases of individuals who joined the force prior to 1914. Many of these individuals were probably retired by 1934, and those among them who were suicide-prone would probably have, in the majority of cases, committed suicide much earlier.

Table 1

Number of Policemen Who Entered Force

| Year | Number |
|---|---|
| 1922 | 780 |
| 1923 | 434 |
| 1924 | 1,062 |
| 1925 | 1,637 |
| 1926 | 948 |
| 1927 | 776 |
| 1928 | 133 |
| 1929 | 885 |
| 1930 | 720 |

Of the thirty-seven suicidal policemen who joined the force from 1925 to 1927, at least seven portrayed aggressive and impulsive personalities, and, in most instances, sexually delinquent patterns with serious maladjustments in their marital relations were evident. An additional five cases were "good" policemen but had disturbing marital discord in their homes. At least fifteen, and very probably more, of this group, manifested prior to their suicides obvious psychotic behavior—in some instances so diagnosed by a police surgeon. Of those five policemen in the suicide list who committed murder before their suicide, four are found in this three-year period. Alcoholism was extreme in a majority of the thirty-seven cases.

The suicide rate in the Department for the six-year period from 1928 to 1934 was 0.47 per thousand, whereas from 1934 to 1940 it was 0.84 per thousand. Subtracting these 37 cases from the total of 93 yields 56—almost the same rate as the six-year period just before the striking rise in the rate. It thus appears that the high rate is due in part to this unstable group who entered the force in droves, relatively speaking, during 1925, 1926, and 1927, with a frequency of almost 12 to 1 as compared with all the other years, especially when coupled with the changes that occurred in the Department after 1933.

One glaring example is to be seen in the case of the patrolman whose pre-police record showed charges of assault and battery and one charge of a technical homicide. The normal possibilities of his getting on the force were slim. But as one friend of his said, "The great Jimmy Hines took care of that and saw to it that he got well set after, too." This individual became one of our most aggressive and brutal patrolmen. He was known to "beat them up first and stand on ceremony later," not infrequently seriously beating and abusing innocent people; but he was never officially charged with doing so. This patrolman, further, had the kind of home life, sex delinquency, and alcoholism that would have clearly shown him to be an unstable character. With the demise of Jimmy Hines, and that regime, he saddened. Often he tried for a promotion to the detective division, but always with no success. He complained, "My anchors are not heavy any more," meaning that he had no more political weight to throw in the proper direction.

Some of the policemen interviewed said sadly—in off-the-record statements—that "those were the days when we didn't worry and didn't give a damn." The wives of some of the deceased regretfully remarked, "Our weekly income in those days was nice and fat; one hundred to two hundred dollars was not unusual sometimes."

Not only were the financial returns and the protection within a functioning machine satisfying, but the psychological and social gratifications and benefits of being a "cop" were of special significance. The immature or unstable personalities who previously had been without vocational status, without any element of achievement or prestige, and with little security as men in their own right, suddenly found themselves in a new and exalted position. They became the "guardians of the law," the "protectors" of their fellowmen. The gun, badge, and police club became the symbols of their power. The aggressive personality was given a glorified outlet, and the proper, submissive, or inadequate person now considered himself "a man." Some became hypermoralistic. The aggressive, exploitative person, with his impulsive and essentially delinquent personality, acquired, with the donning of the police uniform, social license and the approbation of his superiors for aggressive and, in some instances, brutal behavior. The patrolmen on their posts not infrequently said, "On this beat, I am the law." Policemen interviewed have remarked, "In those days we weren't sissies; we treated them rough and got credit for it." In a certain instance, a policeman was criticized by a judge for having authoritatively and abusively handled a prisoner who was innocent of a mild charge. The patrolman in the open courtroom shouted angrily at the judge that he, the policeman, would not be made a fool of, and further, that the judge was a "Goddamn fool." The patrolman had "pull" and nothing ever came of this incident.

This aspect of the attitude toward policemen was evident in their acceptance in the courts. Judges regarded them with some concern and not infrequently avoided arousing their antagonism. In their communities, they were proud to let everyone know that they were policemen. They had nothing to fear. They were occasionally able to dispense minor favors in connection with the law. They could also assert their hostilities and exploit their position as policemen without worrying about citizens' complaints and subsequent punishment from headquarters. If by chance they were brutal, neglectful, or unfaithful to their wives, they had little to fear, because their wives' complaints to headquarters had only incidental effect —in many cases, none whatsoever. Their status remained unaltered.

The policemen themselves often committed violations of the law—violations which were condoned and which in some cases gained much approbation from superior officers. One of our cases, a member of a special squad, resorted frequently to illegal and often brutal methods, on occasion so foul as to evoke great disapproval from his own fellow workers. Despite this, no charges were brought against the man and he continued in favor with his superior officers. His behavior became so "queer" that in the last year of his life his co-workers thought he was "going crazy."

Free license to obtain gratification through aggressive behavior made them feel like "big shots." To deprive a man of his gun was unusual unless he was truly violent or disgracefully dismissed. Because of the political influence exerted by the officer, dismissals were extremely difficult to put through and were therefore infrequent. An officer who was brought into the complaint room could easily influence the higher authorities so that his fine was light or the charges were dropped altogether.

All these means of gratification and avoidance of punishment or censure were such as to enable an unstable personality, a delinquent, an inadequate person, or even a serious neurotic (and, in a few instances, a psychotic) to continue on the force. And, further, through his position as a policeman, he could acquire approved and protected outlets for his psychological and social maladjustments.

With a change in political regime, such as occurred in 1934, these incompetent, dishonest, or mentally unstable or psychologically ill individuals were the first to feel the resultant insecurity. Whereas those who had adjustable and secure personalities accommodated themselves to the new demands, in many instances with great pleasure, the others—whose protectors were shorn of power and whose jobs became more exacting of efficiency and allegiance—suddenly found themselves feeling anxious, fearful, and, on occasion, insecure. The insecurity and anxiety had a contagious effect. The job—previously the source not only of material benefit but of psychological self-glorification—now took on the ever-present threat of completely berating, humbling, and eventually "knocking a man down and throwing him out."

Fear of dismissal from the force terrified the insecure person and made him suspicious of everyone around him. With the return of the "confidential squad" came the fear that its men were trailing him to revive his past sins in order to punish or "break" him. In the station house, the attitude that predominated may be expressed by a statement often heard in various forms. To quote one: "I keep my mouth shut, and my nose out of others' business—and I'll see to it that they keep their noses out of my affairs. I do my job, turn in, and say nothing. We trust no one."

Of the trial room, in which he formerly felt safe because of his protector, he now came to say: "Once you're inside that room you are guilty before you say a word. The fact that you're there, they assume, means you are guilty, and you have a fat chance of proving yourself innocent." It was claimed that dismissals from the force that before the change in regime had been less than one a month suddenly jumped to an average of five or more. In the station house one not infrequently heard the remark, "If I got broken, I'd take the gas pipe [suicide]."

An atmosphere such as just described became to the fearful, anxious, unstable, or insecure personality a hammering reminder of his impotence, with its eventual threat of his destruction.

Under the new regime, patrolmen complained that the judges who had formerly respected them as administrators of the law now treated them as humble servants and, in some instances, berated them. "Now the judges love to make us feel like damn fools." The patrolmen's superior officers—partly because of their own anxiety and hypercautiousness—did not trust any of them. To the patrolmen's complaints that they were often treated as though they were playing hookey from school, the commanding officer's reply was that the patrolmen "are a bunch of kids and have to be treated that way."

Citizens complaining of a patrolman's improper behavior now obtained hearings from his commanding officers, and the patrolman was often endangered by the threat of charges from headquarters. Even complaining "cranks" and "kids" received a hearing. In other words, the patrolman was reminded on all sides that he was the "servant of the people" and not the law himself. One alert officer said, "Now the public can and does hate cops—and don't cops know it."

Irregularities in the patrolman's marital life, formerly considered "private" by him and therefore free of criticism from his superiors, now constituted a disturbing threat. If he became wayward, his wife could exert a real power over him. If he abused her, took a mistress, or disturbed her in any real sense, a formal complaint to his commanding officer received immediate response. Such complaints brought reprimands, unofficial punishment, and, in some extreme cases, dismissal from the force for "behavior unbecoming a police officer." Although most frequently the patrolman's fellow workers and captain sympathized with him, headquarters frowned upon and unofficially punished marital disharmony. Wives of the patrolmen were quick to learn of the authorities' attitude. The result was an added threat to the already anxious and insecure patrolman. In many cases, especially among those of the aggressive policemen, the wife exercised her new-found privilege. Sometimes the captain, in order to protect the patrolman, would attempt to handle the situation and would demand absolute obedience to a prescribed mode of living. The wife had the upper hand now. One of our cases had to report at regular intervals to his captain about the nature of his home life. Another was ordered to return to his home even though he was living with a mistress and was seeking a separation from his wife. A number of men were kept in fear by their wives' threats that their mistress relationships would be revealed to headquarters. One threatened in this way shot and killed his wife and then himself. Another whose wife complained of his "playing around with other women" was transferred—according to his captain, for no reason—from a favored post to a difficult and unimportant assignment. Divorce was considered almost impossible. Why this was so will become clear in our subsequent discussion of the problem of police marriages.

Another change that came with the new regime was in relation to the gun. Whereas formerly free use of the gun or club used to be overlooked, it was now censured. The "cowboys" who both on and, in many instances, off duty, fired their guns recklessly and unnecessarily, or both, numbered at least eighteen among our ninety-three cases. It was not uncommon for some of them to shoot at street lamps, play at their own improvised target practice, and jestingly threaten bartenders with guns if they were refused a drink. There was a case in which the patrolman fired his gun in anger at another patrolman and was never brought up on charges. All of this appeared to be different with the change in regime. Now suspicion of dangerous or careless behavior could mean deprivation of the gun. As one who was deprived of a gun remarked, "I felt so ashamed, so helpless. I was not a cop any more." The gun is more than an implement of the policeman's trade; it is a symbol of his power. Guns may be taken away during periods of suspension or even of censure. To many this deprivation was the greatest possible disgrace.

Because supplementary incomes became impossible or dangerous under the new regime, homes and personal equipment that had previously been purchased in the expectation of such income had now become distressing liabilities. It has frequently been stated that at least 50 percent of New York City's police lived in Queens, where most of them own their own homes. Payments on mortgages and installments on equipment and furniture had been calculated on the basis of the supplementary income. With its discontinuance came additional concern, which, however, was a nuisance factor rather than a cause in the disturbed personality of the suicidal policemen. In fact, significant debts were a negligible factor among the ninety-three cases.

In summary, all the deprivations listed above, frustrations, and ego-deflationary situations, combined with the more exacting demands for honest police work, disturbed the depth of the personality of the insecure, unstable, and immature policeman, who was so thoroughly affected that it made his whole living plan one of evident maladjustment. These maladjustments varied in their manifestations according to the original type of the personality in its self-indulging days before the change in regime. The "breakdowns" were predominantly psychotic among the passive and insecure but "good cops" and were explosively delinquent and, in some instances, murderous among the aggressive, immature personalities with their bases of disturbed marital life, serious alcoholism, and complete dependence for primary gratification on an organization that had allowed them to exploit aggressive personality patterns.

One must not overlook the fact, however, that it was the original unstable, insecure, and immature core of the policeman's personality that was at fault and not the new regime and its exactions. To repeat, the disappearance of the loose police organization and its involved political affiliations that had previously provided outlets that enabled this type of individual to function and the substitution of a stringent system forced upon him impotence and destruction of his whole living program. Should he seek meaning and fulfillment in his family and through the usual means of everyday life and relationships, he failed again, because these sources had never been utilized and the relationships had never been built on the basis of a sound, mature personality. In the vernacular, he had placed all his eggs in one basket (the Police Department and gratification as a policeman), and the bottom fell out.

With the change, the hostile and aggressive policeman who formerly functioned with social license suddenly began to feel like a frustrated child. No one would support him, and everyone was against him or was unsympathetic. Some "took it out" on themselves by extreme alcoholism and illness; others, by aggressive and murderous acts—all eventually leading to so much pent-up murderous hostility as to eventuate in suicide. The latter type was vividly illustrated in the case of the policeman who waited for hours to kill the sergeant he hated. When the sergeant failed to appear, the patrolman killed himself.

## Statistical Background

Some statistical data for the six-year period reported in this chapter (1934–1940), as well as the six-year period preceding that interval (1928–1933), are relevant. Table 2 presents these data.

What is most striking about these data is the increase in the number of suicides and in the suicide rate within the New York Police Department subsequent to 1934. In the period 1928–1933, there were 51 suicides, or about 8 per year, with an average rate of 46.9 per 100,000. In the interval from 1934 to 1939, there were 93 suicides or about 15 per year with a rate of 84.5 per 100,000. It is important to note that this marked increase in rate within the Police Department was not reflected in any general change in suicide rate in the country, which was the same for both of these six-year periods.

Some further comparisons can be made between the New York Police Department suicide rate and the suicide rate in the general popu-

Table 2

Suicide Data—New York Police Department—1928–1939

| Date | Enrollment of Department | Suicides per year | Rate per 100,000 | U. S. Bureau of Census rate for civilian population |
|---|---|---|---|---|
| Jan. 1, 1928 | 16,801 | 10 | 59 | 13.6 |
| Jan. 1, 1929 | 17,577 | 2 | 11.8 | 14.0 |
| Jan. 1, 1930 | 17,017 | 9 | 52.8 | 15.7 |
| Jan. 1, 1931 | 18,595 | 11 | 59.6 | 16.8 |
| Jan. 1, 1932 | 19,315 | 7 | 36.2 | 17.8 |
| Jan. 1, 1933 | 19,275 | 12 | 62.2 | 15.9 |
| 1928–1933 | 108,580 | 51 | 46.9 | 15.2 |
| Jan. 1, 1934 | 18,922 | 10 | 52.8 | 14.9 |
| Jan. 1, 1935 | 18,268 | 18 | 98.5 | 14.3 |
| Jan. 1, 1936 | 17,842 | 17 | 95.2 | 14.2 |
| Jan. 1, 1937 | 18,045 | 16 | 88.6 | 14.9 |
| Jan. 1, 1938 | 18,358 | 18 | 98.0 | 17.5 |
| Jan. 1, 1939 | 18,645 | 14 | 75.0 | 15.5 |
| 1934–1936 | 110,080 | 93 | 84.5 | 15.2 |

lation. Taking the point of the highest suicide incidence in the country in the year 1913 as a base line for individuals aged 25 through 34, for the period 1934 to 1939 the suicide rate for the New York Police Department was 38 per 100,000, whereas for the general population it was 20; for ages 35 through 44, the New York Police Department rate was 50, whereas for the general population it was 32; and for ages 45 through 54 the New York Police Department rate was 70 per 100,000, whereas for the general population it was 48.

## Overview of Psychological Problems

A detailing of the lives of these ninety-three policemen, especially before their acceptance by the Police Department, may furnish significant clues to the understanding of the act of suicide. A surprisingly large number—63 of the 93 (67 percent) manifested some behavior trait that indicated mental imbalance. The majority of this group were obviously psychotic, of either the depressive or paranoic type. Two-thirds of the cases included in the group of psychotic, prepsychotic, or seriously neurotic types were essentially passive individuals who were frequently of the quiet, reliable, and, in many cases, inadequate or inconsequential personalities whose suicide on superficial examination seemed to have no obvious cause. However, the majority of them during most of their lives had been good examples of "home men," "good cops," and superficially adjusted personalities. They had generally been well-liked, most often just "one of the gang"; most of them had not been extreme alcoholics, and they had exemplified a superficially satisfactory marital adjustment. In periods ranging from a few months to a few years before their suicides, a disintegration of personality developed. Their fellow policemen recognized in only a few instances that their friend was under some strain or stress. Those who became extremely alcoholic, the "rummies," were protected by their fellow workers because of their previously good reputations. Camaraderie that is usually restrained came to the fore after the breakdown, and the good cop or good fellow was helped on all sides. Superior officers, police surgeons, and fellow policemen did not want to see him lose his job. Consequently, his benefactors, because of both their desire to help and their ignorance of the nature of his severe mental illness, nursed him along instead of encouraging him to go on the sick list. This procedure was very evident. It was usually not until their mental illness had become very severe that they were treated as "queer" or "sick."

Others of this group, who had for years been the good cops, suddenly developed irritable, suspicious, or despondent behavior. An examination of their home life betrayed a psychopathy which must have been quiescent and of long standing and which had burst forth in a psychosis just before the suicide.

One-third of this mentally unstable and psychotic group were of an overtly aggressive, impulsive, and reckless nature. There was a high percentage of alcoholics among them. Those in the passive group had been predominantly functioning policemen who had had some degree of adjustment prior to their mental breakdown and eventual suicide, whereas in the aggressive group the life plan had been one of maladjustment in relation to work, family, and self.

The incidence of alcoholics was higher and the extent of indulgence in alcohol was greater in the aggressive group. Among them, 70 percent were severe alcoholics whereas only 36 percent of the passive group were.

Whereas 64 percent of the aggressive group were most frequently involved in marital discord, only 26 percent of the passive group failed to make an acceptable marital adjustment. Further, of the aggressive group only one could have been called a good cop with regard to character and efficiency as a policeman, whereas 57, or 70 percent, of the passive group had been respected as good cops by their commanding officers.

## Aggressive Personality Group

Two-fifths of the total group coming within this aggressive, assertive personality type showed a lower incidence of psychotic or prepsychotic trend than did the passive group. However, during their life activity prior to the suicide, they did manifest a greater personality disorganization. Persistent and severe alcoholism, greater marital discord, loose sexual living, and precarious security as a policeman were so vividly the pattern that a frequently heard statement from or about these men was "the digging of their own graves." Often they themselves felt that this grave-digging process was inflicting harm on their friends or family, and the suicide itself was reacted to by these relatives with an awareness that the suicide was the final *coup de grâce* of aggression. Many widows commented, "Why did he do this to me?" "How could he leave us this way?" etc. Just over half this group showed in their suicide anger or aggression toward their wives, and often in their suicide notes expressed unrestrained hostility toward them. Some even forbade their wives to attend the funeral. A large number of these actually committed the act after a violent argument with, or following a series of frustrations by, their spouse. A number were threatened by the wife with exposure in police headquarters of their extramarital sexual behavior, wife-beating, excessive drinking, and, in a few instances, irregular police behavior. The frequency of murder threats in this group was high. Examples were:

One young policeman, alcoholic, with a bad record on the force, had been carrying on extramarital sexual relations. He impregnated a girl and married her in a pompous church ceremony, set up another home, and tried to keep the secret from both wives while living with each. The first wife discovered the bigamy but was restrained from revealing it for fear her husband would shoot her as he had often threatened. Her mother, however, betrayed him. He pulled his gun and wanted to shoot both the woman and her mother. Then, telling his wife that his suicide was inevitable, he was further angered by her taunting refusal to believe that he would do it. He shot himself then and there.

Another patrolman, when threatened by his wife with exposure of his various mistress relationships, shot and killed her and then himself. He was known in his district as "king of the beat;" in the station house his fellow patrolmen were afraid of his temper but flattered him by calling him "stud horse."

One patrolman, on the force for ten years, married twice, frequently up for disciplinary charges, often intoxicated while on and off duty, beat and abused his wife and was always accusing her of infidelity. He himself was suspected of considerable extramarital sexual activity. On at least one occasion, in a fit of temper, he shot at a fellow patrolman. His suicide occurred after he shot and killed a policeman who refused to drink with him.

Other cases of this nature can be enumerated. At least half (eighteen) and probably more of the aggressive group were known to have recklessly fired their guns or threatened frequently to fire and kill. At least five had murdered someone just before their suicide.

This picture of maladjustment had been evident long before they joined the Department: Vocational status had been one of considerable insecurity; jobs had been in the unskilled and semiskilled fields and had been held for only a short time; economic status had been low; alcoholism was not infrequent. In a number of cases minor delinquencies were evident, whereas in a few cases actual arrests for assaultive behavior were on record.

## Mental Status

Of the 93 cases, 63 cases (67 percent) showed evidence of disturbed mental status. Although known as such at the time by the medical department, the outstanding majority were neither diagnosed nor treated as mental cases. In fact, only a relatively few were referred to the psychiatric specialists for further diagnosis. Some cases are:

A patrolman, thirty-seven, on the force for twelve years, the last two of which he was assigned to light duty because of a fractured arm, was in regular contact with the police surgeon. The patrolman was alcoholic, lived in constant marital discord, and was known as a sex delinquent. Both he and his wife had often threatened, and at least once had attempted, suicide. About a year before his suicide he disappeared. Upon return to his precinct some days later, he claimed that he had suffered amnesia and had "found his mind" when he regained awareness in a distant city.

His family said that before his suicide, he frequently saw "enemy agents after him because he was a G-man." On at least two occasions he shot at these illusory followers. He often dressed his ten-year-old son in a police uniform in order to protect him from "being taken away to war." He accused his wife of being in league with the "spies." There was no mention of any of this behavior in the man's medical record.

Another patrolman, on the force for twenty-five years, single, and extremely dependent on the housewife of the family with whom he boarded, was often miserable for days, convinced that he was being followed or checked on by his superiors. Fearful that citizens were employed as spies by the Police Department, he was surly and suspicious when approached by them and on two occasions accused women on his post of trying to "frame" him. His fellow patrolmen thought him "queer," seclusive, and "unduly suspicious." His medical record lacks an indication of his disturbed mental state.

A young patrolman, the adopted and only child of a widow, was alcoholic during the last few years of his life. Usually, after recovering from intoxication, he was convinced that he had been followed and beaten, and once he was certain he had been dismissed from the force. He recalled, without any foundation in fact, how he had been brought before his superiors and deprived of his gun and badge. He committed suicide when deserted by his fellow patrolman, an intimate companion; previously, his foster mother had threatened to desert him while he was imploring her to give him money for more whiskey.

Another young, single, efficient patrolman, not an alcoholic, always talked of his sexual impotence. He had been seeing a psychiatrist for at least four months, unknown to the police surgeons. With his fiancée he attempted a double suicide. She survived the attempt at monoxide poisoning. He shot and killed himself.

Two other patrolmen, both married, non-alcoholic, efficient policemen with good records, were both worried over gonorrheal infections for which they were seeing private physicians without the knowledge of their police surgeons. During the last months of their lives, they were convinced that they were being laughed at, discriminated against, "framed," and generally persecuted. Neither was known to the medical department as a mental case.

Cases of this type can be enumerated at length, and in almost all instances there was no psychiatric diagnosis. In a few instances, even when seen by a psychiatrist, the patrolman continued on duty. The following is an example:

One patrolman, after firing his gun wildly into space with the claim that he was shooting his "persecutors," was taken to a psychiatric hospital whence he was discharged to the police surgeon with a report recommending his release from the force since he was dangerous and psychotic. He was subsequently returned to light duty however, and within two years he repeated the above behavior, but this time he finished by shooting himself so that his "persecutors" would not get him.

A most tragic and dramatic case was that of the almost fanatically religious, righteous, exceptionally efficient patrolman who shot his wife and three children and then himself. For months before, his friends had said he was "cracking up," but the medical record showed no such indications until two days before the tragedy.

Among these sixty-three cases, at least one-fifth were of the type of personality that could be called "neurotic character." They were known as such by their captains and fellow workers. Quite a number of them were frequently up before their district commanding officers for serious disciplinary charges or extreme alcoholism.

Two, both married, were tried for having had sexual intercourse with minors (a statutory offense). Despite their exoneration, most of the informants and families were of the opinion that they were both guilty.

In this total group of 63 cases, 26 percent showed behavior suggesting depression whereas 17 percent were clearly paranoics. The likelihood, however, is that if more information were available about the remaining cases, the known percentage of psychotics among the total 93 cases would be considerably higher.

The majority, 41 cases (65 percent of the group), comes within the classification of quiet, reliable, conscientious, or passive personality types—those commonly called good cops.

In the group of 63 as a whole, 51 percent had noticeably unhappy or extremely disturbed marital relations; 59 percent were alcoholic; and 49 percent had had a disciplinary charge against them at some time or another. Twenty-eight percent had served on the force long enough to be retired on pension.

## Precipitating Factors, Psychological Background, Clinical Vignettes

The immediate precipitating factors were in many cases difficult to discover. It was not uncommon for many of the informants to greet the interviewer with the statement: "There seemed to be no reason in the world for him to do it . . . he had everything to live for." In other cases, the family angrily refused to accept the verdict of suicide and insisted that it was an accident. In a few cases, the relatives hesitatingly remarked that they thought the policeman had been murdered. Further complicating the difficulties in reconstructing the actual events prior to the patrolman's suicide was the informants' (wife or parents) feelings of guilt over their own behavior before the event.

Of the men who were married, 50 percent manifested varying degrees of hostility toward their wives during their last days—restrained hostility which culminated in impotent anger at the time of the suicide. A reconstruction of the man's behavior, his personal history, and the events of the suicide situation often showed that the suicide had been directed more toward the wife than at first appeared likely. For example, an officer on the force for over twenty years, who had achieved a reputation for brilliant police work, was transferred to a new command which was traditionally of less prestige than was his former post. Everyone linked the transfer to the uncovering of irregularities in his district and said that he had been demoted; the official reason for the transfer was said to have been a need to place him where he could do the most good. Some months afterwards he committed suicide and everyone stated that he had been depressed because of the demotion. A reconstruction of the history made clear a hostile relationship to his wife, anger against whom he had been suppressing for years.

More direct evidence of hostility toward the wife is presented in the following cases:

A patrolman on the force for over twenty-five years and about to be retired committed suicide while on his post. His few close friends claimed that he had done it to prevent his wife from using his pension. The wife was known as an alcoholic and a sex delinquent. The patrolman told his captain that often when arriving home he had had to throw intoxicated men out of his wife's room.

One patrolman had been having quarrels with his wife for years. She was described by him as "dead as a board" during sexual intercourse. During his last few years he became alcoholic and was hounded and nagged by her in her efforts to keep him sober. He entered a phone booth and after reaching his wife on the telephone told her of his intention. While she was talking to him, he shot himself. There is some reason to suspect that he first berated her and blamed her for his intention to kill himself.

A young married patrolman, alcoholic, lived with and had three children by an alcoholic wife with whom he rarely had sexual relations. Quarrelling and open infidelity were accepted by both of them. She refused to grant him a divorce, stating that she had "roped him into the marriage" and was going to "hang on." Once, while intoxicated, he beat her. When he left home the next day, she placed the children in a boarding home and disappeared. He then deliberately went to the station house to secure his gun. He paid off some small debts, went to a friend's house where he spoke angrily about his wife, returned to his home (which he had described as "barren as a barn"), shaved, and then shot himself.

A thirty-two-year-old patrolman had been on the force for about five years, during the last two of which he had frequently been in danger of suspension because of drinking. His marriage to a young woman of another religious faith caused ill-feeling with his mother, who felt that the girl had forced him into the marriage just to spite her. His wife, upon again seeing him intoxicated, deserted him, and he shot himself.

Another case of what is essentially the same situation occurred only after the patrolman, intoxicated, had tried to kill his wife.

It is noteworthy that in the last six cases cited, the patrolmen were all the favorite sons of their mothers, indulged in some cases to an extent which annoyed other children, and all married over parental protest to girls of other religions, with resultant quarrels over religion between themselves and their wives and themselves and their parents and siblings.

There was one officer who had received considerable distinction in administrative police work. He was married to a woman who not infrequently had quarrels with her mother-in-law, an intensely fervent follower of another religion. After his death, the mother and the wife held separate and different religious funeral ceremonies. Six weeks before his suicide his wife became pregnant by him. This, it is claimed, made him very angry toward her. The family and others blamed the suicide on the "stolen pregnancy." There was some suspicion that the man was developing a psychosis of the depressive type.

A forty-two year-old married patrolman with children had frequently quarrelled with his wife, who is reported to have deserted him and gone to her widower brother-in-law. The patrolman went searching for them but found only the brother-in-law. He shot and killed him on the spot, then shot himself.

There were a number of cases (and probably many more which we were unable to ascertain) in which the wives who were dominant individuals nagged the patrolmen for being failures, specifying their inability to get promotions, their big debts, and low standards of living. In these cases the suicides usually occurred in the presence of the wife.

One thirty year-old, recently married, alcoholic patrolman, whose father was a policeman who had committed suicide a few years before, shot and killed himself while his wife and sister were urging him to correct his drinking. He pulled his gun and said, "O.K., I'll get out of your way," and killed himself.

A patrolman at a party with "his girl" announced his engagement to her and within an hour killed himself in her presence—at the event which was supposed to celebrate the engagement.

At least one-sixth of this group of married men who in their suicides manifested obvious anger toward their wives had been for some time before frequently frustrated, occasionally angry, and often forced to implore their wives to give them the means to drink. This does not mean that all this group were alcoholic; in fact, many were complete nondrinkers. Only thirty-seven of the total of ninety-three cases were heavy drinkers. It was only in those individuals whose whole personality was gradually but persistently breaking down that the increased drinking brought forth anger and frustration from their wives.

This fact is well-illustrated by the case of the thirty-two year-old patrolman who was known in his precinct as a sensational and "slashing good" cop. He believed in and practiced the old police philosophy of the "cop with the club is the law." His many irregular police practices, brutal behavior toward citizens, etc., were overlooked because he kept his post under control. He had both gonorrheal and syphilitic infections. He had incessant quarrels with his wife, whom he was forced to marry after he impregnated her. It was openly known that on his post he had sexual relations with many women, prostitutes and otherwise. In his sexual behavior with his wife he demanded perversions which she fought. She finally threatened to reveal all to the police commissioner's office. The patrolman threatened suicide. She taunted him, claiming that she did not care what he did. He first wrote a note leaving all his money and property to his oldest daughter, then shot himself. Within the following year, this twelve-year-old daughter committed suicide by leaping from a window.

The question is often asked why many of these men did not separate or secure a divorce. The answer is complicated by many religious and police department attitudes that will be discussed below.

Whereas 51 percent of the 93 cases expressed in their suicide restrained or direct aggression toward their wives, mothers, or mistresses, 38 percent of the 93 cases were precipitated by an event in direct relation to a superior officer or a departmental order that was to their discredit, causing them demotion or suspension. Most of them, however, although apparently reacting to the departmental situation, had had or were having an incomplete, unhappy, or extremely discordant relation with wife and family.

There is one case in which a patrolman, upon being suspended because of intoxication, went home only to have his wife leave him in anger for his suspension. The relation of the patrolman and his wife had for some two years been one of conflict with frequent threats of separation and one desertion on her part some months before. This patrolman, when intoxicated, "was always shooting a sergeant" and not infrequently boasted of his plan to beat up a certain "hounding" officer. It appears that although he blamed his precarious position on the force on his "persecuting" superiors, it was his relations with his wife, his fear of her disapproval, and her threats of separation that really precipitated the suicide.

We have the case of another patrolman, 37 years of age, married twice, and on the force for seven years. His first marriage was one of much quarrelling, with flaunting infidelity on the part of both. There is, further, an allusion in his record to promiscuous sexual behavior before this first marriage and to an illegitimate child whose support he had to guarantee before he could get on the force.

His first marriage was of a nature suggesting coercion on the wife's part, with resultant discord. His fellow patrolmen frequently claimed that his wife had sexual relations with other patrolmen in her husband's precinct. Divorce followed after much difficulty.

His seven years on the police force were such as to elicit from some men in his station house the remark, "He was no loss to the Department." In his record he is reported to have shot himself while cleaning his gun. From some informed sources this incident appears to have been the result of a quarrel with his wife, concerning which he angrily remarked, "I almost shot her at the time."

Seven months after his divorce and about eighteen months before his suicide, he remarried. His friends claim that he was again disappointed and unhappy in marriage, "since his wife was lavish and she expected him to support her folks."

In his precinct he was surly, irritable, and disliked. He often remarked that everyone was against him. Toward a certain sergeant he was especially angry. He felt hounded by him and not infrequently fearful of being brought up on charges of either drinking or negligent police duty.

On the day of the suicide he felt especially plagued by the sergeant, and after finishing his tour he went to a barroom where he waited for the sergeant to appear. To some people in the saloon he said that he was going to kill the officer as soon as he saw him. For some time he waited impatiently, frequently going to the street to look for him. After a long while he returned to his barroom table and wrote the following note, which he addressed to the same sergeant:

"To whom concerned:

"Goodbye you old prick and when I mean prick you are a prick. Hope you fall with the rest of us, you yellow bastard.

"May the [number of the precinct] get along without you."

Although the note implies that some disclosure about the sergeant's affairs might be made, there has been no such disclosure. However, the sergeant later seemed to have become paranoid.

Any number of cases in which the men were apparently reacting by their suicides to a police situation revealed upon study a series of events having their cause in the total personality and preceding the Police Department incident, which made the latter merely "the last straw." Regardless of the vocation of police work, noticeable immaturity and instability would have resulted eventually in a breakdown.

It is important, however, to point out here that not all the patrolmen were scoundrels, men with unusually disturbed marital relations, drinkers, or undesirable people. The cases just mentioned are nevertheless not in the least an exaggeration of the type of personality on the force that represented nearly 40 percent of all the suicides and 35 percent of the group in which there were indications of possible psychotic breakdown.

The other two cross-groupings were: first, those who were called good cops—who were good family men with excellent police records and happy personal relations with their fellow workers; and second, that small but definite group of cases in which the patrolman, suffering from an incurable physical ailment, preferred suicide. There were about seven cases of this last type, with ten additional instances in which the men only believed they were so afflicted.

As has been stated earlier, the incidence of probable psychotic breakdown of all the cases is higher in this good-cop group. They were occasionally spotted by the police surgeon who too often used the diagnoses of gastric neurosis, neurosis, anxiety neurosis, and neurasthenia and too frequently impatiently urged the patrolman back to duty. Even when the surgeons were more sympathetic, no significant psychiatric treatment was given in any except two cases which were sent to psychiatric sanatoriums.

The incipient mental breakdown or suicidal impulses in the good-cop group were not easy for either the police surgeon or fellow patrolmen to detect. However, most of those close to the man knew that something was wrong with him.

An example is the case of a patrolman, forty-five years of age, who had an excellent record for twenty-two years on the force, was married, had two children, and lived close to a large clannish family. He was the eighth of nine children born of a stern father and capable mother who dominated the whole household. His father died of cancer when the patrolman was twenty-two. He was his mother's favorite. She died of a kidney ailment when he was twenty-seven. As a child and an adult he lived an active, happy life, although somewhat dominated more by the girls of the family than the other boys. He stopped school at sixteen to enter the family trade of stonecutting. He entered the Police Department only after being urged by relatives on the force and passed the police examination despite himself. He was proud of being a policeman and was well-known for his fastidiousness with regard to work, appearance, and family life. Always overprotective of his two daughters, who "adored" him, he blocked their too-intimate contact with boys, saying, "There isn't anything any boy can give you that I can't." His married life was said to be "very happy."

After an appendectomy, eight years before his suicide, he developed what he and others called "writer's cramp." He was very sensitive about this and always borrowed others' pens and pencils, with the thought that he could control his writing better with them. Some months before the suicide he angrily tossed a pen to the floor, saying, "Damn it, my writing is like a kid's." Between his thirty-eighth and forty-fifth year four of his siblings died, the last death, nine months before his suicide, being that of his favorite sister.

Three months later "he just seemed to mope around the house." He suffered from constipation and feared cancer. His medical record had a notation of a gastric neurosis for which he received the usual medical treatment. The last six months of his life he worked at his job but was said "to be in a fog." The night before his death, while trying to write a note, he very angrily threw his pencil away again, saying that his was child's writing. The next morning, after shaving and inquiring about his daughter who had just started her first job, he shot and killed himself.

This case is presented at greater length because it is a good example of the life and work of so many of the group who were spoken of as reliable, passive, and good policemen.

There was one patrolman, thirty-seven, single, on the force for nine years, who had not only a good police record but a reputation among his fellow workers for being a good friend and worthwhile person.

He shot himself after writing a note leaving his considerable savings to his sister and close male friend. In the note he said that he suffered from such severe headaches that he could not go on, and further, that "before I do something that may hurt someone else, this is the best way out."

His father had been committed to an insane asylum repeatedly after sexually attacking his own daughter (the patrolman's twin sister) when she was about twelve years of age. A few days before the patrolman's suicide, he visited his father in the institution. Upon his return home he was said to have been exceptionally depressed at finding his father so insane as to be unable to recognize him.

The headaches that the patrolman suffered so severely were unknown to his police surgeon, and the medical record shows no awareness of the man's physical or mental condition.

His suicide was one that evoked from all who knew him the statement, "We would never believe it. . . . He had everything. . . . There was no reason for his doing it."

The record of one particular patrolman, thirty-three, single, on the force for nine years, was good. He was the second of seven children of poverty-stricken parents who struggled for life in a foreign section of the city, of which they were all an integral part. His oldest sister married. His father became alcoholic, and the patrolman, after some adventures in the armed services, took over the responsibility of the household. In a quiet and very paternal way he helped his family and friends. After some years he became engaged to a girl but appeared to have had a conflict about whether he could care for his mother and siblings as well as his wife if he were to marry. The engagement was broken. Some claim that the girl had been unfaithful to him. Some weeks after the termination of his engagement there appeared behavior changes—most noticeable were insomnia, fatigue, and loss of appetite. When friends urged him to go on vacation, he was very upset and said that the precinct could not spare him. He remarked that his mother did not cook his food right and once implied that it might be poisoned. He himself suspected that he was "going crazy like my sister," who was a schizophrenic in a state hospital.

Four days before his death, he saw a police surgeon who diagnosed his difficulty as gastric neurosis and, according to the family, ordered the patrolman back to police duty. The night before his suicide he wrote two notes: one asked forgiveness for his suicide intention and added that "Every moment is torture, please forgive me for what I'm going to do. I know it's horrible, but it's the only way out." The other note was in the form of a formal bequest of his money and belongings to a "beloved sister" in order to enable her better to care for his "beloved mother."

He then shot himself in the stomach and lived for two days, during which time he gave no reason for his suicide, asked to see his former fiancée, and also arranged with an undertaker (a friend) who was to have supplied automobiles for his wedding to use the same cars for his funeral.

There are a great many other cases of this type—some married or about to be—and almost all with no significant psychiatric diagnosis or treatment.

In a few cases in which the patrolman was thought to be acting queerly, his family and friends hesitated to have him see the psychiatrist, or "nut doctor," as the average policeman called him. To most police families and men on the force, referral to the psychiatrist or neurologist meant almost certain discharge from the Department. Not only was there a reluctance to refer a man to what was felt to be his "doom," but in most instances his breakdown was never recognized.

One patrolman who was always known as "dopey," but who functioned well enough to get by, complained of feeling dizzy, of having noises in his head, and of insomnia. When seen by the police surgeon two days before his suicide, he was diagnosed as suffering from anxiety neurosis and was asked to appear two days later (the day of the suicide) before a department specialist in psychiatric cases.

The morning of his death he read the Bible, appeared disturbed by all noises, and when the doorbell rang rushed to the cellar, crying, "That's the end—they won't get me," and shot himself.

Another young patrolman, married, with a good Department record, despite heavy drinking while off duty, was abnormally suspicious of his very attractive wife, toward whom he at least once had fired his gun with the apparent intention of killing her. The officers of the precinct in which he lived knew of this incident but tried to handle it "off the record," as though the patrolman had merely fired his gun accidentally. After a quarrel with his wife, whom he accused of infidelity, he shot and killed himself. There were suspicions that he suffered from a paranoic psychosis. His medical and police record were completely without any indication of signs of unusual mental behavior despite the fact that he was on sick report for the month before his death, seeing a police surgeon occasionally for treatment of a fractured right index metacarpal bone.

One case of a thirty-nine year-old married patrolman provides an instance of an individual whose "moody" and depressed behavior was so apparent that both family and coworkers had him referred to a police surgeon, who in turn sent him to a psychiatrist. He was diagnosed as "suffering from a marked attack of melancholia and not fit for duty." Eight days later another specialist stated that the patrolman suffered from "a mild emotional depression" and recommended the routine of duty as better than sick leave. Within ten days after his assignment to light duty, he shot himself while guarding a "raided premises."

His wife, who was seriously ill and who had for three years been a semi-invalid, died two weeks later.

This man's character was that of a compliant, dutiful policeman, quiet and unobtrusive among his friends. A depressed personality, he seemed to have a great sense of wanting to do the right thing.

This is one of the few instances on record of the mental disturbances being so aggravated as to bring the patrolman to a psychiatrist. But, as is evident even in this instance, the authorities were always too reluctant to recognize the seriousness of the man's illness, because it could mean causing him to lose his job. Although policemen are quite commonly suspicious of each other and are careful to keep their private affairs secret, they become overprotective when a fellow worker is in difficulty. In fact, in some instances, even serious misdemeanors are covered up, and this overprotective relationship holds for the attitude of superior officers toward the men in the ranks as well as for the attitude of the patrolmen toward one another.

One manner of handling the mentally or physically ill patrolman was to take him away from regular duty. This most frequently meant placing him on the duty called "raided premises," which usually consisted of guarding raided houses or hotels used by prostitutes. The purpose appeared to be that of keeping prostitutes from again inhabiting the place. The patrolman sat quietly by himself in one spot for a full eight-hour shift. In other instances, the recipient of light duty was given a simple errand or clerical job. In the case of both assignments, the average policeman felt much contempt for the job and condescending sympathy for those assigned to it. Some of our cases avoided and feared these assignments, saying, "I'll be damned if I'll cut paper dolls all day." As one said, "It's the next step to the nut house." One patrolman who felt that he was being "discriminated" against refused an inside assignment with the words, "That's no job for a man." In his disturbed behavior he thought people were claiming that he was "not a man."

Another of the cross-groupings was that of those who committed suicide while suffering from a serious physical ailment, in some instances apparently incurable. There were only seven cases that are undeniably of this class. All but two involved men who had been on the force for more than twenty years and who were in a position either to retire or serve a very short time before retirement on life pensions. Further, they were of the good-cop type, performing their duty with good records. The home situations and personal adjustments in all but one case were apparently satisfactory, which again seemed to indicate that the suicide was predominantly related to the physical ailment. Of the seven, three had cancer and two others showed signs that made the physicians suspicious of its existence. Of the remaining two, one suffered from a progressive paralysis and the other had very serious diabetes. Their illnesses were known by the Department some years before the suicides, and the men were frequently under special treatment. Because the ailments were not the result of injuries sustained while on duty, the men received only half-pay while on the sick list.

Men of this group at first resisted revealing their illness to the police surgeon for fear of being dropped from the force. When their illness became known, however, they apparently accepted the limitation of their police activity but in their personal lives began to develop depressions, feeling that they were now worthless and burdens.

An example is the case of a patrolman who had been on the force for twenty-four years with a good but colorless record. He was married and had three daughters. It is interesting to note that he had several automobile accidents shortly after he was married and again a few weeks before the birth of his second daughter. Seven years before his suicide, he was in another accident while driving a police car and suffered severe injuries to his spine and head. After six months of hospitalization he returned to duty.

About six years later he developed a paralysis in both legs, and the department surgeon presented a differential diagnosis of "polycythemia, thrombosis, anterior spinal artery, and/or destruction of cord at 6-7 dorsal segment." He was hospitalized, and in the course of 2½ years became increasingly worse. When he discovered that the physicians considered his condition hopeless, he deliberately planned suicide and strangled himself with a bell cord which hung over his bed.

The next case in this group is that of a forty-nine year-old, married police lieutenant who had been on the force for twenty-two years. He had a good police record and a satisfactory personality and family adjustment. He was of slightly higher intelligence and had more initiative than the average policeman. When he was forty-two, seven years before his suicide, a lump on his neck was diagnosed by a police surgeon as "cervical adenitis." It was painful at intervals, grew steadily worse, and frequently made him irascible. A few years later it was diagnosed as cancer, and with the onset of psychological symptoms he was sent to a neurological hospital. Discovering his condition to be hopeless and driven to desperation by the incessant pain, he deliberately planned suicide, first writing a long letter of adoration to his wife.

There were sixteen additional cases of men who either feared physical illness to the point of depression or actually had physical difficulties that were complicated by and probably secondary to the involved and disturbing psychological picture. In many instances, the psychological situation was such that even if the man had been completely without the organic difficulty, a disturbed-behavior picture would have emerged.

A case of this type is that of a forty-six year-old patrolman who had been on the force for twenty-three years. His background before acceptance by the Police Department appears to be cluttered with deliberate falsifications and indications that he was an aggressive, wandering person. He was an army sergeant, private detective, and, supposedly, a law student. Efforts to verify his law-school enrollment met with failure. In order to further his own ends, he had frequently falsified both his name and age. He claimed to have been an only child whose parents had been dead since he was very young.

As a policeman, his assaultive behavior had gotten him into many difficulties, out of which he squirmed rather successfully. Known as a clever person, "Beau Brummel," and "ladies' man," he boasted of his fine clothes, "flashy" car, and long line of conquests of any women he desired. On occasion, women brought charges against him for his forward, "vulgar," or insulting behavior.

One year after he was placed on the force he married under conditions that suggest coercion—a "shotgun" affair. Within four years he married a second time. He had not divorced his first wife but did agree to pay her a weekly stipend. He boasted of his role as an unmarried man among his fellow workers, and if ever seen with his wife, he introduced her as a "girl friend" and described her as a "steady piece of good lay."

Many of his fellow patrolmen in the precinct knew him as one who frequently had sexual relations with two or three women a day (according to his stories). Despite his braggadocio character, he was popular with the men and was frequently unusually helpful to policemen in need.

His medical record shows a long continuation of entries of grippe, fatigue, gastroenteritis, insomnia, indigestion, and headaches. Just three months before his death, he had pain from an "old hernia," and a herniotomy seemed advisable. Some claimed that he suffered severely from sinus infections. Others heard him talk of "bad blood." The dapper, glib, jovial person became depressed. There are reliable indications that he saw private doctors and kept his condition a secret from his police surgeon. About six weeks before his death, he did see his police doctor and was diagnosed as suffering from a "neurosis," but there was no further elaboration. Eleven days before his suicide, he returned to duty but appeared "worried." One day after paying his bills, he dressed in his uniform and went to the lavatory; while sitting on a toilet, he shot himself.

One of this group of sixteen cases in which the physical symptoms were so severe but in which the psychological picture seemed the most probable cause of the suicide was of a fifty-nine year-old patrolman who had been on the force for over twenty-five years.

He was the youngest son of immigrant parents. He hated his father's stern disciplinary methods, and at the time of his father's death, when the patrolman was about twenty-eight, he stated that he felt no grief for he had always hated him. He adored his mother.

Shortly afterwards, at twenty-four, the patrolman was married to a girl of eighteen. Their sexual relations were always inadequate: she was frigid and he suffered from ejaculatio praecox. They had three children by the time he was twenty-nine. The patrolman had become by this time a steady drinker, and members of his family were suffering financial difficulties.

After his older brother died of a rectal disease, the patrolman developed oral abscesses and bronchitis. He was given an inside job. He was then about forty-six. At fifty-three he claimed he suffered from severe headaches, kidney stones, and stomach aches. His medical record, however, shows no real basis for these complaints. He may have been seeing a private physician.

He became melancholy and acted as if he were "tired of living." He continued drinking and suffered from insomnia and alternate constipation and diarrhea. He occasionally had bleeding from the rectum and feared dying as had his brother. His police medical record still gave no indication of his condition.

One day after he treated the family to a special meal, for which largess his wife scolded him, he shot himself. He left a note that he was sorry for his act and gave financial difficulty as the reason. The family owed only $50.

The majority of the entire list of ninety-three cases had frequent entries of gastroenteritis, indigestion, constipation, fatigue, and many of insomnia.

Syphilis, gonorrhea, and prostate difficulties were more frequent than reported. The men feared dismissal if they reported these diseases.

Some whose medical records had absolutely no reference to these ailments were discovered to have been for years under the care of private physicians from whom the men usually concealed both their names and vocation. In a great many cases, fellow workers suspected venereal disease, but verification was often difficult. In the cases that were verified the disease did not appear to have been a disturbing factor and had existed for from four to fifteen years. In these cases, obvious character disorders or psychoses preceded the suicide.

We have previously cited a case in which a married patrolman, alcoholic, father of three children, shot himself when his wife, who was also an alcoholic, deserted him and placed their children in a boarding home.

This patrolman's medical record had frequent entries of indigestion (gastric disturbances from alcohol—"hangovers") but no reference to any condition even suggesting venereal disease. His wife, however, claimed that he did have such a disease and that he was treated for it throughout their married life. She further stated that because of it, sexual relations were rare and only took place when they both were intoxicated. As a result, both husband and wife had frequent extramarital sexual relations.

Another case was that of a most efficient patrolman who was on a "special privilege" squad of the Department. Although he joined the force after Wasserman tests were uniformly administered, he contracted gonorrhea and infected his wife. He had her treated for it without allowing her to know what the ailment was. At twenty-nine, seven years after his marriage and six years after joining the force, he suffered from an obvious paranoic psychosis and shot himself. At the time, he was secretly being treated for his venereal infection by a private physician; his police doctor knew nothing of it. Two days before his death he went on sick report. The police surgeon reported that he seemed physically unfit for duty because of influenza. He expressed a desire to return to duty as soon as possible. He was accordingly given a slip telling him to return to duty at midnight. The next day he wrote a series of notes, speaking of nervous breakdowns and people framing him and ending, "That clammy feeling on my hands was a weak heart from nervous prostration and mental fatigue from loss of sleep. Bury me as cheap as is possible."

A few months after his death, his wife was institutionalized with the diagnosis: dementia praecox.

Another case, already cited as an example of an aggressive patrolman with an unusually disturbed marital background, also suffered from venereal diseases for which he was treated, under an alias, for many years. This case was also unknown to the medical department. There were many more instances of this situation and indications of a great number that we were unable to verify.

## Retrospective Postscript

I am writing these following remarks in 1967. Thirty years ago, when the Committee for the Study of Suicide began its activities it was no doubt a revolutionary and unique event. A press release by the committee in 1936 explained:

The fact that there appears to be a definite relationship between the number of capital crimes and suicide in any given country or community, that contrary to common belief suicide appears greater among primitive races than among civilized races, the fact that suicide is apt to increase in time of peace rather than in time of war and in periods of prosperity rather than during economic depressions—these are the most important of the considerations which have determined the shaping of the plans for the coming year now announced by the Committee for the Study of Suicide.

The psychoanalytic conceptualizations, according to which an intimate and inverse relationship exists between murderous instincts and self-destructive drives, were then a new scientific discovery that needed further clinical validation. The study of suicide among policemen had special appeal to the committee. The assumptions that suicide represented a displacement of externally directed homicidal impulses was thus one of the main factors which led the committee to focus its scientific interest on policemen as a group. It was expected *a priori* that here one would find a greater rate of suicide than in the general population, inasmuch as the policeman's role is to use sanctioned power and aggression in the enforcement of law and order. The policeman is permitted to kill and receives praise from his superiors, peers, and even the public for carrying out these acts.

But, on the other hand, he is also expected to refrain from killing and from other violent behavior. The aggressive and controlling drives, which are no doubt the primary motivations for his choice of occupation, are often in collision with the command to refrain and repress, therefore causing tremendous conflict within him. This conflict of the policeman and the vicissitudes of aggression offered a great challenge and opportunity to the Committee for the Study of Suicide.

The recent data made available to me through the cooperation of Chief Inspector Sanford D. Garelik of the New York City Police Department indicate that the number of police suicides has declined: 1960, nine; 1961, five; 1962, six; 1963, four; 1964, four; 1965, seven; 1966, three. According to Table 3 the relative proportions, as compared with the officially accepted rates (approximately 10 suicides per 100,000 general population per year) are still somewhat high.

As one can see, however, these figures differ from year to year, the highest rate occurring in 1960, the lowest in 1966. It may be conjectured that this decline reflects in part an improvement in the emotional makeup of individuals who enter the police force and in part an improvement in the

Table 3

Total Number of Policemen on the Force
(As of January 1, Each Year)

| | |
|---|---|
| 1960 | 23,805 |
| 1961 | 23,515 |
| 1962 | 24,374 |
| 1963 | 24,827 |
| 1964 | 25,432 |
| 1965 | 25,897 |
| 1966 | 27,030 |
| 1967 | 27,429 |

sociopsychological climate in which the policeman finds himself after he joins the force.

The improved "emotional stability" is possibly due in large measure to more differentiated recruitment policies. Of course, the quality of leadership undoubtedly has something to do with this change. Detailed data concerning these factors must await more intensive study of the recent cases. On the basis of available statistics, in at least one more important respect the recent picture resembles the earlier one: The use of firearms is still the predominant method of police suicide. Of the thirty-eight cases (1960–1966), thirty-one involved the use of a gun.

As we know, the overdetermination of the suicidal act is particularly evident in the specific method of self-destruction. An individual does not merely want to kill himself; he wants to kill himself by a specific method, and there are cases where persons who have been thwarted in their suicidal attempts then abandon their plans. There is, of course, also a wide range of differences with regard to the sadistic quality of the suicidal act. Apparently, the wish to inflict a severe injury on one's own body plays a role in the choice of the method of suicide.

Today, in 1967, at least a few things are less questionable than they were thirty years ago. There has been, indeed, an upsurge of interest in the field of suicide prevention in the last decade. Numerous publications have been circulated and suicide prevention centers are being organized in many cities throughout the country. On the other hand, we are still confronted by the same basic problems and the same basic challenges as we were thirty years ago. With further research in depth perhaps we may hope to find reliable diagnostic criteria and enhance a prophylaxis of suicide.

**Part IV**

# TAXONOMIC AND FORENSIC ESSAYS

Clear definition and meaningful classification of self-destructive phenomena are crucial both to comprehensive current understanding and to solid future advances in the prevention of self-destruction in man. We must always press for improved conceptualizations, believing that there are few things as practical as good theory. This section contains chapters concerned with definition, classification, and theory-building, and the importance of having several diverse disciplines converge on common areas of investigation.

Lawrence Kubie, in his chapter, reminds us that "many goals other than self-destruction may play a determining role in suicidal efforts." Among these determinants he discusses the roles of fantasies, concealed purposes, acts of deliberation, preconscious or unconscious motivations, and "mixed constellations of these inarticulate, contradictory and conflicting determinants." Throughout this chapter, he focusses on the all-important differences between fantasy and action. His paper also contains a semantic warning that the word "suicide" has many roots and purposes and that "death" is not always the univalent objective of "suicidal" behavior.

Even in this volume written by individuals representing many disciplines, Theodore Curphey's contribution presents a somewhat novel but obviously important point of view. Representing the profession of pathology, Dr. Curphey not only espouses his own specialty but, moreover, he persuasively presents for our consideration the usefulness of multidisciplinary approaches to the certification and understanding of deaths. He illustrates his chapter from his own vast experience as a chief medical examiner-coroner. It may very well be that Dr. Curphey is the first psychodynamically-oriented coroner in the world concerned, appropriately, with all aspects of sudden and unexpected deaths, and especially with the application of the "Psychological Autopsy" procedure in the accurate certification of death.

Kresten Bjerg, writing from the vantage point of a student of phenomenology, constructs a model which "is meant as an illustration of the different causal aspects found in a variety of suicidal situations," using over 700 suicide notes (on deposit in the files of the Suicide Prevention Center) for his analysis. Through his model, he attempts to "make a diagrammatic representation of essential recurring traits of the life spaces" of individuals who have committed suicide. Students of Kurt Lewin will be especially interested in Bjerg's topological presentation of self-destructive life-space.

Halmuth Schaefer's chapter reports some first experiments in a paper which may well stimulate, surprise, and provoke many readers. Students of comparative psychology as well as of human nature will be interested in the implications of these studies related to the topic of infrahuman self-destruction. In his chapter, Dr. Schaefer kindly indicates that some of the impetus for his study came from discussions with me; perhaps this is the place to say that I can claim no credit at all for the directions in which his own imagination and initiative have taken him.

The final chapter is built around the following hypothesis: Within a person there are discernible relationships between his self-destructive behaviors and the patterns of his temporary and his partial "deaths," especially as seen in the nuances of his sleep behaviors. The chapter, after suggesting a set of concepts as substitutes for our current notions of "death" and "suicide" and examining some relationships between time of life and type of crisis, reports data gathered daily over a year from seven individuals, relating their sleep behaviors to their day-to-day changes in self-destructive status.

# 20. Multiple Determinants of Suicide*

LAWRENCE S. KUBIE

Although continuing interest in this ancient problem of suicide has been expressed in a series of fairly recent researches and reports on this topic,[1] the study of the determinants of suicidal behavior is hampered by serious difficulty in sampling. Since the completed suicide can no longer speak, his motives can never be studied directly; at best they can be reconstructed retrospectively. To what extent, then, are we justified in applying to those who succeed in dying that which we learn from the study of those who survive, when we cannot be sure that the latter are not a weighted sample? It is nonetheless important to survey the survivors, because any effort to anticipate and forestall suicide must take into account the goals and the clinical settings of all who make the attempt. This is especially true because among those who die, some do so only by accident. In this connection, the "psychological autopsies" on equivocal "suicide-accident" deaths which are conducted at the Suicide Prevention Center are revealing.[2] The procedure has been described in *The Cry for Help*.[3]

Many goals other than self-destruction may play a determining role in suicidal efforts.[4] As examples:

The suicidal attempt may express a fantasy of returning to infancy for the purpose of living life over again. In describing several such efforts, one patient put it, "I wanted to go right back to the very edge of obliteration *but not over the edge*. Then I could start afresh."

* This chapter is revised and adapted from an editorial on "Multiple Determinants of Suicide" which appeared in *The Journal of Nervous and Mental Disease*, 138:3–8, 1964. 

The concealed purpose may be a longing to change sides, e.g., to change from man to woman or from woman to man.

Another version of this goal may be a hidden need to obliterate a congenital defect by growing up all over again without it: in one patient a huge facial birthmark, in another a harelip, in a third a deformed hand and arm.

Other suicidal efforts evolve out of a fantasy of joining someone who has died. This fantasy need not be of death, but it may be linked either to a concomitant hidden denial of the reality of death in general or of the other's death or else to a hidden belief in spiritual and/or corporeal immortality. Thus it may mean *living* together in perpetuity.

Many suicidal efforts are acts of deliberate and conscious rage, or they may arise out of an unconscious need for vengeance. Quite regularly, these are accompanied by a concealed fantasy of living on to relish the suffering which has been caused.

Contrariwise, some suicidal attempts are acts of self-punishment and self-mutilation to expiate profound guilt feelings, which may be conscious or deeply buried.

Alternatively the goal may be to propitiate and thus to avoid punishment.

Another preconscious or unconscious goal may be to avert the possibility of yielding to forbidden impulses.

Mixed constellations of several of these inarticulate, contradictory, and conflicting determinants are frequent. Their recognition is more than an academic exercise. Because they may betray themselves in different ways, may be accompanied by varied affects, and may give different warning signals, it is important to keep these varied and multiple determinants in mind, watching to see which are regular and which exceptional, and also to ascertain their correlations with age, sex, national origin, education, cultural level, religion, and the like. The signals which may warn of an impending act are necessarily different when the act itself, however uniform its outcome, expresses such widely varied constellations of inner needs. Even when on the surface the symptomatology appears to be constant, the subtler hints (such as their manifestations in moods, dreams, and fantasies) will not be identical. Thus a search for some simple rule of thumb as a constant warning is hardly likely to succeed.

Related to this general issue is a problem which runs through all of psychopathology. What is it which determines the boundary between fantasy and action, between dream and somnambulism, between obsession and compulsion, between wishing to injure somebody and actually going out to injure him, between fantasies of suicide and an actual suicidal effort? This difference between the symbolic representation of an impulse and the active execution of the impulse is one of the more general problems of all psychopathology, yet it is one that is least explored and least understood.

The layman tries to dispose of this by assumptions about simple quantitative differences: "If he wants to die hard enough he will succeed." This is convenient. It puts the blame squarely where we feel most comfortable with it—on the shoulders of the patient. It also serves the self-inflating purpose of making us feel superior by nurturing the illusion that we have understood and explained something when in fact we have only redescribed it in circular terms.

The psychoanalyst uses the same fallacious illogic when he translates the same type of reasoning into the allegorical language of investments of libido, cathexis, narcissism, or masochism.

One unanticipated phenomenon associated with suicide is the resentment that is generated when the drive toward suicide is lost through therapy. Thus one male patient who had made repeated suicidal attempts, and who in a real sense began to get well, became furiously angry and felt deprived because suicide was no longer a way out for him. This is an informative aspect of the problem and one which has been little explored.

The types of psychopathological soil out of which suicidal efforts can arise are many and varied. In patients who are subject to recurrent bouts of relatively mild anxiety or depression, sudden intensification may precipitate suicide efforts. Not infrequently this occurs when a hidden fear of insanity suddenly erupts into consciousness. This is one reason why it may occur as a patient is on his way to his initial psychiatric consultation, or immediately after a first consultation, and this even when the consultation itself has been reassuring.

Sudden terror of recurrence of psychosis: I have known suicide to be attempted out of a sudden terror that a previous psychosis was about to return. In one patient this occurred after a dream in which some of the symptoms of a prior psychotic episode had been reexperienced.

Initial panics: Perhaps the most unpredictable suicidal effort may occur without warning when an initial experience of panic occurs in a seemingly calm and undisturbed life. As an example, a man of exceptional strength had stood up sturdily to every kind of external stress until one final straw, intrinsically minor, touched off his first experience of blinding terror. For this he was wholly unprepared; and it led to a nearly fatal effort at self-destruction.

"Recovery" to face impossible situations: Paradoxical and tragic suicidal efforts may occur in a patient who is recovering from a psychosis out of a fear of "getting well," when "getting well" means to the patient that he must return to an unacceptable situation from which he can see no escape other than suicide—especially since the alternative path back into psychosis has been blocked by therapy.

Expiation of death wishes: Suicidal efforts may be attempts to expiate death wishes. This seems more likely to occur in someone who throughout life has been a dedicated supporter of everyone in trouble. Such a man was in fact a compulsive do-gooder, whose benevolence effectively concealed a profound jealousy and hate, which had their roots in a secret sense of having been wronged. His strongest death wishes were directed against a mean, ungrateful, overtly paranoid, and crippled sister. Only once did these death wishes break through in overt form, i.e., in a dream in which the sister had drowned in spite of the dreamer's heroic efforts to rescue her. After a day of brooding, his suicidal attempt occurred the following morning.

Confirmation of painful illusions concerning self-image: A suicidal effort occurred in a professional woman who thought of herself as painfully plain. Actually she was very attractive; but for various reasons she could not allow herself to believe this and violently rejected the idea. On one occasion she imagined that she recognized herself in the account of a male patient who was described in an article written by a friend who happened to be a dermatologist. Her debased self-image and her conviction of the unalterability of her imagined deformity, plus the feeling of public exposure, were so painful that they led to an effort to end her life.

Anniversary reactions: Suicidal efforts can occur on the anniversary of the natural death of a parent, or of his death through suicide. Indeed, suicidal efforts seem not infrequently to follow the patterns of suicidal attempts by father, mother, older brother, or older sister. It will be essential to make precise statistical investigations into the relative incidence of suicidal efforts, both successful and unsuccessful, in successive generations, starting with the direct progenitors but including collaterals of both the same and the opposite sex.

Psychosis vs. neurosis: There are no adequate data on the relative incidence of suicides in states of psychotic decompensation as compared with their incidence in the neuroses. Therefore any assumption that suicidal efforts imply psychosis is fallacious, or at least premature.

Escaping delusional persecution: Among the several kinds of suicidal efforts known to occur in psychotics are efforts to escape delusional persecution. Other efforts may occur during states of partial trance, with and without pseudohallucinatory experiences or vivid hypnagogic reveries, sometimes in response to dreamlike "orders."

Delirious suicides: Behavior with suicidal consequences may also occur in delirious states. These are easily recognized when the deliria are florid; but many deliria are so muted that they are overlooked, particularly in post-operative, toxic-infectious, or pharmacogenic states; and occasionally after ECT or psychosurgery. They may be related to but not identical with the suicidal "accidents" that are noted below as occurring during "blackouts" with automatic repetitive acts.

Accidental suicide through toxic perseveration: Automatic repetitive behavior with blackouts can simulate purposive suicide, even to the point of death or near-death. This may happen in various states of intoxication, notably under the influence of a combination of alcohol and barbiturates. Not infrequently, even in the absence of any suicidal intent this results in the unwitting ingestion of more and more pills and alcohol, over the brink of death. How often this occurs is not known; but it probably occurs more often than is generally recognized; and it must be regarded as an "accidental suicide."

Ticklike suicides: There is another form of tenaciously repetitive suicidal behavior which constitutes a special problem in that the suicidal action acquires the independent, clocklike automaticity of a tick. In two patients known to me these automatic repetitive acts had resisted the most skillful and intensive analytic therapy by various experienced colleagues who represented different schools of theory and techniques. After a few ECT the insights that had been acquired during analysis but had remained unused suddenly became accessible for use; and the ticklike suicidal drive disappeared permanently.

Depressive response to success: Of particular significance are the suicides that occur as acute depressive responses to success. Suicides of this type have been recorded among graduate students in various fields and among scientists, writers, painters, musicians, lawyers, and financiers.

A suicidal purpose masked by an hysterical pseudoeuphoria: A not infrequent suicide is carried out from behind a mask of "*belle indifférence*," a mask which sometimes forms only after the decision to commit suicide has been reached *in secret*. Because it is not easy to differentiate between this *belle indifférence* and the genuine lifting of a depression, the family, the family physician, and the psychiatrist are often fooled by it.

Social and cultural variables: Interacting with these complex and varied intrapsychic determinants are many social, cultural, and religious variables, such as the different values placed on life, death, and afterlife in different faiths and cultures. Not all men expect to be punished for suicide or for efforts at suicide; but even when punishment is expected the influence of the anticipation of punishment will not be uniform. For instance, the threat of punishment in afterlife does not deter the man who has a profound conscious or unconscious need for punishment. Instead it provides him with an added incentive for suicide.

Some questions about warnings: Many questions about the evaluation and recognition of warning signals remain unanswered. For instance, what does "thinking about suicide" indicate? What is its significance when it is sporadic or obsessive, sad, angry, or fearful, or when it is under delusional influences? What does thinking about suicide indicate when the patient thinks silently and does not talk about it, or when he speaks of it freely and frequently or only occasionally, or when he shows a consistent affect, a varying affective state, or no affect at all when he talks about suicide? What of those who talk as a magical way of warding it off; or those who talk out of rage to threaten or else to allay panic because they are afraid that their foot may slip, i.e., that the suicide may occur "accidentally on purpose"? (Among these are the precipice-walkers who flirt with suicide.)

Since dreams are visual samples of the condensed preconscious processes of the sleeper, will the study of the dreams of those who have attempted suicide furnish clues that have not yet been adequately explored?

Presuicidal disturbances may occur in all metabolic functions (such as eating and excreting) that influence weight, sleep, and the like. These too require detailed study if they are to be used as clues.

Related to this is a practical question: do the precautions that hospitals usually take against suicide actually protect? Does hospital experience give conclusive evidence as to whether suicidal precautions prevent suicidal efforts or encourage them? How often do such precautions merely thwart the suicidal effort by preventing its success? Or do they serve primarily the natural emotional needs of the staff, such as the need to allay their own anxieties and their own guilt? Or do they serve to avert criticism of the younger men by the administrative hierarchy, who in turn need protection against criticism from trustees and from public authorities or families? Finally, to what extent are the evaluations of precautionary measures influenced by the need to protect hospitals from damage suits? In varying degrees all of these needs are valid; but we cannot allow them to bias our scientific judgment about the efficacy of precautionary measures. As a matter of fact, without fully documenting their views, some hospital authorities have claimed in personal communications that when suicidal precautions were discontinued the suicide rate dropped, in one instance to zero for nearly twenty years.

There are some incomplete recent data which suggest that the use of tranquilizers may lead to premature discharge from hospitals, which among other unhappy consequences may increase both the relapse rate and the incidence of post-hospital suicides. These possibilities merit further investigation.

It would seem doubtful that we could gather so many threads into any single cohesive pattern of motivation, affect, conflict, need, impulse, symbols, and warnings. Since each symbol is itself multivalent, it is more likely that the search for any one set of determinants of suicide will not succeed and that no universal warnings exist. At most there may be certain recurring settings which signal danger; but within each of these settings, and with or without warnings, the suicidal constellation will range from abstract preoccupation through timid and innocuous gestures to determined and final acts. Consequently no warning can be consistently meaningful; and to confine every such patient as a suicidal risk might well defeat all therapeutic effort. Indeed we may be forced to choose between evils. We must ask whether we even want to aspire to the prevention of every suicide if such an effort would render us therapeutically impotent?

In conclusion: The mixed purposes which lead to any action rarely have a simple and direct relation either to the immediate goal or to the remote consequences of the act. Nevertheless the assumption is usually made that whatever happens is what we "really" sought, whether we knew it or not. We find this assumption both in the vernacular of the street and in sophisticated psychoanalytic theory, although it has been shown repeatedly that this is not true, not even for those activities which meet our biogenetic needs.[5] Even here conscious, preconscious, and unconscious goals play a larger role than does biochemistry in determining what we do. If this is true for our basic bodily processes and needs and for their derivatives, then it is hardly likely that the underlying purpose of every suicidal effort is death, especially when man is rarely able to accept realistically the prospect of his own obliteration, of actually ceasing to exist. He can contemplate the deaths of others with relative ease, but the contemplation of his own death remains a remote, elusive, unreal, and abstract concept.

The study of those who have failed at suicide makes it possible to penetrate the verbal mask that is embodied in the stereotype "suicide" and reveals that suicidal efforts can have many roots and purposes, among which the concept of death may play a minor role, if any. Only rarely is death the single or major goal.

Students of suicide have been unduly influenced by the uniformity and finality of the end result. They have assumed that suicide is invariably the expression of an impulse to put an end to living. If this were uniformly true it would be relatively easy to recognize warnings of its imminence, to begin appropriate preventive maneuvers, and to understand and describe its dynamics. These would be viewed as different facets of a process with one single goal. But since suicide can occur at the end of many different roads, there is no one goal and no one warning. Once achieved, however, death is a single state which reduces all complexities to a single common denominator. It is this which has misled psychoanalysts and others into treating the multivalent objectives of suicidal behavior as though they could all be characterized by the one word "death."

This summary of a few clinical observations on suicidal efforts and their unconscious and/or preconscious goals is neither complete nor exhaustive. It is intended as a challenge to us to investigate the problem of suicide with a clear understanding of its many aspects and of its peculiar difficulties.

## REFERENCES

1. For example: L. I. Dublin, *Suicide: A Sociological and Statistical Study* (New York: The Ronald Press Company, 1963); N. L. Farberow and E. S. Shneidman, *The Cry for Help* (New York: McGraw-Hill Book Company, 1961); K. A. Menninger, *Man Against Himself* (New York: Harcourt, Brace and World, Inc., 1938); P. Sainsbury, *Suicide in London: An Ecological Study* (London: Maudsley Monograph Series No. 1, 1955); E. S. Shneidman, and N. L. Farberow, *Clues to Suicide* (New York: McGraw-Hill Book Company, 1957); E. Stengel, and N. G. Cook, *Attempted Suicide: Its Social Significance and Effects* (London: Maudsley Monograph Series No. 4, 1958).
2. R. E. Litman, E. S. Shneidman, N. L. Farberow, N. D. Tabachnick, and T. J. Curphey, "Investigations of Equivocal Suicides," *Journal of the American Medical Association,* **184**:924–929, 1963.
3. Farberow and Shneidman, *op. cit.*
4. E. S. Shneidman, "Orientations Toward Death: A Vital Aspect of the Study of Lives," in R. W. White (ed.), *The Study of Lives* (New York: Atherton Press, 1963), pp. 200–207.
5. L. S. Kubie, "Instincts and Homeostasis," *Psychosomatic Medicine,* **10**:15–30, 1948; also in S. Lorand, (ed.), *Yearbook of Psychoanalysis, 1949* (New York: International Universities Press, Inc., 1950), vol. V., pp. 157–188; L. S. Kubie, "Influence of Symbolic Processes on the Role of Instincts in Human Behavior," *Psychosomatic Medicine,* **18**:189–208, 1956.

# 21. The Forensic Pathologist and the Multidisciplinary Approach to Death

THEODORE J. CURPHEY

The very opportunity offered to contribute to a volume of essays on self-destruction represents one more step in the historic continuum of the role of the pathologist in the fight against disease. As a prelude, one might do no better than to quote from Lester J. Evans's Preface to Samuel Bloom's recent book *The Doctor and His Patient: A Sociological Interpretation*. Evans says: "Medicine is in the midst of a period of transition and challenge, not unlike the situation it faced one hundred years ago. In response, it is again reaching outside itself, but now, secure in its century-old partnership with the natural sciences, it seeks the added collaboration of the behavioral sciences."[1]

The investigator in the field of forensic pathology is primarily concerned with matters of sudden and unexpected death and faces certain problems that are centered in the field of the behavioral sciences. As a result, he welcomes the opportunity to be associated with such a distinguished group of behavioral scientists as are represented in this volume. He thus embodies, in the presentation of certain aspects of self-destruction peculiar to his special interest, the spirit of Evans's words in seeking the added collaboration of the behavioral scientist in the study and clarification of this most important problem.

The heterogeneity of professional backgrounds of the contributors to this volume aptly reflects the current approach to the study and the solution of so many of our problems in the broad field of scientific investigation. The day is long since past that any major contribution to knowledge was typically made by the lone investigator in a separate discipline. The progress made in the field of medicine, especially in the past half-century, is well known; and if one views this progress in retrospect, it becomes immediately evident that it has been in great measure attained by the multidisciplinary attack on those medical problems that deal largely with the soma rather than the psyche of the sick human being.

The challenging thought here is whether there is any room for the multidisciplinary approach in an attack on the problems of mental illness. One need only cite as evidence the progress that has resulted from the recent psychopharmacological studies as a consequence of the entrance of the pharmacologist and the biochemist into the field. This interdisciplinary approach has blazed the trail, and its success points to the need for involving other disciplines in a larger assault on the total problem. This is especially true if we are to reduce the morbidity and mortality of attempted or accomplished suicide.

It is a cardinal principle in scientific investigation that before one seeks for a solution of any problem, one must first outline its boundaries and then concentrate one's attack on specific areas that lie within its confines—the difference between the precision of the rifle and that of the shotgun. It would seem that with limited exceptions, our approach to the problem of suicide in the past has been with the shotgun rather than the rifle.

For example, a very fundamental question deals initially with the true incidence of suicide, whether in this or any other country. It is generally agreed that the present statistical evidence leaves much to be desired because of the dissimilarity in methods of reporting suicidal deaths and the wide spectrum in which the individuals responsible for the certification lie, ranging from the lay coroner with no scientific training, little personal interest, and a definite emotional bias conditioned by the social mores of his environment, on the one hand, to the forensic pathologist, on the other hand, who certifies these deaths on the basis of the findings of the pathologist, the toxicologist, and the trained lay investigator who is at the scene of the death. Because of the current state of statisical confusion, a prime prerequisite would be to document with a greater degree of accuracy the true incidence of suicidal deaths.

There are, however, other specific areas that are inestimably more important than the statistical frequency of suicide; joint study offers great opportunity for obtaining new insights into old problems. One of the most promising at this time is the multidisciplinary approach involving the collaboration of the pathologist with the behavorial scientist, especially the psychologist, the psychiatrist, and the psychiatric social worker—members of the staff of the Suicide Prevention Center.

Such studies have been in progress in Los Angeles County since 1958.[2] In each year since 1958, the medical examiner's office in Los Angeles County has certified approximately 1,000 cases of suicide. Of these, approximately 30 percent were cases of death due to drug intoxication and about 60 percent were cases of death from gunshot wounds; the remaining 10 percent of the cases were ascribed to hanging, cutting, carbon monoxide, etc., methods which by and large offer no problem of accurate certification as to mode of death, except possibly in the instance of carbon monoxide poisoning.

The method of handling a case of suspected suicide by the interdisciplinary approach in our office is as follows:

After the acceptance of a case, a police officer is notified and proceeds to the scene of the death. After his investigation, he submits a report to our office. A report is also prepared at the scene by a nonmedical investigator from our office who is also charged with the removal of the case to either the central office or to an outlying mortuary in the County of Los Angeles. This latter report, as would be expected, is more detailed than is the police report if the death is nonviolent or noncriminal.

By this approach, the medical examiner is now supplied with the pertinent facts of the case derived from two different sources having different investigative viewpoints. This provides the basis for his decision as to whether to perform an autopsy or to release a certificate on the strength of the investigative data, but only after the body has been examined to rule out external evidence of injury. It would be better if the medical examiner obtained all or part of this information through a personal visit to the scene, but this is not possible at present because of the shortage of trained personnel; and indeed it is a moot question in some quarters as to the actual need for this as a routine practice.

The present procedure then entails (1) the review of the two reports, (2) the performance of an autopsy when indicated, including if necessary a microscopic study of all or certain key organs in the case, and (3) a toxicological study when indicated, following which a cause of death and the mode of death is arrived at by the pathologist. If a suicide note is found, the handwriting expert is asked for an opinion, and if the note is authentic, the case is certified as "suicide" without further consultation. An estimated 20 to 30 percent of suicides leave notes. If no note is found and the facts suggest a probable suicide or if the case is equivocal as to mode of death, then consultation is requested from the "death investigation team" of the Suicide Prevention Center.

In another group of cases where the pathologist is unable to determine from the documentary and laboratory evidence whether the appropriate mode of death is accidental, suicidal, or in rare instances even natural, then the file is submitted to the psychological team for their study. By far the largest single group of such cases are those associated with drug ingestion, chiefly barbiturates and/or tranquilizers.

The psychological study typically consists of interviewing persons who knew the deceased, e.g., the spouse, grown children, neighbors, employers, physicians, etc., in an attempt to reconstruct the life style of the deceased. In their investigation they try to obtain relevant information about any psychiatric idiosyncrasies or prodromal clues to suicide that the victim may have voiced. Following this they make a scientific extrapolation of the victim's behavior over the days preceding his death, using all the information they have obtained.

To emphasize the nature of their study, they have coined the descriptive term "psychological autopsy" as a connotation of its post-mortem nature and its scientific content. The psychological autopsy focuses on what is usually the missing element, namely the *intention* of the deceased in relation to his own death.

The types of information gathered by the suicide team fall under the following headings: (1) Anamnestic or life history details (such as history of previous suicide attempts); (2) psychiatric-psychological data (such as indices of depression and agitation; for example, recent loss of appetite, loss of interest, or change in habit patterns); (3) communication information, i.e., indications of morbid content of thought as exemplified in such statements as, "I can't go on," "Life isn't worth much," or, "I'm a worthless person"; and (4) nonpsychiatric information which may not be primarily psychological in nature but which nevertheless frequently appears in the course of certain investigations, where the scene of the death is personally viewed by a member of the team and where material evidence found at the scene throws additional light on the mode of death, e.g., discovery of a small mophead stuffed in the drain of a bathtub, indicating that the victim had made careful preparation for death by ensuring that there was sufficient water in the bathtub in which to drown.

Following the collection of all this information, members of the team discuss the case by the conference method, and then a written report with their final opinion is prepared. This report is in the nature of a confidential communication to the medical examiner. This report is subsequently discussed in detail in seminar fashion with the chief medical examiner and his staff in person at regular staff conferences. Following this, a certificate on the cause and mode of death is then issued.

It is important to recognize that in their expression of opinion, the consultants confine themselves to their special fields of training and interest, and by the very nature of the cases submitted to them for study, they are called upon to say only whether they think the mode of death is suicide or not. If there is psychiatric or psychological evidence to support their determination, they elaborate on it in their written opinion. If, on the other hand, the available investigative and medical evidence, coupled with their special study, leads to an equivocal opinion, then the mode of death is considered as "undetermined." In this latter group the difficulty arises in resolving the question as to whether the mode is either accidental or suicidal, in which case the mode is certified as "accident-suicide-undetermined." Incidentally, the majority of these indeterminate cases are instances where barbiturate intoxication is the cause of death and where alcohol is found in sufficient amounts in the blood as to raise the question whether the victim was under the influence and might have accidentally taken an overdose as a consequence.

In this same connection, we encounter a rare case where there is a documented history of addiction to barbiturates and where, as a consequence, not only the mode but also the cause of death is in question. With our present scant knowledge relative to the interpretation of blood levels in barbiturate addicts, we are reluctant to accept as prima facie evidence of lethal intoxication in an addict those blood levels that we now associate with deaths from barbiturate intoxication in the nonaddicted individual. A real problem further develops when one is confronted with a case showing a high concentration of barbiturates in the blood and no documented history of addiction, and where, unfortunately, no autopsy has been performed but the case is certified as one of barbiturate intoxication. Following this, the family protests the certification and produces medical evidence to show that the deceased was in fact an addict and raises the question whether the death might not indeed have been from natural causes.

The problem is further complicated when psychological investigation of the life style of the deceased in such a case fails to yield any evidence that favors the probability of suicide. Under these circumstances then, one is forced to admit that both the cause and the mode of death are undetermined because of failure to perform an autopsy to rule out a possible natural death. Fortunately, this type of case is rarely encountered, but this rarity might be more fancied than real, because in so many of these drug deaths the on-the-scene interrogation frequently fails to go into the possibility and extent of addiction.

The following case abstracts are presented to illustrate various aspects of the problems alluded to above.

*Case* 1. A fifty-year-old female was found dead in her bed. Her last visit to her physician was four days before her death. He refused to issue a death certificate. The case was reported to the medical examiner as a natural death. The deceased had been treated previously by another physician for a back injury received in an auto accident many years before. No further information was supplied by the investigating police officer. The autopsy showed old surgical scars in the lumbosacral, upper midline, and low midline abdominal regions as well as an old healed gastrojejunostomy. Moderate pulmonary edema was also present. Toxicological examination of blood revealed the absence of alcohol, barbiturates 1.5 mg % with phenobarbital absent, and glutethimide (Doriden) 2.1 mg %. The cause of death was certified as acute drug intoxication and the mode as "accident-suicide-undetermined." As is the practice in this type of case, consultation was sought with the death investigation team. The psychological autopsy revealed a long history of barbiturate addiction to relieve the severe pain as a result of her back injury. The physician who had treated her for her back injury reported that she had been previously treated by three psychiatrists and had complained of intolerable pain and had stated on several occasions that she could not go on much longer. She had admitted to a suicide attempt fifteen months prior to her death when she was hospitalized and then later changed her story and said that it was an accident. Her past history included a considerable number of traumatic experiences, namely, her first husband burned to death in her presence, her mother reportedly died in an explosion in the operating room during a gastric operation, and her father was a chronic alcoholic who was sadistic and beat both the deceased and her mother. She also stated during her psychiatric interviews that she was unhappily married. Prior to the suicide attempt she had been hospitalized for an acute psychotic break from which she recovered rapidly. On the basis of the foregoing, the consulting team recommended certification of the mode of death as "probable suicide" and an affidavit to correct the mode was subsequently forwarded to the State Bureau of Vital Statistics.

*Case* 2. A fifty-seven-year-old female who, according to the police officers, was found dead floating face down in a bathtub with her left leg sticking out of the tub. No other pertinent information was recorded in the police report. The autopsy revealed acute pulmonary edema and moderate arteriosclerosis of the cardiovascular system. Toxicological examination showed a blood barbiturate level of 2.2 mg % phenobarbital and 0.25% alcohol. The cause of death was certified as asphyxia due to drowning, with acute alcoholic intoxication as a contributory cause. The mode was listed as accident-suicide-undetermined and was referred to the suicide team for consultation. The psychological autopsy established a definite suspicion on the part of her personal physicians that the deceased and her husband were addicted to alcohol. The husband reported that the deceased had been a social drinker until about two years before her death when she began to imbibe quite heavily. She had never spoken of depression or suicide. He stated that on the night of her death when he went looking for her to tell her that it was about time for her favorite television program, he found her dead in the bathroom and it looked as though she had placed one foot in the tub and had fallen on her face into the tub full of water. Both faucets were on and the water was going out of the overflow. She had removed her watch, and her bathing suit was lying across the bed as though she had planned to put it on after her bath in order to have a dip in the pool with him before dinner. He said that they often swam before dinner and that she often took a hot bath to sober up. The husband further related that she had fallen on her face while intoxicated at least four times during the past year. On the basis of the above findings, the recommendation of a mode of "probable accident" was made, following which an affidavit to correct the death certificate was issued by the medical examiner's office.

*Case* 3. A twenty-three-year-old single woman was found unconscious in a garage by friends, with marks of a beating about her head. She was admitted to the hospital and died in profound shock shortly after, with a diagnosis of intracranial hemorrhage vs. drug overdosage. The case was investigated by the homicide detail of the police department which provided no pertinent information at the time of the autopsy. Following the autopsy and the toxicological findings, they later reported that the victim was a prostitute and a drug addict with a known police record, that she had attempted suicide in the past with barbiturates, that she had been in a mental institution, that the beating had been administered by one of two male suspects associated with her and some other girls during an evening of debauchery and sexual intercourse, and that one of the men had been "rolled" of his wallet. The autopsy revealed recent superficial injuries to the face and body, with the presence of two black eyes, contusion and swelling of the lips, and contusion and superficial hemorrhage of the left side of the chin and neck. Fatty metamorphosis of the liver, a condition frequently found in chronic alcoholism, was also present. It was felt by the pathologist at the time that none of these findings caused or contributed to her death. The toxicologist reported no evidence of alcohol in the blood but a barbiturate level of 4.6 mg %, 1.2 mg % of which was phenobarbital. The cause of death was certified as acute barbiturate intoxication and the mode as accident-suicide-undetermined, and the case was referred for psychological consultation.

The psychological autopsy confirmed the police report of previous suicide attempts, the last attempt being about two months before her death. These attempts were always with pills. She was a known narcotic and pill addict. She had been committed to a state hospital for treatment of her addiction six months before her death and was under treatment there for about three months. She had seen a psychiatrist about six weeks before her death and was under treatment at the time of her death. Her parents reported that she was known to have said that her hospitalization was her last chance for rehabilitation and that she felt that her treatment there was a failure. On the basis of their investigation, the consultants recommended a certification of "probable suicide." An affidavit was subsequently issued to amend the death certificate.

*Case* 4. Parenthetically this case is presented to highlight the controversial question of the part so-called "automatism" plays in deaths from drug intoxication. Following routine nonpsychological investigation of a case showing at autopsy significant values of alcohol and barbiturates together present in the blood, and lacking a suicide note, the family invariably claims that the mode of death is accidental, postulating that the victim while under the influence of alcohol was either unaware of the number of pills he took in a single dose or had lost count of the number he took in repeated doses. That the latter circumstance can exist is illustrated by the following case.

A fifty-year-old male was found dead in a motel room. A nearly empty whiskey bottle and a vial containing eleven white capsules were found on a nearby desk. An envelope addressed to the Los Angeles police was found containing a handwritten note apologizing to the police for causing them "all this trouble." Another note addressed to his wife in part stated: "As I write I will take sleeping pills. I also have a bottle of Scotch which I wash down the pills with. If my letter gets silly you will know it is because I am getting drunk." From here the writing becomes less legible and after several more lines the note ended, "I am now going to take four more pills. I just lost count." The autopsy showed pulmonary edema and chronic disease of the gall bladder with gallstones. The toxicologist reported a blood alcohol level of 0.26% associated with a barbiturate value of 0.7 mg %, with phenobarbital excluded. The capsules found at the scene turned out to be a cold remedy containing acetanilid, phenacetin, and codein. The death was certified as acute ethanol and barbiturate intoxication and the mode of death was certified as "suicide."

This case demonstrates that it is indeed possible to lose count of the number of pills taken while under the influence of alcohol, but it cannot be cited as supporting the theory of automatism. On the contrary, the suicide note establishes the fact that the repeated pill-taking was based on a conscious motivation. Because of the interest of the consulting psychiatrists and psychologists in the theory of automatism, the case was brought to their attention. Provided with the note and the toxicology report they made a retrospective study to see whether any prodromal symptoms and change in his life style existed that would have provided them with enough evidence to certify the mode if the suicide note had been lacking. Their study resulted in establishing the fact that the deceased had had a recent change in character and change in his life style associated with a separation from his wife, that he had neglected his business, gambled, drank excessively, and had disappeared for about two months, returning extremely depressed after writing a series of bad checks. None of this information was available in the police report. The summary of the psychiatrist who studied the case stated in part: "If we had not had a suicide note from this man, the findings of the blood test would have suggested accidental death in an alcoholic. However, the psychological autopsy would have corrected this impression and produced the correct certification of suicide. I consider this case to have worked out as a validation of the method of psychological autopsy."

*Case* 5. A sixty-year-old male was found dead by his wife in his pickup truck in his garage. The police report failed to state whether the doors to the garage were closed and whether the ignition switch was on. The case was investigated by the medical examiner's office and it was found that the deceased had left home at about 6 A.M. to look for work. At approximately 9 A.M. his wife noticed the truck in the garage, and went out to check it, and found her husband dead, slumped over the steering wheel. She stated that the deceased had been seen by a physician four months previously and was told he had an enlarged heart. Autopsy revealed a markedly enlarged heart, weighing 650 grams (normal is 350–400 grams), with left ventricular hypertrophy as well as the presence of fatty metamorphosis of the liver. The toxicologist reported the finding in the blood of 0.25% of alcohol and 95% of carbon monoxide saturation. The cause of death was acute carbon monoxide intoxication with a contributory cause of acute alcoholism. The mode was listed as "accident-suicide-undetermined." The case was referred for psychological consultation. On interview the wife stated that the deceased was an alcoholic and drank increasingly during the period of five months prior to his death. During this period, which began with the loss of his job, he showed typical signs of a severe depression. The consultant felt that these facts would be indicative of suicide, but he learned from the wife that there were no doors on the garage and that the ignition key was turned off—findings that are unusual in suicide from carbon monoxide. The final psychological opinion on the basis of the evidence as to the mode was "accident-suicide-undetermined." This case indicates the difficulty frequently encountered in determining the mode when the primary cause of death is associated with acute alcoholic intoxication irrespective of whether it is a case of asphyxia from drowning, carbon monoxide intoxication, or ingestion of a barbiturate when no suicide note is found at the scene.

It should be apparent that the foregoing cases illustrate the value of a more comprehensive study of the problem of suicide with special reference to those circumstances peculiar to deaths from drug intoxication. As the study has taken shape, it has become more and more obvious that the solution of the problem does not lie simply in the interdisciplinary approach to the study of the individual case; on the contrary, it has seemed that the more precise the approach by the multidisciplinary route the more are the problems that present themselves for resolution. For example, it seems to us that the two most pressing problems that now deserve study are (1) the proper evaluation of the blood barbiturate level in the addicted individual with respect to what is to be regarded as the lethal dose level, a matter of fundamental importance bearing on the metabolism of the drug as to whether it differs in the addicted and nonaddicted individual, and (2) the interpretation of the combined ethanol and barbiturate blood level as it relates to synergism, automatism, and suicidal intent.

When these matters have been further investigated by the toxicologist and the psychologist, the knowledge gained should be valuable in contributing to the precision now needed in certifying these deaths as to cause and mode, for without this knowledge we are forced to conclude that currently we work in an area of uncertainty that calls for greater refinement if we are fully to discharge our professional responsibilities in relation to this thorny problem of suicide.

In retrospect, two general impressions and practical implications from the investigations by the death investigation team of equivocal deaths seem to have emerged:

1. The serious limitations faced by the coroner or medical examiner when problems of certification are resolved on superficial or incomplete evidence or on impressions and preconceived opinions—rather than on the objective accumulation of all the possible facts, including histological, toxicological, and psychological data—seem to be well documented. The

medicolegal agency must avoid fictitious accuracy if it expects to enjoy the confidence of the other agencies and interests in the community. Altogether too many certificates of death fall within this category of fictitious accuracy; more especially are they in those jurisdictions where there is no semblance of the scientific method in studying the case material. In fact, it may be that one good criterion by which to evaluate the scientific accuracy of a medicolegal office is, paradoxically, the percentage of equivocal deaths annually certified as of undetermined cause or mode. Parenthetically it might be stated that even after their intensive investigations, the death investigation team will not infrequently recommend an "accident-suicide-undetermined" certification, indicating that the equivocal nature of the matter was not resolved. One practical result of such realistic certification is the increased accuracy and validity of statistics for modes of death.

2. In addition, the real therapeutic benefits that often occur as the result of team members' contacts with the bereaved survivors of the deceased which deserve mention. Team members report that on several occasions the surviving widow or surviving grown child has indicated to them, at the conclusion of their interviews, that the sessions had been a helpful and therapeutic experience for them. Because of their special skills, they are alert, in their interviews with survivors of persons who have committed suicide, for evidence of extreme guilt, serious depression, and the need for special help on formulating plans for solving specific problems, such as caring for children whose parent has committed suicide. Since we noted this phenomenon, the medical examiner's office has, in some few cases, referred distraught survivors of suicide victims to members of the death investigation team specifically for supportive interviews, even when the suicidal mode of death was not in doubt. Far from being "ghoulish" or untoward, these investigations, sensitively conducted, have been welcomed by professionals and by the community.

This chapter has emphasized some changing concepts in the field of forensic medicine and pointed out, at least implicitly, the opportunities offered to those working in this field to help shape the pattern of future development of this speciality. With the increasing infusion of scientific methods into this field in the past half-century, we are now at the stage where the investigation of sudden or unexpected deaths calls for new approaches, using the skills and knowledge of a broad spectrum of specialties —just as the physician uses many specialties in the diagnosis and treatment of the live patient—in making final judgments concerning the psychosomatics of a man's death.

## REFERENCES

1. New York: Russell Sage Foundation, 1963.
2. T. J. Curphey, "The Role of the Social Scientist in the Medicolegal Certification of Death from Suicide," in N. L. Farberow, and E. S. Shneidman (eds.), *The Cry for Help* (New York: McGraw-Hill Book Company, 1965); R. E. Litman, T. J. Curphey, E. S. Shneidman, N. L. Farberow, and N. D. Tabachnick, "Investigations of Equivocal Suicides," *Journal of the American Medical Association*, **184**:924-929, 1963; and E. S. Shneidman, "Sample Investigations of Equivocal Suicidal Deaths," in Farberow and Shneidman, *op. cit.*

# 22. The Suicidal Life Space: Attempts at a Reconstruction From Suicide Notes

KRESTEN BJERG

Why would anybody commit suicide?

There are those answers provided by the students of the phenomena and there are those provided by the suicidal persons themselves. We are here going to focus on the latter, the experiential causes of suicide.[1]

For any action taken by an individual there exists a matrix of phenomenal causality. When I am doing something—closing a door, writing a letter, applying for a job, divorcing, jumping from the tenth floor, or whatever human beings engage in during their lifetime—it is only on very rare occasions that I would not be able to give at least some answers to the question: "Why do you do that?" My answers can be of all kinds. I might reply: "Because I feel like it," "Because I have to," "Because I can't stand not doing it," or "Because I planned to," "Because she has been nagging me for 20 years," "Because this will bring me a profit of one hundred dollars," "Because this is the only way out," etc.

Such experienced causes for action—such easily emergent phenomenal causes—have never been subjected to a systematic study *per se*, either inside or outside the context of suicide.

The present inquiry represents an attempt at making some kind of order out of the chaos with which the matrix of phenomenal causality is presented to us today.[2]

It is a matter of course that I am thereby not dealing with a *direct* illumination of causal relationships. My interest in the topic, however, stems from a deep-seated conviction about the value of careful descriptions of conscious phenomena in the investigation of dynamic processes. What

I am concerned with here, then, are the reasons present in a given person's mind at the time of a specific act or decision.

The verbalized reports of such phenomena will most often have to be retrospective and usually even a solicited communication to someone (and thus distorted). Especially, this last factor introduces a source of error of considerable magnitude. It may be that no reason or only one reason was experienced simultaneously with the decision or the act. This will not prevent the subject from reporting a variety of reasons, which are essentially post-factum rationalizations. Also, we can often suspect that reasons which are not seen fit for communication are excluded.

One way of overcoming some of these obstacles, or at least reducing some of their consequences, is to examine many accounts of reasons from a multitude of "unsuspicious" people engaged in the same act.

## Materials

Because of the particular nature of the subject, there are only limited opportunities of obtaining phenomenological data pertaining to genuine suicide.

Suicide notes, however, represent a unique type of material when the limited amount of information contained in some notes is counterbalanced by the immediacy of the notes and the possibility of studying many notes.[3] In this case, the materials consist of a large collection of suicide notes compiled by Shneidman and Farberow in collaboration with the Los Angeles County Coroner's Office and previously analyzed by them.[4] The collection includes 706 notes left by persons who committed suicide in Los Angeles County during the years 1944 to 1953.

Although suicide notes do not necessarily contain stated reasons for the suicide, this is more often the case than not. Of the 706 notes inspected, only 138, or less than 20 percent, did not contain any stated causes for the act. They were either wills, or contained practical instructions, statements of identity, or names of relatives to be notified. The remaining 568 notes constitute the basic material for the present analysis. There are exactly three times as many notes written by males as by females, representing an age range of from thirteen years to ninety-six years. The notes are thus fairly representative of a general sample as far as sex and age go.

## Method

Inspecting the notes, I have considered whatever looked like a statement of reason, an explanation, a cause, or a purpose for the act of suicide. A total of approximately four thousand statements was thus collected. It was then attempted, through repeated inspection, grouping, and regrouping of the statements—first with a smaller sample, then with a larger, and, finally, with the total sample—to reach some kind of an ordering of this apparent diversity. It was the aim of the analysis to take account of the more evident differences and similarities among the "causes." The purpose was to reach a number of categories which could form the basis for a generalized model reflecting the varieties of suicidal situations.

The analysis presented the author with a number of difficulties, none of which could be solved in an entirely satisfactory way. These had to do with the premise, inherent in the purpose of the study, that whatever categories were arrived at they should not so much be of a specific, concrete, contentual character, but should rather highlight generalized, abstract, or structural aspects of the "matrix of phenomenal causality." Another premise was that, as far as possible, a "natural" taxonomy (as exemplified by Aristotelean and Linnean procedures) would be desirable.

The search for abstract categories tended to defeat the purpose of a "natural classification," so the easily delineated, outer circumstances such as debts, unemployment, sickness, jealousy, persecution, etc., had to be discarded as main taxonomic clues. On the other hand, there was the bias present in all attempts at a "natural" classification, namely, that the criteria for items being different or alike should ultimately rest on the implicit or explicit concepts already at the disposal of the classifier whether he liked it or not. Thus, the formation of abstract categories was prone to be influenced by the hypothetical constructs of psychological theories familiar to the author.

The process of classifying, therefore, became a hazardous steering between the Scylla of specificity and the Charybdis of making inferences about hypothetical constructs.

## Model

The admittedly somewhat arbitrary compromises resulted in the delineation of a set of categories representing various types of phenomenal reasons for killing oneself.

All categories except a few were found represented in three temporal modes, so that a given cause could be found that belonged to the remembered past, the present, or the anticipated future.

On the basis of these categories, which are delineated below, a model was developed. This model is meant to be an illustration of the different causal aspects found in a variety of suicidal situations. It constitutes an attempt to make a diagrammatic representation of essential recurring traits of the life spaces ultimately referred to by the suicide notes.

Symbols from the Lewinean topology have been used wherever possible. The model is presented as both a very specific and a very generalized instance of the Lewinean field theory. It is specific because it attempts only to represent certain (namely causal) aspects of a certain (namely suicidal) situation; it is generalized because it does not attempt to represent any one individual suicide situation or even any one type of suicide situation but contains a variety of the elements found in diverse, and not necessarily overlapping, suicide situations.

The model, represented in Fig. 1, contains three parts, corresponding to the three temporal modalities of causes.[5]

However, the Lewinean concept of life space has had to be slightly altered in order to be applied to the present problem. It has been necessary to distinguish between life space in a narrow sense and life space in a wide sense.

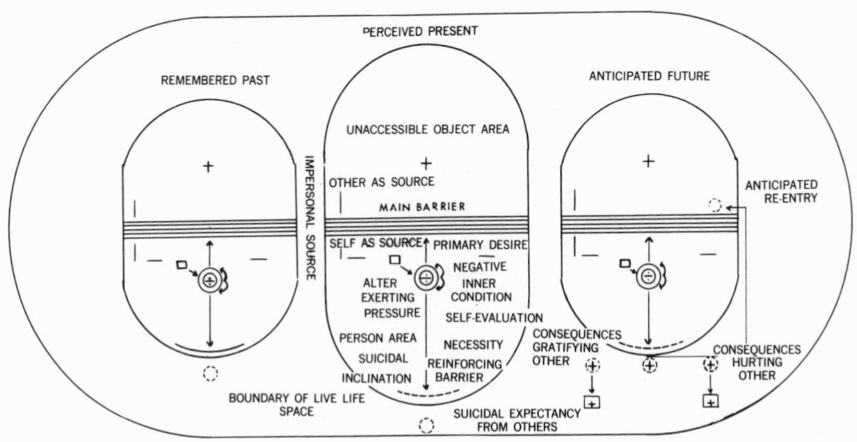


Figure 1
THE MODEL

In the narrower sense, represented by the heavy ovals, we are referring here to the space within which the person is *living*. In the wider sense, we are referring to the space within which the individual is *acting*—even when he is dead! The extended field indicated by the larger oval includes parts of the life space of others, or a specific other, to be influenced by the suicidal person after his death. It also leaves the person a potential avenue of locomotion, after his death, around and past any barrier which joins the boundary of the life space.[6]

The presence of the barriers (in the model, simplified as one barrier), a person region, and a vector pointing toward a positively cathected area are all topological notions treated by Lewin in great detail on several occasions.[7]

The concept of barrier has here been elaborated, so that the experienced *source* of the barrier is indicated by "hinges" either pointing toward the person or the object side of the barrier or indicating an impersonal source from the outside.

The person area itself is qualified in two ways: by the (negative) quality of its perceived inner condition; and by its (positive and negative) self-reflective evaluation.

The model contains two different vectors: A primary, or proactive, vector pointing toward the primary goal area of the upper part of the life space; and a second, presumably reactive vector, pointing toward the boundary of the *life* space. Additional concepts are: (1) Barriers reinforcing the *life*-space boundary; (2) Another person, represented as a square, exerting a pressure on the person in the direction of the reactive vector; and (3) Positively cathected areas in the extended life space, representing either an experienced suicide expectancy from others or the location from which beneficient or malicious pressure can be exerted on others. One final concept, symbolized by the arrow pointing around and past the main barrier, represents anticipated reentry into the *life* space.

That so many new concepts have had to be added to the already well-developed topology of Lewin in order to take account of some of the salient facts pertaining to suicide is notable. It is possible that a more sophisticated picture could be developed by the differentiation of levels of relative reality in the model, but the data at hand did not encourage such an attempt. It seems possible, however, that the discrepancy between strictly Lewinean models and the one at hand mirrors not only the author's biases but also some unique and distinctive features of the inner world of suicidal persons.

The model shares many of the weaknesses of a "composite picture" in that no single case is characterized by more than a few fragments of it. It can well be seen as a somewhat dubious enterprise thus to add together numerous individual situations into one single picture. Individual differences are overshadowed, and a fictitious homogeneity is suggested. This seems justified, however, in view of the advantages of the model: It can be used to illustrate peculiarities of various suicidal persons and situations; it may help us to conceptualize more adequately within this area; and it might even suggest some therapeutic steps conducive to the prevention of suicide in individual cases.

## Findings

The only "supporting evidence" which can at this time be given for the model is the actual appearance in the suicide notes of the various categories of "causes" on which it is based.

In light of this I shall go into some detail in qualifying and quantifying the categories and subcategories developed in order to illuminate the significance of the various elements of the model. This seems a necessary prerequisite to the main discussion of its possible applications.

1. A great variety of statements, representing 81 percent of the notes, had the common trait that they seemed to refer to the person's seeing himself as having a desire (other than suicidal) which could not, cannot, or will not be fulfilled.[8] There were three distinct types of such statements:

*a.* The frustration of the desire was seen in 40 percent of the notes as originating from an impersonal or nondescript source: "I have been in ill health since last May," "There is no hope," "There was no chance of recovery," "I can't hear," "I'm too lonely," "There is no end to housework," "Life up to now has given me very little pleasure," "Broke, flat, in trouble," "I don't have a friend," "With unemployment coming up," etc. Most frequent in this category are statements pertaining to illness and isolation.

*b.* Forty percent of the notes contained examples of frustration of a desire seen as originating from another person, group, or institution. Alleged injustice, mistreatment, rejection, and loss were here the frustrations most commonly referred to. There are, within this category, a majority of statements reflecting a clearly extrapunitive attitude: "I have no babies, you have taken them away," "I hope nobody hurts you like you have me," "I have been treated like a dog," "I have heard so many lies in this trial that I am sickened," "Mother has made a sucker out of me,"

"I am tired of being a henpecked husband." Such statements were found in 33 percent of the notes. A lesser part of the statements in which the source of frustration is the same are impunitive insofar as the blame is not explicit: "I would rather have you back than anything else in the world," "With him gone I have nothing," "This could have been a happy day if George would have been here," "I cannot live without Dad," "I can never quit loving you so I shall take this way out," "I loved you very much but you never quite felt that way about me," etc. Such statements were found in 13 percent of the notes.

*c.* Thirty-seven percent of the notes contained statements of frustration seen as originating from the person himself. Blaming one's own destructiveness or self-destructiveness and referring to one's own incapacities, one's being a burden, etc., are here the most common examples. Approximately half these statements have a clearly intrapunitive aspect (21 percent): "I did wrong when I walked out on you," "This is all my own fault," "I am no good to myself or anyone else," "Forgive me for all the misery I have caused you," "I am afraid I will start killing innocent people," "I ruined my life," etc.

Still reflecting the self as origin, but with less intrapunitive attitude, are the other half of the statements (23 percent): "I am sorry I couldn't take it," "You have all tried everything to help me be myself again, but it's no use," "I am such an anxiety and burden to you," "I can't build myself up," "Knowing this it would be terrible to subject you to all the sacrifice you would be called upon to make."

As can be seen from Table 1, which gives the distribution among the three temporal modes for all categories, impersonal frustrations seem preponderant in the present and future tense, frustrations from others in the past and present tense, frustrations from oneself in the past tense. In general, unfulfilled desire as a cause is not so much an anticipated as a remembered and a present strain. For the sake of simplification the results for the extrapunitive-intrapunitive distinction are left out of the table.

2. An inner condition of intolerable character is a type of cause found in 59 percent of the notes. It can be remembered, acute, or anticipated. The statement can, at the same time, refer to the source of frustration. It can refer specifically to a lack of motivation. It can refer clearly to an anticipated panic or be more concerned with the continuation of a present crisis. Although such aspects have been take into account, as can be seen in Table 1, the pervading similarity among all these statements is quite evident: "I have been at the verge of a nervous breakdown for a month," "My main spring has been broken," "I'm lost and frightened," "I am all mixed up," "I can't stand being without her," "A state of mind

Table 1

Frequency of the various categories of causes
as expressed in percentage of notes where category appeared
(N = 568)

| Name of Category | Past | Present | Future | Any Tense |
|---|---|---|---|---|
| *Urge frustrated, any source* | 45.7 | 47.8 | 28.9 | 81.3 |
| Impersonal Source | 11.3 | 25.5 | 17.6 | 40.0 |
| Other as Source | 25.9 | 21.1 | 6.5 | 40.3 |
| Self as Source | 22.9 | 12.0 | 10.6 | 36.6 |
| *Intolerable Inner Condition* | 14.4 | 42.4 | 25.3 | 58.6 |
| In General | 14.4 | 31.0 | 4.2 | .... |
| Specified Cause | .... | 8.4 | .... | .... |
| Lack of Motivation | .... | 9.1 | .... | .... |
| Interminable Condition | .... | .... | 22.2 | .... |
| *Evaluation of Self* | 6.9 | 9.5 | 4.0 | 16.5 |
| Positive | 2.7 | 0.2 | 1.6 | .... |
| Negative | 4.9 | 9.3 | 2.6 | .... |
| *Inclination Toward and Desirability of Suicidal Reaction* | .... | .... | .... | 38.0 |
| Desire and Desirability | 2.6 | 5.8 | 9.5 | .... |
| Urgency, Unavoidability | 3.3 | 8.6 | 19.2 | .... |
| Absence of Barriers | 3.9 | 2.8 | 1.0 | .... |
| *Expectation from Others* | 1.2 | 2.1 | 3.5 | 6.2 |
| *Somebody makes me do this* | 3.9 | 2.6 | 0.2 | 6.2 |
| *Worthwhile Consequences* | .... | .... | 20.9 | 20.9 |
| Harmful to Somebody | .... | .... | 4.2 | .... |
| Beneficial to Somebody | .... | .... | 17.4 | .... |
| *Anticipated Re-entry in Life-space* | .... | .... | 6.7 | 6.7 |
| *Any Category* | 57.2 | 74.6 | 64.6 | 100.0 |
| | | | | All three tenses 29.0 |

where I don't give a damn," "I am not strong enough to stand it," "I can't stand no more," "I can't go on like this."

As to the temporal distribution within this category, the impressive fact is the preponderance of the category in the present (its acuteness) and the frequency of its being expected to go on (its interminable character).

3. Evaluation of oneself was found as a causal aspect in 17 percent of the notes. "I was never really fit for life," "I have been a sham and a fake," "I am just a fat old woman now," "I am worse than a murderer," "I'll always be a misfit," "I would be a failure as a husband." All are negative evaluations and represent the most common type of self-evaluation.

There are, however, also a few examples in which the evaluation is positive and still can be seen as a causal aspect: "I was a good woman until I started going with John," "I have put my house in order with a balanced sheet," "This is the only decent thing to do." It seems in these instances that the recovery of a past, positive self-evaluation, the upholding of such an evaluation, or the achievement of it through atonement is seen as a worthwhile cause.

It seems significant, on inspection of the distribution of the three temporal modes within these categories in Table 1, to note that negative evaluation of self is typically formulated as something present and positive evaluation almost exclusively as something remembered or anticipated.

4. The inclination toward or the desirability of suicide is mentioned in 38 percent of the notes.[9]

*a.* There are the simple statements of wish, desirability, and direct gratification anticipated: "I have wanted it for a long time," "It seems at long last that I know what I want," "I'll be out of my misery and that will be merciful," "I only hope this is fatal, then I can rest."

*b.* There are statements that are concerned with the compulsive, inevitable nature of reacting this way, the trying to withstand the compulsion, and the overriding preference of this to other alternatives: "I have fought this for some time, but can't beat it," "I have put this off as long as I can," "I must go," "I can't help it," "It is what I have to do," "It's the only way out."

*c.* There are statements that are concerned with the reaction as a plan, the realization of which depends on the presence or absence of potential barriers.

As a reason of the past, this comes out as a statement to the effect that there has been a plan to react (with suicide) the moment that certain specified conditions are present or absent, or, more generally, that there has been long premediatation and planning: "I have been planning this for years, since my mother died, but Jim needed me," "This is a deliberate and long premeditated suicide," "I decided to end everything at the first opportunity," etc.

As a reason of the present, we are dealing here with the explicit absence of barriers: "Nothing holds me back anymore," "I don't hurt anyone," "I have reached the end of my rope," "I am only going now to a death that would come sooner or later anyway."

The future tense of this category takes the form that it may become too late for the reaction; that, whereas there are presently no barriers present, such may be anticipated to be present later on: "Jack will be back and want his gun," "I may have a harder time later," "I may get too much pain or so weak that I can't go this easy way."

The distribution among the temporal modalities points to the importance of the *anticipated* gratification, the *anticipated* unavoidability of the reaction (no viable alternatives are expected) but the *remembered* planning.

5. Six percent of the notes contained reference to the person's perceiving that another expected him to react suicidally. "I know this is what you have been hoping for a long time," "This is what you wanted," "I am at the verge of ending my life, which Jim wishes I would do," "I took the pills for you," "I hope you are satisfied," "I hope you are happy in your heart," "I hope this makes you happy," etc.

Although, of course, statements such as these have a clearly hostile content, they do appear as statements of cause or motive, and there is no good reason not to include them with other causes. The results within the temporal modalities suggest that the anticipated fulfillment of others' expectations carries more weight than the remembered expectation, as it has been going on in the past.

6. Another 6 percent of the notes refer to a slightly different type of "influence" than the one described above. These are statements about one's being forced to, made to commit suicide through the influence of somebody else. "You drove me to this," "Bill is the cause of this," "See what you are making me do," "You have killed me," "I hope you are never allowed to forget what you (will) have done to me," etc.

That this category is almost never represented in the future tense is consistent with its definition.

The remaining three categories are, by definition, limited to the future tense. They are concerned with the anticipated consequences of the suicide, i.e., acting in the extended life space.

7. Four percent of the notes contain statements to the effect that the contemplated suicide or its consequences will hurt or frustrate someone else: "You will suffer a lot for just what you have done to me," "You will know, after I am gone, that I spoke the truth," "I hope you have my last breath on your mind forever," "Let this be a lesson for

people who box in on other people's affairs," "I hope that each time you pass a cemetery you will have memories of one who is there," etc.

8. That the consequences of the contemplated suicide are anticipated to be of benefit to someone or to prevent another from suffering is found in 17 percent of the notes: "Everyone will be better for it," "This way he can be free," "All menace to their well-being will have disappeared," etc.

It is beyond doubt that most of the examples in this category have a hostile undertone. However, this is not always so. "Everyone will be better for it" and "Perhaps in the end it will be all for the best" are examples within this category of the hostility's (if it is there) being almost suppressed.

9. Seven percent of the notes, finally, contained statements indicating an anticipation that the suicidal reaction eventually would, or might, bring about the satisfaction of a primary desire now frustrated: "I believe we will meet later under much more favorable circumstances," "I hope one day we will meet in heaven," "This is the only way we could keep our happiness whole," "I hope this brings the peace we once had," "I am going to meet my dad," "This is an experiment in metaphysics," "I will be released in the kingdom," "Hope to see you again some-day," etc. All these statements contain more than a mere anticipated satisfaction. They all more or less explicitly stand for some degree of belief in an afterlife, a continuation of experience, a continued satisfaction of desires, a reentry into the live *life* space, as it is perhaps most vividly described in the following excerpt from a note: "Somewhere out in the great beyond I know that I'll find peace—a winner on every horserace and a love that will never cease—out where the stars shed their pale blue light, out where it's always eternal night, out where my soul can roam in the light—that's where I will find peace."

This, then, represents the "supporting evidence" for the model. It is evident that the cake could have been cut in many other ways. On the other hand, the author feels that this order, in spite of its many apparent shortcomings, is better than none.

## Implications of the Model

The remainder of this chapter will be devoted to a series of excursions into some fourteen potential applications of the model. In each, we shall be concerned with (1) hypotheses furnished by the model,

(2) suggestions for reinterpretation of known phenomena, and (3) the meaning of contemporary techniques used in dealing with the suicidal patient. The issues brought forth in the following paragraphs could be discussed in relation to any suicidal person. In some suicide cases, many of them may be relevant; in other cases, only a few. It is my belief, however, that at least one of the problem areas will be relevant to any genuine case of suicide.

1. A suicidal person may be characterized by lacking an ability to restructure his temporal life space, so that he is not sufficiently able to revise his views of the past, change his conception of the present, and conceive of adequate futures for himself.[10] One possible explanation for this would be a confused distinction among these very temporal aspects. Therapy can help in restructuring the past through induced recall, interpretation, and confrontation. It can offer new concepts and make use of self-confrontation, corrective emotional experiences, etc., in the restructuration of the present. As regards the future, it can offer imagination, point at resources not thought of, and revise unrealistic anticipation.

2. A suicidal person might be characterized by rigidity of object-choice. This might consist both in the choice of specific kinds of objects (for example, of a frustrating nature) and in the rigid persistence of a fixation to a given object. In dealing with any given patient, one would have to reexamine the basic characteristics of the object—what makes it valuable—and explore possible substitutes. This must lead one inevitably into areas not covered by this model, namely into the values held by the individual and the hierarchial organization of such values. The rigidity of object-choice might thus be alleviated, in some instances, through some revision of the patient's value system.

3. Confusion about the origin of barriers and, perhaps, even a specific self-defeating proclivity to set up such barriers in front of a primary central object might be characteristic of a suicidal person. One will have to attend closely to the source of barriers in the person's life in general as well as in the specific instance. I may alleviate the situation, in some instances, if I can convince the patient that he himself is not the source of the frustrating barrier. If the object can be seen as the source, this may help to minimize its cathexis. In other instances the demonstration of self as source, where others were thought to be the source, may open the possibility of self-examination, motivational analysis, etc., and thus bring about some restructuring.

4. Most often we meet, in the suicidal person, an extreme degree of impermeability of the main barrier caused by interpersonal, physical, or intrapsychic conditions. It is also possible, however, to imagine circum-

stances in which fluctuations in permeability would be detrimental to survival. For example, the availability sometimes of a given object might reinforce that object as being positively cathected, while the intervening *un*availability in itself might be a sufficient precipitator of suicide. Examples of such fluctuation are teasing, by an alter, fluctuations in health, or cyclic depressive features making for repetitive revolving between initiative and self-defeating incapacity. The common character of all these is that they give the person a taste of the cake but do not permit him to eat it. Therapeutically, a reassessment of the realistic permeability of the given barrier is a matter of course. Our alternative hypothesis, however, might suggest that increase in permeability is not necessarily desirable. It is usually desirable to move—or remove—the barrier and thereby genuinely increase the motility of the individual. If this cannot be done, however, the model would seem to suggest that one might do better to increase its impermeability as a prerequisite for a devaluation of the inaccessible object-area.

5. A specific expansiveness of the inaccessible object-area, to include a larger and larger part of the life space, may prove to be fatal. What we are referring to here is basically what is meant by the term "monomania." Such "expansiveness" is, in suicidal patients, perhaps most often related to close symbiotic relationships where the alter takes on a great majority of object-functions in the person's life. This occurrence is not basically different from what goes on in more healthy instances of "romantic love" and is characterized by the subordination of most other objectives to the role of being merely in close relationship to the primary love object. If everything one does is subordinated to one's love for another human being (or some similar, highly focused sentiment), one can function extremely well as long as the primary object is available or is at least somehow within reach. In fact, the expansiveness of the object-area is not likely to make itself felt too much before the moment the primary object becomes unavailable. Then, suddenly, the significance of all other objectives shrinks to nothing, and almost all areas of one's life space have become unreachable because one's wish to move into them presupposed an availability of the primary love object.

It is evident that the therapeutic objective must be to dissociate as many areas as possible from their ties to the primary love object. There are good reasons to believe that the process of grieving is nature's way of dealing with this problem. However, we do not as yet know of any way to induce this process when it does not occur spontaneously or bring it to a successful termination whenever it lingers.

6. Another aspect of this same problem is the contraction of the

area outside the barred-object area. The expansion of one necessarily brings about a contraction of the other. However, in some instances there may actually be a special affinity for a confined position in a person who, by thus restricting his locomotive freedom, wards off more grave dangers. In a way, such a position could be seen as giving an excuse for not showing one's incapacities and thus rationalizing passivity, dependency, inefficiency, or lack of autonomy. The therapeutic implications of this hypothesis for therapy would be of an interpretative nature, consisting in part of a demonstration of the secondary gains involved.

7. There might be a special proclivity in some suicidal persons to develop and sustain an inner state of crisis, highly autonomous and independent of whatever originally brought it about. Speculations about a "metacritical" state were introduced, for example, by Shneidman.[11] The whole notion of such an autonomous inner state is closely related to phenomena described as shock, depression, anaclitic depression, and the grief reactions referred to earlier. Even some of the speculations about the nature of schizophrenia presuppose analogous "vicious circles."[12] Common to all of these are their evident somatic manifestations.

The demonstration, to the patient, of the autonomous character of the process is actually one of the main strategies in suicide-prevention work. One often points out to a patient that he is in an acute state of mind, a depressive crisis where he is not able to perceive himself and his own problems without distortion. The somatic character of this state is emphasized, in such instances, and the patient is admonished to postpone important decisions until it has subsided. That psychopharmocological agents are going to play an increasing role in this area is evident. One might also consider, however, the possibility of making phenomenological investigations of this state, and thereby perhaps making new inroads in its clarification and treatment.

8. The remembered decision probably carries great weight in determining the outcome of a given situation. It takes a very special kind of flexibility to alter major decisions once they are made, and the suicidal decision is certainly no exception to this general rule. We might even assume that those who actually do commit suicide are characterized by less such flexibility than those who do not. The flaw in determination of the person who arranges his suicide attempt in such a way that makes it more or less bound to fail is, seen from this viewpoint, a sign of healthy flexibility. The "courage" which, the saying will have it, goes into killing oneself is, from this same viewpoint, to be characterized more as stubbornness.

The clear and unfaltering differentiation between past and present seems the most important therapeutical goal in this area. What we ultimately can strive for is to move the suicidal person from a position of having made a decision to one of contemplating which decision will be the best to make. We may, however, run into a major obstacle here which has to do with the fact that any state of decidedness sometimes—and with some persons—is better than undecidedness. This is probably the best rationale for the technique of activating the patient—favored, for example, at the Suicide Prevention Center. Instead of just trying to cancel a decision to react suicidally, it is also attempted to substitute for it other reactions, so that the patient is not left powerless in a vacuum.

9. That the succumbing to a hostile alter can be a major aspect in suicide has long been known. When another person is given such an important role that he has attributed to him the power of chasing the person out of his own *life* space, this points to a serious lack of autonomy, absence of voluntary control, or a specific, passive, object-like quality of the self. Therapeutical suggestions relative to this point would be concerned with an analysis of the inherent positive cathexis of "the aggressor" and the dependency needs and reliance on environmental forces of the patient.

10. The willingness to comply with perceived expectations can be as dangerous as it can be useful. In the suicidal person, it may mirror some of the same fundamental problems suggested in the previous paragraph but have a more active and initiating quality, so that it can be described as "aggression through compliance": "I'll do what your attitude seems to suggest I should do, so that you can see that your attitude was wrong." These are the dialectics of the suicide, but also those of the adolescent rebellion or the marital dispute. There is only one significant difference, namely, that the compliance in the suicidal case consists in trespassing the boundary of the *life* space. The therapeutical analysis of the "aggression through compliance" might consist of (1) a reevaluation of the perceived expectation involved; (2) a distinction-making between actual expectation and what *seems* suggested by a given attitude; and (3) a clarification of the aggressive aspects of the reaction.

11. The degree of permeability of the *life*-space boundary and the degree of permeability of barriers reinforcing that boundary are, of course, crucial to an evaluation of suicidal potential. The first would correspond to the person's inherent concepts of life and death, the cultural norms of proper time, place, and mode of trespassing from the first state to the second; the second would correspond to more specific social, material, and self-imposed barriers between the two. As to the cultural image of suicide,

we are within an area in which the therapist can effect little change. That future research within this relatively unknown field may prove to be very illuminating is, on the other hand, most probable. As to the social, material, and intrapersonal barriers, it is very possible that although the relative unavailability of means (to suicide) might be a deterrent, the limited availability might be a precipitating factor. Even if we assume that the suicide rates can be decreased by limiting the access to guns, barbiturates, ropes, and razor blades, it is very probable that a person's knowing that his opportunity to kill himself has been less than it is at the present, or that it will be less than it is now, can dispose him toward killing himself at this very moment. It might thus be life saving, in some instances, to point out to a person that he will always have the opportunity to commit suicide and that the absence of a barrier is only an apparent reason for acting.

12. The very real phenomenological existence of an extended life space is seldom given the acknowledgment that it deserves. It is not only the suicidal person but almost everyone, especially within a materialistic culture, who tries to connect with a post-mortem world. It is important in therapy to clarify whether or not such action in a post-mortem world is existentially true for the person. Only thus can we deal adequately with that person's subjective situation.

13. The belief in the possibility of reentry into the *life* space can evidently be dangerous for survival. The main thing to be stressed therapeutically is that the belief in a post-mortem life space does not justify belief in reentry. It can be a matter of argument whether one will choose either the narrower *life* space or the extended life space as one's frame of reference, but it *cannot* be doubted that trespassing the boundary of the *life* space is an irreversible process. It must be acknowledged, however, that we are here fighting an often culturally built-in incapacity which may be modified only in connection with a general revision of a life philosophy.

14. The last point to be made is the conception of suicide as an instance of "leaving the field" behavior. We might here dare to make two hypotheses: (1) Suicide may, in some instances, be a symptom of a general tendency to leave the field, any field, on the slightest provocation. The pointing out and interpretation of such a trend, together with offering alternative coping mechanisms, may, in such instances, prove life saving; and (2) It is also possible, however, to think of suicide as in some instances being an *avoidance* of leaving a *specific* field. Thus, it is conceivable that some persons may regard their own suicide as a freezing of the present sentiment or attitude, thus eminently staying in the present posi-

tion and only transposing it to a level where it is all "extended life space" or "post-mortem world."

The list of problem areas is not exhausted here. We ought to mention the problem of self-evaluation and its close relationship to the state of crisis. It might also have been feasible to consider the topology of suicide in terms of an approach-avoidance concept: Is the person mainly avoiding life or approaching death? Or we could have focussed on the relative degree of structuration of areas in the suicidal life space in order to illuminate the fatal oversimplifying dichotomizing that takes place.

All of this and much more can be used to exemplify how the proposed model might stimulate and integrate ideas in the field of suicide research and suicide prevention.

I am not assuming that all of this can be deduced logically from the model. The model is primarily meant to be of heuristic value. It is, of course, not meant to be finite, i.e. a model which, once it is exhausted, or once limitations in its applicability are demonstrated, has to be discarded.

On the contrary, the model, in its imperfect and hastily designed form, almost invites additions and changes. For example, the author is quite sure that many more concepts from Lewin's topology could be incorporated and put to use. It is also evident that new empirical findings will suggest other additions.

The topology of suicide is concerned with the mapping of a vastly unknown territory.

## REFERENCES

1. The present research was carried out under a fellowship at the Center for the Scientific Study of Suicide, Suicide Prevention Center, Los Angeles, California in 1962 and 1963. The author wishes to express his gratitude for extremely favorable work conditions, help, suggestions, and inspiration offered by secretarial as well as professional staff of the SPC. Special thanks are due to the project director, Edwin S. Shneidman, under whose liberal sponsorship the CSSS was inaugurated in 1962.
2. It goes without saying that I am here referring only to the experienced causality of *one's own* behavior. Phenomenal causality in other areas, such as "moving objects," "natural events," and "other people's behavior" have been amply illustrated by such eminent scholars as J. Piaget, *The Child's Perception of Physical Causality*, trans. M. Gabain (New York: Harcourt, Brace & World, 1932); A. Michotte, *La Perception de la Causalité* (Lou-

vain: Institut Superieur de Philosophie, 1946); F. Heider, *The Psychology of Interpersonal Relations* (New York: John Wiley & Sons, Inc., 1958); F. From, "Apperception: A New Approach to a Forgotten Problem," *Acta Psychologica*, **16**:254, 1959; etc.

3. A list of references to studies of suicide notes would include the following: Capstick, A., "Recognition of Emotional Disturbance and the Prevention of Suicide," *British Medical Journal*, **1**:1179–1182, 1960; Gottschalk, Louis A., and Goldine C. Gleser, "An Analysis of the Verbal Content of Suicide Notes," *British Journal of Medical Psychology*, **33**:195–204, 1960; Hayakawa, S. I., "Suicide as a Communicative Act," *ETC.*, **15**:46–50, 1957; Morgenthaler, W., "Letzte Aufeichnungen von Selbstmördern," *Beiheft zur Schweizerischen Zeitschrift für Psychologie und Ihre Anwendungen*, no. 1 (Berne: Hans Huber, 1945); Osgood, Charles E., and Evelyn G. Walker, "Motivation and Language Behavior: A Content Analysis of Suicide Notes," *Journal of Abnormal and Social Psychology*, **59**:58–67, 1959; Shneidman, Edwin S., and Norman L. Farberow, "Some Comparisons between Genuine and Simulated Suicide Notes in Terms of Mowrer's Concepts of Discomfort and Relief," *Journal of General Psychology*, **56**:251–256, 1957; Shneidman, Edwin S., and Norman L. Farberow. Appendix to their *Clues to Suicide* (New York: McGraw-Hill Book Company, 1957); Shneidman, Edwin S., and Norman L. Farberow. "A Socio-Psychological Investigation of Suicide," in Henry David and J. C. Brengelmann (eds.), *Perspectives in Personality Research* (New York: Springer, 1960); Tuckman, Jacob, Robert J. Kleiner, and Martha Lavell, "Emotional Content of Suicide Notes," *American Journal of Psychiatry*, **116**:59–63, 1959; Wagner, Frederik F., "Suicide Notes," *Danish Medical Journal*, **7**:62–64, 1960; and Wolf, H., "Suicide Notes," *American Mercury*, **24**:264–272, 1931.
4. See Edwin S. Shneidman and Norman L. Farberow, *Clues to Suicide* (New York: McGraw-Hill Book Company, 1957).
5. This concept is consistent with Lewin's writings, as exemplified by his paragraph on "the psychological past, present and future as parts of a psychological field at a given time" in his paper, "Defining the Field at a Given Time," *Psychological Review*, **50**:292, 1943, and his topographical model representing "the psychological time dimensions" in his "Behavior and Development as a Function of the Total Situation," in Leonard Carmichael (ed.), *Manual of Child Psychology* (New York: John Wiley & Sons, Inc., 1946).
6. See Shneidman's concept of the "post-self," in his "Suicide, Sleep, and Death: Some Possible Interrelationships among Cessation, Interruption, and Continuation Phenomena," *Journal of Consulting Psychology*, **28**:95–106, 1964.
7. See especially Kurt Lewin, *A Dynamic Theory of Personality* (New York: McGraw-Hill Book Company, 1935); and his *Principles of Topological Psychology* (New York: McGraw-Hill Book Company, 1936).
8. Many statements were found in which the desire was present only as a suppressed premise. However, it seemed justified to infer the presence of

such a premise in these cases. When somebody asserts: "I lost control and struck you," "All the trouble I have caused you," or "You would prefer the company of almost anyone to mine," there can be no doubt in the reader's mind that there is a suppressed premise such as: "I have a desire not to have struck you," "I have a desire not to have caused you trouble," or "I have a desire that you should not prefer others' company." Such inferences are taking place on the level of logic and do not represent psychological hypothesizing.

9. It may seem strange to view this as a *cause*. However, although what we are here looking for are the causes for the suicidal inclination and reaction, the experienced desire or desirability of the reaction is, phenomenologically, also a cause in itself.
10. It must be noted here that although our model apparently only represents *one* anticipated future, it contains information pertaining to at least two, namely the suicidal and the (hypothetical) nonsuicidal. Our assertion here is that both of these might be restructured and that several alternative nonsuicidal futures might be suggested.
11. See Shneidman, "Suicide, Sleep, and Death . . . ," *op. cit.*, pp. 103–104.
12. See S. A. Mednick, "A Learning Theory Approach to Research in Schizophrenia," *Psychological Bulletin*, **55**:316, 1958.

# 23. Can a Mouse Commit Suicide?

Halmuth H. Schaefer[1]

That man and lower animals have much in common, as Darwin pointed out, was first accepted only so far as physiological and anatomical functioning was concerned. Even a layman could be convinced that the mechanism of blood circulation works in essentially much the same way in dog as in man. The possibility that behavioral repertoires of man and lower animals could be similarly and equally fruitfully compared was not—and is not even now—as readily admitted.

As a consequence we are much more in the dark today about the behavioral functioning of man than we are about the intricate mechanisms of his kidneys, heart, or nervous system. However, in relation to this fact there are several circumstances we might consider. First of all, it is well to remember that the hesitance to accept Darwin's anatomical argument was not as speedily overcome as may seem at times. Many years after Darwin stated his theories, men were publicly condemned for subscribing to them. There seems to be a strong reluctance in many of us to yield the central position we like to think that we occupy in nature.

Second, it is also true that when the concept of evolution was introduced there was more factual information about the anatomy of organisms available than there was about the behavior of organisms.

Finally, naturalists sympathetic to Darwin's views and interested in behavior began to endow lower animals with many of man's psychological attributes in an attempt to show that evolution applied to this sphere as well. Unlike Aesop who wrote, tongue in cheek, about the cunning, love, greed, or valor of his charming creatures, these naturalists told us seriously that we should not be surprised that rudiments of emotions as we know them in ourselves could also be found in lower animals. As they argued in this way, buttressing their case largely with anecdotal bits of evidence, they violated, of course, Morgan's canon of parsimony, which states that in no case should we use a higher psychological faculty for explaining a certain behavior where a faculty lower on the ladder of psychic functioning would suffice.

When Morgan's canon was applied to the reasoning of the turn-of-the-century naturalists much of what they said was discredited; but unfortunately, attempts to investigate and to analyze behavior were subsequently abandoned as well.

It is not improbable that these factors—the brevity of time since we began to study animals in trying to understand man, the lack of factual information about animal behavior, and the absence of a proper technology to study behavior—account for the absence of what we like to consider as hard-core, scientific knowledge of the behavior of man, including such acts as committing suicide. It may well be that these factors more readily explain the paucity of laboratory research on death, dying, and suicide than does the oft-cited taboo which is believed to surround these. There are other taboo areas on which—even against clearly discernible odds—much has been published and openly discussed.

Since Darwin's day, however, a technology for the study of behavior has developed which so far has proved to be astonishingly successful. Based on much painstaking laboratory work and especially on the formulations of Skinner it is possible at this time to cite general laws which the analysis of behavior has yielded. Superficial acquaintance with these laws has led some to conclude that it is not within their nature to touch upon typically human concerns. Yet, it is no small matter to show that organisms that have in common their condition of being alive are governed to the extent to which we know this now not by separate and different principles but by essentially the same principles. As examples, one might cite such simple laws as those which state that a reinforcer may be used to strengthen a response, that extinction of a response after continuous reinforcement is more swift than after variable ratio reinforcement, or that punishment will suppress but not change the rate at which a given response is emitted. It is also evident that the sophisticated application of the analysis of behavior to such divergent areas as mental health, crime, and human learning has been successful when compared with traditional approaches.

Suicide is one behavior—generally considered solely human—which to the best of my knowledge has not been included in the long and versatile list of behaviors that has been dealt with in the experimental laboratories of the behavioral scientist. There is no good reason for the exclusion of this behavior from such study. We can use operation of a lever by an animal in the same way in which we are using language in a human: We can let a human subject push a button or say or write "yes" and push another button or say or write "no" in response to questions such as "Do you fear the election of this candidate?" "Do you think this product is tastier than that one?" and others. Since responses other than verbal ones suffice here, there is no need to exclude animals from similar questioning about feelings, fears, or wishes they might have about relevant aspects of their environment.

Suicide requires what we like to call intent. Intent, in turn, implies the possibility of making a choice. The study of both intent and choice is entirely within the realm of the experimental analysis of behavior. Moreover, such analysis can study these conditions directly and not via the detour of self-descriptive verbal statements.

Some time ago, while talking shop about some work I was doing with mice as experimental subjects, Professor Shneidman asked me half jokingly whether I thought that a mouse could commit suicide. We wondered out loud for awhile what one could mean by this. He pointed to the absence of a generally satisfactory and generally applicable definition of suicide by humans as a possible obstacle in the way of utilizing animals for study. We readily agreed that anecdotes about horses foundering and dying after their master is slain in battle, dogs refusing to eat after their young master leaves for college, pelicans who open their chest to feed their starving young with their heartblood, or lemmings who, following their leader, march into the sea to drown by the thousands do not make for convincing sources in a study of suicide.

There is, of course, a good deal of statistical, actuarial, survey-type material on suicide, but nobody has ever *experimented* with suicide. The obvious reason for this is that such experimentation with humans is out of the question. To use animals as research subjects in such a study had simply never been thought of. It was, perhaps, the absence of such research which unconsciously was underlying the question of whether mice can commit suicide. If taken in that way that question would really be: Is it possible to experiment with suicide?

It struck me at once that one lead to experimentation in this area could be found in Shneidman's ingenious distinction between death and cessation. In writing on death and suicide Shneidman has made the intriguing observation that there is a simple functional difference between physiological death and cessation of being.[1] The example he likes to give is that of a young man who, in driving a car at high speed, hits another car and is thrown head-on to the pavement. By some medical fluke this man is kept "alive," i.e., his heart is kept beating and his lungs are kept operating for several weeks. But the electroencephalogram never shows anything but deep sleep, he never once opens his eyes again, he never says anything, or, if we like, regains consciousness after he hit the pavement. That instant when the young man hit the pavement, Shneidman calls his moment of "cessation." The instant his heart stopped beating is his "termination."

It should be evident now what is of interest to the experimentally oriented psychologist here: The same fluke which kept alive this man for many months could also have brought him back to consciousness. Indeed, all of us experience temporary cessation daily (which Shneidman calls "interruption") as we fall asleep. Many of us experience interruption as we "pass out" (without "passing on") because of acute pain or drug injection. There is no evidence whatever to justify the assumption that occasions of ceasing differ in quality as a function of some future event, i.e., awakening or not awakening again. Hence, there is no reason why entirely controlled experiments with regard to interruption, for example, could not be conducted on humans that could tell us something about cessation. Since lower animals, too, cease, there is no reason why research that could tell us something directly about ceasing could not be carried out on them.

With lower animals it should be possible to conduct experiments that involve physical death. To begin with, our experimentation should be concerned with basic questions such as: Can this animal, our subject, discriminate between life and death, or even more basic, can he discriminate between a live or dead fellow member of his species?

These questions must be answered before we can proceed to experimental arrangements in which we might attempt to induce lower animals to kill themselves or find some other behavior which enables them to deal with that arrangement.

Once the question of suicide can be related to discriminations, the behavioral scientist can be of considerable help, since discriminations for him are a very amenable class of procedures for analysis. He would reason somewhat like this: Intent implies making a choice or, technically, the "ability to make a discrimination." In intending suicide the organism must—before it proceeds to anything else—be able to discriminate between the state of being alive and that of being dead and, more important, between environments (stimuli) that are lethal and others that are not. An organism can tell us in many ways whether it can make these discriminations: If it is man, he can say "no, I don't want to step on this hot third rail." But even if he never spoke we could observe that he discriminates as, in many trials, he carefully engages in many behaviors which avoid his contact with this lethal third rail.

With nonspeaking animals we should rely entirely on observation of the animal in the presence of lethal situations. If an animal had a choice between entering two compartments, one of which is lethal, and never enters the lethal compartment, we would be justified in saying that the animal discriminates between these two compartments.

Inherent in the technical use of the term discrimination is the experimenter's ability not only to show convincingly that a given organism *can* discriminate but also to establish such a discrimination in an organism. Rather than rely on verbal self-descriptive repertoires about an organism's ability to discriminate, the experimenter proceeds as follows: Suppose we wish to ask a mouse whether he can tell a triangle from a circle. We arrange it so that both of these shapes take on meaning for him. We project, for example, a triangle against a wall in his cage and while this triangle is shown, a lever which sticks through the wall can be operated by the mouse to produce a pellet of food. In its crudest form we might simply let the animal live in such a cage for a while without making any attempt at "training" him. Sooner or later he will operate the lever. At the time the triangle happens to be on the wall, the lever will be functional and the animal will receive a pellet. Food pellets can function as reinforcers if the organism has been deprived of them for some time. Consequently, the animal will now press this lever more frequently. In very short order, instead of pressing the lever three or four times per day he will press it as many as two hundred times in ten minutes.

He will press the lever indiscriminately whether the circle or the triangle shows on the wall of his box. But, while the circle shows, the lever responses go unreinforced and the animal extinguishes his high rate of responding. These processes—reinforcement in presence of the triangle, extinction in the presence of the circle—alternate, and very soon we have a situation where the animal emits few if any responses in the presence of the circle and responds immediately and at a high rate when the triangle appears.

His differential rate of responding is, of course, a way of our knowing that he perceives circle and triangle as different. We say that he can now discriminate between circle and triangle. Many other stumuli could serve instead of the circle and the triangle. We could, for example, arrange for a dead animal to be present (visible through a window) whenever the lever is nonfunctional and a live animal to be there whenever the lever is functional.

What would such an experiment prove? Certainly nothing about the animal's ability to describe or respond to what we commonly call knowledge of life and death. Such an experiment would prove no more and no less than that an animal can or cannot discriminate between two other animals, one living, one dead.

There is a subtlety in the last statement which might escape one on first glance. When I described the experiment to one of my assistants,[2] he said at once, "Oh, he'll just discriminate then between movement and no movement!" This is, indeed, correct. Lack of movement is one of the stimuli by which we too make our discrimination of death—but not of cessation.

There are other stimuli by which we also judge: discoloration of the skin and body temperature, to mention but the major ones. It is remarkable how behavioral procedures force one to recognize similarities in behavior between man and lower animals. Absence of movement in a body that typically moves is a stimulus for us which controls our self-descriptive behavior as we say "This man looks dead." As soon as we try to think of an experiment which would arrange for the same discriminative contingencies with a lower animal, we at once say that he "*only*" responds to lack of movement, implying that we, of course, respond to more than that.

Because it is relatively easy to conduct and to have the matter on record, my assistants and I ran the simple live-versus-dead-fellow discrimination experiment anyway. The result was that the animals (we ran only three subjects on this discrimination schedule) learned to discriminate between a live and a dead mouse in the observation chamber in about the same time that they would have learned to discriminate between a dark and a white patch of material, the presence and absence of a light, or any other pair of stimulus conditions.

Typically, discrimination experiments are run fully automated. The experimenter programs the presentation of the stimuli and the corresponding schedules of extinction and continuous reinforcement. In this case we could not very well do that. Manually we had to place a live mouse in the observation chamber when the lever was functional and a dead one when the lever was not functional. A timer informed us when to switch from one schedule and stimulus to the other. Since we had found previously that the formation of a discrimination is much accelerated if movement of the response lever in the presence of the negative stimulus (in this case the dead mouse) resets the timer that determines the length of the extinction period, we used that arrangement here, too. Typically one schedules the reinforcement and extinction periods to be of about one-minute duration each. In the beginning the animal pressed frequently during the extinction period and thus reset the timer, which resulted in long extinction periods (up to 60 minutes in one case). During training the animals received all their food during the experimental sessions. Whenever the stimulus appeared in the presence of which the lever was functional the "observer mouse" learned quickly to respond at a high rate. For this he was reinforced with a food pellet for every lever response. Soon the observer mouse also learned not to press the lever any more in the presence of the other stimulus (the dead mouse). This difference in the rate of responding, then, told us that the animal was in fact discriminating. He had answered our basic question "Can a mouse tell the difference between a dead and a live fellow mouse?" with an equally simple "Yes I can and do here in this situation."

The result of this experiment certainly confirmed a good deal of anecdotal evidence that "animals can tell." In western rodeos a typical task is to ride a horse evenly over a cowhide. Horses apparently prefer to walk *around* cowhides lying in the sand rather than *over* them. They, too, are discriminating, although it is impossible to say what the stimuli are that they are discriminating. A cowboy once told me that these horses were showing respect for the dead. Perhaps they are, but it is equally possible that they have learned that dead cows are putrid things that will squirt smelly stuff on you if you step on them. It is hard to know.

In addition, this exercise prepared us to think more seriously about the possibility of an experimental procedure which might bear more directly on the question which occupied me: Could one show that animals can discriminate between lethal and nonlethal environments? Obviously recognition of lethal environments cannot be learned by an organism other than by observation of their effect on others. Just as for recognizing dead or live species members, there may be innate components for discriminating between "good" and "lethal" environments, as when ducklings take cover from a flying hawk but not from a flying goose. But this does not alter the contention that it is only those animals who display the discrimination who are still alive, i.e., who never experienced the effect of the lethal situation on themselves. It also is of little interest for our present purposes to know whether the discriminative behavior was acquired culturally (involved language perhaps) or by direct observation. What is of interest is whether an animal can discriminate between a lethal and a nonlethal situation and whether, having formed the discrimination, he will then avoid the lethal environment when given a chance to choose between it and a nonlethal environment.

We first worked with an apparatus which used observer and experimental animals and consisted of a small observation room suitable to accommodate a single observer mouse. This room overlooked (through a clear Plexiglass window) three other rooms, arranged like a T maze as shown in Fig. 1. The central room (*a*) served as the starting place for the "experimental mouse." The other two rooms were the "death" chamber (*b*) and the "life" chamber (*c*), respectively. They could be located either to the right or left of the observer and were different in that the death chamber always contained a grid floor and solid, painted walls. The experimental animal, once released from the starting chamber, could do one of three things: he could stay where he was, move into the life chamber, or go into the death chamber. Doors closed after he entered either chamber.

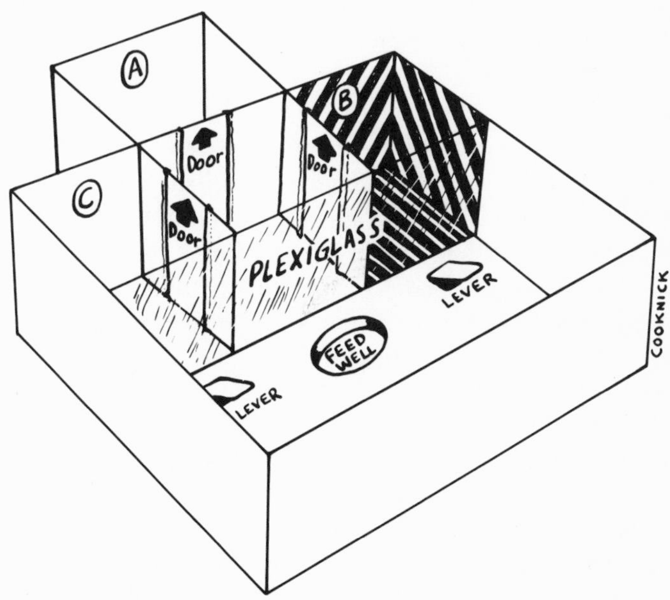

The observer mouse had to tell us what went on in these three chambers by pressing appropriate levers. He was deprived of food and merely had to learn a discrimination much as was described for the training of discrimination between dead and live mice.

The location of the death chamber was changed from one side to the other according to a schedule determined by the occurrence of odd and even numbers in a table of random numbers.

As long as the experimental animal stayed in the starting chamber—it rarely did so for longer than a few seconds—or went into the life chamber, one of the two levers in the observation chamber produced pellets for our observer mouse. However, as soon as the experimental animal entered the death chamber, it was quickly and painlessly killed by high-voltage, low-frequency current applied through the grid floor and the other lever in the observation chamber instantly became functional. If the observer mouse were not watching the experimental animal at all, he should make approximately 50 percent wrong responses by pressing the "wrong," i.e., nonfunctional lever. This is about what our observer mouse did during the first session. During that session he had a chance to observe a total of 4 experimental mice and gave a total of 135 lever presses, 51 percent of which were "errors."[3] During the next session he made fewer, though not significantly fewer, errors (46 percent). But with the next session his error score became significantly smaller than would be expected had chance prevailed, and it remained so throughout the subsequent sessions.

During these observation sessions many experimental mice were used. We were conducting at that time a genetic study in our laboratory and had a considerable surplus of animals. Nevertheless, it was clear that we could not afford to run large numbers of observer mice.

The question was now whether our skilled observer mouse would enter the death chamber if he were given the choice that the experimental animals he had observed previously had been given. Before he ever had been called upon to function as observer, this mouse had fairly well alternated between entering the life chamber and the death chamber. Out of five such experimental runs he had run to the death chamber three times and to the life chamber twice. In this his performance was altogether typical. Ten other mice did very much as he did: fifty percent of the time on the average they went to either chamber.

Now, after his training, our observer behaved differently. *Not once* in the first five times of being placed in the starting box did he run into the death chamber.

At this stage of experimentation we decided that we were still using clumsy apparatus. To change the position of the death chamber required unplugging leads, tightening screws, and so forth. It was not as smooth an operation as would be desirable. It occurred to us that there was really no need to have that many chambers. All we really wanted to know was: Would an observer mouse ever go into a place in which he had seen his fellows come to a violent end? We now designed an apparatus which was much more simple (See Fig. 2). A single chamber was divided by a Plexiglass wall into two compartments: one side had a solid floor and a single lever, the other had a grid floor, nothing else. The experimental mouse was placed in the grid-floor compartment, plainly visible to the

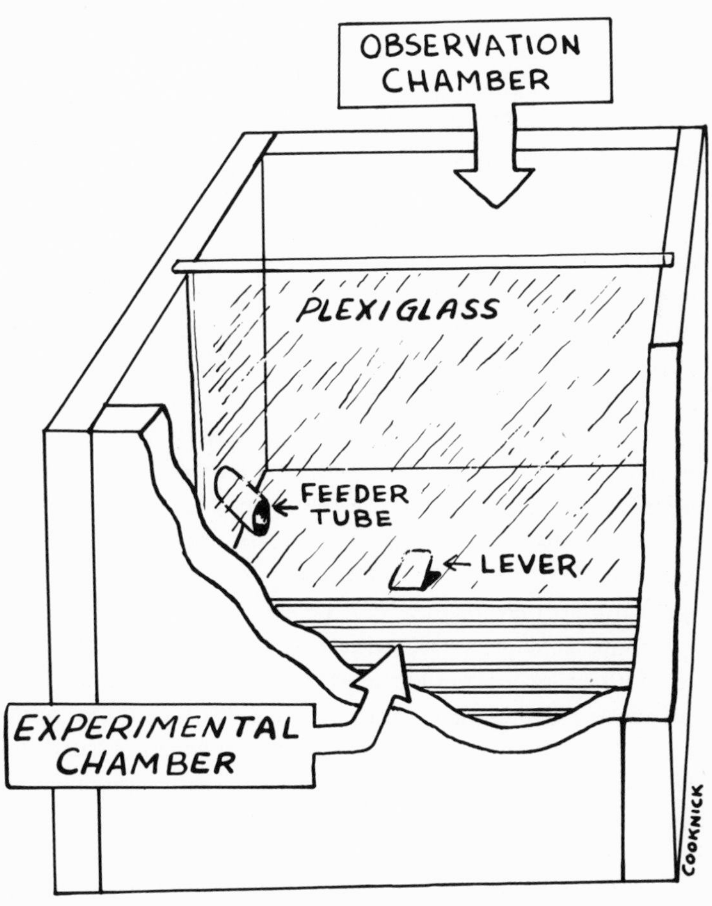

observer mouse. A clock was started at the moment of placing the experimental animal in view of the observer into the grid-floor compartment of the box. If the observer mouse operated the lever he received no food, but the clock reset and started timing again. If the observer did not press the lever while the experimental mouse was scampering about in the other compartment, the clock would run out after two minutes, make the lever functional (for providing food), and also electrocute the experimental mouse. This procedure removed the burden of our having to watch continually while the lever went from the nonfunctional to the functional state. Replacement of an electrocuted animal by a live one had, of course, to be accomplished manually.

The crucial test, as before, was whether the observer mouse would enter the grid-floor compartment once the Plexiglass dividing wall was removed. But when we did that, all animals, even the one animal observer who had learned the discrimination to near-perfection (28 percent error over all trials), at once and without hesitation ran to the grid-floor side of the box as soon as the glass wall was pulled out. This is the present status of our studies at the time of this writing. We are also breeding trapped wild mice for this project and plan to use other species as well.

It is probably well at this point to remind the reader that the experiments cited here are not meant to provide conclusive evidence of any sort (although it should be admitted that they are interesting in their own right); rather, they are cited here merely to demonstrate how one might go about experimenting in the laboratory on a subject that heretofore has not been experimented with. So far we believe we have demonstrated that those animals with which we have worked could certainly tell a live from a dead fellow member of their species. This alone tells us nothing about an animal's feelings about death, but it points the way to experimentation that allows us indirectly to query an animal about such feelings. Such a query reveals that a mouse probably will avoid a place where he saw a fellow mouse being killed. He identifies this place not by spatial location but by appearance. If on the basis of this avoidance behavior we wish to infer the presence of fear of something in the animal we are free to do so, although making this inference adds nothing to our understanding of the existing situation.

It is also apparent that the stimulus situation is quite specific and includes the organism itself. The animals that were run in the simplified discrimination apparatus (Fig. 2) did not hesitate to enter the grid compartment of their box. Were we not in possession of data which show that an animal avoided the death chamber in a differently constructed apparatus, we should suspect that the observer animal did not form discriminations about the environment that prevailed when members of his species died. But we have such data now, and there are other experimental avenues which must be pursued.

If it can be shown that lethal environments are avoided by an organism, it must then be explored how permanent such avoidance remains over the lifespan of the animal. Some data that we have suggest that this avoidance behavior is not permanent. The mouse who avoided the death chamber after having observed his fellows coming to an untimely end in there did, in later trials, enter the death chamber—interestingly enough, he even began to show a slight preference for that chamber.

What the factors are which make for more lasting avoidance still remain to be shown. But suppose that it will be possible to establish such avoidance on a more durable basis. The next step then would consist of establishing conditions which would cause the animal *not* to emit the avoidance behavior any more. If that could be achieved we would, indeed, have caused an animal to commit suicide. The procedures to be followed for this experimental attack would not be unlike those that Masserman developed for exploring neuroses in cats.[4] Masserman, it will be recalled, frustrated his animals and succeeded in inducing cats to drink alcohol when, due to experimental procedure, they were unable to solve a problem that they usually could solve. We like to think that suicide occurs with human beings when an individual is unable to cope with his environment, when he is frustrated. But we also know that this is not generally true, and, most interestingly, there is some indication that if the stress placed on human beings is of extreme intensity, an individual would rather stand up and fight the world than commit suicide. The stress has to be of just a certain degree for a given individual. There is good hope now that this question can be answered by experimentation with animals.

There is no question that some avoidance behaviors exist innately and are permanently displayed. However, it does not necessarily follow that because of their permanence, these behaviors make the study of long-lasting discriminations more easy. We know next to nothing about the ontogeny of these behaviors. A discrimination that we can establish in an organism by proper experimental procedures in the laboratory is easier for us to interpret than is an existing discrimination which we merely can observe and record.

Yet animals who show innate discriminations would be interesting. Discussion of this topic touches on what is often called "fear of death." Here, again, the behaviorist would say that the organism must be able to form discriminations before displaying behaviors from which the outside human observer could infer the presence of such fear. Some contend that animals have not and cannot have fear of death. Yet, when cast in behavioral terms, it is clear to see that any species which could not discriminate and avoid lethal environments would sooner or later vanish. Some of these discriminations must be present when the animal has just been born, as, for example, the "fear" reaction of certain birds to the flying hawk already mentioned.

The pursuit of laboratory controlled studies on death is of primary interest to those who are not satisfied with "fears" or "wishes" as explanations of behavior. Even though many psychologists claim to be behavioral scientists, many of them still "explain" observable behavior through some inner force, such as anxiety, for example.

The tautology involved is not easily evident, but as one asks for a definition of "anxiety" the answer very likely is that anxiety is present (or working) when palms are sweaty. The explanation of sweaty palms as a result of anxiety thus becomes: "Sweaty palms are caused by sweaty palms," a statement which is not satisfactory. It does not help either when, in the fashion of not letting the left hand know what the right hand is doing, one defines anxiety in one instance by one array of observable behaviors (while disregarding some others which are equally present) and in another instance explains the previously disregarded phenomena by anxiety, as defined by the formerly observed behaviors. Yet this tautological explaining is done everywhere. We explain the behavior of a thief through his criminality. Criminality, of course, is inferred to be present in somebody who steals.

In dealing with death, tautological explanations seem to be very prevalent. For example, no less an authority than Menninger uses "wishes" as explanations for suicide.[5] That these explanatory constructs (wishes) take on human characteristics is best witnessed by the fact that the wishes were then split into three separate homunculi with different names and different jobs: the "wish to kill," the "wish to be killed," and the "wish to die." These are given to explain why men commit suicide. Other inner forces are used similarly: Menninger writes in *Man Against Himself*: "In the unconscious we are still animals, and there is no reason to believe that any animal fears death; with us humans it is our intelligence which 'doth make cowards of us all'."[6] The "fear" causes one thing but when that does not happen we invent another homunculus and call it "intellect" and that one now combats the other one, all inside a man's skin and utterly invisible to us. In this particular case fear sometimes wins out over intellect. The ghosts of old are still ruling us; we are still possessed by them. When the intellect wins out we do not commit suicide; if we lose against that other devil, fear, then we murder.

The behaviorist of Watson's day was wont simply to deny the existence of anything he could not subject to experimentation. By "could not" I do not mean because of moral issues but because of the felt nature of the thing involved, in the sense in which William James said that you cannot light a candle to study the darkness. As soon as you do so you have destroyed the condition you wish to investigate. In making this denial the early behaviorist often threw out the baby with the bathwater. In denying the possibility to study wishes, for example, by direct observation the old behaviorist denied equally that there was anything to be studied about what we call wishes. The modern behaviorist does not do this. A concise but thorough statement of the position of modern behaviorism, appropriately entitled "Behaviorism at Fifty," is given by B. F. Skinner in an article in *Science*.[7]

Because this point is so basic to my position and also because experience has taught me that it is the least understood aspect of behavioral science, I would like to quote extensively from a passage from Skinner's article. In talking about mental way stations, as Skinner calls the homunculi with which we are prone to populate the inside of man, he points out that moods, cognitions, and expectancies are typically (and with justification) examined introspectively and descriptions are used in psychological formulations. He says:

> The conditions under which descriptive repertoires are set up are much less successfully controlled. Terms describing sensations and images are taught by manipulating discriminative stimuli—a relatively amenable class of variables. The remaining kinds of mental events are related to such operations as deprivation and satiation, emotional stimulation, and various schedules of reinforcement. The difficulties they present to the verbal community are suggested by the fact that there is no psychophysics of mental states of this sort. That fact has not inhibited their use in explanatory systems.
>
> In an experimental analysis, the relation between a property of behavior and an operation performed upon the organism is studied directly. Traditional mentalistic formulations, however, emphasize certain way stations. Where an experimental analysis might examine the effect of punishment on behavior, a mentalistic psychology will be concerned first with the effect of punishment in generating feelings of anxiety and then with the effect of anxiety on behavior. The mental state seems to bridge

the gap between dependent and independent variables, and a mentalistic interpretation is particularly attractive when these are separated by long periods of time—when, for example, the punishment occurs in childhood and the effect appears in the behavior of the adult.

We believe that any definition of suicide must contain a statement about intent. A person can give us descriptions of the feelings, fears, or wishes that he discriminates within himself. As long as the verbal community agrees that the descriptions of his discriminations are useful, understandable (i.e., they can be made by the listener himself for what he regards analogous feelings, fears, or wishes), and reasonable (i.e., the observable external situation is likely to produce such feelings, fears, or wishes in the listener too), one is likely to overlook the fact that in an experimental analysis of behavior the emergence of a given behavior can be explained directly and without recourse to the verbal self-descriptive repertoire of a person. As soon as we understand this possibility, it becomes evident that experimentation with lower animals is entirely feasible for the exploration of suicide.[8]

It may well be that for human beings there is a wider range of stimuli which may be discriminated about death, but the difference between the richness of discriminative ability in human beings and lower animals is not a generic one. Fear of death varies from one human being to another and from time to time in one human being. To talk about the fear of death is not justified in the light of this. We agree that suicide requires premeditation and intent. Without knowledge about death, without an understanding of the meaning of death, no organism can be said to commit suicide as we use the term. Meaning of death is no more or less than the ability to recognize and think of lethal environments, including weapons, hot wires, and dangerous railroad tracks. By recognition we mean discrimination. The organism shows us that it "has" such recognition, i.e., can make the discrimination by responding appropriately.

Can a mouse commit suicide? To some degree I feel embarrassed at my inability to give an answer at this time. I wish that I were in a position to speak with confidence from experimental data, having followed the steps suggested above. The point, however, is that the techniques described here are novel applications to an old question. It is primarily in the hope of stimulating research in this field that I have presented my experiences so far.

I would expect some to take issue with my rationale in designing this experimentation, but I would hope that criticism and counterarguments would go beyond those which simply insist that man is different from lower animals (a fact which nobody at all denies) who thus do not commit suicide (a conclusion which does not follow from acceptance of that fact). I do hope to have shown that information about suicide from animal sources need not be restricted to the gathering of anecdotal evidence, and that, in general, research on suicide need not be limited to the types of research to which it is now confined.

## REFERENCES

1. E. S. Shneidman, "Orientations Toward Death," in Robert W. White (ed.), *The Study of Lives* (New York: Atherton Press, 1963).
2. I am grateful to Messrs. Robert Moss and Richard Landis and to Miss Lynette Milberg of the Behavioral Research Laboratory at Patton (California) State Hospital for running the mice who provided the experimental evidence for this essay.
3. The terms "errors" is used here following common usage. It is not a technical term. The inappropriate responses were errors from our point of view only.
4. J. H. Masserman, *Behavior and Neurosis* (Chicago: University of Chicago Press, 1943).
5. K. A. Menninger, *Man Against Himself* (New York: Harcourt, Brace & World, Inc., 1938).
6. *Ibid.*, page 18.
7. **140**:951–958, 1963.
8. A. Brion and P. Citrome, "Suicide and Automutilation in Animals," in A. Brion and H. Ey (eds.), *Animal Psychiatry* (Paris: Desclée de Brouwer, 1964).

# 24. Sleep and Self-Destruction: A Phenomenological Approach[1]

EDWIN S. SHNEIDMAN

*"Rightly or wrongly, however, I prefer spiritual insomnia to psychic suicide."*
*e. e. cummings*

At first glance it might appear that the main question for this chapter[2] is Are there, for certain individuals, some instructive parallels between their overt self-destructive behaviors and their withdrawals from their ordinary states of consciousness, expecially their behaviors relating to sleep? But I should reveal at the outset that an additional focus of my concern is with the *uses of time in life*. I shall need to involve such issues as staying awake or going to sleep, remaining alive or letting oneself die, wasting the present moment or integrating it constructively into one's future, living in a way that is appropriate to one's stage in life or being out of phase with one's years. All these and more are uses of time which tie together sleep and self-destructive wakefulness, sufficiently at least so that they can be discussed within the scope of a single chapter.

To me, professionally obsessed with suicide, the topic of sleep as a potentially useful avenue for research into self-destructive behaviors seems to have occurred quite naturally: A kinship between death and sleep is in our folk language. There are many metaphors which tie the two together. A perusal of Bartlett's *Familiar Quotations* leads me to believe that the relationships, even in metaphor, are complicated and tangled. For example: (1) Sleep is seen as the replenisher of life. The most famous quotation in this connection is from *Macbeth*: "Sleep that knits up the ravell'd sleave of care, / The death of each day's life, sore labour's bath, / Balm of hurt minds, great nature's second course, / Chief nourisher in life's feast"; (2) sleep is also seen as "unplugging"[3] from life, as, for example, in the quotation "Slumber awaits to house the mind from care," or from Spenser, "Rest, the gift of Gods, sweetly sliding into the eyes of man, doth drown in the forgetfulness of sleep, the careful travails of the painful day"; and (3) sleep is seen as the brother of death. A quotation from Joseph Conrad—one might also quote Tennyson, Shelley, Hesiod, Homer—will suffice: "The men, women, the children; the old with the young, the decrepit with the lusty—all equal before sleep, death's brother." Still, the familial relationship between sleep and death is not too clear; but if they are siblings, sleep must then be viewed as the cryptic brother of death, the closeness of the relationship depending upon how inimical to life or self-destructive is the intention of the sleeper.

On the topic of sleep, there is a vast contemporary technical literature, especially on the biochemical, physiological, and electrophysiological (EEG, REM) correlates of sleep. As an example, Nathaniel Kleitman's 1963 revision of *Sleep and Wakefulness* lists more than 4,300 references.[4] Other recent books on sleep by Oswald, Murray, Wolstenholme and O'Connor, and Luce and Segal, to name four, testify further to the current efflorescence of interest in the subject.[5]

But if there has been an awakening of interest in sleep, there continues to be a semi-somnambulistic state in respect to the investigation of the psychological aspects of sleep, especially the phenomenology of sleep. In the plethora of current observing and measuring, there is a relative dearth of direct questions about a person's own sleep experiences—his attitudes, sentiments, and affect; his subjective feelings on going to sleep, intrasleep, and upon awakening.

In two previous papers, which stand as a theoretical introduction to this present chapter, I attempted to present a tentative scheme for classifying various temporary and permanent (partial and complete) stoppings of consciousness, including the interruption of sleep and the final cessation of death.[6] In this present chapter, I am interested in sleep as both a methodological devise (offering a useful tool for getting at variations in affect, attitudes toward living, etc.) and a conceptual thing-in-itself (offering new ways of viewing the stopping of waking consciousness—including sleep, unconsciousness, and death).

But I need first to ask: Is the concept of "death" necessary? Let us realistically agree that for each individual the actuality of cessation, naughtment, termination, stopping, demise is inevitable, but let us also agree that conceptualizations of death are not themselves inexorable; we invent them to promote personal, religious, or scientific ends. The role of the individual in his own demise is obviously a worthy (although neglected) object of rigorous study. What I mean by "role" will, I hope, become clearer in the following paragraphs. I shall begin by indicating two current conceptualizations which I consider to be inadequate for our purposes—the first because it makes too much of the individual's role in his own death; the second because it makes too little of that role.

The first conceptualization makes too much of the individual's role, by viewing death as an experience. Death, as Bridgman has pointed out, is not an experience.[7] It is neither a common nor a unique experience. It is not an experienceable experience at all, for no one can experience his own death. If he could, he would not be dead. An extension of this notion is that an individual cannot even experience his own dying, for he can never be certain; and the one time he would have been correct, there would then be no "he" to have the validating experience. The muddled thinking about death as experience is based, it seems to me, on the fundamental confusion between (1) the individual as he experiences himself ($I_s$), including experiencing himself as he experiences others—his here-and-now introspective experiences; and (2) the "individual" (physically present, physically absent, alive, deceased, actual, apocryphal, or fictional) as he is experienced by others ($I_o$). It follows, of course, that although we cannot experience our own death we can experience the death of others; that although we cannot experience the survival of our own demise we can, in the living present, experience among other fears and aspirations our own present fears or aspirations in relation to our own "post-self," (i.e., "our" after-death impact, reputation, or influence—our escape from total annihilation).[8]

The second inadequate conceptualization, which makes too little of man's role in his own demise, refers to the current Western classification of the *modes* of death. The four administrative crypts into which each death must now be placed are natural, accident, suicide, and homicide (N-A-S-H). Several points can be made about this classification: its primary purpose is a legal one of assigning responsibility, if not guilt, to man or to God; it is in the tradition of seventeenth century Cartesian thinking, viewing man as a machine (rather than a psycho-socio-biological organism); it ignores or minimizes the role of the individual in his own demise, making him a vessel of the fates. It is of trivial importance to me whether I am invaded by a lethal steering wheel (accident), a lethal virus (natural), or a lethal bullet (homicide), if I do not want any of them in the first place. (The one item on my own death certificate in which I have the keenest interest is the *date*.) The N-A-S-H classification systematically neglects the major teachings of twentieth-century psychodynamic psychology—an omission we cannot afford to make. While cessation is inevitable, modes of conceptualizing death are not.

My own recent attempts to free myself from this conceptual miasma have taken the form of viewing man's living and dying behaviors—one seen as part and parcel of the other—in terms of three dimensions of consciousness in time: alteration, intention, and utilization. Herein, hopefully, may lie the hints of some conceptual parallels between sleep and self-destruction.

1. *Alteration* is the general notion having to do with changes in the presence, absence, or quality of consciousness, including the special cases of death and sleep. Subsumed under alteration are three subconcepts:

*a. Cessation,* defined as the final stopping of the possibility of any further conscious experience—what Melville, in *Pierre* (Bk. XII, Part III), called "the last scene of the last act of man's play."

*b. Interruption,* defined as the stopping of consciousness with the retrospective actuality, and usually the expectation, of further conscious experience. Again from Melville (*Mardi*, chap. 143): "When I sleep . . . I live while consciousness is not mine, while to all appearances I am a clod." An interruption is, to use two contradictory terms, a "temporary cessation."

*c. Continuation,* best defined by James[9] as experiencing, in the absence of interruption, the stream of temporally contiguous conscious events.[10]

What we ordinarily call death is, I propose, better conceptualized in terms of *cessation*. Unconsciousness (coma, inert sleep) are examples of interruption states; continuation has to do with all manners of usual (modal) and unusual (altered) conscious states, including altered continuation such as being intoxicated, drugged, hypnotized, or malingering, being a spy, feigning, and "unplugging" from one's ordinary course of activities. From the point of view of these conceptualizations, the entirety of an individual's ongoing psychological life is made up of *one* series of alternating continuation and interruption states. The stopping of this series, the end, the nothingness,[11] the naughtment[12] of conscious life is inexperienceable cessation.[13] A schematic overview of the interrelations among types of alteration—cessation, interruption, and continuation—admittedly grossly over-simplified—is presented in Chart 1.

CHART I SCHEMATIC CHART OF INTERRELATIONS AMONG CESSATION-INTERRUPTION-CONTINUATION BEHAVIORS

| | ALTERATION BEHAVIORS | | | | | | |
|---|---|---|---|---|---|---|---|
| | I. DISCONTINUATION BEHAVIORS | | | | II. CONTINUATION BEHAVIORS | | |
| ALTERATION STATES | A. FINAL Permanent (Cessation) | C. INTERMEDIAL | B. PERIODICAL Temporary (interruption) | F. PARTIAL CONTINUATIONS AND DISCONTINUATIONS | D. MODAL | G. CRITICAL (Endings) | E. FOCAL Acutely Altered Continuation States |
| RELATED PSYCHOLOGICAL STATES | Naughtment<br>Cessation<br>Death<br>Demise | Near-cessation<br>Trend toward cessation | Sleep<br>Unconsciousness<br>Anesthesia<br>Stupor<br>Fainting<br>Seizures | Sensory Anesthesia<br>Motor paralysis<br>Affectlessness<br>Withdrawals<br>Psychoses<br>Dissociations<br>Fuguestates<br>Amnesias | Modal behaviors together with shifts and changes with age and "stages of man" | Grief<br>Bereavement<br>Mourning<br>Nostalgia<br>Longing | Intoxication<br>Drugged states (LSD, etc.)<br>Hypnosis<br>Anoxia<br>Malingering<br>Role playing<br>Spying<br>Feigning<br>Unplugging |
| CROSS-BEHAVIORAL CONGRUENCIES | 1. *COSMOLOGICAL BELIEFS:* Beliefs about natural and supernatural world; God, prayer, hereafter, reunion, survival after death, etc.<br>2. *MOTIVATIONAL ROLES:* (of individual in his own alteration): Intentioned, subintentioned, unintentioned, and contraintentioned.<br>3. *AFFECTIVE STATES:* especially the sequence and order of both positive and negative affect states.<br>4. *COGNITIVE STYLES:* Individual's idiosyncratic logical styles and his private epistemology (contralogic); ways of concluding.<br>5. *STRUCTURAL FEATURES:* Inexperiencability of death and sleep enforced and middle states; metaphenomena; the postego.<br>6. *PHENOMENOLOGICAL ASPECTS:* Defining the self coded messages; death and sleep as a resource; as a threat to competence, etc.<br>7. *SOCIO-CULTURAL CHARACTERISTICS:* Modal times and places; taboos and sanctions; artifacts and rituals; deviant patterns, class differences. | | | | | | |
| RELEVANT SOURCES OF DATA | Suicide notes<br>Wills<br>Letters written in context of death | Materials reflecting ambivalence, role of chance, and internal debate | "Interruption notes" written in context of sleep, anesthetic, ECT | Conspicuous lacunae in modal communication patterns | Ordinary letters to relatives and friends<br>Diaries<br>Credo statements | Communications re divorce; death of loved one; graduation; leaving job; changing locale | Communications during or about special state |
| | | ANAMNESTIC, INTERVIEW AND DYADIC MATERIALS<br>(POSTSELF) | | | | | |

2. *Intention*: From any individual, at any given moment, it is possible to elicit attitudes, intentions, and orientations toward his own cessation, interruption, or altered and unaltered continuation.[14] Very briefly, the major categories of intention—the over-all role of the individual in his own alteration—can be conceptualized as follows:

*a.* Behavior can be *intentioned*, in which case the individual plays a direct, conscious role in his own alteration of conscious state, such as shooting himself, lying down to go to sleep (and advertently giving himself up to passivity or unvigilance), or having two martinis, in his wish to cease, to interrupt, or to alter his conscious state, respectively.

*b.* Behavior can be *subintentioned*, in which case the individual plays an important indirect role in his own altered behavior, the death or unconsciousness or altered conscious state being owed in some not insignificant part to the actions of the individual which reflect both his conscious and unconscious wishes, as evidenced by his own carelessness, foolhardiness, neglect of self, imprudence, ambivalence, poor-risk gambles, ennui and resignation, mismanagement of drugs, disregard of medical regimen, misuse of alcohol, or his injudicious way of moving into the world. Most deaths, including homicidal deaths,[15] are of this nature.

*c.* *Unintentioned* situations, which the individual plays no significant role in the alteration of his own behavior, the cessation, interruption, or altered continuation owing entirely to unwished-for failures or malfunctions within the body or assaults from without (such as being shot to death, knocked out, or drugged in the absence of *any* participation on the part of the victim).

3. *Utilization*: The conceptual cement between the notions of alteration and intention is provided by the notion of utilization, which refers to the use or employment of life's coin: time. Further, the *use* of each temporal interval (minute, day, year, decade, etc.) is subject to evaluation. This evaluation can be in terms of the role that interval has played in the ongoing life of the individual relative to his own welfare and best interests. Three general types of use of time can be distinguished:

*a.* *Elevative*, i.e., patterns of behavior which expand, restore, enlarge the life, which promote the individual's best interests, which are related to the individual's self-actualization, and which elevate and improve the tone of the life. In short, they are patterns which move the individual toward increased happiness, decreased perturbation, greater maturity, more peace of mind, better interpersonal relationships, self-actualization, etc. Elevative moments are rare in most lives, and only the rare and privileged person lives a predominantly elevative life; but nonetheless the goal of civilization ought to be to increase the proportion of such moments in our lives.

*b. Reductive,* i.e., patterns of behavior which diminish or truncate the individual's life, which subtract from its length or reduce its scope. They demean and limit the life and are inimical to one's general welfare. They are self-defeating and self-injurious and, in general, against one's own best interests. They are seen in such patterns of living as drug addiction or alcoholism. Patterns of multiple business, school, or marital failure and behaviors in which the individual is repeatedly his own worst enemy are other examples of this genre. Stopping one's life—committing suicide—is, by definition, the most self-inimical act that one can do to oneself.

*c. Temporative,* i.e., patterns of behavior which neither elevate one's life nor diminish it but rather have the characteristic of "existing" or getting one through the next temporal interval. Being conscious (i.e., living) becomes simply a way of passing the time. One exists and an hour later one is simply an hour older.[16] The day passes. Where has the year gone? Perhaps a prototypical example of temporative existence is the picture of an individual sitting in his darkened living room on a warm summer afternoon, drinking a can of beer, watching a second-division baseball team lose a game in midseason. In America today, most aspects of spectator sports, most features in the daily newspaper, much of what occupies the mind, is of this time-passing quality. When interruption is neutral, as most sleep is—although some interruptions can be restorative and some can be destructive—it serves a most useful purpose. But it is a major moral question whether or not temporative continuation is, paradoxically, wasteful.

One does not have to be completely misanthropic to believe that Time is a hostile enough force in one's life—"Oh, what quenchless feud is this, that Time hath with the sons of Men!" (*Pierre,* Bk. I, Part II)—without our helping hostile forces along. It may well be that the greatest tragedy of life lies in self-induced wastefulness, specifically in the waste of the moment, in the inimical use of time—whether it is the demeaning of the present moment, the waste of last year, the shortening of one's years, or the truncating of the human aspects of one's total life.

Inimical or reductive behaviors reflect the dark side of the omnipresent balance between developing one's potentialities or neglecting them; and, perhaps, at their root, they represent the dark side of the perennial debate between the forces of life and those of death.[17]

Our special concern with the uses of time implies that time itself is critically important for an understanding of both sleep and self-destruction.

Indeed, sleep may be seen as "time out of life;" and self-destruction, if it is anything, is a reduction of an individual's living time. And if one is concerned with the concept of time, it is not a large conceptual step to an interest in the concept of age.

By age I do not mean exclusively chronological age but rather what might be termed "psychological age" or "philosophic age" or age-in-relation-to-one's-own-death. I am referring not only to the life-phase ages of the subjects in this study but also to my own ages and to the belief that I myself would have written this whole piece differently had I done it ten years ago and that it would be still different were I to do it again ten years from now. (Erik Erikson reflects in the Foreword to the Second Edition of his *Childhood and Society* that his students, in counseling him against an extensive revision, felt that "tampering with an itinerary written in younger years was not one of an older man's prerogatives."[18])

One implication of this notion is that the wide variety of thoughts one finds written about death stem in part from their having been written by men at various phases of their own lives. Dr. Murray's study of Melville and Dr. Litman's essay on Freud in this volume show the progression of an individual's orientations toward annihilation over the broad range of his own psychological history. To the oversimple inquiry, "what did Melville or Freud think about death?" one's first response would have to be the counterquestion, "to what stage of his life are you referring?"[19]

A further implication is that an all-encompassing psychology of suicide is most likely not forthcoming. What is more likely is that we will have psychologies of self-destruction, relating, perhaps, to various stages in life, such as Shakespeare's seven ages of man, Erikson's eight psychosocial stages in the human life cycle, Jung's two main ages of man, Gerald Heard's five ages of man, Sullivan's developmental epochs, Charlotte Buhler's stages in the human course of life, Schachtel's periods in the human metamorphosis,[20] or some newly conceived death-orientations of man. Explanations of self-destruction—even when they take account of multiple causation and even when they include views from several disciplines—will need to be several, resonating to the total range of conceivable psychosocial ages-in-relation-to-death.[21]

One can now relate the concepts of inimical use of time, crisis, and psychosocial age. Inimical or self-injurious patterns of living can be seen as involving one of three kinds of crises: a *failure* of integration at a particular stage of psychosocial development; an untoward *precocity* in development, whereby the individual is inundated by too many experiences too soon; or a *retardation* in development as a psychological person, whereby psychosocial age lags noticeably behind chronological age.

Within the context of this concept of discernible psychosocial stages in the human life cycle, I would propose four ways of conceptualizing self-destruction, focussing on the role of crisis in its *temporal* relationship to the phases of life:

1. A crisis occurring *within* a phase of life: *intra-temporal.*
2. A crisis occurring *between* phases of life: *inter-temporal.*
3. A crisis occurring *out of phase* with life: *extra-temporal.*
4. A metacrisis occurring *independent* of the phases of life: *meta-temporal*

Now a few words of explanation about each.

1. A crisis occurring *within* a phase of life: *intra-temporal.* The concept here is one of a crisis which occurs within a particular phase of life and which is more or less appropriate to the individual's chronological age and his time in life. Although the phases of life have been variously conceptualized by different authors, there is some agreement that these periods include infancy (when the main problem is the distillation of I-ness); childhood (when the main problem is the acquisition of social skills and psychological resources); adolescence (when the main problem is the separation from the family and movement into young adulthood); young adulthood (when the problem is to find and hold love, to find a career, and to establish a family); middle-adulthood (when the task is to accomplish whatever one is going to accomplish in the world); and old age (when the aims include accommodating oneself to one's accomplishments, aging gracefully, setting a good example, and lending a stable and conservative balance to the community, while at the same time accepting inevitable decline).[22]

Each of these ages has, of course, been the subject of special studies—studies relating to the psychology, habits, psychodynamics, conflicts, special problems, crises, ordeals, and even "mysteries" of each age; adolescence and old age have been selected for special study by a number of contemporary students of human personality, and the variable meanings of adolescence in different times and different cultures have become an area of special focus.[23]

In addition to the numerous writings of crisis within an age, there is a further view, that of C. G. Jung, which proposes that the major psychological task within the scope of an entire life is the preparation for and the integration of the shift from the first half (being young) to the second half (being old)—what I would call a "Continental Divide" view of man's life-span. For Jung, the task of the second half of life—a task that should not be undertaken prematurely—is the confrontation with the contents of the unconscious: "as my life entered its second half, I was already embarked on the confrontation of the contents of the unconscious."[24]

Most relevant for our current interest is the growing literature on attitudes toward death at various chronological ages. For example, three chapters on this topic appear in *The Meaning of Death* edited by Herman Feifel:[25] by Maria Nagy (on ages 7 to 10), by Robert Kastenbaum (on ages 14 to 18), and by Feifel (on four groups with mean ages of 26, 36, 40, and 67); and in *Death and Identity* edited by Robert Fulton,[26] in which there are contributions by Irving Alexander and Arthur Adlerstein (on ages between 5 and 16), by Alexander, Randolph Colley, and Adlerstein (on undergraduate college students), and on the aged, in separate chapters by Wendell Swenson, Paul Rhudick and Andrew Dibner, Samuel Schrut, Adolph Christ, and Frances Jeffers, Claude Nichols, and Carl Eisdorfer. Also relevant is a chapter by N. L. Farberow and E. S. Shneidman entitled "Suicide and Age" in their book *Clues to Suicide*.[27]

2. A crisis occurring *between* phases of life: *inter-temporal*. Here the notion is one of a crisis which occurs in the interstices between the major psychosocial ages of man; for example, in the *movement* from adolescence to young adulthood, or in the *change* from middle adulthood to older age. An analogy: It is as though the driver could maneuver down the straight stretches in the road of life (with the kids fighting in the back seat, the baby crawling on his head, and his wife barking directions) without too much difficulty, but, at the *turns* in life's highway, the pressures and demands become too much to handle, and he goes into the ditch.

In a recent book edited by Howard J. Parad, *Crisis Intervention: Selected Readings*,[28] a number of authors discuss crises at "turning points" of life—what I call inter-temporal pivots: Donald C. Klein and Ann Ross' paper, "Kindergarten Entry: A Study of Role Transition" relates to the turn from babyhood to young childhood; and E. E. LeMasters' chapter "Parenthood as Crisis" is concerned with the turn from adolescence to young adulthood.

Interestingly enough, Kurt Lewin, in his classic paper "Field Theory and Experiment in Social Psychology,"[29] sees adolescence not so much as a period of life but as a transition, an extended inter-temporal event, in which the individual occupies the position of "a marginal person . . . during locomotion . . . between . . . *childhood* and *adulthood*." Along these same lines, Lawrence Frank has written of "Adolescence as a Period of Transition."[30]

3. A crisis occurring *out of phase* with life: *extra-temporal*. Whereas

the intra-temporal and inter-temporal patterns of self-destruction relate to individuals who are, for their chronological age, more or less in a temporally appropriate phase of their lives (or are caught between appropriate phases of their lives), extra-temporal self-destruction relates to crises which occur out of phase with life. This group includes individuals who have "too early" savored experiences "beyond their age" and, in this sense, are too old for their years (inappropriately precocious in life development); conversely, it includes individuals who are not "grown up emotionally," who are sheltered not only from experience but from reflection (retarded in life's ways). These individuals are, in terms of their chronological age, out of tune with the modal psychological issues and conflicts that ought to be occupying their psyches. They are way ahead of themselves, or way behind. Experiences that come "too early" (such as having to be one's own parents, having to understand the impact of sexuality, or having to face annihilation) put one out of phase with one's own years. These individuals suffer from "information overload" or what might be called "stimulus inundation."

4. A metacrisis occurring *independent* of the phases of life: *meta-temporal*. Both sleep and suicide can be seen as meta-phenomena, i.e., as secondary reactions to more substantive occurrences. Sleep, for example, can be seen as a resonating (or secondary) reaction to what might be called "unvigilance." (Oswald discusses the role of "vigilance" in sleep.[31]) My own current view of many suicidal acts is that oftentimes they represent meta-crises. That is to say, on the one hand, we hear reported almost every "reason" for suicide (ill health, being jilted, loss of fortune, pregnancy, loss of job, school grades, etc.—some more persuasive than others) and, on the other hand, we hear of the circumstances where "we simply can't imagine why he did it." It may well be that in some cases the substantive reasons (whatever they are) are simply not sufficient causes for the events. What seems to happen in these cases is that the individual becomes disturbed (over ill health, loss of work, etc.) and *then* develops a panic reaction (a meta-crisis to his perception that he is disturbed). He becomes agitated over the fact that he is anxious—or anxious over the fact that he is agitated. At the time of the greatest perturbation, the content which sparked the original disturbance may not be recoverable to his mind. These meta-crises may occur during any phase of life and are thus independent of—i.e., without regard to—the phase itself. Suicide may represent a panic reaction to the individual's feeling that things are getting out of control, a meta-critical act, representing a reverberating crisis, with its own (essentially content-free) autonomy. Erikson provides us with a

quotation which clarifies this notion of the meta-crisis: "This is the truth behind Franklin D. Roosevelt's simple yet magic statement that we have nothing to fear but fear itself, a statement which for the sake of our argument must be paraphrased to read: We have nothing to fear but anxiety. For it is not the fear of a danger (which we might be well able to meet with judicious action), but the fear of the associated states of aimless anxiety which drives us into irrational action, irrational flight—or, indeed, irrational denial of danger."[32]

Even though these thoughts constitute a first presentation,[33] a brief discussion of some of the implications, as seen in the refractory light of the present, might be useful. Two will be mentioned: (1) The type of self-destruction (or inimical behavior) most likely to be found in the various types of crisis; and (2) the varying role of the precipitating stimulus in the various types of crisis.

1. *Types of inimical behaviors.* A wide range of self-destructive patterns can be distinguished, including suicide, accidents, addiction, underachievement, aridity in the life, etc. A *priori*, it might be speculated that *intra*-temporal crises would be most apt to be related to overt self-destruction (suicide); *inter*-temporal crises, to psychologically laden accidents—as Tabachnick has indicated in his chapter in this volume; *extra*-temporal crises, to generally destructive and inimical patterns of ongoing life (such as addiction, underdevelopment, masochistic patterns, etc.; and *meta*-temporal crises, to those seemingly inexplicable (and especially surprising and sudden) overt self-destructive acts.

2. *Role of the precipitating stimulus.* Ordinarily when we think of the nexus of causes for a destructive act, we include, for example, primary causes, sustaining causes, and almost always, precipitating causes. Much of the literature on suicide is limited to the discussion of precipitating causes (ill health, rejection, etc.). I would believe that the role or weighting of the precipitating cause would differ among the four temporal categories of crisis, perhaps as follows: in *intra*-temporal crises the impact of the precipitating stimulus might be relatively greatest, playing a disproportionately heavy role within the total etiological equation; in *inter*-temporal crises, an individual may exhibit a special vulnerability to the nefarious triggering effects of the precipitating cause, especially if an event (which then becomes a precipitating cause) relates to some special characteristics of the two stages the individual is between, e.g., being rejected when one is between adolescence and young adulthood, or suffering ill-health between middle age and older age; in *extra*-temporal situations, the aberrant out-of-phase life style is itself often the self-destruction, so that

the issues attendant on the precipitating causes may be less urgent; and in *meta*-temporal crises the role of the precipitating cause is, almost by definition, only remotely related to the incapacitating metacrisis.

The three notions involved in this section are: (1) inimication, (2) crisis, and (3) psychosocial age. Looking at any two of them may permit us to see more clearly the role of the third. Even at this point it would seem useful to relate self-destruction in man not only to his chronological age but also to his position (intra, inter, extra, or meta) relative to his appropriate psychosocial stage of life. An understanding of the causes of self-destruction and effective action in both primary prevention and individual treatment will, in good part, depend on such comprehensive assessments.

Out of all these thoughts about the possible relationships between cessation and interruption phenomena, I undertook, at the Suicide Prevention Center, a study of the phenomenological aspects of the sleep behavior of a few individuals who have been patients at the Center. For this study, a Sleep Study Form was developed, based in part on liberal borrowings from Kleitman and Murray and Morgan and on the use, almost in its entirety, of Hildreth's Feeling and Attitude Scale.[34] The Sleep Study Form includes forty or more multiple-choice and yes-no items relating to the number of hours of sleep, quality of sleep, record of alcohol and drug intake, attitudes toward sleep, and especially the positive and negative affective states upon retiring and awakening. In addition, there are some items which reflect the individual's "lethality" or suicide potential. The subjects were requested to submit a Sleep Study Form each day for an extended number of consecutive previous nights. Over three years of consecutive daily reports for each of several subjects were obtained.[35]

A *priori*, the Sleep Study Form contains items which tap nightly fluctuations in three separate areas: (1) *interruption*, as exemplified by the hours of sleep, attitudes toward sleep,[36] the affect related to sleep, feelings upon awakening, etc.; (2) *altered continuation*, as exemplified in the use of medication, drugs, pills, alcohol, etc.; and (3) *cessation*, as indicated by items relating to death and suicide. In this last regard, an especially important item is one that will be referred to in this text as the "Lethality Scale," and which reads as follows: "During the last 24 hours, I felt that the chances of my actually killing myself (committing suicide and ending my life) were: absent, very low, low-medium, fifty-fifty, high-medium, very high, extra high (came very close to actually killing myself)."

Although the contents of the Sleep Study Form are primarily phenomenological items, they also include items which might appropriately be subsumed under the *sociology* of sleep. Discussions of the sociological aspects of sleep may be found in Murray, Naegele and especially in Aubert and White.[37] The latter two present a number of attributes which they cite as sociological characteristics of sleep and which, on reflection, can *also* be thought of as characteristics of dying and/or suicidal behaviors. Among the sociocultural parallels between both dying behaviors and sleep behaviors, the following are of especial interest: (1) modal times and locations for both; (2) taboos and sanctions in relation to both; (3) artifacts and rituals in both; (4) elements of social disengagement in both; (5) aspects of communion rites in both; (6) deviant patterns in both; (7) "norms of secrecy" in both; (8) class differences of patterns of expression in both; (9) aspects of "defining the self" in both; (10) coded messages in both; etc.

Sleep Study Form data[38] for seven subjects[39] covering a 365-day period (from September 1, 1964, to August 31, 1965) will be reported in this chapter. Very briefly, the subjects can be initially identified as follows:

1. *Hunilla* is a 22-year-old Negro woman in a stressful marriage, intermittently made more stressful by her husband, by her 10-year-old stepson, by her having children, and by her acting-out sexually, followed by confession and contrition. She made a suicide attempt—her second—during the year.
2. *Oberlus* is a 67-year-old, semiretired physician-inventor, initially very depressed over his dying wife, then subsequently over the death of his wife; extremely lonely; has multiple serious physical complaints.
3. *El* is a 32-year-old homosexual male with a history of several suicide attempts, described by Henry Murray as a daytime Jekyll and a nighttime Hyde and by Evelyn Hooker as a "Modern Everyman" with a marginal hold on life,[40] whose Sleep Study Forms for seven of the twelve months reported in this study were submitted from prison.
4. *Rolfe* is a 44-year-old, embittered, angry, sardonic (this "stinking humanity"), suspicious ("everyone has screwed me"), divorced man who has been thinking of suicide for the past three years to the point of having once developed an elaborate suicide plan. He had been steadily employed as an aircraft assembler for several years but has since retired and has moved to a sparsely populated rural area some distance from the city. During the year he made a suicide attempt.
5. *Jenna* is a 38-year-old divorced nurse with two teenage children who

feels that her life is running down and that she has little to live for and who often thinks of suicide. Her father, a policeman, shot himself when she was nine years old. She is depressed, feels overworked and somewhat hopeless.

6. *Vine* is a 62-year-old divorced salesman who planned to take his life because of financial worries, a bleak future, and general emptiness in his life. He made a serious attempt with Nembutal two years ago. He has successfully belonged to Alcoholics Anonymous for the past 20 years. Superficially, he seems like a prototypical happy-go-lucky Irish-American, but upon examination, he is found to be tormented and depressed.

7. *Robin* is a 45-year-old woman whose marriage to a Japanese man ten years her junior is a source of great difficulty for her. She is both emotionally dependent on him and extremely angry at him, especially for his gambling and his activities with women. When she drinks to excess she tends to become action-prone, and her capacities for physical assault on her husband, or a serious suicide attempt, increase.

For purposes of computer analysis, the data on the Sleep Study Form were converted to 65 items, plus 15 additional items to represent the MMPI profile scores. A composite frequency distribution (for all 7 subjects) within each of the 65 items, for the one-year period September 1, 1964 to August 31, 1965, was prepared.[41] From these data, one can state that the responses of these seven subjects on the Sleep Study Form indicate that their modal sleep pattern had the following characteristics: (1) slept between 7 and 7½ hours per night; (2) turned off lights within a half-hour after getting into bed; (3) got out of bed within a half-hour after awakening; (4) awakened one or two times during the night; (5) used alcohol during the day but not just before bedtime; (6) used medication just before bedtime; (7) went to bed feeling moderately tired and sleepy; (8) looked forward to sleep; (9) went to sleep almost right away (only 1 percent of the responses was "could not sleep for hours," and 3 percent of the responses indicated "had insomnia all night"; (10) viewed sleep as "recharging of my battery" or as "a nice long nap"; (11) slept soundly and more or less continuously; (12) reported dreaming "not at all"; and (13) felt "kind of low," "without too much pep," and "only just about able to keep going" upon awakening in the morning.

Eight tables (one for the combined data and one for each of the seven subjects) of 2,080 Pearsonian correlation coefficients were computed.[42] Using the composite correlations of ±0.60 or higher,[43] some interesting general findings concerning sleep and self-destruction may tentatively be drawn:

1. An interesting negative finding was that there were no correlations of 0.50 or higher between duration of sleep (Sleep Log) and any other items on the Sleep Study Form. (For the record, the correlation between length of sleep and self-destructive lethality was —0.32. To the extent that this finding is a valid one, it would appear that neither excessive sleep nor sleeplessness (insomnia) relate directly to suicidality. This corroborates our clinical impression that in relation to suicide, the prodromal aspects of sleep have much more to do with disturbances in the quality and the nuances of sleep than simply with the quantitative aspects of sleep. This issue is further complicated by the fact that suicidal state or depression seems to affect different individuals in different ways: Some become agitated and have increased difficulty sleeping; others, in the words of one, "take to bed and pull the covers over my head and have no difficulty sleeping for many more than my usual number of hours."

2. Perhaps the most important finding was that scores on the Lethality Scale related to the way in which the subjects perceived or conceptualized sleep (attitudes toward sleep), specifically in terms of the following correlations: Saw sleep as a "temporary death," 0.60; and saw sleep as a "chance to find oneself," 0.65. From comments made by the subjects, it was surprising to see how often sleep was personified—almost reified. Our subjects had rather definite attitudes about what sleep meant for them, and, further, changes in these attitudes toward sleep correlated with changes in their lethality status. These correlations, taken together with the absence of correlations with duration of sleep, tend to emphasize the importance of the qualitative nuances and phenomenological meanings of sleep in relation to mental health. To assess the status of his patient, the clinician might do better than to ask, "How long did you sleep?" He might rather inquire "What did you think of sleep?", "How did you feel before you went to sleep?", and "How did you feel when you awakened this morning?"

3. In the Sleep Study Form, there are four multiple-choice items, typically with ten steps each, from Hildreth's Feeling and Attitude Scale, reflecting affect ("on top of the world" to "wished I were dead"), energy level ("bursting with energy" to "completely worn out"), security and hopefulness ("full of enthusiasm" to "no hope"), and general feeling in life ("never felt better in my life" to "couldn't feel worse"). In the Sleep Study Form, the lead for each of these items was: "After I got up I felt. . . ." The statistical results indicated that these four items correlated highly among themselves (0.67 to 0.80 in the composite data and 0.62 to 0.88 among the individual subjects).

4. There appeared to be a single nexus of intercorrelated items which,

if not directly correlated with one another, were indirectly correlated through a middle term. This cluster was made up of the following: (*a*) negative affects such as depression, worry, loneliness; (*b*) use of sleep as surcease: Sleep as temporary death, sleep as a chance to find oneself, sleep as an escape from the world; (*c*) troubled views of the morning upon awakening; insecurity and negative feelings; and (*d*) elevated lethality.

5. It is interesting to compare our tentative findings with some related findings previously reported in 1937 by Kleitman and his co-workers.[44]

In our subjects, we studied six characteristics which we thought might collectively determine the quality of sleep: (a) the ease of going to sleep; (b) motility during sleep; (c) sleeping continuously; (d) incidence and character of dreaming; (e) the duration of sleep; and (f) the subjective feeling of being well rested on awakening. The most striking feature of the results obtained on 36 subjects with a mean number of 179 nights per subject, was that, with respect to every sleep characteristic, there was a considerable variation from subject to subject, and in the individual, from night to night.

To the extent that the present study is comparable to Kleitman's experiment, our data would seem to corroborate his earlier findings of considerable variation from subject to subject. Specifically, inspection of the data revealed that among all the intercorrelations of 0.60 or higher, 65 percent (40 out of 62) were obtained by only one subject and were not shared by any of the others. That is to say, there were relatively few pairs of items for which three or more subjects showed the same patterns of relationships.

If we turn to those pairs of items where four or more of the seven subjects had 0.60 or higher correlations on the *same* pairs of items, we found that there are eight such pairings: (*a*) number of times out of bed vs. number of times awakened; (*b*) soundness of sleep vs. continuity of sleep; (*c*) depth of sleep vs. continuity of sleep; (*d*) depth of sleep vs. soundness of sleep; (*e*) energy level in the morning vs. affect in the morning (upon awakening); (*f*) over-all feeling in morning vs. affect in morning (upon awakening); (*g*) over-all feeling in the morning vs. energy in the morning (upon awakening); and (*h*) lethality rating vs. fantasies of suicide.

Excluding the first and last of these eight pairs, there appear to be two sets of three pairs each: intensity of sleep (pairs *b*, *c*, and *d*) and morning status and outlook (pairs *e*, *f*, and *g*).

What all this means is that where the subjects agreed with each other, they tended to agree on the internally consistent items within the Sleep Study Form rather than the pairing of an aspect of sleep with another aspect of behavior. It is interesting to compare the eight individual items above with the results of the composite correlations and to note that by and large the two are essentially similar and tend to corroborate each other.

Within the context of these general remarks about the relationship between sleep and self-destruction, I turn now, by way of illustration, to some data from one of our subjects, the 22-year-old woman whom I call Hunilla. Here are some excerpts from the SPC intake interview, done two years before the sleep-study year reported in this chapter:

Mrs. H., a 20-year-old, tall, very attractive, married Negro woman, with a daughter aged two and a stepson aged eight, called on behalf of herself. Mrs. H. said that she had made a suicide attempt three months ago by taking an overdosage of sleeping pills. She called her mother and was subsequently taken to an emergency hospital. She stated that she was not close to her mother, that she was upset by her stepson, that her husband did not understand her, and that she had no outlet for expression.

Patient's husband is 28 years old, has been married before, and did not obtain a divorce before marrying patient. She met her husband when she was 16 years old, became pregnant, and then went to her mother and asked her mother to help her obtain an abortion. Instead, her mother threatened to kill her boyfriend if he did not marry her daughter. The mother then took them to Mexico where they were married. The night before the patient was married, her mother beat her. Patient felt that her mother forced the marriage; nobody had asked her whether she wanted to get married or not. After the marriage, her mother forced her to return to Mexico for an abortion. Patient stated, "You can see that my mother is a very dominating woman, and I can't say no to her even though I know she is in the wrong." Since then the patient has lost four children. Two were stillborn, and two were miscarriages. Patient stated that her two-year-old daughter is her only reason for living.

Patient's parents divorced when patient was two years old. She says she does not recall her father and has never seen him since. Her mother has remarried five times. Patient has an 18-year-old brother who is in a state mental hospital. She said that he went berserk in school one day and stabbed a teacher. Patient stated that she never had a close relationship with any of her stepfathers.

Shortly after she was married, she had an affair with a 40-year-old man in her neighborhood. She stopped seeing this man when he started calling her home. Subsequently, two repetitive patterns of acting-out sexually occurred when she "seduced" older men. On both occasions, she confessed to her husband what had happened. His initial response was that of denial followed by confrontation. She expressed some relief and also some delight that her husband became more attentive, even calling her during the day to make sure that she was home.

Hunilla becomes angry at her husband or her mother but is unable to verbalize her feelings; instead she withdraws, becomes very sullen, and usually deprives herself of something that is important to her, or she may become depressed and suicidal when faced with angry feelings toward her husband. To Hunilla, recounting feelings is the same as acting on them, which throws her into a panic. She related that once, as a child, a boy threw a rock at her and hit her in the stomach. She said she wished that he would fall off of his bicycle and break his neck; while riding his bicycle away, when the neighbors came out, he did fall off and break his arm. She also related other angry wishes that actually happened. She feels that her anger will either destroy someone or herself.

During the year reported in this chapter, Hunilla one night ingested seven sleeping pills in what she termed a "suicide attempt." Within the month in which this episode occurred, one may trace the course of her increasing perturbation as it built up to the crest manifested in her overt episode and subsequently subsided to relatively more tranquil behavior. In a subsequent interview some months later, she stated that two days after she took the pills (on a date when she rated her own self-destructive impulses as being the most lethal), she thought of cutting her wrists and then actually held her husband's loaded gun to her chest, but, as she stated, "I couldn't pull the trigger. I attempted to, but I couldn't do it. I just couldn't get that finger to move, like it got stuck or something."

That this self-destructive crisis was not the usual state of affairs for Hunilla, or even a typical monthly occurrence, is indicated by the fact that whereas the mean monthly lethality rating—within a possible range of 1 to 9—for the month in which this behavior occurred was 6.48, the mean lethality ratings for the previous two months were 3.06 and 2.70, and for the subsequent three months were 2.82, 3.09, and 2.70.

When I examined the intercorrelations among Hunilla's Sleep Study Form items for the year, especially the correlations $\pm 0.70$ or higher, I discerned these four groupings of items: (1) soundness of sleep, depth of sleep, and continuity of sleep; (2) the occurrence of dreaming and crying during the night; (3) high correlations among various aspects of feeling and outlook in the morning upon awakening; and (4) lethality ratings and feelings upon awakening. When Hunilla indicated that on the night she took an excessive number of sleeping pills she approached sleep in a "matter-of-fact" way, she meant, as she explained to me later, that

basically I didn't care about going to sleep. I didn't want to go to sleep, but at the same time I wanted to be free of these problems and things I was having, but I knew that sleep would not prevent or solve these problems . . . sleep means to me nothing, absolutely nothing . . . just means the end of the day thing, it's something I don't like. I dislike going to bed. I wish there was, sometimes, daylight all the time. I just don't like sleep because I don't like the way I feel when I get up. Very seldom do I have a decent night's sleep.

Six days after she ingested the pills, Hunilla completed an MMPI—one of a series of monthly MMPI's which she had previously and has subsequently completed. For the readers' interest, the data from this series (of eleven) MMPI's, each completed by Hunilla approximately one month apart, are presented in Table 1. The MMPI completed within a week after the pill-taking episode is indicated by an asterisk. The changes that month in profile scores in the F, Pd, Mf, Pa, Pt, and Sc scales, as well as the changes in subsequent months, especially in the D and Hy scales, may be of special interest.

In terms of the theoretical framework of this chapter, her ingestion of seven sleeping pills (together with her contemplation of cutting her wrists and her putting a loaded gun to her chest but being unable to pull the trigger) did not have death (cessation) as the goal, but rather temporary surcease (interruption)—"I would like to sleep forever"—or, probably more accurately, an alteration of her living conditions (altered continuation)—"I can't go on this way." Our evaluation of her behavior over these days would place her lethality rating (the probability of her actually killing herself) in the middle range rather than at the extreme end of the continuum.

Further, in terms of our previous conceptualizations relating to psychosocial age, Hunilla appears to be out of phase with her own chronological age: She is both 30 and 15 but not centrally 22. Apropos of this point, in a recorded conversation with me she said:

I see myself more as a mature woman—in some sense, middle-aged—more than a young adult. And there are times when I feel more like an adolescent. It's sort of odd to me, but this is the way I feel . . . I have very few 20-year-old friends; I just can't cope with people my own age . . . I was brought up around older people, and I basically just didn't care for people my own age. People my own age always seemed silly. I was always

Table 1

Hunilla's MMPI Scores
September, 1964, to August, 1965

| | ? | L | F | K | Hs | D | Hy | Pd | Mf | Pa | Pt | Sc | Ma | Si |
|---|---|---|---|---|---|---|---|---|---|---|---|---|---|---|
| September 1 | 50 | 47 | 64 | 49 | 48 | 52 | 45 | 67 | 42 | 64 | 68 | 66 | 63 | 64 |
| October 2 | 50 | 46 | 70 | 51 | 53 | 63 | 53 | 88 | 47 | 70 | 78 | 86 | 60 | 67 |
| November 1 | 50 | 43 | 76 | 55 | 62 | 69 | 59 | 90 | 51 | 67 | 91 | 91 | 74 | 71 |
| December 21 | 50 | 43 | 85 | 44 | 64 | 69 | 61 | 86 | 47 | 76 | 76 | 95 | 70 | 69 |
| January 18* | 50 | 53 | 104 | 54 | 62 | 67 | 70 | 68 | 66 | 91 | 98 | 109 | 75 | 62 |
| February 7 | 50 | 43 | 87 | 44 | 82 | 78 | 80 | 93 | 47 | 82 | 97 | 101 | 75 | 68 |
| March 1 | 50 | 43 | 80 | 48 | 82 | 75 | 78 | 88 | 64 | 70 | 99 | 100 | 75 | 64 |
| April† | | | | | | | | | | | | | | |
| May 8 | 50 | 43 | 90 | 47 | 76 | 76 | 80 | 95 | 47 | 76 | 98 | 100 | 78 | 68 |
| June 16 | 50 | 43 | 90 | 42 | 80 | 75 | 80 | 90 | 50 | 79 | 98 | 98 | 75 | 68 |
| July 8 | 50 | 46 | 90 | 42 | 78 | 80 | 75 | 86 | 47 | 85 | 95 | 101 | 75 | 68 |
| August 4 | 50 | 46 | 89 | 42 | 78 | 76 | 79 | 90 | 47 | 79 | 96 | 98 | 78 | 69 |

* This MMPI was completed six days following her suicide attempt.
† This MMPI is lost somewhere in my office—probably on my desk.

that way. Even at 15, I was dealing with people 21, 22 years old—people five to ten years older than I was. . . . Sometimes I think I am much closer to death than my life span is supposed to be . . . like I'll live five years more, and then I'll be gone. I just can't see myself still living after that. I'll be worn out completely at 30; in other words, at 30 I'll feel like 50 or 60. At other times, I feel like an adolescent. Usually that occurs when I begin to gain weight; I don't like to gain weight—I like to look young so I begin to attempt to be young—such as listening to rock 'n' roll records and drinking cokes all day and different things of this sort, things that a teenager would actually do, not a married woman. I mostly pick up teenage talk and teenage attitudes, becoming just a little bit babyish. I want to be older, I want to be younger; it's a combination . . . wanting to be 18 and wanting to be 30. You can't be both, but that's the way I feel.

One is reminded of the section in Harry Stack Sullivan's *The Interpersonal Theory of Psychiatry* entitled "Disasters in Timing of Development Stages" in which he speaks of preadolescent individuals ". . . driven to establishing relationships with a chronologically younger [or older] person," and he warns that the latter especially ". . . does entail very serious risk to the personality." In general, on this point, Sullivan believes:

The changes which take place at the thresholds of the developmental eras are far-reaching; they touch upon much of what has already been acquired as personality, often making it somewhat acutely inadequate, or at any rate not fully relevant for the sudden new expanding of the personal horizon.[45]

In the *Cemetery* scene of the Make-A-Picture-Story (MAPS) Test, Hunilla chose a sad-looking male and a sad-looking little girl and then told the following story, again illustrating the gap in her conceptualization of the ordinary sequence of generations:

The grandfather and his granddaughter are standing at his wife's grave and he misses her very much as he hasn't anyone now that she is gone. The little girl feels the same way, as her parents are dead and her grandparents are taking care of her. The old man is a very religious person, and he consoles himself that his wife has a better life now. The girl does not understand this. [Title?] Alone in Grief.

In our terms, Hunilla's self-destructive crisis might be thought of as an extra-temporal crisis in a young woman out of phase with her life's years. In her, the crisis represents an ambivalent cry for help that has the paradoxical tones of an appeal from a nymph-matron who is suffering from a decade of temporal vacuum around her actual age. Simultaneously, she is yearning for a future of more stability, and she is looking backward to a past of less responsibility. She is struggling to master the tasks appropriate to her time in life (sexuality, work, marriage, family), but she is handicapped by a chaotic and preformed view of death seen alternatively as either a child might view death or as an older person might conceive of death. She is too young for her age and too old for her years; a temporal orphan not adapted to her own time in life.

Sleep has a special "time-out" quality and plays a unique role in human life in that it is an interruption usually used constructively to restore and to replenish (elevative), often used to escape or simply to exist (temporative), but, in its very nature, very rarely used to destroy or denigrate one's own existence (reductive).

In unusual instances, inimical use of sleep can be employed—for instance, to be in bed asleep when one in his own best interests "ought to be" up and doing; but even in such cases sleeping has something of an overdetermined defensive function which may, in the long run, be essentially protective of the stability and welfare of the individual.

Thus, sleep itself is rarely self-destructive; rather than view it as "death's brother," we tend to view sleep, in our research sleep subjects at the SPC, as the silent therapist of disturbance, gyroscopically moving with the individual's perturbation, balancing it, leveling it, and all the while reflecting the ups and downs in the total life. Troubled sleep is part and parcel of troubled wakefulness; this is particularly true if by "sleep" we include in our thinking both pre-sleep and post-sleep—especially the attitudes and feelings upon lying down and upon arising.

It seems appropriate for me to conclude this brief phenomenological study of sleep with a short personal note. How do *I* sleep? As a beginning, I would say that I sleep well, and, characteristically for me, when I sleep I do so rather intensely. But when I seem to be most life-oriented, that is, when I have some favorite projects under way, I sometimes have considerable difficulty falling asleep. I lie awake, occupied with thoughts and plans, unable to achieve that necessary state of restful unvigilance or to give myself up to the cerebral passivity of sleep. For example, during the month or so when the preparation of this volume on self-destruction was at its peak, I not unexpectedly did not sleep as much as I usually do. I hope now that it is not too evident that I then should have slept a good deal less.

## REFERENCES

1. This study was part of a larger Comprehensive Suicide Prevention Program, supported by National Institute of Mental Health Grant MH-00128, administered through the University of Southern California School of Medicine.
2. In at least one aspect, this final chapter of this book is the converse of the opening chapter, the one by Professor Murray: *this* chapter contains a statement by *me* about *him*. My declaration can be brief: Almost everything I have thought and written in the last several years, especially since my stay with him at Harvard in 1961 and 1962, has been an acknowledgment of my debt to him. I am acknowledging it again now in presenting this chapter. His direct and indirect influence on both the formal and substantive elements of my thought should, I trust, be manifest. That I am an imperfect student will be too painfully clear for me to need to elaborate.
3. By "unplugging" I have in mind the ways in which individuals temporarily move out of the mainstream of their lives—taking a vacation from their ordinary patterns of continuation behaviors. I can try to define what I have in mind through some examples: darting into a movie; watching the late-late TV show; "burying oneself" in a novel—what the English call "having a good read"; going on a *wanderjahr*; having a transient affair; indulging in a hobby; spending a weekend in Las Vegas; etc. When unplugging behaviors are not too inimical to the life pattern of the individual, they can be seen as useful safety valves.
4. Revised and enlarged ed.; Chicago: University of Chicago Press, 1963.
5. I. Oswald, *Sleeping and Waking* (Amsterdam and New York: Elsevier Publishing Company, 1962); E. J. Murray, *Sleep, Dream, Arouse* (New York: Appleton-Century-Crofts, Inc., 1965); G. E. W. Wolstenholme and M. O'Connor (eds.), *The Nature of Sleep* (Boston: Little, Brown and Company, 1960); and Gay G. Luce and J. Segal, *Sleep* (New York: Coward–McCann, 1966).
6. "Orientations Toward Death: A Vital Aspect of the Study of Lives," in R. W. White (ed.), *The Study of Lives* (New York: Atherton Press, 1963); reprinted in *International Journal of Psychiatry*, **2**:167–200, 1966; and "Suicide, Sleep and Death: Some Possible Interrelations among Cessation, Interruption and Continuation Phenomena," *Journal of Consulting Psychology*, **28**:95–106, 1964.
7. "There are certain kinks in our thinking which are of such universal occurrence as to constitute essential limitations. Thus the urge to think of my own death as some form of my experience is almost irresistible. However, it requires only to be said for me to admit that my own death cannot be a form of experience, for if I could still experience, then by definition it would not be death. Operationally, my own death is a fundamentally different thing from the death of another in the same way that my own

feelings mean something fundamentally different from the feelings of another. The death of another I can experience; there are certain methods of recognizing death and certain properties of death that affect my actions in the case of others. . . . My own death is such a different thing that it might well have a different word, and perhaps eventually will. There is no operation by which I can decide whether I am dead; 'I am always alive.' " Percy W. Bridgman, *The Intelligent Individual and Society* (New York: The Macmillan Company, 1938), p. 168. See also Bridgman's *The Way Things Are* (Cambridge, Mass.: Harvard University Press, 1955), pp. 234–235.

8. A further discussion of the "post-self" can be found in my paper "The Deaths of Herman Melville," in H. P. Vincent (ed.), *Melville and Hawthorne in the Berkshires* (Kent, Ohio: Kent State University Press, 1967).
9. "Within each personal consciousness, thought is sensibly continuous. . . . the only breaches that can well be conceived to occur within the limits of a single mind would either be *interruptions, time*-gaps during which the consciousness went out altogether to come into existence again at a later moment; or they would be breaks in the *quality*, or content, of the thought, so abrupt that the segment that they followed had no connection whatever with the one that went before." William James, *Principles of Psychology* (New York: Dover Publications, Inc., 1950), vol. 1, p. 237. (Originally published by Henry Holt and Company, Inc., 1890).
10. The concept of continuation is a complicated one. It contains within itself a number of subconcepts including (1) one's modal (or unaltered) continuation state; (2) altered continuation states, in which the person remains conscious but is in an unusual-for-him (e.g., drugged or intoxicated) state; (3) truncated continuation states, in which there is a symbolic death of part of the self, such as the death of certain feelings or the stopping of major segments of the inner or outer life; (4) uncontinuation states, by which I mean the continuation of the stream-of-unconscious events, the other-than-waking conscious life that occurs especially during sleep and is manifested especially by dreams; and (5) discontinuation or "stoppings" in the human condition that we can refer to as "endings." These are, so to speak, conclusions of phases of life; they are the breaking off of relationships and living patterns. They are the closing off of aspirations. They involve irreparable losses (in a way, over and above the manner to which we become habituated to the loss of temporal units). Examples of such endings would involve at least the following: moving from a home; graduating from school; leaving or losing a job; being discharged from military service; divorcing a spouse; terminating a friendship; experiencing the death of a loved one; losing a limb or an organ; having property destroyed or stolen, etc.
11. "We start then, with nothing, pure zero. But this is not the nothing of negation. For *not* means *other than*, and *other* is merely a synonym of the ordinal numeral *second*. As such it implies a first; while the present pure zero is prior to every first. The nothing of negation is the nothing of death, which also comes *second to*, or after, everything." Charles

Hartshorne and Paul Weiss (eds.), *Collected Papers of Charles Sanders Peirce* (Cambridge, Mass.: Harvard University Press, 1931–1958), vol. VI, p. 148.

12. A. K. Coomaraswamy is quoted as saying: "Our head is ourself, and to cut off one's head is self-abandonment, self-denial, and self-naughting." In J. M. Plumer, "Suicide and Sacrifice," *Art Quarterly* (Autumn, 1947), pp. 254–261.
13. The term "cessation" was used in this present sense by Bridgman in at least two places (*The Intelligent Individual and Society*, pp. 168 and 225): "It seems plausible in the first place to suppose that the idea of the soul arose because of the inability of people to imagine the meaning of a cessation of their own consciousness. One almost had to invent a life after death in order to make the ordinary forms of thought possible." And: "Or the idea of the sacredness of life is pushed to cover suicide, and it is made an unpardonable crime to presume to send one's own soul before its maker. If one has succeeded in divesting oneself of supernatural ideas about death, and thinks of death as being cessation, he will find any such argument as this just silly and will therefore not be appealed to by it."
14. A basic assumption in this entire scheme is that an individual's orientations toward cessation are *bi-phasic*; that is, any adult, at any given moment, has (1) more or less long-range, relatively chronic, pervasive, habitual, characterological orientations toward cessation as an integral part of his total psychological makeup (reflecting his philosophy of life, need systems, aspirations, identifications, conscious beliefs, etc.); and (2) is also capable of having acute, relatively short-lived, exacerbated, clinical, sudden shifts in his orientation toward his own cessation. Indeed, this is what is usually meant when one says that an individual has become "suicidal." It is therefore crucial in any complete assessment of an individual's orientation toward cessation to know both his habitual and his at-that-moment cessation orientations. (Failure to do this is one reason why previous efforts to relate "suicidal state" with psychological test results have been barren.) In individuals in their "normal" (i.e., usual-for-them) state, their habitual and their current orientations toward cessation will be the same.
15. See, for example, John M. Macdonald, *The Murderer and His Victim*. (Springfield, Ill.: Charles C Thomas, Publisher, 1961); and M. E. Wolfgang, "Suicide by Means of Victim-Precipitated Homicide," *Journal of Clinical and Experimental Psychopathology*, **20**, 335–349, 1959.
16. "Most of life is so dull that there is nothing to be said about it, and the books and talk that would describe it as interesting are obliged to exaggerate in the hope of justifying their own existence. Inside its cocoon of work or social obligation, the human spirit slumbers for the most part, registering the distinction between pleasure and pain, but not nearly as alert as we pretend." E. M. Forster, *A Passage to India*, chap. 14.
17. In this connection, one is reminded especially of the profound paragraphs of that remarkable octogenarian Frances Wickes, in her book *The Inner World of Choice* (New York: Harper & Row, 1963), especially a passage on pages 289–290.

18. New York: W. W. Norton & Company, Inc., 1963.
19. In this connection, it is interesting to note that Eugenio Montale ("An Introduction to *Billy Budd* (1942)," *Sewanee Review*, 68:419–422, 1960), mentions, but dismisses as "sterile," the "daring interpretation" that the three principal figures in *Billy Budd* might be seen "as narcissistic projections of the three ages of the author."
20. From *As You Like It*, II.vii; *Childhood and Society*, chap. 7, "Eight Stages of Man"; *Modern Man in Search of a Soul*, chap. 5, "The Stages of Life"; *Five Ages of Man*, part II, "The Personal Psychological Story of Man: The Five Ordeals"; *The Interpersonal Theory of Psychiatry*, chap. 16, the section entitled "Disasters in Timing of Developmental Stages"; *The Interpersonal Theory of Psychiatry*, chap. 12, "Meaningful Living in the Mature Years," in Robert W. Kleemeier (ed.), *Ageing and Leisure: A Research Prospective into the Meaningful Use of Time*; and *Metamorphosis* (the entire book); respectively.
21. All this is not unrelated to Weisman and Hackett's concept of "an appropriate death." (Avery D. Weisman and Thomas P. Hackett, "Predilection to Death: Death and Dying as a Psychiatric Problem," *Psychosomatic Medicine*, **23**:232–256, 1961.). This involves the capacity to see inner consistency in all of an individual's acts and ambitions so that, beyond any specific point, further living would be defeat or a pointless repetition of the old. The concept of an appropriate death is essentially a romantic or poetic one. That is to say that within the life span of an individual, there are certain dramatic heights or crests when death itself at that time gives an appropriate and self-consistent tone to the life style of the person and might even heighten his "post-self" impact by, for example, making his memory more treasured. Another way of stating it is that there are "right times to die" in a person's life—that dying either before or after these high points is either preclimactic or anticlimactic. Considering what was going on in the person's life, his general life style, and where he was in his own life, one can evaluate the appropriateness, from the point of view of history, of the time and manner of an individual's death in terms of this concept of "an appropriate death." In this sense, how would one rate the death of President Kennedy? Ernest Hemingway? Adlai Stevenson? Marilyn Monroe?
22. It may be that my own use of the concept of life phases is closer to that of Shakespeare's than to that of Erikson's, or somewhere between the two. In Shakespeare's concept, one can almost concretely see individuals growing from phase to phase (infancy, childhood, adolescence, young adulthood, middle adulthood, older age, and senescence), whereas in terms of Erikson's phases, one usually cannot, except under certain rather dramatic and exceptional conditions. Erikson's stages represent a rather complex conceptualization of how the functional interaction between child and society is crystallized into psychological structure, habits, attitudes, or strengths and weaknesses.
23. In this regard, the following books are of especial interest: Edgar Z. Friedenberg, *The Vanishing Adolescent* (Boston: Beacon Press, 1959);

Yehudi A. Cohen (ed.), *Social Structure and Personality: A Casebook* (New York: Holt, Rinehart and Winston, Inc., 1961); Ruth Benedict, *Patterns of Culture* (Baltimore: Penguin Books, Inc., 1946 [originally published in 1934]); J. H. van den Berg, *The Changing Nature of Man: Introduction to a Historical Psychology* (New York: Dell Publishing Co., Inc., 1964).

24. *Memories, Dreams and Reflections,* (New York: Pantheon Books, a Division of Random House, Inc., 1961), p. 200. To this, Jolan Jacobi [*The Psychology of Jung* (London: Routledge & Kegan Paul Ltd., 1942)] has added: "The individual's psychological situation is different at every age. At the beginning of life he must struggle out of infancy, which still is wholly imprisoned in the collective unconscious, to the differentiation and demarcation of his ego. He must get rooted in real life and, first of all, master the tasks—sexuality, profession, marriage, descendants, ties and connections of all kinds—that it imposes on him. Therefore it is of the greatest importance that he acquire the tools for his establishment and adjustment by means of the highest possible differentiations of his constitutionally superior function. Only when this task, which constitutes that of the first half of life, is fully accomplished, should the experience of and adjustment to the internal be added to the adjustment to the external. Once the construction and reinforcement of the personality's attitude with respect to the outer world are completed, energy can be turned to the as yet more or less unheeded inner psychic realities and can therewith bring human life to true perfection" (p. 140). And: "The activation of the archetype of the soul-image is an event of fateful significance, for it is the unmistakable sign that the second half of life has begun" (p. 113).
25. New York: McGraw-Hill Book Company, 1959.
26. New York: John Wiley & Sons, Inc., 1965.
27. New York: McGraw-Hill Book Company, 1957.
28. New York: Family Service Association of America, 1965.
29. In *Field Theory in Social Science* (New York: Harper & Row, 1951).
30. In *Adolescence*, 43d Yearbook of the National Society for Studies in Education (Chicago: University of Chicago Press, 1944), part I.
31. Oswald, Ian, *op. cit.*, pp. 20–21 and 42–65.
32. *Op. cit.*, p. 407.
33. A more complete explication of these notions will be published in a separate book, *Suicidology: The Study of Self-Destruction*, to be published by Prentice-Hall, Inc.
34. N. Kleitman, F. J. Mullin, N. R. Cooperman, and S. Titelbaum, *Sleep Characteristics* (Chicago: University of Chicago Press, 1937); Henry A. Murray and Christiana D. Morgan, "A Clinical Study of Sentiments: I and II," *Genetic Psychology Monographs*, **32**:3–149 and 155–311, 1945; and Harold M. Hildreth, "A Battery of Feeling and Attitude Scales for Clinical Use," *Journal of Clinical Psychology*, **23**:214–221, 1946.
35. It may be worth mentioning that each subject was then sent one month's Sleep Study Forms at a time, with stamped, return-addressed envelopes,

and was asked to mail a form to the Suicide Prevention Center each day. Each subject was paid $1 for each form and $10 for completing an MMPI on the first day of each month: $485 per annum per subject. The payment was thought useful to maintain the subject's incentive and to give the enterprise a businesslike character.

36. One subject in our sleep study—a 50-year-old, college-educated man (not listed among the subjects included in this chapter) spontaneously wrote the following: "To me at least, I have no significant attitude (or set of attitudes) toward the concept of SLEEP-PLUS-BED-PLUS-PRIVACY-PLUS-DARKNESS-PLUS etc., etc. (Mainly of course just SLEEP-PLUS-BED.) Our language does not at the moment supply us with a portmanteau word to cover this concept. Categories such as 'escape from the work-a-day world' or 'temporary death' do not supply the meaning I have in mind. If I speak of SLEEP as a *refuge*, which is the nearest one-word description of my attitude that I have come up with to date. I am not reifying SLEEP, but I come close to reifying the concept of SLEEP-PLUS-BED, and perhaps properly so, since BED at least is a *res*, and is a very important part of the concept. I look forward to sleep both as a period of oblivion and as a time for dreaming. I am quite serious when I say that to me SLEEP-PLUS-BED is a *wonderfully pleasant way to pass the time* (particularly during periods of depression), and that this is its main attraction to me . . . more so than *refuge*, or *return to the womb*, or *the protected place*, or *the private place*, although I give you all these labels as additional truths."
37. Murray, *op. cit.*; Kaspar Naegele, "Sociological Observations on Everyday Life: First and Further Thoughts on Sleep" (unpublished manuscript, University of British Columbia, 1961); and V. Aubert and H. White, "Sleep: A Sociological Interpretation," *Acta Sociologica*, fasc. 2 and 3: **4**: 46–54 and 1–16, 1959; respectively.
38. The following types of data were available in addition to the daily Sleep Study Forms: MMPI completed on the first of each month; Suicide Prevention Center intake interview, progress notes, and summaries; lethality ratings; and, for some subjects, TAT, MAPS test, autobiographies, and special in-depth interviews.
39. Several other subjects participated for varying periods of time. In one particularly tragic case, a 65-year-old widow, who had made a death-pact with her husband, committed suicide some months after his death, 42 days after she had begun the Sleep Study Forms. She submitted forms until the very night she took a lethal dose of barbiturates. What was especially remarkable about her Sleep Study Forms was that she slept fully (i.e., 7 to 8 hours per night) but not "well" up to the night of her suicide, her disturbance being manifested in the items relating to feeling and mood and hopelessness.
40. Murray, Henry A., "Commentary on the Case of El," *Journal of Projective Techniques*, **25**:404–411, 1961; Hooker, Evelyn, "The Case of El: A Biography," *Journal of Projective Techniques*, **25**:252–267, 1961.
41. One measure of consistency of these percentages was obtained. The com-

posite data were run at 10 months (303 days) as well as at 12 months (365 days). The percentages for each item for the ten and twelve months were almost identical; the mean difference of percentage point between the two for all categories was less than one percentage point, 0.63.

42. In relation to the statistical computations, I wish to acknowledge my indebtedness to Mrs. Elaine Fielder, Research Volunteer at the Suicide Prevention Center, who collated and processed all the Sleep Study Forms, to Miss Jan Kramer, Research Technician at the Suicide Prevention Center, who was my administrative right hand in this sleep study, and to Mr. Leonard W. Staugas and Mrs. Cleo B. Nelson of the Western Research Support Center, Veterans Administration Hospital, Sepulveda, California, whose interest and help to me were indispensable.
43. Mr. Staugas wrote the following *caveat emptor*: "Essentially, you have 365 samples of behavior on each individual, taken over twelve months time. Although it is subject to all the limitations of the usual paper-and-pencil techniques, if repeated sampling increases reliability, your approach should maximize this effect. We have also computed the intercorrelations among 80 items of your original questionnaire, using the questionnaires available for each individual. There are no published tables of significance that can be used to determine how large a correlation should be before one could say that it is significantly higher than would be expected by chance. This is due to the fact that such tables were constructed to determine the significance level of correlations based on independent observations.

    "I think that the approach you suggested, where you list those pairs of variables which have correlations of .6 or higher, is a good one. In attempting to point out similarities and differences between the seven individuals in your study, you can make use of the fact that the same pair of variables did or did not correlate highly in the two individuals.

    "The word 'highly' is used in a somewhat subjective sense. If the correlation between a pair of variables for one individual was .7 and between the same variables for another individual was .2, you might say that these individuals responded differently to the two questionnaire items. However, you would not say this in any rigorous statistical sense. When comparing such correlations, you should also take care to examine the table of 'N's' to make sure that the correlations are not based on a very small sample."
44. N. Kleitman, F. J. Mullin, N. R. Cooperman, and S. Titelbaum, *Sleep Characteristics* (Chicago: University of Chicago Press, 1937).
45. (New York: W. W. Norton & Company, Inc., 1953), pp. 258 and 228.

# Index